The Chemistry Of Paper-making, Together With The Principles Of General Chemistry; A Handbook For The Student And Manufacturer

Griffin, R. B. (Russell B.)

Nabu Public Domain Reprints:

You are holding a reproduction of an original work published before 1923 that is in the public domain in the United States of America, and possibly other countries. You may freely copy and distribute this work as no entity (individual or corporate) has a copyright on the body of the work. This book may contain prior copyright references, and library stamps (as most of these works were scanned from library copies). These have been scanned and retained as part of the historical artifact.

This book may have occasional imperfections such as missing or blurred pages, poor pictures, errant marks, etc. that were either part of the original artifact, or were introduced by the scanning process. We believe this work is culturally important, and despite the imperfections, have elected to bring it back into print as part of our continuing commitment to the preservation of printed works worldwide. We appreciate your understanding of the imperfections in the preservation process, and hope you enjoy this valuable book.

THE CHEMISTRY

OF

PAPER-MAKING

TOGETHER WITH THE

PRINCIPLES OF GENERAL CHEMISTRY

A HANDBOOK FOR THE STUDENT AND MANUFACTURER

BY

R. B. GRIFFIN AND A. D. LITTLE

NEW YORK
HOWARD LOCKWOOD & CO
1894

Entered according to Act of Congress, in the year 1894, by HOWARD LOCKWOOD & CO.
in the office of the Librarian of Congress at Washington.

PREFACE.

A CONSIDERABLE part of this book has been devoted to the elementary facts and principles of general chemistry and to processes of chemical analysis which are, in the main, well known, in the hope that the strictly technical portion might thus be rendered more available to the large body of paper-makers whose knowledge of the science is limited. For this reason the Introduction treats briefly of chemical theory, while Part I contains a short account of the different elements and a reference to their more important compounds. In Chapter VIII the various analytical processes which are employed in the examination of paper-making materials are given at some length.

Among the numerous authorities consulted special mention should be made of Goodale's "Vegetable Physiology," Sargeant's "Report on the Forest Trees of North America," Schubert's "Die Cellulosefabrikation," the very complete reports of the State Board of Health of Massachusetts in connection with the subject of water, and files of "THE PAPER TRADE JOURNAL" and Hofmann's *Papier-Zeitung*. The excellent plate of fibres is from the valuable little book by Dr W Herzberg entitled "Papier-Prüfung," in which also may be found many of the facts relating to the German methods of paper-testing. The numerous papers and reports of Cross and Bevan on cellulose, fibres, and the processes of paper-making have been freely drawn upon

This opportunity is taken to thank collectively the many friends in the paper trade who have kindly contributed the results of their experience and permitted the publication of analyses made in our laboratory for them. Valuable assistance has also been received in various ways from Messrs. A. Wendler, E. C. Albree, J. L. Hecht, George T. Cooke and Dr. Frederick Fox.

The death of my friend and partner deprived me of his co-operation when the book was only partially completed, and has at many points obliged me to forego that fullness of treatment which his aid would have rendered easy.

A. D. LITTLE

BOSTON, August, 1894

CONTENTS.

	PAGE
INTRODUCTION — Principles of Chemical Theory	3

PART I

GENERAL CHEMISTRY

The Non-Metallic Elements	25
The Metallic Elements	62

PART II

THE CHEMISTRY OF PAPER-MAKING.

CHAP		
I	Cellulose	103
II	Fibres	117
III	Process for Isolating Cellulose	151
	Rag Boiling	151
	Treatment of Picker Seed and Picker Waste	153
	Esparto	157
	Straw	158
	Manufacture of Wood Fibre.—	
	The Soda Process	161
	The Sulphate Process	178
	The Sulphite Process	179
	Theory	182
	History	185
	Preparing Wood	188
	Liquor-making	190
	Digesters and Linings	232
	Boiling	250
	Recovery of Gas	261
	The Waste Liquor	270

IV Bleaching	275
V. Sizing and Loading	301
VI Coloring	320
VII Water	329
VIII Chemical Analysis	348
IX Paper-testing	420
X Electrolytic Processes	452
Appendix	463
Index	503

THE
CHEMISTRY OF PAPER-MAKING.

THE CHEMISTRY OF PAPER MAKING.

INTRODUCTION.

Physical and Chemical Change.—The action of force upon matter gives rise to changes which are called physical or chemical, according as the identity of the substance acted upon is preserved or lost. In grinding wood, each particle of the pulp remains a bit of wood; in beating stock or forming a sheet of paper, the identity of the cellulose is not affected. Rosin may be melted or broken down to powder, but its character as rosin remains the same. Iron may be forged, rolled, filed to dust, or drawn to wire along which an electric current passes, but in each case the product of the process is iron. All of these changes are non-essential ones so far as the identity of the substances is concerned. The composition of the substances has been unaffected and the changes are physical ones.

If rags are boiled for some hours with acid, glucose is formed. Rosin is heated with soda, and a size which is different from either is prepared. Iron rusts in the air or burns in the forge or dissolves in acid, and the products would never be confounded with the metal. These are chemical changes, the identity of the materials involved in them has been lost, and new and different substances have appeared. The changes have affected the ultimate constitution of the substances, and they are no longer what they were. It is with such changes that the science of *Chemistry* has to deal.

Conservation of Energy and Matter.—Chemistry, in the modern sense, began with the recognition, by Lavoisier, of the fact that matter is never destroyed but only takes on new forms. If a piece of charcoal is burned in a sealed globe large enough to contain sufficient air for the combustion, the weight of the globe remains the same although the charcoal has disappeared. So in any chemical change the weight of the products of the reaction is always equal to the weight of the substances first concerned in it.

This law, first formulated in regard to matter, has more recently been shown to be equally true of energy or force. Energy is never created or destroyed, but only passes from one form of energy into its equivalent in some other form or forms of energy. When coal is burned, the energy of chemical attraction is transformed into the energy of heat, which may become in succession the energy of steam, of a moving piston, of electricity in motion, to be again transformed into light and heat. These changes are obscure, the force which is available for our uses becomes less with each transformation, and careful experiments which take into account many minor changes are necessary to show that the total amount of force remains the same through each successive change.

Weight and Volume. — Weight, as the term is used in chemistry, means about the same as the term "mass" in physics; that is, it is used to denote the quantity of matter which a body contains as compared with the quantity contained in some other body which is taken as the unit weight. The volume of a body is the space which it occupies, and volumes are given in terms of some unit of volume. Much of what chemistry has to teach rests upon the accuracy of our determinations of these two functions of matter, and it is therefore of the first importance that the units employed should be as definite and convenient as possible. For this reason the French system of measurement, known as the metric system, has been universally adopted by chemists, and the student should familiarize himself with it at the first opportunity. This need require very little time, as the system is extremely simple. The tables will be found in the Appendix.

Specific Gravity. — The specific gravity (or Sp. Gr.) of a substance is the ratio between the weight of a given volume of the substance and the weight of the same volume of some other substance which is selected as the standard. Water, at its temperature of greatest density, $4°$ C., is the substance usually taken for the standard in determining the Sp. Gr. of liquids and solids, and we therefore mean in saying that the Sp. Gr. of sulphuric acid is 1.84, of lead 11.36, of alcohol 0.792, that these substances are respectively 1.84, 11.36, and 0.792 times as heavy as water at $4°$ C., volume for volume. In some cases, for greater convenience, water at the ordinary temperature, 15° C., is taken as the standard, but where this temperature has been adopted the fact is usually stated in giving the Sp. Gr. Various tables of Sp. Gr. will be found in the Appendix.

The specific gravity or vapor density of gases and vapors is usually referred either to hydrogen, because it is the lightest of them all, or else to air, because it is most convenient. In this book, unless otherwise stated, the standard is hydrogen.

The Atomic Theory. — The facts of chemistry are best explained upon the theory, first propounded in its present form by Dalton, that all matter is composed of extremely minute particles called *Molecules*. A molecule is the smallest particle of a substance which can exist and still remain that substance. The molecules are themselves believed to be composed of still smaller, indivisible particles called *Atoms*, and these particles or atoms are the ultimate units with which chemistry deals and upon which chemical forces are exerted. The molecules of a compound substance contain two or more different kinds of atoms, which, by their association and arrangement, give rise to the properties which distinguish the substance. When, therefore, by any chemical process the molecule is broken up, the atoms composing it arrange themselves in other groups, and new substances result. The molecules of those simpler forms of matter, called by chemists *Elements*, contain atoms of only a single kind, but, except in one or two instances to be referred to in due course, the association of two or more atoms in the molecule is necessary to establish the qualities which characterize the elementary substance; and if the integrity of the molecule is impaired, the atoms group themselves with other atoms to form new molecules, and again new substances are formed.

Properties of Matter. — The different kinds of matter exhibit the widest possible range of qualities. The words hard, soft, light, heavy, crystalline, ductile, brittle, elastic, volatile, call to mind as many distinct qualities. The physical properties, like those named, depend mainly upon the relations of the molecules to each other in the substance. Chemical properties are those exhibited by a substance in its relations to other substances. Thus a substance may be inflammable or non-inflammable, acid or alkaline, soluble or the reverse, in various liquids. Chemical properties depend upon the number and kind of atoms which compose the molecule, and upon their arrangement within the molecule.

States of Matter. — Matter may exist as a solid, a liquid, or a gas, and a very large number of substances may be made to assume one state or the other at will. All gases may be reduced to liquids and even to the solid form by the combined action of cold and pressure. The essential difference between the three states is found in the amount or range of movement which the molecules of a substance possess. The molecules of a substance are not packed together like the cells in a honeycomb, but are separated by spaces which are undoubtedly great in comparison with the size of the molecules. The whole great group of molecules which constitutes a body is held together, in a solid or liquid, by the force called *Cohesion* excited between the molecules, and which in its final terms is probably similar in kind to the force which holds the sun and planets together. Like the stars, the molecules and atoms are in ceaseless motion. In a solid this motion is so limited by cohesion that the molecules preserve their positions relative to each other, and resist any force tending to displace them. In a liquid the molecular motion is so much greater that the cohesive force is nearly overcome. Still liquids have a definite surface, and when conditions permit assume a spherical form. In a gas the molecules move still more freely, and there is no cohesion between the molecules. The molecules of a gas tend to diffuse equally in all directions.

Differences in what we call the temperature of a body are differences in the momentum of the moving molecules. These differences are measured in an arbitrary way by the thermometer. When we heat a body we expend force upon it to increase the momentum of its molecules, and conversely, when a body is cooled, the momentum of its molecules is gradually distributed among those of the cooling agent.

Change of State. — Bearing the facts of the last two paragraphs in mind, it becomes evident how, through the action of heat, a solid body may be converted into a liquid and finally into a gas; and also how the volume of a substance increases as its temperature rises.

In order to bring about this change from the solid to the liquid state, or from the liquid to the gaseous state, it is necessary to move the molecules apart sufficiently to limit in the first case, and entirely overcome in the second, the force of cohesion. This is accomplished by the power supplied by heat. In other words,

INTRODUCTION

heat is absorbed during both these changes. Ice at zero centigrade may be heated for some time, and the result is water at zero. Water at 100° C. requires much heat to convert it into steam at 100° C. The heat thus absorbed is given out again when the molecules resume their former positions, and is therefore called *Latent Heat*. Different substances have different latent heats. Similarly, equal weights of different substances require different quantities of heat to produce the same rise of temperature. Water requires more than almost any other substance, and the quantity of heat needed to raise one kilogramme (2.2 lbs.) from 0° to 1° C. is called one *unit of heat*. It is the moving force developed by 423 kilogrammes falling one metre (3 ft. 3⅜ in.). The *Specific Heat* of a substance is the proportion between the quantity of heat needed to raise the temperature of a given weight of the substance through one degree and the quantity of heat needed to raise the temperature of an equal weight of water through one degree.

Gas Pressure. — Since the molecules of a gas are free to move in straight paths, it follows that the molecules are constantly bombarding the walls of any containing vessel. These blows, by their aggregate effect, produce the phenomena of gas pressure. If the rapidity of motion is increased by heat, the impacts are more violent and the pressure rises. If the volume of the vessel is decreased, more molecules strike the walls and the pressure similarly rises. The power of the steam-engine is derived from the blows delivered against the piston by the infinite number of molecules of water as their motion is arrested by its face.

Compounds and Elements. — By the processes of chemical analysis nearly every known substance may be made to yield two or more simpler bodies. Substances which may be thus decomposed are termed *Compounds*. About seventy substances are known to chemists which have so far resisted all attempts to resolve them into anything simpler. Such simple substances are called *Elements*. The elements exhibit every diversity of character. Some, like oxygen and chlorine, are gases; others, like bromine and mercury, are liquids at ordinary temperatures. The great majority are solids. Only about one-half of them are of common occurrence.

The Law of Ampère. — Various experimentalists have shown that all gases expand and contract equally under the same variations of temperature and pressure. From this fact it follows, as a mathematical consequence, that *equal volumes of all gases, under the same conditions of temperature and pressure, contain the same number of molecules.* This deduction, which is of great importance in the theory of chemistry, is called the Law of Ampère

Atomic Weights. — In order that chemical calculations may be accurately performed, it is of the first importance that the relative weights of the atoms composing the different elementary substances should be accurately determined, since combination takes place between atoms. Hydrogen is the lightest of all known substances, and the weight of the hydrogen atom is therefore taken as the unit in which the weights of all the other atoms are expressed. The atomic weight of oxygen is given as 16 — this means that an atom of oxygen is 16 times as heavy as an atom of hydrogen. The molecular weight of a substance is the sum of the weights of the atoms which compose the molecule, and is of course dependent upon the number and kind of atoms which the molecule contains. A table giving the atomic weights of the different elements will be found in the Appendix

Although these weights are only relative weights, they are none the less real, and many of them have been determined with the most refined accuracy. Their value rests upon data of several kinds, and which are in large measure independent of each other First, the law of Ampère gives us a means of finding the molecular weight of any substance which can be brought into the state of gas We know by the results of chemical analysis that the molecule of hydrogen contains two atoms, and that its molecular weight is therefore 2 Since equal volumes of different gases contain the same number of molecules, it follows that the molecular weight of any substance is equal to twice its specific gravity in the state of gas. For example, oxygen is 16 times as heavy as hydrogen, volume for volume, that is, the Sp Gr of oxygen is 16, and the oxygen molecule must weigh 16 times as much as the hydrogen molecule. $16 \times 2 = 32$, the molecular weight of oxygen.

Second, by analysis of the different compounds of an element, and comparison of the results, we are able to find those compounds in which the element enters into combination in smallest proportion, and such compounds are therefore believed to contain only

INTRODUCTION.

one atom of this element in a molecule of the compound. Thus twice the Sp. Gr. of hydrochloric acid gas gives 36.5 as the molecular weight, and 36.5 parts of the acid by weight yield one part of hydrogen. None of the immense number of hydrogen compounds yield on analysis less than one part by weight of this element, where amounts which are proportional to the molecular weight of the compounds are taken for analysis. Some give two, three, four, or more times this quantity, and are therefore believed to contain two, three, four, or more atoms of hydrogen in the molecule, as the case may be.

Third, we find, for example, that one volume of hydrogen combines with one volume of chlorine to form two volumes of hydrochloric acid gas; therefore one molecule of hydrogen combines with one molecule of chlorine to form two molecules of hydrochloric acid. This acid contains the smallest proportion of chlorine which enters into combination, as well as the smallest proportion of hydrogen; that is, one molecule of the acid contains an atom of hydrogen and an atom of chlorine. It follows, then, that if one molecule of hydrogen forms, with one molecule of chlorine, two molecules of the acid, the molecule of each element must contain two atoms. Twice the Sp. Gr. of chlorine gas is 71, which is the weight of this molecule containing two atoms. The weight of the single atom is therefore 35.5, and no compound of chlorine is known which does not give this quantity or some multiple of it, when an amount proportional to the molecular weight of the compound is analyzed.

Fourth, the relations of the atoms to heat furnish another means by which the atomic weights may be checked, since it is true that the quantity of heat required to raise the temperature of an atom one degree is the same for all atoms. We believe that 16 grammes of oxygen contain as many atoms as one gramme of hydrogen, since an atom of oxygen is believed to be 16 times as heavy as one of hydrogen. If this belief is correct, it should require the same amount of heat to raise the temperature of a gramme of hydrogen one degree as to raise the temperature of 16 grammes of oxygen one degree, and experiment proves that such is the case.

The Law of Definite Proportions. — Chemical combination always takes place in definite proportions, and such proportions appear whether we regard the weights of the substances concerned or their volumes in the state of gas. In this fact is found one of the strongest proofs of the correctness of the atomic theory, for the fact can only be explained upon the assumptions that combination takes place between atoms and that the atoms have definite weights. Two volumes of hydrogen combine with one volume of oxygen to form two volumes of steam, and the law of Ampère points out the simple numerical relation existing between the number of molecules of each substance and consequently between the number of atoms concerned. If by accident or design any excess of either gas is present, it remains unchanged. Since the atoms have definite weights, combination between them must always take place in a definite proportion by weight. A molecule of water always contains two atoms of hydrogen, and one atom of oxygen and 18 parts by weight of water must therefore always yield two parts by weight of hydrogen and 16 parts by weight of oxygen.

Mixtures and Chemical Compounds.—The facts of the last paragraph enable us to determine whether a substance under examination is a mixture or a chemical compound. The proportions of the different substances which enter into a chemical compound are always fixed and definite, and the compound itself is different from either or any of its components. Heat, moreover, is usually developed when substances combine chemically. Mixtures may take place in all proportions, no heat is developed unless there is some accompanying chemical action. and the properties of the mixture bear some obvious relation to those of its ingredients. Simple mechanical means are usually sufficient to separate a mixture. Gunpowder, for example, is a very perfect mixture of sulphur, nitre, and charcoal. The proportion of each varies with the country and purpose for which the powder is made. The separate particles of each component may be distinguished under the microscope. Mere washing with water will remove the nitre, and the sulphur may be dissolved in bisulphide of carbon, leaving the charcoal by itself. When the powder is exploded. chemical compounds are formed which differ completely in their character from any of the ingredients of powder, and if more charcoal, for example, is present than was needed to form these compounds, the excess will remain as charcoal until it reaches the air.

Chemical Symbols.—In order to represent the constitution of substances as clearly and concisely as possible, chemists have adopted a system of notation in which the initial letter of the

INTRODUCTION

Latin name of the different elementary substances is made to represent one atom of the element. Thus one atom of hydrogen is represented by H, one atom of sulphur, by S; one atom of oxygen, by O. Where several elements would otherwise have the same symbol, an additional letter is added to avoid confusion. C stands for one atom of carbon; Cl, for an atom of chlorine; Na, for an atom of sodium (*natrium*). A table of the elements, giving their symbols and atomic weights, will be found in the Appendix.

When it is wished to represent several atoms of the same kind, the appropriate figure is placed to the right of and below the symbol; thus, H_2 represents two atoms or a molecule of hydrogen; S_6, six atoms of sulphur. The composition of a compound substance is shown by grouping together the symbols of its component atoms with the figures showing the number of each kind of atom: thus, HCl stands for one molecule of hydrochloric acid, and shows that the molecule is composed of an atom of hydrogen and an atom of chlorine; H_2O stands for water or a molecule of water, which contains two atoms of hydrogen and one of oxygen; H_2SO_4 stands for a molecule of sulphuric acid, which is composed of two atoms of hydrogen, one of sulphur, and four of oxygen.

In order to represent several molecules of the same substance it is customary to use a large figure on the line and to the left of the symbols which represent a single molecule; thus, $2\,Na_2CO_3$ stands for two molecules of soda-ash. Parentheses and a small number to the right are sometimes used for the same purpose; thus, $(Na_2CO_3)_2$ but this form is usually limited to cases where the symbols or formulas of several different molecules are grouped together, and the small number outside the parenthesis indicates that everything inside the parenthesis is to be multiplied accordingly.

Since the atoms have definite weights, the symbol which represents the number and kinds of atoms in a molecule also represents the proportion by weight in which each element occurs in the molecule; and since the mass of a compound is made up of similar molecules the symbol also stands for the kinds and proportions of the elementary substances composing the compound substance. For example, in the case of the symbol Na_2CO_3 just given for soda-ash, a reference to the table of atomic weights shows that the atomic weight of sodium, Na, is 23; of carbon, 12;

of oxygen, 16. The proportion by weight in which the different elements occur in the molecule is then —

Sodium, Na	$23 \times 2 = 46$
Carbon, C	$12 \times 1 = 12$
Oxygen, O	$16 \times 3 = 48$
	106

The molecular weight of soda-ash (sodium carbonate) is therefore 106, and in the molecule there are 46 parts by weight of the metal sodium, 12 parts of carbon, and 48 parts of oxygen. Any quantity of sodium carbonate is merely an aggregation of similar molecules, and therefore the proportions by weight which are true of the molecule are also true of any quantity of the compound.

Chemical symbols, furthermore, indicate the proportions in which combination by volume occurs when the substances are in the state of gas; for, bearing the law of Ampère in mind, each molecule represented by the symbols represents a unit volume of the gas.

$$\underset{\text{2 mols of hydrogen}}{2\,H_2} + \underset{\text{1 mol of oxygen}}{O_2} = \underset{\text{2 mols of steam}}{2\,H_2O}$$

or two volumes of hydrogen combine with one volume of oxygen to form two volumes of steam.

The Law of Multiple Proportions. — Among the compounds of chlorine there are four which are known to have the composition represented by the formulas: —

$$HClO,\ HClO_2,\ HClO_3,\ HClO_4$$

These are the only known compounds of chlorine which contain these three elements and no other. Nearly all the elements combine with each other in more than one proportion, but there is always in such cases a simple numerical ratio between the proportions in which the elements occur in the different compounds. If we select the compound containing the least of one of the elements which combines thus in several different proportions, the proportions in the other cases are simple multiples of the proportion present in the one selected. In the case given above there is present in each compound 35.5 parts by weight of chlorine, while the amount of oxygen is, as the compounds are successively considered, 16, 32, 48, 64 parts by weight, and these numbers bear the same ratio as 1, 2, 3, 4. This law of multiple proportions, though first shown by the results of chemical analysis, is an evident consequence of the fact that combination always takes place between atoms.

Chemical Equivalents. — The same quantity of any acid which is needed to neutralize 40 parts by weight of caustic soda will neutralize 28 parts of lime or 20 parts of magnesia, and the same quantity of any of these alkalis which will neutralize 36.5 parts by weight of gaseous hydrochloric acid will neutralize 49 parts of sulphuric acid or 63 parts of nitric acid. Quantities of different substances which are found by experiment to stand in this relation to each other are termed chemical equivalents.

Quantivalence. — A reference to the symbols given below, which of course represent the composition of the compounds as determined by analysis, reveals an important fact: —

HCl	Hydrochloric acid
H_2O	Water
H_3N	Ammonia
H_4C	Marsh gas

We find, that whereas an atom of chlorine, Cl, combines with or fixes one atom of hydrogen, H, an atom of oxygen, O, fixes two, an atom of nitrogen, N, fixes three, and an atom of carbon, C, fixes four of hydrogen. This attractive or atom-fixing power, which varies with the atoms of different elements, is termed the quantivalence of the atom. An atom which either combines with or replaces a single atom of hydrogen is called a univalent atom; one which combines with or replaces two atoms of hydrogen, or another univalent substance, is termed bivalent; if the fixing power extends to three or four atoms of a univalent substance, the atom is trivalent or quadrivalent, as the case may be.

The quantivalence of the atoms is believed to be due to a sort of polarity, the attractive power of each pole being sufficient to hold in the molecule a single univalent atom. These poles or bonds are often represented by short lines radiating from the symbol of the atom, and the symbols given above are then written thus: —

$$H-Cl \quad\quad H-O-H \quad\quad H-\underset{\underset{H}{|}}{\overset{\overset{H}{|}}{N}} \quad\quad H-\underset{\underset{H}{|}}{\overset{\overset{H}{|}}{C}}-H$$

Just as the two poles of a magnet may neutralize or satisfy each other, so, under certain circumstances, two of these atomic poles may satisfy each other, and the same atom may in its different combinations exhibit different atom-fixing powers. Thus we have:

Ammonia
$$H-N\begin{array}{c}H\\|\\|\\H\end{array}$$

Chloride of ammonia
$$\begin{array}{c}H\\H\diagdown\ |\\ N-Cl\\H\diagup\ |\\H\end{array}$$

and the two chlorides of phosphorus: —

$$Cl-P\begin{array}{c}Cl\\|\\|\\Cl\end{array}$$

$$\begin{array}{c}Cl\\Cl\diagdown\ |\\ P-Cl\\Cl\diagup\ |\\Cl\end{array}$$

Manganese and fluorine form four compounds, and the proportions and quantivalence of the atoms in each case are shown in the symbols given below: —

$$F-Mn-F$$

$$F-Mn-F\begin{array}{c}F\\|\\|\\F\end{array}$$

$$\begin{array}{cc}F&F\\|&|\\F-Mn-Mn-F\\|&|\\F&F\end{array}$$

$$\begin{array}{cc}F&F\\\diagdown&\diagup\\F-Mn-F\\\diagup&\diagdown\\F&F\end{array}$$

Since whenever the quantivalence varies, two poles must either neutralize or free each other, the atom-fixing power is either always even or always odd, and a comparison of all the symbols given under this head brings out this fact. Symbols, like those immediately above, are called *Graphic* Symbols, and they are much used to represent, as clearly as may be, the arrangement of the atoms in the molecule.

Nomenclature. — The number of substances known to chemistry is so immense that their study is greatly facilitated by a system of naming them, which not only arranges them in groups, but indicates their composition. The names of all the more recently discovered metals end in *-ium* or *-um*, as sodium, potassium, platinum. The names of various groups of non-metallic elements have distinctive endings, as car*bon*, bor*on*, silic*on*; chlor*ine*, brom*ine*, iod*ine*, fluor*ine*. In many cases, however, both among metals and non-metals, old names persist, as iron, silver, sulphur, phosphorus. Compounds of oxygen and another element are called *oxides*, similar compounds of sulphur are called sulph*ides*, and most of the non-metallic elements form with another element compounds whose names end in *-ide*. Thus chlorine, bromine, iodine, fluorine form chlor*ides*, brom*ides*, iod*ides*, fluor*ides* respectively. The proportion of the non-metallic element present is indicated by the prefixes *di-* (or *bi-*), *tri-*, *tetra-*, *penta-*, as appears in the examples below —

Manganese dioxide	MnO_2
Phosphorous trioxide	P_2O_3
Tin tetrachloride	$SnCl_4$
Phosphorous pentoxide	P_2O_5

The different atom-fixing power of an element is often indicated by the endings *-ous* and *-ic* of its Latin name. Thus iron (*ferrum*) forms ferrous chloride, $FeCl_2$, and ferric chloride, Fe_2Cl_6. Tin (*stannum*) forms stannous chloride, $SnCl_2$, and stannic chloride, $SnCl_4$; and in such names *-ous* indicates the lower degree of atom-fixing power or quantivalence, and *-ic* the higher.

Compounds of the metals with oxygen, or oxides of the metals, are called *Bases*, and the same term is applied to compounds of the metals with oxygen and hydrogen or hydrates of the metals. The bases possess, in a more or less marked degree, those properties which are termed alkaline. They unite with acids to form *Salts*.

Compounds of the non-metallic elements which contain hydrogen which may be replaced by a metal are termed *Acids*. Hydrochloric acid, HCl, for example, contains an atom of hydrogen, which may be replaced by a metal, like sodium, to form, in this case, sodium chloride, NaCl, common salt. Sulphuric acid contains two atoms of hydrogen, which may be thus replaced by two univalent atoms like sodium to form sodium sulphate, Na_2SO_4, or by one bivalent atom like zinc to form zinc sulphate, $ZnSO_4$. An acid is termed monobasic, dibasic, and so on, according as it contains one, two, or more hydrogen atoms which may be thus replaced. Whether the hydrogen atoms can be replaced by a metal depends on their position in the molecule. Acetic acid, $C_2H_4O_2$, is a monobasic acid; while oxalic acid, $C_2H_2O_4$, is a bibasic acid. This difference is shown in the graphic symbols of these compounds: —

$$\text{Acetic acid} \qquad\qquad \text{Oxalic acid}$$

$$H-O-\overset{\overset{O}{\|}}{\underset{\underset{H}{|}}{C}}-\overset{\overset{H}{|}}{C}-H \qquad H-O-\overset{\overset{O}{\|}}{C}-\overset{\overset{O}{\|}}{C}-O-H$$

It will be noticed that three of the hydrogen atoms in acetic acid are shown in a different relation to the carbon atoms than that occupied by the other one, and we find by experiment that these three atoms can be replaced by a non-metallic element like chlorine, but not by a metal. The graphic symbol is deduced from the results of such experiments. In the molecule of oxalic acid, however, both hydrogen atoms occupy the same position relative to the molecule that the atom of hydrogen which can be replaced by a metal occupies in acetic acid. Both of these atoms can be replaced by a metal, but not by a non-metal like chlorine.

This illustrates again the general truth that the properties of a substance depend quite as much upon the arrangement of the atoms in the molecule as upon the number and kind of the atoms themselves.

Compounds which contain no hydrogen, but which unite with the elements of water to form bases or acids, are called *Anhydrides*, the word meaning, without water. Sulphuric anhydride, SO_3, for instance, is a snow-like solid which combines with water, H_2O, to form sulphuric acid, H_2SO_4.

When the same elements combine in different proportions and form more than one acid, the suffix *-ous* is used to indicate the lower stage of oxidation, and *-ic* to indicate the higher. We have chlor*ous* acid, $HClO_2$, which forms chlor*ites*, and chlor*ic* acid, $HClO_3$, which forms chlor*ates*. In case there are other acids the prefixes *hypo-* and *per-* are added, the first to indicate the lowest and the last the highest stage of oxidation. Thus we have *hypo*chlorous acid, $HClO$, which forms hypochlorites, and *per*chloric acid, $HClO_4$, which forms perchlorates.

Reactions and Equations. — The changes which occur when two or more substances react upon each other chemically, or when one is decomposed by heat or otherwise, may be represented by chemical symbols arranged in the form of equations. Caustic soda and hydrochloric acid combine to form sodium chloride and water, and the reaction may be written —

Caustic soda + Hydrochloric acid = Sodium chloride + Water
$$NaOH + HCl = NaCl + H_2O$$

Upon examining this equation, and any properly written one, we find that the sum of the atomic weights of the factors on one side is the same as the sum of the atomic weights of the products on the other. The same number of atoms of each kind also must appear on each side of the equation.

It must be borne in mind that these equations are not arbitrary formulas which the atoms are expected to follow, but that they are written to express what, so far as we know, actually does occur; and such an equation, to be useful, must take into account the known relations and chemical properties of all the substances concerned and their components.

When there are several possible reactions, that one, if any, in which a gas is evolved, or an insoluble substance formed, is the one most likely to occur. Solution in a liquid, by overcoming the cohesion of the molecules and leaving them more free to move within range of each other's influence, promotes chemical change and often determines the course of the reaction. A rise of temperature has the same effect in promoting chemical activity, because it means that the moving power of the molecules is increased. At the instant in which an atom is liberated from one combination, and before it has entered into another, the atom is said to be in the *nascent state;* and since all its affinities are during that instant unsatisfied, its chemical properties are thus intensified. For example, in the reaction of sulphuric acid upon zinc, —

$$Zn + H_2SO_4 = ZnSO_4 + H_2,$$

two atoms of hydrogen are liberated which ordinarily combine at once to form the molecule of hydrogen, H–H; but if another substance is present upon which the just liberated atoms can react before mutually satisfying each other, they are likely to so react much more powerfully than after their union in the molecule H–H.

When an electric current is passed through water the following decomposition occurs:—

$$2 H_2O = 2 H_2 + O_2$$

When limestone, calcium carbonate, $CaCO_3$, is heated, it splits up into caustic lime, CaO, and free carbonic acid gas, thus:—

$$CaCO_3 = CaO + CO_2$$

Such reactions, in which a substance is separated into two or more simpler ones, is called an *Analytical Reaction*, and analytical processes are those which seek to separate a substance into its constituents, or to otherwise determine what its constituents are. Synthetical processes are those by means of which a substance is transformed into another more complex one by the addition of new atoms in the molecule. The following are examples of *synthetical reactions*:—

$$S_2 + 2 O_2 = 2 SO_2,$$
$$H_2 + Cl_2 = 2 HCl$$

There is another very common form of reaction in which certain of the atoms merely exchange places in different molecules. For example, in the manufacture of Pearl Hardening—

Calcium chloride + Sodium sulphate = Sodium chloride (2 mols) + Calcium sulphate, Pearl hardening

$$CaCl_2 + Na_2SO_4 = 2 NaCl + CaSO_4$$

Stochiometry.— When the chemical symbols and reactions are understood, ordinary chemical calculations require only the application of the simplest rules of arithmetic, and can usually be solved by the rule of proportion. The following rules will be found useful. The relations upon which they depend have been already discussed in the preceding sections.

1. *The molecular weight is equal to the sum of the weights of the atoms composing the molecule.*

2. *The percentage of any constituent in the molecule is found by multiplying the weight of the constituent by 100 and dividing by the weight of the molecule*, or,

$$\text{Wt. of constituent} : \text{Wt. of Mol} = x : 100$$

3. *The proportion of any ingredient in a mass of a compound is the same as the proportion of the ingredient in a molecule of the compound.*

4. *In any chemical reaction the total weight of the products is equal to the sum of the weights of the substances first concerned.*

5. If any chemical operation is expressed in the form of an equation, and the molecular weights of all the substances concerned are then written below their respective formulas, the following rule will be found sufficient for most problems:—

As the molecular weight of the substance given is to the molecular weight of the substance required, so is the weight (in pounds, grammes, etc.) of the substance given to the weight of the substance required.

In case the equation shows that more than one molecule of a given substance is concerned in it, the molecular weight of that substance should be multiplied accordingly, for the purposes of the above rule.

EXAMPLES

1. What is the molecular weight of common salt?
Symbol of common salt is NaCl.
Ans. Na = 23, Cl = 35.5, NaCl = 58.5.

2. What is the molecular weight of caustic soda, NaOH? *Ans.* 40

3. What is the molecular weight of sulphuric acid, H_2SO_4? *Ans.* 98

4. What is the molecular weight of carbonate of soda, soda-ash, Na_2CO_3? *Ans.* 106

5. What is the molecular weight of bisulphite of lime, $H_2CaS_2O_6$?
Ans. 202

6. How much chlorine is contained in 1170 lbs of common salt?
Since NaCl = 58.5, every 58.5 lbs of salt contain 35.5 lbs. of chlorine
Ans. 710 lbs

7. What per cent of sulphur is there in sulphurous acid gas, SO_2?

$$S = 32, \quad O = 16, \quad SO_2 = 32 + 16 + 16 = 64$$
$$\text{Wt. of S } 32 \text{ : wt. of } SO_2 \ 64 = x : 100.$$
$$\frac{32 \times 100}{64} = x.$$
Ans. 50%

8. What is the per cent of alumina, Al_2O_3, in pure crystallized potash alum, $K_2Al_2S_4O_{16}, 24\ H_2O$?

$Al_2\ 27.4 \times 2 = 54.8$
$O_3\ 16\ \times 3 = 48$
Mol wt., $Al_2O_3 = 102.8$

$K_2\ 39.1 \times 2 = 78.2$
$Al_2\ 27.4 \times 2 = 54.8$
$S_4\ 32\ \times 4 = 128.0$
$O_{16}\ 16\ \times 16 = 256.0$
$\overline{517.0}$
$24\ H_2O\ (2+16) \times 24 = 432.0$
Mol wt potash alum $= 949.0$

$\dfrac{102.8 \times 100}{949} = \%\ Al_2O_3$

Ans. 10.94%

9. How much water, H_2O, is there in 2000 lbs of crystallized potash alum?

Ex. 8 shows that $24\ H_2O = 432$, while the molecular weight of potash alum is 949.

$432 : 949 = x : 2000$ .... Ans. 910.4 lbs

10. How many pounds of sulphurous acid gas will be formed by the combustion of 420 lbs of sulphur, supposing the loss of sulphur as ash, and by sublimation, to amount to 10 per cent?

420 lbs less 10% = 378 lbs available.
$S\ 32 : SO_2\ 64 = 378 : x$ .... Ans. 756 lbs

11. The formula of Pearl Hardening, or crystallized sulphate of lime, as it occurs in paper, is $CaSO_4, 2\ H_2O$. In burning the paper to determine the amount of filler, this combined water ($2\ H_2O$), which really adds so much to the weight of the paper, is driven off, so that the formula of the ash as weighed is $CaSO_4$. What correction should be applied to the per cent of ash found in order that it may show the amount of Pearl Hardening really in the paper?

Mol wt., $CaSO_4, 2\ H_2O = 136 + 36 = 172$,
$CaSO_4 = 136$

136 parts of ash, $CaSO_4 = 172$ parts of filler, $CaSO_4, 2\ H_2O$

$\dfrac{172}{136} = 1.26$, therefore every 1% of ash = 1.26% of filler,

and per cent of ash should be multiplied by 1.26 in order to obtain per cent of filler in paper.

12. How many pounds of pure sulphuric acid, H_2SO_4, are needed to dissolve 100 lbs of zinc, the reaction being —

$Zn + H_2SO_4 = ZnSO_4 + H_2$?
65   98

The proportion, then, is $65 : 98 = 100 : x$ .... Ans. 151 lbs

INTRODUCTION 21

13. If in burning 420 lbs of sulphur to make sulphite liquor 10 per cent of the sulphur is converted into sulphuric acid, how much lime will this neutralize in forming the useless sulphate of lime? The reaction may be considered for the purposes of the problem —

$$CaO + H_2SO_4 = CaSO_4 + H_2O.$$
$$56 \quad\quad 98$$

Ans 73.5 lbs

14. The formula of soda-ash is Na_2CO_3, of soda crystals, Na_2CO_3, $10\ H_2O$. One molecule of each combines with the same amount of rosin. If 40 lbs. of Na_2CO_3 are required to make a certain quantity of size, how much Na_2CO_3, $10\ H_2O$ will be needed to make the same amount? *Ans* 108 lbs

15. Lime, CaO, in contact with water slakes to form calcium hydrate, CaH_2O_2. How much lime would be required to causticize 2000 lbs of soda-ash, Na_2CO_3, according to the reaction —

$$Na_2CO_3 + CaH_2O_2 = CaCO_3 + 2\ NaOH?$$

Ans 1056.6 lbs

16. 560 kilos of lime are required to make a certain quantity of sulphite liquor. How many kilos of limestone, carbonate of lime, $CaCO_3$, will be required to make the same amount of liquor? One molecule of lime will make as much liquor as one molecule of limestone. *Ans* 1000 kilos

PART I.
GENERAL CHEMISTRY.

Part I.

GENERAL CHEMISTRY.

THE NON-METALLIC ELEMENTS.

OXYGEN.

Symbol, O — Atomic weight, 16 — Molecule, O_2 — Molecular weight, 32

OXYGEN is by far the most important of all the elementary chemical substances, as well as the most abundant, both in the free state and in combination with other substances.

Free oxygen is a colorless, tasteless, and odorless gas. It forms in the free state about one-fifth by measure and about one-quarter by weight of dry air. In combination with hydrogen as water it constitutes eight-ninths of the weight of the latter substance, and in combination with various substances it has been estimated to constitute about one-eighth of the total weight of the entire globe. In the free or gaseous state oxygen is necessary to respiration, the germination of seeds, the growth of plants, the decay of vegetable substances, and the commencement of putrefaction in animal matters. It is also necessary for the support of combustion, though it is itself uninflammable. Oxygen is the most magnetic of all gases; the daily variations of the magnetic needle are probably caused by the effect of heat in changing the magnetic properties of the gas. Oxygen is only slightly soluble in water, 100 volumes of water dissolving 2.99 volumes at 15° C. and 4.11 volumes at 0° C. under the ordinary pressure of the atmosphere.

The weight of oxygen, as compared with an equal volume of dry hydrogen, or its specific gravity, is 15.96. Pure oxygen may be prepared by heating many of its compounds — as manganese dioxide, MnO_2, or potassium chlorate, $KClO_3$ — in a closed vessel to a temperature sufficiently high to decompose the compound, when oxygen will be given off and may be collected by suitable means. It may also be obtained through the decomposition of water by means of the electric current. When a clear solution of bleaching-powder, to which have been added a few drops of a solution of any cobalt salt, is heated to about 80° C., oxygen is easily and regularly evolved in considerable quantity. If the solution is milky, or if a paste made with bleaching-powder and water is used with the cobalt solution, it is necessary to add a little paraffin oil to prevent frothing. Oxygen was first prepared by Priestley in 1774 by heating mercuric oxide, HgO.

The process of union, or of combination of oxygen directly with another substance, is called combustion or oxidation; and the products of such combustion are called *Oxides*. The weight of the products of combustion is always equal to that of the substance burned plus the weight of the oxygen consumed (combined or fixed) in the process. Combustion may be either dry, as in the burning of coal in a grate, or moist, as in the combustion (destruction) of coloring-matters in the process of bleaching. In the latter case the oxygen of the bleaching-powder, $Ca(ClO)_2$, combines with the coloring-matters to form eventually dioxide of carbon or carbonic acid, CO_2, and water. Combustion, whether moist or dry, is always attended with sensible increase of temperature, varying directly with the rapidity of the chemical combination. Conversely, sensible increase of temperature always increases the rapidity of combustion. This explains the phenomenon of spontaneous combustion. This only takes place with easily combustible substances and those which by their physical conditions expose a large surface to the action of the oxygen of the air, as, for instance, oily waste or fur. When a mass of waste saturated with an easily combustible oil is thrown carelessly in a warm place where it is exposed to the air, combination of the oxygen with the oil at once begins and heat is developed. This in turn increases the rapidity of the combination, which generates more heat, until after a time the mass becomes hot enough to smoulder and then burst into flame. If, however, the supply of oxygen is limited, as is the case when the waste is enclosed in a tight case, the combustion will be limited to the consumption of the oxygen within the case, and the heat can never rise to the inflaming-point. Spontaneous combustion can never occur in such materials loosely exposed or spread out to the air, since in that case the currents of air and large radiating surface exposed keep the temperature always below the inflaming-point by carrying off the heat as fast as it is generated. Mineral oils have no tendency to spontaneous combustion, and when present in a mixed oil greatly lessen the danger from this source. When the proportion of mineral oil reaches 30 per cent. there is no danger.

When sparks from an electric machine are passed through ordinary oxygen. three volumes of the gas are condensed into two, the gas at the same time acquires a peculiar odor, and has its characteristic chemical properties intensified in a marked degree. The same change may be brought about in several other ways. This condensed oxygen is called allotropic oxygen or *ozone* When heated to 290° C. it is instantly converted into ordinary oxygen. Ozone is produced in nature by the action of the air on gums and resins, but is instantly decomposed by contact with putrescent matters. The gradual deterioration of rosin-sized paper is believed to be due in part to the effect of ozone, formed by the action of the air upon the rosin size. Ozone may often be detected in minute quantities in the air of the country, and especially in the vicinity of pine forests, but is almost never present in the air of thickly settled towns.

It is a very energetic bleaching agent, and many attempts have been made to produce it on a manufacturing scale for that purpose, but none have met with commercial success.

HYDROGEN

Symbol, H — Atomic weight, 1. — Molecule, H_2 — Molecular weight, 2

Hydrogen is a colorless, tasteless, and odorless gas. As usually prepared, however, it always contains slight traces of other substances which impart to it various odors more or less disagreeable, and characteristic of the different impurities. It is the lightest of all known substances, and on that account the weight of the hydrogen atom is taken as the unit or standard of atomic weights. A given volume of the gas weighs only 0.0691 as much as an equal volume of air. Hydrogen is inflammable when heated in air. combining with the oxygen to produce hydrogen oxide. H_2O, water. The hydrogen flame produces very little light, being of a faint bluish color, but a very intense heat.

By leading hydrogen and oxygen gases. under pressure, through separate tubes and allowing them to mix in the proper proportions at the point of ignition, a heat may be produced second only to that of the electric arc. This flame, known as the oxyhydrogen flame, and the instrument for its production as the oxyhydrogen blowpipe, is made use of in the production of the calcium light, which was the most powerful light known previous to the invention of the electric light. In the production of the calcium light the flame from the oxyhydrogen blowpipe is directed upon a cylinder of compressed lime, raising the latter to such an intense heat that it emits a dazzling white light.

The oxyhydrogen blowpipe, or more often one in which air is used in place of oxygen, is also invaluable to the plumber, who employs it in fusing together two pieces of lead into a single piece, the operation being technically called lead-burning.

Hydrogen when mixed with air or oxygen in any quantity, as in a flask or bottle, forms a mixture which will explode with terrific force when fire is brought into contact with it. For this reason one should always be sure, when using the gas that it is coming from the generator pure, or unmixed with air, before applying a light to the stream of gas.

Hydrogen is but slightly soluble in water. Iron, at a red heat, is penetrated by hydrogen. The gas is not poisonous, and may be breathed, when pure, for a short time, without ill effects. It has a curious action, however, on the organs of speech, raising the pitch of the voice very noticeably after a few inspirations.

Hydrogen occurs chiefly in combination with oxygen as water; it also occurs in the larger number of organic bodies with oxygen and carbon, and sometimes nitrogen; and with carbon alone in the mineral oils. It forms the chief element, as shown by the spectroscope, in the atmosphere of many of the stars.

Hydrogen may be obtained by the electrolysis of water, or by passing steam over red-hot iron, the oxygen of the water uniting with the iron to make oxide of iron, and leaving the hydrogen free.

Certain metals, notably sodium and potassium, have the power of decomposing water at ordinary temperatures, with the formation of an oxide of the metal and free hydrogen. The easiest as well as least expensive method of preparing hydrogen in quantity is by the action of a metal, preferably zinc, on muriatic or sulphuric acid diluted with water. In this case the metal takes the place of hydrogen in the acid, forming chloride or sulphate of the metal, and free H_2, as shown in the equation —

$$H_2SO_4 + Zn = ZnSO_4 + H_2$$

This latter is the method used by plumbers in preparing hydrogen for use in lead-burning.

The most common, as well as the most important, compound of hydrogen is water, hydrogen oxide, H_2O.

Water is a clear transparent liquid, colorless in small quantities, but of a blue tint in large masses.

At $0°$ C. ($32°$ F.) it crystallizes or freezes. At $100°$ C. ($212°$ F.), and 760 millimetres (30 inches) barometric pressure, it is changed into an invisible colorless gas called steam, having the same elasticity as the air. Increased pressure raises the boiling-point as does also the presence of solids in solution. Water has its maximum density at $4°$ C. ($39\frac{1}{5}°$ F.), at which temperature one cubic foot weighs 997 ounces avoirdupois and one American gallon $8\frac{1}{3}$ lbs. One volume of water will produce 1320 volumes of steam at $100°$ C. and 760 millimetres barometric pressure. Water is the most universal solvent known, nearly all substances being dissolved by it in greater or less degree.

Hydrogen also forms one other compound with oxygen which deserves brief mention; namely, hydrogen peroxide, H_2O_2. This is a liquid heavier than water, and was discovered by Thenard in 1818. It begins to give off oxygen at $20°$ C., and at $100°$ C. is at once converted into water, giving off one-half the oxygen it contains. Half its oxygen appears to be very loosely held in the molecule, and is consequently very ready to unite with other oxidizable substances. On this account it has been proposed as a bleaching agent, and used as such with considerable success, but on account of the difficulty and expense attending its preparation on a large scale it has never come into extended use.

It is somewhat employed for restoring old engravings.

NITROGEN

Symbol, N — Atomic weight, 14 — Molecule N_2 — Molecular weight, 28

Nitrogen, discovered in 1772 by Rutherford, is a gas without color, taste, or odor. It is lighter than air, its specific gravity being 0.972 compared to air, or 14 compared to hydrogen. Dry atmospheric air is a *mixture* of nitrogen with oxygen in the proportion of about four-fifths nitrogen and one-fifth oxygen by volume. Nitrogen is distinguished more for its negative than its positive qualities. It combines directly with but few of the elements, and, in these cases even, its combination is effected with considerable difficulty. Nitrogen is uninflammable. It is neither combustible in the air, like hydrogen, nor is it a supporter of combustion, like oxygen.

Nitrogen may be easily obtained by passing air over red-hot copper, the oxygen of the air combining with the copper to form copper oxide, CuO, leaving the nitrogen practically pure. Only two compounds of nitrogen are of sufficient importance to be mentioned here, — ammonia and nitric acid. The former, nitrogen hydride or ammonia, NH_3, is a colorless gas of strong pungent odor and totally irrespirable. It is very soluble in water and alcohol, water at 15° C. dissolving 727 times its own volume of the gas, forming the ammonia water ("stronger ammonia") of commerce. A pressure of $6\frac{1}{2}$ atmospheres condenses the gas at the ordinary temperature to a colorless liquid, which, when it is allowed to evaporate by the removal of the pressure, produces intense cold. This property of anhydrous liquid ammonia is taken advantage of in machines for producing ice.

Ammonia is obtained in the incomplete combustion of organic substances containing nitrogen and hydrogen. It is obtained commercially as a by-product in the manufacture of bone charcoal and illuminating gas. Ammonia is a strong alkali, and as such receives many useful applications in the arts.

Oxides of Nitrogen.

Nitrogen forms five different compounds with oxygen, —

$$N_2O, \quad N_2O_2, \quad N_2O_3, \quad N_2O_4, \quad \text{and } N_2O_5$$

Only the last-mentioned, nitric anhydride, N_2O_5, is of interest in this connection. Nitric anhydride is a brilliant colorless crystalline solid. When brought into the presence of water, H_2O, it unites with it to form nitric acid, HNO_3, according to the equation —

$$N_2O_5 + H_2O = 2\,HNO_3$$

Nitric acid, sometimes called "aqua fortis," is a fuming corrosive liquid heavier than water. It boils at 85° C. and freezes at −40° C. It stains the skin yellow and rapidly destroys its substance. It unites with alkalis and metallic bases to form, for the most part, crystalline solids soluble in water, called nitrates. Potassium nitrate, KNO_3, is "saltpetre," and sodium nitrate, $NaNO_3$, is "Chili saltpetre." The latter is brought from Chili in large quantities, and forms the chief source of nitric acid. The acid is obtained from the nitrate by distilling the latter with sulphuric acid. Nitric acid acts energetically upon most of the metals, dissolving them to form nitrates. It transforms glycerine into nitro-glycerine and cellulose into guncotton. Gold and platinum are not affected by pure nitric acid, and iron is only attacked by the dilute acid, the strong acid so affecting the surface of iron as to render it what is called passive, and while in this state it entirely resists the action of the weaker acid.

CARBON

Symbol, C — Atomic Weight, 12

Pure carbon occurs in nature as the diamond. In this form it is usually colorless, of very high refractive power and great brilliancy when cut or polished. The diamond is the hardest of all known substances; it does not conduct electricity and is incombustible at the highest heat attainable by the blowpipe. Heated in the voltaic arc, it swells up, takes the appearance of coke, becomes a conductor of electricity, and is slowly consumed.

Graphite or plumbago is, so far as chemists have been able to determine, another natural form of pure carbon. Graphite occurs either massive or crystallized in six-sided plates, which have a metallic lustre. It is friable and almost greasy to the touch and leaves a black mark on paper — the mark of a common lead-pencil — although its ultimate particles are very hard. It is an excellent conductor of electricity. Graphite is frequently employed in conjunction with grease as a lubricator for machinery. Lignite, stone coal, and coke are all more or less pure varieties of carbon.

Lampblack is an artificial variety of nearly pure carbon.

Compounds of Carbon.

Carbon unites with hydrogen to form a long series of compounds — gaseous, liquid, and solid — called hydrocarbons, interesting examples of which are the gases, naphthas, and oils obtained from petroleum. These are all hydrocarbons, varying chemically only by the different numbers of carbon and hydrogen atoms which go to form the molecule in each.

Carbon and Oxygen

Carbon unites with oxygen in two different proportions, forming carbon monoxide, CO, and carbonic anhydride or carbonic acid gas, CO_2. The first product of combustion is always carbonic anhydride, but when this subsequently passes over red-hot coals it gives up a portion of its oxygen and is reduced to the monoxide. Carbon monoxide is a colorless, odorless gas about as heavy as air. It is very poisonous when inhaled, and burns in the air with a blue flame, forming carbonic anhydride. The same product is formed when the monoxide comes in contact with metallic oxides, which give up their oxygen with production of the metal. The monoxide thus plays an important part in the operation of the blast furnaces used for smelting iron ore. When steam is passed over red-hot coals, carbon monoxide and hydrogen are formed. Together they constitute almost the entire portion of the so-called water-gas.

Carbonic acid gas is also a colorless gas, one and a half times heavier than air. It has a faintly acid taste and odor. It sometimes collects in mines, where it is called choke-damp. It is formed during the fermentation of liquids, and by its escape causes the effervescence noticed in such liquids. It is always present in small amount in the air, and cannot properly be called a poison, although it becomes injurious if breathed in excessive amount. Plants absorb it, retaining the carbon, which enters into their structure, and breathing out oxygen when in the sunlight. Animals reverse the process, absorbing oxygen and eliminating carbonic acid gas.

Carbonic anhydride is uninflammable and does not support combustion, since it is already fully burned. Water at 15° C., and at the ordinary pressure, dissolves its own volume of the gas, and an additional volume for each 15 lbs. increase of pressure. Water so charged forms the ordinary soda-water. By a pressure of $38\frac{1}{2}$ atmospheres ($38\frac{1}{2} \times 15$ lbs.) at 0° C., the gas may be condensed to a colorless liquid, lighter than water, and may then be frozen, by its own evaporation, to a snow-like solid. Carbon dioxide, as it is also called, is a product of the wet or dry combustion of all bodies containing carbon. It is evolved in large quantities from the kilns in which limestone is burned, and from the top of the limestone towers used in making sulphite liquor.

In presence of water carbonic anhydride forms the true carbonic acid, which unites with bases to form carbonates. Almost all the carbonates, except those of potassium, sodium, and ammonium, are nearly or quite insoluble in water, although rather soluble in water containing carbonic acid. Marble is nearly pure carbonate of calcium. All carbonates give off their carbonic acid with effervescence, on the addition of one of the stronger acids.

Combustion. — All combustion, in the ordinary sense of the word, as already noted under **Oxygen**, is a process of combination with oxygen. In the pure gas such combination, once started, proceeds with uncontrollable energy until the combustible body is consumed, but in ordinary cases the supply of oxygen is drawn from the atmosphere, where one-quarter by weight of oxygen is diluted with three-quarters of inert nitrogen. The following reactions serve to illustrate the more typical cases of combustion, and indicate the resulting products: —

Combustion of hydrogen		$2 H_2 + O_2 = 2 H_2O$
"	of carbon (charcoal)	$C + O_2 = CO_2$
"	of marsh gas	$CH_4 + 2 O_2 = CO_2 + 2 H_2O$
"	of alcohol	$C_2H_5OH + 3 O_2 = 2 CO_2 + 3 H_2O$
"	of sulphur	$S_2 + 2 O_2 = 2 SO_2$
"	of phosphorus	$P_4 + 5 O_2 = 2 P_2O_5$

The ordinary combustibles, like coal, wood, petroleum, and illuminating gas, are compounds of carbon and hydrogen, and form by their burning carbonic acid gas and water. The light and heat developed during combustion are due to the rushing together of the atoms under the attractive force of chemical affinity. The amount of heat developed varies greatly with different combustibles, and depends upon the kind of atoms composing their molecules, and the extent to which the affinities of these atoms are already satisfied. The number of heat units developed by the combustion of one kilogramme of several different substances is given on the following page: —

Hydrogen	34462
Alcohol	7184
Sulphur	2221
Charcoal	8080
Dry wood	3654
Soft coal	7500
Gas coke	8047

If a flame like that of an ordinary candle is inspected closely, the existence of three distinct zones, as shown in Figure 1, may be detected. The innermost, dark zone, consists of gas formed by heat from the melted wax drawn up by the capillary action of the wick. The two outer zones shut off the inner one from the oxygen of the air, and there is consequently no combustion within this zone. The middle zone is the one from which most of the light is derived. There is here not sufficient air for complete combustion, and the minute particles of carbon are rendered incandescent by the heat. The flame at this point is a *reducing* one, because the white-hot carbon and partially burned gases possess so strong an affinity for oxygen that many metallic oxides give up their oxygen and are reduced to the metal if this portion of the flame is brought to bear upon them. The carbon and gases are completely burned to CO_2 and H_2O in the outer zone, in which, of course, an excess of oxygen is present; and the action of the flame at this point is an *oxidizing* one, since conditions are favorable for the oxidation of a metal brought within it.

Fig 1

Carbon unites with both oxygen and hydrogen to form a large class of organic substances called carbohydrates, of which sugar, $C_{12}H_{22}O_{11}$, starch, and cellulose $(CH_{10}O_5)_n$, are notable examples. Many of these substances, as, for instance, starch and cellulose, have the same number of the elementary atoms in the molecule, so that their percentage composition, or the proportion of C, H, and O, is the same in each. In these cases the different character of the substances is supposed to be due to a different arrangement of the several atoms in the individual molecule.

Many of the carbohydrates are valuable food substances, being burned in the system by means of the oxygen inhaled, and furnishing fuel, so to speak, for the fires of life. Any superabundance above what may be required for keeping up the animal heat and energy is either voided unchanged or is transformed into fat and stored as such in the body, according to the vigor of the individual system. The number of the various compounds in the organic world into which carbon enters is almost infinite, and the study of the carbon compounds, or organic chemistry, forms a science in itself.

Probably no other element, if we except oxygen, takes part in the formation of such a variety of compounds of the highest use to man as carbon.

Carbon and Nitrogen.

When air is passed over potassium carbonate mixed with charcoal, and contained in a red-hot tube, the nitrogen of the air unites with carbon to produce a colorless and extremely poisonous gas called cyanogen, C_2N_2, which has the odor of peach blossoms or bitter almonds. Cyanogen is 1.8 times as heavy as air. It is easily condensed by cold and pressure into a colorless liquid. Water dissolves four times its volume of the gas. When heated in the air cyanogen burns with a beautiful pink flame, producing carbon dioxide and free nitrogen. Cyanogen unites directly with hydrogen to form cyanhydric or "Prussic" acid, CNH, a colorless transparent liquid most intensely poisonous. When inhaled, even in very minute quantities, it produces headache, giddiness, etc. The hydrogen in prussic acid may be replaced by metals to form cyanides. Cyanogen, under certain conditions, may be made to unite with iron and potassium to form ferrocyanide and ferricyanide of potassium.

The ferricyanide of potassium is red, and is commonly known as red prussiate of potash. Its solutions, when mixed with those of ferrous salts (see Iron) yield a blue precipitate. Ferrocyanide of potassium, or yellow prussiate of potash, occurs in beautiful yellow crystals. It gives a white precipitate with ferrous salts, which turns blue on exposure to the air. With ferric salts which contain more oxygen, the precipitate is the ordinary Prussian blue.

SULPHUR.

Symbol, S — Atomic weight, 32 — Molecule, S_2 — Molecular weight, 64

Sulphur is a pale-yellow, brittle solid of specific gravity 2.045. It occurs native in Sicily, and on the shores of the Mediterranean

Sea, in Japan, and in Utah, and some other parts of the western portions of the United States. The principal commercial source of sulphur is Sicily, though considerable quantities reach the Pacific coast from Japan, and an occasional cargo of Japanese sulphur may be found in New York. The deposits in our own country, although very extensive and of high-grade ore, remain at present in an undeveloped condition. In Sicily the sulphur is found mixed with earth, and to prepare it for export large heaps of the sulphur-bearing earth are formed around a central opening and covered with turf, air channels being left near the bottom of the heaps. Some brushwood is laid at the bottom in building the heap. When the mound is finished the brushwood is fired, and the heat from this melts a portion of the sulphur, which runs toward the central hole, and there accumulates, to be drawn off from time to time into pans, where it is allowed to cool. Only a small quantity of wood is used to start the heap, since as soon as the sulphur begins to melt a portion of it is ignited and serves to heat the pile. The amount of air admitted through the air channels is carefully regulated so as only to allow enough sulphur to be burned to keep up the very moderate heat required.

In England considerable quantities of sulphur are now being recovered by the Chance process, in an almost chemically pure state, as a by-product in the Leblanc process of soda manufacture. Chance treats the waste sulphide of calcium with carbonic acid to expel the sulphur as sulphuretted hydrogen, H_2S. By carefully regulating the supply of air this is then burned in accordance with the reaction —

$$H_2S + O = H_2O + S$$

into watery vapor and sulphur.

Sulphur melts at 114° C. (238° F.) to a thin, amber-colored fluid. On further heating, the liquid thickens and turns dark, until at about 240° C. it is very nearly black, and so thick and tenacious that the vessel containing it may be inverted without the sulphur running out. At a still higher temperature it again forms a thin liquid, and at 446° C boils and gives off vapors or sublimes. This sulphur vapor, when condensed or sublimed, forms a fine crystalline powder, known in pharmacy as "Flower" or Flowers of Sulphur.

Native sulphur is found crystallized in the form of octahedrons, and when crystallized from solution in carbon disulphide, sulphur always takes this form. When, however, sulphur is melted and allowed to cool, it crystallizes in the form of oblique prisms, having a specific gravity of 1.98.

A third modification of sulphur appears when that substance, at a temperature of about 250° C., or in the second liquid stage is poured slowly into water. It then appears as an elastic ductile solid, soft and resembling in a marked degree crude caoutchouc or rubber. On exposure to the air, however, this modified sulphur soon loses its amorphous form, and returns to the ordinary prismatic variety.

Sulphur is insoluble in water, and only very slightly soluble in alcohol. It is somewhat more soluble in ether and the essential oils generally, and in petroleum naphtha. It is abundantly soluble in carbon disulphide, CS_2; in sulphur dichloride, S_2Cl_2, benzene, coal-tar naphtha C_6H_6; and in boiling turpentine spirit, $C_{10}H_{16}$.

Sulphur burns readily in the air, with a beautiful blue flame, producing sulphur dioxide, SO_2, sulphurous acid gas.

Four qualities of sulphur are recognized by the trade. "Firsts" consist of large, shining pieces of amber color; "seconds" are not so shining, but are still purely yellow; "thirds" are of a dirtier color, often inclining to red or brown, and both these latter qualities contain much powder. "Recovered" sulphur, so called from its method of preparation from alkali waste, is equal in color to firsts and contains only a trace of impurity. Unlike the other grades, which are shipped in bulk, recovered sulphur is usually shipped in bags. The total ash of commercial Sicily sulphur is rarely over 2 per cent., and often only 0.5 per cent.

Compounds of Sulphur.

SULPHIDES

Sulphur unites directly with most of the metals, when heated with them, to form sulphides. Copper, for example, when heated to redness in vapor of sulphur, unites with the latter to form copper sulphide, CuS. Many of the sulphides of the metals are found in nature, and sometimes, as in the case of lead sulphide, galena, PbS, and mercury sulphide, cinnabar, HgS, form the most valuable ores of the metals. Iron pyrites, FeS_2, and copper pyrites, $FeCuS_2$, are valuable minerals, both for the sulphur they contain and also for their metal. Both minerals occur as golden-yellow masses, or crystalline grains, so often mistaken for gold that they have received the name of "Fool's gold." By roasting iron pyrites and many other native sulphides, with free access of air, all the sulphur may be burned out of the mineral, going off as sulphurous acid gas, SO_2, which may be utilized for various purposes, as the making of "sulphite liquors" for the manufacture of sulphite pulp, etc. Iron pyrites, often containing more or less copper, is the sulphide usually chosen for this purpose on account of its larger content of sulphur than many others, and of the ease and completeness with which the sulphur may be burned out in a properly constructed furnace.

Most of the native sulphides are insoluble in dilute acids. When, however, artificially prepared sulphides, as sulphide of iron, FeS, are treated with dilute hydrochloric or sulphuric acid, HCl, or H_2SO_4, the metal is dissolved to form a metallic chloride or sulphate, while the sulphur of the sulphide and the hydrogen of the acid are simultaneously freed from the former combinations, and unite to form hydrogen sulphide, sulphuretted hydrogen, H_2S. Sulphur and hydrogen combine directly only when both are in what is called the nascent condition; that is, at the instant of their liberation from some previous combination.

Nearly all the sulphur which abroad enters into the manufacture of sulphuric acid is derived from iron pyrites, containing more or less copper, and usually a small amount of arsenic. Pyrites furnish the cheapest source of sulphur, but require for their burning a much more elaborate and expensive plant than the element itself, and a considerable quantity of fine brown dust is carried along with the gas. For these reasons sulphur has usually been preferred by sulphite mills, although in a few instances pyrites have been introduced. The content of sulphur in the different ores varies from 27 to about 50 per cent., good ores usually carrying about 45 per cent.

Hydrogen Sulphide, H_2S, is a colorless gas of an extremely offensive odor. It possesses narcotic properties. It is somewhat heavier than air. Water dissolves, at the ordinary temperature, a little more than three times its volume of the gas. By a pressure of 17 atmospheres H_2S may be condensed to a liquid. It is usually formed in the decay or putrefaction of organic substances which contain sulphur either in their own composition or that of a compound of sulphur mixed with them. This fact explains the fetid odor sometimes noticed in sulphite pulp, or soda pulp, which has been allowed to remain in the drainers or other unventilated place for some time before it is properly washed. In both cases the liquors left in the pulp contain compounds of sulphur, and the commencing decay of organic substances in the pulp, or of the pulp itself, begets a change in the sulphur compound, which results in the production of H$_2$S. The darkened color of such ill-smelling pulp may be accounted for in two ways, either by the presence in the solution of traces of metals which would be transformed into black sulphides by the H$_2$S formed, or the presence of organic matters in the pulp, other than cellulose, may determine the decomposition of a portion of the H$_2$S formed with the production of a dark color by the precipitation of free sulphur. Pure cellulose is not darkened by H$_2$S, but if left in contact with H$_2$S, in the presence of air, for any considerable time, sulphur is precipitated in it by the decomposition of the H$_2$S, and it takes on a more or less dark color.

Hydrogen sulphide, or sulphuretted hydrogen, burns with a blue flame to form water and sulphurous acid gas. It forms one of the most valuable reagents to the analyst, as by its aid he is able to separate the common metals from all other substances.

Sulphur and Oxygen.

Sulphur unites with oxygen in a great variety of proportions to form oxides of sulphur, or, as they are termed, sulphur anhydrides, which in turn unite with the elements of water to form sulphur acids, or with metallic oxides to form sulphur salts. The following is a list of the various oxides of sulphur, with their corresponding acids:—

$SO + H_2O = H_2SO_2$	Hyposulphurous acid
$SO_2 + H_2O = H_2SO_3$	Sulphurous acid.
$S_2O_2 + H_2O = H_2S_2O_3$	Thiosulphuric acid [1]
$SO_3 + H_2O = H_2SO_4$	Sulphuric acid
$S_2O_4 + H_2O = H_2S_2O_5$	Di-thionic acid
$S_3O_4 + H_2O = H_2S_3O_5$	Tri-thionic acid
$S_4O_4 + H_2O = H_2S_4O_5$	Tetra-thionic acid.
$S_5O_4 + H_2O = H_2S_5O_5$	Penta-thionic acid

[1] Often improperly called hyposulphurous acid.

Only the first four of these are of common occurrence or use in the arts. These we will consider in the natural order of their manufacture from sulphur. When sulphur is burned with free access of air, it combines with oxygen, as we have already said, to form sulphur dioxide, SO_2, called sulphurous anhydride, or **sulphurous acid gas.** This is the starting-point for the manufacture of all the oxygen compounds of sulphur. Either sulphur may be used or pyrites, which gives up its sulphur as SO_2 on heating in air. When the latter is employed as the source of sulphur, a furnace for burning it must be used, in which more or less elaborate mechanical appliances are necessary to facilitate the handling of the ore and the removal of the burned cinder, called "Blue Billy." In the burning of sulphur only the simplest appliances are necessary. A furnace as satisfactory as any for this purpose consists simply of a cast-iron retort, with a flat bottom and arched top, one end being open, and a pipe leading from the crown of the arch near the closed end for the escape of the SO_2 formed. The front, or open end, is fitted with a sliding iron door, which may be raised or lowered to regulate the admission of air. The sulphur is fed in through this door on to the bottom of the retort, and once ignited needs no other fuel to keep it burning. Water is allowed to trickle continuously upon the top of the retort in order to keep the heat below the boiling-point of sulphur, and prevent its "subliming," or going away in vapor without burning, as in this event it would be deposited in the cooler portions of the pipes, to cause trouble by clogging. In the manufacture of "sulphite liquor" for reducing wood, the gas is usually led through tanks containing milk of lime or magnesia, as will be described under the **Sulphite Pulp Process,** which see.

Sulphurous acid gas, SO_2, properly called sulphurous anhydride ("without water"), is a colorless, pungent, suffocating gas, of a specific gravity, compared with air, of 2.21. So long as sulphurous anhydride is kept from contact with moisture, it remains an inert gas, having no effect upon metals or other dry substances with which it may come in contact.

Sulphurous anhydride may be readily prepared for laboratory experiments by heating metallic copper with strong sulphuric acid. The reaction is represented by the equation —

$$Cu + 2\,H_2SO_4 = CuSO_4 + H_2O + SO_2$$

THE SULPHITES

Water at 0° C. will absorb 79.8 times its volume of SO_2, and 39.4 times its own volume at 20° C. Sulphurous anhydride is condensed into a liquid by a temperature of $-17.8°$ C., and by increased pressure it may be liquefied at considerably higher temperatures. Liquid SO_2 may be obtained in syphons similar to those in which Seltzer and other carbonated waters are sold.

Sulphurous anhydride combines with one molecule of water to form sulphurous acid, H_2SO_3, as before shown on page 39, and then becomes an extremely active substance. It attacks and rapidly corrodes most of the metals, dissolving or combining with them to form sulphites. Copper, zinc, tin, aluminum, and iron are rapidly eaten away by solutions of sulphurous acid. Lead, however, and alloys of that metal with antimony resist its action almost entirely. Certain alloys in which copper forms the greater part of the metal, resist the action of sulphurous acid to a very considerable extent. All of them, however, yield to the action of the acid more or less rapidly.

Sulphurous acid is able to decompose the oxides, hydrates, and carbonates of the alkali metals, and metals of the alkaline earths forming *sulphites* of the metals, and water, in the case of the oxides and hydrates; and sulphites of the metals, water and carbonic acid in case of the carbonates, thus:—

$$Na_2O + H_2SO_3 = Na_2SO_3 + H_2O,$$
$$2\ NaHO + H_2SO_3 = Na_2SO_3 + 2\ H_2O,$$
$$Na_2CO_3 + H_2SO_3 = Na_2SO_3 + H_2O + CO_2,$$
$$CaO + H_2SO_3 = CaSO_3 + H_2O,$$
$$CaCO_3 + H_2SO_3 = CaSO_3 + H_2O + CO_2$$

Bisulphites, preferably called Acid Sulphites.— Sulphurous acid, H_2SO_3, like all the oxygen acids of sulphur, is a bibasic acid; that is, it contains two atoms of *basic* hydrogen, or hydrogen so situated with reference to the other atoms in the molecule that it may be replaced by an equal number of atoms of a univalent alkali metal as sodium, or by a single atom of a bivalent alkaline earth metal, as calcium or magnesium. There are, in consequence, two series of sulphites: the neutral or normal, or monosulphites, mentioned in the preceding paragraph, in which compounds both the hydrogen atoms are replaced by a metal, and the bisulphites, or acid sulphites, in which only one of the hydrogen atoms in the molecule of acid is replaced by a metal. The bisulphites therefore retain much more of the acid character than do the normal sulphites. This difference in the structure of the two molecules may be shown thus:—

Normal sodium sulphite
$$\begin{array}{c}Na-O\\Na-O\end{array}\!\!>\!S=O$$

Sodium bisulphite
$$\begin{array}{c}H-O\\Na-O\end{array}\!\!>\!S=O$$

Normal calcium sulphite
$$Ca\!<\!\begin{array}{c}O\\O\end{array}\!\!>\!S=O$$

Calcium bisulphite
$$\begin{array}{c}H-O\\ \quad\;\,O\\Ca\\ \quad\;\,O\\H-O\end{array}\!\!>\!S=O$$

Sulphurous acid
$$\begin{array}{c}H-O\\H-O\end{array}\!\!>\!S=O$$

The contracted or empirical formula of the bisulphites named is for sodium bisulphite, $HNaSO_3$; for calcium bisulphite, $H_2CaS_2O_6$. It will be noticed that, because calcium is a bivalent metal, two molecules of sulphurous acid unite with one atom of calcium in forming the bisulphite.

The bisulphites are formed when only sufficient of the base is added to a solution of sulphurous acid to half neutralize the acid, or more commonly in practice, as in the manufacture of sulphite liquors, by first bringing sufficient acid into contact with the base to form the normal sulphite, and then continuing the addition of sulphurous acid until the normal sulphite is converted into the bisulphite. They may also be formed by adding to the normal sulphite enough of a stronger acid than sulphurous to displace one-half the sulphurous acid, thus:—

Sulphuric acid + Sodium sulphite (2 molecules) = Sodium sulphate + Sodium bisulphite (2 molecules)
$$H_2SO_4 + 2\,Na_2SO_3 = Na_2SO_4 + 2\,HNaSO_3$$

A similar reaction takes place, to some extent, in sulphite digesters, when, during the boiling operation, a portion of the sulphurous acid is oxidized to sulphuric acid; although, if the sulphite liquor contains only bisulphite at the start, the sulphurous acid displaced appears as free sulphurous acid, and increases the gas pressure.

The acid sulphites (bisulphites) of the alkaline earth metals are what are called loose or unstable chemical compounds, being easily broken up or decomposed into the neutral salt and free acid by heat alone, the acid being volatilized. Acid sulphite of magnesium is less easily decomposed than the corresponding calcium salt, but both are so unstable that their solutions cannot be evaporated without decomposing the salt. Neither of these salts has been isolated, and indeed many good authorities hold the opinion that acid sulphites of the alkaline earth metals do not exist, the so-called bisulphite solutions of these bases being simply solutions of the neutral sulphite in aqueous sulphurous acid. Certain facts in our own experience with these solutions, however, make us strongly of the opinion that these salts are formed and do exist in the so-called bisulphite solutions. Certainly there is no theoretical reason why they may not be formed.

The acid sulphites of the alkali metals are definite compounds, and can be crystallized from their solutions. Both the neutral and acid sulphites of the alkali metals are very soluble in water. Neutral sulphite of magnesia is much less soluble, while that of calcium is nearly insoluble. Neutral sulphite of magnesium separates from solution in coarse, sandy crystals, while that of calcium forms a fine, granular precipitate when SO_2 gas is passed into lime-water. It often forms coral-like crusts on the containing vessels, and, when precipitated by heat from the solution of the acid sulphite, often concretes in hard, stony masses. It frequently appears in the bottom and on the sides of digesters used for "cooking" wood with bisulphite of lime, sometimes forming a scale an inch or more in thickness.

All the bi- or acid sulphites appear to be soluble in water. The addition of any of the stronger acids to a sulphite causes the liberation of SO_2, often with effervescence. The acid sulphites form soluble, and many of them crystallizable, compounds with certain organic substances called aldehydes and ketones, and to this fact is probably due, in part at least, their efficiency in reducing wood to fibre.

Sulphurous acid, both free and in combination, is very ready to take on more oxygen and be changed into sulphuric acid. Hence it is called a reducing agent, since it can reduce certain other compounds from a higher to a lower state of oxidation, being itself, at the same time, oxidized. This property gives it its value as an antichlor, it being more easily oxidized by the "bleach" than is the fibre.

This reducing action is of first importance in the sulphite process for making pulp, since, on account of it, any oxidation and consequent weakening of the fibre is prevented, while the incrusting matters of the wood are so little changed by the process of solution that there is good reason to believe that they may be made to yield valuable by-products.

Sulphurous acid also possesses marked bleaching power, which depends on the fact that the acid forms colorless compounds with the coloring-matter. These compounds may often be broken up, and the color restored, by treatment with alkali. The sulphurous acid bleach is not a permanent one, like that obtained by the use of hypochlorites, which destroy the coloring-matter. The acid is used for bleaching wool and straw. It also gives a fictitious color to sulphite pulp. Such pulp, after washing, is often as white as it is after bleaching with bleaching-powder, although this first color is not very permanent.

The moist gas and also the sulphites and bisulphites are very destructive to the lower forms of life, preventing fermentation and destroying disease germs. They are much employed as disinfectants.

Hyposulphurous Acid, H_2SO_2. — When aqueous sulphurous acid is poured upon zinc, best in the shape of clippings or zinc dust, the metal dissolves, but no hydrogen is evolved. The nascent hydrogen formed combines at once with an atom of oxygen, which it takes from the molecule of sulphurous acid, with formation of hyposulphurous acid and water. Thus —

$$H_2SO_3 + H_2 = H_2SO_2 + H_2O$$

When the zinc is added to a solution of a bisulphite, as, for instance, bisulphite of soda, the reaction is as follows: —

$$3\,NaHSO_3 + Zn = NaHSO_2\,(\text{hyposulphite of soda}) + Na_2SO_3 + ZnSO_3 + H_2O$$

Hyposulphurous acid has never been isolated. It is produced in the decomposition of sulphurous acid by the electric current, but is such an unstable compound that it reoxidizes to sulphurous acid almost immediately. All its salts are very unstable, contact with the air very rapidly changing them, through absorption of oxygen, to the acid sulphites. The hyposulphites are extremely powerful reducing agents; that is, they act powerfully in withdrawing oxygen from other compounds of this element, reducing them to a lower state of oxidation. They are even capable of reducing indigo to the soluble and colorless form, and have been commercially applied for this purpose.

Calcium hyposulphite is the salt usually chosen for this purpose on account of the comparative ease of its preparation, and because it is the most stable in solution of these compounds. Only one of the hyposulphites has been obtained in the solid, or crystallized, form; namely, sodium hyposulphite. This salt may, by the exercise of great care in the manipulation of a somewhat lengthy process, be crystallized from its alcoholic solution, and may be preserved for some time, if carefully kept from contact with the air.

Thiosulphuric Acid, $H_2S_2O_3$. — This acid is, like the preceding, not known in the free state; any attempt to separate it from one of its salts resulting in the breaking up of the acid into sulphurous acid and free sulphur, which is precipitated. The only one of its salts which possesses any interest is sodium thiosulphate. $Na_2S_2O_3 . 5 H_2O$, the *commercial* name for which is "hyposulphite of soda." This salt is largely used in photography, and also in bleacheries as an "antichlor" to destroy any trace of "bleaching chlorine" remaining in the bleached material. Its use for the latter purpose is, however, to be discountenanced in favor of the sulphites, since the former leaves free sulphur in the fabric by its decomposition, which is liable to work injury, while the sulphites are merely changed to comparatively harmless sulphates.

Thiosulphate of sodium is easily prepared by heating a solution of sodium sulphite for some time with powdered sulphur, evaporating the solution and crystallizing out the salt. It forms large, colorless crystals readily soluble in water, and of a cooling saline and sulphurous taste.

The crystals contain five molecules ($5 H_2O$) of water of crystallization.

Sulphuric Acid, H_2SO_4; commercial name, "Oil of Vitriol." — This acid probably holds the place of highest importance in the arts of any known acids. It is formed from sulphurous acid by the addition of an atom of oxygen to the molecule of the latter,

$$H_2SO_3 + O = H_2SO_4.$$

This is always accomplished slowly, by natural means, whenever sulphurous acid is exposed to the action of atmospheric oxygen

The first step in the manufacture of sulphuric acid is always the burning of sulphur (generally in pyrites) into sulphurous anhydride, and its combination with moisture into sulphurous acid. The rapid oxidation of the latter into sulphuric acid is accomplished by the aid of nitrous fumes, produced by heating nitre; oxygen from the air, and steam. Sulphurous anhydride from burning sulphur, nitrous fumes, steam, and air are introduced together into large chambers made of 7 lb. sheet lead.

The entire course of the reactions which take place in the chambers is not definitely known. A very small amount of the nitrous fumes is, however, found to be sufficient to cause an almost unlimited amount of H_2SO_3 to be oxidized to H_2SO_4, the nitrous fumes which consist of a mixture of several oxides of nitrogen, apparently acting simply as carriers of oxygen, alternately giving up a portion of their oxygen to the sulphurous acid, and renewing their supply from the air present in the chamber. The H_2SO_4, as it is formed, falls as a fine rain, and collects on the floor of the chamber, diluted with the condensed water from the excess of steam always present in the chamber. This dilute acid is known as "chamber acid," and usually contains about 50 to 60 per cent. of real H_2SO_4.

This chamber acid may be concentrated to a gravity of about 1.78, and containing about 70 per cent of H_2SO_4, by evaporation in leaden pans, when it is technically called B. O. V. (brown oil of vitriol). Beyond this point the acid begins to attack the lead, and must then be further concentrated in vessels of glass or platinum. The metal is most used on account of the liability of glass to breakage and the disastrous effects of the acid when this occurs. The concentration may be continued until oil of vitriol is obtained, having a gravity of 1.84, a boiling-point of 338° C., and containing 100 per cent. H_2SO_4.

Sulphuric acid, H_2SO_4, is a colorless and odorless, heavy liquid, of an oily appearance. It freezes at −26° C. It chars wood and other organic bodies. It has a great affinity for water, absorbing more than its own volume from the air when exposed for some time. A very dilute solution of H_2SO_4 has the property of changing cellulose and starch into glucose when heated with them for some hours, and more rapidly under high pressures. Sulphuric acid of 1.60 specific gravity will, at a temperature of 50° C., dissolve cellulose, without charring, to a nearly colorless solution, which may be diluted with water without precipitation. This property of the acid furnishes an easy method for the estimation of total cellulose compounds in woody materials, since the non-cellulose compounds are neither charred nor dissolved by acid of the above strength.

Sulphuric acid unites with bases to form sulphates, all of which are soluble in water except the sulphates of barium, strontium, and lead. Sulphate of lime is only moderately soluble, one part of the crystallized salt, $CaSO_4 . 2 H_2O$, requiring 400 parts of water at 15° C. for solution.

Quite a number of sulphates are of natural occurrence, as heavy spar (barium sulphate, $BaSO_4$), gypsum (calcium sulphate, $CaSO_4, 2 H_2O$), celestine (strontium sulphate, $SrSO_4$), and Epsom salts (magnesium sulphate, $MgSO_4, 7 H_2O$).

"Nordhausen," or fuming, sulphuric acid, which is H_2SO_4, containing sulphurous anhydride, SO_3, is obtained by distilling dry ferrous sulphate (copperas), $FeSO_4$. It is useful as a solvent for indigo blue, and is mainly consumed in the manufacture of indigo extracts, carmines, etc.

Sulphuric anhydride, SO_3, may be obtained pure, as a mass of white, silky needles, by passing SO_2 and O through a red-hot porcelain tube filled with spongy platinum, and condensing the vapors in an air-tight receiver, surrounded with ice.

Solid SO_3 has a specific gravity of 1.916. It melts at 18.3° C., and boils at 35° C. When thrown into water it hisses like a red-hot iron, and dissolves, forming H_2SO_4. SO_3 is soluble in all proportions in pure H_2SO_4.

The remaining acids of sulphur — namely, the di-, tri-, tetra-, and penta- thionic acids — and their salts are of no commercial value. They are all unstable acids, which are known only in combination. None of them have been obtained in the free state. They are formed to some extent, in the sulphite process, through the action of sulphurous acid upon sulphur vapor when overheating of the furnace occurs. The dithionates decompose on heating into SO_2 and a sulphate, but the decomposition of the higher sulphur acids is attended with separation of sulphur, and their presence in sulphite liquors is, on this account, very objectionable.

Sulphur and Nitrogen.

Sulphur forms a single compound with nitrogen, S_2N_2, obtained by passing dry ammonia gas through a solution of sulphur dichloride, S_2Cl_2, in carbon disulphide. It forms golden-yellow crystals, insoluble in water. It explodes when heated to 157° C. Of no practical interest.

Sulphur and Carbon

When vapor of sulphur is passed over red-hot charcoal, the two combine to form carbonic sulphide, or carbon bisulphide, CS_2. This is a colorless, very inflammable liquid, of specific gravity 1.66, boiling at 88° C. It has a very high refracting power. When pure, CS_2 has a not unpleasant ethereal odor; but, as usually met with, it possesses a very repulsive odor, reminding one of rotten cabbage.

Bisulphide of carbon is of considerable importance in the arts as a solvent of sulphur, phosphorus, iodine, and rubber or caoutchouc. It is also a free solvent of fats and oils, and is employed in the manufacture of certain acid-proof paints from asphalt, and petroleum residues.

SELENIUM

Symbol, Se — Atomic weight, 79.5.— Molecule, Se_2 — Molecular weight, 159.

Selenium is a reddish-brown solid, of specific gravity 4.3. It melts above 100° C., and boils at 343° C. When heated in the air, it has an extremely disagreeable odor of decayed horseradish. In its properties and combinations selenium presents a very close analogy to sulphur. Selenium has never been found native. It was discovered by Berzelius in 1817. It is of no importance in the arts.

TELLURIUM

Symbol, Te — Atomic weight, 128 — Molecule, Te_2 — Molecular weight, 256

This substance also presents a close analogy to sulphur, but in appearance approaches very closely to the metals, being lustrous like silver. The specific gravity of Te is 6.26. It melts below a red heat. It occurs rarely native in Hungary, but chiefly in combination with other metals as Tellurides. Both selenium and tellurium often occur in Japanese sulphur. Tellurium was first discovered by Müller in 1782. Like selenium it is of no commercial importance.

CHLORINE

Symbol, Cl — Atomic weight, 35.5 — Molecule, Cl_2. — Molecular weight, 71

Chlorine is a yellowish-green gas of specific gravity 2.47 compared with air. It is uninflammable and irrespirable. Water at the ordinary temperature, 15° C., dissolves 2.3 times its own volume of the gas; it also combines with water at 0° C. to form a solid crystalline hydrate of chlorine, $Cl_2, 10 H_2O$. A pressure of 90 lbs. at a temperature of 0° C. condenses the gaseous chlorine into a yellow liquid 1.33 times as heavy as water.

Chlorine was discovered by Scheele in 1774. It never occurs native, but always in combination with a base as a metallic chloride.

Sea-water contains the chlorides of potassium, sodium, calcium, and magnesium, each in considerable amount. Chlorine has a very strong affinity for the metals generally. Many of them when placed, in a finely divided condition, in an atmosphere of chlorine, combine with it so rapidly as to be raised to vivid incandescence by the heat of the chemical action. It also has a great affinity for hydrogen, with which it combines to form hydrochloric acid, HCl. Many hydrogen compounds are at once decomposed by chlorine in solution with the formation of HCl and free oxygen. Chlorine is a powerful disinfecting and bleaching agent, in the presence of light and moisture. Its effect, in these instances, is explained by its decomposition of water, when the liberated oxygen destroys the identity of the disease germs in the one case, or the coloring-matter in the other. It may be termed a powerful secondary oxidizing agent, since, though not itself an oxidizer, it produces an oxidizing action through the agency of the elements of water.

Chlorine and Hydrogen.

Hydrochloric Acid. — Chlorine, as already stated, is eager to combine with hydrogen, atom for atom, both being univalent, forming chloride of hydrogen, or hydrochloric, commercially called muriatic, acid, HCl.

This is a colorless, incombustible gas, of specific gravity, compared with air, of 1.27. It is of intensely acid taste, and pungent, irritating odor. It may be condensed by a pressure of 40 atmospheres, at 10° C., to a colorless liquid. The hydrochloric or muriatic acid of commerce is, however, merely a solution of the gas in water, which will dissolve, at 0° C., 500 times its own volume of the gas. Ordinary muriatic acid is yellow from the presence of chloride of iron, and it frequently also contains some sulphuric acid. Pure hydrochloric acid is colorless, and if evaporated on a piece of glass or porcelain leaves no residue. Hydrochloric acid is prepared commercially by treating chloride of sodium, common salt, with sulphuric acid, the torrents of hydrochloric acid which are given off being a by-product from the first stage of the Leblanc process for the manufacture of soda. The gas is condensed by passing up through towers, down through which a stream of water falls. (See **Manufacture of Alkali**.)

Hydrochloric acid is a monobasic acid. It combines with the metals in general to form metallic chlorides, with the liberation of hydrogen. With the metallic oxides, it reacts to form metallic chlorides and water. A single molecule of HCl requires but one atom of the alkali metals, which have a valency of 1 for its saturation, while those metals whose valency is 2, as the alkaline earth metals calcium and magnesium, require two molecules of the acid for each atom of the metal. This appears in the following reactions: —

$$Na_2O + 2\,HCl = 2\,NaCl + H_2O.$$
$$Mg + 2\,HCl = MgCl_2 + H_2.$$

Chlorine and Oxygen

Chlorine cannot be made to unite with oxygen directly, but by indirect means three different compounds of these two elements may be formed: —

Chlorine dioxide or peroxide	ClO_2
Hypochlorous anhydride	Cl_2O
Chlorous anhydride	Cl_2O_3

On theoretical grounds there is some reason to believe that the two following unknown compounds might exist —

Chloric anhydride	Cl_2O_5
Perchloric anhydride	Cl_2O_7

Chlorine dioxide is an unstable, dark-yellow gas, and its preparation is attended with danger, on account of the tendency of the gas to decompose spontaneously, often with explosive violence. Its odor suggests those of chlorine and burned sugar. *Euchlorine*, which has powerful bleaching properties, was at one time considered a distinct oxide of chlorine, but is now known to be a mixture of free chlorine and chlorine dioxide. It is prepared by treating potassium chlorate with hydrochloric acid, and is a more active decolorizer and disinfectant than chlorine itself.

The anhydrides of chlorine, as such, possess little practical interest; but, by combination with the elements of water, the corresponding acids, known as the oxy-acids of chlorine, are formed, and these are, in some cases, of the highest importance. Thus:—

$Cl_2O + H_2O = 2 HClO$ . . Hypochlorous acid, two molecules.
$Cl_2O_3 + H_2O = 2 HClO_2$ . . Chlorous acid, " "
$Cl_2O_5 + H_2O = 2 HClO_3$. Chloric acid, " "
$Cl_2O_7 + H_2O = 2 HClO_4$. Perchloric acid, " "

Hypochlorous Acid, HClO. — The first of the oxy-acids of chlorine, or that containing the least oxygen, is hypochlorous acid. Free HClO is formed when hypochlorous anhydride, Cl_2O (formed as a yellow-colored gas by treating mercuric oxide, HgO, with chlorine), is passed into water. One volume of water will dissolve 200 volumes of the gas. Free HClO is also formed when a dilute solution of hydrochloric acid is submitted to electrolysis with platinum electrodes. In this case the water and HCl are simultaneously decomposed by the electricity, the chlorine and oxygen appearing at the positive electrode, where they unite with each other and combine with water to form HClO, while hydrogen escapes as gas at the negative electrode. Thus:—

$2 HCl + 2 H_2O$, electrolyzed, become $2 HClO + 2 H_2$

Hypochlorous acid is a very unstable compound, the oxygen atom being apparently very loosely held in the molecule. The presence, in a solution of this acid, of almost any oxidizable substance is sufficient to determine the reduction of the HClO molecule to a molecule of HCl, while the other substance present passes to a higher state of oxidation. On this account hypochlorous acid is a very powerful bleaching agent, giving up its oxygen with great readiness to the coloring-matter of the material to be bleached, either forming with it colorless, soluble compounds, or ultimately burning it to carbonic acid gas and water. Free hypochlorous acid being, however, so difficult of preparation, and of so little stability, that it cannot be preserved for any length of time in solution, plays no important part in the arts. It unites with the alkali and alkaline earth metals to form hypochlorites, which are much more stable compounds than the free acid. Common bleaching-powder, for example, which consists (at least when dissolved) of calcium hypochlorite, $CaCl_2O_2$, mixed with varying proportions of calcium chloride, $CaCl_2$, and calcium hydrate, CaH_2O_2, may be preserved for a considerable time, with only slow deterioration. (See **Bleaching**.) Even in solution, the oxidizing or bleaching action of the hypochlorites is much less rapid than that of the free acid, as may be shown by the addition of acetic acid, for example, to a solution of calcium hypochlorite, and observing the action of portions of the solution, before and after the addition of acid, upon two portions of unbleached pulp. The acetic acid in this case combines with the lime, leaving the hypochlorous acid free. Nor do all the hypochlorites act as oxidizing or bleaching agents with the same energy and rapidity, aluminum hypochlorite being probably the most rapid in its action, while sodium hypochlorite is probably the slowest. The magnesium salt acts more rapidly than the calcium salt. (Compare **Electric Bleaching, Chap. X**.) The mode of action of the hypochlorites in the process of bleaching is the same as in the case of the free acid; namely, the transference of the oxygen of the acid to the organic coloring-material, the hypochlorous acid, in both cases, being the bleaching agent, or, better, furnishing the bleaching oxygen.

Manufacture of Bleaching-Powder.—Chlorine is usually prepared for use in the arts by the action of hydrogen chloride, HCl (hydrochloric or muriatic acid), on dioxide of manganese, the equation for the reaction being—

$$MnO_2 + 4 HCl = MnCl_2 \text{ (Manganous chloride)} + 2 H_2O + Cl_2$$

By "Weldon's Process," which consists in treating the solution of manganous chloride with hot milk of lime or magnesia, and blowing hot air through the mixture, the manganese may be reconverted into manganese dioxide to be used afresh in the manufacture of chlorine. "Deacon's Process" for the manufacture of chlorine consists in passing a mixture of gaseous hydrochloric acid and air over copper sulphate, heated to about 370° C. By the electrolysis of many of the metallic chlorides in a fused state, or strong solution, chlorine is obtained at the positive electrode, and the metal at the negative (**Part II, Chap X**)

Bleaching-powder, "chloride of lime," or properly, calcium hypochlorite, is prepared by passing chlorine over slaked lime, exposed in shallow layers to the action of the gas. The absorption chambers are usually 60 feet long, 18 feet wide, and 7 feet high. They are built sometimes of large flag-stones, but more generally of 8-lb. lead, supported by a framework of scantling. The floor is made of brick, laid in tar cement over a sheet of lead. Where the Deacon process is worked the chambers are divided into sections fitted with shelves, upon which the lime is placed; but in other cases the lime is spread upon the floor in a layer from four to five inches deep, and is then raked into furrows.

The chlorine is admitted to the chambers, and is at first rapidly absorbed by the lime with evolution of heat. After the lime is nearly charged the supply of gas is shut off, so that the chlorine remaining in the chambers may be gradually taken up. This requires four or five days, and the entire treatment about a week.

The quality of bleaching-powder depends very much upon that of the lime from which it is made, and in order to secure the best bleach the lime must be especially pure. A "fat lime," or one which slakes easily, is best for the purpose as it absorbs chlorine more quickly and keeps best. Iron and manganese are, of course, objectionable in the lime, on account of the color which they impart to the bleaching-powder, and they are also said to impair the keeping qualities of bleach in which they occur.

Clay and silica injure the quality of bleach, since they cause it to settle slowly and imperfectly; while bleach containing magnesia has an increased tendency to take up water and become pasty through the formation, according to Lunge, of magnesium chloride.

In order to prepare bleaching-powder it is necessary that the lime contain some water. Partially slaked lime may be imperfectly chlorinated, but the best results are obtained when dry chlorine is used and the slaked lime contains 2 to 4 per cent. excess of water. The temperature at which absorption takes place has a decided influence upon the strength and quality of the product, through the formation of chlorate at the higher temperatures. The best authorities prefer a temperature not above 40° to 55° C. Hurter gives as the maximum 40°, Bobierre, 50°; Sheurer-Kestner, 55°. The experiments of Schappi, who used moist chlorine, gave at —

Temperature °C	Available chlorine per cent	Temperature °C	Available chlorine per cent
−17	2.30	40	41.18
0	19.88	45	40.50
7	33.24	50	41.52
21	35.50	60	39.40
21 (25°)	39.50	90	4.26
30	40.10		

Good bleach should be a pure white powder, containing some lumps if the test is high, and having a faint odor of hypochlorous acid. It should become tough when kneaded with the fingers. The lumps should not contain a core of lime, but should be converted to bleach throughout, and should break down easily between the fingers. The formula usually given for bleaching-powder is $CaCl_2O_2$, but the latest experiments of Lunge point to the formula $CaOCl_2$. There is usually present also a little calcium chlorate, chloride, and free lime.

Chlorous Acid, $HClO_2$. — This acid, containing one more atom of oxygen in its molecule, is formed by the action of nitric acid on potassium chlorate. It is never met with ordinarily in the free state, as it is a dangerous compound. In combination with bases, however, as chlorites, it is of not infrequent occurrence. Chlorites are formed by the electrolysis of solutions of the alkali and alkaline earth chlorides, under regulated conditions. They are bleaching agents of less energy than the hypochlorites, and are of little importance.

Chloric Acid, $HClO_3$. — This acid is of no importance in the free state. Its chief salt of commerce is potassium chlorate, $KClO_3$. A solution of this salt does not bleach in the cold, but on heating, with the addition of a mineral acid, it oxidizes organic matter with great energy. The dry salt forms powerful explosive mixtures with sulphur, phosphorus, many of the minerals, and organic matter generally. A mixture of sugar and chlorate of potassium, powdered separately, and cautiously mixed to avoid friction, will be set on fire by a drop of strong sulphuric acid. Potassium chlorate is formed by passing a stream of chlorine gas through a warm solution of caustic potash. Chlorates are also formed by the electrolysis of solutions of the chlorides, under certain conditions of strength of solution and current, and especially of temperature of solution, elevation of temperature favoring their formation at the expense of that of the hypochlorites. Chlorate of lime occurs in small and varying percentage in bleaching-powder.

Perchloric Acid HClO₄ — This is a colorless, volatile liquid, and is a very powerful oxidizing agent. It forms perchlorates. Neither the acid nor its salts are of any importance except as chemical reagents.

Chlorine and Nitrogen

Chlorine combines with nitrogen to form a single compound, which we mention here simply on account of its extremely dangerous character. It is an oily liquid, heavier than water. It explodes spontaneously, and with extreme violence, below 100° C. Its formula is probably NCl₃. It is formed by the action of chlorine gas on a strong solution of chloride of ammonia, sal ammoniac, and also when such a solution of sal ammoniac is electrolyzed.

Chlorine and Sulphur

Chlorine combines directly with sulphur, forming —

Sulphur chloride	S₂Cl₂
Sulphur dichloride	SCl₂
Sulphur tetra-chloride	SCl₄

These compounds are all liquids of some value to the chemist, but having few practical applications.

BROMINE

Symbol, Br — Atomic weight, 80 — Molecule, Br₂ — Molecular weight, 160

Bromine is a deep-red liquid of specific gravity 2.976. It freezes at −24½° C., and boils at 63° C. It volatilizes rapidly at ordinary temperatures in red fumes of a very disagreeable odor, and extremely irritating to the mucous membrane of the throat and eyes. Bromine is little soluble in water, more readily in alcohol and ether. Bromine was discovered by Balard in 1826. It is contained in combination with alkaline bases, in sea-water, and in the water of many mineral springs. It never occurs native.

Bromine resembles chlorine very markedly in all its properties, forming throughout analogous compounds. In chemical activity, however, it is somewhat less energetic. It finds many uses in the arts and in medicine; but, aside from its close relation to chlorine, is of little interest to the paper-maker.

IODINE

Symbol, I — Atomic weight, 127 — Molecule, I_2 — Molecular weight, 254.

Iodine bears great resemblance in its chemical properties to chlorine and bromine, but differs from both in being, at ordinary temperatures, a solid crystalline substance, of a steel-blue color and metallic lustre. It has a specific gravity of 4.95. Iodine melts at 107° C., and boils at 175° C., the vapor having a deep violet color. It volatilizes quite rapidly at ordinary temperatures. Iodine is very slightly soluble in water, but easily in alcohol and in a solution of potassium iodide.

It was discovered by Courtois in 1811, in the ash of sea-weeds. It occurs usually as sodium iodide in sea-water and in many mineral springs. Iodine never occurs native. It is of great value both free and in combination in medicine, and finds many uses in the arts.

Its compounds are all analogous to those of chlorine and bromine. A solution of iodine in potassium iodide is of great value in the sulphite pulp process, since it furnishes a ready means of determining the total amount of sulphurous acid in the bisulphite solution used. (Compare **Analysis of Bisulphite Liquors**.)

FLUORINE.

Symbol, F — Atomic weight, 19 — Molecule, F_2 — Molecular weight, 38.

Fluorine is an extremely energetic and corrosive gaseous element, never found native. It forms, with hydrogen, hydrofluoric acid, HF, corresponding to hydrochloric acid, and is interesting from its property of dissolving or etching glass; hence it must be preserved in leaden or gutta-percha bottles. Hydrofluoric acid is a dangerous substance to handle, owing to its injurious action on the throat and lungs. The chief natural compounds of fluorine are calcium fluoride, or fluorspar, CaF_2, and sodium-aluminum fluoride, or cryolite, 3 NaF, AlF$_3$. The latter is the raw material from which "Natrona" alum and "Natrona" bicarbonate of soda are made. It is obtained from Greenland.

These four elements — chlorine, bromine, iodine, and fluorine — are often classed together as the chlorine group, from their similarity in their chemical characters, and in the formation and nature of their compounds.

They are also sometimes denominated the halogens, and their compounds the halogen compounds. It is interesting to note in this connection how the chemical activity of the members of the group falls as the atomic weight rises.

BORON

Symbol, B — Atomic weight, 11 — Molecule, B$_2$ — Molecular weight, 22

Boron is a solid element, never native, and of no interest except in combination. It has a valency of three, one atom being the equivalent of three atoms of hydrogen in combining power. Thus it forms with chlorine, BCl$_3$, boron chloride, and with fluorine, BF$_3$, boron fluoride. The latter is interesting as being one of the few reagents which give a direct qualitative reaction with cellulose, which is blackened by boron fluoride.

Boron always occurs in nature combined with oxygen as boracic acid (or boric acid), H$_3$BO$_3$, either free or in combination. Boracic acid is soluble in three parts of boiling water, from which it crystallizes on cooling in pearly, mica-like scales, requiring 25 parts of water at 18° C for solution. Boracic acid is soluble in alcohol, and when alcohol containing it in solution is burned the acid imparts a green color to the flame.

The chief salt of boracic acid is borax, sodium biborate, Na$_2$B$_4$O$_7$, 10 H$_2$O, which is found native in large quantities in California and certain other places. Borax is of considerable use in the working of iron and many other metals, from its property of dissolving or forming a flux with many metallic oxides when fused with them. Borax possesses marked detergent qualities, owing largely to the power of its solutions of dissolving and partly saponifying fatty matters. It also, when in solution, forms a ready solvent for shellac, one part of borax being sufficient to render soluble about five parts of shellac. Alum and lime salts precipitate the gum.

Solutions of boracic acid and its salts possess quite marked antiseptic properties, and on that account are of considerable importance. They also possess medicinal properties.

SILICON

Symbol, Si — Atomic weight, 28

Silicon never occurs native, but combined with oxygen as silicic anhydride, SiO_2, or silica, it is one of the most abundant of minerals. The elementary substance was first isolated by Berzelius in 1823. It may be prepared with some difficulty in two forms,—amorphous silicon, a brown powder heavier than water, and a non-conductor of electricity, and crystalline silicon, a steel-gray sub-metallic crystalline substance of specific gravity 2.49, and which is a conductor of electricity. By electrolysis of certain compounds of silica, in a state of fusion with metallic compounds, alloys of silicon may be obtained. They, however, present more of the characters of a solution, if we may so term it, of the silicon in the metal than of true homogeneous alloys. Rock crystal, or quartz, is pure silica, SiO_2. Amethyst, agate, flint, carnelian, onyx, etc., are nearly pure silica, colored by small quantities of metallic oxides. By fusion with carbonate of soda, silicate of soda is formed, which is a substance having the appearance of glass, but soluble in water, hence called soluble glass. Ordinary glass is a more or less pure silicate of lime, containing some soda and some metallic oxides, as manganese, lead, and iron oxides.

Ordinary clay is a mixed silicate of alumina, lime, magnesia, etc., usually containing other metallic silicates, which give it color. Kaolin, or china clay, is very nearly pure silicate of aluminum, the impurities being varying amounts of silicates of lime and magnesia. It contains no iron or other colored metallic oxides.

The value of a clay for a paper-maker's use is largely dependent on the proportion of silicate of alumina it contains, and its freedom from iron oxide, sand, and grit.

Silicon forms compounds with chlorine, bromine, iodine, and fluorine, $SiCl_4$, $SiBr_4$, SiI_4, and SiF_4. They are solely of interest and use to the chemist.

PHOSPHORUS

Symbol, P — Atomic weight, 31 — Molecule, P$_4$ — Molecular weight, 124

Phosphorus is a translucent, slightly yellow substance of specific gravity, 1.83, and resembling wax in appearance. It possesses a peculiar odor suggestive of garlic. It melts at 44° C., and boils at 290° C. It is insoluble in water, somewhat soluble in ether, turpentine, and oils. It is freely soluble in carbon disulphide.

Phosphorus was discovered by Brandt in 1669. It takes its name from two Greek words meaning "light-bearer," and was so called on account of its property of emitting light when exposed to the air.

It is never found native, but in combination with lime is widely distributed in nature. It forms an essential element in the composition of the bones, blood, brain, and other portions of the animal economy, and is always necessary to the development of seed in plants.

Although in combination with oxygen it is so essential to animal life, yet in the free state it forms a virulent poison, excepting in a single one of its amorphous forms. This latter modification, known from its color as red phosphorus, is prepared by heating ordinary phosphorus in an atmosphere of carbonic anhydride for thirty or forty hours, at a temperature of 230° to 240° C. It then forms a red powder, insoluble in all media. It is non-poisonous, and does not, like ordinary phosphorus, need to be preserved under water, as the red variety does not inflame below 260° C. Phosphorus is prepared from calcium phosphate, by distillation with charcoal, the vapors of phosphorus produced being condensed and the resulting phosphorus preserved under water. On account of its inflammability phosphorus is a very dangerous substance, and must be kept under water and handled with extreme care.

Phosphorus forms a great variety of compounds of extended use in medicine and in the arts, but none have any immediate bearing on the art of paper-making, and on that account may be omitted here.

Phosphorus combines directly with metals, when heated with them, to form phosphides of the metals, and in many cases the phosphides may be alloyed directly with other metals. When present in very small quantities the phosphides serve to impart to metals characters quite distinct from those of the pure metals.

In most cases the presence of phosphorus in a metal is objectionable, while in a few instances, as, for example, in "phosphor bronze," it imparts very useful properties to the metal or alloy. Phosphor bronze is an alloy of copper and tin, and contains a small amount of phosphide of tin, which gives the alloy marked acid-resisting quality, besides increasing its strength and toughness.

ARSENIC

Symbol, As — Atomic weight 75 — Molecule As_4 — Molecular weight, 300

Arsenic is sometimes found native, but more commonly occurs in combination with metals and sulphur as sulpho-arsenides. Arsenicum, as it is frequently written, occupies the border line between the non-metallic substances and the metals. In its physical characters, and in its combinations with sulphur, it approaches more nearly the metals; while in the formation of anhydrides, As_2O_3 and As_2O_5, and their corresponding acids, H_3AsO_3 and H_3AsO_4, as well as in most of its other chemical characters, it plays the part of a non-metal. Pure arsenic is a steel-gray substance, having a bright, metallic lustre. It tarnishes rapidly in the air. Its specific gravity is about 5.8. Heated in the air, it burns with a bluish flame. Nearly all the compounds of arsenic are extremely poisonous. The common arsenic of the shops, or white arsenic, is arsenious anhydride, As_2O_3. Paris green is aceto-arsenite of copper.

The common rat-poisons and potato-bug poisons are nearly all preparations of arsenic. Some of the compounds of arsenic are of great use in the arts. In the manufacture of aniline colors many of the most brilliant and beautiful shades are best obtained by the use of compounds of arsenic. In these colors it is the aim of the manufacturer to remove the arsenic in a subsequent process of the manufacture. Unfortunately the removal is often incomplete, and numerous cases of arsenical poisoning, more or less acute, have occurred from the presence of arsenic in the colors of wall-paper or in the dye of carpets or clothing. The presence in wall-paper of the equivalent of a quarter of a grain of white arsenic per square yard is considered dangerous.

Arsenious acid in solution, either in hydrochloric acid or dissolved in water as arsenite of soda, is readily oxidized by chlorine, or a hypochlorite, into arsenic acid, and so furnishes the analyst with a ready means of determining the "available chlorine" in a solution of bleaching-powder (Compare **Analysis of Bleaching-powder**)

The preceding fifteen elements comprise all the non-metallic elements at present known. The oxides of all these elements are called anhydrides, and unite with water to form acids, either mono-basic, di-, tri-, or tetra- basic, according as they contain respectively one, two, three, or four atoms of hydrogen, which may be replaced by a metal.

THE METALLIC ELEMENTS.

THERE are at least forty-nine known metals. Many of them are, however, of small importance, and indeed have been but little investigated.

All the metals combine with oxygen to form oxides, which in turn may unite directly with anhydrides (oxides of the non-metals) to form salts. The oxides of the non-metals (anhydrides) unite with water to form acids, while the metallic oxides unite with water to form hydroxides, sometimes called hydrates or bases. Acids and hydroxides unite to form metallic salts, with the elimination of water; thus, hydrochloric acid, HCl, and sodium hydroxide, NaHO, unite to form sodium chloride, NaCl, and water, H_2O —

$$HCl + NaHO = NaCl + H_2O.$$

A few of the metals form both acid and basic oxides, standing as it were on the dividing line between the non-metals and the metals.

A very large proportion of the oxides are insoluble in water, and also most of the metallic salts, with the exception of the chlorides, nitrates and sulphates, which are nearly all soluble in water.

The metals are all good, though not equally good, conductors of heat and electricity. They are all opaque substances, capable in the mass of receiving a more or less polished surface, and they exhibit a peculiar lustre, termed metallic. They show various degrees of hardness, from the consistency of putty to the hardness of steel. The brittleness of metals is much increased by lowering of temperature. All exhibit a considerable degree of tenacity, or resistance to a breaking strain. Many of the metals are malleable, that is, may be extended under rollers or beaten into sheets. In the latter regard gold takes the first rank. Gold leaf may be made only $\frac{1}{280000}$ of an inch in thickness.

The specific gravity of the metals varies greatly, lithium being the lightest, specific gravity 0.59, and osmium the heaviest, specific gravity 22.48.

Many of the metals occur in nature in the form of crystals. The metals combine together under the influence of heat to form alloys the melting-point of the alloy often being below that of any of the constituent metals. The alloys appear, in some respects, to be true chemical compounds, but are not in general so regarded. Alloys of mercury are called *Amalgams*.

THE ALKALI METALS

The alkali metals are six in number: —

Potassium	Symbol, K	— Atomic weight,	39.1
Sodium	Symbol, Na —	"	23
Lithium	Symbol, Li —	"	7
Cæsium	Symbol, Cs —	"	133
Rubidium	Symbol, Rb —	"	85.4
[Ammonium]	Symbol, NH$_4$ — Combining		18

The alkali metals all have a valency of 1, that is, are capable of replacing the hydrogen of an acid atom for atom. Their hydroxides are very soluble in water, and their solutions are strongly alkaline to test paper, and caustic and destructive in their action upon animal substances. Their carbonates are soluble in water, and these solutions are also alkaline.

POTASSIUM

Symbol, K — Atomic weight, 39.1 — Specific gravity, 0.865

Potassium is a brilliant, bluish-white metal, which melts at $62\frac{1}{2}°$ C., and volatilizes at a red heat in green vapors. It is never found native, but its compounds are widely distributed, being found in mica, feldspar, all fertile soils, sea-water, and in large quantities in the salt deposits at Stassfurt, Germany. The metal oxidizes so rapidly that it has to be preserved under naphtha or some other liquid which contains no oxygen. When thrown upon water it decomposes the latter, uniting with the oxygen, and dissolving as hydroxide, KHO, and setting free the other atom of hydrogen. So much heat is developed in the reaction that the hydrogen takes fire, its flame being colored violet by the vapor of potassium. This violet-colored flame furnishes a ready test for the metal.

Potassium oxide, K$_2$O, is the potash of chemists. It is formed by the dry oxidation of potassium. It unites with water molecule for molecule ($K_2O + H_2O = 2 KHO$) to form *potassium hydroxide*, or hydrate, KHO, commercially called caustic potash. This is a hard, grayish-white solid, which dissolves very readily in water, with development of much heat. It attracts moisture from the air so rapidly as to become liquid in a short time. This action is called *deliquescence*. Potassium hydrate is a very caustic and powerful base. It precipitates the metals as hydrates from nearly all solutions of metallic salts. It forms compounds with all the acids, many of these compounds being of great importance. With fats and oils it forms hard soaps, while soda forms soft soaps.

Potassium carbonate, K_2CO_3, is very similar to soda-ash, which is sodium carbonate. The crude potassium salt is obtained from wood ashes by leaching them and evaporating the solution, and is called crude potashes. It is mainly used in the manufacture of glass and soap.

Potassium nitrate, KNO_3, is saltpetre, an important ingredient in gunpowder, of which it forms about three-fourths the weight. Its use here and in fireworks is due to the readiness with which it gives up its oxygen.

Potassium chlorate, $KClO_3$, is, like saltpetre, a white, crystalline salt, largely used in fireworks and matches to supply oxygen. It is also used in medicine.

Potassium chloride, KCl, much resembles common salt; the bromide, KBr, is a valuable medicine. The ferrocyanide, yellow prussiate of potash, forms with iron (ferric) salts the well-known Prussian blue.

Potassium tartrate is "cream of tartar."

SODIUM

Symbol, Na — Atomic weight, 23 — Specific gravity 0.972

Sodium is a beautiful crystalline metal, of silver-white appearance. It fuses at 97.6° C., volatilizes at a red heat, and greatly resembles potassium in all its properties. Sodium never occurs native, but in combination it is of universal occurrence. Potassium and sodium correspond very closely in all their chemical combinations, the chemical activity of the latter being, however, somewhat weaker than that of the former.

Sodium hydroxide, or *caustic soda*, NaOH, is a white, fusible, deliquescent solid, very soluble in water, though less so than caustic potash. It is a powerful alkali.

The most commonly occurring salt of sodium is the chloride, NaCl, or "common salt." It is obtained by the evaporation of sea-water, the water of salt springs and wells, and is also mined as rock salt. Common salt crystallizes generally in cubes. It is soluble in $2\frac{1}{2}$ times its weight of water at $15\frac{1}{2}°$ C. It fuses and volatilizes at a red heat. Hydrochloric acid is made by distilling sodium chloride with sulphuric acid, $2\,NaCl + H_2SO_4 = Na_2SO_4 + 2\,HCl$. Glauber's salt is crystallized sodium sulphate $Na_2SO_4, 10\,H_2O$. Soda-ash is more or less pure anhydrous, or dry, sodium carbonate, Na_2CO_3. "Soda crystals," or "washing-soda," is crystallized sodium carbonate, $Na_2CO_3, 10\,H_2O$. Common baking-soda is sodium bicarbonate, $NaHCO_3$. (For description of processes of manufacturing soda-ash, etc., see **Manufacture of Alkali**.) Borax is sodium biborate, $Na_2B_4O_7, 10\,H_2O$. Borax is found native in California. It is soluble in 12 parts of cold, and in one-half part, or one-half its weight of boiling water. Borax when heated swells up, loses its water of crystallization, and finally, at about a red heat, melts to a clear glass. It is of great value as a flux in metal working.

Sodium nitrate, $NaNO_3$, is found native in Peru and Chili, and is imported from these places in large quantities. It has very nearly the same properties as saltpetre, KNO_3, but cannot be substituted for the latter in gunpowder, since it attracts moisture. Saltpetre is made from sodium nitrate by what is called double decomposition between that salt and potassium chloride. When solutions of the two salts are mixed in the proper proportions an interchange of acids and bases occurs, and potassium nitrate and sodium chloride result —

$$NaNO_3 + KCl = KNO_3 + NaCl$$

The normal salts of sodium are all soluble in water, with the single exception of pyr-antimonate of sodium, $Na_2Sb_2O_7 \cdot 6\,H_2O$.

The compounds of sodium are the most useful in the variety and extent of their applications of any of the salts of the alkalis.

Manufacture of Alkali. — The manufacture of soda-ash from common salt, by the Leblanc process, depends primarily upon the following reactions —

	Common salt	Sulphuric acid	Acid sodium sulphate	Hydrochloric acid
(1)	$NaCl$ +	H_2SO_4 =	$NaHSO_4$ +	HCl

			Sodium sulphate	
(2)	$NaCl$ +	$NaHSO_4$ =	Na_2SO_4 +	HCl

(3) By heating sodium sulphate, Na_2SO_4, with carbon in the form of coal and with chalk, calcium carbonate, $CaCO_3$, the various reactions shown below are set up, which result in the production of black-ash, from which sodium carbonate may be extracted by lixiviation. These phases of reaction (3) may be regarded thus —

(a) $5 Na_2SO_4 + 10 C = 5 Na_2S + 10 CO$.
              Carbon   Sodium sulphide   Carbon monoxide

(b) $5 Na_2S + 5 CaCO_3 = \mathbf{5\ Na_2CO_3} + 5 CaS$
                                                   Calcium sulphide

(c) $2 CaCO_3 + 2 C = 2 CaO + 4 CO$
                          Caustic lime

Reactions (1) and (2) on page 65 are carried out in iron pots, set in a furnace, and containing the charge of salt, upon which the sulphuric acid is run. The torrents of hydrochloric acid gas which are evolved pass out of the furnace and up through scrubbers, or towers, filled with flints, down which a stream of water trickles. The gas is absorbed by the water, forming commercial muriatic acid, which flows from the bottom of the tower. The sodium sulphate, or salt cake as it is technically termed, is removed from the pots and made up into what is called black-ball, with coal, lime, and limestone or chalk. This mixture is furnaced, and under the influence of heat the various phases of reaction (3) are set up, and black-ash, yielding in different works from 23 to 45 per cent. of sodium carbonate, with a much smaller and varying percentage of caustic soda, is obtained. The carbonate and caustic are removed by washing the black-ash with water, and the solution is either subjected to minor operations to purify the subsequent product, or is run down at once to obtain the commercial soda-ash. For the preparation of caustic soda the black-ash liquors are usually treated at once with lime, air is blown through the mixture to decompose sulphides, etc., and the caustic liquor decanted and evaporated. In many works the caustic is produced at once in the furnace by somewhat increasing the quantity of coal added to the mixture of salt cake and limestone, and lixiviating the ball-soda at once with water at 50°.

The hydrochloric or muriatic acid obtained in reactions (1) and (2) above is decomposed as described under **Chlorine**, for the manufacture of bleaching-powder, or more rarely of potassium chlorate.

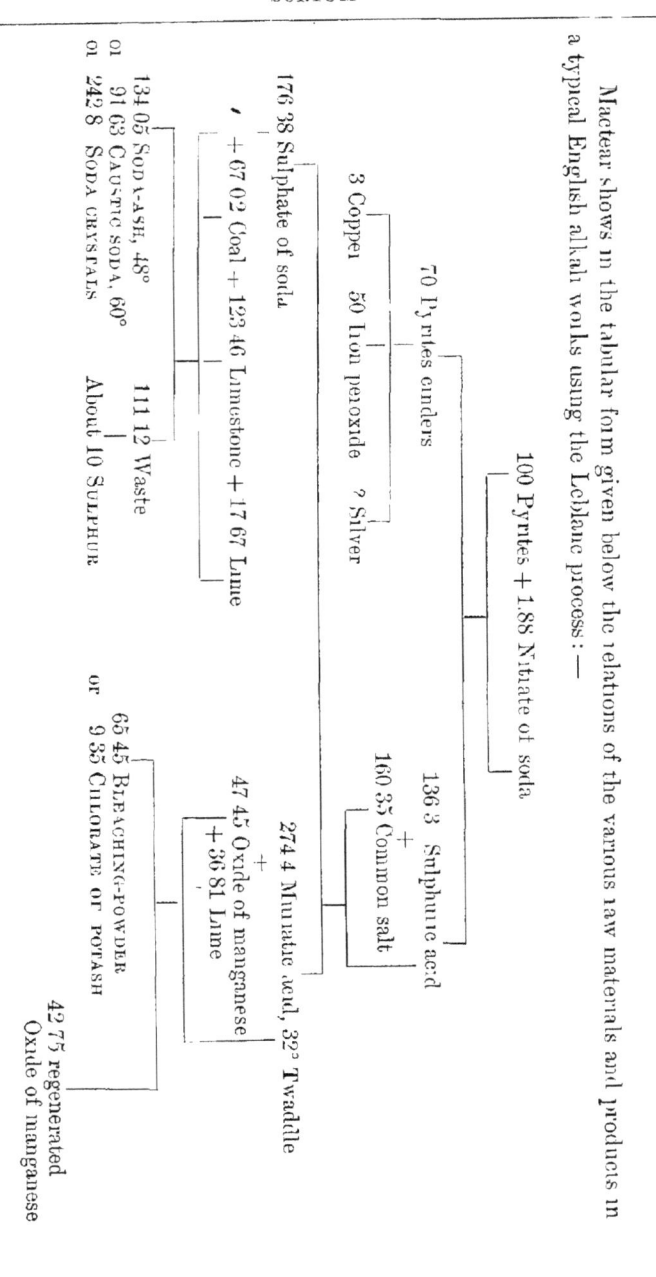

SODIUM

Mactear shows in the tabular form given below the relations of the various raw materials and products in a typical English alkali works using the Leblanc process:—

```
                    100 Pyrites + 1.88 Nitrate of soda
                                  |
              ┌───────────────────┼───────────────────┐
         70 Pyrites cinders              136.3 Sulphuric acid
              |                                 +
         50 Iron peroxide                 160.35 Common salt
        3 Copper                                |
         ? Silver                               |
                                                |
         176.38 Sulphate of soda ────────────── ┘
         + 67.02 Coal + 123.46 Limestone + 17.67 Lime
              |
         ┌────┴─────┐
    134.05 Soda-ash, 48°    111.12 Waste
    or 91.63 Caustic soda, 60°
    or 242.8 Soda crystals    About 10 Sulphur

                                  274.4 Muriatic acid, 32° Twaddle
                                         +
                                  47.45 Oxide of manganese
                                         + 36.81 Lime
                                         |
                                  65.45 Bleaching-powder
                                  or 9.35 Chlorate of potash
                                         |
                                  42.75 regenerated
                                  Oxide of manganese
```

A large and increasing quantity of high-grade soda-ash is now manufactured by the Solvay or ammoniacal process, which depends upon the fact that if common salt is dissolved in ammonia water, and a current of carbonic acid gas passed through the solution, ammonium chloride is formed and sodium bicarbonate precipitated. The bicarbonate is then washed free from the solution, and upon ignition yields the carbonate. The ammonia is recovered by heating the ammonium chloride with lime, the chlorine combining with the lime to form calcium chloride, which is a waste product. On account of this loss of chlorine no bleaching-powder is made by this process.

LITHIUM

Symbol, Li — Atomic weight, 7 — Specific gravity, 0 59

Lithium is a white, lustrous metal, discovered by Arfwedson in 1818. It is the lightest solid known, being only about one-half as heavy as water. It is fusible at 180° C., and volatile at a red heat. It occurs as chloride in many mineral springs, and as silicate or fluoride in not a few minerals. It is of no importance other than as a medicinal agent.

CÆSIUM

Symbol, Cs — Atomic weight, 133.

RUBIDIUM

Symbol, Rb — Atomic weight 85 4

Both these metals were discovered by Bunsen and Kirchoff in spring waters in Hungary. They are present also in a few minerals. Traces of cæsium have also been found in the ashes of tobacco, beetroot, coffee, and grapes. Both are very rare metals, and form no compounds of any commercial importance

AMMONIUM

Symbol, NH_4 — Combining weight, 18

Ammonium (a compound of hydrogen and nitrogen, not to be confounded, however, with ammonia, NH_3) is not in reality a metal, but in many of its combinations so nearly plays the part of an alkali metal, and its compounds are so similar to the corresponding compounds of potassium and sodium, that they may be best considered here.

Ammonium unites with water to form ammonium hydrate or hydroxide, NH_4OH, the common ammonia water, which possesses all the alkaline properties, though in less degree, of a solution of potassium or sodium hydrate.

It unites with acids to form ammonium sulphate $(NH_4)_2SO_4$, chloride $(NH_4)Cl$, carbonate $(NH_4)CO_3$, etc., strictly analogous to the corresponding salts of the alkali metals.

Ammonium is often carelessly mistaken for hydrogen nitride, or ammonia, NH_3, but it should never be, as it is entirely distinct. Ammonia, NH_3, never enters into combination with acids to form salts, these compounds always being formed from ammonium, NH_4. Ammonia by contact with water is changed into ammonium hydroxide $(NH_4)OH$, which then may perform all the functions of any other alkaline hydroxide.

Ammonium, NH_4, is a good type of what is called a *Radicle*; that is, an unsaturated group of atoms, which in combination plays the part of a single atom. The number of such groups or radicles known to organic chemistry is very large, and in many cases, by the coalescence of two groups of the same kind, a stable molecule is formed, so that the radicle can exist in the free state. Cyanogen, $-C \equiv N$, is such an organic radicle, the molecule of free cyanogen being $N \equiv C - C \equiv N$.

METALS OF THE ALKALINE EARTHS.

Barium Symbol, Ba — Atomic weight, 137 — Specific gravity, 4.000
Strontium Symbol, Sr — "   " 87.5 — "   " 2.540
Calcium Symbol, Ca — "   " 40 — "   " 1.578

These metals all decompose water at the ordinary temperature. They form oxides of an earthy nature. These combine with water (slake), forming hydroxides, which dissolve somewhat in water, forming alkaline solutions. All are strong bases. Their carbonates are insoluble. Their bicarbonates and most of their other salts are soluble in water. One atom of each can replace two atoms of acid hydrogen.

BARIUM.

Symbol, Ba. — Atomic weight, 137. — Specific gravity, 4.000.

Barium is a silver-white metal, which melts below a red heat and oxidizes readily. It may be obtained by the electrolysis of fused barium chloride.

Barium oxide or caustic baryta is obtained by calcining barium carbonate, $BaCO_3$, at a red heat. It combines eagerly with water, with the development of much heat, and forms barium hydroxide or hydrate, BaH_2O_2. The hydroxide is soluble in 20 parts of cold or two parts of boiling water.

The solution is strongly alkaline. Barium hydrate and all the soluble salts of barium are very poisonous, their antidotes being sodium or magnesium sulphate.

The soluble salts of barium are the chloride, $BaCl_2$, $2 H_2O$, nitrate, BaN_2O_6, chlorate, $BaCl_2O_6$, the acetate, $BaC_4H_6O_4$, $3 H_2O$, and the thiosulphate, BaS_2O_3, H_2O. Barium sulphate, $BaSO_4$, is insoluble. It is frequently employed as an adulterant of white lead in paint, and to some extent as a filler in paper. It is found native as "Heavy spar." Barium carbonate is also found native as "Witherite." The soluble salts of barium impart a green color to the colorless flame of alcohol or of the Bunsen gas-burner.

Barium oxide, when heated in a current of dry air, takes on a second atom of oxygen, the peroxide, BaO_2, being formed. At a still higher temperature the peroxide is reduced to the original barium oxide, BaO, oxygen being at the same time liberated. This reaction has been made use of in the preparation of oxygen on the large scale, the barium oxide being alternately brought to the lower and higher temperature in retorts, which are first connected with a source of air, and then with gas-holders. The Brins, who have developed the process in the commercial way, prepare a solution for bleaching paper stock by saturating hydrochloric acid with oxygen.

Barium peroxide is also interesting as furnishing a means for preparing hydrogen peroxide, H_2O_2. Thus, when barium peroxide is treated with water and hydrochloric acid, barium chloride and hydrogen peroxide are formed —

$$BaO_2 + 2\ HCl = BaCl_2 + H_2O_2,$$

both products remaining in solution.

When sulphuric acid is employed barium sulphate is precipitated, and a pure solution of hydrogen peroxide in water is obtained, which may be used for bleaching or other purposes.

STRONTIUM

Symbol, Sr — Atomic weight, 87.5 — Specific gravity, 2.54.

Strontium is a yellow metal, somewhat harder than lead. In its properties and reactions it is very similar to barium. Its hydroxide, SrH_2O_2, is somewhat less soluble than barium hydroxide, while most of its compounds are more soluble than the corresponding barium compounds. Strontium compounds impart a crimson color to flame. They find their chief employment in the manufacture of "red fire." The hydroxide forms a comparatively insoluble compound with sugar (sucrose), and hence affords a means of separating the latter from the uncrystallizable sugar of molasses.

CALCIUM.

Symbol, Ca — Atomic weight, 40 — Specific gravity, 1.578

Calcium is never found native, but its compounds, especially the carbonate, silicate, and phosphate, are widely distributed, and are of great use and value. The metal calcium is prepared with considerable difficulty, and is of no importance as a metal. It is of a light-yellow color, about as hard as gold; is malleable and ductile. It tarnishes slowly in dry air, and decomposes water rapidly at the ordinary temperature. When heated in oxygen it burns with a magnificent rose-red flame. Like barium, it forms two oxides, CaO and CaO_2, the former only being of importance. Calcium oxide, CaO, is ordinary "quicklime." It is a white, caustic, earthy substance, infusible when pure. When heated in the oxyhydrogen flame it glows with an intense white light, rivalling the light of the electric arc. Calcium oxide combines with water with the development of great heat, and "slakes" into calcium hydroxide or hydrate, CaH_2O_2. The latter substance is a strongly alkaline base, soluble in 700 times its weight of cold water, but much *less soluble* in boiling water.

A clear saturated solution of calcium hydrate is the lime-water of pharmacy, and water containing more CaH_2O_2 than it is able to dissolve is called milk of lime. Calcium hydroxide forms the basis of mortars and cements. The hardening or setting of mortar is brought about by the combination of the lime with the carbonic acid of the atmosphere to form carbonate of lime, aided by the silica of the sand used, which forms silicate of lime to a small extent.

"Hydraulic lime" is lime which contains free *soluble* silica. Such lime, when moistened, first slakes and then in a short time sets to a hard mass through the combination of the lime with the soluble silica, forming stone.

This setting will take place even under water. Hydraulic lime is employed in the manufacture of Portland cement, and gives the cement its valuable properties. Calcium hydrate is capable of many useful applications, as in causticizing soda (compare Soda-ash), preparing indigo for coloring, as a "base" in the sulphite pulp process, and in the manufacture of bleaching-powder, etc.

Calcium oxide, CaO, is prepared by calcining, or burning, limestone, calcium carbonate, $CaCO_3$, in a kiln. The heat decomposes the calcium carbonate, driving off the carbonic acid as gas, CO_2, while the stone is changed into quicklime, CaO. Marble and chalk are nearly pure calcium carbonate, while ordinary limestone contains varying amounts of magnesia, iron oxide, alumina, silica, etc. A lime for building purposes may contain quite considerable amounts of impurities other than magnesia without seriously injuring it. On the other hand, a lime for sulphite liquor making may contain almost any amount of magnesia, though moderate amounts of other impurities are objectionable; while lime intended for the manufacture of bleaching-powder must be very nearly pure CaO.

Calcium hydrate is a strong base. Some of the salts of calcium are extremely soluble in water, as the chloride, $CaCl_2$, nitrate, CaN_2O_6, and the chlorate, $CaCl_2O_6$. A larger number are moderately soluble, as the hypochlorite, $CaCl_2O_2$, sulphate, $CaSO_4$, etc.; while not a few are almost absolutely insoluble, as the carbonate, $CaCO_3$, the sulphite, $CaSO_3$, and the phosphate, $Ca_3P_2O_8$. In some cases the insoluble salts of calcium may combine with a second equivalent of the acid, as the carbonate, to form bicarbonate, and the sulphite to form bisulphite, the latter salts being largely soluble. The so-called "hard" waters often contain calcium bicarbonate. In this case boiling removes the "hard" quality, the second equivalent of carbonic acid being liberated by the heat, and the lime precipitated as the insoluble carbonate. Bisulphite of lime solutions are decomposed in a similar way by boiling, with the precipitation of calcium sulphate. Other soluble salts of lime produce "hardness" in water, which remains after boiling, and hence is called "permanent hardness."

Selenite, gypsum, anhydrite, and alabaster are all different natural forms of calcium sulphate, $CaSO_4$. "Pearl hardening," "pearl pulp," and "crown filler" are artificial sulphate of lime, prepared for use as "fillers" in paper. Crystallized sulphate of lime, $CaSO_4$. $2 H_2O$, is soluble in 400 times its weight of water, or one pound in about 48 gallons, at the ordinary temperature. It is less soluble in hot water. At 100° C. sulphate of lime loses three-fourths of its water of crystallization; at about 260° C. still more is lost, and it becomes plaster of Paris. When the latter is moistened it again combines with water, increases in bulk, and sets to a hard mass. If heated much above 260° C., plaster of Paris recombines with water only very slowly.

Calcium phosphate, $Ca_3P_2O_8$, forms the greater part of bone. It is also found native in Canada as apatite, and in South Carolina as "phosphate rock." Coprolites, supposed to be the fossil excreta of prehistoric animals, are nearly pure phosphate of calcium. These are all largely used in the manufacture of artificial fertilizers or superphosphates.

THE MAGNESIUM GROUP

					Melting point
Magnesium	Symbol, Mg	— Atomic weight, 24	— Specific gravity, 1.743		
Zinc	Symbol, Zn	" " 65.2	" " 7.146	—412° C
Cadmium	Symbol, Cd	" " 112	" " 8.604	—228° C
Glucinum	Symbol, Be	" " 9.3	" " 2.100	—900° C

These metals all have a valency of 2. They all burn when heated in the air, and are all volatile. They each form but a single oxide. Their carbonates are insoluble in water, but are dissolved by solution of ammonium carbonate. The metals of this group decompose water only very slightly. They dissolve in hydrochloric acid with evolution of hydrogen.

MAGNESIUM.

Symbol, Mg — Atomic weight, 24 — Specific gravity, 1.743

Magnesium is a white metal, malleable and ductile. It is never found native. It oxidizes slowly in damp air. It burns rapidly when heated in the air, with a brilliant white light, which may be employed instead of sunlight in photography. Magnesium oxide or magnesia, MgO, is formed when magnesium is burned. It is prepared on a large scale by calcining carbonate of magnesium, $MgCO_3$, in the same manner as limestone is calcined. Magnesia resembles lime, but its hydroxide, MgH_2O_2, is much less soluble than hydrate of lime. It forms combinations similar to the corresponding lime compounds, but its basic properties are less strong than those of lime, and most of its compounds are largely soluble in water. Epsom salts is magnesium sulphate, $MgSO_4$, 7 aq [1] This is soluble in three times its weight of water. Many of the salts of magnesium are of importance in pharmacy. Magnesia forms the base for the manufacture of bisulphite liquor in the Ekman process for the manufacture of pulp. Silicate of magnesium, with small proportions of other metallic silicates, forms a very important class of minerals. Meerschaum, talc, soapstone, serpentine, and asbestos are mainly magnesium silicates.

ZINC

Symbol, Zn — Atomic weight 65.2 — Specific gravity 7.146.

Zinc is a bluish white, hard, lustrous metal. It is rarely found native, the best ore being calamine, zinc carbonate, $ZnCO_3$. Zinc is brittle at low temperatures, but becomes malleable and ductile between 100° and 150° C. It melts at 412° C., and boils at 1040° C. It oxidizes very slowly in the air, and hence is employed for coating or "galvanizing" iron to protect it from rust. It is readily attacked by chlorine and all the mineral acids, and dissolved by them. Zinc forms the electro-positive element in most electric batteries, the wire leading from it forming the negative pole. It is capable of replacing most other metals in solution, itself being dissolved, while the metal originally in the solution is, at the same time, deposited in the metallic state. Zinc heated in the air burns with a greenish blue flame, forming oxide of zinc, ZnO. This is yellow while hot, but on cooling becomes white. Zinc hydroxide is a white, gelatinous substance, insoluble in water, but

[1] The abbreviation Aq for *aqua* (water) is frequently used to represent a molecule, H_2O, of water which is present as such in association with some other molecule.

dissolved by solution of potash or ammonia. Metallic zinc is obtained from the oxide by heating with charcoal —

$$2\,ZnO + C = 2\,Zn + CO_2.$$

Chloride of zinc, $ZnCl_2$, dissolved in water, forms "Burnett's disinfecting solution" of pharmacy. Cellulose or paper treated with a strong solution of zinc chloride is changed into a transparent, parchment-like substance, vegetable parchment. Sulphate of zinc, "white vitriol," $ZnSO_4$, 7 aq., is employed in calico-printing as a mordant. Zinc carbonate or "zinc white" finds considerable use as a substitute for white lead in paint.

CADMIUM

Symbol, Cd — Atomic weight, 112 — Specific gravity, 8 6

Cadmium is a metal much resembling zinc and also tin. It accompanies zinc in many of its ores. It melts at 228° C., boils at 860° C., and is more volatile than zinc. It tarnishes but little in the air, but when strongly heated burns to cadmium oxide, CdO. Its salts resemble the corresponding salts of zinc, but the metal is of little importance either in the metallic state or in combination.

GLUCINUM

Symbol, Be — Atomic weight 9 3 — Specific gravity, 2 1

Also called beryllium from its being the principal constituent of the beryl. It is a white, malleable metal. Called glucinum from the Greek word γλυκύς, meaning sweet, on account of the sweet taste of solutions of its salts. Its salts resemble both those of zinc and aluminum, but are of no importance. The emerald is a double silicate of beryllium and aluminum.

THE EARTH METALS.

Aluminum	Symbol, Al —	Atomic weight,	27.4
Yttrium	Symbol, Y —	" "	92.0
Erbium	Symbol, E —	" "	168.9
Lanthanum	Symbol, La —	" "	139.0
Didymium	Symbol, D —	" "	144.7
Cerium	Symbol, Ce —	" "	138.0

These metals are all capable of replacing three atoms of hydrogen in combination. Their oxides are earths, and are reduced to the metallic state only with great difficulty. From solutions of their salts ammonium sulphide precipitates the metal as hydroxide.

ALUMINUM

Symbol, Al — Atomic weight, 27.4 — Specific gravity, 2.6

Aluminum is a bluish white, malleable, and ductile metal, first prepared by Wöhler in 1827. It is a good conductor of electricity, and is very sonorous. It fuses at about 450° C. It does not tarnish in the air, but when heated in oxygen it burns with a bluish white light, forming the oxide, Al_2O_3. It dissolves in acids, with the exception of nitric acid, with moderate facility. Solutions of potassium and sodium hydroxides also dissolve it readily with the liberation of H_2. The metal is never native, but the oxide and silicate are found in abundance, the latter forming the principal part of clay. Corundum and emery are native Al_2O_3.

The sapphire and ruby are also oxide of aluminum, tinted with small amounts of other metallic oxides. Bauxite is a hydrous oxide of aluminum, containing more or less iron oxide. Aluminum possesses properties which would render it a very valuable metal for many industrial purposes. The difficulty of reducing its ores has, however, up to the present rendered its cost too high to admit of its application to any but a few special purposes.

The price of the metal has however, been reduced about one-half within a couple of years, but it still remains at about $0.65 per pound.

The salts of aluminum are easily prepared from many of its natural compounds, and are of great value, especially to the paper manufacturer.

Aluminum hydroxide, Al_2O_3, $3 H_2O$, is precipitated as a nearly colorless, translucent jelly when a solution of any aluminum compound is mixed with a hydrate of an alkali, or alkali-earth metal Hydrate of aluminum, on strong ignition, loses its combined water, and is converted into the oxide or alumina, Al_2O_3. Hydrate of aluminum or aluminum hydroxide is a moderately strong base. It is entirely insoluble in water, but dissolves readily in acids to form the corresponding salts. Aluminum chloride, Al_2Cl_6, is not of much importance. Aluminum acetate is of considerable use as a mordant for fixing the colors, and obtaining different shades in dyeing and calico-printing. By far the most important of the alumina compounds are the alums. Alums, properly so called, are the crystallized double sulphates of aluminum and an alkali Thus potash alum is $K_2Al_2 4 SO_4$, 24 aq., and contains 10.92 per cent. of alumina, Al_2O_3, and 45 51 per cent. of combined water Soda alum is $Na_2Al_2 4 SO_4$, 24 aq, and contains 11 23 per cent. of alumina, and 47 11 per cent of combined water. Ammonium alum is $(NH_4)_2Al_2 4 SO_4$, 24 aq., and contains 11 35 per cent. of alumina and 47 63 per cent. of combined water. These percentages, of course, represent what the *chemically* pure crystals of these alums contain, and not the "commercially pure" article. Sulphate of alumina, $Al_2 3 SO_4$. 18 aq, is largely used in paper-making instead of true alum, since in the partly dried form in which it appears in market it is stronger in alumina than the true alums, and at the same time cheaper This may contain from about 15 to about 30 per cent. of alumina, according to the completeness with which the combined water has been driven off in the manufacture.

Among the insoluble salts of aluminum may be mentioned cryolite, the double fluoride of aluminum, and sodium, which is found in large quantities in Greenland, and is employed as a source of alumina in alum manufacture, clay (silicate of alumina) and bauxite (hydrate of alumina) are also employed in the manufacture of alum and aluminum sulphate.

The turquoise is a hydrous phosphate of aluminum.

Manufacture of Alum. — As already indicated, the term "alum" in paper-making has come to be almost entirely restricted to sulphate of aluminum, or concentrated alum, as it is often called. This material is in this country generally prepared from bauxite. The pulverized mineral is added to sulphuric acid of 50° B, contained in lead tanks. The reaction is very violent, much heat is developed, and considerable frothing occurs After the mixture has cooled down it is diluted with water, and allowed to stand to deposit silica and other impurities. The clear liquor is decanted and run into tanks heated by steam passing through coils of lead pipe The evaporation is continued until a portion of the liquor taken up on a stick or rod solidifies in cooling The concentrated material is then run off upon a stone table, where it solidifies, and is subsequently broken up and packed Zinc is sometimes added while the alum is in the liquid state, and by its action while dissolving nascent hydrogen is liberated and reduces any iron present to the ferrous state, thereby improving the color of the product. If sodium bicarbonate is added just before the mass is poured, the liberated carbonic acid produces the structure found in porous alum.

In order to produce true potash or ammonia alum, sulphate of potash or sulphate of ammonia is added to the clear liquor decanted after treatment of the bauxite with acid The concentration is not carried so far as in the manufacture of sulphate of alumina, and the alum solution is run into wooden tanks to crystallize The tanks are then knocked down to obtain the crystals.

When clay is used as the source of alumina, it is moderately heated to drive off water, convert the iron to oxide, and render the whole mass as porous as possible.

The powdered clay is added gradually to sulphuric acid of 50° B., and the whole heated nearly to boiling in lead tanks The mixture gradually thickens, and is run out into iron pans to solidify. The sulphate of alumina is washed out with water, and cleared by standing The liquor is then treated in the same manner as that obtained from bauxite

A large quantity of alum for paper-makers' use is made in this country from cryolite. By ignition of cryolite with limestone, aluminate of soda and calcium fluoride are formed. The former is soluble in water, and may be washed out From this solution carbonic acid gas precipitates the alumina. which is then dissolved in sulphuric acid to form sulphate of alumina Another method is to boil the cryolite with milk of lime Aluminate of soda and calcium fluoride are formed, and upon addition of a further quantity of powdered cryolite the alumina is precipitated and treated with acid as before.

In England alum is largely manufactured from the bituminous shale containing iron pyrites and found lying above the coal measures. The shale is heaped up and roasted, by which operation the pyrites are converted into ferrous sulphate and sulphuric acid, both of which react upon the clay, forming sulphate of alumina. This may either be dissolved out with water, or the roasted material may be transferred to covered pans and heated to about 110° for two days with sulphuric acid of specific gravity 1.35, while ammonia gas is passed into the mixture for the production of ammonia alum. Potassium sulphate or chloride, or more often a mixture of both, added to the lye from the roasted shale yields potash alum.

YTTRIUM,

Erbium, lanthanum, and didymium are all rare metals, found principally in Sweden. They never occur native. None of their compounds have any industrial importance.

CERIUM

Is a little-known metal discovered by Klaproth in 1803. It forms two basic oxides, Ce_2O_3 and CeO_2, and consequently two classes of salts, ceric and cerous respectively. Cerium oxalate forms a medicinal agent of some importance. Apart from this use cerium is of no industrial importance.

THE IRON GROUP

Iron (*Ferrum*)	Symbol, Fe —	Atomic weight,		56
Manganese	Symbol, Mn —	"	"	55
Chromium	Symbol, Cr —	"	"	52.2
Cobalt	Symbol, Co —	"	"	58.8
Nickel	Symbol, Ni —	"	"	58.8
Uranium	Symbol, U —		"	120

This group includes the distinctively magnetic metals, and also non-magnetic uranium. These metals all decompose water at a red heat. Hydrogen sulphide does not precipitate them from their *slightly acid* solutions.

IRON (Ferrum).

Symbol, Fe — Atomic weight, 56 — Specific gravity, 7.844

Iron very rarely occurs native. It is sometimes present in the metallic state in meteorites, and is found in a mica slate at Canaan, Connecticut. Pure iron is an almost silver-white metal, malleable, ductile, and very tenacious. It is the most magnetic of all substances. It remains unchanged in dry air, and when immersed in *pure* water. In damp air it rusts or oxidizes. Heated in oxygen, it burns with vivid incandescence, forming the magnetic oxide, Fe_3O_4. Dilute sulphuric and hydrochloric acids dissolve it readily with evolution of hydrogen, forming protosulphate, $FeSO_4$, and protochloride of iron, $FeCl_2$, respectively. Dilute nitric acid also dissolves it, but the strong acid not only fails to dissolve it but renders it "passive," or incapable of being acted upon by other acids, until, by appropriate means, its passive condition is altered. Bar iron, the purest commercial form, contains from 0.2 to 0.4 per cent. of carbon. At a white heat it softens, and may be welded by hammering or by strong pressure. In electric welding a small portion of the iron is brought to a white heat by the concentration on it of a very powerful electric current, and the two surfaces are united by strong pressure. Iron melts at about 1530° C.

The chief ores of iron, in the order of their value, are magnetic iron ore or magnetite, Fe_3O_4, which occurs both massive and crystalline, and from which the purest iron is made by reduction of the ore with charcoal alone; "specular" iron ore, Fe_2O_3, and red hæmatite, $2 Fe_2O_3, 3$ aq. This last occurs in two forms, fibrous and compact. By roasting it loses its water of combination and becomes Fe_2O_3, which is then readily reduced to iron by coal.

"Spathic" iron ore, carbonate of iron, $FeCO_3$, occurs in yellowish crystals, and also massive. By roasting, carbonic anhydride, CO_2, is driven off and the FeO oxidized to Fe_2O_3. "Clay ironstone" is the chief ore of Great Britain. It is an impure carbonate of iron and is reduced in the blast furnace. Blast furnace treatment is in outline as follows: The ore is mixed with limestone and small coal and charged into the top of the furnace, the fires of which are urged by a strong blast of air. The ore and the limestone first roast in the cooler portions of the furnace, and become Fe_2O_3 and CaO. As the mass sinks down the lime and silica of the ore unite to form a fusible slag, while the coal, at the high temperature, burns at the expense of the oxygen of the Fe_2O_3, reducing the latter to Fe, which sinks to the bottom of the furnace in a fluid state, and is drawn off from time to time by the removal of a plug and allowed to flow into furrows in a bed of dry sand to cool. These bars when broken up form "pig iron."

There are many minor reactions taking place all the while in the furnace, which we have not space to notice here. "Pig iron" contains from 1 per cent or less to 5 per cent. and even more of carbon, partly or wholly combined with the iron, as well as small amounts of sulphide and phosphide of iron. These must be removed by different processes of refining, in order to obtain "wrought iron." The presence in cast iron of a small amount of sulphide or arsenide renders it "hot short," or brittle at a red heat, while a small amount of phosphide renders it brittle at the ordinary temperature, or "cold short." Steel contains from 0.7 to 1 7 per cent of combined carbon, which gives it its special properties.

Iron forms four oxides, two of them, FeO, the protoxide, and Fe_2O_3, the sesquioxide, being basic; Fe_3O., magnetic oxide, having neither basic nor acid properties. and consequently forming no compounds; and FeO_3, an acid oxide. The last, however, cannot be isolated, since when freed from combination it immediately evolves oxygen and deposits ferric hydrate. Ferrous oxide, FeO, is very unstable, both in its free state and in most of its compounds, absorbing oxygen very readily and passing into the ferric state. Most of the ferrous salts are soluble in water. Ferrous sulphate, "green vitriol,' $FeSO_4$, 7 aq., is also commercially called "copperas." It takes this name from the fact of its becoming reddish brown, coppery, on exposure to the air. It is a sea-green, crystalline substance, very soluble in water. Solutions of the salt rapidly absorb oxygen and deposit basic ferric sulphate.

Ferrous bicarbonate. FeC_2O_5. ($FeO\ 2\ CO_2$), occurs in mineral waters, called "chalybeate" waters. Such waters. on exposure to the air, absorb oxygen and deposit ferric hydrate, $2\ Fe_2O_3\ 3\ H_2O$. A brown bulky precipitate of hydrate, having the composition $Fe_2H_6O_6$, is obtained when ammonia is added to solutions of ferric salts. Ferric oxide or sesquioxide of iron, "iron rust." is Fe_2O_3. It combines with acids to form ferric salts. Most of these are very soluble. Ferric chloride, Fe_2Cl_6, may be obtained by sublimation in brown scales, which very rapidly absorb water from the air and deliquesce, or liquefy, to an orange-red solution. Ferric nitrate,

$Fe_2 6 NO_3$, 12 aq., is very soluble. In conjunction with tannins it forms a black dye. Ferric oxide may take the place of alumina, Al_2O_3, in the formation of ferric alum: thus $K_2Fe_2 4 SO_4$, 24 aq., is potash ferric alum. Ferric oxide has received a curious application in the manufacture of caustic soda from soda-ash, sodium carbonate. When ferric oxide is furnaced at a low red heat with soda-ash, a compound of the iron and soda, probably sodium ferrate, Na_2FeO_2, is formed, from which hot water extracts sodium hydrate, NaHO, leaving ferric oxide, which has but to be dried to be again ready for use in the same operation.

Ferrous salts are very readily changed into the corresponding ferric salts by means of oxidizing agents, as by boiling with nitric acid, or, in the cold, by hypochlorites, etc : and, conversely, ferric salts are readily changed to ferrous salts by reducing agents, such as nascent hydrogen, hydrogen sulphide, sulphurous acid, etc.

MANGANESE.

Symbol, Mn — Molecular weight, 55 — Specific gravity, 8 01

Manganese is a grayish white, brittle metal, never occurring native. It was discovered by Gahn in 1774. The metal oxidizes rapidly in the air, and decomposes water slowly at the ordinary temperature. It is prepared from manganous carbonate, $MnCO_3$, by heating to whiteness in a smith's forge with charcoal. The metal alloys readily with iron to render the latter harder and more elastic. Manganese occurs in a variety of combinations. Its most valuable ore is pyrolusite, MnO_2.

Manganese forms two basic, two indifferent, and two acid oxides. Manganese oxide, MnO, is an olive-green substance, which when ignited in the air absorbs oxygen and is changed into brown manganous-manganic oxide. Manganous oxide is a powerful base. Most of its salts are pink or rose red.

Manganic oxide, Mn_2O_3, occurs in a natural form as manganite. It is a feeble base. It may be substituted for alumina and ferric oxide in alums and other compounds. This oxide gives a violet color to glass, and the color of the amethyst is also due to the same substance.

Manganous-manganic oxide, Mn_3O_4, is formed by the ignition of any of the other oxides of manganese with free contact of air. It is not basic.

Manganese dioxide or peroxide, MnO_2, is the most useful ore of manganese. It is not basic. When strongly ignited it gives off oxygen, and is converted into Mn_3O_4. When heated with sulphuric acid it also evolves oxygen. When heated with hydrochloric acid chlorine is given off, and manganous chloride is formed according to the equation —

$$4 HCl + MnO_2 = Cl_2 + MnCl_2 + 2 H_2O.$$

Manganic acid, H_2MnO_3 (the anhydride being MnO_2), is green. The manganates are very unstable. Their solutions, as well as those of the permanganates, form powerful disinfectants.

Permanganic acid, $H_2Mn_2O_7$ (anhydride, $Mn O_6$), is scarcely known except in combination. Potassium permanganate, $K_2Mn_2O_7$, is a dark purple salt, crystallizing in needles. It yields up a portion of its oxygen very readily to oxidizable substances, being at the same time reduced to MnO_2 or MnO. Its use as a bleaching agent has been proposed, and as such it is very effective under favorable conditions, but the expense of the substance and of its use has hitherto prevented its extensive employment for this purpose.

Solutions of permanganates form very efficient deodorizers and disinfectants. The oxides of manganese and many of its salts find extended application in the arts.

COBALT

Symbol, Co — Atomic weight, 58.5 — Specific gravity, 8.95

Cobalt is a reddish white, brittle metal, difficultly fusible. It is magnetic and very tenacious. It was discovered by Brandt in 1733. The best ore of cobalt is the arsenide, As_2Co, or speiss-cobalt. Cobalt forms two oxides, cobaltous oxide, CoO, of a greenish color, and cobaltic oxide, Co_2O_3, which is black. The former is used as a pigment. "Smalt" is a glass colored blue by cobaltous silicate. The salts of cobalt are blue, pink, and red. Unsized paper which has been impregnated with a solution of cobalt chloride is blue in dry weather, but turns pink when exposed to a moist atmosphere. Such papers, made up into various fanciful articles, are sold in France as a sort of weather indicator.

NICKEL

Symbol, Ni — Atomic weight, 58.8 — Specific gravity, 8.8.

Nickel is a hard, bluish white, difficultly fusible metal, capable of receiving a high polish. It is tenacious in a high degree. Nickel nearly always accompanies cobalt in its ores. It also resembles the latter in many respects. The chief ores of nickel are the arsenide or "Kupfer-nickel," As_2Ni_2, the diarsenide, As_2Ni, and the arsenio-sulphide, $AsNiS$. The metal is obtained by the ignition of nickel oxalate in a wind furnace, or by reducing the oxide by ignition with carbon. Nickel is magnetic at the ordinary temperature, but loses this property at 350° C. It is not easily acted on by acids, with the exception of nitric acid. "German silver" is an alloy of copper, zinc, and nickel, being practically $Cu_5Zn_3Ni_2$.

Nickel forms one basic oxide, nickel oxide, NiO, and an indifferent oxide, nickel peroxide, Ni_2O_3. The caustic alkalis precipitate nickel hydroxide, NiH_2O_2, from solutions of nickel salts, as a bulky, light green precipitate, insoluble in potash and soda, but soluble in ammonia to a blue solution. The latter solution has the property of dissolving silk, while it does not dissolve cellulose.

CHROMIUM

Symbol, Cr — Atomic weight, 52.2 — Specific gravity, 6.81

Chromium is a steel-gray metal, more intractable than platinum. It was discovered by Vauquelin in 1797. It is insoluble even in aqua regia.[1] Never native. The metal may be obtained by strong ignition of the oxide with charcoal in a wind furnace. Chromium forms two basic oxides, chromous oxide, CrO, and chromic oxide, Cr_2O_3. The latter is a green, earthy substance, often employed as a pigment and to give a green color to porcelain and glass. It gives to the emerald and to serpentine their characteristic colors. Chromic oxide may replace alumina in the formation of alums.

Chromium also forms an acid oxide, CrO_3, chromic anhydride, which forms brilliant dark red deliquescent prisms. Chromic acid, H_2CrO_4, is the most important compound of chromium. With potash it forms neutral chromate, K_2CrO_4, yellow, and the

---

[1] This is only true of the crystallized metal obtained by Frémy.

bichromate or red chromate, $K_2Cr_2O_7$. Chromic yellow or canary yellow is neutral lead chromate, $PbCrO_4$. It is formed when a solution of a chromate is added to a solution of acetate of lead. Orange mineral is basic lead chromate, $PbCrO_4$, PbO.

The compounds of chromium, in which the latter takes the part of base, are of little importance. They are all remarkable, as well as the chromates, for the beautiful colors of the salts themselves, and also of their solutions.

URANIUM

Symbol, Ur. — Atomic weight, 120. — Specific gravity, 18.4.

Uranium is a steel-gray, slightly malleable metal, never found native. It is not oxidized at ordinary temperatures, but burns when strongly heated. In its chemical properties, as also in most of its compounds, it bears a close analogy to iron and manganese. The ores of uranium are of rare occurrence, and the element is of little practical importance.

THE TIN GROUP

Tin (*Stannum*)	Symbol, Sn. — Atomic weight,			118.
Titanium	Symbol, Ti. —	"	"	50
Zirconium	Symbol, Zi. —	"	"	89.5
Thorium	Symbol, Th. —	"	"	231.5

TIN

Symbol, Sn. — Atomic weight, 118. — Specific gravity, 7.292.

Tin is a lustrous, white, malleable metal, never found native. It possesses but little ductility. It has a slight but peculiar odor. When a bar of tin is bent it emits a peculiar crackling sound, called the "cry" of tin. Tin melts at 228° C. When strongly heated in the air it burns into stannic oxide SnO_2. At ordinary temperatures it tarnishes slowly. Hydrochloric acid dissolves tin slowly, forming stannous chloride, $SnCl_2$. Boiling sulphuric acid dissolves it to stannic sulphate. Nitric acid does not dissolve tin, but changes it into insoluble metastannic acid, $H_2Sn_5O_{11}$, 4 aq. Tin is a very valuable metal for many purposes, both in the pure form and as alloyed with other metals. Pewter is four parts tin and one part lead. Common solder is usually equal parts tin and lead. Bronze is an alloy of copper and tin "Phosphor bronze" contains a little phosphide of tin, to which its peculiar properties are due

Tin forms two oxides: stannous oxide, SnO, a black, crystalline substance which rapidly absorbs oxygen, and becomes stannic oxide, SnO_2; stannous hydroxide, SnH_2O_2, is white and gelatinous, very soluble in solutions of caustic potash and soda. It is a powerful base.

Stannic oxide, SnO_2, is a yellowish white, insoluble substance This is found as cassiterite or tinstone, and forms the chief ore of tin

Stannic acid, H_2SnO_3, is formed as a white gelatinous precipitate, by adding ammonia to a solution of stannic chloride. It is insoluble in ammonia, but forms compounds with the alkali and alkali earth metals, called stannates Stannate of soda is Na_2SnO_3, 3 aq

Stannous sulphide, SnS, is a bluish gray substance, formed by fusing together tin and sulphur. The same substance is precipitated as a brown rated sulphide by passing hydrogen sulphide into a solution of stannous chloride "Mosaic gold" is stannic sulphide, SnS_2. The soluble salts of tin are largely used in dyeing as mordants.

TITANIUM

Symbol, Ti — Atomic weight, 50 — Specific gravity, 5 3.

Titanium is a rare element, never native. The chief ore is titanic anhydride, TiO_2, occurring as "Rutile," "Brookite," and "Anatase." Titanium forms comparatively few compounds, and is of little interest. It was discovered by Gregor in 1791.

ZIRCONIUM

Symbol, Zr — Atomic weight, 89 5 — Specific gravity, 4 15

Zirconium is a black amorphous powder, assuming some lustre under the burnisher. It resembles silicon and titanium, and under certain circumstances antimony.

THORIUM

Symbol, Th — Atomic weight, 231.5 — Specific gravity, 7.7 to 7.9

Thorium is a metal discovered by Berzelius in 1828. The metal dissolves easily in nitric acid, and slowly in hydrochloric acid. It forms one oxide, which is white and very heavy. Thorium is of no importance in the arts.

MOLYBDENUM

Symbol, Mo — Atomic weight, 96 — Specific gravity, 8.62

Molybdenum is a white, brittle metal, very difficultly fusible. It takes its name from the Greek word μολύβδαινα, a piece of lead, which its chief ore, molybdenite, resembles.

It forms two basic and one acid oxides. The basic oxides are molybdous oxide, MoO, black, and molybdic oxide, MoO_2, dark brown. In solutions of salts of molybdic oxide, alkalis precipitate molybdic hydroxide. The latter is readily soluble in acids giving red-colored solutions. Nitric acid changes molybdic oxide to molybdic anhydride, MoO_3, which may unite with water to form molybdic acid, not known, however, in the free state. Neither the metal nor its salts are of much technical importance. Some of the molybdates of the alkalis are useful in the laboratory for the detection and separation of phosphoric and arsenic acids and the precipitation of certain alkaloids.

TUNGSTEN (Wolfram)

Symbol, W — Atomic weight, 184 — Specific gravity, 17.6

Tungsten is an iron-gray metal, nearly infusible. Its most common ore is wolfram, tungstate of iron and manganese. It is a difficult metal to obtain in the free state, but may be alloyed with some difficulty with other metals by simultaneous reduction of the oxides. It forms a variety of compounds with oxygen, some of them exhibiting acid, and others basic properties. Sodium tungstate possesses the property of rendering cotton fabric, etc., uninflammable.

THE ANTIMONY GROUP

Antimony	Symbol Sb —	Atomic weight,	122.0
Arsenic	Symbol, As —	"	75.0
Bismuth	Symbol Bi —	"	210.0
Vanadium	Symbol, Va —	"	51.3
Niobium	Symbol, Nb —	"	94.0
Tantalum	Symbol Ta —	"	182.0

ANTIMONY

Symbol, Sb — Atomic weight, 122 — Specific gravity 6.75

Antimony is a brilliant, bluish white metal, crystalline, and so brittle that it may be powdered in a mortar. It melts at 450° C., and in the air burns brilliantly with the formation of antimonous oxide, Sb_2O_3. Strong hydrochloric acid dissolves the metal slowly, forming antimonous chloride, $SbCl_3$. In chlorine gas the metal takes fire, and burns to $SbCl_5$. Nitric acid converts it into antimonic acid, $HSbO_3$. Antimony alloys readily with most other metals. Type metal consists of two parts lead, one part tin, and one part antimony, the latter being added to give hardness and stiffness to the type, and also to cause the metal to expand in cooling, and so take the fine lines of the mold. "Britannia metal" is nine parts tin and one part antimony. Antimonous hydride, or stibine, H_3Sb, is formed when hydrogen is liberated by zinc and acid in the presence of any compound of antimony. It is a colorless, fetid gas, which burns with a greenish flame to water and antimonous oxide, or, when the supply of air is insufficient, to water and antimony.

Antimony forms with chlorine antimonous chloride, $SbCl_3$, antimonous oxychloride, $SbClO$; and antimonic chloride, $SbCl_5$. Antimonous sulphide, Sb_2S_3, is of a beautiful orange color. Antimonic sulphide, Sb_2S_5, is also orange red.

Antimonous oxide, Sb_2O_3, occurs native as "white antimony ore." It is a gray white crystalline powder, becoming yellow on heating. It is soluble in hydrochloric acid, and in tartaric acid solution to form chloride or tartrate of antimony. The latter is the "tartar emetic" of the pharmacists. When heated in the air antimonous oxide burns to antimonous antimonate, Sb_2O_4.

Antimonic anhydride, Sb_2O_5, is a pale yellow, tasteless, insoluble powder. United with water it forms antimonic acid, $HSbO_3$.

$$Sb_2O_5 + H_2O = 2\,HSbO_3$$

It forms antimonates with the basic oxides. Metantimonic acid is $H_4Sb_2O_7$. Metantimonate of sodium is interesting as being the only compound of sodium with an inorganic acid which is insoluble in water.

Antimony and its compounds bear a close analogy to the corresponding forms of arsenic. These two metals appear to stand, as it were, on the border line between the metals and the non-metallic elements. Antimony, however, has the metallic character more distinctly than arsenic. Both have the property of rendering other metals with which they are alloyed hard and brittle.

Arsenic has been previously noticed under the non-metallic elements

BISMUTH

Symbol, Bi — Atomic weight, 210 — Specific gravity, 9.79

Bismuth is a beautiful crystalline metal, of a reddish white hue. It melts at 264° C. When strongly heated in chlorine gas bismuth burns with a bluish flame, forming the terchloride, $BiCl_3$. Bismuth has the property of lowering to a remarkable degree the melting-point of alloys of which it forms a part. Fusible metal is an alloy of eight parts bismuth, five parts lead, and three parts tin. This alloy melts at 98° C.

Similar alloys, made in such proportions that they fuse at some particular temperature, are used as safety plugs in boilers and for certain joints in automatic sprinklers. Except in such alloys metallic bismuth is little used. It forms four oxides. Some of its salts are medicines of importance, especially the nitrate, which is also used for giving a colorless iridescent glaze to porcelain.

VANADIUM

Symbol, V — Atomic weight, 51.3 — Specific gravity, 5.5

Vanadium is a very rare metal, discovered by Sefstrom in 1830, and never found native. In its combinations with oxygen it is analogous to nitrogen, forming five oxides,— V_2O, V_2O_2, V_2O_3, V_2O_4, and V_2O_5. The highest of these, V_2O_5, forms with water vanadic acid, HVO_3, and the salts of this acid are the only compounds which have received any industrial application. Vanadium in solution is remarkable for its affinity for cellulose, this substance being able to abstract vanadium from a solution containing only one part of the metal in a trillion.

Blitz has patented a process for reducing wood to pulp by the use of a solution of sodium sulphide, containing, to every cord of wood, fifteen grains of vanadate of ammonia dissolved in hydrochloric acid. We cannot believe that the efficiency of the solution is in any way increased by this homœopathic addition.

NIOBIUM

Symbol, Nb — Atomic weight, 94 — Specific gravity, 4.06

Niobium is a rare element, never native. It is sometimes called Columbium, on account of its having been first discovered by Hatchett in columbite in 1801. It greatly resembles phosphorus in its combinations.

TANTALUM

Symbol, Ta — Atomic weight, 182

A rare metal, about whose properties little is known. Discovered by Ekeberg in the mineral called tantalite.

THE LEAD GROUP.

	Symbol	Atomic weight	Specific gravity	Fusing-point
Lead	Pb	207.0	11.38	325° C.
Thallium	Tl	203.6	11.86	294° C
Copper	Cu	63.4	8.95	1091° C
Gallium	Ga	68.0	5.90	30.1° C
Indium	In	113.4	7.40	176° C

LEAD (Plumbum).

Symbol, Pb — Atomic weight, 207 — Specific gravity, 11.38

Lead is a bluish-colored metal, soft, malleable, and ductile, but little tenacious. It tarnishes slowly in moist air. It is acted upon to a considerable extent by *soft* water in the presence of air and carbonic acid, also by water containing chlorides and nitrites. Hard water and that containing sulphates does not attack lead. Hence lead poisoning need not be feared from the use of water which contains sulphates. Lead oxidizes rapidly when melted in the air, forming the yellow oxide, PbO, litharge. On further heating litharge takes on more oxygen and becomes red lead or minium, Pb_3O_4, sometimes called "orange mineral." At a still higher temperature red lead loses oxygen, and is changed back to litharge. Two other oxides of lead are known: the suboxide, Pb_2O, which is black, and the peroxide, PbO_2, which is brown.

Lead is never found native. Its chief ores are galena, lead sulphide, which usually carries more or less silver sulphide, and the peroxide known as "heavy lead ore," or puce lead. Lead expands with heat, like other metals, but is peculiar in that it does not return to its former dimensions on cooling, a bar or sheet of the metal growing continually larger and correspondingly thinner with each successive heating and cooling. On this account in a boiler lined with lead the lining soon becomes too large for the shell, and either breaks or wrinkles at the weakest points after a certain number of heatings and coolings.

Dilute sulphuric and hydrochloric acids have scarcely any action on lead. Chemically pure lead is, however, attacked to a greater extent than that containing traces of other metals. It resists the action of sulphurous acid perfectly, and consequently is of great value in the sulphite process.

Nitric acid dissolves it readily, forming nitrate of lead. $Pb(NO_3)_2$. Strong sulphuric acid scarcely attacks lead at moderate temperatures, but at about 300° C. it dissolves it so rapidly as to almost produce explosion. Sulphate of lead, $PbSO_4$, is a white, insoluble substance. It is formed when sulphuric acid or a soluble sulphate in solution is added to the solution of a soluble lead compound. Hence Glauber's salts, sulphate of soda, or "Epsom salts," sulphate of magnesia, are the antidotes for lead poisoning. "Sulphuric acid lemonade," which is water soured by sulphuric acid and flavored with lemon, is used by workmen employed in white lead works as a preventive of lead poisoning. Sulphate of lead is frequently employed as an adulterant of "white lead," which is the basic carbonate of lead, PbH_2O_2, $2 PbCO_3$. The normal carbonate is $PbCO_3$.

All adulterants of white lead injure its qualities as a paint

Nitrate of lead $Pb(NO_3)^2$ is a white crystalline substance soluble in eight parts of water. Acetate or "sugar" of lead, $Pb(C_2H_3O_2)_2$, 3 aq., is soluble in twice its weight of water. Chromate of lead, chrome yellow, $PbCrO_4$, is formed when a solution of bichromate of potash or soda is added in excess to a solution of acetate of lead as a beautiful yellow precipitate entirely insoluble in water. By boiling the yellow chromate of lead with limewater, a portion of the chromic acid combines with the lime, leaving basic lead chromate, Pb_2CrO_5 (or $PbO, PbCrO_4$), which is an orange red, almost approaching vermilion. This is also sometimes called orange mineral. Flint glass is a silicate of lead and potash. "Paste" for imitation gems is also a silicate of potash and lead, containing more lead than flint glass.

THALLIUM

Symbol, Tl — Atomic weight, 203.6 — Specific gravity, 11.86.

Thallium is a soft, malleable, crystalline metal, between lead and silver in color. It was discovered by the aid of the spectroscope, in 1861, by Crooks. Thallium melts at 294° C. It tarnishes in moist air. Heated in oxygen to 315° C., it burns with a green light. It greatly resembles lead in its properties, and also in its compounds. It has found scarcely any useful applications. Thallium compounds are poisonous.

COPPER (Cuprum)

Symbol, Cu — Atomic weight, 63.4 — Specific gravity, 8.95.

Copper is a metal of a rich reddish color, often found native, notably near Lake Superior, where it occurs sometimes in masses of tons' weight, and often containing native silver. Copper is one of the most useful of metals. It is malleable, ductile, and tenacious to a high degree. Next to silver it is the best conductor of heat and electricity. It corrodes but slowly, and only superficially, in moist air. Seawater, however, acts upon it rapidly. Copper melts at 1091° C. Heated to redness in the air it oxidizes rapidly, forming first red cuprous oxide, Cu_2O, and then cupric oxide, CuO.

Dilute hydrochloric and sulphuric acids attack copper scarcely at all in the cold. Sulphurous acid (moist) corrodes it rapidly.

Nitric acid attacks it immediately. Boiled with strong sulphuric acid, copper is slowly dissolved as copper sulphate, and at the same time sulphurous acid gas, SO_2, is given off according to the equation —

$$Cu + 2 H_2SO_4 = CuSO_4 + SO_2 + 2 H_2O.$$

This reaction furnishes a convenient means of preparing sulphurous anhydride, SO_2, in the laboratory. Chlorine gas combines rapidly with copper, so that copper foil immersed in chlorine takes fire or becomes incandescent from the heat generated by the rapid chemical combination. Copper alloys readily with many of the metals. Brass is an alloy of zinc and copper; bell metal and bronze, tin and copper, etc.

Copper burns with a green flame in the oxyhydrogen flame. Its salts also impart a green color to flame.

Copper forms two basic oxides: cuprous oxide, Cu_2O, red; cupric oxide, CuO, black. The former occurs native as "ruby copper ore." It gives a ruby color to glass. The cuprous salts are colorless in solution. They are few in number, and of little importance in the present connection.

Cupric oxide or, as ordinarily spoken of, copper oxide, CuO, is black, and forms with acids green or blue salts. Ordinary "bluestone," or "blue vitriol," is cupric sulphate, $CuSO_4$, 5 aq. It is soluble in four parts of water, forming a blue solution. At 200° C. all the water of crystallization, or combined water, is driven off, and the salt becomes white.

Cupric chloride, $CuCl_2$, 2 aq., forms green deliquescent needles.

Cupric acetate, $Cu(C_2H_3O_2)_2$, H_2O, crystallizes in green prisms. Verdigris is a mixture of several basic cupric acetates, and occurs in both a green and blue variety.

Insoluble salts are the carbonate, the arsenite and arsenate, and the aceto-arsenite, the latter being known as "Paris green."

Cupric oxide is soluble in oils and fats, which may become poisonous through its presence. It, however, colors them green. It also gives a green color to glass.

Ammonia, added in small quantity to solutions of cupric salts, precipitates the copper as cupric hydrate, CuH_2O_2, of a light greenish blue color. Excess of ammonia redissolves the cupric hydrate to a beautiful deep blue solution. Copper is precipitated from its solutions by iron, zinc, and many other metals, either in a spongy form or as a coating or plating on the surface of the immersed metal. An easy test for the presence of copper in a solution is to immerse in it a piece of polished steel, as a knife-blade when, if even a small amount of copper is present the steel will, after a short time, show the characteristic color of copper.

Copper forms the best material for conductors and pipes of a paper-mill, as the alum used serves to keep the inside of the pipes clean and bright, and slime is less likely to find a lodgment than on other metals

GALLIUM

Symbol, Ga — Atomic weight, 68 — Specific gravity, 5 9

Gallium is a hard, white metal, resembling aluminum and zinc. It was discovered by Lecoq de Boisbaudran in a zinc blende in 1875. It melts at 30.1° C. Heated to redness it only oxidizes on the surface. Gallium oxide may be substituted for alumina in alums

The metal and its compounds have yet found no practical uses. It is of infrequent occurrence.

INDIUM

Symbol, In — Atomic weight 113 4 — Specific gravity 7 42

Indium is a rare metal, never found native It was discovered in 1863 in a German zinc ore. It is a white metal, malleable and ductile It melts at 176° C. When heated to redness in the air it burns with a beautiful violet-colored flame, forming indium sesquioxide, In_2O_3, which is yellow Zinc or cadmium (metallic) immersed in a solution of indium replaces the latter and precipitates metallic indium.

THE SILVER GROUP

SOMETIMES CALLED THE NOBLE METALS

	Symbol	Atomic weight	Specific gravity	Fusing-point
Silver	Ag	108.0	10.53	916° C
Mercury	Hg	200.0	13.59	38.8° C
Gold	Au	196.6	19.34	1037° C
Platinum	Pt	197.1	21.53	1460° C
Palladium	Pd	106.5	11.80	1360° C
Rhodium	Rh	104.3	12.10	
Ruthenium	Ru	104.2	11.40	
Osmium	Os	199.0	22.48	
Iridium	Ir	198.0	21.15	

SILVER (Argentum)

Symbol Ag — Atomic weight, 108 — Specific gravity, 10.53

Silver is frequently found native both in the crystalline and massive forms. It is the whitest and most lustrous of all the metals, also the best conductor of heat and electricity. It does not tarnish in pure air. Its oxide is reduced to metal by heat alone. Silver melts at 916°. When melted the metal will absorb twenty-two times its bulk of oxygen *without combining* with it. On cooling the absorbed oxygen is discharged often with some violence, causing "sprouting" and "spitting" of the metal.

Silver has a great affinity for sulphur, being rapidly blackened and converted into sulphide of silver by free sulphur or soluble sulphides. Sulphuric and hydrochloric acids scarcely attack silver at all. It is, however, rapidly attacked by nitric acid, and dissolved with the formation of nitrate of silver, $AgNO_3$. Silver readily alloys with other metals. Silver coins are usually alloys of silver and copper or nickel.

Silver forms three oxides, only one of which is basic: —

Argentous oxide, Ag_4O, a very unstable compound.

Argentic oxide, Ag_2O, which is a brown substance, a powerful base. It is soluble in ammonia, and slightly soluble in water. At a low red heat it is decomposed into metal silver and oxygen.

The peroxide, Ag_2O_2, is formed in dark gray needles by the electrolysis of silver nitrate.

Argentic sulphide, Ag_2S, occurs native as "silver glance." The same substance is formed when hydrogen sulphide or an alkaline sulphide is added to a solution of silver.

Nitrate of silver, $AgNO_3$, is made by dissolving silver in dilute nitric acid, evaporating the solution, and crystallizing. It thus forms colorless anhydrous tabular crystals. The crystals melt at 219° C., and the mass may then be cast into sticks, which form the "lunar caustic" of pharmacy. Nitrate of silver is very soluble in water, and readily so in alcohol. Other soluble salts of silver are the sulphate, Ag_2SO_4; silver alum, $Ag_2Al_2\ 4\ SO_4$, 24 aq.; acetate, $AgC_2H_3O_2$; fluoride, AgF, and the double cyanide of silver and potassium, $2\ KCN\ AgCN, H_2O$. The latter is the salt commonly employed in silver-plating.

All the soluble silver salts are irritant poisons. Their antidote in all cases is common salt, NaCl.

All salts of silver, except those enumerated above, are nearly or quite insoluble in water. The chloride, bromide, and iodide of silver are peculiarly sensitive to light, turning nearly black on short exposure to sunlight.

The art of photography depends upon the sensitiveness of the silver salts to light. The "plate" is prepared by spreading a film of albumen, collodion, or gelatine, carrying the bromide and iodide of silver, upon glass. When the plate is exposed to light, as in the camera, obscure chemical changes take place which affect the subsequent solubility of the salts in the fixing or reducing bath. The extent of the change is proportional to the amount of light falling upon different portions of the plate. The image is subsequently developed by contact with a reducing agent, as, for instance, a solution of ferrous sulphate, which converts those portions of the silver salts which have been affected by light into metallic silver. The image is fixed or rendered permanent by washing out the undecomposed silver salts by a solution of sodium thiosulphate ("hyposulphite of soda"). If, now, paper, similarly prepared to the glass plate, is exposed to light under this "negative," the silver salts are blackened where the light comes through the negative, and the "positive" picture so obtained may be fixed by washing in a bath of sodium thiosulphate. Paper made for photographic purposes should be free from acid, antichlors, and bleach, since these affect the sensitive silver salts.

MERCURY (Hydrargyrum).

Symbol, Hg — Atomic weight, 200 — Specific gravity, 13.59

Mercury is the only metal known which is fluid at the ordinary temperature of the air. It freezes or solidifies at $-38.8°$ C. Mercury is rarely found native, more frequently as cinnabar, mercuric sulphide, HgS. It does not tarnish, and its oxides are reduced by heat alone, hence it is called a "noble metal." It boils at $357°$ C., and may be readily distilled.

Mercury readily alloys with other metals. Alloys of mercury are called amalgams. It amalgamates with gold with extreme facility, dissolving the latter almost as readily as water dissolves sugar. Advantage is taken of this property in the extraction of gold from gold-bearing quartz, the gold being dissolved out from the powdered rock by means of mercury, and the resulting amalgam distilled in iron retorts, when the gold remains in the retort and the mercury in the receiver may be used again. The amalgam of tin and mercury is employed for "silvering" mirrors. At $300°$ C. mercury slowly oxidizes, forming mercuric oxide, HgO. Hydrochloric acid does not attack mercury. Nitric acid dissolves it in the cold to mercurous nitrate, $Hg_2N_2O_6$, and, when heated, to mercuric nitrate, HgN_2O_6. Heated with sulphuric acid, sulphurous acid gas, SO_2, is given off, and the metal is dissolved to mercuric sulphate, $HgSO_4$.

Mercury forms two oxides, both basic. Mercurous oxide, Hg_2O, is black and unstable. It forms with acids mercurous salts. Mercuric oxide, HgO, is a red crystalline powder. Mercuric oxide forms with acids mercuric salts.

Calomel is mercurous chloride, Hg_2Cl_2. Corrosive sublimate is mercuric chloride, $HgCl_2$. The former is almost entirely insoluble in water and alcohol, while the latter is very readily soluble in both. All the soluble salts of mercury, as well as such other of its compounds as may become in any degree soluble in the system, are violent acrid poisons. Their antidote is raw egg albumen, or white of egg. True vermilion is an artificial mercuric sulphide, Hg_2S. Mercuric iodide, HgI_2, is also of a vivid scarlet color. "Turpeth mineral" is yellow, and consists of basic mercuric sulphate, $HgSO_4 \cdot 2HgO$.

All the mercuric salts are powerful destroyers of organic life, and hence are frequently of the highest use as disinfectants. One part of corrosive sublimate in 5000 of water has been found to destroy instantly all forms of bacteria.

GOLD (Aurum)

Symbol, Au — Atomic weight, 196.6 — Specific gravity, 19.34

Gold is always found native. It is very widely distributed, but occurs only in comparatively small quantities. It is a bright yellow, lustrous metal, the most malleable and ductile of all the metals. Gold leaf is often only $\frac{1}{200000}$ of an inch in thickness. It melts at 1037° C. It does not tarnish in the air, and its oxide is reduced by heat alone. It is not attacked by any single acid, but is readily dissolved as auric chloride, $AuCl_3$, by aqua regia (hydrochloric acid three parts, to nitric acid one part). It is also attacked by chlorine, bromine, and iodine.

Pure gold is a very soft metal, and hence is alloyed with a percentage of copper, which renders it much harder and better able to resist wear. As a conductor of heat and electricity, gold is not so good as silver and copper.

The compounds of gold are of little importance, since they are only used for a few special purposes, as, e. g., gilding porcelain, etc.

PLATINUM.

Symbol, Pt — Atomic weight 197.1 — Specific gravity 21.53.

Platinum is a white, lustrous metal, resembling tin in appearance, very malleable and ductile. It was discovered in 1741. It does not tarnish in the air, and is attacked by no single acid. Aqua regia dissolves it slowly as platinum chloride. It is also attacked and dissolved slowly by chlorine, bromine, and iodine in presence of water. Platinum always occurs native and alloyed with palladium, osmium, iridium, rhodium, and ruthenium. It has been found in greatest quantity in the Ural Mountains, but even there it is by no means abundant. It has been found also in Brazil and Ceylon. Platinum melts at 1460° C. Platinum possesses qualities which render it an extremely useful metal, but the sparseness of its distribution in nature, together with the difficulty of working, renders its cost so high as to prohibit its use in all but exceptional instances.

Platinum appears to be the only metal which is able to resist the chemical action which takes place at the positive electrode in the processes for electric bleaching

The stills or retorts used in concentrating sulphuric acid are of platinum. Vessels made of this metal are of the greatest use to the chemical analyst, since it resists the action of nearly all chemicals as well as great heat.

PALLADIUM

Symbol, Pd — Atomic weight, 106 5 — Specific gravity, 11 8.

Palladium was discovered by Wollaston in 1803 It occasionally occurs native, but usually forms one-half to one per cent. of the platinum ores. It is a white, lustrous metal, similar to platinum, but much harder. It melts at 1360° C. It is dissolved readily by nitric acid and aqua regia. Palladium has the curious property of absorbing hydrogen equal to 982 times its own volume, forming apparently an alloy with it. Mercury also, under certain circumstances, alloys with hydrogen to form hydrogen amalgam. These reactions seem to indicate that hydrogen is in reality a metal Palladium occurs only in very small quantities, and as yet no considerable economic use has been found for it.

RHODIUM

Symbol Rh — Atomic weight, 104 3 — Specific gravity, 12 1

This is a rare metal, of no industrial importance, found alloyed with platinum in its ores, usually to the extent of about one-half of one per cent.

RUTHENIUM

Symbol, Ru — Atomic weight, 104 2 — Specific gravity, 11 4

A very rare metal discovered in 1845 Never native, but always alloyed with other of the platinum metals Of no industrial importance.

OSMIUM

Symbol, Os — Atomic weight, 199 — Specific gravity, 22.48

A rare metal, also of the platinum family, discovered in 1803. It is a bluish white, very infusible metal. It takes its name from the Greek word ὀσμή, meaning smell, on account of the pungent, irritating odor of its oxide, OsO_4, whose vapor is extremely irritating and poisonous. Osmium is the heaviest substance known.

IRIDIUM

Symbol, Ir — Atomic weight, 198 — Specific gravity, 21.15

Iridium was discovered in 1803. It sometimes occurs native, but usually as an alloy with osmium. It is a very hard, white, brittle metal. It is frequently used for making the points of gold pens. It is very rare, and of scarcely any importance in the arts. It takes its name from the Latin word *iris*, the rainbow, from the rapid changes of color due to different stages of oxidation which occur when the metal is heated.

Part II.

THE CHEMISTRY OF PAPER-MAKING.

Part II.

THE CHEMISTRY OF PAPER-MAKING.

CHAPTER I

CELLULOSE ($C_6H_{10}O_5$)

The physical features of the ordinary forms of cellulose are familiar to every paper-maker, since it forms the basis of all that he produces. It is essentially vegetable in its origin, and forms so large and important a part of the structure of all plants that it has been said that in the vegetable world the formation of cellulose may be considered as synonymous with growth. Cellulose also occurs to a limited extent in the animal kingdom, and has been found in the brain, in diseased human spleen, the skin of silkworms and of serpents, and in the mantles of certain molluscs.

Cotton-wool, filter paper, and, in general, any vegetable fibre which has undergone the usual chemical processes of paper-making consist mainly of cellulose, with which are associated various other substances in greater or less amount. Pure cellulose is most readily obtained by treating cotton-wool or white filter paper with a boiling one per cent solution of caustic soda, then with cold dilute hydrochloric acid, and after that with ammonia. The fibre should be carefully washed with water after treatment with each of these reagents, and finally exhausted with alcohol and ether. Thus obtained, cellulose is a white, translucent body, of Sp. Gr. about 1.45, and which preserves the form and general character of the fibres from which it was prepared. It resists the action of chemical reagents to a remarkable degree, as is shown by its wide use in the laboratory in the form of filter paper. Cellulose has, however, a powerful attraction for certain salts in solution, and water containing them may be so filtered through a mass of cellulose as to have the dissolved salts completely removed. This attractive power is so strong in the case of vanadium compounds that cellulose will separate them from solutions containing only one part of the salt in a trillion.

Solutions of iron and alumina salts in contact with a quantity of pulp may have a considerable portion of the base fixed upon the fibre. Where iron is present, the color may thus be seriously affected. The process of mordanting cotton goods depends upon this affinity of cellulose for metallic bases.

The formula for cellulose, $C_6H_{10}O_5$, does not indicate the presence of any mineral constituents, but even its most carefully purified forms leave an appreciable amount of ash. In cotton this is usually from 0.1 to 0.2 per cent., though Herzberg gives a figure as high as 0.41 per cent., and bleached filter paper which has been washed with both hydrochloric and hydrofluoric acids leaves sufficient ash to render a correction for its presence necessary in very careful chemical work.

The various reactions of cellulose prove it to be closely related to the sugars, starch, dextrin, glucose, and other members of that group of bodies which, including cellulose, are termed carbohydrates. The formula of cellulose is the same as that of starch, and, like starch, cellulose can be readily converted into dextrin and glucose. (See, also, **Cellulosic fermentation**, p 116.)

The only known liquid in which cellulose dissolves without undergoing chemical change is Schweitzer's reagent, as it is called, though it is stated (Life of John Mercer, London, 1886) that its action was first studied by Mercer. This reagent may be prepared in various ways. Our own experience has led us to prefer the following method: cupric hydrate is precipitated by adding a solution of caustic soda to a cold solution of copper sulphate until nearly all the copper is precipitated. The hydrate is then carefully washed, and may be preserved under water in a glass-stoppered bottle. As the reagent is needed for use, it is made by dissolving the hydrate in ammonia of Sp Gr 0.900 until a saturated solution is obtained. When treated with Schweitzer's reagent, cellulose at first swells up and becomes gelatinous, but finally dissolves completely to a thick syrupy solution. Erdmann and other chemists have contended that no true solution is formed, but recent experiments by Cramer on the osmotic properties of the solution prove that the cellulose is really dissolved. From this solution it may be precipitated in gelatinous flocks by the addition of acids, many salts, and, it is generally said, by simply diluting it largely with water and allowing the solution to stand in a closed vessel for eight to ten days. We think it doubtful if complete precipitation is obtained in this way, and we have allowed such dilute solutions, containing less than 0.25 gram of cellulose per litre, to stand in glass-stoppered jars for more than a month without causing any precipitation. The precipitate, as usually formed, contains, in addition to cellulose, considerable copper hydrate, which gives it a blue color, and which may be removed by washing with water, dilute acid, and then with water again. When a solution of lead acetate is used to precipitate the cellulose, the precipitate contains both cellulose and lead oxide in varying proportions; while by digesting the same solution with finely divided lead oxide a definite compound of cellulose and lead oxide ($C_6H_{10}O_5$, PbO) is obtained. Metallic zinc, added to the solution of cellulose in Schweitzer's reagent, throws down the copper, which is replaced by zinc, forming a colorless solution similar in its properties to the original one.

A practical application of the action of Schweitzer's reagent upon cellulose has been made on the large scale in the manufacture of the so-called Willesden papers and products. The reagent is prepared in quantity in a series of towers, loosely packed with copper scrap, over which strong ammonia is allowed to trickle, while air is drawn up through the towers. When a web of paper is passed through this solution, the fibres become superficially softened, and may be pressed into a continuous mass, or several sheets may be pressed together. No attempt is made to wash out the solution, which dries to a green varnish, coating the fibres, and rendering them waterproof and very durable. Canvas and rope cordage are similarly treated.

A solution of iodine, prepared by dissolving one gram of iodine and five grams of iodide of potash in 100 c.c. of water, stains cellulose blue under certain conditions, and is used for its recognition under the microscope. If Iceland moss or some of the lichens and algæ containing cellulose in its less compact forms are merely boiled with water, the cellulose is disintegrated, and the blue color is obtained on adding the above solution of iodine. With a fresh solution, cellulose in its denser forms, as in cotton and other purified fibres, merely develops a yellow color, which may shade into brown, but if the fibres are first treated with sulphuric or phosphoric acid, or zinc chloride, they are then stained blue with iodine. It would seem, therefore, that although this blue coloration is generally spoken of as characteristic of cellulose, it really depends not upon cellulose, but upon other bodies, whose presence is the result of the treatment to which the cellulose has been subjected. Schultze's solution of iodine gives a blue with cellulose at once, and may be prepared by dissolving zinc in hydrochloric acid so long as there is any action, evaporating the resulting solution of zinc chloride to a syrup, saturating with potassium iodide, and then adding enough iodine to color the whole brown. It may be used of various degrees of strength, but it is to be observed that the zinc chloride would exert a powerful action upon the cellulose, so that in this case also the blue coloration is probably due to modifications of the cellulose rather than to that substance itself and iodine.

Concentrated sulphuric acid, Sp. Gr. 1.60, dissolves pure and thoroughly dry cellulose, a syrupy and almost colorless solution being obtained, which, on dilution with water and boiling, is converted into dextrin and glucose. If the boiling is continued for a long time, about five hours, only glucose, or similar reducing sugars, is obtained. As the glucose can be readily fermented, with consequent production of alcohol, it is thus possible to make both glucose and alcohol from such materials as sawdust and rags. Starch, under the same conditions, acts similarly and gives the same products. With more concentrated acid, especially if it be hot or if the cellulose is damp, there is a breaking down of the cellulose molecule, and, at the same time, more or less decomposition of the acid. Gases are evolved, in which carbonic and sulphurous acids may be recognized, and the liquid becomes black from the separation of carbonaceous matters. These are precipitated on pouring the acid into a considerable volume of water, and may be easily removed by filtration, leaving a golden colored liquid, whose color darkens when the acid is neutralized with ammonia. When treated with acid of the strength previously given, Sp. Gr. 1.60, or even with somewhat weaker acid, the cellulose first becomes gelatinous and more transparent. If the mixture is poured into water before the solution is complete, white flocks resembling hydrate of alumina are obtained, which dry to a horny mass. The substance composing them differs little from cellulose in composition, and is termed amyloid, from its resemblance to starch. Its composition is given as $C_{12}H_{22}O_{11}$. It is difficult to determine just when the cellulose is entirely dissolved, owing to its transparency, and it is usually stated that precipitation of amyloid occurs at once on diluting the clear solution. We find in our own experiments, using various strengths of acid, that when a clear solution is obtained there is no precipitation of amyloid upon dilution until a considerable time has expired, when at best only a small proportion of the cellulose is recovered in that form. The loss is probably due to the formation of dextrin. Amyloid forms the outer coating of the parchment paper which is largely used in dialyzing apparatus and for many of the purposes to which animal parchment was applied.

Parchment paper is prepared by dipping unsized paper for a few seconds into sulphuric acid diluted with one-quarter to one-half or more its bulk of water, to which glycerine is sometimes added. After removing the paper it is washed with water, then with dilute ammonia or other alkali, and finally with pure water again. On the large scale the paper is treated in the web in a continuous way, passing into the acid, as into a vat for glue sizing, then between rollers, or " doctors," to remove the excess of acid, and from there into the dilute ammonia and water. Thus treated, the paper acquires a remarkable toughness and many of the properties of animal parchment. It undergoes a considerable linear shrinkage during the treatment (20 per cent.), and suffers some loss of weight (Cross and Bevan). The action of a concentrated solution of zinc chloride, about 65° Bé. upon cellulose is similar to that of sulphuric acid. The so-called vulcanized fibre is formed of sheets of paper which have been treated with zinc chloride, then pressed together, and washed for a long time in running water to remove the chemical.

The formation of parchment paper by means of sulphuric acid was first noticed by Poumarède and Figuier in 1847, from whom it received the name Papyrin. No practical application of their discovery was made until it was extended and patented by Gaines in 1857.

The process has quite recently received an ingenious application, which would seem to make any alteration in the denomination of a bank note or other paper money impossible. The denomination is printed in large numbers in the centre of the bill, the numbers being preceded and followed by a star or other device, thus —

—✯1000✯—

Strong sulphuric acid or a solution of chloride of zinc is used in place of ink, and transforms the paper, which is generally tinted, into transparent vegetable parchment at the points where it is deposited, so that after washing and drying the numbers seem to be formed by a tough transparent membrane inserted in a colored sheet. The effect is highly artistic and as the fibrous structure of the paper is destroyed at the points where the chemicals were deposited, it is practically impossible to alter the characters.

When cellulose is heated in a sealed tube to 180°, with six to eight times its weight of acetic anhydride, it dissolves to a thick syrup. On pouring this into water white flocks of triaceto-cellulose are precipitated, which have the composition represented by the formula —

$$C_6H_7(C_2H_3O)_3O_5$$

The compound dissolves in strong acetic acid, but is insoluble in water, alcohol, and ether. Alkalis easily remove the acid with recovery of the cellulose. This reaction is similar to the one taking place when oils are treated with alkali, when glycerine is set free, and soap formed, and it therefore indicates that cellulose, like glycerine, may be considered a triatomic alcohol. This view is confirmed by the fact that it has been found impossible to prepare compounds containing more acetic anhydride than the above, no matter how great an excess of the anhydride is used or how long the heating is continued. It is to be noted also, in this connection, that by the action of nitric acid upon cellulose nitro-substitution products are formed similar in many of their properties to the nitroglycerines.

The action of nitric acid upon cellulose was first studied by Pelouze, who observed in 1838 that it resulted in the conversion of the cellulose into an explosive substance. Schonbein, in 1846, announced the discovery of an explosive cotton, but kept its method of preparation secret. It was independently discovered soon after by Böttger and Otto, by the latter of whom the method was published. Several disastrous explosions of large quantities of the material as at first made caused it to be considered utterly unfit for use, until von Lenk and Abel pointed out the precautions necessary to secure the production of a material of constant composition, and which remained perfectly stable under all ordinary conditions. Knop had previously shown that a mixture of nitric and sulphuric acids gave better results than nitric acid alone, and the explosive called guncotton is now prepared as follows. Loosely spun yarn or cotton wool is first purified by boiling in a dilute solution of carbonate of potash to remove resinous, gummy, and waxy matters or oil. It is then carefully washed with water and dried, after which it is placed in a mixture of one part of nitric acid, Sp. Gr. 1.5, and three parts sulphuric acid, Sp. Gr. 1.85, and allowed to remain twenty-four hours. Great pains are taken to keep the mixture cool. The nitrated cotton, after washing, is removed to a beating-engine, where it is washed again and reduced to pulp. It is then ready to be pressed into hexagonal blocks or into cylinders.

The composition of guncotton was determined by Crum, who gave it the formula —

$$C_{12}H_{14}(NO_1)_6O_4,$$

or that of a hex-nitrate of cellulose. Guncotton is also called Pyroxylin, though this term is usually extended to comprise the other nitrates of cellulose as well. Its general appearance is the same as that of the cotton from which it was prepared, but it is harsher to the touch, and its fibres, viewed under the microscope by polarized light, do not show the brightness and play of color exhibited by ordinary cotton. It becomes strongly electrical on being rubbed, crackling and emitting sparks, and is phosphorescent in the dark (Gaiffe). It is slowly soluble in acetone, but insoluble in water, methyl alcohol, glacial acetic acid, Schweitzer's reagent, alcohol, or ether, or in mixtures of the last two liquids. Weak acids and alkalis do not affect it. Strong sulphuric acid dissolves it slowly, and upon heating the solution carbonic acid and nitric oxide are given off, though there is no blackening. It dissolves rapidly in strong potash lye when heated to 70°, with formation of ammonia, nitrous acid, oxalic acid, and other bodies of acid character. The alkaline solution precipitates silver from an ammoniacal solution of the metal, and the reaction has been utilized in a process for silvering mirrors. Alkaline solutions of moderate strength remove more or less nitric acid from guncotton on warming, the proportion of acid removed varying with the strength of the solution (Eder). A solution of potassium sulphydrate in dilute alcohol converts the nitrate into the original cotton, potassium nitrate and some ammonia being formed. Ferrous sulphate and ferrous acetate or a solution of stannous oxide in caustic soda have the same effect. In contact with sulphuric acid and mercury, guncotton gives up its nitrogen as nitric oxide. These reactions, like that with acetic anhydride, indicate that cellulose is analogous, in many of its chemical relations, to the alcohols.

Concentrated sulphuric acid displaces the nitric acid in guncotton even in the cold. A method of estimating the nitrogen in pyroxylins is based upon the fact that when they are boiled with ferrous sulphate and hydrochloric acid the nitrogen is set free as nitric oxide (Eder).

Besides guncotton, which contains six NO_3, there have been prepared several other lower nitrates of cellulose, containing successively five, four, three, and two NO_3. They differ from guncotton mainly in being less explosive, and in the fact that they are soluble in a mixture of alcohol and ether. The penta-nitrate, $C_{12}H_{15}O_5(NO_3)_5$, is best prepared, according to Eder, by dissolving guncotton in hot nitric acid, about 90° C., then cooling to 0°, when it is precipitated as the penta-nitrate on addition of sulphuric acid. The precipitate is washed with a large amount of water, and further purified by being dissolved in a mixture of alcohol and ether, from which the pure nitrate is thrown down on addition of water. By the action of strong solutions of potash upon the penta-nitrate a portion of the acid is removed, leaving di-nitrate of cellulose.

The extent to which the nitration of the cellulose is carried when in contact with the mixed acids depends upon the strength of the acids employed and upon the time for which it is exposed to their influence. Thus, by shortening the time of immersion to a few minutes, or by the use of weaker acids, a mixture of the tetra-nitrate, $C_{12}H_{16}O_6(NO_3)_4$, and tri-nitrate, $C_{12}H_{17}O_7(NO_3)_3$, is obtained. These are readily soluble in a mixture of alcohol and ether, in acetic ether, and in methyl alcohol. The solution in ether-alcohol mixture is called collodion, and the tetra- and tri-nitrates are termed collodion pyroxylins.

The di-nitrate, $C_{12}H_{18}O_8(NO_3)_2$, is the result of the action of a hot dilute mixture of nitric and sulphuric acids upon cellulose. It dissolves in the solvents mentioned in the preceding paragraph. All of the higher nitrates are finally reduced to this body when treated with alkaline solutions; but if the action is carried too far, there is a further decomposition with production of a brown gummy mass. The mono-nitrate has not been formed.

Celluloid and zylonite are prepared by treating the lower nitrates, collodion pyroxylins, with camphor, either melted or as spirits of camphor. This reduces the pyroxylin when hot to a plastic condition, in which it can be readily worked and moulded into a great variety of articles, and which permits the incorporation of coloring matters and other substances.

Celluloid in the mass burns about as readily as paper, and with a smoky flame. It cannot be exploded by any ordinary means. The camphor present may be removed by ether. Thin, transparent plates and rolls of celluloid are now much used in photography, as their flexibility and lightness give them great advantage over glass. In this form celluloid flashes up quickly and burns without smoke.

Collodion — the solution of pyroxylin in ether-alcohol mixture — rapidly dries on exposure to the air, and forms a tough, lustrous varnish. It is largely used in surgery as a covering for wounds, in photography as a vehicle for the silver salts, and in the match manufacture for rendering the tips of matches waterproof. Pure sulphite fibre or unsized paper made therefrom is sometimes used instead of cotton in the preparation of both celluloid and collodion.

The nitrates of cellulose and their reactions have received a new interest for the paper-maker through their recent application in the process of manufacturing artificial silk. This product, which resembles silk only in its physical properties, was first shown at the Paris Exposition of 1889, where it attracted much attention. It is prepared by the following process of M. de Chardonnet: —

Cotton or pure chemical fibre is nitrated and dissolved in a mixture of thirty-eight parts ether to forty-two parts alcohol to form collodion. This is placed in a copper vessel, and forced by air pressure through capillary glass tubes into water. In Fig 2, *A* shows the glass tube through which the collodion passes. *B* is a second tube surrounding the first, and supplied with water through the inlet *C*. The collodion solidifies upon contact with the water, forming a smooth thread, which is carried

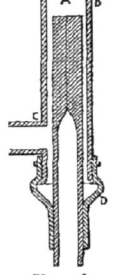

Fig. 2

forward by suitable mechanical arrangements through a drying chamber to the bobbins. J. H. du Vivier, Br Pat. 2570, A. D 1889, prepares three solutions as follows: —

1. A 12.5 per cent. solution of gutta percha in carbon bisulphide.
2. A 5 per cent solution of isinglass in glacial acetic acid
3. A 7 per cent. solution of pyroxylin in glacial acetic acid.

These are mixed in such proportion that the resulting solution contains —

> 4 parts nitrocellulose,
> 1 part isinglass,
> ½ part gutta percha,

to which is added a little castor oil and glycerine. The thread coming from the capillary aperture is led first through a bath of soda, then into one containing albumen and finally into a solution of bichloride of mercury to coagulate the albumen. It then passes through the vapor of carbon bisulphide on its way to the bobbins, and may be treated with ammonia and alum in order to sufficiently impregnate it with alumina to prevent its burning readily. The combustible nature of the nitrocellulose renders the soda or other chemical bath necessary, as the nitric acid is thereby removed in greater part. Chardonnet employs a bath of nitric acid of Sp Gr. 1 32, the temperature of which is slowly allowed to fall from 35° to 25°, by which means, it is stated, the fibre is denitrated and reduced to the condition of ordinary cellulose.

This new fibre promises to have an important bearing on the textile industries, as it compares favorably with silk as to strength, while surpassing silk in lustre and beauty It may be dyed brilliantly in any color

Cellulose and Chlorine. — Dry chlorine has no effect upon cellulose. but when moisture is also present. as when the gas is passed into water containing cellulose in suspension, the cellulose is rapidly oxidized and carbonic acid evolved A similar action is observed when cellulose is heated with a solution of bleaching powder or other hypochlorite. Cross and Bevan have lately shown that in ordinary bleaching there is often some chlorination of the cellulose The extent of the chlorination appears to depend somewhat upon the base present. and is stated by them to be conspicuously less when hypochlorite of magnesium is used instead of bleaching powder. We find, in electric bleaching. that fibre caught and held against the positive electrodes where it is subject to the action of nascent chlorine is after some weeks converted into a yellow, gummy substance, all fibrous structure being lost. By acting upon guncotton in a sealed tube with phosphorous penta-chloride Baeyer has indirectly prepared a compound of cellulose and chlorine, which was obtained as a viscous liquid which mixed readily with alcohol and ether.

Cellulose and Oxygen; Oxycellulose. — The action of oxidizing agents upon cellulose has been studied by Witz, who finds that their first effect is to convert the cellulose more or less completely into a white, friable substance, containing less carbon and more oxygen than cellulose, and for which he has proposed the name oxycellulose. The frequent tendering of cotton cloth in bleaching, or in boiling with milk of lime, is due to partial conversion into oxycellulose. When cotton or linen cloth is wet with a solution of bleaching powder, and exposed for some time to the air, there is a gradual loss of strength and change of composition as indicated above. Kept in a very slightly acidulated solution of bleaching powder for several days, the fibre is so completely changed to oxycellulose that it readily rubs down to a white powder. When converted into oxycellulose, no reducing agent, as antichlor, will restore the fibre to its original condition.

Oxycellulose has a powerful attraction for basic aniline dyes, though not for those of acid character, and the greater readiness with which fibre may be colored after bleaching is due in part to the superficial formation of this substance. Many aniline blacks are dyed upon cloth which has been partially converted into oxycellulose and which are consequently lacking in strength.

Vanadium salts are often used in the preparation of fast aniline blacks, and oxycellulose has the remarkable property of forming compounds with vanadium even in solutions containing only one part of the element in 1,000,000,000,000. By converting portions of a fabric into oxycellulose by the action of oxidizing agents, the cloth may be dyed topically by dipping in a basic dye.

Fehling's solution is reduced by oxycellulose, which is colored red by the precipitated copper oxide. We have noticed the formation of oxycellulose in parchment paper held in the wooden frames of dialyzing apparatus used for glue solutions, the change seeming to have been induced by contact with the slowly decaying wood. Upon boiling such paper with Fehling's solution the copper oxide was deposited in streaks, coinciding with the position of the softer portions of the grain of the wood. The paper was unaffected where it had not touched the wood.

Through the action of more powerful oxidizing agents than those which bring about the formation of oxycellulose, cellulose is split up into a number of simpler molecules. Treatment with strong permanganate or bichromate of potash gives glucose, dextrin, and formic acid among the decomposition products. Hot chromic acid burns cellulose in the wet way, carbonic oxide and carbonic acid being formed. Upon this reaction Cross and Bevan have based a method of ultimate analysis. Certain metallic oxides, notably iron rust, in contact with moist cellulose, convert it into glucose and a gummy substance which changes to glucose on boiling with dilute acid.

Hydrocellulose. — When cellulose is moistened with any dilute mineral acid and then dried, or when it is exposed for some time to their vapor, it is changed to a friable substance having the composition $C_{12}H_{22}O_{11}$, and named by Girard, hydrocellulose; by Witz, hydracellulose. Girard has shown that the modification thus brought about in cellulose is one of true hydration, since pure cotton treated for five days with pure dry hydrochloric acid gas showed no trace of change, while it was rapidly converted to hydrocellulose in the presence of moisture and the acid. Liquid organic acids also modify cellulose considerably, but not to so great an extent as do mineral acids. Hydrocellulose is soluble in warm potash lye. It absorbs oxygen when heated, even at so low a temperature as 50°, and after being kept for some hours at 80° to 100° in contact with the air is converted into dark ulmic compounds, which are soluble in water. Hydrocellulose does not, like oxycellulose, attract basic aniline dyes, but both these substances, like cellulose, form explosive nitrates when treated with the mixed acids.

In the process of removing burrs from wool, and cotton fibre from mixed goods, the materials are moistened with dilute sulphuric acid and dried, by which treatment the cellulose is converted into hydrocellulose, which from its brittle nature may be separated by mechanical means. It is sometimes dissolved out by weak alkali, the wool in either case being unaffected. A strong solution of aluminum chloride has recently been used to replace the dilute acid in the "carbonizing" process.

Water at High Temperatures. — The effect of heat upon cellulose is greatly increased by the presence of water, the cellulose being partially decomposed with formation of carbonic acid and dark brown products of acid character. Mulder was the first to observe the formation of a small quantity of glucose at the same time. By extracting pure filter paper, under pressure in a Muncke's digester, Tauss obtained yellow extracts passing into brown on exposure to the air, and depositing on evaporation a black resinous precipitate, soluble in alkalis. Three hours' treatment at 75 pounds pressure gave an extract containing, per 100 grams of cellulose, 1.385 grams total solids, of which 0.1285 grams were glucose or similar reducing sugars. Cellulose, under about 300 pounds pressure, was completely changed to a jelly-like mass, which could be powdered after drying. Its composition was then the same as that of hydrocellulose, $C_{12}H_{22}O_{11}$.

The manufacture of chemical fibre by the soda process proves that the action of hot and moderately strong solutions of the alkalis has, at most, only a superficial action upon cellulose. Concentrated solutions, Sp. Gr. about 1.3, cause cellulose to swell up and become transparent in much the same way that it does in the preparation of parchment paper. Cloth thus treated and washed free from alkali is said to be Mercerized, from Mercer, who first prepared it. The cloth shrinks considerably in the operation, but acquires additional strength. The mercerized cellulose also shows a greater tendency than before to absorb water. Gladstone, using soda-lye of Sp. Gr. 1.342, has noted the formation of a compound of soda and cellulose, $C_{12}H_{20}O_{10} + NaOH$, which is resolved by carbonic acid or even by washing with water. When equal parts of potassium hydrate and cellulose are moistened with water and heated in a closed vessel, hydrogen, methyl alcohol, and wood-spirit are driven off, while carbonic, formic, and acetic acids are found in combination with the potash. Heated in contact with the air the main product is oxalic acid.

Cellulose is decomposed by various fermentative processes, especially those going on in the digestive canal. It is dissolved with liberation of marsh gas, by the fluid from the vermiform appendix of the rabbit. In the rumen and large intestine of herbivora it is decomposed into fatty acids and gases, consisting mainly of carbonic acid and hydrogen. This has been shown in the laboratory by Tappeiner, who placed cotton-wool in flasks with Nageli's salt solution and asparagine. Upon addition of fluid from the rumen, fermentation set in, with evolution of volatile acids, hydrogen and carbonic acid.

In nature, when the supply of air is somewhat limited and moisture is present, cellulose gradually decays with formation of large quantities of marsh gas and the dark brown or black amorphous substances which constitute vegetable mould or humus. This consists mainly of acid products, soluble in alkaline solutions. Among them have been recognized ulmin and ulmic acid, humin and humic acid. This decomposition has an important bearing on the character of the soil, not only through the mechanical action of the evolved gases in loosening the soil, but by the power possessed by humus of fixing atmospheric nitrogen in a form suitable for plant life (Storer).

A peculiar fermentation, called **Cellulosic fermentation**, which Durin first observed in beet juice possesses much interest in connection with the study of cellulose. It is there due to a ferment very similar to diastase, but may be induced in solutions of cane sugar through the influence of certain fatty seeds, as rape and colza. It results in the formation of hard, white, warty lumps, which exhibit all the reactions of cellulose, while from the mother-liquor there is precipitated, on the addition of alcohol, another body, similar to cellulose in composition, but tough and glutinous. Upon placing some of these lumps in a solution of cane sugar the formation of cellulose continues at the expense of the sugar, the solution finally containing only a trace of that substance. It has been shown in case of many plants whose juices are rich in sugar, that as the cellulose increases, the sugar lessens in amount, and there is little doubt that in general cellulose is formed in the living plant from sugar and substances of similar composition in the sap. Such food as the plant stores or holds in reserve is elaborated in the form of starch, which may be then, possibly by the action of ferments, converted into sugar or its isomers, to be dissolved and carried by the sap.

CHAPTER II.

FIBRES

The Vegetable Cell. — The unit of structure in the plant is the vegetable cell. All living cells consist essentially of protoplasm, which in the higher plants is surrounded by a wall of cellulose, produced by the protoplasm at the limiting film, and laid down in close contact with the film. The protoplasm is to be regarded as the actual basis of the life of the plant, as indeed it is the actual basis of all life. Chemically considered, it belongs to the group of albuminous bodies, and is closely similar in appearance and composition to the albumen which forms the white of egg. Under the microscope the protoplasm is seen to maintain a constant circulation, which is rendered visible by the granules in its substance, and by means of which nutritive matters are brought from the outside to the denser portion, called the nucleus, while the waste products are carried to the surface of the mass.

The green color of plants is due to the presence at certain points of a peculiar coloring matter called chlorophyll, or, more properly, chlorophyll pigment, which is associated with certain of the denser or more differentiated portions of protoplasm, called chlorophyll granules. The coloring matter is developed only through the action of light. It is soluble in alcohol, the solution appearing green in transmitted and blood-red in reflected light. The chlorophyll granules are the agents by which, under the influence of light, the plant decomposes the carbonic acid always present in the atmosphere, and assimilates the carbon needed for building up the plant-structure.

It is only in very young cells that the cell-wall consists of pure cellulose, and even here it contains a trace of mineral matters. With increasing age various changes in the wall take place, either through degradation of the cellulose itself, or more generally by the infiltration of other substances upon it. Through the deposition of silica upon or within the cell-wall the wall may be so hardened and stiffened that the change is called mineralization.

Calcium salts are sometimes so deposited, and well-defined crystals of the oxalate or carbonate are not unfrequently formed within the cell.

Either with or without these mineral matters there is often a deposition upon the cell-wall of suberin, or cork substance. The cell thereby gains greatly in elasticity and such suberized cells are, as would be expected, much less permeable to water and gases than the normal cells.

Lignin.— By far the most important change which, from our present point of view, occurs in the cell-wall is that known as lignification, and caused by the formation and infiltration upon the wall of a substance somewhat analogous to cellulose and called lignin. Lignin, which probably consists of several closely related substances, forms by far the greater portion of the incrusting matters which it is the object of several of the preparatory processes of paper-making to remove. These changes do not always extend throughout the cell-wall, but often only definite layers or strata of the wall are thus affected. The numerous researches of Cross and Bevan have led them to regard the lignified cell-wall as a chemical whole, from which by appropriate processes cellulose may be reduced. We are ourselves disposed to adhere to the older view, which considers the incrusting matter as something laid down in intimate contact with the cellulose of the wall, which itself remains unchanged, and reappears when the incrusting matters are removed by solvents. Contrary to the statement of Erdmann, and in support of our belief, we find that Schweitzer's reagent readily removes the cellulose from lignified wood-cells. The solution dissolves over 35 per cent of beech, spruce, gumwood, and birch after they have been extracted with water, alcohol, and ether. After boiling the extracted and washed residue with dilute hydrochloric acid enough more of the wood is dissolved by the Schweitzer reagent to bring the total quantity removed to over 60 per cent. of the dry wood.

Compared with cellulose lignin is harder and more elastic and absorbs relatively little water. The hardness of wood is generally in proportion to the amount of lignin it contains. The acetic acid produced in the distillation of wood appears to be derived chiefly and the wood-spirit wholly from lignin. Alkaline solutions dissolve lignin at a temperature of 130° C with formation of acid products. Fused with caustic potash it is converted into ulmic acid. Treatment with oxidizing agents, as chlorine, bromine, chromic acid, permanganate of potash, or dilute nitric acid, converts lignin into resinous acids, soluble in dilute alkali, or the oxidation may even proceed to the formation of carbonic acid and water.

A solution of aniline sulphate in water or alcohol stains lignin yellow; nitric acid produces a yellowish brown coloration; phloroglucin gives a rose-red stain when the specimen has been previously treated with hydrochloric acid; a solution of indol produces a similar effect upon lignified tissues which have first been moistened with dilute sulphuric acid, made by mixing one part of strong acid with four of water. All of these reagents are of much value for detecting the presence of incrusting matters in paper-making fibres, or in the finished product. Comparative tests may easily be arranged to show the thoroughness with which the boiling operation has been conducted in the manufacture of wood fibre, the depth of color produced by the reagent being in a measure proportional to the amount of incrusting matter still remaining in the fibre.

The chemical composition of lignin is still a matter of some doubt. It is known to contain more carbon than cellulose, and Fremy gives the formula $C_{18}H_{20}O_8$, while Schuppe finds it to be $C_{19}H_{18}O_8$. Although, as previously stated, lignin is probably made up of several analogous bodies, it may, for practical purposes, be regarded as a single substance, and will be so referred to by us. Payen distinguishes four different components, thus: —

Lignose. — Insoluble in water, alcohol, ether, and ammonia; soluble in caustic soda and potash.

Lignin. — Insoluble in water and ether; soluble in alcohol, ammonia, caustic potash, and soda.

Lignone. — Insoluble in water, alcohol, ether; soluble in ammonia, caustic potash, and soda.

Lignireose. — Soluble in all the above reagents, but only slightly so in water.

Their percentage composition, according to the same author, is as below: —

	Carbon	Hydrogen	Oxygen
Lignose	46.10	6.09	47.81
Lignin	62.25	5.93	31.82
Lignone	50.10	5.82	44.08
Lignireose	67.91	6.89	25.20

The thickening of the cell-wall, which is the result of the deposition of lignin upon the cellulose, and which, up to a certain point, accompanies increase of age, does not in most cases take place uniformly over the entire surface of the wall. As a consequence, depressions or markings, having in different instances the form of pits, lines, rings, or spirals, appear in the gradually thickening wall, and often become so distinct and characteristic as to afford one of the best means for the identification of the fibres in which they occur. Diffusion of sap and water or gases proceeds with greatest freedom at these thinnest portions of the wall.

The formation of gums and resins, although not wholly understood, is doubtless due to changes of degradation in the cell-wall. The products may either be found as minute, irregularly shaped drops within the cell itself, or in the spaces formed by the breaking down of several cells, or, as in the case of spruce and other coniferous trees, in distinct receptacles, known as resin-passages. The resins are soluble in alcohol and in alkaline solutions, and are stained yellow by tincture of alcannet root. They may be distinguished under the microscope by their appearance and these reactions.

Protoplasm is found only in the living cells, and these are at the points of growth. Where protoplasm is absent, growth has ceased, and such older lifeless cells generally contain only air more or less highly rarefied. In some cases they contain water or a few granules. Their usefulness to the plant has by no means ceased, however, for from them the plant-structure derives in the main its strength and stiffness. The different plant-cells present an almost infinite variety of form, but, except in case of those which serve as a means of identification for the fibres which they accompany, we shall endeavor to confine ourselves to those long-drawn, pointed elements of the bast and wood, which are properly called *fibres*, and which alone, with the single exception of cotton, possess a practical interest for the paper-maker. They are derived from the ordinary primitive cells by progressive growth and change of form.

The fibres which are commonly used in paper-making may be divided, according to their relations to the plant from which they are derived, into four classes.

1. Seed-hairs, as cotton, which is the only representative of the class.

2. Bast-fibres, as linen jute, manila, adansonia

3 Those derived from whole stems or leaves, and associated with various vessels and cells not properly fibres, as straw, esparto, sorghum, bamboo.

4 Those derived from wood

1 Seed-Hairs

Cotton (*Gossypium*) — All of the many known varieties are derived from the three species, *G. Barbadense*, sea-island cotton, which has a very soft, silky staple nearly two inches in length; *G herbaceum*, upland or short staple cotton; *G arboreum*, which sometimes attains the height of a small tree.

The cotton fibre consists of a single slender cell or hair, the hairs forming the covering of cotton seeds. The length of the fibre varies from 2-5 cm, diameter, from 0 012–0 037 mm The widest are found in upland cotton of short staple; the average for sea-island cotton is 0 023 mm The ripe fibre presents the appearance of a collapsed tube spirally twisted, the unripe cells show little or no twist. See Plate I. 24-29 Ordway mentions a single fibre which had a breaking weight of 149.4 grains.

Schunck has found in raw cotton two coloring matters: (*a*) soluble in alcohol, insoluble in ether; (*b*) insoluble in cold alcohol, soluble in boiling alcohol, both containing nitrogen He has also found a wax similar to carnauba wax; pectic acid; albuminous matter, and a solid crystalline fatty acid All of the above are soluble in solutions of the alkalis and alkaline carbonates Muller has analyzed the raw fibre with result as below.—

	Per cent
Water	7 00
Cellulose	91 35
Fat	0 40
Aqueous extract (containing nitrogenous substances)	0 50
Ash	0 12
Cuticular substance (by difference)	0 63

2. Bast-Fibres.

The term *bast* was first applied to the inner bark of the basswood, and later was extended to include the inner bark of other plants. The long, tough cells found in such barks were called

THE CHARACTERISTICS OF BAST-FIBRES.—GOODALE.

Name of Fibre	Reaction with Cupr-ammonia Schweitzer's reagent	Reaction with iodine and sulphuric acid	Reaction with aniline sulphate	Length of raw fibre, cm	Width, mm	Length of the bast-cells composing the fibre, mm	Width of the bast-cells composing the fibre — Limits of err, mm	Average size, mm
Raw flax fibre (*Linum usitatissimum*)	Soon attacked and almost entirely dissolved	Colored blue	Remains uncolored or nearly so	20–140	0.4–0.62	20–40	0.012–0.026	0.015–0.012
Raw hemp fibre (*Cannabis sativa*)	Clean fibre dissolved	Greenish blue to pure blue	Colored faint yellow	100–300	—	10+	0.015–0.028	0.016–0.019
Raw jute (*Corchorus capsularis*)	Bluish color and more or less distinct swelling	Yellow to brown	Golden yellow to orange	150–300	0.3–1.4	0.8–4.1	0.010–0.021	0.016
Raw espaito fibre (*Stipa tenacissima*)	Bright green	Rusty red	Egg-yellow	10–40	0.9–5	0.5–1.9	0.0009–0.015	—
Bromelia kaiatas	Bluish color and marked swelling	Reddish brown	Golden yellow	120	1.5–1.2	1.4–6.7	0.027–0.042	—
Raw fibre of aloe (*Aloe perfoliata*)	Bluish color and feeble swelling	Reddish brown	Golden yellow	40–50	0.75–1.05	1.3–3.7	0.015–0.024	—
New Zealand flax (*Phormium tenax*)	Bluish color and more or less distinct swelling.	Varies with purity of fibre, being yellow, green, or blue	Remains uncolored or nearly so	80–110	0.42–1.2	2.5–5.6	0.008–0.019	0.013
China grass (*Boehmeria nivea*)	When "cottonized" quickly acted upon, and almost completely dissolved	Copper-red to blue	Remains uncolored or nearly so	—	—	Up to 220	0.010–0.089	0.050
Ramie fibre (*Boehmeria tenacissima*)	When "cottonized" quickly acted upon, and almost completely dissolved	Copper-red to blue	Remains uncolored or nearly so (hardly perceptible yellow)	—	—	Up to 80	0.016–0.126	—
Coir (*Cocos nucifera*)	Perceptible swelling and pronounced blue color	Reagent not applicable, on account of color of fibre	Not applicable, on account of the color of the fibre.	15–33	0.5–30	0.4–0.96	0.012–0.020	0.010
Agave (*Agave Americana*)	Swells, and becomes somewhat blue.	With iodine solution, yellow, on the addition of sulphuric acid, greenish or brownish	Yellow	100	.10–.40	1.02–2.2	0.015–0.021	0.017
Manila (*Musa textilis*)	Blue color and feeble swelling	With iodine solution, yellow, on the addition of sulphuric acid, golden yellow to greenish	Pale yellow	730	0.10–.28	2.0–2.7	0.012–0.04	0.029

bast-fibres. Similar cells occur, however, throughout other portions of many plants, and all such cells are now collectively termed bast-fibres or liber-fibres. By far the greater number of the fibres in use throughout the world belong to this class

The walls of bast-fibres are generally much thickened through lignification, and crystals are often present in the cavity. The thickening is often very uneven and may cause projections of the wall, within the cell. There are also in the different fibres such considerable variations in the extent of lignification, and in the kind and quantity of foreign substances deposited on and in the wall, that the behavior of the fibres with reagents is often sufficiently characteristic to serve roughly for their identification.

The length of the single fibres is seldom sufficiently great to permit their use in textile manufactures, and their peculiar value for such purposes lies in the fact that as they occur in the plant they are associated together to form bundles, which often attain great length. We shall reserve the name filaments for these bundles, to distinguish them from the ultimate fibres of which they are composed. The fibres are generally firmly attached to those immediately above and below them by partial identity of their walls, or by incrusting matter, and in most cases a chemical treatment is necessary to effect their separation from each other. The separation of the filaments from the body of the plant is brought about in various ways, one of the most common being the well-known retting process applied to flax.

See table on page 122.

According to the report by Cross and Bevan, on Indian fibres and fibrous substances exhibited at the Colonial and Indian Exhibition, London, 1886, to which we are indebted for much of our material relating to these fibres, there are in India over 300 fibre-bearing plants, of which over 100 yield strong and useful fibres, regularly employed by the natives of that country. As we shall give in many cases the results of the chemical examination of the fibres by these chemists, reference should be had to the subjoined scheme, on page 124, which was followed in their investigations.—

Moisture   Hygroscopic water or water of condition

SEPARATE PORTION TAKEN FOR EACH DETERMINATION BELOW RESULTS CALCULATED IN PERCENTAGE OF DRY SUBSTANCE

Ash . . . . . Total residue left on ignition
Hydrolysis (a) . . Loss of weight on boiling raw fibre five minutes in one per cent solution of caustic soda
" (b) Loss of weight on continuing to boil one hour
Cellulose . . . White or bleached residue from following treatment: (1) Boil in one per cent caustic soda five minutes; (2) exposure to chlorine gas one hour; (3) boil in basic sodium sulphite.
Mercerizing . Loss on treating one hour with 33 per cent. solution of caustic potash, cold.
Nitration . Weight of nitrated product obtained by treatment with mixture equal volumes nitric and sulphuric acids, one hour in the cold.
Acid purification . . Raw fibre boiled one minute with acetic acid (20 per cent), washed with water and alcohol, and dried.
Carbon percentage . The carbon in the fibre from above determined by combustion.

Linen (fibres of flax plant) (*Linum usitatissimum*). — The plant yields 7.9 per cent. of fibre, which is separated by a fermentative process termed *retting*, and is then called flax. The fibres (Plate I, 51-56) are thick-walled tubes, showing knots or septa at intervals, and often creases. The internal cavity is of very small relative diameter. Filaments run entire length of stem. Bleached with more difficulty than cotton. Muller gives the following analyses of two samples of heckled Belgian flax: —

Cellulose	81.99	70.55
Fat and wax	2.37	2.34
Aqueous extract	3.62	5.94
Pectous substances .	2.72	9.29
Water	8.60	10.56
Ash	.70	1.32

The figures obtained by Cross and Bevan on a sample of heckled Irish flax are as follows: —

Moisture	9.1
Following percentages are on dry basis.	
Ash	1.6
Hydrolysis (*a*)	13.3
" (*b*)	22.1
Cellulose	80.2
Mercerizing	8.4
Nitration	125.0
Acid purification	4.3
Carbon percentage	43.2

As they occur in bleached linen cloth the fibres are nearly pure cellulose.

Jute (*Corchorus capsularis* and *C. olitorius*). — Filaments obtained by retting and maceration of stem. Jute butts and cuttings are the stumps. Much of the fibre received by paper-makers in the form of gunny bags.

The fibres (Plate I, 7–10) are primarily bound together, forming filaments containing 6–20 fibres. As ordinarily used in paper-making, with only partial bleaching, the fibres are not completely separated, and the resulting stock is therefore especially long and strong. Fibres are thick-walled, highly lignified, contain much coloring matter; section is polygonal.

Jute, as the type of lignified fibres, has been carefully studied by Cross and Bevan, who regard it as a chemical whole, termed by them ligno-cellulose, which splits up into cellulose, as one product, upon treatment with appropriate reagents. They find evidences of lignification in even the youngest fibres. The fibre is easily chlorinated by the moist gas or chlorine water, and then becomes bright yellow, which changes to magenta in solution of sodium sulphite.

Composition of raw fibre (Muller). —

	First Quality	Cuttings or Butts
Cellulose	63.76	60.89
Fat and wax	0.38	0.44
Aqueous extract	1.00	3.89
Non-cellulose or lignin	24.32	20.98
Water	9.86	12.40
Ash	0.68	1.40

From a sample of unusually good quality Cross and Bevan obtained figures as below: —

Moisture 10.3

Following percentages are on dry basis

Ash	1.2
Hydrolysis (a)	15.0
" (b)	18.0
Cellulose	75.0
Mercerizing	16.0
Nitration	125.0
Acid purification	1.0
Carbon percentage	46.5

Hemp (*Cannabis sativa*) — Filaments run entire length of stem, separated from bark by process of retting. Fibres (Plate I, 57–62) much resemble linen; fine hairs, however, project from the septa or knots. Walls very thick, not highly lignified.

Composition of raw Italian hemp (Muller): —

Cellulose	77.13
Fat and wax	0.55
Aqueous extract	3.45
Pectous substances	9.25
Water	8.80
Ash	0.82

Many other plants yield fibres to which the name hemp is applied, but they are usually distinguished as sunn hemp, manila hemp, etc.

Manila — Manila hemp — (*Musa textilis*) — Filaments separated by the natives in the Philippine Islands by drying and scraping the outer sheath (leaf petioles) of the stem of the plant, which is a species of banana; further purified by beating and washing. Each tree produces only about one pound of fibre.

Ultimate fibres much shorter than in hemp; cavity much more conspicuous; number of fibres in section of filament much greater; section of fibre more or less polygonal.

Composition of raw fibre (Müller):—

Cellulose	64.07
Fat and wax	0.62
Aqueous extract	0.96
Lignin and pectous substances	21.60
Water	11.73
Ash	1.02

Figures obtained by Cross and Bevan.—

Moisture	10.5 per cent

Following percentages are on dry basis

Hydrolysis (b)	13.5 per cent
Cellulose	58.0 "

Sunn Hemp (*Crotalaria juncea*).— Filaments, which contain 20-50 fibres, separated from stem by retting as with jute. Fibres 3-5 mm. long, polygonal, cavity small, show spiral markings. With iodine and sulphuric acid fibre is colored a mixed blue and brown; shows yellow stains or streaks with sulphate of aniline. Sunn is not a true hemp, but is derived from a plant of the pea family.

Composition of raw fibre (Muller).—

Cellulose	80.01
Fat and wax	0.55
Aqueous extract	2.82
Pectous substances	6.41
Water	9.60
Ash	0.61

New Zealand Flax (*Phormium tenax*).— Name flax misleading; filaments are separated from the leaves, which, when air-dry, yield 49.5 per cent of cellulose (Cross) and which attain a length of 1-2 metres. Fibres nearly white, soft, lustrous, not highly lignified; walls not so thick as in true flax, smooth; no knots, cavity much larger than in flax (linen).

Percentage of cellulose in the raw fibre variously given from 67 to 86.3, the higher figure being more probably correct.

Ramie (*Boehmeria tenacissima*).— Fibres stiff; lustrous like silk, take brilliant colors; sometimes single; average in filament three; section ovoid to polygonal, cavity large. Separated with some difficulty from plant. After separation bleach easily.

Percentage of cellulose 75 (Cross)

China Grass—Rhea—(*Boehmeria nivea*) — Not a grass but like ramie a shrubby plant, the filaments being derived from the inner bark. General characteristics of ultimate fibres similar to those of ramie, but in this species the maximum length is much greater. This is the longest fibre (ultimate cell) known, the length reaching 220 mm. (8.66 inches) in some cases. The stiffness of the fibre is its great drawback.

Coir — Cocoanut fibre — (*Cocos nucifera*). — Filaments separated from the husk of the cocoanut by soaking for months in water and then carding. Has been pulped by Ekman in one hour, by boiling under pressure with bisulphite of magnesia. Mainly used for mats, probably never in practice as paper-stock. Mixed with clay it has been used as an exterior coating for sulphite digesters

Adansonia (inner bark of baobab or monkey-bread tree) (*Adansonia digitata*) — Has attracted some notice from English papermakers. Makes a strong paper which takes a high finish. The composition of the bast as exported varies, as shown below —

Cellulose	49 35	58 82
Fat and wax	0 94	0 41
Aqueous extract	13 57	7 08
Pectous substances	19 05	15 19
Water	10 90	13 18
Ash	6 19	4 72

Paper Mulberry Tree (*Broussonetia papyrifera*). — The fibres of the inner bark are used by the Japanese in making their peculiar paper. Fibres are separated by scraping, soaking, and maceration in water; are bleached in the sun, and sometimes further purified by boiling in weak lye. The bark yields a glutinous substance which acts as a size

The fibres are 6–20 mm long, soft, lustrous. According to Vétillart, they appear under the microscope nearly transparent; have longitudinal marks or striæ, and are often flattened on each other and convoluted like a ribbon; the points are fringed and terminate in a round end. They have a tendency to curl up into rings.

As they occur in Japanese paper the fibres are usually unbroken.

The bark yields 62 5 per cent. of unbleached or 58 per cent. of bleached fibre (Routledge).

Agave — Aloe — Century plant — (*Agave Americana*). — Filaments separated from leaves, by maceration or scraping, large, white, lustrous, stiff, fibres 2-6 mm. in length (Cross and Bevan), or 1.02-2.2 mm. (Goodale); walls thick, cavity conspicuous, section polygonal, ends either tapering or forked.

Sisal hemp or heniquen is derived from *Agave rith*, common in Yucatan and Mexico. About one and a quarter pounds of fibre are produced yearly by each plant. Largely used for cordage, bags, etc., and comes in these forms to the paper-mill.

Cross gives the following figures on *Agave keratta* from the West Indies: —

Moisture	15.5
Following percentages are on dry basis	
Ash	1.4
Hydrolysis (*a*)	10.0
" (*b*)	20.0
Cellulose	75.8
Mercerizing	11.0
Nitration	109.8
Acid purification	0.4
Length of ultimate fibres	2–8 mm

3. *Fibres derived from whole stems and associated in the pulp with cells and vessels not properly fibres.*

The fibres in this class, although bast or libriform fibres, are separated by treating the whole stem by a chemical process. The resulting pulp consists of the ultimate fibres, — the filaments being broken up in the process of treatment, — and cells from the epidermis and other portions of the plant.

Straw (the stems and leaves of the various cereals). — Straw pulp consists of the ultimate bast fibres and accompanying cells, freed from the incrusting and other matters by a chemical process. The bast cells or fibres form the greater portion of the pulp. They are comparatively short and fine; at nearly regular intervals the wall appears somewhat thicker than elsewhere, and drawn together (Plate I. 30, 31). The fibres and the accompanying cells are stained blue by iodine solution, but these thickened portions show a reddish brown coloration. The dimensions of the fibres from different straws are given below: —

	Length	Width
Wheat	0.152–0.449 mm	0.018–0.024 mm
Rye	0.086–0.345 "	0.012–0.016 "
Barley	0.103–0.224 "	0.012–0.014 "
Oats	0.186–0.448 "	0.012–0.017 "

The most characteristic feature of straw pulp is the occurrence of epidermal cells (Plate I. 37, 39, 41) with serrated or toothed edges. These cells show great differences in size, and the proportion of length to width varies from 1·1 to 10:1. The differences are sufficiently marked and constant to enable the different varieties of straw to be distinguished in the pulp. Associated with the epidermal cells are others from the pith (Plate I. 35, 36), which aid in the recognition of this pulp. These cells vary in shape from the nearly round to an oval or much more elongated form. The width is usually great in comparison to the length. Portions of vessels and other elements occasionally occur (Plate I. 32, 33, 34, 40).

ANALYSES OF STRAW (WOLFF & KNOP)

	Winter wheat	Winter rye	Winter barley	Oats
Water	14.3	14.3	14.3	14.3
Ash	5.5	3.2	5.5	5.0
Albuminoids	2.0	1.5	2.0	2.5
Carbohydrates, etc	30.2	27.0	29.8	38.2
Crude fibre	48.0	54.0	48.4	40.0
Fat etc	1.5	1.3	1.4	2.0

The percentage of pure cellulose in dry straw is given by Cross and Bevan as below: —

Oat straw	52.0
" "	53.5
Wheat	49.6
Rye	53.0

Arendt has exhaustively investigated the composition of different parts of the oat plant at different periods of growth. The straw contains 30–40 per cent of water when fully ripe, much more if cut earlier. Straw is of best quality if cut before ripening is completed. When about a foot (0.31 m.) high both stem and leaves contain about 23 per cent. of crude fibre on the dry substance; at commencement of ripening the stem contains 36–41, and the leaves 29–33 per cent of fibre. the proportion being in each case lowest in the upper part of the plant.

Straw yields a white wax soluble in alcohol and solutions of caustic alkali. The amount of ash, which is often more than half silica, ranges from about 3–7, or in exceptional cases as high as 12 per cent on the dry straw. The strongest straw yields the most ash.

Esparto — Alfa — Spanish Grass. — The rush-like leaves of *Stipa tenacissima* and *Lygeum spartum*, which grow wild in Spain and Northern Africa. Spanish esparto is considered the best.

The bast fibres occur in bundles or filaments, which are resolved into ultimate fibres by the method of treatment. Fibres (Plate I. 43, 49) similar to those of straw, but shorter, more even, and with cavity nearly closed. Serrated cells (Plate I 47, 48) common, but smaller than those of straw. Esparto pulp is distinguished from straw pulp by the presence of small, tear-shaped cells (Plate I 45 Z) and the absence of the oval cells.

Muller gives the composition of esparto as below: —

	Spanish	African
Cellulose	48 25	45 80
Fat and wax	2 07	2 62
Aqueous extract	10 19	9 81
Pectous substances	26 39	29 30
Water	9 38	8 80
Ash	3 72	3 67

The analyses of Cross and Bevan give: —

	Cellulose, per cent on dry basis
Spanish	58 0
Tripoli	46 3
Arzew	52 0
Oran	49 6

In paper esparto fibre is tougher than straw. The yield of air-dry fibre on the dry plant is from 45–55 per cent.

Bamboo (*Bambusa*).—About 170 species are described by Munro. *Bambusa vulgaris* being the one most generally distributed. Mr Thomas Routledge, who first worked esparto in England, published in 1875 a pamphlet, calling attention to the value of bamboo as a source of paper-stock, and printed upon an excellent paper made from that material. Microscopical examination of this paper shows the pulp to possess the general characteristics of that from straw. The bast fibres are short, fine, with thick walls; seriated cells numerous and of various shapes and sizes; numerous ovoid cells from the pith, some nearly square, all pitted. Cells similar to those found in esparto (Plate I 45) and to those shown in Plate I. 33, 34, were also noticed. The proportion of these different cells to the fibre present is very large, and from their small size many must be lost in working the pulp

The bamboo has been known to attain a height of forty feet in forty days, and Routledge estimates the yield per acre at forty tons of green stems, or six tons of paper-stock per annum When the stems are cut before maturity, they are easily reduced by crushing and boiling with caustic soda.

Bagasse and Sorghum.—The crushed stalks and diffusion chips of the sugar cane and sorghum have been often proposed and occasionally used as a raw material for paper-making They are easily reduced by boiling with weak soda, and the resulting pulp is much like that from straw On account of the large proportion of pith the yield of fibre is only about 25 per cent on the dry stalk, and the samples which we have seen were so badly specked by fragments of seed hulls as to be useless for making any but the cheapest papers.

4 Wood.

The cells or elements which make up the woody tissue of plants exhibit great diversity of form and markings, as is shown in Figs 3 and 4 taken from Sanio. Those which especially deserve consideration as furnishing a raw material for paper-making are the true wood fibres and the *tracheids* Many of the other cells are, however, of interest, as they serve in some cases to identify the wood from which they were derived. The wood fibres or libriform cells never show true spiral markings, and the pits, which rarely occur in the cell-wall, are not especially noticeable In certain of them,

FIBRES.

called septate cells, the cavity instead of being continuous throughout the whole length of the cell, as in most cases, is divided into two or more compartments by partitions perpendicular to the longer axis. The length of the wood fibres and the extent to which their cell-wall is thickened by lignification show great variations in different plants. Some of the longest have a length of 2.0 mm., while others are as short as 0.14 mm. Their arrange-

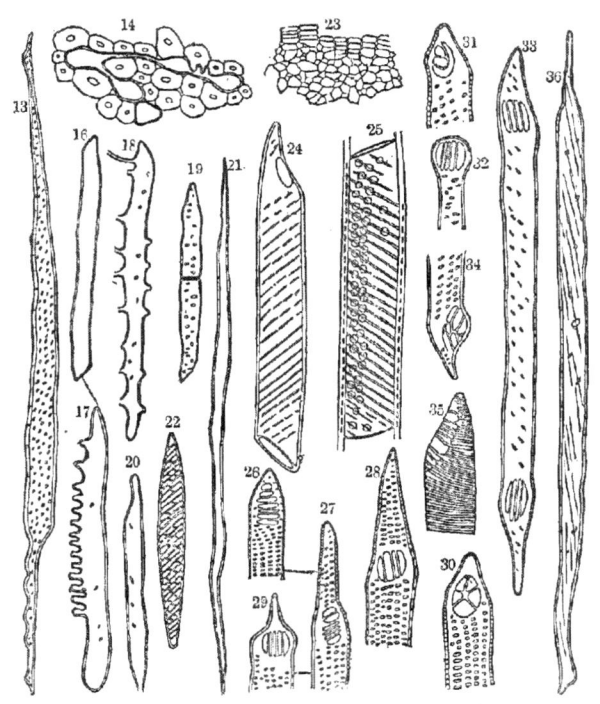

FIG. 3. — WOOD ELEMENTS FROM VARIOUS PLANTS.

ment in the plant stem also varies in different cases, being sometimes radial, and in other instances showing an irregular grouping. Chemical pulp made from poplar consists almost entirely of true wood fibres.

For the practical purposes of paper-making tracheïds are to be regarded as fibres, since they possess the same elongated shape and tapering ends. They are, however, to be distinguished from the libriform fibres by the numerous large and well-defined markings, which from their shape are called bordered pits or discoid markings. These markings arise with the gradual thickening of the cell-wall until finally they assume the appearance shown in Figs. 5, 6, and 7.

The wood of cone-bearing or coniferous trees, like spruce, fir, and hemlock, consists entirely of tracheïds, and the discoid markings

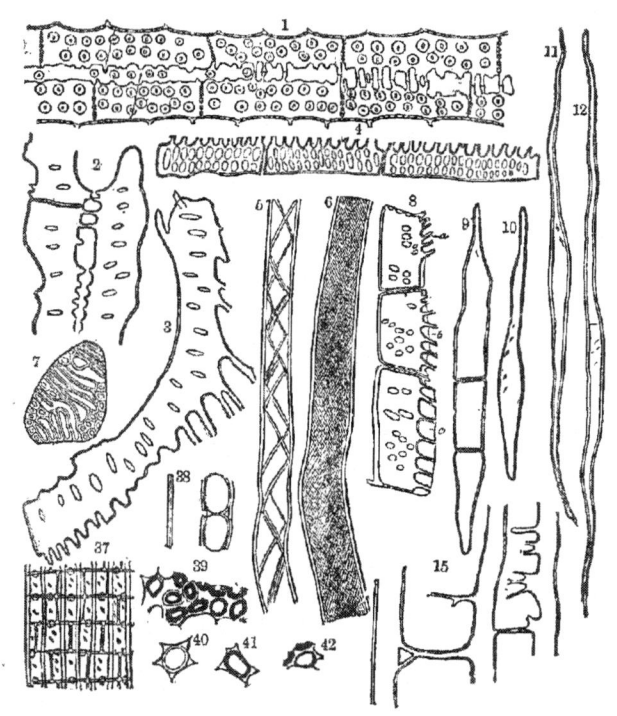

FIG. 4.—WOOD ELEMENTS FROM VARIOUS PLANTS.

are very apparent when sulphite pulp, made from these woods, is examined under the microscope. They are even more readily seen in ground wood. These tracheïds are much longer than the libriform fibres occurring in the wood of other trees, but in the common case, in which both tracheïds and fibres occur in the same wood, the fibres are always the longest elements in the particular wood considered.

Growth of Wood. — Growth in the widest sense takes place by the division of cells. A single cell is converted into two by the formation of an excessively thin membrane of cellulose. This

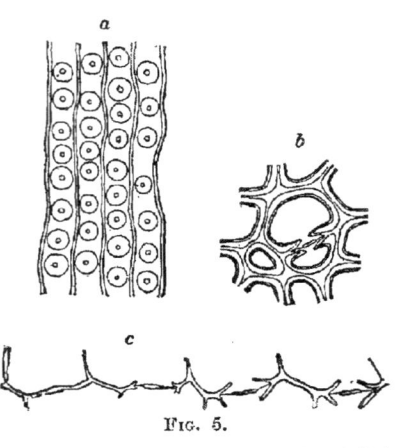

Fig. 5.

Bordered pits or discoid markings of the wood cells (tracheïds) of Pinus laricio: *a*, aspect of radial walls; *b*, a transverse section; *c*, development of the markings in Pinus sylvestris (Sanio).

single membrane is at first a common wall for the two adjacent cells, but as growth proceeds and the thickness of the membrane increases it commonly splits into two adjacent walls. The growth of wood depends upon the activity of a thin layer of tissue lying immediately under the bark, and called the cambium layer. The cells composing this layer are filled with protoplasm, and by their subdivision and growth new wood is formed upon the old wood in concentric rings or layers. As growth altogether ceases during winter, and as the character of the wood produced varies periodically at different seasons of the year, these

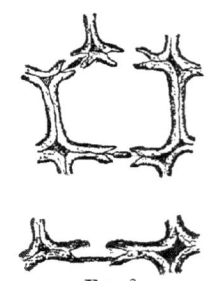

Fig. 6.

Pinus sylvestris. Transverse sections of perfect and nearly perfect discoid markings (Strasburger).

rings become visible, and serve as a register of the annual growths. The fibres and tracheïds formed during the spring have comparatively thin walls, and are somewhat larger than those formed during the autumn.

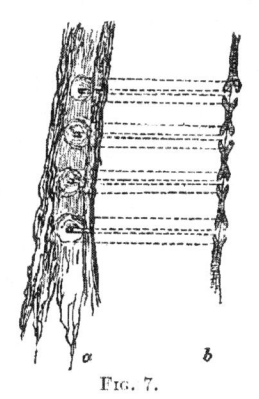

Autumnal wood is somewhat more dense and contains more incrusting matter than spring wood. A section through the wood shows that the autumnal fibres are considerably flattened by the pressure of the bark, which is greatest at this time, while the section of the fibres formed in the spring is nearly square, as shown in Fig. 8.

FIG. 7.
Portion of wood-cell (tracheïd) showing bordered pits: *a*, aspect of radial wall; *b*, section through wall (Herzberg).

Sap and Heart Wood. — The wood of comparatively recent growth, or sap-wood, often called from its color alburnum, contains a larger proportion of sap and putrescible matters than the older and harder heart-wood or duramen, so called on account of this greater hardness and durability. The difference in color and hardness is not always evident, as, for example, in the fir and sweet buckeye. Each year a ring of sap-wood passes over into the condition of heart-wood, and then takes no further part in the activity of the plant. It becomes darker by the infiltration of coloring-matter. The thickness of the sap-wood is practically constant, while that of the heart-wood increases with each succeeding year. Heart wood is for most purposes of much greater value than sap-wood, and when ground into pulp should be less likely to deteriorate with age than pulp made from sap-wood. There is, however, a prejudice among pulp-makers in favor of sap-wood, or for the younger trees in which it is present in greatest amount, and it is quite probable that such wood, because of its smaller content of lignin, would be less brittle under grinding, and would therefore yield a longer fibre.

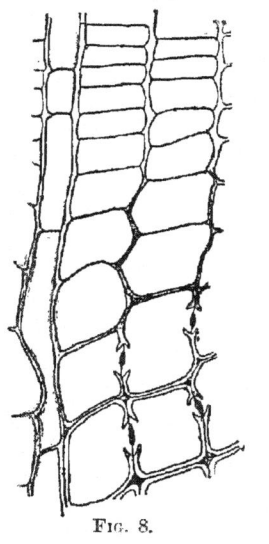

FIG. 8.

The cells in the earliest annual rings are considerably smaller than those in the succeeding rings, and the increase in size proceeds regularly until after a number of years a maximum is reached and maintained in the rings formed afterward.

This fact is brought out in the following table by Sanio, quoted by Goodale, based on measurements of tracheids of *Pinus sylvestris* —

Number of the annual ring	Medium length of the tracheids	Medium width of the tracheids
1	0.95 mm	0.017 mm
17	2.74 "	
19	3.13 "	
31	3.69 "	
37	3.87 "	
38	3.91 "	
39	4.00 "	
40	4.04 "	
43	4.09 "	
45	4.21 "	
46	4.21 "	
72	4.21 "	0.032 mm

All wood contains in the cell cavities a large amount of air and water, the former being highly rarefied. According to Sachs, 100 c.c. of freshly cut fir consists of

Mass of cell-walls	24.81 c.c.
Water	58.63 "
Air cavities	16.56 "

A determination by ourselves of the amount of water in green spruce as received at the mill gave 37 per cent. by weight. It is much larger in growing or freshly cut wood.

Gelesnoff determined the water in entire trees each month for a year. Scotch pine gave a maximum (January) of 64.0 per cent., and a minimum (May) of 55.3 per cent.; average for the year 61.1 per cent. Aspen gave a maximum (March) of 56.6 per cent., and a minimum (May) of 48.9 per cent.; average for the year 52.8 per cent. Birch gave a maximum (May) of 65.9 per cent., and a minimum (December) of 43.5 per cent., average for the year 49.2

The hardness and density of wood is largely dependent upon the amount of lignin which it contains. The lignin not only tends to harden the cell-walls, but also by its presence lessens the space within the cells which might otherwise contain air. The following table, compiled from the reports of the Tenth United States Census, gives the density, ash, and fuel value of the woods commonly used for pulp-making. The determinations were made by Mr. S. P. Sharples, under direction of Professor Sargeant:—

Botanical Name	Common Name	Specific gravity	Weight of cubic foot in pounds	Ash, per cent	Heat units evolved by combustion of one kilogramme of dry wood
Pinus Strobus	White pine	0.3485	21.72	0.12	4272.69
Pinus Banksiana	Gray pine of Canada	0.4761	29.67	0.23	—
Picea nigra	Spruce	0.4087	25.47	0.30	3919.37
Abies grandis	Fir	0.3545	21.97	0.19	—
Abies Fraseri.	Balsam	0.3565	22.22	0.54	—
Larix Americana	Tamarack	0.7024	43.77	0.27	4182.04
Populus grandidentata	Poplar	0.4632	28.87	0.45	—
Populus tremuloides	Aspen	0.3785	23.59	0.74	4292.31
Populus monilifera.	Cottonwood	0.4494	28.00	0.65	4242.15
Salix nigra	Willow	0.4456	27.77	0.70	—
Fagus ferruginea	Beech	0.7175	44.71	0.54	3895.04
Acer dasycarpum	Maple	0.5269	32.84	0.33	—
Betula alba	White birch	0.6160	38.05	0.29	4073.05
Betula papyrifera	Paper birch	0.6297	39.24	0.23	4101.41
Æsculus glabra	Buckeye	0.4542	28.31	0.86	—
Liquidambar styraciflua	Sweet gum	0.5615	34.99	0.48	4016.46
Taxodium distichum	Cypress	0.4084	24.45	0.40	4739.73
Tsuga Canadensis	Hemlock	0.4097	25.53	0.48	4208.58
Castanea vulgaris	Chestnut	0.4621	28.80	0.13	4092.96
Tilia Americana	Basswood	0.4525	28.20	0.55	—
Robinia pseudacacia	Locust	0.7257	45.22	0.23	3890.02

The heaviest wood found in the United States is black iron-wood, *Condalia ferrea*, which has a specific gravity of 1.3020, and is also remarkable for its large amount of ash, 8.31 per cent. The lightest is *Ficus aurea*, which has no common name. Its specific gravity is 0.2616, and ash 5.03 per cent. Both trees are found in Florida.

Resins. — Although, as previously pointed out, the formation of resins is not fully understood, they are known to be immediately derived from the oxidation of essential oils which occur in the tree. If the resins contain gum or mucilage, they are termed gum-resins, while if they are mixed with the essential oils, they are variously called oleo-resins, turpentines, or balsams. The term oleo-resin is the more comprehensive one, and only such oleo-resins as contain benzoic or cinnamic acid are, properly speaking, balsams. The well-known but misnamed Canada balsam is a true turpentine. The oleo-resins are generally viscous liquids, like honey, but sometimes occur as soft solids.

The resins are insoluble in water, difficultly soluble in hot bisulphite solutions, readily soluble in alcohol and alkaline solutions. They are to be regarded as mixtures of several analogous bodies, and various substances of acid character are recognized among their components. Sylvic acid, with others, is found in common rosin. Rosin, often called colophony, is the residue left on distilling off the volatile oil (spirits of turpentine) from the turpentine obtained from Southern pine. The color of rosin ranges from light yellow to dark red, the darker color being, at least in part, a result of the increased temperature to which the rosin was exposed in order to drive off all the spirits of turpentine. The specific gravity of rosin is usually about 1.083, but the very light-colored varieties may have a specific gravity of only 1.040, while that of the darkest specimens may run as high as 1.100. One hundred parts of refined rosin will completely neutralize about eighteen parts of caustic potash, KOH. According to Sargeant, the fuel value of resinous woods is about 12 per cent. higher than that of those containing little or no resin, but the statement is evidently a general one.

The quality of a wood for pulping, especially by the acid processes, depends largely upon its freedom from any excessive quantity of resin, and nearly as much upon the evenness with which the resin is distributed. If the resin is mainly localized at certain points or rings, the other portions of the wood may be reduced with comparative ease, while the more resinous portions still remain hard, and largely increase the proportion of chips and shive in the pulp. Ulbricht has studied the distribution of resin in the spruce fir, *Abies excelsa*, with the result shown below. He includes as resin all matter soluble in alcohol and not in water.

PARTS OF RESIN PER 100 OF WOOD.

	Sap wood	Heart wood	Entire wood
Winter	1.966	2.299	2.213
Spring	1.781	2.041	1.911
Summer	1.987	2.235	2.100
Autumn	2.024	2.158	2.137

We have made determinations of the quantities of material removed from the following woods by water, and by a successive treatment with ether and alcohol, with results as shown. The figures give per cents. on the dry basis:—

	Water — removes gums, mucilage, sugars, tannin, etc.	Ether.	Alcohol.	Total removed by ether and alcohol — includes resins, oils, waxes, etc.
Spruce	4.83	1.67	1.61	3.28
Poplar	4.80	0.85	1.00	1.85
Cottonwood	4.69	0.79	2.04	2.83
Sweet gum	3.39	0.30	0.55	0.85
Beech	2.14	0.38	0.55	0.93
Yellow birch	1.88	0.32	0.65	0.97
Cypress	4.22	0.81	0.94	1.75

The analyses of a number of European woods has been carried much farther by Müller, and from his results we select those of especial interest.

PROXIMATE ANALYSES OF WOODS.

HUGO MÜLLER (*Die Pflanzenfaser*).

	Water.	Soluble in water.	Soluble in alcohol and benzine.	Cellulose.	Incrusting matter.	Incrusting matter for every 100 of cellulose.
Black poplar	12.10	2.88	1.37	62.77	20.88	33.3
Silver fir	13.87	1.26	0.97	56.99	26.91	47.2
Birch	12.48	2.65	1.14	55.52	28.21	50.8
Willow	11.66	2.65	1.23	55.72	28.74	51.6
Scotch pine	12.87	4.05	1.63	53.27	28.18	52.9
Chestnut	12.03	5.41	1.10	52.64	28.82	54.7
Linden	10.10	3.56	3.93	53.09	29.32	55.2
Beech	12.57	2.41	0.41	45.47	39.14	86.1
Ebony	9.40	9.99	2.54	29.99	48.08	160.3

Bark and Knots. — Simultaneously with the production of a layer of wood, through the activity of the layer of cambium tissue surrounding it, there is formed on the outside of this tissue a layer of bark, which serves as a protective envelope to the stem. Cork cells, or those upon whose walls has been deposited suberin or cork substance, are admirably fitted on account of their impermeability to protect the underlying tissues and occur, often in layers, in the bark. Associated with them, more especially in the inner bark, are the long bast fibres which give strength to the bark. As the bark increases in thickness, the outer layers become more or less completely cut off from the underlying tissue by layers of cork cells, and, as a result, this outer portion dries up and dies, becoming sometimes deeply fissured as the trunk expands with growth. The bark is often rich in tannin and coloring matters; that of hemlock containing 13–16 per cent of tannin; and, on account of the permanence of these colors and the slight extent to which suberin is affected by reagents, the bark is only slightly acted upon by the chemical processes for pulping wood; indeed, in the sulphite process hardly at all, and, if present with the chips, remains to form black or brown specks in the pulp.

An experiment to determine the shrinkage of pulp wood in barking gave result as follows: one cord of green spruce, containing 37 per cent moisture, and cut in four-foot lengths, weighed 4440 pounds; after barking the weight was 3570 pounds.

Knots are formed at the point where a branch makes out from the stem, and consist of the dead and dried tissue, usually very dense and highly charged with coloring matters. They are partially reduced by the soda process, but entirely resist the action of the reagents employed in the sulphite process, which usually fails even to soften them appreciably.

The woods most commonly employed in the United States for the manufacture of ground wood and chemical fibre are spruce and poplar. A number of other woods are used, however, in considerable, though varying, amounts, as the factors of price, length of fibre, ease of reduction, and relation of the mill to the source of supply may determine in particular cases. We shall consider briefly these different woods, with reference to their occurrence, general features, and availability for pulp-making. Their specific gravity, ash, and fuel value have already been given. The statements regarding the occurrence and general character of the several woods are taken from the exhaustive Report on Forest Trees, by Professor Sargeant, in the reports of the Tenth United States Census. The scientific names by which the different species are designated by different authors show a lack of uniformity almost as great as that which prevails in common usage regarding the common names. We have therefore followed the nomenclature of the report to which we have just referred. The species given by no means comprise all those which are or may be used, but are to be considered as typical of the different sorts of wood employed. Thirty-five species of pine (*Pinus*) are enumerated in the report quoted as found in the United States

Black Spruce (*Picea nigra*). — Newfoundland, northern Labrador to Ungava Bay, Nastapokee Sound, Cape Churchill, Hudson Bay, and northwest to the mouth of the Mackenzie River and the eastern slope of the Rocky Mountains, south through the northern states to Pennsylvania, central Michigan, Wisconsin, and Minnesota, and along the Alleghany Mountains to the high peaks of North Carolina

Wood light, soft, not strong, close, straight grained, compact, satiny: bands of small summer cells thin, resinous, resin passages few, minute; medullary rays few, conspicuous: color, light red or often nearly white, the sap-wood lighter

Easily reduced to a strong, long-fibred pulp by the sulphite process, with somewhat more difficulty by the soda process, pulp made by the latter process bleached with difficulty. We have made the following analyses of different samples of the ground wood: —

	A	B	C
Moisture	11.31	11 48	11 26
Ash	0.32	0 25	0 30
Cellulose	52 96	53 08	52 98
Lignin, etc., by difference	35.41	35 19	35 46
	100.00	100 00	100 00

Gray Pine (*Pinus Banksiana*). — Bay of Chaleur, New Brunswick, to the southern shores of Hudson Bay, northwest to the Great Bear Lake, the valley of the Mackenzie River, and the eastern slope of the Rocky Mountains between the fifty-second and sixty-fifth degrees of north latitude; south to northern Maine, Ferrisburg, Vermont (R. E. Robinson), the southern shore of Lake Michigan, and central Minnesota.

Wood light, soft, not strong, rather close grained, compact, bands of small summer cells not broad, very resinous, conspicuous, resin passages few, not large; medullary rays numerous, obscure, color, clear light brown or, rarely, orange, the thick sap-wood almost white

Reduced to pulp with somewhat more difficulty than spruce; fibres long as in spruce.

White Pine— Weymouth pine — (*Pinus strobus*) — Newfoundland, northern shores of the Gulf of Saint Lawrence to Lake Nipigon and the valley of the Winnipeg River, south through the northern states to Pennsylvania, the southern shores of Lake Michigan, "Starving Rock," near La Salle, Illinois, near Davenport, Iowa (Parry), and along the Alleghany Mountains to northern Georgia.

Wood light, soft, not strong, very close, straight grained, compact, easily worked, susceptible of a beautiful polish, bands of small summer cells thin, not conspicuous, resin passages small, not numerous nor conspicuous, medullary rays numerous, thin: color, light brown, often slightly tinged with red, the sap-wood nearly white.

Requires more severe treatment than spruce, but yields very long, strong fibre.

White Fir (*Abies grandis*). — Vancouver Island, south to Mendocino County, California, near the coast, interior valleys of western Washington Territory and Oregon south to the Umpqua River, Cascade Mountains below 4000 feet elevation, through the Blue Mountains of Oregon (Cusick) to the eastern slope of the Cœur d'Alene Mountains (Cooper), the Bitter Root Mountains, Idaho (Watson), and the western slopes of the Rocky Mountains of northern Montana (Flathead region, Canby & Sargeant)

Wood very light, soft, not strong, coarse grained, compact; bands of small summer cells broader than in other American species, dark colored, resinous, conspicuous, medullary rays numerous, obscure; color, light brown, the sap-wood rather lighter

Requires somewhat more severe treatment than spruce, but yields very long, strong fibre.

Balsam (*Abies Fraseri*) — High mountains of North Carolina and Tennessee.

Wood very light, soft, not strong, coarse grained, compact, bands of small summer cells rather broad, light colored, not conspicuous; medullary rays numerous, thin; color, light brown, the sap-wood lighter, nearly white.

Occasionally reduced by the sulphite process; unbleached fibre carries considerable pitchy material, which is likely to cause trouble in mill, and which interferes with bleaching. General character of fibre similar to spruce.

For the purposes of his process Mitscherlich considers balsam and spruce identical.

Hemlock (*Tsuga Canadensis*). Nova Scotia, southern New Brunswick, valley of the Saint Lawrence River to the shores of Lake Temiscaming, and southwest to the western borders of northern Wisconsin; south through the northern states to New Castle County, Delaware, southeastern Michigan, central Wisconsin, and along the Alleghany Mountains to Clear Creek Falls, Winston County, Alabama (Mohr).

Wood light, soft, not strong, brittle, coarse, crooked grained, difficult to work, liable to wind-shake, and splinter; not durable; bands of small summer cells rather broad, conspicuous; medullary rays numerous, thin; color, light brown tinged with red, or often nearly white, the sap-wood somewhat darker.

General character of pulp similar to spruce, but wood is reduced with more difficulty, and is likely to cause chips if mixed with spruce.

Larch — Tamarack — Hackmatack — (*Larix Americana*). — Northern Newfoundland and Labrador to the eastern shores of Hudson Bay; Cape Churchill, and northwest to the northern shores of the Great Bear Lake and the valley of the Mackenzie River within the Arctic Circle; south through the northern states to northern Pennsylvania, northern Indiana and Illinois, and central Minnesota.

Wood heavy, hard, very strong, rather coarse grained, compact, durable in contact with the soil; bands of small summer cells broad, very resinous, dark colored, conspicuous; resin passages few, obscure; medullary rays numerous, hardly distinguishable; color, light brown, the sap-wood nearly white.

Reduced by sulphite process with some difficulty; fibre somewhat sticky from pitchy material, and requires a large amount of bleach. Wood if mixed with spruce is likely to cause chips. Length of fibre comparable to spruce.

Poplar (*Populus grandidentata*). — Nova Scotia, New Brunswick, and west through Ontario to northern Minnesota, south through the northern states and along the Alleghany Mountains to North Carolina, extending west to middle Kentucky and Tennessee.

Wood light, soft, not strong, close grained, compact, medullary rays thin, obscure, color, light brown, the sap-wood nearly white.

The wood most commonly used by mills working the soda process, never used by sulphite mills, though easily reduced by that process. Pulp from both processes very easily bleached. Fibre short and soft, associated in the pulp with much wider pitted cells (Plate I. 19).

Aspen (*Populus tremuloides*). — Northern Newfoundland and Labrador to the southern shores of Hudson Bay, northwest to the Great Bear Lake, the mouth of the Mackenzie River, and the valley of the Yukon River, Alaska; south in the Atlantic region to the mountains of Pennsylvania, the valley of the lower Wabash River, and northern Kentucky; in the Pacific region south to the valley of the Sacramento River, California, and along the Rocky Mountains and interior ranges to southern New Mexico, Arizona, and central Nevada.

Wood light, soft, not strong, close grained, compact, not durable, containing, as does that of the whole genus, numerous minute, scattered open ducts; medullary rays very thin, hardly distinguishable, color, light brown, the thick sap-wood nearly white.

Much resembles poplar in character of pulp and ease with which wood yields to treatment.

Cottonwood (*Populus monilifera*). — Shores of Lake Champlain Vermont, south through western New England to Chattahoochee region of western Florida, west along the northern shores of Lake Ontario to the eastern base of the ranges of the Rocky Mountains of Montana, Colorado, and New Mexico.

Wood very light, soft, not strong, close grained, compact, liable to warp in drying, difficult to season; medullary rays numerous, obscure, color, dark brown, the thick sap-wood nearly white.

Much resembles poplar in character of pulp and ease with which the wood yields to treatment.

Sweet Gum (*Liquidambar styraciflua*) — Fairfield County, Connecticut, to the valleys of the lower Ohio, White, and Wabash Rivers, south to Cape Canaveral and Tampa Bay, Florida, southwest through southern Missouri, Arkansas, and the Indian Territory to the valley of the Trinity River, Texas; in central and southern Mexico.

Wood heavy, hard, not strong, rather tough, close grained, compact, inclined to shrink and warp badly in seasoning, susceptible of a beautiful polish, medullary rays numerous, very obscure; color, bright brown tinged with red, the sap-wood nearly white.

Easily yields to chemical processes a pulp of short fibre, much resembling poplar.

Cypress (*Taxodium distichum*). — Sussex County, Delaware, south near the coast to Mosquito Inlet and Cape Romano, Florida, west through the Gulf States near the coast to the valley of the Nueces River, Texas, and through Arkansas to western Tennessee, western and northern Kentucky, southeastern Missouri, and southern Illinois and Indiana.

Wood light, soft, close, straight grained, not strong, compact, easily worked, very durable in contact with the soil; bands of small summer cells broad, resinous, conspicuous; medullary rays numerous, very obscure; color, light or dark brown, the sap-wood nearly white.

Easily reduced to pulp by sulphite process, unbleached fibre rather dark in color, and woolly, bleaches readily, and then much resembles spruce.

Beech (*Fagus ferruginea*). — Nova Scotia and the valley of the Restigouche River to the northern shores of Lake Huron and northern Wisconsin, south to the Chattahoochee region of western Florida and the valley of the Trinity River, Texas, west to eastern Illinois, southeastern Missouri, and Madison County, Arkansas (Letterman).

Wood very hard, strong tough, very close grained, not durable in contact with the soil, inclined to check in drying, difficult to season, susceptible of a beautiful polish; medullary rays broad, very conspicuous; color varying greatly with soil and situation, dark red, or often lighter, the sap-wood nearly white.

Rather more difficult to reduce than poplar; fibres somewhat shorter, pulp soft, easily bleached.

Silver Maple (*Acer dasycarpum*). — Valley of the Saint John River, New Brunswick, to Ontario, south of latitude 45°, south to western Florida, west to eastern Dakota, eastern Nebraska, the valley of the Blue River, Kansas, and the Indian Territory.

Wood light, hard, strong, brittle, close grained, compact, easily worked; medullary rays numerous, thin.

More difficult to reduce than poplar; fibres somewhat shorter; pulp soft, easily bleached; rarely used, and only by soda mills

Bass Wood (*Tilia Americana*). — Northern New Brunswick, westward in British America, to about the one hundred and second meridian, southward to Virginia, and along the Alleghany Mountains to Georgia and southern Alabama, extending west in the United States to eastern Dakota, eastern Nebraska, eastern Kansas, the Indian Territory, and southwest to the valley of the San Antonio River, Texas.

Wood light, soft, not strong, very close grained, compact, easily worked; medullary rays numerous, rather obscure; color, light brown, or often slightly tinged with red, the sap-wood hardly distinguishable

Very easily reduced, and yields by soda process pulp similar to poplar

White Birch (*Betula alba*). — New Brunswick and the valley of the lower Saint Lawrence River to the southern shores of Lake Ontario; south, generally near the coast, to Newcastle County, Delaware.

Wood light, soft, not strong, close grained, liable to check in drying, not durable; medullary rays numerous, obscure; color, light brown, the sap-wood nearly white

Easily reduced; pulp much resembles poplar.

Paper Birch (*Betula papyrifera*) — Northern Newfoundland and Labrador to the southern shores of Hudson Bay, and northwest to the Great Bear Lake, and the valley of the Yukon River, Alaska, south in the Atlantic region to Wading River, Long Island, the mountains of northern Pennsylvania, Clear Lake, Montcalm County, Michigan, northeastern Illinois, and Saint Cloud, Minnesota, in the Pacific region south to the Black Hills of Dakota (R Douglas), the Mullen Trail of the Bitter Root Mountains and Flathead Lake, Montana, the neighborhood of Fort Colville, Washington Territory (Watson), and the valley of the lower Fraser River, British Columbia (Engleman & Sargeant)

Wood light, strong, hard, tough, very close grained, compact, medullary rays numerous, obscure, color, brown tinged with red, the sap-wood nearly white

Somewhat more difficult to reduce than poplar. Pulp easily bleached and similar to poplar.

Buckeye (*Æsculus glabra*) — Western slopes of the Alleghany Mountains, Pennsylvania, to northern Alabama, westward through southern Michigan (rare) to southern Iowa, eastern Kansas to about longitude 97° west, and the Indian Territory.

Wood light, soft, not strong, close grained, compact, difficult to split, often blemished by dark lines of decay; medullary rays obscure; color, white, the sap-wood darker.

Said to be occasionally used in pulp-making.

Black Willow (*Salix nigra*) — Southern New Brunswick and the northern shores of Lakes Huron and Superior, southward through the Atlantic region to Bay Biscayne and the Caloosa River, Florida, and the valley of the Guadalupe River, Texas; Pacific region, valleys of the Sacramento River, California, and the Colorado River, Arizona.

Wood light, soft, weak, close grained, checking badly in drying; medullary rays obscure; color, brown, the sap-wood nearly white.

Said to be occasionally used in pulp-making.

Locust (*Robinia pseudacacia*) — Alleghany Mountains, Pennsylvania (Locust Ridge, Monroe County, Porter), to northern Georgia; widely and generally naturalized throughout the United States east of the Rocky Mountains, and possibly indigenous in northeastern (Crowley's Ridge) and western Arkansas and the prairies of eastern Indian Territory.

Wood heavy, exceedingly hard and strong, close grained, compact, very durable in contact with the ground; layers of annual growth clearly marked by two or three rows of large, open ducts; color, brown or, more rarely, light green, the sap-wood yellow.

Said to be occasionally used in pulp-making

Chestnut (*Castanea vulgaris*). — Southern Maine to the valley of the Winooski River, Vermont, southern Ontario and southern Michigan, south through the northern states to Delaware and southern Indiana, and along the Alleghany Mountains to northern Alabama, extending west to middle Kentucky and Tennessee.

Wood light, soft, not strong, coarse grained, liable to check and warp in drying, easily split, very durable in contact with the soil; layers of annual growth marked by many rows of large, open ducts medullary rays numerous, obscure; color, brown, the sapwood lighter

Said to be occasionally used in pulp-making

FIBRES.

The following table, from the report for 1890 of the chief of the Division of Forestry, gives interesting figures regarding the use of the various woods in pulp-making: —

States	Number of mills	Kinds of wood used	Mechanical	Soda	Sulphite	Good	Fair	Limited	Declining	Poor	Remarks
Maine	12	Spruce only or chiefly	16-20		11-13	5	20	1			
	7	Spruce and poplar	15-20	10							
	1	Spruce, poplar, and pine		10 3							
	1	Poplar									
New Hampshire	13	Spruce only or chiefly	18-24	5		10	11	2	2		1 gets supplies mostly from Canada
	2	Spruce and poplar		10							2 get supplies partly from Canada
Vermont	11	Spruce only or chiefly	18-20				11		4	1 1	1 gets supplies mostly from Canada
	5	Spruce and poplar	20-23								
	1	Poplar and pine	20								
Massachusetts	4	Spruce only or chiefly	15-22			10	5			3	2 supplies from Northern Vermont and New Hampshire
	4	Spruce and poplar	17-18								
Connecticut	1	Spruce								1	Supplies from New Brunswick and Nova Scotia
New York	52	Spruce only or chiefly	15-22			13	34	7	8	2 2	1 supplies mostly from Canada
	4	Spruce and poplar	16-20								15 supplies from Canada or distant points
	1	Spruce and hemlock				11					
	1	Spruce, hemlock, bass				10					
	3	Spruce, poplar, and pine									
	2	Poplar	14	9							
	1	Poplar, bass, pine, and spruce		10							
	1	Spruce and pine									
Pennsylvania	2	Spruce only or chiefly	19-20			1		1			
	1	Spruce and poplar				10				1	Supply from West Virginia and Nova Scotia
	2	Poplar		10						2	Supply from Maryland and Virginia
	2	Poplar, bass, pine		9-10			2				
	2	Poplar, bass, pine, maple		7-12			2				
	1	Hemlock, pine, beech, bass		10		1					
	1	White pine	19			1					
Maryland	2	Spruce only or chiefly	18			10	1	1			Spruce from West Virginia and Canada
	1	Poplar		10		1					
Delaware	1	Poplar						1			
Virginia	2	Poplar	20				2				
West Virginia	4	Spruce only or chiefly	17		10 5	2	2				
North Carolina	2	Pine	10					2			
South Carolina	1	Cypress and gum						1			
Georgia	3	Pine	20-27				3				
	1	Cypress and gum					1				
	1										
Kentucky	1	Spruce, buckeye, and maple	18					1			
Ohio	2	Spruce only or chiefly	17				2				
	1	Cottonwood and bass		9	10		1				

States	Number of mills	Kinds of wood used	Range of yield, per cord, in hundreds of pounds			Number of mills reporting supplies				Remarks
			Mechanical	Soda	Sulphite	Good	Fair	Limited	Declining	Poor	
Indiana	3	Aspen	16			1	1			1	
	1	Spruce and poplar	16				1				
	2	Poplar, spruce, pine	12					1		2	
	1	Aspen, poplar, cottonwood	10							1	
	1	Cottonwood	20					1			
	1	Basswood		9		1					
Michigan	4	Spruce only or chiefly	16		8–10	1	2			1	1 supply all from Canada
	3	Poplar	16–20	15		2		1			
	4	Poplar, pine, tamarack, spruce, and balsam				4					
	1	Aspen, pine, poplar, spruce, and bass	14						1		
Wisconsin	4	Spruce only or chiefly	16–18		9–10	1	2		1		
	15	Spruce and poplar	13–15		9–10	5	5	2	1	2	
	4	Spruce, poplar, pine	10–12			1		1	2		
Minnesota	1	Spruce only or chiefly	15					1			
Oregon	1	Cottonwood				1					
California	1	Tamarack and fir	17			1					

CHAPTER III.

PROCESSES FOR ISOLATING CELLULOSE

Rag Boiling. — In order to free the rags from the dirt and other impurities with which they are generally associated as received at the mill, they are put through a preliminary mechanical treatment, and are then boiled, usually under pressure, with alkali. The preliminary treatment involves the threshing, picking, cutting, and sorting of the rags, opening seams to facilitate removal of dirt, carefully removing all buttons, metallic fasteners, rubber, and such foreign materials, a final cutting by machinery into pieces about two inches square, and dusting. Such severe treatment is, of course, unnecessary in the case of new cuttings, which contain merely a moderate admixture of starch, clay, and similar substances employed in sizing and filling, and such rags are often put directly into the engine and beaten up when strength is especially desired.

The object of the boiling operation, to which all other rags are subjected, is to bring the grease, dirt, and other impurities into such condition that they may subsequently be easily removed by washing, and to destroy or so affect the coloring-matter as to facilitate the process of bleaching. Lime is only slightly soluble in water, 1 part, in the cold, dissolving in 425 parts of water, but it forms, with the acids of the grease, insoluble soaps, and as these are precipitated, fresh portions of the alkali pass into solution. In the case of soda, the soaps formed are soluble, and therefore more easily washed out; but the action of this base, in strong solution, upon the fibre is more severe, and it is believed to occasion greater loss.

The rotaries commonly employed are of the well-known cylindrical, horizontal type, turning about once a minute, and of various dimensions. They are fitted with manholes and with steam-pipes, the latter passing through the trunnions and curving below them. The rotary is packed with rags, and milk of lime is run in through a sieve, which may be made of a piece of Fourdrinier wire, water is added in amount sufficient to come above the journals, or even in some cases to fill the boiler two-thirds full, the manholes are closed, and in the best practice the rotary is allowed to run for half an hour before steam is admitted. The lime used should contain as little iron as possible and is best suited for this purpose when the content of magnesia is small, since this base is practically insoluble in water, and is much less powerful in its action than lime. The lime should slake readily and completely, and should be so kept as to avoid air-slaking. We give below an analysis of an excellent grade of lime for this purpose: —

	Per cent
Silica, etc., insoluble in acid	0.01
Iron and alumina (Fe_2O_3 and Al_2O_3)	0.28
Lime (CaO)	92.81
Magnesia (MgO)	2.28
Moisture, carbonic acid, etc. (by difference)	4.62
Total	100.00

The proportion of lime used, as well as the pressure and time of boiling, depends very much upon the character of the rags treated and the amount and kind of dirt which they contain. From 5 to 18 per cent of lime on the bale weight of the rags are the extremes, the general tendency being toward the higher limit. For No. 3 cottons and blues about 15 per cent of lime is used; for shivy linen 15 to 18. A pressure of 60 to 80 lbs. of steam is usually carried, and the time of boiling extends from twelve to eighteen hours, though the details of treatment vary not only with the stock, as just stated, but also in different mills. The paper-maker is governed by the stock he has and the paper he has to make. The better grades of rags require less time, pressure, and lime, and are in many mills boiled in open bleaches.

In emptying the rotaries the practice also varies. Some superintendents blow the pressure down completely before opening the bottom blow-off to run off the liquor prior to opening the manholes; while others, as we believe with good reason, reduce the pressure to 20 or 30 lbs., and blow the liquor off under this pressure through the bottom valve, claiming thereby to carry away more dirt. An objection to this procedure is found in the danger of losing some fine fibre in the blow-off. As soon as the liquor has left the rags, they are dumped upon the floor to drain. The emptying is performed with as much expedition as possible, in order that the liquor, which contains substances more readily soluble in hot than in cold water, may carry these off before it cools. The rags are softened if they are allowed to remain piled up on the floor for several days.

Japanese rags are washed and spread upon the grass at the country of shipment, and seed hulls thus derived may cause

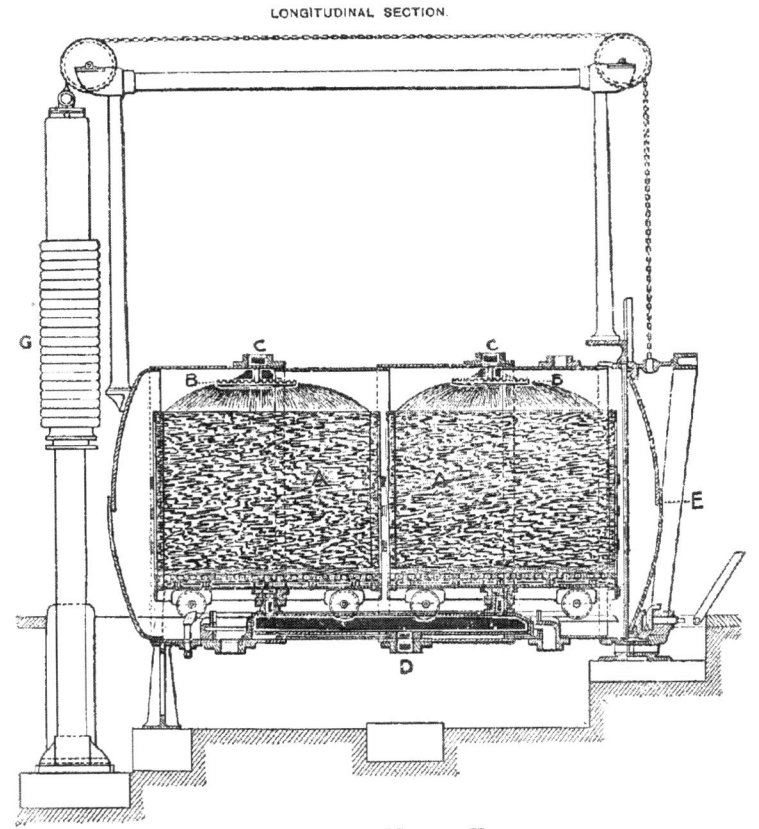

LONGITUDINAL SECTION.

Fig. 9.—The Mather Kier.

trouble. They may be reduced by the addition of 1 per cent. of soda-ash on the weight of the rags. Such addition of soda-ash, in the proportion of 1 to 5 per cent., greatly increases the efficiency of the liquor in its action upon certain colors, as for instance red, which is usually difficult to destroy, and which may even leave a tinge of that color in the bleached half-stuff. Japan blues give a bluish tinge suitable for white papers, while the darker shades of natural may be as well made from city rags, which are usually darker than those from the country. Such considerations are

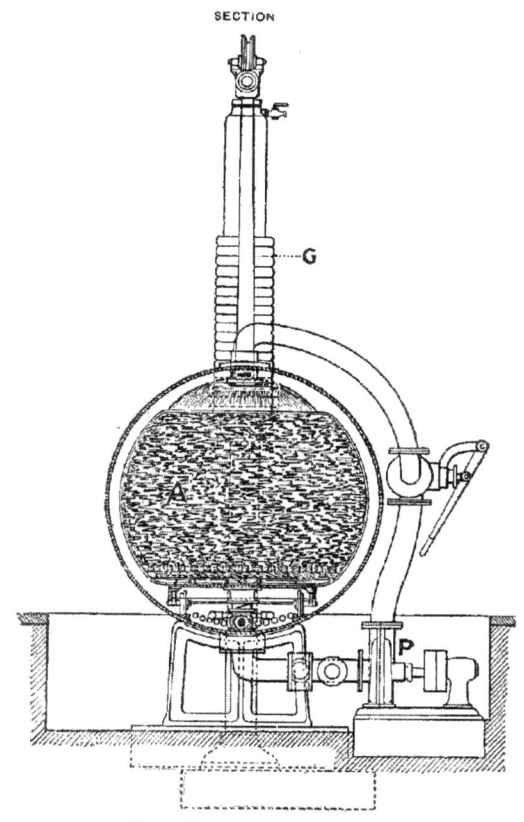

FIG. 10. — THE MATHER KIER.

borne in mind by the superintendent in sorting and mixing the rags prior to boiling.

The Mather Kier. — This well-known apparatus, which is shown in Figs. 9 and 10, was originally designed for the bleaching of textiles, and its adoption by the leading bleachers of cloth all over the world has demonstrated its value in this direction. It has lately been applied to the boiling of rags for paper-making at the mill of W. Joynson & Son in England, and the results there secured are such as to merit the attention of American paper-makers.

The kier consists of a horizontal boiler closed in front by a door, E, which is the full diameter of the kier. This door is balanced by the counterpoise, G, and is raised, lowered, and set up against the seat by hydraulic power. On the bottom of the kier are tracks upon which can be run in two cars, A, A, containing the cloth or rags. Owing to the construction of the kier and the mode of operation the amount of liquor required is very small. The liquor is drawn from the bottom of the kier through D by the pump, P, and is discharged upon the rags through the inlets, C, C, above the spreaders, B, B.

The results obtained in the treatment of rags in practice are best set forth in the report of Messrs. Cross and Bevan, which is given in large part below. —

A kier was erected last year [1888] at the works of Messrs W. Joynson & Son, St Mary Cray, where it has been in continual use for six months. Its dimensions are 8 feet long by 7 feet in diameter, and it is adapted to hold two wagons. In order, however, to economize time, six wagons are employed by Messrs Joynson, four either being filled or washed, while the other two contain rags in process of treatment in the kier. The cut and dusted rags are delivered automatically from a shoot direct into the wagons. The average weight taken by each wagon is 16 cwt, the full kier charge being therefore 32 cwt. The running of the wagons into the kier and the closing of the patent door occupy only some two or three minutes. As soon as this is completed, the rags are saturated with about 750 gallons of caustic-soda solution, which is delivered from a tank above the kier, and is circulated by means of a centrifugal pump. Steam is turned on until the pressure reaches 10 lbs per square inch, and the process continued for from two to three hours according to the nature of the material. The steam is blown off, which occupies about fifteen minutes, the door opened, the wagons removed, and another pair run in, the three latter operations occupying only ten minutes.

The rags, after being withdrawn from the kier are washed by causing cold water to flow on to the top of the wagons. By performing this operation outside the kier a considerable saving of steam is effected, only one heating up of the kier being required. Arrangements are provided for washing the rags by upward displacement by which a further economy of water is effected.

The kier in use at Messrs Joynson's is capable of doing at least 40 tons of rags per week; it has, in fact, for some time past been used for treating the whole of the rags used in the mill. It is equally well adapted with certain slight modifications of treatment, for all classes of rags, from new linen and cotton pieces to unbleached linen.

The labor required is one man for "treading" the rags into the wagons, one man for tending the kier, mixing the liquors, etc., and one man for emptying the wagons. Where circumstances permit, the wagons can be hoisted and transferred direct to the side of the breaking engines, thereby saving the labor of emptying into trucks.

The following are among the further advantages claimed for the kier, and substantiated by the result of the extended trial by Messrs. Joynson & Son:—

1. The rags, being stationary during the steaming, are never "knotted," as is the case with revolving boilers; they can therefore be rapidly filled into the breakers without danger to the breaking rolls.
2. A notable improvement in the color of the rags, after treatment, both before and after bleaching. This would enable the paper-maker to use rags of somewhat lower quality without affecting the color of his paper. If an improved quality of pulp is not so much desired as economy of chemicals, a saving of about 25 per cent of the latter can be effected. It amounts on the average to 1s. 3d. per ton of rags for soda, and about 2s. for bleaching-powder. It has, however, been found more advantageous to forego this saving and aim at improved quality of pulp instead.
3. Economy of water for washing purposes, 1000 gallons being sufficient for one ton of rags as against four or five times this amount by the ordinary process.
4. Saving of steam for heating and maintenance of steam pressure. This has been found to amount to about one-third of that required by the best system of treatment in revolving boilers, or about 6d. per ton of rags, with coal at 15s. per ton.
5. Improved strength of fibre. It has been abundantly proved in the case of cotton and linen textiles that a notable increase in strength is obtained by the use of the kier as compared with any other form of boiler. It may fairly be assumed therefore, that the fibres suffer less damage from the action of the alkali in the case of rags also.
6. An enormous saving in the space occupied. A kier 8 feet long by 7 feet diameter occupies with turntables, rails, etc., for four extra wagons, engine for driving pumps, etc., a ground space of 727 square feet. To this should be added the space occupied by the overhead tanks for the caustic soda, making a total of 843 square feet. The ground space occupied by six boilers, required to treat the same amount of rags would amount to 1440 square feet. In addition to this a top floor of equal area would be required for filling. Together these amount to 2880 square feet, as against 843 square feet required for the kier.

Treatment of Picker Seed and Picker Waste. — These two raw materials require about the same treatment. They are boiled, either in rotaries or open tubs, with rather weak lye. About 125 lbs. of soda-ash and 150 lbs. of lime are used to the ton of stock. Treatment in the rotary requires about 65 lbs. pressure if the boiling is to be completed in about eight hours. Twelve hours in the open tub gives a stock which bleaches better than that obtained by boiling under pressure. In either case the stock is much improved by being allowed to stand from six to eight days to soften. The same treatment applies to **Cotton Waste**.

Treatment of Esparto.—On account of the high price of this material it has never successfully come in competition with poplar

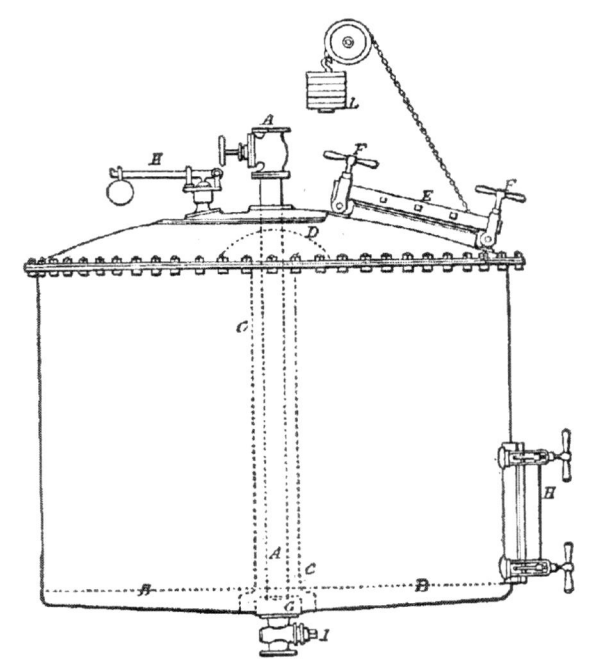

FIG. 11.—VOMITING BOILER.

fibre in this country, but on the Continent, and especially in England, it forms one of the most important sources of paper-stock. The grass is first picked over by hand to remove root ends, weeds, etc., and is then shaken and dusted. It is packed into the boiler without cutting, as is the case with straw. The details of the boiling operation vary much in different mills. In a few cases open vomiting-tubs are used, but the general practice is to treat, under pressure, in vertical boilers. In rotaries the fibre is likely to roll up into small balls, which make lumps in the paper. The pressures carried vary from 5 to 50 lbs., and the time of boiling is from one and a half to six hours. Caustic-soda liquor is always used. Routledge gives 10 per cent. of soda as the necessary amount. In one of the best English mills the practice is to use 16 lbs of caustic per 112 lbs of grass, and to boil from one and a half to two hours at 40 lbs. pressure.

One of the best types of boiler for esparto is shown in Fig. 11. It is a vomiting-boiler, the steam, which is admitted through A, passing to the bottom of the boiler before escaping. It then drives upward through the vomit-pipe, C, carrying with it the liquor which has worked below the false bottom, B, B, and which is then discharged under the hood, D, which acts as a spreader. E is the manhole for filling, the manhole plate being secured by the clamps, F, F, and balanced by the counterpoise, L. The boiler is emptied through H K is a safety-valve.

The washing of the pulp and recovery of the liquors are generally conducted as in soda-pulp mills in this country, but we have been in at least one English mill where no attempt at recovery was made. In many others the old-style pan evaporators are in use, but they are being replaced by the far more economical multiple-effect Yaryans. The ash in esparto is over 3 per cent., and consists largely of silica, which forms silicate of soda in the furnacing of the liquors, and thus reduces somewhat the per cent. of ash recovered. A recovery of about 80 per cent. is claimed. Recent experiments seem to show that it is impossible to recover over 85 per cent. under the best conditions. The yield of fibre is about 50 per cent., and it is bleached to good color with 7 per cent. of bleaching-powder

Treatment of Straw. — The similarity between the plant substance of straw and that of esparto is sufficiently close to render substantially the same methods of treatment applicable to both. Straw is, however, rather more highly lignified, and on that account requires the employment of somewhat higher pressures, or of stronger solutions In the preliminary treatment, the straw is picked over by hand to remove weeds, etc, and is afterwards dusted and cut into small pieces one to two inches long Care is taken to avoid the presence of seeds or seed hulls in the material ready for the boiler, as these are reduced with difficulty, and are likely to form specks in the pulp.

PROCESSES FOR ISOLATING CELLULOSE

The different processes for treating straw show considerable variation in their details, according to the kind and quality of the straw itself, and the purpose for which the product is to be used. They nearly all show in their general principles a close resemblance to the process of Melher, patented in 1854, and which consisted in cooking the straw, for about three hours, at a pressure of 70 lbs., with a solution of caustic soda contained in a rotary digester heated by indirect steam. 16 lbs. of caustic were used per 100 of straw.

Most of the straw pulp made in this country is prepared for use in strawboard by boiling the straw with lime. Abroad the straw is more commonly treated for the production of the pure fibre. The following methods are among those used in Germany:—

1. A charge of about 700 kilogrammes of straw is packed into a rotating spherical digester of 235 cm. diameter. Liquor is used which contains about 13 per cent caustic soda figured on the weight of the straw, and the digester is rotated cold from one to three hours. The boiling is carried on from six to eight hours, at about 40 lbs. pressure.

2. A charge of 1000 kilogrammes of straw is extracted from one to three hours with warm water, which is then drained off and the leaching repeated. The mass is then drained and packed into a cylindrical rotary. The lye is made by dissolving 10 to 14 per cent. caustic-soda, calculated on the gross weight of the straw, in only enough water to well wet but not to cover the straw. The cooking is carried on from four to six hours, at a temperature of about 150° C. After dumping, the pulp is washed for eight to twelve hours with warm water.

3. A charge of 1000 kilogrammes more or less of straw is packed and tamped into bags holding 40 to 60 kilogrammes each. The bags are tied up and packed in a cylindrical rotary. The cooking is carried on from four to eight hours with a caustic liquor standing 5° to 8° Bé. The pressure varies from 75 to 120 lbs. These variations in treatment are rendered necessary by the quality of different straws and the character of pulp desired.

4. In order to obtain a strong, creamy white fibre for use in fine writing-papers the straw is cut very small, and carefully cleaned from all weeds. Small spherical or cylindrical rotaries are used. The straw is first cooked for five to eight hours, at about 60 lbs. pressure, with 13 to 17 per cent of lime, and sufficient water is

used to keep the straw covered. It is then dumped into washing-engines fitted with granite plates, and carefully washed and beaten in order to remove all the lime with as little injury to the fibre as possible. The stuff is kept in drainers for about four days in order to make it soft and porous, and is then cooked for about five hours, at 40 lbs. pressure, with a soda lye containing 6 per cent. of caustic soda on the weight of the straw.

The mechanical preparation of the straw before cooking and the treatment to which it is afterwards subjected have at least as much to do with the quality of the product as the details of the boiling operation.

Some manufacturers find an objection to the use of rotary boilers, in the liability of the short fibres to roll up into little balls, which are likely to make spots in the paper. Partly on this account, and partly because of a real or supposed economy of soda, vomiting-boilers are in use in some mills abroad, especially in England.

In order to pack the greatest amount into the rotary the digester is, in some cases, filled with the chopped straw, and then run for a few moments with a portion of the liquor, so that the straw may soften and pack down sufficiently to admit a considerable additional quantity. The English practice in boiling shows the variations noticed elsewhere. According to Cross and Bevan the proportion of caustic is from 10 to 20 per cent. of the weight of the straw, and the boiling is carried on from four to eight hours, at pressures ranging in the different mills from 10 to 50 or even to 80 lbs.

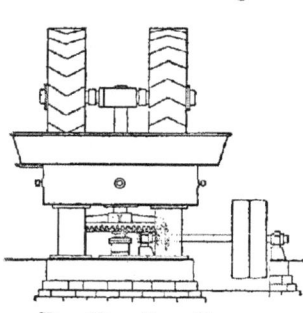

FIG. 12.— EDGE-RUNNER.

Glaser, British patent No. 938, A. D. 1880, subjects the straw pulp obtained by the usual process of cooking to the action of chlorine gas, in leaden or stone chambers, for several hours. A very complete isolation of the cellulose is thus secured, but the pulp has afterwards to be bleached in the ordinary way in order to free it from all products of the chlorine treatment.

Considerable rye straw is still treated in France by the following method for the manufacture of a coarse pulp: The straw is cut quite short in a cutting-machine. It is then transferred into large, rectangular brick wells, and just covered with dilute milk of lime. A covering of heavy boards weighted with stones is put on, and the whole allowed to remain from two to four weeks. The mass of pulp is then removed and worked under edge-runners (Fig. 12) for not less than an hour. As the knots are not softened, especial care must be taken to have the grinding well done. The product is harder than that from straw which has been treated in the usual way.

On account of the considerable proportion of silica present in straw, it has been generally assumed that this material would not easily lend itself to treatment by the sulphite process. Practical experience has, however, shown that this is not the case, and this process has recently been applied to the preparation of straw pulp with excellent result.

THE MANUFACTURE OF WOOD FIBRE

The Soda Process. — The efficiency of this process depends partly upon the direct solvent and saponifying power of the alkali at high temperatures, and partly upon the secondary reactions, by means of which the acid products resulting from the resolution of the wood are brought into the liquor as salts of soda. Mere treatment in the cold with dilute alkali is sufficient to dissolve an appreciable portion of the incrusting matter of wood, and the solvent power of the alkali is greatly enhanced as the temperature rises.

Poplar is used far more than any other wood in the soda process, but considerable quantities of pine, spruce, and hemlock are consumed in making longer fibred stock, while such woods as maple, cottonwood, white birch, and basswood are not infrequently made to replace poplar. Maple, birch, and basswood, however, give so short a fibre when used alone that they are generally mixed with poplar.

On account of the great solvent power of the alkaline solution, comparatively little pains are necessary in the preparation of the wood. The bark is removed, but no attempt is made to take out knots or portions which are stained or rotten. The process reduces small fragments of bark and knots to pulp. Whole knots are somewhat softened, but are easily removed by the screens. The wood is always chipped in the well-known manner, and the chips in the best practice are either sent through a willow duster or blown against a wire netting to remove the dirt which collects upon the piled wood.

The digesters used in this process are all of well-known forms. The most common type is probably a horizontal cylindrical rotary, about 22 feet long by 7 in diameter, and holding about three cords of wood. Such digesters are usually heated by coils supplied with steam through the trunnions, and revolving with the boiler. A few spherical rotaries are used, a common size being 12 feet in diameter, with a capacity of about five cords. Many mills use upright digesters, a few of which are heated by a steam-jacket, as in the Marshall boiler, a few by direct fire, but by far the greater number by live steam. It is very difficult to keep an iron shell tight in which alkaline solutions are boiled, as such solutions soon work their way through crevices which would be tight to water. Leaky digesters have in the past been a source of much annoyance in this process, but at the present time comparatively little difficulty from this cause is experienced. The Marshall jacketed boiler rested its claims chiefly upon the fact that the pressure in the jacket was always kept higher than that in the digester, so that in case of any leak in the digester walls there was a passage of steam inward rather than a passage of liquor outward. A welded digester is now upon the market, which would seem to make further trouble from leakage unnecessary.

The strength of liquor used varies from 8° to 15° Bé at 60° F., according to the pressure and time of boiling and the manner in which heat is applied to the digester. Where heating is effected by jackets, coils, or direct fire, the liquor ordinarily stands from 12° to 14° Bé, and contains, when properly causticized, from 6 to 9 per cent of caustic soda, NaOH. With live steam allowance has to be made for condensed water, and it is necessary to use less liquor, but of higher test. With indirect heat in rotaries about 700 gallons of liquor are used to a cord of wood. Upright digesters require considerably more, or enough in any case to cover the wood as soon as it becomes well soaked and settles down.

As much wood as possible is put into the digester, and in some cases mechanical devices for tamping and packing the wood are employed.

The boiling operation is a simple one. Full pressure is reached as soon as possible, and is maintained to the end of the cook. Watt and Burgess are said to have used a lye of 12° Bé, at a pressure of 60 lbs. but the later experience has been that even 75 lbs. is not sufficient to ensure a good cook, and the tendency now is toward the adoption of pressures above 100 lbs. With 90 lbs. as a minimum the present practice generally calls for 100 to 110 lbs. pressure. The time of boiling is eight to ten hours. As the pressure is increased, the strength of the liquor may be somewhat diminished. Thus Houghton, in the early days of the process, used a lye of 4° Bé, at pressures which reached 180 lbs.

The practice necessarily varies with the character of the wood to be treated, and where 11° Bé gives good results with poplar, maple cottonwood, or basswood, a lye of 15° Bé is needed for spruce, pine, or hemlock. The experiments of Tauss have shown that an increase in the time of boiling is only a partial equivalent for the use of such stronger liquors.

The pulp obtained at the close of the cook is of a grayish brown color, while the liquor is a dark, rich brown, and has a somewhat empyreumatic odor. It contains very little alkali which is not in combination with the acid products from the wood. The contents of the digester are dumped or blown into one of a series of iron washing-tanks, with drainer bottoms, and the pulp is there subjected, after most of the liquor has drained off, to a thorough and systematic washing. It is extremely important to remove the last traces of black liquor with as little expenditure of water as possible, because even a small quantity of such liquor left in the pulp renders bleaching very difficult; while, if a large quantity of water is used, the cost of concentrating the liquors in the recovery process becomes excessive. For these reasons the pulp in the different tanks is washed with the liquor coming from the tank before it in the series, and the moderate quantity of fresh water which finishes the washing of one lot of pulp passes in succession through four or five tanks, in each succeeding one of which the quantity of black liquor in the pulp is greater, until finally it passes through the pulp which has just come from the digester, and is brought up to about one-half the strength of the original liquor.

Well-washed poplar pulp made by this process bleaches easily with 12 to 14 lbs. of bleaching-powder to the hundred, and then consists of almost entirely pure cellulose. An appreciable portion of the cellulose present in the wood is dissolved during the boiling and the yields are consequently lower in this than in the sulphite process. Differences of treatment and inaccuracies in the measurement of wood make the yields reported by the different mills vary to a considerable extent, as is shown by the table on page 149.

Unbleached spruce pulp is soft and strong, but the coloring-matter derived from the decomposition of the non-cellulose portion of the wood so nearly approaches tar or ulmic compounds in character that it can only be bleached to good color by an oxidizing treatment so severe as to attack and weaken the cellulose itself. For this reason most of the spruce pulp is used in papers of such grades or tints that its color is no objection.

Recovery of Soda. — In the early days of the process no attempt was made to recover the soda from the waste liquors, but the nuisance caused by their discharge into running streams, and the large quantity of ash required, soon led to the adoption of various methods of reclaiming. The character of the waste liquor and the combinations in which the soda exists therein are such as to render recovery especially easy from a chemical point of view. The organic acids with which the soda is combined, as well as the organic matter present in other forms, represent nearly one-half the fuel value of the original wood, and furnish by their combustion a supply of heat which, if utilized in a properly constructed apparatus, is nearly or quite sufficient to effect the concentration of the weak liquors up to the point where they may be ignited. After the ignition in the presence of so much carbonaceous matter, the soda remains as carbonate in the black ash.

Among the bodies which have been recognized in the black liquor are sodium formate, oxalate, and acetate, together with dark-colored products similar to ulmic acid. Sugar and bodies like sugar are not present. According to Tauss the proportion of substances which are precipitated by alcohol and acids becomes greater as the pressure or the concentration of the lye is increased.

Where the original boiling liquor was strong, and where much care is taken to wash the pulp in a systematic manner, it is possible to bring the mixture of waste liquor and wash water up to a gravity of 6° to 9° Bé. at 160° F. The higher gravity is very rarely reached, and in some mills the liquors going to the evaporator do not stand over 3° to 4° Bé at the same temperature. The following analysis of a partially concentrated liquor indicates in a general way the proportion between the organic and inorganic constituents of liquors of this class: —

Black liquor standing 11½° Bé at 115° F.

	Per cent
Water	83.51
Organic matter	5.96
Caustic soda	8.60
Black ash waste	1.93
Total	100.00

In order to maintain a continuous combustion of the organic matter, the liquor must be concentrated by evaporation until it stands at least 30° Bé. at 130° F., and it is desirable to bring up to 40° Bé. or even higher.

In the earliest systems of recovery the evaporation was conducted in open pans frequently arranged one above the other to avoid undue loss of heat, but the volume of liquor to be concentrated is so large that such crude forms of apparatus, in which only a small proportion of the heating power of the combustible is made efficient, have now been almost entirely replaced by forms in which the principles of multiple-effect evaporation are embodied.

The boiling-point of water depends, as is well known, upon the pressure under which evaporation takes place, and is rapidly lowered as the pressure is diminished. Under the ordinary atmospheric pressure of 14.7 lbs. the boiling-point is 212° F.

The lowering of the boiling-point of water by diminution of pressure is shown by the following table: —

The temperature of water boiling —	° F.
at atmospheric pressure is	212
under 5 ins. vacuum is	195
" 10 " "	185
" 15 " "	160
" 20 " "	150
" 25 " "	130
" 26 " "	120
" 27 " "	112
" 28 " "	100
" 29 " "	72
" 29½ " "	52

166 THE CHEMISTRY OF PAPER-MAKING.

Other liquids follow a similar rule, but have different normal boiling-points; while, in case of water-holding substances in solution, the boiling temperature for the different pressures is increased.

When water is boiled under the ordinary atmospheric pressure, the resulting steam, like the water, has a temperature of 212° F., and the large quantity of heat necessary to convert the water into steam has been expended in bringing about that complete separation of the molecules which constitutes the essential difference between steam and water. That portion of the heat which was thus consumed or converted into the energy of steam is termed latent heat, and reappears when the steam is condensed. The total

FIG. 13. — THE YARYAN EVAPORATOR.

heat present in a pound of steam at 212° F. is represented by 1146.1 thermal units, and of this quantity 964.3 thermal units are in the form of latent heat. This series of facts is made use of in multiple-effect evaporation in the following way: The effects, as they are called, are pieces of apparatus so arranged that the steam or vapor from the liquid boiling in the first effect can be carried over and used as the heating agent in the second effect. The boiling-point of the liquid in the second effect, and consequently the temperature of the vapor issuing from it, is lowered by the maintenance of a partial vacuum in the second effect. The vapor from this effect is in the same way used as the heating agent in the third effect, in which the boiling-point of the liquid there present is still further reduced by the maintenance of a higher vacuum. Three or four effects are the number which are ordinarily used in practice, but there is in theory no limit to the number which might be used. Each additional effect within practical limits increases, in a numerical ratio, the quantity of liquor evaporated by given weight of combustible, because in each effect after the first the vapor from the preceding one is made to give up its latent heat to the liquor in that effect.

Many different types of multiple-effect evaporators have been devised, but at the present time nearly all the work of evaporating soda liquors in this way is done by the apparatus known as the Yaryan evaporator, from its inventor. Figure 13 shows a triple-effect Yaryan evaporator, as ordinarily designed for soda liquors, and Fig. 14 gives a section through one effect. Each effect consists of a boiler shell surrounding a number of independent

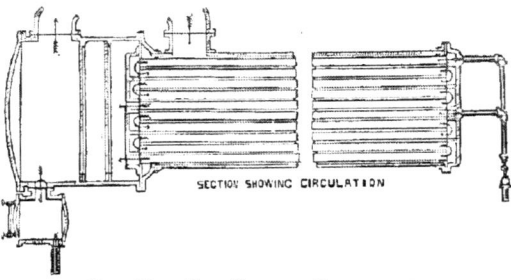

FIG. 14. — THE YARYAN EVAPORATOR.

pipes arranged in coils parallel with the length of the shell. The pipes are three inches in diameter, and the liquor is admitted into each coil through an independent supply tube of relatively small diameter, and at the back of the apparatus. The tubes in the first effect are heated by steam under a pressure varying in different mills from 10 to 45 lbs., and which is admitted into the shell or jacket which surrounds the coils. The small stream of liquor entering at the back end of a coil is exposed to the action of heat, partly as a spray and partly as a thin film lining the interior of the tube. Under the influence of the partial vacuum maintained in the separating-chamber in which the coil ends, the liquid moves forward through the coil with considerable velocity, and is thus continually exposing fresh particles to the action of the heat. Five lengths of pipe constitute a coil, and the liquor, in passing through one effect, has therefore to travel a distance equal to about five times the length of the shell, or 60 feet. The mixture of vapor and liquor issuing from each of the independent coils is discharged into the separating head or chamber, which forms the front of the effect, and there strikes a series of dash-plates or partial partitions, the openings through which alternate in such a way that the vapor and liquor strike upon each plate in succession, and are at last well separated, the liquor falling into the drum below the separator, and the vapor passing over into the shell or jacket of the second effect. The partially concentrated liquor from the first effect is delivered into the coils of the second effect through the supply tubes at the back, and on its passage through the coils is heated by the vapor given off during its concentration in the first effect. As the temperature of this vapor is lower than that of steam first used, the boiling-point of the liquor in the second effect is reduced by the maintenance of a slight vacuum. The liquor passes in succession through each of the effects, and the vapor from each effect passes over into the shell of the next one, where it is used as the heating agent, each effect being under a higher vacuum than the one preceding, in order to compensate for the gradual fall in the temperature of the vapor. The vacuum is maintained by means of a condenser and pump, while, by another pump, the concentrated liquor is removed from the last effect. The liquor enters the apparatus in a continuous stream at from 3° to 8° Bé., and in a few moments has passed through the entire system of pipes and been discharged at a density of 35° or more. 42° Bé. is reached at times, but it is difficult to pump liquor standing as high as 40°. The efficiency of the Yaryan is said to be due in part to the much greater rapidity with which liquids absorb heat when in motion, as compared with the rate of absorption when they are at rest. Jelinck gives the following figures in this connection : —

Velocity of the liquid per second in metres	Calories absorbed per square metre
0.312	22.7
0.640	33.6
1.020	46.9
1.640	69.9

The Yaryan evaporator, in connection with the Warren rotary furnace, has practically revolutionized the recovery of soda, since the expense is not only greatly diminished, but on account of the small cost of evaporation the washing can be carried further and a considerably greater percentage of soda recovered. Under the best present practice about 2100 gallons of liquor come to the Yaryan per ton of pulp produced, but in some cases the volume reaches 3200 gallons per ton.

The Gaunt multiple-effect evaporator, which is a more recent type of apparatus, has been lately applied to the concentration of soda liquors. The liquor to be evaporated and the heating agent occupy, in this apparatus, positions which are just the reverse of those in which they stand to each other in the Yaryan; that is, the liquor flows by gravity over the outside of the pipes in a thin sheet, and the vapor from which heat is derived is inside the pipe. Where three or four effects are used, they are arranged one above the other. The first effect is the highest one, and the liquor falling through this collects in the bottom of the effect, and flows into the slotted liquor-supply tube of the second effect, which is immediately below, and so down through the series until it reaches the bottom of the last effect, from which it is removed by pumping. The first effect is heated by direct or exhaust steam, which is let into the tubes under a slight pressure, and the vapor formed as the liquor falls over the tubes expands into the chamber, in which they are enclosed, and passes over into the tubes of the second effect; the vapor from this effect passes into the tubes of the one following, and so on. The amount of vacuum maintained on each effect is regulated by the height of the liquid seal formed by the liquor in the bottom of each effect. The vapor from the last effect passes over to the condenser, which maintains the vacuum.

Partly on account of the thick and tarry nature of the highly concentrated liquors, which retards their motion through an evaporator and makes pumping difficult, and partly because of the tenacity with which the last portions of water are held by the dissolved substances, the evaporation of such liquors cannot be economically carried above 40° Bé. The amount of water still present is too great for the liquors to maintain their own combustion, but when run into a furnace, through which the flames from a fire-box pass, they soon take fire and greatly increase the amount of heat which would otherwise pass from the furnace. The earliest style of black-ash furnace consisted of a pan, over which the flames from the fire-box passed as in the reverberatory furnaces used in the soda manufacture. Such furnaces are still used in a few mills and have openings at intervals along the sides, through which the workman, by means of a long rake gradually moves the burning material from the back towards the front of the pan, at which point it is withdrawn after the ignition is complete. In this country such furnaces have been almost entirely superseded by the Warren rotary furnace, which is shown, with its auxiliary apparatus, in Fig. 15. In the drawing, A is the movable fire-box, built of fire-brick, either inside an iron shell or held together by iron rods and bands. It is mounted on wheels resting upon rails, so that it may be easily moved away to give access to the furnace. It is either fitted with grate bars for burning coal or wood, or may be arranged for gas or oil.

The furnace itself, G, consists of an iron shell lined with fire-brick in such a way that the interior is conical, the larger end of the cone being toward the fire-box. The furnace is encircled by iron rails, which rest upon flanged wheels, as shown at L, and is made to revolve by the worm and gear and gear and pinion shown at M. The concentrated liquor is admitted to the furnace in a regulated stream at J, and gradually works its way forward, being exposed to more and more intense heat, until practically all the organic matter has been destroyed, and the ignited black ash falls out at N into an iron cart or conveyer. In order to utilize the waste heat from the furnace, a boiler, O, is set up in such relation to it that the hot gases pass under the boiler and then through the tubes. By this arrangement a quantity of steam may be generated nearly sufficient to carry on the whole process of evaporation up to the point where the liquors enter the furnace. A considerable proportion of the heat still remaining in the gases is taken up by the concentrated liquor in the tank, H, mounted over the boiler.

The throat of the furnace is protected by the water-jacket, K, fastened to the back of the fire-box, and projecting a short distance into the furnace. This jacket is filled with concentrated liquor from the tank H. The colder, and therefore heavier, liquor flows in at the bottom of the jacket, through the pipe F, and being expanded by the heat becomes lighter, and is forced back into the tank through the pipe E, as fresh portions of the colder liquor pass down F. In this way a constant circulation and rapid heating of the liquor in the tank are secured. Those portions of the pipes, E and F, which are fastened to the jacket are of smaller diameter than the portions coming from the tank, and project into them

THE MANUFACTURE OF WOOD FIBRE.   171

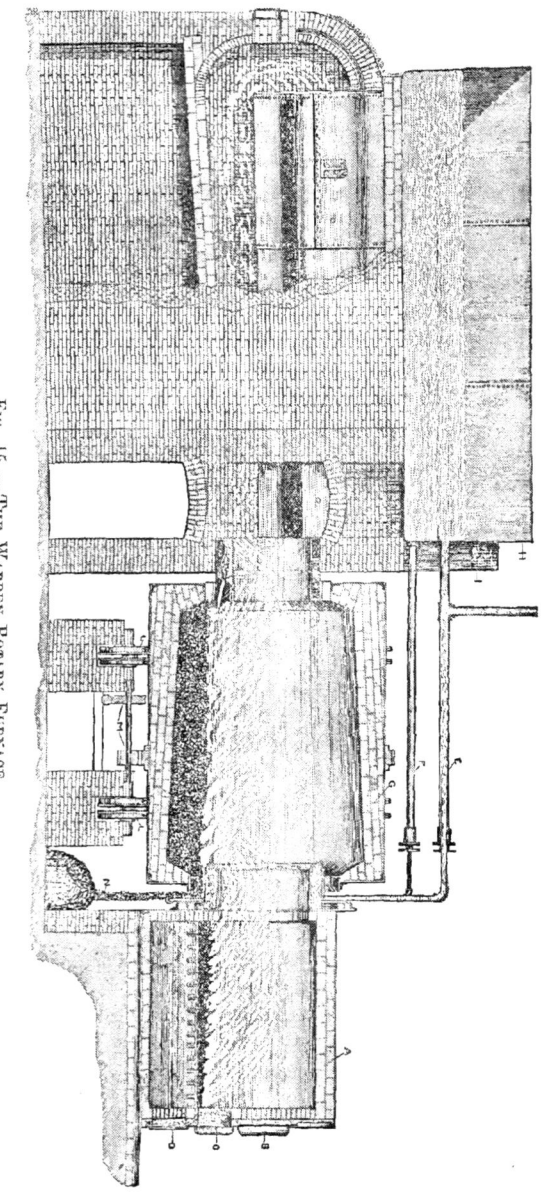

FIG. 16.—THE WARREN ROTARY FURNACE.

through stuffing-boxes, so that the fire-box may be moved back without breaking the connection.

We are indebted to Cross and Bevan's "Paper-making" for the following cuts and description of the Porion evaporator, which is one of the most economical of the large class of evaporators in which the liquors are not treated in multiple effect. It is shown in sectional elevation and plan in Figs. 16 and 17. It is largely

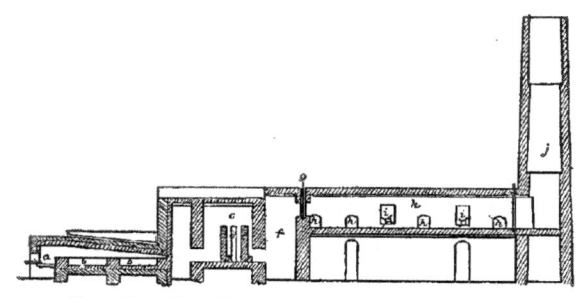

Fig. 16. — The Porion Evaporator — Section.

used on the Continent and also in England and Scotland. It consists of a large chamber, k, the floor of which is slightly inclined from the chimney shaft, and through which the waste heat from the furnace, a, passes.

The liquor to be evaporated is run in at the end nearest the chimney from the tank placed above the chamber, e. A number of cast-iron fanners, i, dip into the liquor and revolve rapidly, usually

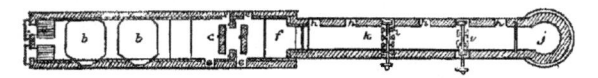

Fig. 17. — The Porion Evaporator — Plan.

at the rate of about 300 revolutions per minute, producing and filling the chamber with a very fine spray, thus presenting a very large evaporating surface.

Between the furnace and the evaporator are placed the chambers c and f. In c a number of brick walls, d, are so placed that the flames from the furnace are intercepted and broken up. The object of this is to give time for all the products of combustion to be thoroughly burned up, which would not be the case without the "small consumer," as these chambers are called. This part is an addition to the original evaporator, and was devised by Messrs. Menzies and Davis. The liquor, after having been concentrated in the chamber, k, runs into a trough placed alongside the doors, h, and flows into one or the other of the furnace beds, b, where it is still further concentrated, and the residue ignited by the flames from the fires at a. The draught can be regulated by the damper, y, and also by one placed near the shaft, j. The doors, e, in the smell-consuming chamber are for the purpose of cleaning out. The fanners, i, are worked by a small steam-engine not shown in the drawing. The temperature of the gases near the chimney should not be higher than about 85° C. By running the fanners at a very high speed the temperature of the gases may be still further reduced, thus showing the completeness of the evaporation.

This form of evaporator is open to the objection that the whole of the sulphur in the coal employed for the furnaces finds its way into the recovered soda. It combines with the alkali to form sulphite of soda, part of which is decomposed in the furnace with formation of sodium sulphate, sulphide, and other sulphur compounds. The same objection, of course, applies, though perhaps in a less degree, to all systems of evaporation in which the flame is in contact with the liquors to be evaporated.

The Porion evaporator can be erected at very small cost, and costs but little for maintenance. It is capable of producing three-quarters of a ton of recovered soda per ton of coal with liquors of the usual strength.

A profitable outlet for black-ash waste has recently been opened up by a process for its conversion into carbons for arc lights.

Causticizing. — The strong solution of carbonate of soda prepared from the mixture of black ash and fresh soda-ash is made caustic by treatment with lime in tanks, about 10 feet in diameter by 7 feet in height, fitted with agitators and usually with drainer bottoms. For every 100 lbs. of carbonate of soda in the liquor about 60 lbs. of lime are either thrown directly into the tank or else immersed in the liquor in an iron cage fastened to the side of the tank. The lime soon slakes, and is carried into the liquor, which takes on the appearance of milk of lime. The small quantity of lime, which at first goes into solution, reacts with the carbonate as shown below —

$$CaH_2O_2 + Na_2CO_3 = CaCO_3 + 2\,NaOH,$$

and is precipitated as carbonate of lime, an equivalent portion of fresh lime is immediately dissolved, and the reaction continues until either the lime is exhausted or all the soda causticized. In order to hasten the reaction the mixture is usually heated to about 212° F. by a steam-pipe passing through the bottom of the tank.

The character of the lime used in causticizing is of the first importance if good results are to be secured. It should contain as little silica as possible, since otherwise there will be a loss through the formation of silicate of soda, and the proportion of magnesia should be small because of the great insolubility of this base, which renders it comparatively ineffective.

We give below analyses of two samples of lime, the sample marked No. I. being especially good for causticizing, while that marked No. II. is not at all well suited for the purpose:—

	No. I	No. II
Sand and insoluble material	0.08	3.16
Iron and alumina oxides	0.89	2.67
Lime	94.07	54.04
Magnesia	1.20	36.80
Water, carbonic acid, etc.	3.76	3.33
Totals	100.00	100.00

Solvay, in his British patent of 1879, claims that lime slaked in a solution of calcium chloride gives a granular hydrate which thoroughly causticizes the hot liquors, which are merely run over a layer of the material. The hydrate does not lose its form, and can therefore be very easily and thoroughly washed.

G. Lunge has obtained the following results from experiments to determine how completely sodium carbonate may be converted into caustic soda by treatment with lime. At the ordinary atmospheric pressure the experiments gave the following numbers:—

Per cent Na_2CO_3 in liquor	Specific gravity before causticizing	Percentage of soda made caustic by treatment I	II
2	1.022 at 15° C	99.4	99.3
5	1.052 "	99.0	99.2
10	1.107 "	97.2	97.4
12	1.127 "	96.8	96.2
14	1.150 "	94.5	95.4
16	1.169 at 30° C	93.7	94.0
20	1.215 "	90.7	91.0

Corresponding experiments, conducted under pressure, at a temperature of 148° to 153° C., gave—

Per cent Na$_2$CO$_3$ in liquor	Specific gravity before causticizing	Percentage of soda made caustic by treatment I	II
10	1.107 at 15° C	97.06	97.50
12	1.127 "	96.35	96.80
14	1.150 "	95.60	96.60
16	1.169 at 30° C	95.40	94.80
20	1.215 "	91.66	91.61

From which it appears that there is no appreciable gain when the operation is performed under pressure, and that, as was already held, the best results are obtained from the weaker liquors.

Mills which are located upon small streams sometimes experience considerable difficulty in disposing of the waste-lime mud from the causticizing tanks. This difficulty has been met by the lime reclaimer invented by Mr. George W. Hammond, and shown in section in Fig. 18. The lime-mud is fed at G into the flue, F, which is 24 feet long, and through which the mud is slowly carried forward by means of an Archimedes screw. The nearly dry mud is then discharged into the rotary furnace, C, which is driven by gears as shown at H. The material coming from this furnace is guided by the connecting flue, D, into the second furnace, C', which discharges the recovered lime through the opening B, in front of the fire-box, A. In order to drive off all the water and set free the carbonic acid, a very high temperature and a considerable period of time are necessary, so that very long furnaces are required if the process is to be continuous and the output at all large. In the apparatus erected by Mr. Hammond each furnace is 40 feet long, and the capacity is about five tons of recovered lime per day.

The Hewitt and Mond causticizing process, or the ferric oxide process, as it is called, has been lately introduced in England, and depends upon the fact that when a mixture of ferric oxide and carbonate of soda is strongly ignited the iron acts as an acid to displace the carbonic acid with the formation of sodium ferrate which is so unstable that washing with hot water removes the caustic soda, leaving the ferric oxide in condition to be used again. In practice, three parts of ferric oxide, originally in the form of "Blue Billy," which is the cinder from pyrites burning, are used to every one part of soda-ash.

176   *THE CHEMISTRY OF PAPER-MAKING.*

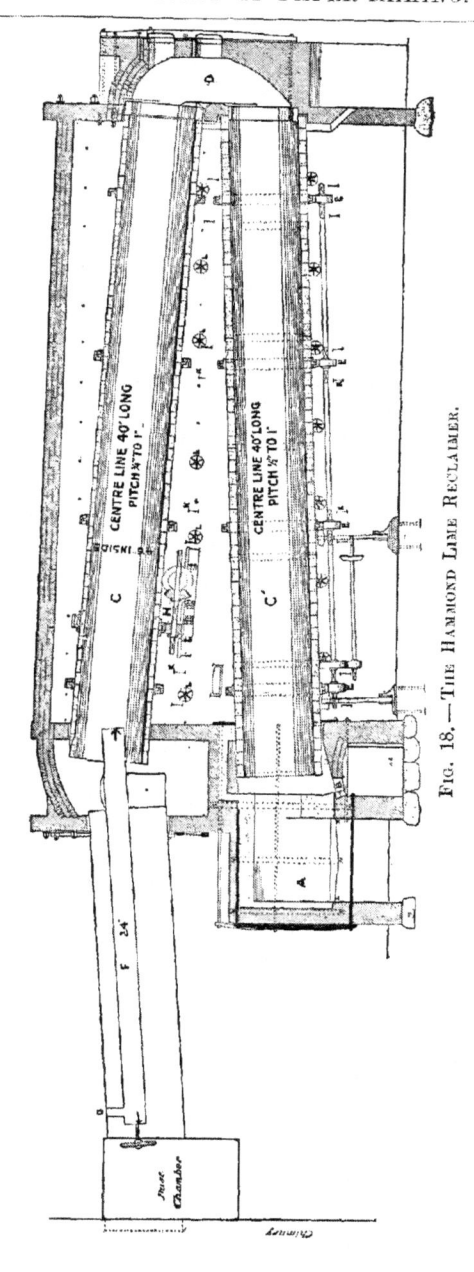

Fig. 18.—The Hammond Lime Reclaimer.

An analysis by ourselves of the "Blue Billy" as used gave figures as below:—

	Per cent
Moisture (loss on ignition)	7.50
Sesquioxide of iron (Fe_2O_3)	65.49
Alumina (Al_2O_3)	0.89
Sand and silica (insoluble in acid)	24.72
Oxides of lead and copper	traces.

A rotary furnace, usually 18 feet long and 10 feet in diameter, is charged with two tons of the mixture of this material and soda-ash, and turned at the rate of one and a quarter revolutions per minute in order to prevent fluxing. About 1400° F. seems to be the temperature necessary for the reaction, and most of the time is consumed in bringing the charge to that heat. The reaction proceeds rapidly after it is once begun. About five charges can be worked in such a furnace in twenty-four hours, with the consumption of seven long tons of coal. The ferrate of soda is removed to tanks fitted with drainer bottoms, and is there leached with hot water in the same systematic way in which black ash is treated. In order to settle out all of the oxide of iron it is necessary to allow the liquors to stand about four days. It is possible by this process to make liquors of a strength of 80° T.

The percentage of soda recovered varies, of course, within considerable limits, according to the efficiency of the apparatus and the care with which the different stages of the process are controlled. Some mills fail to recover more than 60 per cent., while others, in exceptional months, show figures as high as 95 per cent. The average recovery is probably from 75 to 78 per cent., but in the best practice the amount reclaimed runs from 85 to 90 per cent. The percentage of recovery at the Willsborough Mill of the New York and Pennsylvania Company for 1891 is given to us as 89.11 per cent.

The main sources of loss in recovery are:—

Imperfect washing of the pulp.
Volatilization of the carbonate in the furnace, or, which amounts to the same thing, its escape as dust carried into the chimney mechanically by the furnace gases.
Imperfect leaching of the black ash.
Retention of soda in the lime-mud after causticizing.

The greatest loss is likely to occur in washing the pulp, and this can only be kept down by conducting the operation in the most systematic and thorough manner possible. With great care the losses in causticizing and in leaching the black ash need not amount together to more than 1 per cent. An appreciable quantity of soda is undoubtedly lost up the chimney, and it is difficult to either check this loss or accurately estimate its amount. This item is a sort of residuary legatee, to which is credited the balance of loss which cannot properly be charged to the other accounts. In running a soda pulp mill the most careful superintendence is likely to be thwarted unless it is supplemented by careful and frequent chemical tests at every stage of the process. Such tests are fully described in the chapter on **Chemical Analysis**.

The following figures, which are taken from mill records, are of interest as showing the minimum to which the losses at the points indicated have been brought in practice: —

In washing	2 to 3 per cent
Causticizing and leaching black ash, together	0.75 to 1 "
Up chimney	2 to 3 "

The Sulphate Process. — This interesting modification of the soda process was introduced by Dahl, at Danzig, about 1883. In it sulphate of soda is made to replace, in large part, the more expensive carbonate. According to Schubert, the liquor is in the first instance made up from a mixture of three parts sulphate of soda and one part caustic. After cooking the wood, the liquor is evaporated and calcined, and yields a reddish brown ash, which has about this composition: —

	Per cent
Sodium sulphate	16
" carbonate	50
" hydrate	20
" sulphide	10
Various materials	4
	100

The composition of the ash varies, however, according to the treatment, but the solvent power of the liquor made therefrom is not especially affected. The loss in recovery is 10 to 20 per cent. New liquor is then made by adding sufficient sulphate of soda to replace the salts lost, and heating the whole with 20 to 25 per cent of lime. In regular operation the boiling liquors generally contain a mixture of salts composed of about —

37 parts sodium sulphate.
8 parts sodium carbonate
24 parts sodium hydrate.
3 parts sodium sulphide.

The strength of the lyes ranges from 6 to 14° Bé. Iron boilers are used, and the cooking, which requires from thirty to forty hours, is conducted at a pressure of 75 to 150 lbs. The main objection to the process is found in the stench which necessarily arises from the sulphides present in the liquors. Sulphate pulp is of excellent quality, soft and strong. That found in this market is made from coniferous trees, probably spruce and fir. Three grades are common — the unbleached, half-bleached, and bleached.

THE SULPHITE PROCESS.

The first patent involving the use of sulphurous acid in reducing wood to pulp was that numbered 70,485, and issued Nov. 5, 1867, to Benjamin C. Tilghman, then of Philadelphia, and a chemist to whom many branches of technology are much indebted. A supplementary patent, Number 92,229, covering the treatment of fibrous materials at the ordinary pressure, was issued to the same inventor in 1869. These patents form the basis of all the various modifications of the process in operation at the present time. The numerous subsequent patents to other inventors cover merely improvements in apparatus and details of treatment.

Tilghman states that his invention consists in a process of treating vegetable substances which contain fibres with a solution of sulphurous acid in water, heated in a close vessel, under a pressure sufficient to retain the acid gas until the intercellular incrusting or cementing matter existing between the fibres is dissolved, either partially or wholly, as may be desired, and a fibrous product is obtained suitable for the manufacture of paper pulp or of fibres, or for other uses, according to the nature of the material employed.

The following abstract of Tilghman's original patent will serve to indicate how carefully and thoroughly he had worked his process out in the experimental way, and how clearly he perceived all its possibilities. His difficulties, which he later found too serious for him to overcome, were evidently confined almost entirely to the engineering side of the process.

The specification calls for a strong iron vessel of convenient size and shape, lined with lead, and provided with a steam jacket, and with the necessary pipes, cocks, and manholes for filling and emptying the charge; and with gauges, safety valves, and thermometers to indicate height of liquid, pressure, and temperature. This vessel is about two-thirds filled with chips, hemlock or poplar being specified. A solution of sulphurous acid in water, of specific gravity 1.025 to 1.035, in which a quantity of sulphite of lime has been dissolved, sufficient to raise its density to about 1.07 to 1.08, is run in until the amount is sufficient to keep the wood constantly covered by the liquid during treatment. The boiling is conducted for about eight hours, at 260° F., when fresh water is forced in at the top of the digester to wash out the acid solution. It the pulp, upon examination, proved, as was undoubtedly the case, to be imperfectly separated, it was to be again treated with a fresh charge of sulphurous acid and sulphite at a temperature from 260 to 280° F., for three to five hours, as might be necessary. The patentee speaks of the quantity of sulphite of lime deposited during the boiling, and points out that it may be re-used together with the sulphurous acid gas which may be driven off from the waste liquor. He states that the stronger the acid solution, the more rapid is the action at a given temperature. Also, the higher the temperature, the more rapid is the action with a given density of solution; with weak acid and comparatively low temperature, he says, foreshadowing the Mitscherlich process, the effect can be produced by continuing the digestion a sufficiently long time. Sulphurous acid in water at the requisite temperature appears to be the efficient agent in dissolving the intercellular or cementing matter of the vegetable fibrous substance, and where the color of the product is of no consequence, the operation may be performed with the sulphurous acid alone, without the addition of sulphite. In this case a reddish brown color is given to the resulting fibrous product, and the acid solution will be found to contain a quantity of free sulphuric acid, which has been formed during the operation by the oxidation of a portion of the sulphurous acid. This is directly in line with the Pictet process. The presence of a sulphite in the acid solution prevents this reddening effect, and in case of many substances a considerable bleaching of the fibrous product takes place.

Tilghman's idea at this time was that the office of the sulphite was to present a base with which the sulphuric acid could combine as fast as formed, and he therefore naturally supposed that many other of the salts of the weaker acids, such, for example, as the acetates, could replace the sulphites more or less perfectly, in the presence of sulphurous acid. Subsequent experiments and a more complete knowledge of the chemical process have shown this to be incorrect, since the sulphite not only neutralizes the free sulphuric acid, but has also a very important influence in the process depending upon its power of forming double compounds with certain of the derivatives of the wood.

On account of their historical interest and important bearing on the process, we give below in full the claims of Tilghman's first patent. —

The process of treating vegetable substances which contain fibres with a solution of sulphurous acid in water, either with or without the addition of sulphites or other salts of equivalent chemical properties as above explained, heated in a close vessel, under pressure, to a temperature sufficient to cause it to dissolve the intercellular incrusting or cementing constituents of said vegetable substances, so as to leave the undissolved produce in a fibrous state suitable for the manufacture of paper, paper pulp, cellulose, or fibres, or for other purposes, according to the nature of the material employed.

I also claim as new articles of manufacture the two products obtained by treating vegetable substances which contain fibres with a solution of sulphurous acid in water, either with or without the addition of sulphites or other salts of equivalent chemical properties as above explained, heated in a close vessel, under pressure, to a temperature sufficient to cause it to dissolve the intercellular or incrusting constituents of said vegetable substances, one of said products being soluble in water, and containing the elements of the starchy, gummy, and saline constituents of the plants, and the other product being an insoluble fibrous material, applicable to the manufacture of paper, cellulose, or fibres, or to other purposes, according to the nature of the material employed.

I also claim the use and application, in the manufacture of paper, paper-pulp, cellulose, and fibres, of the fibrous material produced by treating vegetable substances which contain fibres with a solution of sulphurous acid in water either with or without the addition of sulphites or other salts of equivalent chemical properties as above explained, heated in a close vessel, under pressure, to a temperature sufficient to cause it to dissolve the incrusting or intercellular constituents of said vegetable substances.

I also claim the use and application of sulphites or other salts of equivalent chemical properties as above explained, in combination with a solution of sulphurous acid in water, as an agent in treating vegetable substances which contain fibres, when heated therewith in a close vessel, under pressure, to a temperature sufficient to cause said acid solution to dissolve the intercellular or incrusting constituents of said vegetable substances

I also claim the recovery and re-use of sulphurous acid and sulphite from the acid liquids which have been digested on the vegetable fibrous substances, by boiling said liquids or neutralizing them with hydrate of lime

Theory of the Sulphite Process. — It is well known that many of the more complex members of the carbohydrate group, to which cellulose belongs, undergo more or less pronounced change upon being boiled with water, especially if the boiling is conducted at the higher temperatures obtained under pressure in a closed vessel. Sugar, which is the typical member of the group, becomes *inverted;* that is, the sugar combines to a limited extent with the elements of water, and the more complex molecule thus formed breaks down into the two simpler ones of dextrose and levulose. Such an action in which, as a result of taking up the elements of water, a molecule is broken down, is called a *hydrolytic* action, and the decomposition itself is called *hydrolysis*. Similar changes as before stated, are brought about through the action of water alone upon the more complex carbohydrates, such as cellulose and its incrusting matters, if not upon all the members of the group, but these changes proceed far more rapidly and completely in the presence of dilute acids. Cellulose itself is comparatively stable under these conditions, unless the temperature is considerably raised, but Tauss and others have shown that it is by no means unacted upon. Lignin, probably from its greater complexity, is broken down with considerable rapidity at temperatures not much higher than that of the boiling-point of water. The products of the decomposition are largely organic acids, and the direction of the decomposition is toward the production of these acids, but among the earlier products there undoubtedly occur a considerable proportion of substances having, at least, the general character of the aldehydes. When the ordinary mineral acids, as sulphuric or hydrochloric acid, act in the dilute form, and at moderately high temperatures, upon wood, the decomposition products rapidly accumulate in the liquor, and undergo further secondary decompositions, the course of which tends toward the production of insoluble, dark-colored, and tarry matters. It is obviously impossible under these conditions to look for the production of cellulose in any condition of purity.

The reaction undoubtedly takes a somewhat similar course when sulphurous acid without any base is used; indeed, this acid is well known to have a decomposing action upon many groups of organic compounds. As a reducing agent, using the word in its chemical sense, the acid retards and limits the secondary changes, but it does not altogether prevent them. The brown color of pulp obtained by the Pictet process is due in part to the products of the changes set up by the sulphurous acid, as well as to those which are induced by the sulphuric acid formed during this process. This is shown by the fact that the addition to the liquor of the very small amount of soda required to neutralize this sulphuric acid does not prevent the browning of the pulp.

The primary action of a bisulphite liquor in resolving wood proceeds upon the same lines as that of a solution of sulphurous acid, but the presence of the base in this combination materially modifies the subsequent course of the reactions. The bisulphites possess the remarkable property of forming, with the aldehydic products of the first stage of the decomposition, true double compounds which are soluble and comparatively stable. Compounds of this class have been found in the waste liquors. It is characteristic of the aldehydes that they pass by oxidation into organic acids, and in spite of the presence of sulphurous acid, which tends to prevent oxidation, there is some formation of these acids. Once formed, they displace the sulphurous acid from an equivalent portion of the base, and form soluble organic salts. By these two actions the bisulphites take up the products of the resolution of the wood, and prevent for the most part the extreme degradation of the products which is characteristic of the water treatment or of the soda process. The combination of the acid products with the base is shown by the steady rise in the gas pressure observed during the last part of a sulphite cook, and which is avoided by blowing off. It is also shown by the composition of the waste liquors. A. Ihl finds that the resinous matter obtained by evaporating these liquors consists mainly of the calcium salts of acids similar to Arabic acid, and that these acids, as indicated above, decompose carbonates, sulphites, and sulphides.

An incidental advantage of considerable importance is obtained by the use of sulphurous acid in connection with a base, and is due to the power of this acid to form with various coloring-matters compounds which are themselves colorless. The practical effect of this latter action is the production of a fibre which may be at first of a color as good as that of well-bleached pulp, although, as in case of all sulphurous acid bleaching, this high color does not persist for any considerable length of time.

Although all the bisulphites act in general in the manner specified above, the character of the liquor is modified in several important particulars, according as one base or another is in combination with the acid. Bisulphite of lime is a very unstable salt which upon being merely heated decomposes; one-half of the acid being set free. The resulting monosulphite is practically insoluble, so that when this decomposition occurs in the boiler, this latter salt is precipitated throughout the pulp, from which it is difficult to remove it by washing. Where lime liquor is used, there is therefore more gas pressure in the digester, and the resulting pulp is comparatively harsh, hard, and transparent. It is also more difficult to make a straight lime liquor of high test than it is to prepare similar liquors from magnesia or soda, but on account of the insolubility of sulphate of lime the former liquors never contain more than three-tenths per cent of sulphuric acid, while soda or magnesia liquors may contain an indefinite amount. In the case of lime liquors, any excess of sulphate over the amount given is precipitated and may be settled out.

Bisulphite of magnesia is somewhat more stable than the corresponding lime salt, and its action on the incrusting matter is milder, but even more effectual. The sulphates or monosulphites which may be present in magnesia liquors remain in solution, and are easily washed out from the pulp. The resulting product is much softer and whiter than any which is ordinarily made with lime without some subsequent treatment. These desirable qualities of magnesia are possessed in a still higher degree by soda. Sodium bisulphite is so permanent that it may be easily obtained and preserved in the crystalline form. The gas has so strong an affinity for the base that liquors of 35° Bé may be made without difficulty. Both the sulphite and sulphate of soda are very soluble, and there is therefore no precipitation either in the liquor apparatus or in the digester. Pulp made with soda liquor is white and soft, and almost entirely free from the last portions of incrusting matter.

It has been held in some quarters that sulphuric acid in considerable amount is formed in the digester during boiling, but numerous experiments by ourselves and others show that in reality this oxidation of the sulphurous acid is very slight, it is obviously so when we consider that making no allowance for the chips and liquor in the digester, but supposing the whole interior to be filled with air at the ordinary temperature and pressure the total amount of oxygen contained therein only amounts to 22 lbs in a digester of a capacity of 1200 cubic feet, a quantity so small when compared to the weight of sulphurous acid in the liquor that it may be disregarded. An additional proof is found in the Pictet-Bielaz process in which it is possible to recover as sulphurous acid 95 per cent. of all the gas originally present in the liquor.

History — Tilghman is said to have spent about $40,000 in experiments at a mill at Manayunk, Pa. He boiled in long ten-inch cylinders, lead lined. Although excellent fibre was obtained, the engineering difficulties proved so serious that the experiments were finally abandoned.

After the failure of Tilghman to put his process upon a commercial footing it was taken up by Fry and Ekman at Bergvik, Sweden, about 1870, after a course of experiments in which nitric and various acids and water alone had been tried as resolving agents. In 1872 the present Ekman process, using a solution of bisulphite of magnesia, was so far developed that these gentlemen had a three-ton mill running on a commercial basis with eight small jacketed digesters. The process was worked secretly until about 1879. It was introduced into England in a small way at Ilford Mills, near London, after which, in 1884, the proprietors of the patent erected a large mill at Northfleet, also near London.

Although in no way essential to his process, Ekman has always favored the preparation of this solution in towers. Those first used at Bergvik were 5 feet in diameter, 14 feet high, and filled above the false bottom with calcined magnesia. They carried at the top sprinklers for distributing and regulating the flow of water.

The next to assist in the development of the process was Mitscherlich, then professor of chemistry at Munden, and a son of the celebrated discoverer of the law of isomerism. He began his experiments at the mill of F. Keferstein, Ermsleben, near the Hartz Mountains, about 1876 and later went to Thode's Mill, near

Dresden. He did not get started on a commercial scale until about 1880 or 1881.

On the 11th of October, 1883, Moritz Behrend, the lessee of Prince Bismarck's mill at Coeslin, disputed the validity of the Mitscherlich patents. He relied chiefly upon the Tilghman British patent. No. 2924, dated Nov. 9, 1866. After a very long trial and examination of technical experts, the German Board of Patents concluded that the Mitscherlich process did not differ from that of Tilghman sufficiently to entitle it to protection.

Francke, in Gothenburg, Sweden. began his experiments about 1879, his attention, it is said, being turned in this direction through the introduction to him of one of Ekman and Fry's chemists. He began work in a commercial way about 1882. His process has so far secured no foothold in this country, and presents few points of interest. The liquor is prepared in towers, and the digester is a horizontal rotary cylinder, lead lined. The lining is held in place by rings of various construction.

The Partington process, which was acquired by the American Sulphite Pulp Company, about 1884, was one of the first to be introduced here. The liquor plant shows a radical departure from those previously used, and will be described in detail under **Liquor Making**. The digesters are spherical rotaries. The various steps taken by Partington in the development of his system for lining these digesters comprise one of the most interesting studies in engineering which the process has shown. They will be discussed at some length in the section given to digester linings.

McDougall was for some time associated with Partington, and his plant in 1887 differed little from the last described, except in the method adopted for lining digesters.

Various other manufacturers in different parts of Europe started almost contemporaneously with these workers. Graham in England. who had been chemist to Ekman and Fry, applied to digester linings a method by which the lead was caused to adhere uniformly over the surface of the iron shell, and worked out a special modification of the Ekman process, which consisted in re-enforcing the strength of the boiling liquor during cooking by fresh charges of gas. Graham's process has not come into practical use, but the digester has been adopted by Ekman, and by some mills in this country. Flodqvist for a time exploited the process in which a liquor containing both bisulphite and phosphate of lime was used, the liquor being made in a series of towers, some of which were packed with limestone and others with the bones which furnished the supply of phosphate. Kellner in Austria, who was at that time associated with Baron Ritter, and who is one of the most skillful chemical engineers who has turned his attention in this direction, had taken out, in 1885, several patents covering a special process, liquor apparatus and digester, which were then in successful operation.

The difficulties occasioned by the use of an acid sulphite had, as early as 1880, led Cross to bring out a process employing an alkaline solution of sulphite of soda in iron digesters, unlined. This reagent has no effect on the iron, but its use necessitates the carrying of considerably higher pressures than where the bisulphite is used, the bleaching action of the sulphurous acid is much restricted, and the cost of chemicals much increased. There is, moreover, according to our own experiments, a precipitation under these conditions of free sulphur throughout the pulp. The Pictet-Brelaz process, on the other hand, which was brought out in 1883, goes to the other extreme, and instead of increasing the amount of base as Cross had done, does away with it altogether, the wood being boiled at a temperature never exceeding 105° C., in a solution carrying from 7 to 8 per cent. sulphurous acid.

The first American paper-maker to introduce the process upon a commercial scale in this country was Charles S. Wheelwright, then of Providence, R.I. The Ekman process was the modification selected, after a visit, in 1882, to the small mill in which it was in operation at Bergvik, Sweden. Although the process as there shown was evidently very imperfect on the mechanical side, the high grade of the product encouraged Mr. Wheelwright and his associates to erect on a large scale the now historical plant of the Richmond Paper Company.

Pulp of the highest quality was made almost from the start; but the mechanical difficulties of working the process on a large scale proved so serious that in spite of his untiring energy, Mr. Wheelwright soon found himself in almost the position of the original inventor, Tilghman.

The towers filled with calcined magnesia, as was the case at Bergvik, gave endless trouble from the difficulty of regulating the flow of water, from the great tendency of the magnesia to soften up and form mud, and finally, from the liability, when the water supply was temporarily stopped, of the whole mass to cake and bind together through the formation of monosulphite of magnesia. These defects in the apparatus frequently made it impossible to secure regular or free draft up through the tower, the output of liquor was small, and both its quantity and composition were irregular. After trials on a large scale, with many different forms of apparatus, those difficulties were entirely overcome by the adoption of the apparatus suggested by Catlin. Obstacles equally serious were encountered in working the digesters, as the engineering problems presented were such that no precedents could be found for guidance. Various forms of digester were designed in succession by Mr. Wheelwright to such good effect that the cost of repairs on linings were in about three years reduced from over $10.00 to about $1.50 per ton of product. Throughout all this period of difficulty the product of the mill was equal, if not superior, to any which has since been produced here or abroad.

Except in a few instances which will be noted, the subsequent development of the process in this country has proceeded upon the lines laid down in Europe, although numerous forms of digesters and liquor apparatus have appeared. Two new systems, those of Schenck and Crocker, have been developed commercially, and the former has been widely introduced. The main novelty of the Schenck process is found in the digester, which is built up in three-feet sections cast from a special bronze. His liquor apparatus differs slightly from that of Partington, and the general method of procedure in the process itself is much the same. The Crocker process differs from all those before mentioned in that it employs a solution of bisulphite of soda prepared by double decomposition by treating bisulphite of lime solution with sulphate of soda.

Preparing Wood.—Owing to the great solvent power of the alkali in the soda process, comparatively little pains are necessary in the preparation of the wood. In the sulphite process, however, all portions of bark and knots which go into the digester are only slightly acted upon by the liquor, and are liable to cause dirt in the pulp. It is a prime necessity, therefore, that all bark should be carefully removed either by draw-shaves or by a barker. This applies as well to the light-colored inner bark as to the outer bark. Wherever, on account of an old wound in the tree, the bark is turned inward, these portions are best cut out by hand, since the use of the barker involves in these cases an unnecessary loss of sound wood. All portions of wood, also, that are decayed or badly stained, must be removed. A difference of opinion exists as to the proper method of handling knots. In some mills it is the practice to remove all knots by boring, but this seems to us objectionable, since it not only involves considerable labor, but is liable to cause fine dirt in the pulp by splitting up portions of the knot into small fragments which will get through the screens. As the sound knots are hardly softened at all by the liquor, the preferable plan, in our opinion, is to make no attempt to remove them until after the wood has been brought to pulp. They are thus left in pieces of such large size that they are readily taken out upon the screen, and all danger of fine dirt from this cause is avoided. Rotten knots break up in the cooking and subsequent operations, and should be cut out. Where labor is sufficiently cheap to admit of its being done, it is well to have the wood coming from the chipper thrown upon an endless belt, by the sides of which boys or girls may be stationed to pick out all knots and unsound chips. This is the universal practice in sulphite mills abroad. Some of these foreign mills go to the further extents of sorting their chips to size. We have failed to discover that this offers any advantages to compensate for the increased cost.

In many mills the wood, after leaving the chipper, is passed between crushing rolls, one running at twice the speed of the other, and both covered with coarse, pyramidal teeth. A toothed scraper under the bottom roll acts as a doctor. The advantage of crushing is that it permits more rapid absorption of the liquor, so that cooks can be made more quickly and with less danger of leaving any of the chips with a hard, red, central portion. The knots, however, are likely to be broken up, and the quantity of wood which can be cooked at one time is somewhat diminished.

All the chips cooked at one time should be of a single kind of wood, and as nearly as possible in the same condition as regards age and moisture. The treatment necessarily varies for different woods, and even for the same wood when dry or green. Where it can be done, it is advantageous to keep the wood in water for some time before chipping, as it is thus all brought to the same state of moisture. Green wood is more easily reduced by the sulphite process than wood which has been seasoned.

Although chips are used in some instances where mills are working the Mitscherlich process, the more general practice is to cut the log into discs 1¼ inches thick by gang-saws. It is claimed that in this way, where the slow method of packing the digester by hand is followed, more wood can be handled at a boiling, and better circulation secured, than where chips are used.

The use of chips, however, involves less time and labor and the yield per cord is greater, as at least 10 per cent of the wood must be lost as sawdust when discs are used. Where the chips are properly handled, the fibre, for all practical purposes, should not have its length or strength impaired.

Spruce is the wood most commonly used in this country for making sulphite pulp, but much of the foreign fibre is made from the Swedish fir. Any of the coniferous woods which are not too resinous to yield easily to treatment may be used in place of spruce; but as each wood has its own peculiarities which call for differences in treatment, it is best cooked separately and unmixed with other woods.

Liquor-Making. — The preparation of the solution used in the sulphite process depends upon, or is influenced by, several general facts which it is well to recall here. When sulphur is heated in the air, it first melts to an amber-colored liquid at 115° C.; as the heating is continued, the melted sulphur gradually darkens in color and becomes very thick and tenacious; at a still higher temperature it partially regains its fluidity; and at about 300° C. begins to vaporize. If this dark, reddish brown vapor is allowed to cool, the sulphur is deposited either in the powdery form as flowers of sulphur, or as a liquid, according to conditions of temperature. Sulphur burns in the air with a blue flame tipped with white, forming sulphurous acid gas, SO_2. This gas is very soluble in water, one volume of water at zero dissolving seventy-nine volumes of the gas. The facility with which the gas is absorbed varies greatly with the temperature and pressure, diminishing rapidly as the temperature rises, while at a given temperature the amount absorbed varies directly as the pressure. The moist gas has a very strong affinity for oxygen, with which, in the presence of water, it combines to form sulphuric acid, H_2SO_4. Since only about one-fifth of the volume of air is oxygen, and since for every volume of oxygen consumed in the first instance by the burning sulphur there is formed only an equal volume of sulphurous acid, the strongest gas which can possibly be made in practice can only contain about 20 per cent SO_2. As a matter of fact, the content of SO_2 rarely reaches 10 per cent. The gas going into the absorption apparatus is therefore so largely diluted with the waste nitrogen from the air and the unconsumed oxygen, that the absorption proceeds at a much slower rate than would be the case could the pure gas be obtained, and there is even a considerable tendency for the waste gases to sweep the free sulphurous acid out of a strong liquor through or over which they pass.

The different forms of apparatus in which the liquor is prepared may be divided for our present purpose into two classes: those in which the gas is brought in contact with water containing the base in solution or suspension, and those in which the gas and water come in contact with the carbonate of the base, which, instead of being minutely subdivided, is present in lumps of considerable size. In the former case the gas is first dissolved by the water forming the true sulphurous acid, H_2SO_3. This acid immediately reacts with the base to form the monosulphite. If the base is soda, the sulphite remains in solution, and the same is true to a considerable extent of sulphite of magnesia. Sulphite of lime, however, is very insoluble, one part of the salt requiring for its solution 800 parts of water, so that when milk of lime is used, the sulphite is precipitated in the crystalline form as fast as it is made. The formation of monosulphite goes on until all the lime is precipitated. As the absorption of gas continues, the monosulphite gradually takes up an additional equivalent of the acid, forming the bisulphite, which is readily soluble. Unless the quantity of base is excessive, nearly the whole of the lime is thus brought into solution. Owing to the great tendency of sulphurous acid to oxidize with the formation of sulphuric acid, and the difficulty of properly regulating the supply of air, there is always formed, in practice, with the bisulphite, more or less sulphate which, being insoluble, remains in the liquor as a white precipitate, which may be readily distinguished from the still more insoluble monosulphite by the yellow color and more granular appearance of the latter. In the second type of absorption apparatus the gas is absorbed by the water as before, and the solution thus formed reacts upon the carbonate which is present in the form of limestone or dolomite, forming sulphite of lime and setting free carbonic acid, as shown in the reaction —

$$H_2SO_3 + CaCO_3 = CaSO_3 + H_2O + CO_2.$$

After a time the surface of the limestone becomes more or less crusted with the sulphite, and as more gas is absorbed this crust is brought into solution as bisulphite. There is, however, in such forms of apparatus a tendency for both these reactions to proceed simultaneously when there is a free supply of gas; that is, fresh portions of limestone are being changed to monosulphite, while at the same time portions of monosulphite are being dissolved by the acid solution. The formation of sulphate of lime proceeds here as in the former case, but considerable portions of it adhere to the limestone as a crust.

The absorption of gas takes place only at the surfaces of contact between gas and liquor, so that, other things being equal, the most efficient apparatus is the one in which the liquid presents the greatest amount of surface to the action of the gas.

Sulphur Burning. — Sulphur is found in the market in three grades, known as firsts, seconds, and thirds, the only differences in the three grades being those of color and in the amount of dirt and ash present. In seconds the ash rarely exceeds $\frac{1}{2}$ per cent. A form of sulphur known as Chance recovered sulphur has been lately put upon the market, and is for all practical purposes chemically pure. The following are analyses made in our laboratory of commercial sulphur: —

	Seconds			Chance recovered sulphur
Moisture	0.01	0.20	0.06	—
Foreign matter, insoluble in carbon disulphide	0.06	0.76	—	0.016
Sulphur	99.93	99.04	99.82	99.984
Ash	—	0.37	0.12	0.012

Thirds usually contain about 1 per cent of foreign matter, but the proportion runs in rare cases as high as 3 per cent.

Seconds and thirds are most commonly used in making sulphite liquors; but in many Eastern mills recovered sulphur is now being used, on account of its greater purity and the fact that because it is shipped in bags it can be handled more easily than the Sicilian sulphur, which comes in bulk. In the West considerable Utah sulphur is now being used.

The dimensions and construction of sulphur furnaces show great variations in different mills. The best styles conform to the following requirements: They should be as nearly air tight as it is possible to make them, except at those points where provision is made for admitting and regulating the supply of air; the pan should be perfectly level, and of such size that not more than 2½ lbs. of sulphur need be burned per square foot of pan surface per hour; the pan should be so supported by foundations as to leave an air-space under its entire length, in order to keep it as cool as possible; and the entire furnace should be so constructed as to avoid as far as may be the danger of overheating.

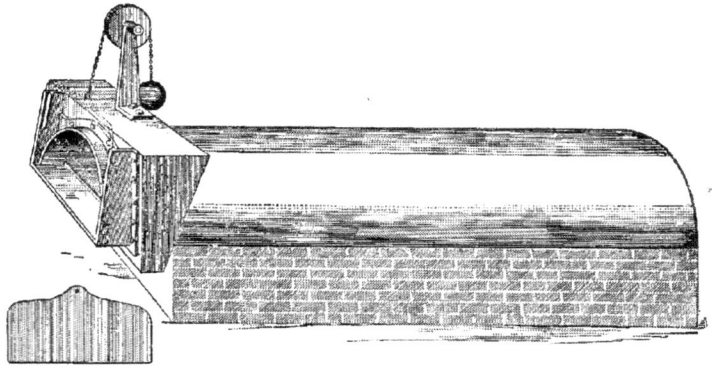

FIG. 19. — RETORT SULPHUR FURNACE.

The retort style of furnace shown in Fig. 19 is in very common use; and where pains are taken to have the door fit closely, this furnace is perhaps as satisfactory as any for plants of moderate size. The body of the furnace is in one piece, and is made of cast iron, an inch, or better, an inch and a half in thickness. It is about 8 feet 6 inches long, and 2 feet 6 inches wide, on the outside; the inside perpendicular being 18 inches. The 8-inch pipe by which the gases leave the furnace is either bolted to the back of the furnace, as high as possible above the pan, or else to the top of the arch near that end. A second casting with guides and bearings for the door is bolted to the perpendicular face which forms the open end of the retort. The retorts are supported by brick foundations which, when properly built, contain an air-space extending along the bottom or pan of the furnace. The retorts are sometimes surrounded by a water-jacket; and in other cases a shower of water is delivered from a sprinkler pipe upon the top of the furnace.

Similar furnaces, but with doors which can be closed air-tight, are used for burning sulphur under pressure, as shown in Fig. 33.

Ekman introduced a furnace built of $\frac{1}{4}$-inch boiler iron, riveted together, and caulked air-tight. The dimensions of the pan are about 2 feet 3 inches by 7 feet, and the height of the furnace about 5 feet. The only novelty in the furnace is found in the layer

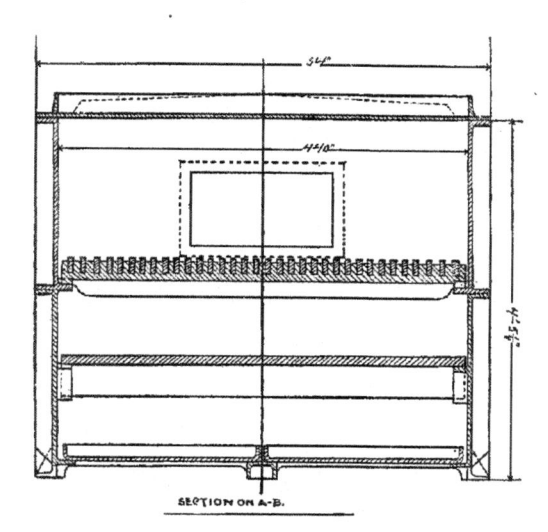

FIG. 20. — MODIFIED EKMAN FURNACE — SECTION.

of broken fire-brick resting on inclined grate-bars. An inclined cast-iron plate extends from the front of the furnace below the grate and just above the door, at a distance about two-thirds of the length of the furnace. The object of the brick, which are loosely arranged in a layer about 9 inches deep, is to cause a more perfect mingling of the air and any sulphur vapor present, thus insuring more perfect combustion and less subliming. The thin iron walls of the furnace radiate heat rapidly, so that it is kept quite cool. Ekman claims to reduce the amount of SO_3 formed about one-half by the use of the fire-brick; but where a furnace is properly run, there should be no vapor of sulphur passing off, and if an excess of air is admitted, much of the SO_3 is formed beyond the furnace in the absorption apparatus.

Figs. 20 and 21 show an improved style of Ekman furnace built of cast-iron in sections which are bolted together. The joints at the flanges are made air-tight by some form of asbestos packing. The layer of brick rests upon wrought-iron grate-bars, which in this furnace are not inclined. The door swings inward, and is so balanced that it closes when left open. The amount of air admitted is regulated by screwing in the handle which passes through the ball counterpoise on the door, so that the end of the handle

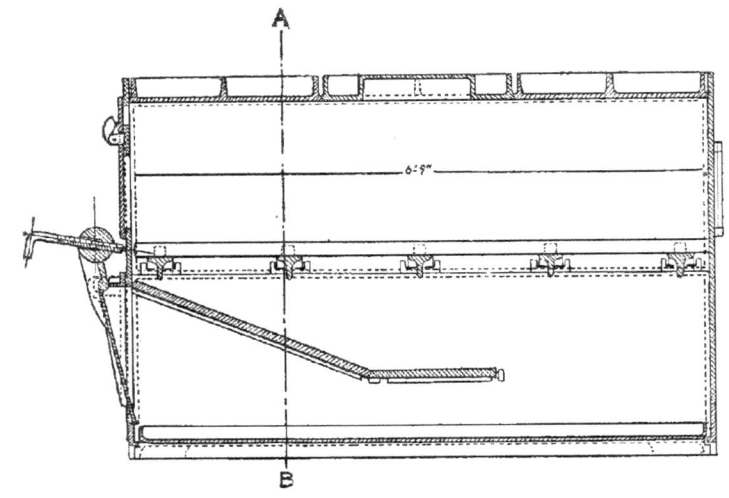

FIG. 21. — MODIFIED EKMAN FURNACE — LONGITUDINAL SECTION.

strikes the furnace and holds the door before the latter has swung completely to. Any desired open space may thus be left below the door. This furnace has two wrought-iron pans.

Furnaces of about the dimensions given in Figs. 20 and 21 are sometimes built with brick walls lined with fire-brick. The back is sometimes in these cases made of an iron plate or casting, and the top and front are nearly always so constructed. Some Mitscherlich mills use a furnace about 2 feet 6 inches wide, 8 feet long, and 7 feet high. The furnace is charged through an 8-inch iron pipe, passing at an angle through the wall, and which is ordinarily kept closed by a flange or cap.

In starting up a sulphur furnace of the usual type sufficient sulphur is thrown in to form, when melted, a layer over the bottom about one inch in depth. A red-hot bolt thrown into the furnace starts the combustion. With retort furnaces, unless working under pressure, the air supply is regulated by the extent to which the door is closed. The open space under the door should never be more than one-quarter of an inch high, and with most of these furnaces sufficient air can generally work its way in through the cracks around the door. In the Mitscherlich and some other furnaces the doors in front are made air tight and the air supply is admitted through a set of air-holes the size of which is regulated by a sliding damper. Some such plan as this is to be recommended in order to properly control the air supply.

The most common way of keeping up the supply of sulphur is for the workman to raise the furnace door and throw in a few shovelfuls as needed. The door is thus opened to its fullest extent at frequent intervals, and each time it is raised there is a great rush of air into the furnace and through the apparatus. In consequence of this the gas is much diluted, even and regular absorption is well-nigh impossible, and an excessive and unnecessary amount of SO_3 is formed. It is much better to give the furnace a considerable supply of sulphur at a time and to make the intervals of charging as few as possible. In working the retorts under pressure they are charged at intervals of about four hours with 200 lbs of sulphur. Kellner, in order to avoid undue excess of air, puts the sulphur in a hopper on top of the furnace, the hopper then being closed at the top and the charge fed in. Mitscherlich feeds through the top or side of the furnace in something the same way. Any hoppers or pipes in this position must be so arranged as to be kept cool, and must have delivery pipes of good diameter, as otherwise there is danger that the sulphur will become so heated as to pass into the thick and tenacious condition. Where a number of furnaces deliver into one gas main they should be charged in regular order, so that the gas may be kept of nearly constant composition

The whole secret of burning sulphur for the preparation of sulphite liquors lies in the proper regulation of the supply of air. In order to convert one pound of sulphur into sulphurous acid there is required just one pound of oxygen, or the amount of this gas contained in 53.81 cubic feet of air. If much more is admitted, and especially if the air is at all moist, there is formed SO_3 and sulphuric acid, which corrodes the pipes and causes a considerable loss of both lime and sulphur. The composition of the liquor under these circumstances is subject to constant variation. When dolomite is used as a base the proportion between the lime and magnesia in the liquor is made to vary as more or less lime is thrown down as sulphate, and where magnesia or soda is used the sulphate causes even more trouble by remaining in solution and giving to the liquor a fictitious strength. Any considerable excess of air is liable also to cause over-heating of the furnace and consequent sublimation of the sulphur. More sulphur is vaporized than can be burned and the unconsumed vapor passes onward with the gas until it strikes the colder portions of the pipes or cooler, where it condenses, clogging the pipes and causing the formation of polythionic acids, as pointed out below.

Sublimation similarly occurs if for any reason the air supply is unduly curtailed after the furnace has become warmed up, since under these circumstances there is not enough air to combine with all the vapor.

Colefax and others have shown that sulphurous acid acts on sulphur at the ordinary temperature even in the dark to form thiosulphuric and polythionic acids. This action takes place still more rapidly at temperatures as high as 80° or 90° C. These acids are very unstable and in most cases decompose on being heated into sulphur, SO_2 and SO_3. The thiosulphates decompose in the presence of stronger acids into sulphur and SO_2. Where these acids are formed, as is the case when sublimation and over-heating occur, a liquor is produced from which, during the boiling operation, sulphur separates out and is precipitated on the pulp. Owing to the insolubility of sulphur it is almost impossible to remove it in this event, and its presence makes trouble when the pulp is used: the sulphur itself rotting the wire cloth and the sulphuric acid formed by oxidation rotting the canvas felts. According to Mitscherlich and others the presence of these higher acids of sulphur will even completely spoil an entire cook.

The conditions under which a burner is working may generally be inferred with sufficient accuracy from the appearance and character of the flame. When the sulphur is burning properly the flame is a lazy blue one, sometimes tipped with white. The occurrence of brown fumes, which are the unconsumed sulphur vapor, indicates that the furnace is too hot, probably because of too much air, and that sublimation is likely to occur.

The furnace must be cleaned as often as any considerable quantity of slag and ash accumulates in the pan, and the cleaning must be done while the furnace is still hot, since the ash will otherwise be so bound together by the sulphur remaining in it that it can hardly be removed at all.

Although sulphur-burning is an apparently simple operation, it requires a considerable degree of skill and careful attention on the part of the workman. Without these, much more sulphur than is needed will be burned, and the excess is more than likely to cause not only loss but trouble all through the process. The workman should aim to keep the gas as strong as possible and to avoid irregularity in its composition. He can only do this by charging the furnace in a regular and methodical way and by admitting the smallest possible amount of air required to burn the sulphur.

Copper or iron pyrites are burned in place of sulphur in many foreign mills, and they have lately been adopted in one or two mills here. Pyrites burners are considerably more difficult to handle than sulphur furnaces, and they can only be worked to advantage where a number of burners are grouped together so that a gas of even composition may be secured. There is considerable liability that the burners may become over-heated locally, and where such over-heating occurs slags form which are difficult to remove and which clog the draft. The most serious objection to the use of pyrites is due to the fine dust which is carried along by the burner gas, and which, unless entirely removed, causes dirt in the liquor and in the pulp. It is usually held back by passing the gas in a very slow stream through long dust flues of large area.

FIG. 22. — FREIBERG PYRITES BURNER.

The ordinary sorts of pyrites are, before being burned, broken either by hand or some form of crusher into pieces of small size, the harder sorts being reduced to the size of walnuts, while the softer kinds may be left in larger lumps. The lumps are burned on grate bars in brick kilns or furnaces of the general construction shown in Fig. 22, and fitted with doors for charging, regulating the supply of air and removing the cinders. Fig. 22 represents two Freiberg burners, one being shown in front elevation and the other in sectional elevation. This furnace is especially adapted for easily burning ores. The burner is charged through the hole in the top and the ore rests upon the triangular grate bars. The round bars just above the grate may be worked back and forth from the front of the furnace and serve both to break up the ore and to support it while drawing cinders. S is the entrance to the gas flue built into the brickwork back of the furnace. A small percentage

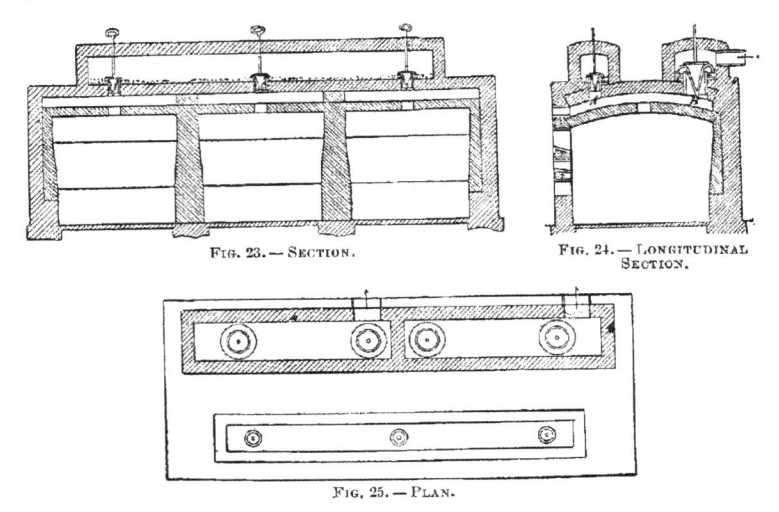

FIG. 23.—SECTION.   FIG. 24.—LONGITUDINAL SECTION.

FIG. 25.—PLAN.

FIGS. 23, 24, 25.—THE MITSCHERLICH PYRITES BURNER.

of copper is usually present in the cinder from iron pyrites and its extraction partially repays the cost of working the pyrites.

The Mitscherlich pyrites burners are shown in sections in Figs. 23 and 24, and in plan in Fig. 25. They are about 1.5 metres square in the clear and are lined with Chamotte brick. The top is a flat arch with a central opening for the escape of the gas into the space between this inner and the upper arch. The upper arch has two openings. Two, three, or more burners, according to the size of the works, are built side by side, or back to back. Two gas flues are built over the burners and the openings through the upper arch make into these flues. Any furnace may be cut out by closing these openings by means of sand lutes, as shown in the drawings. The space between the two arches prevents the burners from becoming too cool.

The grate, which is not shown, is about 0.5 metre from the floor, and is composed of square bars which may be turned by a key from the front in order to shake down cinders. The doors, which are in front, are luted with clay or else smeared all over with this material.

For carrying the gas away from the sulphur furnace iron pipes may be used as far as the cooler, as the hot, dry gas has little effect on this metal. The cooler, and all pipes beyond, should be of lead. It is necessary that the pipes should be free from all curves in which the sublimed sulphur might lodge beyond easy reach, and at all bends or angles crosses should be used to give easy access to the interior of the pipes. The flues from pyrites burners, for a considerable distance at least, are usually built of bricks which have been soaked in coal-tar and which are laid in a mixture of tar and sand. As already pointed out, it is absolutely necessary to lead the gas from pyrites burners through a dust chamber in order to avoid dirt beyond. This chamber, which is usually built high enough to admit a man, is divided by numerous partial partitions so that it forms a long flue through which the gas slowly passes backwards and forwards till it reaches the exit pipe. Similar chambers of smaller size and built of unplaned plank may be used to advantage where the gas is obtained from sulphur. The rough surface of the wood catches the floating sulphur and also removes most of the SO_3. The chamber should be placed between the furnace and the cooler.

The Ritter-Kellner filtering-tower, which is shown in section and plan in Figs. 26 and 27, is also well adapted to hold back sulphuric acid and sublimed sulphur. The tower is built of brick laid in coal tar and sand, and is divided into three compartments, which are covered by a slab of slate. The central shaft has a false bottom, and is nearly filled with limestone, with which the sulphuric acid combines to form sulphate of lime. The tower is washed out from time to time by a copious stream of water.

The means of securing draft through the furnaces and the rest of the apparatus varies with the form of absorption apparatus which is employed. The method employed by Mitscherlich will be discussed when we come to the consideration of the tower. When the gas has to be forced through a volume of liquid some form of direct-acting pump is necessary, and the draft is maintained, either as in the case of the Partington apparatus, by sucking the waste gases from the tanks, or, as in McDougall's system, by forcing air into the furnace. Considerably more power is required in the last case. In other forms of apparatus, like that of Catlin or the later

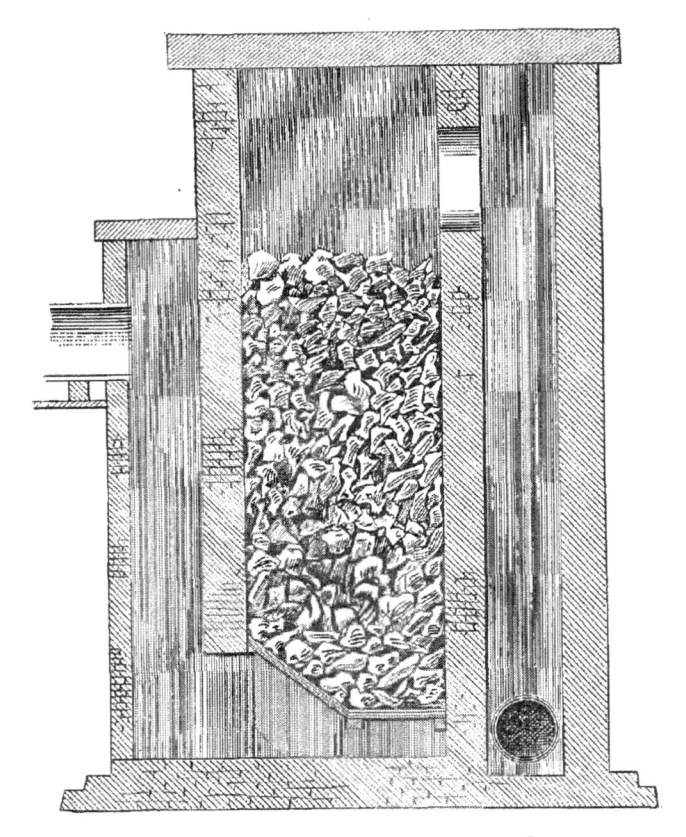

FIG. 26. — THE KELLNER FILTERING-TOWER — SECTION.

form patented by McDougall, an ordinary fan blower may be used, since in these cases the passage of the gas is not impeded. Wherever their use is thus indicated such blowers are to be preferred, as for the same volume of air moved the cost of the blower is much less, while it has fewer working parts, and can be run and maintained more cheaply. The shell should be lined with 6-lb. lead, fastened to the iron by copper rivets, and all rivet heads should be carefully burned over with lead. The wheel and all other internal parts should be of suitable acid-resisting bronze.

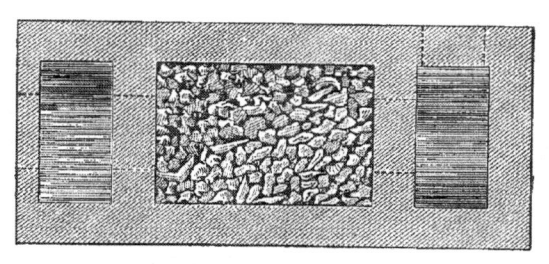

FIG. 27. — THE KELLNER FILTERING-TOWER — PLAN.

The blower is best placed before the coolers, where it takes the hot gas coming from the furnaces.

It has been already pointed out that the rate of absorption and the quantity of the gas dissolved by water are mainly dependent upon the temperature, the quantity of gas absorbed decreasing rapidly as the temperature rises, as shown below: —

Temp.	1 vol. of water dissolves SO_2.	1 vol. of the solution contains SO_2.
0° C.	79.789 vols.	68.861 vols.
20° "	39.374 "	36.206 "
40° "	18.766 "	17.013 "

It is therefore necessary, in order to obtain the best results in liquor-making, that cold water should be used, and that the temperature of the gas should not be above 10° to 15° C. Where the gas is carried in a slow stream through a considerable length of cast-iron pipe exposed to the air, it will generally be sufficiently cool, except on the warm days of summer. In some foreign mills the cooling surface of the pipe is increased very largely by numerous flanges cast on the pipe. It is desirable in most systems to have the liquor plant as compact as possible, and for this reason the cooler pipes are often arranged over the furnace, as in Fig. 33, pages 211, 212. The pipes are then either cooled by water-jackets or by a stream of water trickling over them.

Fig. 28 shows in section a very efficient and compact form of cooler, which is due to Wheelwright. It consists of a tight wooden box about 12 feet long, 3 feet wide, and 3 feet high. Twelve 4-inch lead pipes are arranged in the box as shown, and pass through the ends, where they are flanged over and burned to the half-inch lead with which the ends of the box are covered on the

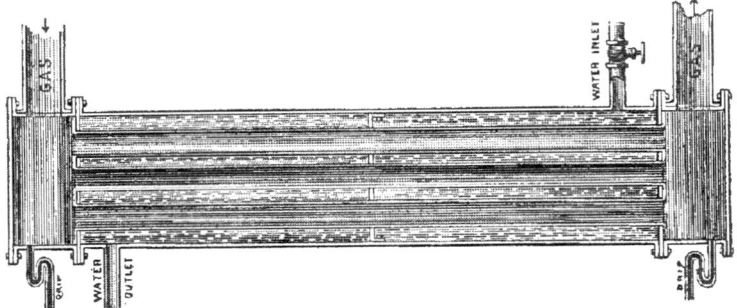

FIG. 28. — THE WHEELWRIGHT COOLER.

outside. A gas chamber, built of half-inch lead and fitted with a trap for condensed sulphuric acid and with a pipe for gas, is bolted to each end of the cooler. The box is kept filled with cold water, which constantly flows in through the supply pipe. This apparatus presents a large cooling surface, and the current of gas moving through the pipes is very slow. It is easily cleaned, and condenses and holds back most of the sulphuric acid.

Still another cooler is shown on page 211 in connection with the Ritter-Kellner liquor apparatus. This is a more expensive form than the one just shown, and on account of the cross tubes in the cooler pipes the latter cannot be readily cleaned. Difficulty from this cause is avoided by the inventors by first passing the gas through a filtering-tower, which keeps back the sublimed sulphur.

Absorption Apparatus. — As already stated in an earlier paragraph, the different forms of apparatus in which the bisulphite solution is prepared may be conveniently considered with reference to two general types, — first, those in which the gas is brought in contact with water holding the base in suspension or solution, and second, those in which the gas and water react upon the carbonate of the base, which is present in lumps of considerable size. To the first class belong the apparatus of Partington, McDougall, Catlin, and others, while in the second class are found the towers of Mitscherlich, Francke, and Kellner, and the modified towers or tank system of the last-named chemist. The later form of Ekman tower combines in a measure the features common to both classes.

The tower, as the oldest and in some respects the simplest form of absorption apparatus, will be considered first. It consists essentially of a high wooden shaft, which may be of various dimensions and which is usually of circular section. To prevent leakage the joints are often stuffed with oakum and painted with tar. Several of these towers are commonly grouped together and surrounded and supported by a scaffolding braced by guy ropes. Near the bottom of each tower is a heavy grating or false bottom. In the high Mitscherlich towers the strain upon the grating is relieved by having the main weight of the stone sustained by two heavy timbers, which pass through the walls of the tower about two feet above the false bottom and which are supported from the outside.

The towers are nearly filled with lumps of limestone or dolomite. In Germany a special form of porous limestone is preferred, but most of the similar material found in this country contains rather too much iron to be well suited to this purpose, and on that account the ordinary dense limestones are commonly made use of here. Dolomite is really the best stone for use in the tower, especially if a dolomite is selected which pits as it is eaten away by the acid.

In all forms of towers the gas from the furnaces enters below the grating and meets, in its ascent, the descending water, which is spread over large surfaces of the stone in a thin film so that the gas is rapidly absorbed. The water is delivered at the top through a large sprinkler arranged to secure even and regular distribution of the water. Many different styles of sprinkler are in use, some mills using the crude rose made of lead, while others have distributing systems of pipe similar to those employed on the Glover and Gay-Lussac towers in the manufacture of sulphuric acid. In other cases the water is delivered suddenly in some quantity at intervals of a minute or two, either by a tilting-tank, as in Fig. 29, or by apparatus embodying the principle of the Tantalus cup, Fig. 30, which empties suddenly as soon as the siphon is primed. The sudden rush and splashing of the water is thought to secure better results

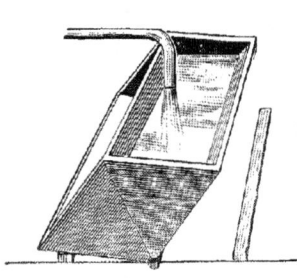

Fig. 29.

in keeping the tower clear. The simplest arrangement of all consists merely of a spreading-stone placed under the pipe from which water is delivered.

Fig. 31 shows in a diagrammatic way one form of the Mitscherlich tower and accompanying draft tubes. The tower is built of wood and varies in height from 100 to 135 feet, and in diameter from 3 to 5 feet. The dimensions of the one from which our figure is taken were: Height, 32 metres over all; height of absorption space, 26 metres; length on each side of tower, 1.2 metres. Several of such towers are usually built together, the whole being surrounded by a scaffolding by which access is gained to the top. As most commonly constructed, the towers have only a single false bottom. The construction shown in Fig. 31, in which the vertical shaft is divided into numerous compartments by a number of false bottoms, is on many accounts preferable; but such towers hold less stone and are more difficult to fill and clean. In either event the tower is filled with limestone either from the top or through the openings marked k. At the top of the tower is a tank holding a considerable supply of water and connected with a sprinkler just below it. The valve controlling the supply of water to the sprinkler is so arranged that it can be worked from the scaffolding around the top of the tower or from the ground. There is also a pipe from the bottom of the tank by which, when desired, the whole body of water can be quickly discharged, in order that the sudden rush of so large a volume of water down through the tower may carry along with it the dirt and small stones which gradually collect there and at the same time wash out much of the sulphate that has accumulated. The leg of the draft pipe nearest the tower is often made of glazed earthenware pipe, while the leg away from the tower is built up of sections of iron pipe. Contrary to the general opinion, these towers do not act like chimneys, for the escaping gases are often not only heavier but colder than the outside air. The proper explanation of the means by which the draft is maintained is this: the specific gravity of sulphurous acid compared to air is 2.25, while that of carbonic acid is 1.53. The gases coming from the burners consist of sulphurous acid mixed with more or less oxygen and sulphuric anhydride and with a large vol-

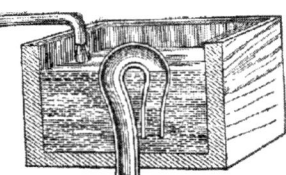

FIG. 30.

ume of nitrogen, and by the time they reach tube *B* they are all well cooled. As result of the reactions which take place within the tower, the sulphurous acid and sulphuric anhydride are absorbed, the former being replaced by about half its volume of carbonic

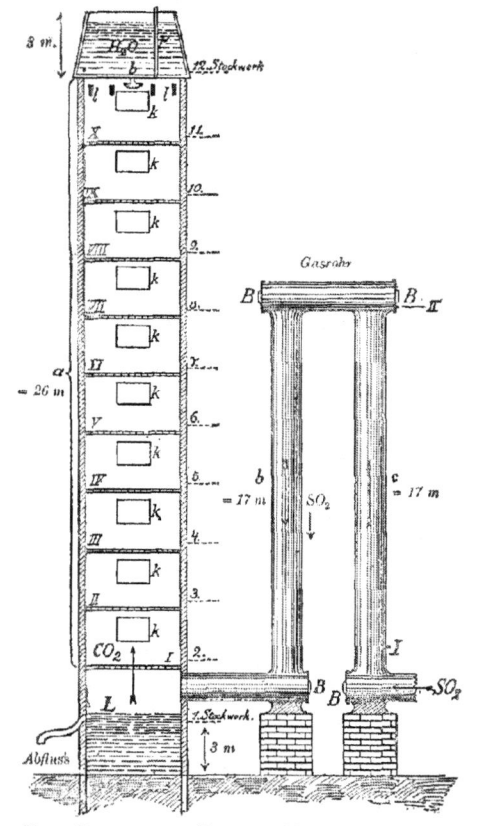

FIG. 31.— DIAGRAM OF DIVIDED MITSCHERLICH TOWER.

EXPLANATION OF TERMS.— *Gasrohr*, Gas-pipe; *Stockwerk*, Story; *Abfluss*, Outlet. Dimensions are in metres.

acid, and the latter by its equivalent of that gas. In spite therefore of the greater height of the tower, the column of gas within it weighs less than the shorter column of gas in tube *B*, so that there is a constant upward flow and escape of gas from the top of the tower. That the gases in the tower are under this slight pressure may be shown by boring into the tower at any point when the draft, instead of being inward, as is the case with the chimney, is from within outward. It is necessary, however, in order to secure this draft, that the tube B should have a length of at least 153 inches for every 225 inches in the height of the tower, and by increasing the length of B over that called for by this proportion the force of the draft may be augmented to any necessary extent. The fall of the heavy column of comparatively cold gas in B draws over continually a fresh supply of hot, and therefore lighter, gas from the burners.

A number of difficulties is likely to arise in working towers. It is hard to secure always an even distribution of the water as it falls through the tower, and similarly to properly spread the gas as it passes upward. Gutters are very likely to form through cutting away of the stone at one point more than another, and any such tendency increases rapidly after the first appearance of the hole. The stone is usually thrown into the tower from the top, but in the process of working the lower lumps of stone are continually eaten away, and being pressed upon by the stone above may pack together and clog the tower as the upper stone falls down. If the stone becomes wedged at any point in the tower, arches are likely to form, and, as the stone below is eaten away, an open space of considerable size may result. Finally the arch breaks, and the stone above, settling suddenly, may so pack together as to impede the draft. Such arches may usually be broken before they cause serious trouble by blows from a heavy mallet against the outside of the tower. Their existence is made evident by the hollow sound given out when suspected portions of the tower are similarly struck, but this involves so much labor as to be hardly practicable. The last traces of gas are almost never absorbed in the tower, and the unabsorbed portion is frequently so considerable as to cause a high percentage of loss. Crusts of monosulphite and sulphate of lime not unfrequently become so extensive as to impede or almost stop entirely the flow of gas. Crusts of monosulphite are especially likely to form if the gas is weak or if the supply of water is curtailed. For these reasons it is necessary to inspect the condition of the stone at frequent intervals, and to either loosen it up by a crowbar, or to remove it altogether and refill the tower with fresh stone. The old stone is piled up in the air and allowed to weather, in order to cause the incrustation to loosen and flake off. These difficulties may be avoided in large part by making the tower somewhat conical in shape, so that the stone in working down comes into a wider and wider space.

The strength and quality of the liquor made in towers depend upon the amount and strength of the gas passing into the tower, the quantity and temperature of water with which the tower is supplied, and the amount and condition of the limestone. The composition of the gas and liquor at different heights in the tower has been studied by Harpf, to whom we are indebted for the following table. The tower from which the samples were taken was divided, as shown in Fig. 31, into twelve sections by false bottoms, ten of the sections containing limestone. The percentage by volume of sulphurous acid in the gas at the different stones on two different days is shown below:—

| | Percentage of SO_2 by volume || Remarks |
	On Oct. 17, 1888	On Oct. 19, 1888	
Draft tube at I	about 5.54	8.92	
First story	—	—	
Second story	4.62	7.52	Beginning of the absorption space.
Third story	3.42	7.42	
Fourth story	2.77	6.25	
Fifth story	2.31	6.96 (?)	
Sixth story	1.95	5.83	
Seventh story	1.57	5.13	
Eighth story	0.92	3.78	
Ninth story	—	2.29	
Tenth story	—	1.29	
Eleventh story	—	1.16	Exit for gases
Twelfth story	—	—	Water reservoir

It will be noticed that there is a continual and quite regular decrease in the percentage of sulphurous acid toward the top of the tower. No tests were made at the first story, as the liquor fell through this to the outlet. The tests of the 17th were made from below upwards, and had to be discontinued at the ninth story, as it had become dark. The tests of the 19th were made in the forenoon in the reverse order, or by starting at the top and working down. The figure obtained at the fifth story is probably erroneous. At the eleventh story the gas escaped into the air, and it will be seen that there was then present 1.16 per cent. of SO_2, or about 13 per cent. of the amount originally present. This of course was lost. The gas is cooled in its ascent so that the absolute volumes change, but each volume of SO_2 absorbed sets free an equal volume of CO_2, so that the proportions of SO_2 in the total volume at the different points are directly comparable.

The composition of the gas and liquor at the different stories on another day is given in the results of the

EXPERIMENTS OF OCTOBER 23, 1888.

	Percentage SO_2 in gases (by volume)	Percentage of SO_2 in liquor (by weight)			Remarks
		Total	Free [1]	Combined [1]	
Draft tube	7 70	—	—	—	
First story	—	—	—	—	
Second story	7 28	3 056	2 608	0 448	
Third story	8 19 (?)	2 662	2 208	0 454	
Fourth story	7 90 (?)	2 848	1 984	0.864	
Fifth story	6 82	3 968	2 688	1 280	(?)
Sixth story	7 18 (?)	1 344	0 832	0 512	
Seventh story	5 59	1 488	0 784	0 704	
Eighth story	4 36	0 672	0 426	0 246	
Ninth story	2 58	0 304	0 192	0 112	
Tenth story	1 90	0 082	0 049	0 033	(?)
Eleventh story	1 27	0 520	0 520	—	Gas exit.
Twelfth story	—	—	—	—	Water reservoir

It should be noted in connection with these tables that in Germany the sulphurous acid present as sulphite of lime, $CaSO_3$ is called "combined acid," while the entire excess over that amount is spoken of as "free acid." This nomenclature has been followed in these tables, although in this country all the acid present as bisulphite of lime is called "combined acid," while the term "free acid" is limited to the amount present in excess of that needed to form bisulphite. The German "free acid" might, perhaps, better be called "available acid," since it is the only portion which is effective in the process.

An examination of the table brings out the fact that the liquor in the eleventh story consisted merely of a solution of the gas in water which forms the true sulphurous acid, H_2SO_3. In the gas

[1] See remarks in text immediately following table

analyses the figures at the third, fourth, and sixth stories do not show the expected decrease in the percentage of SO_2 by volume. This may have been due to inequalities in the gas caused by irregular work at the burners. It will also be noted that the liquor from the fifth story is stronger than any taken lower down. Harpf considers that the difference here found is a real one, due to the fact that the lower stories contained comparatively little limestone, and that there was sufficient oxidation to reduce the strength of the liquor. We have frequently observed a similar loss of strength in case of finished liquors which were exposed for a time to the further action of the gas. In the present case, however, as Harpf suggests, the discrepancy may have been due simply to guttering.

The tower upon which these experiments were made was supplied with gas from pyrites burners, and in other tables given by Harpf the proportion of SO_2 present in the burner gas by volume ranges from 2.30 to 13.30 per cent. The average figure is about 7.5 per cent.

Before taking these samples the liquor flowing from the tower stood 6° Bé. and contained —

	Per cent
Free sulphurous acid	3.232
Combined sulphurous acid	0.768
Total	4.000

while at the conclusion of the tests it stood $5\frac{1}{2}$° Bé. and contained —

	Per cent
Free sulphurous acid	2.944
Combined sulphurous acid	0.896
Total	3.840

Ekman, as already stated, at first prepared the solution of bisulphite of magnesia used in his process in small towers about 5 feet in diameter and 14 feet high. These were filled with calcined magnesia, but as this material even in large lumps rapidly softens up and becomes pasty under the action of the water, while, moreover, it is impossible to calcine the magnesite without producing a large proportion of material too fine to be used in a tower, he was compelled to abandon them and adopt a modified tower working upon quite a different principle. This tower is built of heavy sheet lead, supported by a stout framework of timber, and is about 20 feet square by 60 feet in height. It is filled above the false bottom with flints, and milk of magnesia instead of

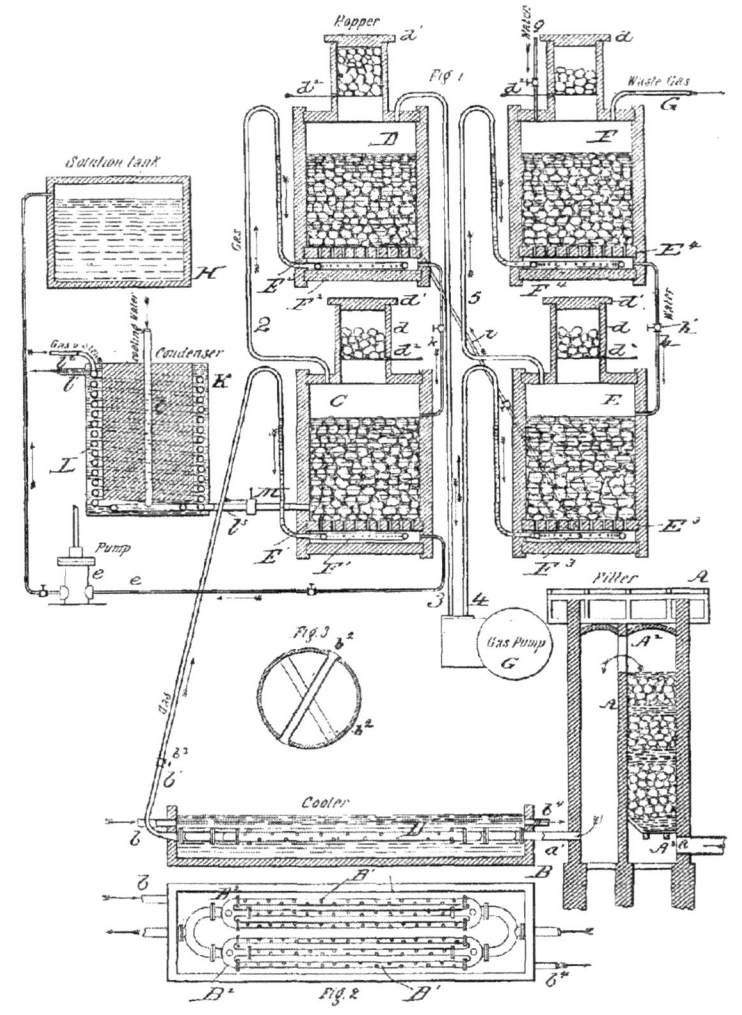

FIG. 32.—RITTER-KELLNER TANK APPARATUS.

water is delivered at the top in an intermittent stream. This is spread in thin films over the surface of the flints and rapidly absorbs the gas, with the formation first of monosulphite and then of bisulphate of magnesia. The chemical reactions in a tower of this form are essentially the same as those occurring in the common form of tank apparatus. As with other forms of towers, there is a considerable escape of sulphurous acid from the top.

Fig. 32 shows a form of liquor apparatus which has been patented and worked by Ritter and Kellner, and which combines in considerable measure the features of both towers and tanks. The portion of the apparatus in which the liquor is made consists of a set of four closed tanks, C, D, E, F, each provided with a perforated

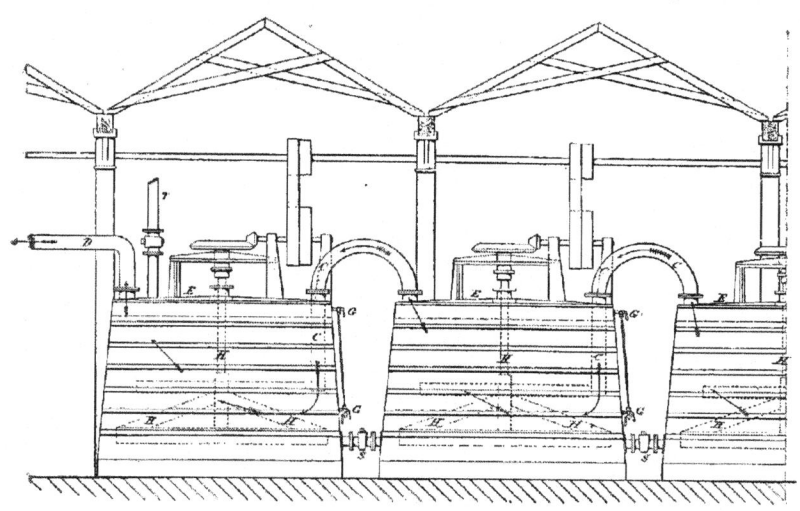

FIG. 33.—McDOUGALL LIQUOR APPARATUS.

false bottom upon which rests the limestone with which the tank is about three-quarters filled. The tanks are filled with water to a point just above the limestone. The gas from the burners after passing through the purifier A and cooler is drawn by the gas pump G up through the tanks C and D in succession, being first delivered through the perforated pipe coiled beneath the false bottom of tank C, and bubbling up through the water on its way to tank D, up through which it similarly passes. As the gas is being continually sucked away from D by the pump, both C and D are working under a partial vacuum. The gas which has been drawn from D is then forced by the pump into tank E below the false bottom, and as it passes upward into pipe 5 it is similarly forced along through F. By this time all the sulphurous acid has been absorbed and the waste gases escape from F through the pipe G. As the liquor-making progresses fresh water is from time to time run in through a pipe in the top of F, from which tank it can be transferred into E as needed, through the pipe h. On account of the pressure in tank E the liquor in E can be transferred to D whenever the valve in the pipe i is open, and from D may be run into C, which like D is under a partial vacuum.

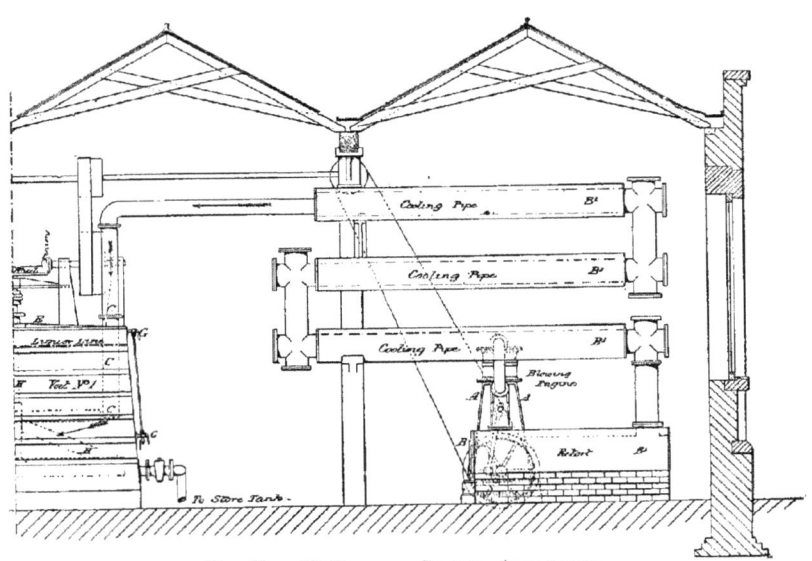

FIG. 33.—McDOUGALL LIQUOR APPARATUS.

The chemical reactions taking place in the tanks are similar to those which take place at what may be called the corresponding stories in the tower. The gas is first absorbed by the water, to form a solution of sulphurous acid, which reacts upon the limestone, setting free carbonic acid and forming in the first case sulphite of lime. The gas passing along through the tanks in series gradually loses all, or nearly all, its sulphurous acid and becomes more and more highly charged with the carbonic acid which passes away with the waste nitrogen. After a time, as the water takes up sufficient gas, the sulphite is dissolved with the formation of bisulphite, and when the liquor in tank C has reached the desired strength it is drawn off and replaced by weak liquor from the tank next in series, the others being similarly emptied and filled, until the last tank is charged again with fresh water.

This apparatus has not, so far as we know, come into use in this country. The novel form of cooler to which reference was made on page 203 should be noticed. Its construction is clearly shown in plan and section in Fig. 2. The cooling surface is greatly increased by numerous cross tubes in the cooling-pipes, as shown at b^2 in Fig. 3. These cross tubes are open at the ends so that the water passes through them. Figs 2 and 3 are sub-figures in Fig 32.

The apparatus patented by McDougall and used with some modification by Partington is shown in Fig. 33, and either in this or its modified arrangement is the type which has been most generally introduced in this country. As used by McDougall it consists of three tight tanks fitted with agitators and with pipes by which the gas coming from the furnace is discharged near the bottom of the first tank and is carried onward through the series, as indicated by the arrows. The tanks are nearly filled with milk of lime, which may be transferred from one tank to the other through the pipes S. G G on each tank are gauges with glass tubes, in which the level of the liquid in the tanks may be seen. The sulphur is burned in the retort under a pressure of 3 to 5 lbs., which is maintained by an air compressor, and the gas passes through a series of water-jacketed cooling-pipes before passing into the first tank. All the tanks are first charged with milk of lime, and as soon as the liquor in vat No 1 comes to test it is drawn off into settling-tanks; the valves between the absorbing-tanks are then opened, and fresh milk of lime is run into the last tank until the level of liquor in all three is again brought to the proper point.

Although a somewhat better absorption of gas is secured, several disadvantages present themselves when sulphur is thus burned under pressure. A great amount of steam is required for the air compressor, and there is difficulty in keeping the tanks tight. Rather more sulphur is burned, and the danger of sublimation and formation of polythionic acids from overheating is considerably increased. The proportion of SO_3 formed is also greater than where the combustion proceeds slowly under the normal or slightly diminished pressure. In a retort working under pressure about 3 lbs. of sulphur are burned per hour per square foot of pan surface

THE SULPHITE PROCESS. 215

In the Partington apparatus, Fig. 34, similar tanks are used, but they are placed one above the other and the gas is drawn through them by a pump connected to the pipe by which the waste gases leave the highest tank. As used by Partington, there is a continuous flow of liquor through the apparatus, fresh milk of lime running constantly in a carefully regulated stream into the upper

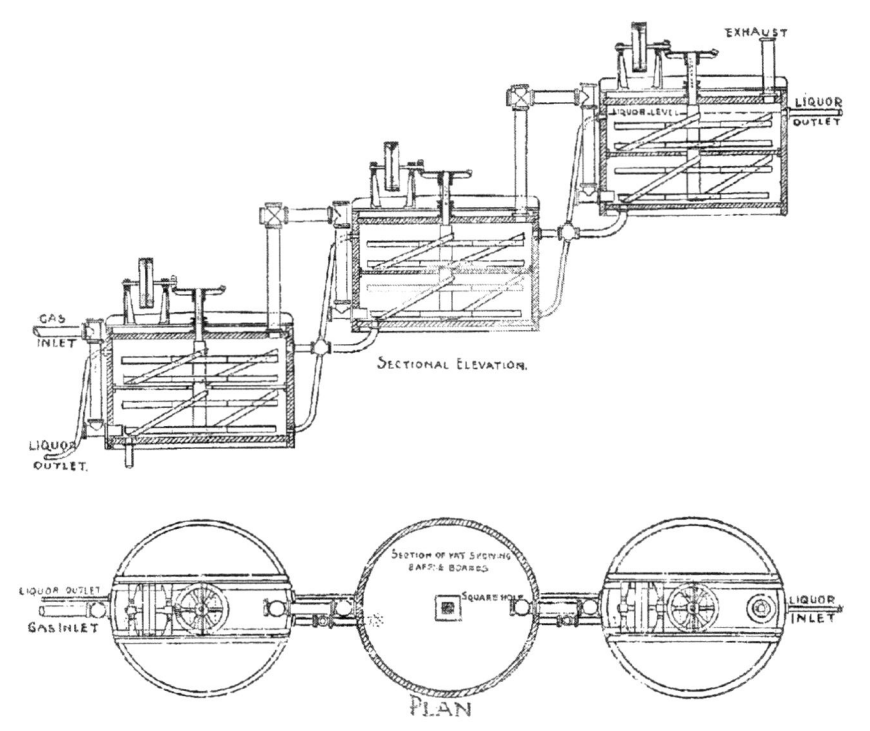

FIG. 34. — PARTINGTON LIQUOR APPARATUS.

tank, while a corresponding amount of finished liquor overflows from the lowest tank nearest the furnaces. In the United States the discharge of liquor from this apparatus has generally been intermittent, the charge in the bottom tank being brought to test and drawn off before the charges in the other tanks are transferred, and fresh milk of lime run into the upper tank.

The liquor apparatus employed by Wheelwright overcomes the

difficulties encountered when the gas is forced through a considerable column of liquid, and is so constructed that the gas has a free passage over the surface of the liquor, which is exposed to its action in thin films. It permits the use of an ordinary fan blower in place of the much more expensive gas pump, and there is consequently a considerable saving of power. The apparatus consists of three horizontal cylinders built of 3-inch Southern pine staves,

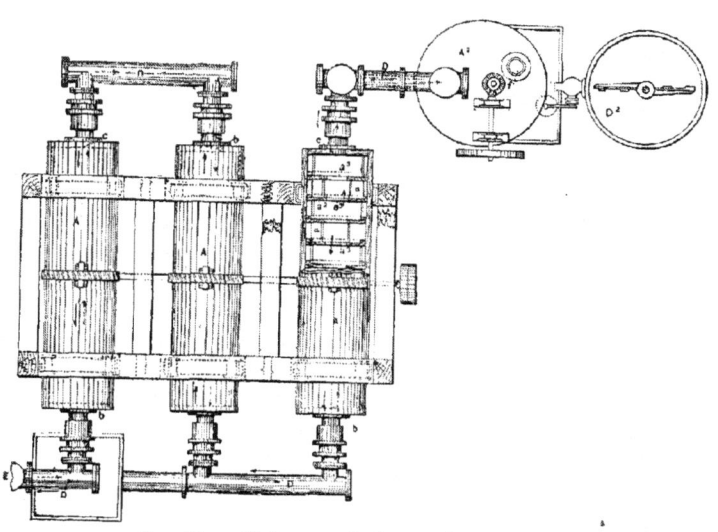

FIG. 35.—McDOUGALL'S LATER APPARATUS.

and placed one above the other. The cylinders are usually about 20 feet in length, and either 5 or 6 feet in diameter. Short and heavy bronze shafts ending inside the tanks in a head, to which the heavy wooden shaft is secured, pass through stuffing-boxes secured to each head of the tank. To the wooden shaft is attached a system of paddles, arranged like those on a stern-wheel steamer. The tanks are filled with milk of lime or magnesia up to the level of the shaft. The gas enters the bottom tank above the surface of the liquor, and passes along over it through the three tanks in succession. The shaft revolves about eighteen times a minute, and as each paddle comes out of the liquor the latter is exposed to the gas, partly as spray and partly as the thin film adhering to the paddle. The conditions for absorption are so favorable that the capacity of this apparatus is practically limited only by the amount of sulphurous acid gas passed through it. With the proper number of sulphur furnaces, 2500 gallons or more of liquor, standing 6° Bé., may be obtained per hour. The only difficulty which is likely to be experienced is due to the tendency of the monosulphite of lime to crystallize upon the paddles in the second cylinder. As patented by Catlin the apparatus is discharged intermittently.

The second and later form of liquor plant employed by McDougall is shown in plan in Fig. 35, and is in principle essentially the same as the apparatus just described. The cylinders marked A are arranged so that they may be rotated by worm and gear; A^2 is a stationary tank of the ordinary form, with an air-tight cover and agitator. Attached to the interior of the vessel A are projections, a, intercepted by transverse partitions, a^2, with central apertures, a^3, to allow of the passage of the gas and liquid through the vessel. These projections as they move carry with them a portion of the liquid and shower it upon the gas, whilst the transverse partitions prevent an immediate flow of the liquid from one end to the other. The level of the liquid is such as to leave a passage for the gas over its surface. D are connecting pipes for the passage of the gas and liquid from vessel to vessel. The milk of lime is stored in the tank D^2, and its flow is regulated by a tap. A continuous current of sulphurous acid gas enters the apparatus at E, and meets successively a shower of liquid in the rotating vessels, while much of the liquid is also exposed to its action as a film upon the partitions. The gas and liquid move in opposite directions, the course of the gas being shown by the dotted arrows and that of the liquid by the full arrows. This apparatus is evidently well adapted to secure a rapid and complete absorption of gas. We

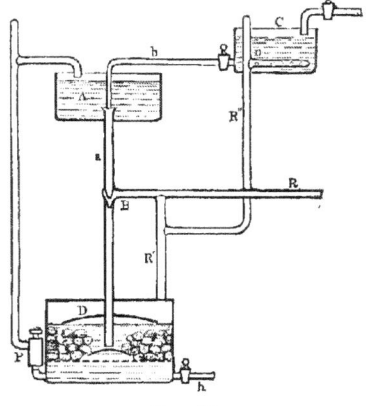

FIG. 36.

have not seen it in operation, but it must be difficult to clean, and, except in the tank next to the furnace, troublesome crusts of monosulphite must be likely to form upon the partitions and projections.

The apparatus shown in Fig. 36 is described in the French patent No. 157,754, quoted by Hoyer and Schubert. A is a water tank, D a tank partly filled with limestone, and C is another reservoir for water. The furnace gases are drawn along the pipe, R, by the action of the injector, B, which works by water from the tank, A. The descending water carries the gas down to D, where it passes up through the liquor in which the limestone is submerged, and escapes through R' and R'' into C, where it bubbles through the water therein contained before making its final exit. A portion of the waste gases is, however, drawn back by B and sent around again. The pump, P, keeps the liquor in circulation by drawing from D and discharging into A. The contents of C are, when necessary, transferred to A, after which C is again filled with fresh water.

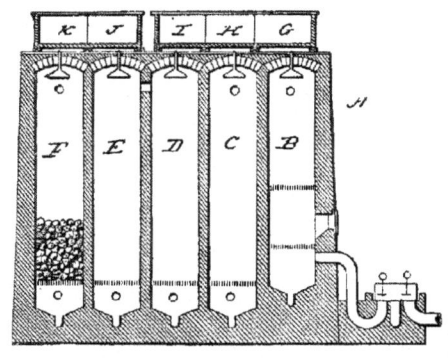

FIG. 37.— RITTER-KELLNER TOWERS.

Frank has employed a tower which is, in its general principles, similar to that of Mitscherlich. The apparatus at first brought out by Ritter and Kellner consists of five towers of moderate height, shown in sectional elevation in Figs. 37, 38, and in plan in Fig. 39. In connection with the towers there is sometimes worked a set of tight boxes filled with lumps of limestone, and shown at

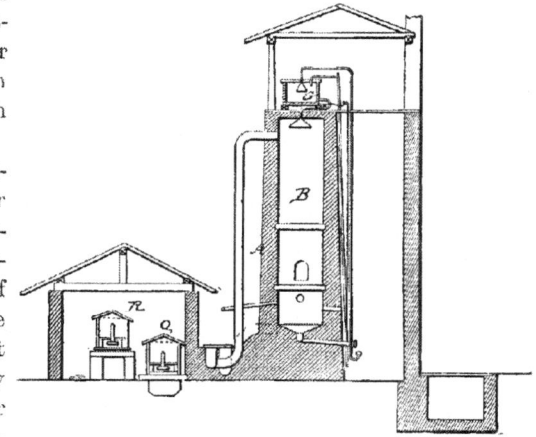

FIG. 38.— RITTER-KELLNER TOWERS.

THE SULPHITE PROCESS.

Q in Fig. 40. A second set of boxes is shown at R, and these may be filled with the carbonate of another base, as magnesite. The gas enters under the false bottom of tower B, and, after passing up through the limestone in the tower, is carried along by a pipe to the bottom of the next tower, and so on through the series. The tower, F, is supplied with fresh water, and the weak liquor flowing from this tower is pumped up and sent through E, D, and C in succession. It is at this stage charged with considerable free acid, and is sent through the boxes Q, where it takes up an additional quantity of lime. From Q it is sent through B, where it meets the strong gas,

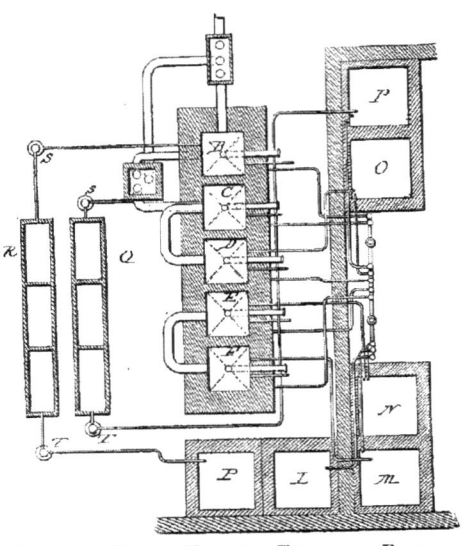

FIG. 39.—RITTER-KELLNER TOWERS.—PLAN.

and after leaving this tower it is sent through the second set of boxes, R, to take up the desired quantity of the second base. When it is desired to obtain a liquor carrying a greater proportion of gas to base than is secured when limestone is used in the towers, certain or all of them may be filled with coke or some substance which is not acted upon by the solution.

The Ritter-Kellner towers are in this country built of wood, and are commonly 5 feet in diameter and about 25 feet high. The use of the boxes, Q, and of coke in any of the towers has, we believe, been generally discontinued as introducing unnecessary complication. As at present worked, the group of five towers may be regarded as a single Mitscherlich tower, built in sections which are placed, for convenience, on the same level. The difficulties in working them are similar in kind though rather less in degree to those encountered with the Mitscherlich tower.

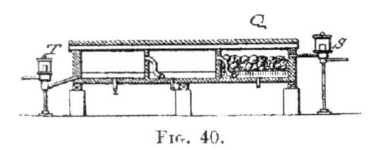

FIG. 40.

The Némethy liquor apparatus, which is shown in plan and in sectional elevation in Fig. 41, is similar in principle to the Kellner apparatus just described, but is rather simpler in detail. The four towers, B, are packed with limestone, as are also the two

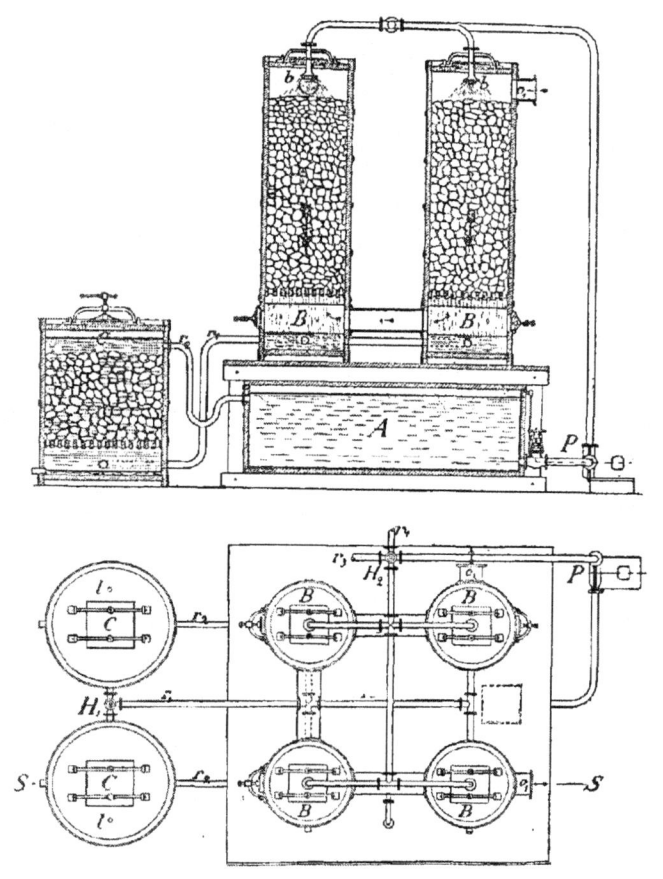

FIG. 41.— THE NÉMETHY LIQUOR APPARATUS.

tanks, C. The gas enters the system at o_1, and passes, as will be noticed, *down* the first tower. It then enters the bottom of the second tower, through which it passes upward. From there it passes down the third tower, and up the fourth, which it leaves at

o_2. Water enters through the branched pipe, H_2, and is delivered at the top of the towers through the sprinklers, b. The liquor flowing from the towers enters the bottom of the limestone tanks through the pipe r_1. Here any excess of SO_2 reacts upon the limestone, while the sulphate of lime settles out as the liquor slowly rises. The clear liquor runs off through r_2 into the storage tank, A. By means of the pump, P, the liquor, if below test, may be again drawn from A and sent through the system.

The Wendler-Spiro liquor apparatus is shown in Fig. 42, in which are the sub-figures 1 and 2. Only the absorption apparatus is here shown. The complete plant comprises also a very large cast-iron retort, which is kept submerged in water, and in which the sulphur is burned under pressure; an air-pump; a subliming box or chamber for holding back sulphuric acid and sublimed sulphur; and a cooler of efficient form.

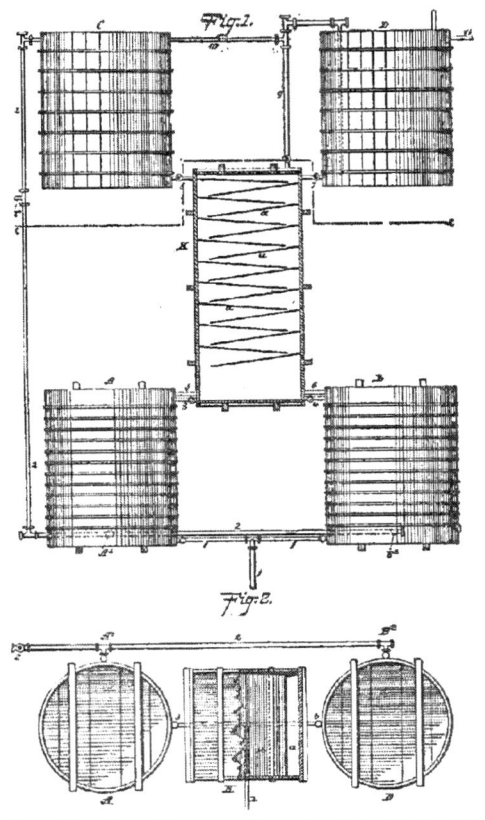

FIG. 42.—THE WENDLER-SPIRO LIQUOR APPARATUS.

Fig. 1 is a sectional view of the apparatus. Fig. 2 is a top view of the lower part of the same, partly in section, the letters A, B, C, and D indicating the vats.

K is the absorption chamber, provided with drip shelves $a\,a$, the vats and the chamber being connected by a system of pipes. The lime-water necessary for the liquor enters the vat D by the pipe 11. The sulphurous acid enters the vats A, B under pressure by the pipe 1, and passes either through A, K, and D, or B, K, and D, the lime-water passing either through D, K, and A, or D, K, and B. The gas cannot be completely absorbed by the liquid in the vats A, B, on account of the rapidity with which it passes through it, and therefore the absorption chamber K, provided with drip shelves a a, is put in, which affords the gas the largest possible plane of attack. It is the object to let the weak liquor, which is still able to absorb a large quantity of sulphurous acid, run as often as possible over the shelves in the saturating chamber K, whereas the strongest liquor, which is unable to absorb much more sulphurous acid, is finally charged with gas in the lower vats. The incomplete liquor passes from A or B through the pipe 2 to C, and from C through K back to A or B. The liquor is completed in either A or B, and then passes through the pipe 2, 2' to the place of consumption. The vat D is used for the reception of lime-water, and the vat C for the reception of the weaker liquor.

The system of piping by which the vats A, B, C, D, and the chamber K are connected is as follows: The gas is conducted to the vats A, B by the pipe 1, and from A, B to the saturating chamber K by pipes 5 and 6, from K to the vats C, D by the pipes 9 and 10—the partial object of 10 being to allow the free flow of the liquid from the vat C when the valve 8 is opened. The liquids are conducted through the pipes 7 and 8 into K, from there by the pipes 3 and 4 to A B, and from these vats they may be carried to the outlet 2' or to the vat C by the pipe 2.

Suppose the vats A and B are already filled with weak liquor. C is empty, and D contains lime-water. The gas enters through the pipe 1 into the vats A and B, and up through the saturating chamber K to D. The valves in the pipes 7, 8, and 9 are then closed, and the valve B^2 in the pipe 2 is opened. Pressure will then increase in A, B, and K until it is sufficient to force the weak liquor from B to C. As soon as this is accomplished, the valve 8 is opened, and the weak liquor is allowed to pass from C over the shelves in the saturating chamber K, and then through the pipe 4 to the vat B. On this passage it will absorb the gas which is in K. The outflow of C is regulated in such a manner that as soon as B is nearly filled the liquor in A will also nearly have absorbed the desired amount of sulphurous acid.

As soon as this is accomplished, the gas is switched over to B, and the outlet valves from K are again closed, and the completed liquor is forced over from B to the pipe 2 2' to the place of consumption. As, meanwhile, chamber K is under pressure of sulphurous acid, the lime which has settled in chamber K will be dissolved, and thus it is possible to obtain a liquor containing an equal percentage of lime, and also in this manner the drip shelves of the chamber K will be kept clean, thus excluding the possibility of an obstruction in the chamber K. When all of the completed liquor has been forced out of the vat A or B, fresh lime-water will be conducted into such empty vat by opening the valve in the pipe 7 and allowing the lime-water to run over the shelves a of the chamber K to the vat A or B. By closing the gas outlet valves of K the weak liquor is forced from A to C. Then by opening the valve 8 the weak liquor is allowed to pass from C over the saturating shelves $a\,a$ of the chamber K to A. After the same liquid from one of the lower vats — say A — has passed over the saturating shelves in K twice, the liquor in the other lower vat — say B — is nearly completed. The gas is then switched over and conducted through the vat A, the outlet valves from K are closed, and the completed liquor is forced from B through the pipe 2 2' to the place of consumption.

In this case the apparatus is worked under gas pressure; but the same effect would be obtained by suction. The circulation of the liquids could likewise be obtained by pumping.

The Behrend liquor apparatus which is commonly used in mills working the Salomon-Brungger process is very similar to the apparatus of Wendler and Spiro, but lacks the absorption box which adds greatly to the efficiency of the latter plant. The Behrend apparatus is in fact practically a Partington plant without agitators, agitation being secured by the upward passage of the gas.

The liquor apparatus of Dr. Frank is shown in plan and elevation in Fig. 43, for which we are indebted to Schubert's "Cellulosefabrikation." Although this apparatus has been in use in many continental mills, it has not, so far as we know, yet found a place in this country. It is, however, to our minds, one of the best which has thus far been devised, and we take pleasure in introducing it to the favorable consideration of American papermakers.

In the figures, A represents a closed sulphur oven in which combustion is maintained by the air-pump B, which is provided with the air-chamber C, to equalize and regulate the pressure. The gas from the furnace passes first into the sublimator D, in which most of the sulphur which may have been carried over is

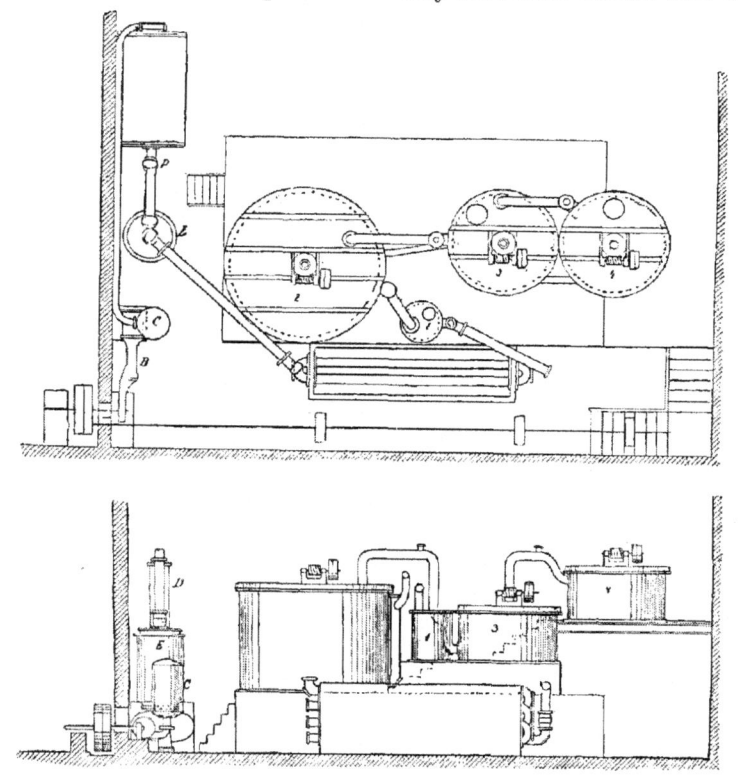

FIG. 43.—DR. FRANK'S LIQUOR APPARATUS.

condensed, the remainder being caught in the dust-chamber E. After passing through the cooler, the gas is sent through the small washing tank 1, which is partially filled with water, to hold back any sulphuric acid which may be present in the gas, and from this washer there may be drawn from time to time a weak sulphuric acid for use about the mill. 2, 3, and 4 are absorption vessels fitted with vertical agitators, and the gas passes through them in the order of their numbers. Tanks 2 and 3 are closed, and work under pressure, but No 4 is generally open, and is the one into which the fresh milk of lime is charged. The milk of lime is made up very strong, and absorption goes on in the last two tanks until the liquor in them is beyond the monosulphide stage and well along toward bisulphite. The charge in 3 is then transferred to 2, being at the same time diluted with sufficient cold water to bring the finished liquor to the proper boiling strength. It will be noticed that, for this reason, tank 2 is made considerably larger than the others. There is, of course, always some heating up of the liquor in the two smaller tanks; but the evil effects of this are corrected by the admission of so large a volume of cold water, which is in the best condition for the rapid absorption of gas. It ordinarily requires only about 3 minutes to bring the monosulphite in solution in tank 2, and finish off the liquor. The air-pump is then stopped, and the combustion of sulphur ceases for the time. The finished liquor is then drawn off, and a fresh charge from 3 transferred to 2, while the tanks 3 and 4 are being refilled with fresh milk of lime. The charging and emptying take about 30 minutes, and the whole operation about 7 hours. The capacity of the apparatus is from 30 to 35 cubic metres for the small size, or from 54 to 60 cubic metres for the large size, for 24 hours. It can be arranged to run continuously, but Dr Frank prefers the intermittent method, as results may thus be better controlled.

In this apparatus, Dr. Frank has used lime, magnesia, and soda, and, where desirable, can bring the test of the liquor up to 10° B. The guarantee given with the apparatus is that 95 per cent. of the sulphur burned shall be brought into the liquor in a form available for use; or, in other words, for every 100 kilogrammes of sulphur burned there shall be obtained in the liquor, 190 kilogrammes of sulphurous acid. In practice, 193 6–194 have been obtained

Dr. Frank, acting upon the theory that the work of the liquor is effected by the free sulphurous acid, advises the preparation and use of liquor with as small a content of lime as possible. This is entirely in accord with our own views, and the point is one which deserves much more careful attention from pulp-makers than it has yet received. It should be borne in mind that by "free acid" Dr Frank has reference to all the gas present in the liquor in excess of that required to form monosulphite with the base present.

In discussing the working of his apparatus, Dr. Frank offers the following as an example of an ordinary factory liquor of 7° Bé, and made in an apparatus other than his own: —

Sample A

	Per cent
Free sulphurous acid	2.35
Combined sulphurous acid	2.00
Total	4.35
Lime	1.75

For comparison with this, he submits a liquor of barely 5° Bé, made in his apparatus, and which pulped the wood in the same length of time as above, without any separation of sulphite. The composition of the liquor was as follows: —

Sample B

	Per cent
Free sulphurous acid	2.382
Combined sulphurous acid	0.874
Total	3.256
Lime	0.764

It will be noticed that this liquor, although of less specific gravity, and containing a smaller total of sulphurous acid, is nevertheless richer in available acid than A. Sample A required 23 kilogrammes of sulphur per cubic metre, while B required only 17 kilogrammes. The ash of the pulp cooked with A was 1.85 per cent, while that from the pulp cooked with B was only 0.36 per cent.

A liquor used at the Krumauer Fabrik, working under the Mitscherlich system, had the composition shown below —

	Per cent
Free sulphurous acid	2.023
Combined sulphurous acid	1.012
Total	3.035
Lime	0.827

and required only 16 kilogrammes of sulphur for a cubic metre. In spite of the fact that less sulphur was used to make this liquor, it is a more expensive liquor than B, which took 17 kilogrammes, because the proportion of free acid in B is so much greater that B is the more efficient liquor, and can therefore be used in less amount.

In these different forms of apparatus in which milk of lime is used, it is perhaps somewhat less trouble to work them in the continuous way, but the quality of the liquor is more easily controlled when the liquor is carried through in separate charges. Each charge can then be tested for strength, and dumped as soon as it comes to test. It is important that the finished liquor should be removed from the absorption tank as soon as possible, as otherwise it is liable to be weakened through the formation of sulphuric acid. It is easier to settle out the last portions of monosulphite than to try to bring them into solution, and considerable time may thus be saved. Besides, the greater portion of the iron which was present in the lime does not go into solution until nearly all the sulphite is dissolved, and there is less danger from contamination from this source when the liquor is drawn off before it is entirely clear.

The quality of the lime used in the preparation of these liquors is of the first importance, and its value for this purpose increases with the amount of magnesia it contains.

The dolomites found at Bowling Green, Ohio, and at several points in the State of New York, are especially good, and carry, in some cases, after burning, over 40 per cent. of magnesia. The lime should, of course, be well burned, should slake easily, and be as free as possible from lime and silica. The following analyses will indicate the general composition of lime well suited for use in this connection: —

Silica, etc.	0.05	0.30	trace
Iron and alumina sesquioxides	0.65	1.54	0.18
Lime	57.09	55.99	57.79
Magnesia	40.88	40.32	40.24
Carbonic acid, water, etc., by difference	1.33	1.85	1.79

If lime which has been improperly burned, or which has become air-slaked, is used, the proportion of base is likely to vary to such an extent as to cause trouble, and such limes are not so readily acted upon by the gas. The usual proportion for making up the milk of lime is 200 lbs of lime per thousand gallons, and this should give a liquor of 9° or 10° T., carrying about 3.50 per cent. of sulphurous acid. The liquor made in towers runs from 7° to 10° T., and usually contains a slightly greater proportion of free sulphurous acid, or acid above that needed to form bisulphite, than the liquor which is made from milk of lime. It is difficult to make a lime liquor in practice of a greater density than 10° T., but where magnesia or soda is used without lime the magnesia liquor can be made in an apparatus like Catlin's to stand 25° T., while the soda liquor can be brought up to 60° T.

The following analysis may be taken as representative of a well-made liquor prepared from dolomite:—

Bisulphite Liquor

Specific gravity at 15° C = 1.0582

	Per cent
Sulphurous acid (SO_2)	4.41
Sulphuric acid (SO_3)	0.13
Lime (CaO)	0.95
Magnesia (MgO)	0.72
Silica (SiO_2)	0.04

Combined as:—

Sulphate of lime ($CaSO_4$)	0.22
Bisulphite of lime (CaS_2O_5)	2.84
Bisulphite of magnesia (MgS_2O_5)	3.04
Free sulphurous acid (SO_2)	0.11

The lime and magnesia in a finished liquor never bear quite the same relation to each other as in the dolomite from which the liquor was prepared. The magnesia is always somewhat in excess, as a portion of the lime is unavoidably thrown out as sulphate and monosulphite. In case any great discrepancy appears, it is evidence that too much air has been admitted to the sulphur furnace, or else that a large proportion of lime is being lost as monosulphite in the sediment. An analysis of the sediment will point to the proper explanation.

Although the loss of both lime and sulphur may easily be considerable, it is so insidious that it will probably be underestimated unless careful daily records are kept of the amounts of lime and sulphur used, the volume of liquor made, and the quantity of each

THE SULPHITE PROCESS.

chemical which analysis shows to be present in the liquor. Good liquor may be made even where large losses occur, since the loss comes wholly upon the lime and the sulphur combined with it, so that as more lime is lost the proportion of the more desirable bisulphite of magnesia in the liquor is increased.

The loss of sulphur is due to dirt and ash, to subliming, escape of gas through imperfect absorption, and, especially, to the formation of sulphuric acid on account of a successive supply of air. The loss from dirt should not amount to more than 2 per cent., and 5 per cent. should cover all loss from moisture, ash, and sublimed sulphur. Unless great care is exercised the loss through formation of sulphuric acid may easily amount to 20 or 30 per cent. There should be no excuse for any loss of sulphur through imperfect absorption of gas. If the lime used has not been freshly slaked, or if it has become air-slaked in storage, a considerable loss will always be found between the lime in the liquor and that weighed off, on account of the absorption of water and carbonic acid from the air. If an inferior grade of lime is used, it is likely to contain considerable silica, which will be left in the sediment. Improperly burned lime carries more or less carbonic acid, and consequently more of such lime must be used to obtain the same strength of liquor. The greater part of the loss of lime is due to failure to bring all the monosulphite into solution, and to the formation of sulphate. The sediment in the storage tanks should be tested before it is thrown away, as it may pay to work it over if the proportion of monosulphite is very large.

It sometimes happens that the sulphite of lime formed in the middle or upper tanks crystallizes upon the paddles of the apparatus instead of going into solution. This crystallization usually takes a peculiar form, which gives the paddles the appearance of having kernels of popped corn stuck over them. The thickness of the deposit may become so great, unless promptly attended to, as to cause the breaking down of the paddles, and, in any case, the power required to drive the apparatus thus incrusted becomes much greater than usual.

FIG. 44. — INCRUSTATION OF $CaSO_3$.

Fig. 44, which is taken from a photograph of a piece of paddle from one of these machines, will serve to give an idea of the thickness sometimes reached by this incrustation. Perhaps the easiest way to remove the deposit is to let down one or two charges of water instead of milk lime. As the gas is dissolved by the water, the sulphite gradually goes into solution.

It is claimed on good authority that the addition of a small amount of Solvay ash to the milk of lime causes much better absorption of the gas, and more rapid settling of the liquor, while it is also said to prevent the precipitation of sulphite of lime in the digester. The ash is added in proportion of 2 to 5 per cent on the weight of the lime, and with it is used about the same weight of common salt. If the desired result is not obtained, the amounts of each are increased in successive charges of liquor, about one-half per cent. of salt being added for each additional per cent. of ash. Soda crystals without the salt are sometimes used in the proportion of 40 lbs. to 1000 gallons of milk of lime. This is equal to about 20 lbs. of anhydrous carbonate of soda.

In the Crocker process, which makes use of a solution of bisulphite of soda, prepared by agitating monosulphite of lime in a solution of neutral sulphate of sodium and then charging the mixture with sulphurous acid, crude acid sulphate of soda is roasted to obtain the neutral sulphate, and the sulphite of lime may be made by adding lime to the waste boiling liquor. This last method is claimed by the patentee as the preferable one; but when the waste liquors are so treated, a large quantity of organic matter comes down with the sulphite and makes the separation difficult.

Pumping. — Rotary pumps, so placed that the liquor flows into them under a slight head, are best used in all cases for pumping sulphite liquors. The pump should never be placed where it is necessary to prime it, or use a foot-valve on the suction-pipe. It is impossible to keep such a foot-valve tight, owing to the crystallization of monosulphite in the working parts. The pump should be built of phosphor-bronze, or other bronze of good acid-resisting quality. In some foreign mills an acid egg similar to those used for vitriol is employed for pumping liquor. The egg is a lead-lined vessel, provided at the top with a pipe through which air may be forced under pressure. The liquor is run into the egg through one pipe until it is nearly full; the valve on this pipe is then closed, and air forced in on top of the liquor, by which means the liquor is driven out through the delivery pipe leading from the bottom of the egg. Steam injectors have been used in some mills in this country for transferring liquor. There is no objection to their use, if the liquor is discharged directly into a closed digester, otherwise considerable sulphurous acid is lost through the heating of the liquor. Where nothing is to be gained by such heating, the use of the injector is too expensive.

Storage Tanks. — The tanks used for storing liquor may be lined with 6-lb. sheet lead for the sides, and 8-lb. for the bottom. No lining whatever is necessary when the tanks are of the ordinary circular form. In such cases, however, the tanks should always be first made tight, with water or steam, before any liquor is admitted. If this is not done, it is impossible afterward to make them tight, on account of the crystallization of monosulphite between the staves. The storage tanks should be covered so as to prevent escape of gas, and access of air, though it is not necessary that the cover should be perfectly air-tight. The tanks should be so placed that the sediment may be easily washed out from time to time. When the liquor is stored in quantity, there is little loss of strength, either through escape of gas or oxidation to sulphate.

In order to obtain clear liquor with as little loss of time as possible, the delivery pipe from the tank should be attached to some form of float, so that, in pumping, liquor would always be drawn from the top. A sufficient length of stout rubber hose may be used inside the tank, and should be attached to the bottom with a lead pipe leading to the pump. The other end of the hose is attached to the float, which may be a box of sufficient size, made of copper, and hermetically sealed. Wood soon becomes so saturated with the liquor as to be useless for the float. The best form of gauge showing the height of liquor in the tank is a glass tube, of a diameter of not less than $\frac{3}{8}$-inch. The fitting which secures the tube to the tank at the bottom should be a cross with a cock on both the horizontal and vertical arms, for convenience in keeping the tube from clogging with the sediment.

The best results in cooking are only obtained where the whole liquor apparatus is so run as to secure liquor of a quality as nearly uniform as possible. This necessitates close attention to the sulphur-burning, air-supply and the strength and quality of the milk of lime. No lime from a new quarry should ever be used until its composition has been ascertained by analysis, and the weight to be used corrected by proper allowance for any impurity it may contain.

Digesters and Digester Linings.— The extremely corrosive action of sulphurous acid and bisulphites upon iron renders some form of lining necessary for protecting the digester shell. All forms of iron are rapidly attacked by the acid, especially at the high temperatures and pressures employed in this process; wrought iron suffers most severely. Corrosion does not proceed regularly over the surface, but instead the iron is deeply pitted. Steel resists somewhat better than wrought iron, and cast iron suffers least of all.

Fig. 45 is from a photograph of a piece of half-inch wrought-iron boiler plate cut from one of the digesters at the mill of the Richmond Paper Company, and shows very well the extent to which the corrosion may proceed. The digester from which the sample was cut had been in use two and a half years, under conditions which it is only fair to say were much harder than any likely to be tolerated now.

The curious irregularity with which the metal was corroded is especially noticeable. The iron was eaten away to a depth of $\frac{7}{32}$-inch for some distance along a line just above the bottom row of rivets on several of the plates. In other places, from $\frac{1}{8}$ to $\frac{3}{16}$-inch of the metal was gone. The average depth to which the shell was corroded was at least $\frac{1}{16}$-inch.

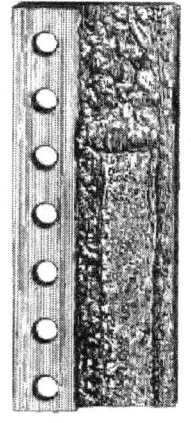

FIG. 45.— CORRODED DIGESTER SHELL.

Lead is the only common metal which resists perfectly the action of the liquor, and its immunity from corrosion is largely due to the almost complete insolubility of its sulphate, which, as soon as formed, makes a protective coating for the metal underneath. The use of lead in this connection is greatly complicated by the peculiar behavior of the metal when subjected to frequent variations of temperature over considerable range. The coefficient of expansion of lead is 0.0000297, while that of iron is only 0.0000123; so that wherever the two metals are held together and subjected to any rise of temperature, there is a constant tendency for the lead to pull away from the iron; or, in the case of a lead lining contained within an iron shell, the tendency is for the lining to grow too large for the shell. This tendency is exaggerated still more by the peculiar fact that when lead has been expanded by heat, it does not, like most metals, resume its original dimensions upon cooling, but, apparently owing to the sluggish movement of its molecules, it covers somewhat more surface than before, being made at the same time correspondingly thinner. This causes the phenomenon known as "crawling," the lead showing a tendency to pull away in one direction from any point at which it is held. If held by bolts, the bolt-hole is gradually changed in form from a circle to an ellipse, while if the lead is secured through the flanges of the digester sections, it gradually crowds out through them.

Owing to this continual movement, cracks are likely to appear wherever the lead makes a turn which is at all short. The crack usually does not come at just the point of turning, but parallel with it, and a little to one side.

Contrary to the usual fact in regard to metals, the acid-resisting qualities of lead are considerably enhanced by the presence in the lead of certain impurities in small amount.

Calvert and Johnson, upon whose researches the following table is based, took lead plates, each 1 metre square, and covered them with 16 litres of sulphuric acid each. After ten days the quantity of lead sulphate formed was determined.

	Specific gravity of acid used	Ordinary lead, grms $PbSO_4$	Virgin lead, grms $PbSO_4$	Pure lead, grms $PbSO_4$
I	1.842	67.70	134.20	201.70
II	1.705	8.35	16.50	19.70
III	1.600	5.55	10.34	16.20
IV	1.526	2.17	4.34	6.84
V	1.746	49.67	50.84	55.00
VI	1.746	51.91	54.75	57.41

The ordinary lead contained: lead, 98.82; tin, 0.40; iron, 0.36; copper, 0.40. The virgin lead: lead, 99.21; tin, 0.01; iron, 0.32; copper, 0.44. In the first four experiments pure acid was used, and at the ordinary temperature; in the last two, commercial acid at a temperature of about 50° C.

Other experiments indicate that small quantities of antimony and copper make lead more resisting; while, when bismuth is present, the lead is more readily attacked.

The whole object of the many ingenious mechanical devices which have been embodied in the lead linings of sulphite digesters is to hold the lead in place, while at the same time localizing and diminishing the tendency to crawl. The thickness and weight of the lead employed varies within wide limits from the 6-lb. lead used in the Mitscherlich process to $\frac{3}{4}$-inch lead, weighing 48 lbs to the square foot, as at one time used in several mills in this country Generally speaking, the thickness of the lead is $\frac{1}{2}$-inch, corresponding to a weight of 32 lbs per square foot

The present rapid introduction of cement linings has so changed the conditions of the sulphite process that lead-lined digesters now have hardly more than a historical interest They have played so important a part in the development of the process, however, and so much skill in chemical engineering has been expended upon their construction, that we shall consider briefly the more important of the different types.

One of the earliest devices for holding the lead in place is found in the rings employed by Frank. These were at first merely formed of lead and antimony cast in half-circles, and burned together inside the digester. In a later form, advantage was taken of the greater expansion shown by brass, and the rings were made of brass covered with lead; the ring thus held more tightly as the temperature in the digester rose. Still later the ring, instead of being continuous, was formed in three segments, held in place by wedges, which could be tightened up as the lead underneath the ring grew thinner The great objection to all forms of ring is found in this tendency to cut and squeeze the lead beneath so rapidly that frequent repairs are necessary. In a modified form, however, rings have been used in several of the most satisfactory lead-lined digesters with which we are acquainted. In these cases the rings were made of wrought-iron strips 2 inches wide, cut in half-circles, and sprung in place inside the digester. They were then covered with $\frac{3}{4}$-inch lead, which was burned to the lining on either side. The rings were placed 18 inches apart through the whole length of the digester.

Partington has employed several different methods for holding the lining in place in his globe-shaped rotaries, and they are all of interest in connection with the study of the development of digester linings. The lead itself is cut in sections having the form of a spherical triangle or lune, each piece being of sufficient size to cover $\frac{1}{12}$ of the interior. In the earlier linings the joints at the junction of the various pieces were burned, so that the lining formed one continuous piece. It was held in place by bolts with large washer-shaped heads, the washer being on the interior and the nut on the outside. These heads were covered with lead of the same thickness as that used for the linings, and the covering was burned around the edge to the lining. Rows of clamps of the form shown in Fig. 46 extended from what may be called the poles of the digester, in lines similar to those

FIG. 46. — CLAMP.

marking parallels of longitude on the globe, and a similar row of clamps passed round the digester equatorially. The heads of the clamps were formed of iron surrounded by cast lead. They were held in place by bolts passing through the digester wall, and secured with a nut on the outside. Makin introduced an improvement (Fig. 47) in these linings by the use of a compound lead and iron plate, formed of a sheet of thin boiler iron perforated with numerous half-inch holes, and

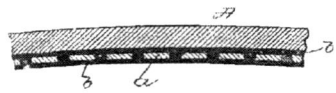

FIG. 47. — MAKIN LINING.

covered with lead, which was cast upon it and secured by the metal which flowed through the holes. An objection was made to this cast lead on account of the numerous pin-holes, which were difficult to avoid in casting the metal, and Makin's lining was next prepared by taking a sheet of lead of the usual thickness used in lining, laying the iron plate upon it, which in this case was perforated in such a way that the holes were considerably smaller at the end next the lead than upon the upper side, and pouring melted lead or solder into these holes. Rolled sheet lead could then be used, and as only one side of the iron was covered, there was considerable saving in the former metal. A somewhat similar lining was adopted by McDougall, who used, in place

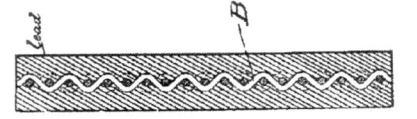

FIG. 48. — G. W. RUSSELL'S LINING.

of the iron plate, stout iron-wire gauze to which the lead was burned. G. W. Russell patented in this country a compound lining, formed by casting lead upon a heavy wire gauze or netting, as shown in Fig. 48.

Fig. 49 represents a digester of the type known as a globe rotary, lined up with the Makin compound plates. As this lining was at first applied, the joints between the sections *b* were covered

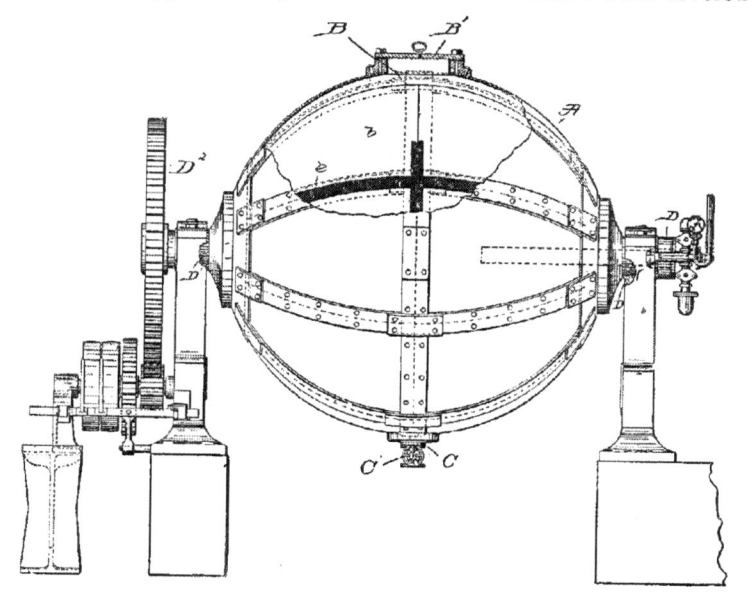

FIG. 49.—PARTINGTON ROTARY DIGESTER.

by strips of sheet lead, shown as a heavy black band at *e*. These strips were soldered or burned to the adjacent edges of the lining.

A later form of the Partington lining made use of the modification introduced by Springer. In this method, which is shown in Fig. 50, the sections of the lining are so placed as to leave a small space between adjacent edges. In the figure, *A* represents the boiler shell, and *a* the compound lead and iron plate, invented by Makin. *C* is an acid-resisting packing of asbestos, or asbestos and rubber, between the edges of the plates. Over the joint is laid a strip of sheet packing, *t*. The sections of the lining are held in place by means of stay strips *B*,

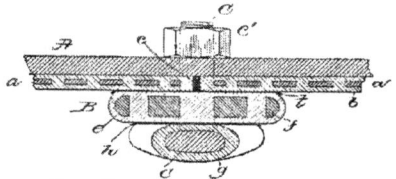

FIG. 50.—THE SPRINGER LINING.

composed of a perforated metal band, e, around which lead has been cast after the method followed in making the lining itself. The stay strips are secured by bolts, which occur at frequent intervals, and whose heads are covered with lead as shown.

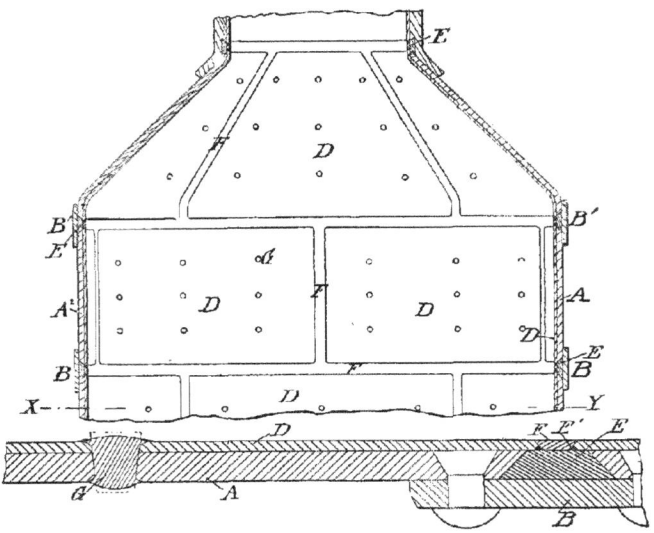

Fig. 51.—The Ritter-Kellner Lining.

The Ritter-Kellner digesters are of upright form, and for holding the lead in position the main reliance is placed in two devices; the first of these consists of a lead, or lead and antimony ring sunk in the digester wall, as shown at E in Fig. 51, and to which the lead is burned. The digester wall between these rings is perforated at various points, and rivets, G, of hard lead are driven in the holes, the lining being burned to them on the inner side. The iron shell presents a perfectly smooth interior, all joints being butt joints, and all rivets counter-sunk.

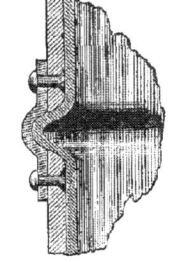

Fig. 52.—Early Ekman Lining.

The earliest form of the Ekman digester which was introduced into this country was of small size, having a capacity of only about 500 lbs. of pulp, and was lined with 16 lbs. lead. At the upper portion of the digester

238   THE CHEMISTRY OF PAPER-MAKING

wall a recess of the form shown in Fig. 52 extended around the digester, and the lead lining was forced into this recess for support. A better method for causing the lining to crack could hardly have been devised, and so far as we know none of these digesters are now in use. The sectional digesters of Wheelwright which succeeded them also gave much trouble in their early form, owing to the cracking of the lead below the flanges, and the difficulty of making joints between the sections. An attempt was made to overcome this by making the lining continuous, and burning it to lead rings which passed between the flanges. We are of the opinion that this is a fairly good form of lining, but at the time of its adoption there was much trouble from collapsing, caused by liquor which had worked its way between the lining and the shell, only to be again converted into steam when the digester was blown off.

The principle of the Wheelwright cast-iron digester, which was designed to overcome the difficulties arising from the expansion and crawling of the lead lining, is illustrated in Fig. 53, which shows a section through one ring. The rings were $6\frac{1}{2}$ or 7 feet in

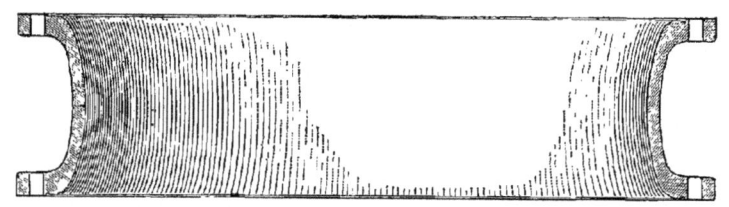

FIG. 53 — WHEELWRIGHT CAST-IRON DIGESTER (SECTION THROUGH ONE RING)

diameter and 2 feet high. The digester was built up of ten of these rings, with top and bottom cone pieces. It will be noted on inspection of the figure that the inner wall of each ring curves outward toward the flanges, so that the lining always lay upon convex curves, while any expansion was at once taken up through the flanges. The joints at the flanges were made tight either by a packing like that of Jenkins or by lead rings placed just inside the bolt holes, at which point a slight depression will be noticed.

The Graham boiler is built up of compound lead and iron plates, and has the lead lining secured to the iron at every point of contact. The compound plates are prepared before the sheets are bent or assembled. The iron plate is cleaned and smoothed very care-tully by an emery wheel. It is then placed over gas jets, and upon it is put a rectangular frame or ledge, the joint between the frame and ledge being made tight by a fireproof packing. The upper surface of the plate which is to receive the lead is moistened by zinc chloride solution, and when the temperature of the plate has been raised by the gas jets to about the melting point of lead, the molten lead is poured on. In this way a very good joint between the two metals is secured, and it is claimed that it is impossible to cut away the lead with a cold chisel without leaving a thin coating of this metal upon the iron plate. An uncoated margin for the joints and rivets is left on each plate, and after the plates are assembled, the unprotected lines along the joints are similarly coated by heating locally with a blow-pipe and running in melted lead.

The difficulties inseparably connected with the use of the best lead linings led to the introduction of digesters built of bronze, capable of resisting more or less perfectly the action of the sulphite solution. The general formula for these bronzes is 9 parts of copper to 1 part of tin; but each manufacturer has his own method of working the alloy, and thus claims to secure special properties.

Martin L. Griffin gives the composition of the Schenck digester metal as below: —

	Per cent
Tin	7.68
Copper	91.28
Zinc	0.89

These digesters are usually built of the cast metal in 3-foot sections, having in some cases a diameter as great as 9 feet; the joints between sections are easily made tight with lead rings, as there is here no lining to be cut. It is undeniably true that all such digesters are acted upon to a considerable extent by the hot liquor, as may be readily proved by taking some of the unwashed pulp, drying and burning it, dissolving the ash in weak acid, and then placing for a moment a polished knife-blade in the solution, when the copper will be deposited upon the iron.

Besides the corrosion which, in spite of chemical testimony, was for a long time denied by the builders of these digesters, they are subject to other and perhaps more serious elements of weakness. Recent tests show that the strength of the metal is, in some cases, reduced fully 40 per cent. by heating to the temperatures reached in practice in these digesters, while the frequent changes of temperature to which they are subjected cause in time a crystallization of the metal, which greatly impairs its power to resist strain. The significance of these facts has been emphasized by several disastrous explosions.

There is some difference of opinion as to the relative merit of the upright and rotary form of digester. Somewhat less liquor can be used in the rotary, and there is no danger of making black chips, as none of the chips remain uncovered for more than a minute or two at a time. The upright digesters are somewhat cheaper to build and keep in operation, and although we have no satisfactory explanation to offer for the fact, we have found it to be generally true, that pulp made in an upright is of somewhat stronger and better quality than that produced in the rotary.

Many forms of blow-off valves are in use on sulphite boilers, and a poor valve causes endless trouble. It may be said, in general, that gate valves are not well suited for use in this position, on account of their great liability to become clogged from

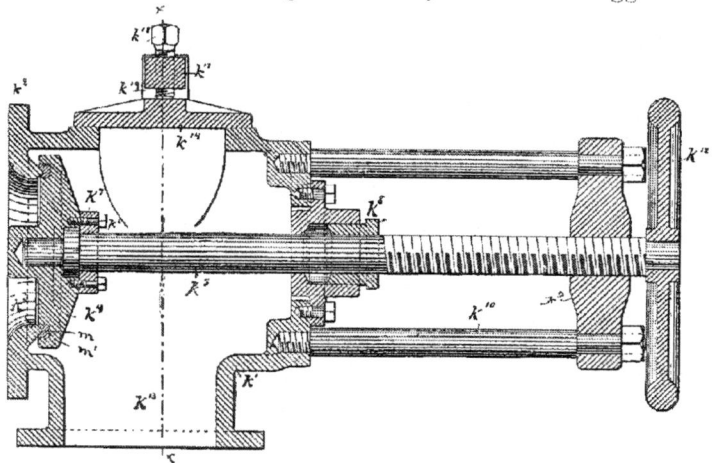

FIG. 54.—CLAPP VALVE.

pulp which has got into the bonnet of the valve or on the seat. Plug cocks are better.

The Clapp valve (Fig. 54) has been used with great success in the soda process, and possesses many points of merit which should make it readily adaptable to sulphite digesters. Its construction and the readiness with which it may be cleaned are apparent from the figure.

The steam-pipes on rotary digesters necessarily pass through the trunnions, and usually follow the curve of the digester for a short distance on the inside. In the upright digesters, steam is always admitted at the bottom, and best through a 3-inch pipe. Various devices have been used for spreading

FIG. 55. — BURNING-IRON.

the steam as it issues from the pipe; but they are objectionable, since the force of the steam is thereby much diminished, and there is considerably more likelihood of clogging the pipe by pulp or incrustation. With the steam-pipe placed at the apex of a properly shaped cone bottom, the chips themselves spread the steam sufficiently, and there is no danger that any of the chips will pack to one side, where the steam will not reach them.

All lead-burning inside the digester is done with a blow-pipe, but joints can be more quickly made with heavy lead by the use of the burning-iron, whenever the seam is horizontal.

Fig. 55 shows the shape commonly adopted for such irons, which usually weigh about 16 lbs. Where much lead-burning of this sort has to be done, it is advisable to employ one of the recently invented irons, which are kept hot by an electric current, since by their use much time is saved, and the plumber's helper can usually be dispensed with.

A good form of plumber's gas-machine for use in lead-burning is shown in Fig. 56. It consists of two cylinders made of heavy sheet lead, or two oil barrels may be taken, and lined up with thin sheet lead. The vessels are connected by a rubber tube at the bottom,

FIG. 56. — GAS MACHINE.

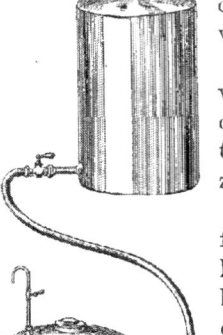

as shown. The lower cylinder has a false bottom, and the space above this is filled with granulated zinc, made by melting the metal and pouring it in water from the height of a few feet. The upper cylinder is filled with dilute sulphuric acid, which, upon opening the cock, flows down into the lower cylinder, and by its action upon the zinc causes the rapid evolution of hydrogen. The gas is led away to the blow-pipe through a rubber tube which is attached to the small pipe leading from the top of the bottom tank. The pressure of the gas may be regulated roughly by the height at which the upper cylinder is placed. The apparatus is self-regulating, because, as soon as the cock in the gas-pipe is closed, the pressure of the gas soon forces the acid up into the higher cylinder, and away from the zinc. The evolution of gas then stops until a new supply is required.

The Mitscherlich Digester is noticeable from its large size, and the fact that it was the first type in which bricks were used as a portion of the lining. These boilers are commonly from 12–14 feet in diameter, and from 36–40 feet long. Those of the smaller size hold about 100 cubic metres of wood and 60 cubic metres of liquor. They have two manholes at the top, and two or three at the bottom, and are mounted on foundation walls at least as high as a man. There is so much expansion in these boilers that they are not fastened directly to the walls, but instead are supported by cast-iron shoes riveted to the shell, and resting upon iron beams. Sometimes rollers are placed between the shoes and the beam, while often the adjacent surfaces are merely planed to give a well-faced bearing.

The Mitscherlich lining consists, first, of a coat of tar and pitch, which offers some protection to the shell, and also acts as a cement to hold the lining of thin sheet lead, which is next applied. Upon the lead are laid two courses of special acid-resisting bricks, formed with tongue and groove, by which they interlock. Portland cement is sometimes used with the bricks, which in any case are laid flat in the first course, and edgewise in the second. In some foreign mills, a second layer of lead is placed between the bricks.

The boilers are heated by a series of hard lead pipes, which cover the lower third of the inside. The pipes are arranged in four sections of coils, each of which is independent of the others. The steam ends of alternate coils are at the same end of the boiler, so that the steam in the adjacent coils is passing in opposite directions. The total length of pipe in a single digester is from 1200–2600 feet. The digesters are fitted with safety-valve, thermometer-tubes, and gauge-cocks to which a tube is temporarily attached to indicate the level of the liquor while charging the digester. There are also cocks by which samples of liquor may be drawn for test during the cook.

Smaller upright digesters in two sizes are offered by the owners of the Mitscherlich patents, the sizes being 16×10 and 24×14.

The expense and difficulty which attend the operation of even the best types of lead-lined boilers have caused the chemists and others engaged in the development of the process to look long and carefully for some other means of protection which should prove more manageable and less costly. One of the earliest attempts in this direction is described in United States patent 351,330, granted to one of the authors. In this case, the interior of a cast-iron digester 6 inches in diameter by 20 inches high was coated with an enamel composed of one part of borate of lead to ten parts of litharge. This enamel has a low fusing-point, is very tenacious, and resists the action of the liquor at least as well as lead. The difficulty of perfectly coating so large a casting proved so great, however, that only one digester thus protected was put in operation, and this developed numerous spots where scale beneath the enamel prevented its adhering to the metal. At about the same time, a white enamel was brought forward by Frambach.

The present greatly improved methods of lining up digesters are the result, in the main, of the work of Pierredon, Brungger, Mitscherlich, Wenzel, and Kellner, in Europe, and of G. F. Russell and Curtis and Jones, in this country.

The Salomon-Brungger Boiler. — About 1883 Brungger, who was chemist in Salomon's mill at Cunnersdorf, was led in the course of some temporary repairs to substitute within a digester a short length of iron pipe for the bronze one by which steam was ordinarily supplied. Upon examining this pipe at the end of the cook, he found it firmly coated with a thin but dense scale of sulphite of lime, which had apparently protected the metal from corrosion. Acting upon this hint, he soon had a digester in operation, in which, by appropriate means, this scale was formed over the entire interior as a substitute for the lead lining previously in use. It is necessary, in order to secure the coating, that the heat be transmitted through the metal to the liquor within; and for this reason digesters of this type are heated by a steam jacket.

In its present form the Salomon-Brungger boiler consists of two distinct parts; an inner shell of welded steel which is from 6 feet 6 inches to 7 feet in diameter, and an outer shell, also of steel, but riveted. The cone and throat of the inner shell are of cast bronze, and to this cone is riveted the outer shell or jacket. In order to allow for differences in expansion, the joint between the two shells at the bottom is made by a stuffing-box. The total length over all is about 30 feet. In all its mechanical features this digester merits the highest praise.

In order to secure the protective coating, the pressure in the jacket is brought to about 40 lbs before the liquor is admitted. The latter upon coming in contact with the hot metal is decomposed in part, and there is deposited over the metal a thin but excessively hard and impervious crust of sulphite of lime, with perhaps some sulphate. It is claimed, and, as we believe, properly, that a crust $\frac{1}{16}$-inch thick (2–3 mm Reuleaux) affords complete protection. There is at most a merely superficial blackening of the shell. No especial reliance is placed upon the acid-resisting quality of the bronze cone, but this, like the steel shell, is protected by the lining. In order to secure protection at this point, the digester is completely filled with liquor up to within a few inches of the manhole cover. With the expansion of the liquor it becomes necessary to blow off a little from time to time, when, in case the liquor falls below the level indicated, sufficient water is pumped in to supply the deficiency. The liquor itself is used clear, and is the ordinary bisulphite solution.

With each successive cook the scale increases somewhat in thickness, while any places which have been laid bare where the lining has flaked off are freshly coated. Too thick a lining is undesirable, not only because the tendency to flake off is much increased with any irregularity in thickness, but also because the thicker scale unnecessarily retards the transmission of heat into the boiler. For this reason it is customary about once a month, or when the scale has reached a thickness of about $\frac{1}{8}$-inch, to remove the scale by hammering. The same result may be attained by the use of a more acid solution, but this necessitates the preparation of a special liquor, and is otherwise objectionable, as there is some danger that the metal may be corroded.

The records of the mill at Cunnersdorf show that whereas in a certain digester 210 boilings were made in a given length of time when working with a lead lining, 300 boilings were made in this digester in the same length of time after adoption of the protective crust.

The Jung and Lindig method of lining depends upon the formation, upon the digester wall, of a coating of the double silicate of iron and lime, protected further by one of silicate of lime. Before applying the lining the inner surface of the digester is first thoroughly cleaned with wire brushes and a strong alkaline solution. This is followed by a wash of dilute sulphuric or hydrochloric acid to remove the alkali, and the excess of acid is rubbed off with waste.

The clean surface of the metal is then painted with ordinary sulphite liquor made from lime, with the result that a thin coat of the double sulphite of lime and iron is formed. After this is dry it is brushed over with a solution of water glass, in order to obtain the double silicate of calcium and iron; and this coat is also allowed to dry, and then repeated. The coating of double silicate so obtained is finally covered with a pasty mass from 1 to 5 centimetres thick, of a mixture of dry calcium monosulphite and water glass. The proportions used are 5 to 30 parts by weight of the monosulphite and 50 parts by weight of water glass. If desired, 100 parts of ground Chamotte, quartz sand, powdered glass, or asbestos powder may be added, according to circumstances. The proportions of the various ingredients may be changed as desired to produce the object in view, which is a solid, adhering, earthenware-like coating, which should become quite hard.

The digester is now ready for the first boiling with sulphite solution, causing the formation of soluble sodium sulphite which goes into solution, and of silicate of lime in the hardened mass. The latter compound is very acid-resisting, and is capable of protecting any metallic surface from the erosive action of sulphurous acid. It is advisable to repeat the coating of monosulphite and water glass, with or without the addition of such bodies as quartz sand, etc., after a few boilings, so as to obtain several layers of silicate. Valves and tubing after being cleaned, as above described, are filled with a solution of bisulphite of lime and well warmed; then emptied, filled up with water-glass solution, emptied, and dried. They are then boiled in a solution of bisulphite of lime, and treated again with water glass, repeating this process until a sufficiently thick coating of silicate is obtained.

The mixture of water glass and monosulphite of lime soon grows hard, and constantly becomes denser and harder, in contact with sulphite solution; further, the coating sticks very closely to the iron or steel, owing to the presence of what corresponds to a rust cement; and finally, the difference between the coefficient of expansion affects only the fifth decimal place, and hence can be assumed to be identical with that of iron.

Cement Linings. — Various linings composed of so-called acid-proof cements are at the present writing being rapidly introduced in this country and abroad. One of the earliest as well as one of the most successful of these cement linings is that of Wenzel. By his method cement blocks are formed in wooden molds made to conform to the curvature of the different portions of the digester, and are then assembled and cemented in place within the boiler. The special cement used is for the most part a mixture of Portland cement and silicate of soda. The thickness of the blocks varies with the size of the boiler and the position for which the block is intended; those for the bottom of the digester being made thicker, to withstand the greater wear. The usual limits of thickness are from 60–200 mm. Rotaries having a diameter of 2.5–3 metres require a lining 80–100 mm. thick, while 70–80 mm. is sufficient for those of 2–2.5 metres diameter. The blocks for a 4-metre Mitscherlich boiler are made 125 mm. in thickness.

After lining by this system, the boiler is heated by steam for several hours, to a temperature of 140°–160° C. By this treatment, cracks are opened in thin or weak places, and are cut out and refilled. The heating is then repeated until no more cracks appear. The lining is finally completed by covering the blocks with a coating of the very fine cement, which is put on to a depth of 4–5 mm. This wears away in two to three months, but may be replaced in a few hours.

Wenzel, in some cases, first lines the digester with iron wire lath, upon which the cement lining is then formed.

Kellner has several recent patents for cement linings, among them being the British patents numbered 6951, 15,930, 15,931, all issued in 1890. Kellner's cements are made of ground slate and silicate of soda, or of powdered slate and glass and Portland cement, and they are either put on in the plastic condition, or in the form of blocks or slabs. In one case the digester is first lined with the mixture of ground slate and silicate of soda, and after this has set, a second layer, composed of one part ground slate, two parts ground glass, and one part Portland cement, is applied. Kellner has also patented in this connection the use of a lining composed of slabs of tempered glass laid upon such a cement backing.

G. F. Russell, at Lawrence, began experiments with cement linings, applied directly to the shell in the plastic state, about 1888. In the earlier linings, a mixture of Portland cement and sand was used, but the sand was found to detract, if anything, from the durability of the lining, and his present excellent results are obtained by the use of Portland cement alone. This is in most cases reinforced by a facing of special brick or tile, as shown in Fig. 57. The usual thickness of the cement lining is about four

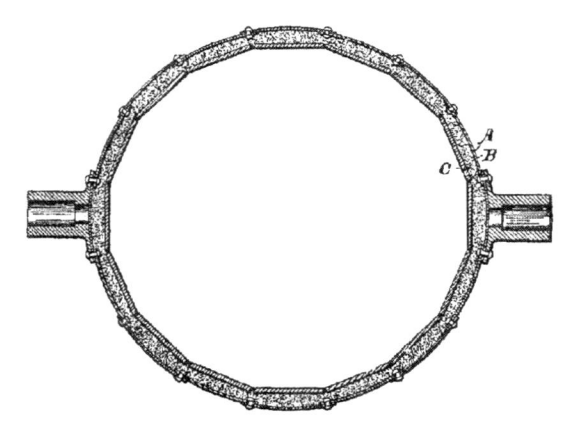

FIG. 57. — RUSSELL LINING.

inches. Where an old digester is relined by this method, this, of course, involves a serious curtailment of production; but since the introduction of these linings the general tendency has been to build the new digesters of very much larger size. The shape of the upright digesters has also been materially changed to good advantage. In place of the well-known cone at top and bottom, the top is now formed by gradually drawing in the shell in a gentle curve, starting nearly from the centre, as shown in Fig. 58, which is taken from one of the digesters recently built for the Waldhof Zellstoff-Fabrik. The dimensions given are in millimetres. Some digesters of this type building in this country have the bottom formed after the same manner as the top here shown. These

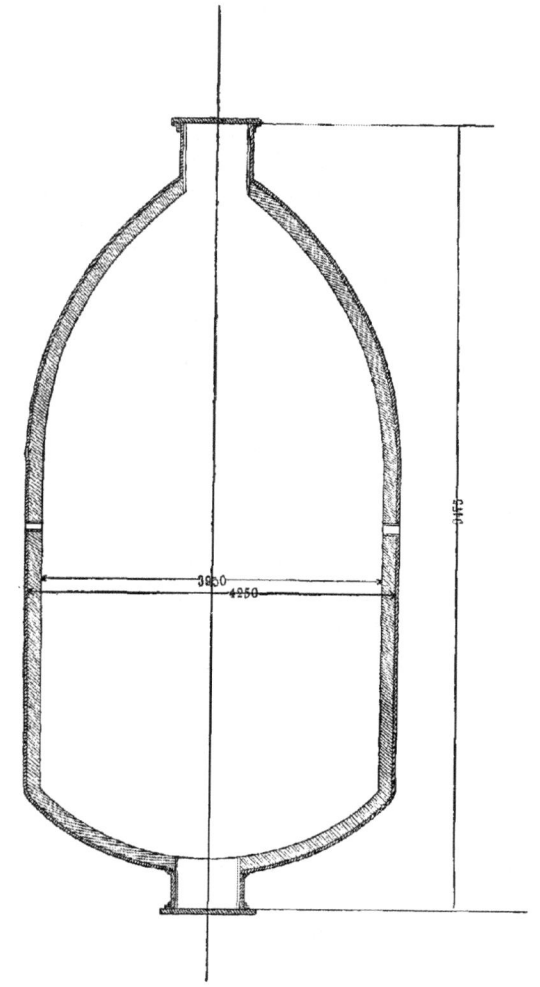

Fig. 58. — Cement-lined Upright Digester.

forms of construction possess the advantage of much diminishing the tendency which the older forms had to spring slightly under pressure, and so open cracks in the cement where the cones joined the body of the boiler. The throat at either end may be protected by a bronze or lead sleeve passing down flush with the lining. Either metal beneath the lining or bronze or lead and antimony pipes passing through it is likely to cause cracks, due to the greater expansion of the metal.

All cement linings are more or less porous when first applied, but in use soon fill up with sulphate and sulphite of lime. They then become practically impervious to the liquor, and afford complete protection to the shell beneath. Such liquor as may work through a crack is quickly rendered harmless through reaction with the lime salts composing the cement. If the lining is built up in layers, the joint between the fresh and partially set cement is likely to be defective, and the crystallization of lime salts within the lining at this point will often cause the outer layer to loosen and flake off. This is avoided by grouting the plastic material in between the digester wall and a movable backer.

Neither Portland cement nor any of the more complex mixtures which have in some cases been adopted resist entirely the action of the liquor. There is, moreover, a gradual erosion of the lining, caused by the friction of the chips and pulp. From these causes, and from occasional flaking off, there is always more or less of the cement in the pulp as discharged from the digester, but the particles are, in nearly every case, so heavy that passage through a short sand-settler is sufficient to hold them back. Such trouble as may be due to this cause is in large measure obviated by facing the lining with well baked brick or tile.

In the selection of these bricks, attention should be had to the following points: They should be very hard and dense, and should not absorb more than 2 per cent. of their weight of water, after being immersed for twenty-four hours in that liquid. They should contain no considerable amount of iron or manganese, and should be hard baked and very well annealed. Several brands of paving and other special brick which meet all these requirements are now made in this country. Bricks which are soft or under burned are very apt to split and crack under the changes of temperature to which they are subjected, and then to come away in the pulp These troubles at their worst are slight in comparison with those which attend the working of lead linings, while the cheapness of cement linings and the readiness with which such slight repairs as they require may be effected are sufficient to ensure their general introduction.

The pulp-digester invented by Messrs. Curtis and Jones, and first put in operation at the mill of the Howland Falls Pulp Company, embodies several novel and valuable features, and has a remarkable record for durability and successful work in practice. The essential novelty of this apparatus is found in the lining, which is composed of blocks of artificial stone so shaped that they lock into each other when in place. This stone is preferably composed of Portland cement and ground glass or quartz, to which sometimes is added a percentage of soluble glass. The density and acid-resisting qualities of these materials are greatly augmented by the process to which they are subjected in the manufacture of the stone.

The objection to the continuous cement lining, applied in a plastic state, is that it is impossible to make the lining of uniform density. Hence, it is often defectively porous in spots, and thus liable to be permeated by the acid. This is avoided in the present instance by subjecting the blocks to pressure during the molding operation, which makes them uniformly dense and strong. The blocks are then exposed for a time to an atmosphere of carbonic acid gas, by which their power of resisting the acid and the mechanical attrition of the pulp is very greatly increased. Digesters thus lined have been in operation for a year without showing appreciable signs of wear, and without entailing any expense for repairs. They are at the present time being rapidly introduced.

Boiling. — In spite of the many different systems under which the sulphite process is worked, the process of boiling is carried on by all of them, with one exception, in practically the same way, so far as strength of liquors, temperatures, and time are concerned. The exception noted is found in the Mitscherlich process, which will for that reason be considered by itself, after taking up the processes in which boiling is conducted at comparatively high pressures and concluded in a comparatively short time.

It is customary, in charging the digester, to fill it as completely as possible with the chips, since, before the full pressure is reached, the chips will settle sufficiently to be entirely covered with the liquor. The liquor should be run in as rapidly as possible; and a 6-inch pipe is none too large for this purpose, as much time may be needlessly wasted through the use of a small pipe. About 2500 gallons of liquor is the proper amount for a digester carrying 2 cords of chips. The strength of the liquor may vary consider-

THE SULPHITE PROCESS.

ably, if the temperature is regulated to correspond, but, in general, liquor of 10° T., carrying about 3½ per cent. sulphurous acid, gives the most satisfactory results. It is very important that the pressure should not be run up too fast, and at least four hours should be taken in reaching full pressure. If the heating is forced at the commencement of the cook, the steam, striking the cold liquor, causes a violent hammering which may seriously strain the digester; but a more serious objection is found in the effect upon the pulp. When the pressure is hurried, a high temperature is reached before the liquor has had time to penetrate to the interior of the chips. The wood inside is more or less burned in consequence, and the pulp is filled with chips showing a hard, red or brown central portion. Wherever such red chips are found in the pulp, the cause may be attributed to getting up pressure too fast. The liquor prevents the oxidation of the wood, and it is necessary that the wood should be thoroughly permeated before there is any considerable rise of temperature. The maximum pressure carried may range from 65 to 85 lbs., the higher pressure being only safe when the liquor is strong in sulphurous acid. The pressure, however, affords a very unreliable indication of the conditions under which the operation is being carried on, and in all cases the main reliance should be placed upon the temperatures as shown by the thermometer. The temperature is the real factor in the disintegration of the wood, and the pressure carried, except so far as it indicates temperature, is of comparatively slight importance. It may be due in a large part to gas set free during the boiling, and in some cases, where much condensed water is formed, the pressure may be almost wholly hydrostatic. In most mills, the thermometer is placed on top of the digester, or in the blow-off pipe; and,

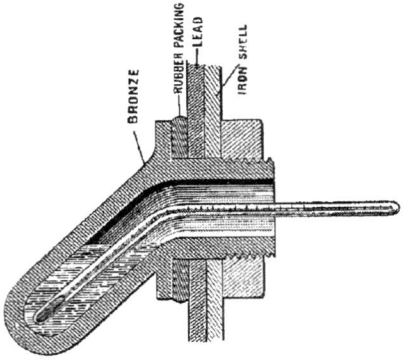

Fig. 59. — Side Oil Bath.

while in these places it may give comparative readings which are of value, the true temperature of the digester is probably somewhat higher than that shown. The proper place for the thermometer is about one-third of the way down on the digester wall. An oil bath may be easily arranged there for its reception by passing a drop tube of bronze through the digester wall and lining, as shown in Fig. 59. A still better arrangement, however, is made possible by the recent introduction of what is known as the Standard thermometer. That portion of the instrument carrying the metallic spring passes through the digester wall, while the dial and pointer on the outside show the temperature as upon a steam gauge. By a slight modification this thermometer can be made to indicate the gas pressure in the digester as well as the temperature. It is only necessary to have printed on the dial the steam pressures corresponding to the various temperatures. The difference between the pressure shown on the thermometer and that shown by the steam gauge is due to gas. An electrical attachment may be applied to these thermometers, by means of which the temperature carried may be indicated at the office, or in any part of the mill. In the quick cooking processes, the best results in boiling are secured when the highest temperature carried is from 300° to 312° F.

As the boiling progresses, the effect of heat and the reactions going on inside the digester is to cause more or less gas to leave the liquor, and the amount of gas pressure increases with some regularity to the end of the cook. With a properly built digester this gas pressure is no detriment, provided the temperature is watched and carried to the proper point. It is the custom in most mills, however, to blow this gas off at intervals, which are more frequent in the last stages of the process. There is an impression in some quarters that if this is not done the gas will burn the pulp; but this is quite erroneous, since it is the high temperature and the absence of sufficient gas which causes burning. If so much gas pressure is observed that blowing off becomes necessary, it merely proves that the liquor was too strong at the start, and that the manufacturer has gone to the expense of putting an unnecessary amount of gas into the liquor, only, in most cases, to waste it in the boiling operation.

There is also great danger, if too much gas is blown off, that the pulp will be burned; in fact, wherever burned pulp is obtained when the temperature has not been allowed to rise above 320° F., it may be inferred that the liquor was originally too weak or that too much gas was blown off.

Unless, however, dry and hot steam is used, so much condensed water may form in the boiler, that blowing off is necessary in order to keep down the volume of liquor and prevent a hydrostatic pressure.

We have already pointed out the great insolubility of the monosulphite of lime, as well as the fact that it is easily held in solution when the extra equivalent of gas necessary to form the bisulphite is present. Bisulphite of lime is a very unstable salt from which the extra equivalent of sulphurous acid may be easily driven off by heat, with formation of the monosulphite. As sulphite liquors rarely contain more than a very small percentage of sulphurous acid above the amount needed to form the bisulphite, it is evident that when, during boiling, any of this gas is blown off, an equivalent amount of monosulphite of lime is deposited in the digester, where it either causes trouble through rendering the pulp very difficult to wash, or, quite commonly, by the formation of a hard incrustation around or in the steam and blow-off pipes. We have seen the inside diameter of a 3-inch steampipe reduced by such incrustation to less than $\frac{1}{2}$-inch, while elsewhere in the lower portion of the digester, the scale was $\frac{3}{4}$-inch thick.

In order to lessen these difficulties, Kellner heats the bisulphite solution in a separate vessel, from which it is run hot into the digester. Much of the monosulphite is thus precipitated outside the boiler, and may be redissolved for further use by the sulphurous acid blown off during treatment of the wood. British patent No. 12,970, A.D. 1891.

Strainers have been used in various digesters and for different purposes. In some cases a strainer bottom of iron covered with lead is placed on a slant within a foot or two of the bottom of the digester. In this case the digester discharges through a pipe at the side near the bottom, and steam is admitted under the false bottom. The strainer here serves to spread the steam, and is by some thought to secure a better circulation of the liquor, but its value in this position is very doubtful. In some digesters abroad a strainer was formerly placed inside the digester, and about one-quarter the way down, and the digester was only filled with chips up to the strainer, which carried a central piece which was removed during filling. The object of the strainer in this position was to prevent the chips from rising to the surface of the liquor, where they might carbonize and form black chips which seriously impaired the value of the pulp. The output of the digester was, however, greatly curtailed, and the black chips are now avoided quite as certainly by taking proper care to have sufficient liquor in the digester. Some form of strainer is always necessary in the top of the digester to prevent the pulp from being carried into the blow-off pipe. Sometimes a hemisphere of hard lead is burned to the manhole plate around the entrance to the blow-off, while often instead of this a larger hemisphere rests on a ledge in the neck of the digester. In either case the metal of the strainer is punched with numerous $\frac{1}{4}$-inch holes.

Much stress was formerly laid upon the importance of thorough circulation of the liquor during boiling, and various devices have been employed to secure this circulation, among them may be mentioned the injector placed in a pipe leading from the bottom of the digester under a perforated false bottom, and discharging through the manhole plate at the top. When the injector is working properly, the liquor is drawn from the bottom of the digester, carried round through the pipe, and discharged on top of the pulp. We have worked digesters fitted with this appliance for several months without perceiving the slightest benefit from its use, and are satisfied that no advantage offsetting the additional expense is to be derived from any of the methods for securing circulation, such as outside pumps or vomiting pipes in the interior of the digester. No such devices are now, in fact, used in this process.

Although it is, of course, desirable to discharge the digester as soon as possible after the reduction of the wood has been completed, there is no danger of injuring the pulp through keeping it too long in the digester, provided always that the liquor is of proper strength, and that it has not been unduly weakened by blowing off. We have in several cases, where, owing to a breakdown in another portion of the mill, it was inconvenient to blow a digester off at once, kept the digester under pressure for twenty-four hours or more after the cooking was completed, and in no case has the pulp been injured in the least, either as regards strength or color.

With a working pressure of 75 lbs. and liquor carrying 3.50 per cent. of sulphurous acid, the best results are obtained when four or five hours are taken in reaching full pressure, and sixteen hours for the entire cook. There is considerable difference of opinion regarding the relative merits of the systems using high pressure for a short time, and those working at lower pressures for a longer time. In our opinion the disintegration of the wood is more complete, and the pulp softer and of purer quality, when the boiling is conducted at high temperatures, provided that the liquor is sufficiently strong to prevent burning. The use of strong liquor involves, however, more gas pressure, so that unless the boiling is carried on by the thermometer the temperatures reached may run lower than if a weaker liquor is employed; and the pulp will consequently be harsh and imperfectly cooked, and will require, if subsequently bleached, a large proportion of bleaching powder.

It would seem, on theoretical grounds, more desirable to heat the digester either by a steam jacket, or by coils of pipe, than with live steam, since in the latter case the liquor necessarily becomes much diluted. This condensed water introduces an uncertain factor in the working of the process, since its amount will necessarily vary from day to day with the temperature and dryness of the steam, and the temperature of the air outside. With proper care, however, and especially if a non-conducting jacket is employed, these objections are not serious, and the greater convenience of the live steam has caused its general adoption. A good jacket of this description is made by plastering the digester over with clay mixed with cocoanut fibre.

The amount of condensed water formed in a lead-lined digester of moderate size, or about $6\frac{1}{2}$ feet in diameter, during a single boiling is much larger than it would be at first sight supposed. Under ordinary conditions, in summer, we have found this amount to be as large as 1000 gallons, and during the cold winter of the Northwest we have frequently known the amount to be so great as completely to fill the digester. In such cases it is, of course, impossible to heat the liquor by any further addition of steam, and the cook can only be completed by allowing the pressure to fall until most of the dilute liquor can be run off, and then making a fresh start with new liquor. The advantage of the thermometer is very apparent in a case like this, as when the digester is filled with water the pressure remains at the proper point, and the true condition of affairs is only shown by the steady dropping of the temperature. In the case mentioned above the mill was practically heated by radiation from the digesters, and the trouble was overcome by boxing them in so that they were shut off from the rest of the mill. If the liquor has been unduly weakened by the condensed water, although not necessarily to the point indicated above, the fact may usually be ascertained by the raw and chippy condition of the pulp.

The introduction of cement linings has practically eliminated the difficulties due to condensed water and loss of heat through the digester wall. Considerable condensed water is, of course, still formed, and there is still some loss of heat by radiation, but both factors are by these linings greatly reduced in value, and, which is of far more importance, they are made to have a nearly uniform value for each cook.

It is desirable to have the connections between the generating boilers and the digesters as short as possible, to avoid loss from condensation of steam and reduction of the steam pressure. Where a number of digesters are fed from the same steam-pipe, its area should be several times greater than that of all the pipes leading from it, or else, as our tests in practice have shown, the digesters at the farther end of the pipe will receive steam under considerably lower pressure than those nearer the boilers. All steam-pipes should be well trapped, and steam as dry as possible should be used for cooking, in order to keep down condensed water.

The steam-pipe leading into the digester is often led up to the top of the digester, and then back and into the bottom, to form a trap, and is fitted with two check-valves, — one placed on the horizontal arm of the steam-pipe, near the digester, and the other on the vertical arm of the trap. The object of these precautions is to prevent any of the liquor from being forced from the digester into the generating boilers, as may easily happen if the gas pressure is considerable in the digester, when, for any cause, the steam pressure has been allowed to fall in the boilers. Considerable danger to the boilers may be apprehended, if the liquor finds its way into them, as the acid rapidly attacks the iron, while the sulphite of lime is likely to form scale.

Boiling by the Mitscherlich Process. — After the digester has been packed with chips or blocks, which are levelled off, so that none shall be uncovered by the liquor, wet steam is admitted into the boiler, and the steaming continued from eight to twelve hours. Care is taken to avoid any pressure in the boiler, as, if the temperature is allowed to rise above 102°, the wood is in danger of burning. The water, condensing, flows away as brown liquor

The object of the steaming, and subsequent admission of cold liquor, is to bring the liquor, at the start, well into the pores of the wood, so as to prevent floating and burning.

The liquor used stands from 5°–7° Bé, and after the steaming is finished, this is drawn into the digester by the partial vacuum which forms as the digester cools, and more rapidly as the cold liquor is injected. The flow of liquor is continued until it comes to within about 15 inches of the top of the digester. Steam is then admitted into the lead coils, and the temperature of the digester contents is brought to 110° C. in as short a time as may be, although, on account of the large size of the digester, this may require twelve hours or more. This temperature is maintained for about twelve hours, and is then gradually increased to 117°–120° C. The pressure on the digester should, according to Mitscherlich, be at no time allowed to exceed 45 lbs. The quantity of gas blown off, and the length of the boiling operation, is governed by tests made upon samples of liquor taken from the digester. For these tests, tubes are used which are 200 mm long, closed at one end, and graduated into $\frac{1}{8}$, $\frac{1}{16}$, $\frac{1}{24}$, and $\frac{1}{32}$ of their length. A mixture of strong ammonia and water in equal parts is poured into the tube up to the $\frac{1}{32}$ mark, and the balance of the tube is filled with liquor, and the tube well shaken.

All the bisulphite of lime present is thus converted into monosulphite, and precipitated; and from the volume and character of precipitate, conclusions as to the progress of the operation are drawn. The higher the precipitate stands in the tube, the more bisulphite there is in the liquor. The liquor grows darker as the cooking is prolonged, and the precipitate, which is at first light and fine, becomes coarse, and settles rapidly. When after a few moments' standing, the precipitate fills only $\frac{1}{16}$ the length of the tube, gas is blown off from the digester in moderate quantity, and at $\frac{1}{24}$ the amount blown off is increased sufficiently to bring a temperature down to 110°. The completion of the cook is indicated when the precipitate sinks to $\frac{1}{32}$.

The course of a Mitscherlich cook and the very long time required to carry it through are well brought out in the following tables from Schubert.[1] It will be noticed that the total time of boiling is reckoned from the commencement of what is taken as the first stage of the pulping operation, i.e. from the time of reach-

[1] Die Cellulosefabrikation

ing 108°. For any comparison with a quick cook the time taken to reach this temperature should, of course, be added to the so-called total time as given.

BOILING NO. 207.— IN A HORIZONTAL DIGESTER.

		Pressure in atmospheres	Temperature, °C
April 23	11 30 A.M.	0 00	45
	8 P.M	0.60	72
April 24.	1 A M	0 75	85
	6	1 00	96
	11.30	1 50	105
	2 30 P.M	1.75	108
	6 30	2 00	112
April 25	1 A M.	2 50	115
	6	2.80	116.5
	9	3 00	119
	12 M	2 80	120
	3 P M	2 25	119
	10	2 10	118

Remarks

Filled April 22, from 1 30 to 11 P M., 88 cubic metres wood in disks, 9 cubic metres wood in chips

Steamed from midnight to 8 A M April 23

Acid of 5° Bé. run in from 8 to 11 30 A M

After 27 hours temperature reached 108°
After 48 5 hours temperature reached 116° } 21 5 hours
After 58 5 hours boiling finished at 118° } 10 hours
Total time of boiling .   31 5 hours

Highest pressure, 3 atmospheres. Highest temperature, 120° Cellulose, very fair.

BOILING No 20 — IN A HORIZONTAL DIGESTER

		Pressure in atmospheres	Temperature, °C
June 2	6 A.M	0 0	40
	11	0 5	73
	4 P M.	1 0	97
	12	2 0	108
June 3	5 A M	2 7	116
	7	3 0	118
	12 M	3 0	118
	10 P M	3 0	118
June 4	8 A M	3 0	118
	1 P M	3 0	118

Remarks

Filled June 1, 1 P.M. to 3.30 A.M., with 60 cubic metres of wood.
Steamed from 3.30 A.M to 3.30 P.M June 2.
Liquor of 5.5° Bé. pumped in from 4.30 P.M to 6 A.M.

After 18 hours reached 108° } 7 hours
After 25 hours reached 118° }
After 55 hours finished at 118° } 30 hours

Total time of boiling . . 37 hours.

Cellulose, good.

BOILING No. 101 — IN AN UPRIGHT DIGESTER

			Pressure in atmospheres At top	At bottom	Temperature, °C At top	At bottom
Aug. 2.	4.30	P.M.	0 0	0 0	30	40
Aug. 3.	9	A.M.	0 3	0 3	87	87
	11		0 4	0 3	89	89
	1	P M	1 0	0 4	96	95
	3		1 2	1 0	102	99
	6		1 3	1 2	106	103
Aug. 4.	6	A.M.	2 4	2.3	120	115
	8		2 4	2 3	122	116
	10		3 0	2 4	122	117
	12	M	3 0	2 4	122	117
	2	P M	3 0	2 4	122	117
	4		3 0	3 0	122	117
	6		3 0	3 0	122	117
Aug. 5.	6	A M	3 0	3 0	122	117
	7.30		3 0	3 0	122	117

Remarks.

Filled Aug. 1, P.M , with wood of mixed sizes.
Steamed Aug 2, from 1 A.M. to 1 P M
Liquor of $5\frac{1}{2}°$ Bé. pumped in from 2.15 to 4.15 P.M.

After 28 hours reached 108° }
After 30 hours reached 114° } 9 hours
After 37 hours reached 118° }
After 63 hours finished at 118° } 26 hours

Total time of boiling . 35 hours

Emptied on morning of Aug 6
Cellulose, fine.

This boiler was 4 metres diameter, and 9 metres high, and contained 60 cubic metres of wood in disks.

It was formerly considered established as a fundamental law in this process, that the pressure in the digester should never exceed 45 lbs., and if a temperature of 114° was reached, gas was at once blown off. Now, however, the boiling operation is shortened as much as possible, and by bringing the pressure from 3.4 to 3.5 atmospheres, and the temperature to 120° C., no evil results are experienced, and the time is cut from seventy-five to eighty-five hours down to fifty-eight hours or less; of which only thirty-two are properly consumed by the boiling. It is usual in Germany to hold the pressure up to the very end, and in this country it is often slowly and regularly raised during the last hours.

The body of pulp contained in one of these digesters is so great that there is danger of burning as soon as the liquor has been run off, and it is therefore customary to let in cold water and wash the pulp two or three times in the digester. Even then the pulp is still so hot that all manholes are opened, and holes punched up through the stuff to create a draft of air. The pulp is finally *shovelled* out of the digester.

The actual time consumed by one cook from the time of filling to that of blowing off is, as shown by the tables previously given:—

    No. 20 . 80½ hours
        101 . 87 "
        207 . 72 "

In addition to this the time required for discharging the liquor, cooling, washing, emptying, and for repairs, is at least from eighteen to twenty-four hours, making a grand total of ninety to one hundred hours, and allowing only seven or eight cooks per month at best.

It is customary after each boiling by the Mitscherlich process to inspect the digester for the location of any leaks or weak places in the cement. Such affected portions may, in most cases, be quickly repaired by cutting out the cement and repointing. A considerable incrustation of sulphite of lime forms on the lead coils during each cook, and is usually removed by rapping with a mallet. This is likely to dent the pipes, and a better way is to use a scraper. Any leaks in the coils cause trouble through deposition of sulphite within the pipe. A stream of weak hydrochloric acid sent through the coil will remove this, unless the deposit at any point is sufficient to close the coils.

The standard Mitscherlich digesters with 40 × 14 shell carry from 22 to 25 cords of wood at a charge, and yield from 10 to 14 tons of fibre at a boiling. So much time is lost, however, in washing, emptying, and charging up, that these digesters rarely show in continuous working a better average output than 3000 lbs. per twenty-four hours.

Leaving breakdowns out of account, there is hardly an excuse when good pulp has once been made by any process, and the conditions governing that boiling are fully known, for failure to produce pulp of similar quality, since the same conditions must invariably produce the same results. The trouble usually arises from imperfect knowledge of the conditions, and every care should be taken to learn and govern them as accurately as possible. A few of the first importance may be pointed out. It is absolutely necessary, in order to obtain pulp of uniform quality, to use with the same kind of wood liquor of good and always uniform quality. There should be no variation in the time taken for reaching pressure, or in that during which the pressure is maintained; the condensed water and consequent dilution of the liquor should be kept at a definite and regular amount by preventing radiation as much as possible, and by using steam of uniform pressure. The amount of gas blown off, if any, must also be controlled, and should not vary from day to day. Failure to make good pulp usually results from disregard of these conditions, which can all be readily controlled. There are certain others which necessarily introduce some uncertainty in the process; one of these is the variation in the condition and moisture of the wood used.

Recovery of Gas. — At the time of the present writing, 1893, no attempt is made in any mill in this country other than those working the Mitscherlich process, to recover the large proportion of sulphurous acid which is blown off previous to the dumping of the digester, although the gas may be utilized by a very simple apparatus, which is regularly in use abroad. The best form of apparatus for this purpose consists of a tower filled with flints or broken brick. The gas and steam from the blow-off are admitted to the tower under the false bottom, while a shower of water is kept up at the top of the tower. This water, as it passes down the tower, absorbs the gas and is somewhat heated by the steam; as it progresses, more gas is absorbed until the water becomes saturated, while through condensation of the steam the temperature of the water is soon raised to a point where it can no longer hold the gas in solution. This liberated gas, passing upward with that still coming from the digester, soon increases in quantity to such an extent that the water falling down is not sufficient to dissolve it, and there is constantly delivered from the top of the tower a stream of pure gas, while from the bottom of the tower hot water is drawn, to be used in washing or for other purposes. The amount of sulphur thus saved is usually not less than 20 per cent.

In the Mitscherlich process the waste gases are blown through a pipe leading from one of the upper manhole plates to a lead coil immersed in water. All the digesters are connected with this coil, which in turn is connected to one of the towers. The steam carried over by the gas is condensed and the pure gas passes on into the tower. Such recovered gas, being undiluted with atmospheric nitrogen, is better suited for the preparation of strong liquors than the original furnace gas. It may be made to yield a liquor standing 12° Bé.

Dr. Kellner has also used the coil and tower for recovering the gas blown off during the cook. For recovering that discharged

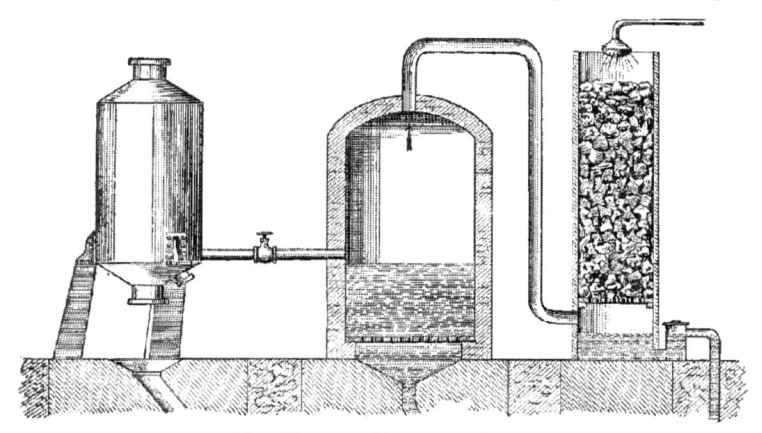

FIG. 60. — KELLNER RECOVERY APPARATUS.

with the liquor after the cook is finished, he has employed the apparatus shown in a diagrammatic way in Fig. 60.

At Northfleet, England, the simple plan is adopted of blowing off the gas into a six-inch pipe laid on the ground, and leading to the tower. The pipe has a pitch toward the mill, and the condensed water flows back, while the gas goes forward.

Various means are adopted in the different mills to get the pulp out of the digester. That which now finds most favor is to blow it out under a pressure of about 30 lbs. The digester is thus emptied perfectly clean in a few seconds, and the pulp is so well disintegrated that no subsequent treatment in the beating engine is necessary to fit it for the market. It is urged against this method, that there is danger of breaking up the knots and uncooked chips, thus causing shive and dirt, while at the same time unnecessarily straining the digester. The danger to the digester is practically nothing, and there is certainly less danger of breaking up the knots in this way than by running the pulp for several hours under the roll of the beating engine. Where the pulp is simply allowed to run out of the digester, considerable time is lost, and a large amount of water must be pumped into the digester before the pulp is all out. This water is in most cases cold, and the sudden admission of it in so large a volume strains the lead severely. The practice of washing the pulp in the digester before discharging must be condemned, as the whole product of the mill is curtailed, while an expensive piece of apparatus is employed in doing work which can be much more efficiently done in apparatus costing only a fraction as much.

The Mitscherlich stamping mill, as used in foreign mills, is shown in

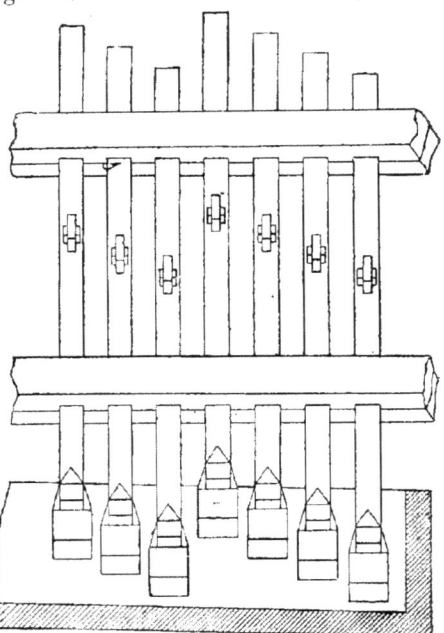

FIG. 61.—MITSCHERLICH STAMP MILL.

side view and sections in Figs. 61 and 62; on about seven of the frames A is laid or carried the shaft B, bearing numerous cams, the shaft turns about ten times in a minute; there are two stout beams, D D' and C C', which hold the frames together, and also serve as guides for about 60 stamps, which reach nearly to the bottom of the stamping trough E; the trough is 15 metres long, and rises about 0.6 metres in this distance; the stamps are lifted by teeth, which engage the cams; the teeth of the three or four adjacent stamps are arranged as in Fig. 61, so that these stamps, instead of falling together, follow each other. This action, and the flow of water through the trough, passes the stuff along; the action of the mill is largely a rubbing one, on account of the different motion of the adjacent stamps: in some mills the wood is broken up by a heavier stamping machine before boiling. This saves subsequent stamping, and makes somewhat shorter cooks possible. The stuff is also worked under edged runners, and these are commonly employed to reduce knots and chips to a pulp suitable for coarse papers. The unreduced remainder is roughly screened from the fibre by rotating drums similar to rag dusters.

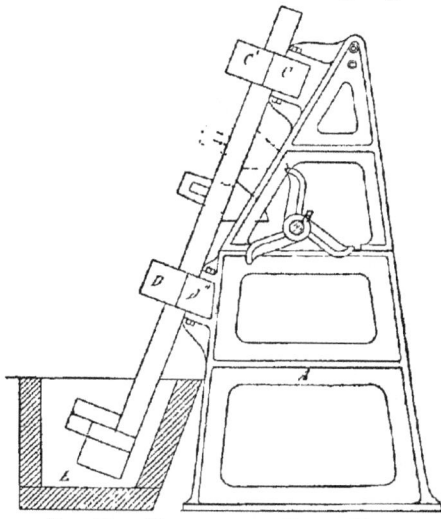

FIG. 62 — MITSCHERLICH STAMP MILL

If the digester has been blown off into a drainer, the most convenient method of washing the pulp is to flood it two or three times with water. It should be observed, however, that the pulp forms in itself a most efficient filter, so that, in case the wash water carries any considerable amount of suspended organic matter, this will be fixed upon the pulp, and more will be lost than gained by prolonging the washing. In some mills the washed pulp is transferred, with little labor, from the drainer to the chest, in readiness for the wet machine, by directing a powerful stream of water against the mass of pulp in the drainer, and washing it out in a sluiceway, from which a pump throws it over into the chest. In other mills the drainers themselves consist merely of large chests with a wooden chimney for the escape of gas, and an agitator. In this case no attempt is made to wash the pulp in the drainer, but it is pumped direct into the washing-machine. The drainers should always be protected before blowing off, by a foot or two of water let into the bottom, to break the force of the pulp as it strikes the drainer bottom

The washing-machine just referred to, although not in common use, is very efficient, and consists merely of a trough provided with three or four washing cylinders, with a corresponding number of back-falls. The first cylinder removes a large proportion of the water from the pulp, and, as the pulp is thrown over the back-fall, it meets a copious stream of fresh water from a pipe behind the washer; and the same operation is repeated as many times as there are washers while the pump passes along the trough

Washing in the engine is conducted after the ordinary method, which is too well known to require comment further than to point out the great danger of breaking up chips and forming shive, unless the engine roll is well raised

Thorough washing, although always desirable, must be insisted upon wherever the pulp is to be bleached; for monosulphite of lime requires a large amount of water for its complete removal, and, if present in the pulp, may greatly increase the consumption of bleaching powder, as it is one of the most efficient antichlors in use. When present in excessive quantity, it may be best removed, and the pulp considerably benefited, by washing with dilute hydrochloric acid

The further handling of the unbleached pulp belongs to the practical paper-maker rather than to the chemist

The bleaching of this pulp and of the other paper-making fibres will be considered in a separate chapter; but we may here point out that it is desirable, before bleaching sulphite pulp, to remove all large shives by thorough screening, as, in the bleaching process, these shives are broken up into smaller ones, which it is very difficult to remove, and which injure the appearance of the paper, though they may readily escape notice in the wet pulp

Well cooked and bleached sulphite pulp should be soft, strong, and of pure color; the frequent failures to meet these requirements are due either to imperfect cooking, which leaves the pulp harsh and hard, or to defects in the method of bleaching, which, especially when hot bleach is used, may lower the color and injure the strength, by chlorination and oxidation of the fibre.

The conditions which affect unfavorably the quality of the finished pulp have been already pointed out in some instances, but may be conveniently considered together. Poor color may be due to imperfect cooking, which has failed to remove the necessary amount of incrusting matter, or it may be caused by unduly weakening the liquor by blowing off too much gas. If the proper cooking temperatures are maintained the color of the pulp improves as more gas is present in the liquor. Raw pulp is, of course, due either to insufficient time or too low a temperature, and the latter may be caused by working with too strong a liquor, in which case the large amount of gas pressure makes it difficult to bring up the temperature to the proper point, or, if very wet steam is used, or if the digesters radiate an undue amount of heat, the quantity of condensed water formed in the quick cooking digesters may be sufficient to fill the digester and prevent the admission of the necessary steam. Black chips similar to charcoal are found in the pulp when any of the wood has remained uncovered by the liquor, and a simple remedy for them is found in more liquor or less wood. If the whole body of the pulp is burned, it means that the liquor was too weak for the temperatures carried. If too much gas is blown off the liquor may be weakened during the boiling to an extent which permits the pulp to burn, and burning is especially likely to occur if the liquor is drained off and the cooked pulp allowed to remain in the hot digester for more than a few moments before water is run in. After the pulp has been cooked, it may be kept in the digester under pressure for almost any length of time, if the liquor contains a good supply of gas. Chips which are well cooked upon the outside, but which have a hard, red or brown centre, are formed when the temperature has been raised so rapidly that the liquor did not have time to penetrate into and protect the interior of the wood before the temperature was high enough to burn such unprotected portions. Any great precipitation of monosulphite of lime in the pulp, where it makes trouble by causing specks, is due either to the use of a liquor containing little or no free sulphurous acid above that needed to form bisulphite, or else to the formation of such a liquor in the digester, by blowing off too much gas. The objectionable red coloration which some sulphite pulp takes on after washing is the result, so nearly as we can determine, of the oxidation of portions of incrusting matter, which have not been removed during cooking, and can generally be avoided when the cooking is made more thorough. Strangely enough, however, the pulp from poplar wood, which is very easily reduced by the sulphite process, frequently develops this color in a way much more marked than spruce. The color is a purer one, and often approaches a delicate pink. Dirt and specks, of course, find their way into the pulp from various sources. Fragments of bark which have not been removed in the preparation of the wood, fragments of knots which have been broken up by the boring machine or in the treatment of the pulp subsequent to boiling, and shives formed by the breaking up of uncooked or partially burned chips, are the most common causes of dirt, but lumps of monosulphide left by imperfect washing, iron scale from water pipes, sulphide of copper from pipes and fittings, coal, black sand, and fragments of brick, all frequently find their way into the product.

The unbleached sulphite fibre, owing to the numerous systems employed for its production, shows even wider variation in quality than the bleached fibre. As found in the market, it may be either a harsh and somewhat transparent very strong fibre, or one nearly as soft and white as the bleached pulp. Spruce is the wood most preferred in this country for making this pulp: abroad, the Swedish fir and pine are both used, as well as spruce, and several of our common woods readily yield a strong fibre. We give below a very complete analysis, made by ourselves, of a sample of sulphite fibre made from spruce by the Mitscherlich process.

ANALYSIS OF UNBLEACHED SULPHITE PULP

(*Mitscherlich Process*)

	Per cent
Moisture, loss at 100° C.	9.000
Extractive organic matter, soluble in very dilute hydrochloric acid	0.516
Extractive organic matter, soluble in very dilute alkali	1.505
Resin	0.060
Cellulose	80.800
Mineral matter:	
a Removable by very dilute acid	0.758
b Not removable by very dilute acid	0.742
Lignin, by difference	6.619
	100.000

Mineral matter
   a contains —   Per cent

	Per cent
Silica (SiO_2)	0.009
Iron sesquioxide (Fe_2O_3)	0.031
Sulphate of lime ($CaSO_4$)	0.333
Sulphite of lime ($CaSO_3$)	0.004
Carbonate of lime ($CaCO_3$)	0.261
Carbonate of magnesia ($MgCO_3$)	0.025
Carbonate of soda (Na_2CO_3)	0.095
	0.758

  b Ash of washed pulp contains —   Per cent

	Per cent
Silicate of soda (Na_2SiO_3)	0.042
Iron sesquioxide (Fe_2O_3)	0.010
Sulphate of lime ($CaSO_4$)	0.158
Carbonate of lime ($CaCO_3$)	0.050
Carbonate of magnesia ($MgCO_3$)	0.029
Carbonate of soda (Na_2CO_3)	0.453
	0.742

Total mineral matter in sample	1.500
Oxygen and carbonic acid lost on burning (calculated)	0.398
Calculated ash to be obtained from sample	1.102
Actual ash obtained by burning	1.084

Our analyses in the following table, although much less complete than the one given above, will serve to point out the variations in quality likely to be found in unbleached sulphite fibre. They are all of pulp made from spruce wood.

ANALYSES OF UNBLEACHED SPRUCE SULPHITE FIBRE

(Quick Cooking Process)

Moisture, loss at 100° C	6.15	6.70	6.57	6.45
Mineral matter (ash)	1.00	0.45	0.33	0.65
Hydrocellulose, etc (soluble in alkali)	2.53	2.26	4.25	1.52
Cellulose	85.32	89.74	88.12	81.51
Non-cellulose ("lignin") by difference	5.01	0.85	0.73	9.87

In studying these analyses, it will be noticed that the proportions of cellulose and of the incrusting matter remaining with it vary greatly in the different samples. This is a point of much practical importance, especially when the pulp is to be bleached, since all this incrusting matter must be destroyed by the bleaching powder. If the incrusting matter is present in large amount, the consumption of bleach becomes excessive, and the pulp shows great shrinkage.

We have made in our laboratory a large number of determinations showing the yield and character of pulp obtained by the sulphite process from different wood. In these experiments we have used a digester (Fig. 63) built of bronze, lead-lined, and holding about 12 litres. A drop tube, passing from the top nearly to the bottom of the digester, was utilized as an oil bath for carrying the thermometer, while pressures were shown upon an ordinary gauge.

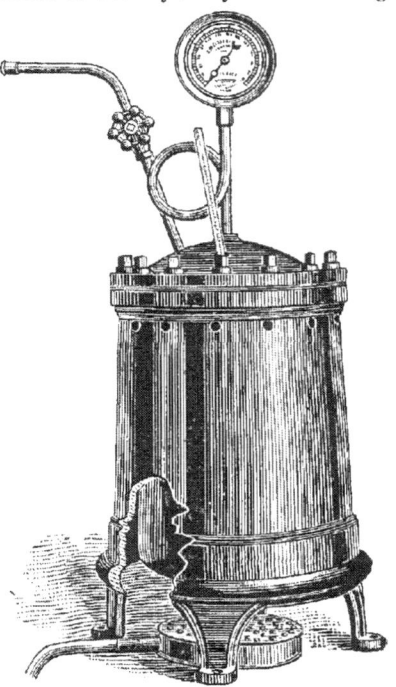

FIG. 63. — EXPERIMENTAL DIGESTER.

The accompanying table gives the results of these experiments. The figures give the per cent. of fibre obtained from the dry wood.

Spruce	50.75
Poplar	55.18
Cottonwood	50.80
Gum	45.73
Beech	42.80
Birch	53.80
Maple	52.61

Fungoid Growth on Fibre. — The black specks having the appearance of mildew, and which sometimes appear on unbleached fibre which is stored for a considerable length of time when in moist condition, have been carefully studied by Herzberg, whose examination proves them to be due to a fungoid growth upon the fibre. The sample of pulp examined was prepared by the Ritter-Kellner process, and was disfigured by numerous black spots, varying in size from that of a pin head to that of a pea.

The appearance was quite different from that occurring in straw cellulose which has been stored in damp places. Microscopical examinations demonstrated the existence of a fungoid growth, twining around the cellulose fibres as ivy does around a tree. The brown color of its mycelium caused the patches of it to be visible to the naked eye as dark specks. It was thought that the germs had been derived from the river water used in the manufacture, spring water not being available, but it is more likely that they came from the air, finding a good soil on the moist cellulose.

Calcium sulphite was recognized on the spots by Frank's method with iodine solution, and if this be viewed as the cause of the growth, the obvious remedy is to avoid its presence in the finished product; on the other hand, the acid juices of the growth itself will tend to liberate sulphurous acid from the calcium sulphite, and arrest its development. Thorough drying is an efficient preventative, and where this is impracticable the use of a very weak solution of zinc chloride is said to act as a reliable antiseptic in killing the germs.

It was observed that a paper made from pure rags and highly sized with rosin developed a fungoid growth when kept in a warm, damp place. There is no direct evidence to show whether the germs are derived from the water or air. Adequate nutriment for the mould is supplied by size of animal origin, and even when rosin is used the accompanying starch may prove sufficient.

The Waste Liquor. — The waste liquors from a well-conducted sulphite boiling are of a light golden-brown color, and contain, in solution, or in combination with the bisulphite, about 50 per cent. of the weight of the dry wood. If lime is added to such liquors, a considerable portion of this organic matter is thrown down, and monosulphite of lime produced. The addition of a soluble alkali like soda determines the precipitation of the organic matter in brown flocks. On account of the action of the sulphurous acid in preventing oxidation, the organic matter in the solution has not undergone great chemical change, but exists in somewhat the same condition, as far as its chemical relations are concerned, as in the incrusting matter of the wood, and it is probable that, with the further development of the sulphite process, methods will be worked out by which this large amount of waste material may be utilized. The most obvious direction for such methods to take will be toward the preparation of glucose, alcohol, and oxalic and pyroligneous acids, since well-known processes are now in operation for making these compounds from similar materials.

The waste sulphite liquors have been found to contain, besides calcium sulphite and sulphate, mannose, galactose, and vanillin, and to yield, upon distillation with sulphuric or hydrochloric acid, furfurol or furfuramide, proving that pentaglucoses are present. Of these xylose [1] has been found.

According to Cross and Bevan, the double compounds of the aldehydes and bisulphites in the waste liquor are not broken up by dialysis, and are precipitated unchanged by alcohol, or alcohol and ether.

Mitscherlich has shown that there exists in the solution a compound apparently similar to tannin, at least so far as its power to precipitate glue goes, and he has based upon this fact a method involving the use of spent sulphite liquors in sizing paper. In Germany the farmers in the neighborhood of the sulphite mills find that the waste liquors are of considerable value in preventing the escape of ammonia when sprinkled upon compost heaps.

Dr. W. Buddeus, in the *Papier-Zeitung* of March 19, 1891, has an interesting summary of the results obtained by an investigation of the composition of the waste liquor and the substances derived therefrom. We give his results somewhat in detail: —

The waste liquor was neutralized with ammonia, the lime was precipitated by ammonium carbonate, and the carbonate of lime thus formed was separated by filtration. The dark brown filtrate was evaporated, and the dried residue distilled. The residue contained 7.2 per cent. ammonia as salts. Water and a yellow-colored oil were obtained in the condenser, and finally a crystalline sublimate appeared on the walls of the tube. The gases escaping were caught in the gasometer. The oil, at first, had an odor like mercaptan, but this disappeared on heating slightly. This odor was, without doubt, due to organic sulphur compounds which were present in traces. The oil and water were, after this heating,

[1] Xylose, the sugar of wood, melts at 144° C., and is dextro-rotary. Upon boiling with dilute sulphuric acid, it yields wood gum.

distilled with steam. The distillate was shaken out with ether, then dried, and the ether evaporated over calcium chloride. A brown oil remained, which boiled at 130° C., and which colored a fine chip, moistened with hydrochloric acid, a strong carmine, and which was therefore believed to be pyrrol. Pyrocatechin was also obtained in the distillate, as was proved by color-tests with iron salts, and its reduction of Fehling's solution.

The gases were carbon moxide, hydrogen, marsh gas, and sulphureted hydrogen. 400 grammes of the residue yielded 180 grammes of coke, 30 litres of gas, and 200 grammes of distillate.

Mucic and saccharic acid could not have been present as such in the liquor, because they are formed by the oxidation of carbohydrates, and the action of the liquor is a reducing one. Pyrrol is formed by the distillation of ammonium salts of these two acids. The only way of accounting for pyrrol is the presence of succinic acid, which is very probably present owing to the occurrence of resins in the wood. Ammonium succinate changes readily by splitting off of water into ammonia succinamide, which by heating with reducing agents gives pyrrol.

The presence of pyrocatechin is due to that of dioxybenzoic acid (1, 3, 4), which is in the liquor as dipyrocatechuic acid. The decomposition of this by distillation with ammonia is a source of tannic acid and pyrocatechin. There is, according to Dr Buddeus, no tannic acid present in the liquor, which will give a blue-black color with ferric chloride, because the tannin in wood is reduced by cooking with sulphurous acid. The reduction is probably to dipyrocatechuic acid, but by treating with ammonia and distilling, tannic acid is eventually formed. Sulphites are oxidized to sulphates when the tannin is reduced. It may be, therefore, that the difficulty of pulping wood rich in tannin by the sulphite process is due to the action of the tannin, which renders the sulphurous acid ineffective.

According to Schubert, the greatest difficulty with which German manufacturers of sulphite pulp have to contend, is found in the disposal of the waste liquor and wash waters. The laws there are far more stringent than in this country in respect to the pollution of streams, and the number of water-courses of considerable size is also comparatively small. No practical method is known for eliminating the sulphurous acid and organic matter in the waste liquor.

The evaporation of the liquor offers no solution of the difficulty, and the product is of absolutely no value as fuel. The waste liquors are in Germany often run off in open liquor ponds, where they are allowed to soak in the ground. These ponds in time develop a very unpleasant odor and seriously contaminate the wells of the neighborhood. The impure wash waters, when allowed to run in small streams, set up conditions which seem peculiarly adapted to the growth of algæ.

According to the experiments of Dr. Weigelt-Reufach, liquors containing from 0.6 to 0.75 per cent of sulphurous acid require dilution with fifteen hundred times their volume of water in order to render them harmless to fish and other forms of animal life. The action of the sulphurous acid is, of course, to lower in the water the proportion of dissolved oxygen which the fish cannot breathe. The precipitated resins and gummy matters are themselves injurious, not so much on account of any poisonous quality, as of their action in coating over the gills and shutting off the supply of oxygen, as pointed out by Dr. Frank.

It is of course evident that nearly as much material from the wood is carried away in the waste liquors as is obtained as pulp, and the quantity of organic matter thus discharged by a large mill is therefore very great. The waste liquor from a Mitscherlich boiling contained per litre, —

Sulphurous acid	3.86 grammes,
Sulphuric acid	7.33 "
Chlorine	0.29 "

and by evaporation of one litre, and drying at 110° C., yielded 109 grammes of residue. which on ignition left 19 grammes of ash containing, —

Sesquioxide of iron	0.02 grammes.
Lime	10.30 "
Magnesia	0.30 "
Potash	0.28 "
Soda	0.10 "
	11.00 grammes.

There were, therefore, in the liquor 90 grammes of organic matter per litre, or 90 kilogrammes per cubic metre, or 5400 kilogrammes per charge of 60 cubic metres.

Traces of sulphurous acid gas are almost constantly present in the atmosphere within or immediately around a sulphite mill, and where apparatus or methods are defective the proportion of gas is likely to be so great as to become a source of much annoyance. Even small quantities of the gas produce, when inhaled considerable irritation of the mucous membrane of the throat and lungs. In consequence of this irritation the tendency to take cold is increased, and if the irritation persists, a chronic cough or bronchitis may be established. The effects of the gas upon plants and animals have been carefully studied by numerous observers, whose conclusions are by no means in harmony with each other. There seems to be no doubt, however, that even small proportions of the gas are injurious to both animals and plants, but we are inclined to think that much of the ill effect which has been charged to the gas alone has been caused by the practice, which was at one time common of blowing the digesters off into the open air, so that all the neighboring vegetation was covered with a film of condensed liquor in which free sulphuric acid was afterwards developed by oxidation. This practice is now happily done away with everywhere.

According to Schroeder both deciduous and evergreen trees absorb sulphurous acid through their leaves from air containing as little as one five-thousandth of the gas by volume. The leaves retain it mostly, but a small portion penetrates into the leaf stalks and bark, where it may be found either as sulphurous or sulphuric acid. Evergreen trees are less sensitive in this respect than others.

Stöckhart finds that a distance of 630 metres is sufficient to protect all vegetation if the vapors, even in large quantity, escape from a chimney 82 feet high.

Dr. Ogata has made a series of experiments on animals in Pettenkofer's laboratory. He finds that different animals differ greatly in their susceptibility to the action of the gas; frogs being most sensitive, then mice, rabbits, and guinea pigs, in the order named. As little as 0.04 per cent. affected all the animals mentioned. A mouse died after two hours' exposure to an atmosphere containing only 0.06 per cent.; a guinea pig after seven hours' exposure to an atmosphere containing 0.24 per cent. The poisonous effect seems to be due to the action of the sulphurous acid on the blood, which absorbs the gas and oxidizes it to sulphuric acid.

Hurt claims, however, that air containing even as much as 4 per cent. of the gas has no permanent ill effect on the health of human beings, but one-tenth of that amount occasions difficulty of breathing (Wagner).

CHAPTER IV.

BLEACHING.

None of the commercial processes for separating cellulose which have been thus far considered yield this material in a state of complete purity. It is always associated with a portion of the lignin or incrusting matter originally present in the raw fibre, and various coloring-matters may also be present. The lignin is more or less modified by the treatment to which the fibre has been subjected, and the coloring-matters may be either those which have survived this treatment, or those which have been developed as a consequence of it. The coloring-matter properly so-called usually forms only a small proportion of the foreign material, so that most of the work of the bleaching agent is spent in the destruction of lignin and those derivatives of lignin which were formed and left upon the fibre in the processes of reduction. The process of bleaching, by which these impurities which cover up the natural white of the pure cellulose are removed, is essentially a process of oxidation, and depends for its success upon the fact that the substances associated with the cellulose are more easily oxidized and split up into soluble products by an oxidizing agent than the comparatively stable cellulose which forms the basis of the impure fibre. The destruction of these impurities may be brought about through the action of almost any of the well-known oxidizing agents, and many of them have been applied for this purpose with more or less success. Practically, however, all bleaching is effected by the use of chlorine, or compounds of chlorine, which in the presence of moisture, set up reactions by which oxygen is liberated. Of these compounds the hypochlorite of calcium, "chloride of lime," or ordinary bleaching-powder, is by far the most important.

The commonly accepted and probably the true theory of hypochlorite bleaching is, therefore, that the destruction of the coloring-matter is due primarily, not to the action of the chlorine, but to that of oxygen which is set free in the decomposition of water brought about by the chlorine, which unites with the hydrogen of the water to form hydrochloric acid. Bleaching, therefore, becomes a form of burning or wet combustion, in which the coloring-matters are oxidized by the liberated oxygen, the final products of the oxidation being carbonic acid and water; while the cellulose, being freed from the foreign matter with which it was at first associated, appears in its natural, uncolored condition. Dry chlorine has no bleaching action whatever, as may be shown by placing a piece of litmus paper, or a piece of cloth dyed a delicate tint, in a jar filled with the dry gas. If care has been taken to exclude all moisture, there will be no change in the color after several hours' exposure to the gas; but upon the addition of water the color is instantly discharged. Chlorine does not, as a rule, destroy mineral colors, or the blacks and grays produced by lampblack or deposited carbon.

Chlorine was first applied to bleaching by Berthollet in 1785, who employed a solution of the gas in water. Tennant in 1798 patented a liquid bleach, which was a solution of calcium or sodium hypochlorite, prepared by passing the gas into milk of lime or a solution of caustic soda. This bleaching agent was necessarily difficult to transport and keep, and in 1799 he introduced a great improvement by preparing a solid bleaching agent by passing the chlorine gas over slaked lime, which absorbed it with formation of hypochlorite of calcium.

Despite the obvious advantages offered by the use of bleaching-powder, its introduction was very slow, and there are doubtless many paper-makers in this country whose recollections go back to the time of gas bleaching. In working this method chlorine gas was generated at the mill by the action of sulphuric acid upon a mixture of peroxide of manganese and common salt in a stone or stoneware retort fitted with earthenware pipes, through which the gas was conducted to the moist pulp stored in the drainer. The inconvenience and disadvantages of this early method were so great that it has now been wholly discarded in favor of the more manageable bleaching-powder.

The method of preparation of ordinary bleaching-powder has been described in Part I., and the various methods for testing its value will be found in the chapter on **Chemical Analysis**. As ordinarily manufactured it is white powder having a somewhat pungent but not disagreeable odor of chlorine. If very strong, it usually contains some lumps. When exposed to the air it rapidly absorbs moisture, and is converted into a sticky mass, or even into a gray mud. The exact chemical composition of bleaching-powder has been a matter of some controversy, but the formula $CaOCl_2$ proposed by Lunge is now being generally accepted. The commercial value of the material depends upon the amount of chlorine present as hypochlorite, this chlorine being commonly called "available chlorine." In the freshly manufactured article the percentage of available chlorine may be as high as 41; but as found in our markets, and owing to the deterioration which always takes place in storage, the percentage of available chlorine is rarely above 37, and anything over 36 is usually accepted as satisfactory.

The strength of bleaching-powder is estimated in France in degrees, which represent the number of litres of chlorine gas at 0° C. and 760 mm. pressure which can be liberated from one kilo of the sample. The relation which these degrees bear to the percentage of effective chlorine is shown below:—

French degrees	Per cent. effective chlorine	French degrees	Per cent. effective chlorine
65	20.65	100	31.80
70	22.24	105	33.36
75	23.83	110	34.95
80	25.42	115	36.54
85	27.01	120	38.13
90	28.60	125	39.72
95	30.21	130	41.34

One litre of chlorine weighs 3.18 grammes, and the percentage may therefore be calculated by multiplying the French degrees by 0.318.

The deterioration of the strength of bleaching-powder is very rapid when the powder has been wet, as sometimes occurs on shipboard, and we have tested samples containing less than 28 per cent. of available chlorine. In rare cases the powder is liable to sudden decomposition, in which oxygen is liberated, and instances are on record in which casks of bleach have exploded from this cause.

The best series of experiments which have come under our notice having for their object the determination of the rate at which bleaching-powder deteriorates in storage are those of Pattinson, which extended over a year, and were concluded in 1886. He took 3 casks of the usual size, each containing about 6 cwt. of bleaching-powder; 12 bottles of each kind of powder were filled at the same time, the casks sealed, and both casks and bottles stored in a cellar. A maximum and minimum thermometer was placed near them, and a careful record of the temperature made for each working day of the year. The record shows the temperature to have been uniform and comparatively low during the entire year, the highest being 62° F., and the lowest 38° F. One bottle from each of the 3 sets of 12 was opened and tested each month, and a sample was also withdrawn and tested from each of the 3 casks. The results of the experiments show a gradual and regular loss of available chlorine during the time over which the tests were made. The average loss in the cask samples was about a third of 1 per cent. greater than in the bottle samples, as the casks were necessarily not air-tight. A complete analysis of each of the cask samples was made at the beginning and also at the end of the experiment. These analyses are given in the table below.—

COMPOSITION OF BLEACHING-POWDER

	January 29, 1885			January 5, 1886		
	A	B	C	A	B	C
Available chlorine	37.00	38.30	36.00	33.80	35.10	32.90
Chlorine as chloride	0.35	0.59	0.32	2.44	2.42	1.97
Chlorine as chlorate	0.25	0.08	0.26	0.00	0.00	0.00
Lime	44.49	43.34	44.66	43.57	42.64	43.65
Magnesia	0.40	0.34	0.43	0.31	0.36	0.38
Silicious matter	0.40	0.30	0.50	0.50	0.40	0.50
Carbonic acid	0.18	0.30	0.48	0.80	1.18	1.34
Alumina, peroxide iron, oxide manganese	0.48	0.45	0.35	0.40	0.40	0.37
Water and loss	16.15	16.33	17.00	18.18	17.20	18.89
	100.00	100.00	100.00	100.00	100.00	100.00
Total chlorine	37.60	38.97	36.58	36.24	37.52	34.87

The small quantity of chlorine found as chlorate at the beginning of the experiments ceased to exist in this combination at the end, and from tests made it was found that all the chlorate had disappeared in May, or about four months after the casks were filled. The amount of chlorine existing as chloride had slightly increased. It is not often the bleaching-powder can be stored where so low a temperature as 60° F. can be maintained for any length of time, especially in the summer months, when, as previous experiments have indicated, the greatest loss of available chlorine takes place.

Bleaching-powder should be stored in as dry a place as possible, or, better, in one that is both dry and cool; and if any casks are damaged, they should be the first ones selected for use, as deterioration is likely to proceed more rapidly in them than in sound casks.

The rate at which the powder deteriorates is largely influenced by the quality of the cask in which it is packed. The soft woods are considerably affected by the action of the powder, and shrink badly when exposed to the sun. In any subsequent exposure to rain, therefore, the water readily finds its way into the cask. Ash and other hard woods may be properly used for staves; but the best casks are built of oak staves one inch in thickness. The pores of oak are very close, and almost impervious to the air, and if, as was formerly the usual case, the staves had previously been used for raw sugar or molasses casks, they are still better fitted to preserve the bleach. Many makes of bleach arrive in casks with staves $\frac{7}{8}$-inch or $\frac{3}{4}$-inch in thickness, but thicker staves are to be recommended.

For the preparation of the hypochlorite solution, one-half the contents of the cask are dumped into about 1000 gallons of water in an agitator tank which is built of iron and well painted with red lead. Agitation of the mixture is continued until all lumps are broken up. The agitator is then stopped, and the greater portion of the mud allowed to settle, after which the cloudy liquid standing above is drawn out into shallow tanks to complete the deposition of sediment. The mud remaining in the agitator is again treated with a fresh quantity of water, and the weak liquor thus obtained is drawn off into another tank, and used in the first treatment of the next lot of bleaching-powder. The mud should be tested from time to time for available chlorine, as unless the washing is thoroughly performed a considerable loss may occur.

We are indebted to Hoffmann's Handbook for the following analysis of the mud from chloride of lime solutions. On account of the variation in the quality of bleaching-powder, however, this analysis cannot do more than indicate in a general way the character of the mud.

ANALYSIS OF DRY MUD FROM BLEACHING-POWDER SOLUTION.

Hydrate of lime (CaH_2O_2)	59.28
Carbonate of lime	27.81
Chlorite of calcium	5.98
Oxide of iron and alumina	1.00
Water	5.42

Only the clear solution prepared as above should be used for bleaching, not only because it acts more quickly than a cloudy one which contains considerable free lime, but also in order to avoid dirt. Many of the black specks noticed in paper are due to dirt in the bleach. When from this source, they generally consist of iron oxide, and traces of copper may be found in them. The best strength of liquor for storage and for economy, and thorough washing of the mud, is about 5° Bé. The hydrometer gives, of course, only a rough approximation to the strength of the bleach, since both the chlorate and chloride of calcium affect the instrument quite as much as the hypochlorite, but as a rough rule it may be stated that 1° Bé. averages about 0.47 per cent. available chlorine in the solution.

The bleaching of paper-stock is performed either in chests or engines. Rags and jute are bleached in engines, wood and similar fibres more commonly in chests. The difficulty of securing thorough agitation and evenness of color in chests is an objection, and their use requires a larger plant to do the same amount of work.

The amount of bleaching-powder actually consumed in bringing stock to color depends mainly, of course, upon the thoroughness with which the non-cellulose has been removed by the previous treatment. On this account the results obtained by different mills in bleaching the same fibre show considerable variation. It is to be noted, moreover, that the mills base their figures upon the weight of bleach in the cask, and that considerable losses may occur in mixing the bleach and washing the mud. The following may be taken as the usual quantities of bleaching-powder required per 100 lbs. of the different fibres.

	Lbs
Rags	2–5
Straw	7–10
Esparto	10–15
Soda Poplar	12–15
Soda Spruce	18–25
Sulphite Poplar	14–20
Sulphite Spruce	15–25
Jute	10–20

The full proportion of bleach in the form of a 5° Bé. solution is usually added after the stock has been well beaten up. It is best to have the stuff as thick as possible without interfering with thorough agitation. The general tendency is to add considerably more bleach than the stock requires. This has the effect of hastening the operation, but the loss in the drainage water may be great.

We have frequently tested the liquor in the chest, in order to determine the proportion of chlorine present after the pulp had come to color, and have found in many cases that it amounted to one-quarter or more of that originally introduced.

The bleaching of rags is a comparatively easy operation, since the preliminary treatment has removed nearly all the material other than cellulose. The half-stuff is always bleached in the engine, and requires from 2 to 5 per cent. of bleaching-powder. A small amount of acid is often added when color is nearly reached, and in the best practice the stock is dumped into drainers, and there gradually brought to full color by the last portions of bleach remaining in the stock.

Wood fibre is bleached either in engines or chests, the latter practice being more common. The pulp is sometimes dumped into the drainer after a treatment of about two hours in the engine with strong bleach solution. Bleaching in the chest requires from six to sixteen hours, according to the character of the pulp, and, on account of the difficulty of securing thorough agitation, is less likely to give an even color, especially when the stock during bleaching is heated by steam.

After the pulp has come to color the action of the bleach should be arrested as soon as possible, either by washing or the use of an antichlor, as otherwise the cellulose itself is likely to have its strength and quality impaired through the continued oxidizing action of the hydrochlorite.

The operation of bleaching is frequently accelerated by heating the mixture of pulp and bleach liquor by means of a steam pipe passing to the bottom of the chest or engine. Considerable care is necessary in order to avoid over-heating; and if the temperature much exceeds 100° F. the chlorine is likely to attack the cellulose, forming organic chlorides, which remain with the fibre and cause the color to go back. This chlorination of the fibre is likely to occur when a considerable proportion of lignin is present, and it is claimed that where, as in the case of soda poplar pulp, the lignin has been entirely removed, a considerably higher temperature may be maintained without injury to the stock. Although there is an undoubted saving of time by hot bleaching, the experiments of Cross and Bevan indicate that the consumption of bleach is increased about 20 per cent., in order to secure the same result as regards color.

The admission of steam into the bottom of a deep chest introduces a danger which it is difficult to avoid. If the movement of the pulp is slow, or if the stuff is very thick, the mixture in the lower portion of the chest may, on account of the imperfect circulation, easily become so hot as to injure the pulp, while the temperature at the surface may be much below this point. Such local over-heating is a common cause of uneven color in the fibre bleached in chests.

In order to free the cellulose from traces of chemicals which are likely to affect its permanence, all pulp should be washed after bleaching, even though the active chlorine has been "killed" by the use of an antichlor. Small traces of free acid or of chlorides cause paper to deteriorate rapidly through the formation of hydrocellulose in the first instance, and on account of changes set up by reactions which are less perfectly understood in the second. Chloride of alumina, even in small amounts, is known to have a very destructive effect upon cellulose, and would be formed on the addition of alum to pulp containing chloride. Traces of bleach seriously impair the strength of pulp by converting it into the brittle oxycellulose. This action is well shown if a piece of cotton is dipped into a dilute solution of bleach, and then squeezed nearly dry and exposed to the air, when it will be found to undergo a gradual disintegration.

The presence of traces of bleach in the stock may be readily detected by the use of iodide of starch paper or solution. The latter is made by boiling up as much starch as would go on a ten-cent piece with five or six ounces of water, and adding a few crystals of iodide of potash. The paper is prepared by dipping pieces of filter paper into the mixture. The paper is somewhat more sensitive if used at once, but it may be dried and preserved for future use. If a drop of liquor containing bleach is brought in contact with either the solution or the paper, iodine is liberated, and forms immediately with the starch a deep blue compound. Two precautions should be observed in making this test; if the bleach liquor is very strong, there may be sufficient chlorine present to destroy the blue, while, on the other hand, the chlorine may sometimes be so nearly exhausted that no test for it can be obtained from the liquor, although the blue color appears when a drop of the starch reagent is allowed to fall upon the pulp itself from which the liquor has previously been squeezed.

A yellowish discoloration is sometimes noticed on the top and edges of wet bleached pulp which has been kept for some time. This is due generally, if not always, to imperfect washing, by which all the calcium chloride is not removed after bleaching. The evaporation going on at the exposed portions, aided by the capillary action of the pulp which continually brings more water from the interior of the mass, gradually concentrates the solution of chloride which may at first be extremely dilute, until it is strong enough to act upon the fibre and form these colored decomposition products. The water extract from such yellow portions is found by us to be dark colored and bitter. It contains calcium chloride in considerable amount. The residue left after evaporating the extract yields, on treatment with alcohol, a light brown solution which gives a copious yellow precipitate with a neutral alcoholic solution of lead acetate; the substances present in the extract seem to be nearly allied to caramelane.

The time required and difficulty experienced in removing the last traces of bleach from the pulp by washing has led to the use of various chemicals for the purpose of neutralizing any hypochlorite left in the stock. Such chemicals are called, from their office in this connection, Antichlors.

Sodium thiosulphate, $Na_2S_2O_3$, $5 H_2O$, commonly called "hyposulphite of soda," is the antichlor most used. It is dissolved in water, and added in small quantity to the engine after the pulp has come to color. When brought into contact with bleach liquor, the following reaction occurs:—

$$2(Ca(ClO)_2) + Na_2S_2O_3 + H_2O = 2 CaSO_4 + 2 HCl + 2 NaCl,$$

in which the products are calcium sulphate, or Pearl Hardening, hydrochloric acid, and common salt. Every 409 parts of active bleaching-powder (35 per cent.) here requires 248 parts of the hyposulphite. This is the reaction as usually given and as it commonly occurs, but if the solutions employed are very dilute, the decomposition may take place in another direction, viz.:—

$$Ca(ClO)_2 + 4 Na_2S_2O_3 + H_2O = 2 Na_2S_4O_6 + 2 NaCl + 2 NaOH + CaO.$$

The use of hyposulphite of soda is open to the objection that the products of either of the above reactions are nearly as prejudicial in the paper as the traces of bleach which might remain after washing. If more than a small quantity of antichlor is used, the stock should afterwards be washed. Sodium sulphite, Na_2SO_3, which neutralizes the bleach after the manner shown, —

$$Ca(ClO)_2 + 2 Na_2SO_3 = CaSO_4 + NaSO_4 + 2 NaCl,$$

has been used abroad as a substitute for the hyposulphite, and is to be preferred, and not only because it is more efficient weight for weight, but because the products of its action are less likely to have an injurious effect upon the paper, in case they are not thoroughly washed out.

Calcium sulphite, $CaSO_3$, is used to a considerable extent in this country under the name of Hosford's Antichlor. It is found in the market in the form of a very fine, smooth powder, nearly white, and showing a granular structure under the microscope. On account of the slight solubility of the salt, the reaction, —

$$Ca(ClO)_2 + 2 CaSO_3 = CaCl_2 + 2 CaSO_4,$$

upon which its value depends, proceeds rather slowly. Any excess of this antichlor goes into the paper to make weight, and is quite unobjectionable, except possibly in the presence of very delicate colors. The chloride of calcium resulting from the reaction should, however, be removed by washing, since, when present even in traces, it hastens the deterioration of the paper. Kellner has advocated the addition of sulphite of lime to the stock, on the ground that it retards the aging and yellowing of papers which have been heavily sized with rosin, or which contain ground wood.

The ordinary sulphite liquor used in the manufacture of wood pulp forms, as will be readily inferred from the last two paragraphs, a very efficient antichlor. As the sulphites are in solution, the action of the liquor is rapid, and its use in many cases tends to brighten the color, though this effect is not likely to be permanent. Any considerable excess of the liquor is to be avoided unless the pulp is to be afterwards washed, as otherwise there is danger that traces of free sulphuric acid may be formed in the paper through the oxidation of the bisulphite, and cause a rapid deterioration in the strength of the fibre, besides corroding the wire and rusting the dryers of the paper-machine.

The mixture of calcium thiosulphate and polysulphide, made by boiling together milk of lime and sulphur, has been proposed as a cheap and effective antichlor; but since a considerable proportion of free sulphur is precipitated by the action of the bleach upon the mixture, its use is not to be recommended. The sulphur is left in the fibre in such a finely divided condition as to be slowly changed into sulphuric acid by ordinary atmospheric influences, and as a result there is a gradual conversion of the fibre into the brittle hydrocellulose. The free sulphur is also likely to cause rotting of the wire through formation of metallic sulphides.

Lunge recommends the use of hydrogen peroxide as an antichlor. It removes the oxygen from the hypochlorite, and is at the same time decomposed into water and free oxygen. Its use offers none of the objections which can be urged against the other antichlors on account of the products which they leave in the paper, and the durability of the bleached stock is rendered more assured. The reaction is a noteworthy one, inasmuch as it furnishes an instance of one powerful oxidizing agent being reduced through the action of another oxidizing agent.

In many cases, and especially in sulphite pulp, which before bleaching contains a considerable proportion of only slightly modified incrusting matter, it is much easier to obtain a cream or slightly yellow tone in the bleached fibre than the pure white, which is desired. This color is largely due to the yellow tint of the insoluble chlorinated compounds formed by the action of bleach upon the ligno-cellulose, and on that account is an evidence of the presence in the pulp of compounds which considerably impair its quality, aside from the mere question of color. It is possible by the judicious use of blue, the color complementary to yellow, to mask this undesirable appearance of the pulp and greatly improve its apparent color. This practice is not uncommon in case of pulp which is offered for sale, but the improvement in color is quite fictitious and serves only to disguise the true quality of the pulp. In extreme cases the sophistication is apparent to the eye, or may be detected at once by the bluish tint observed on looking through a sheet of the suspected pulp. If the quantity of blue used has been more carefully proportioned, its presence may nevertheless be usually detected by rolling the suspected sheet into a tube and looking through it, or by looking into a fold of the pulp as into a partly opened book. In each of these cases the blue is intensified by the multiple reflections of the light before reaching the eye.

Even when a yellow tint is not apparent in the bleached fibre, it often contains an appreciable quantity of chlorinated cellulose. We have found in bleached sulphite pulp of good color between 5 and 6 per cent of this material. The same pulp, after warming to 100° F. for eight hours with weak bleach solution, contained 10 per cent. of the chlorinated cellulose, an increase of about 5 per cent., while a portion treated with the same bleach solution in the cold for the same time showed an increase of the chlorinated cellulose of only 2 per cent.

To show still further the action of warm bleach solution, we treated a sample of pure cellulose with dilute bleach solution at a temperature of 140° F. for four hours. The sample, after thorough washing and drying, showed a loss of $6\frac{1}{2}$ per cent., while the dried sample was found to contain 19 per cent. of chlorinated cellulose soluble in very weak soda. One-quarter of the cellulose, then, in this experiment had been changed, and nearly one-tenth (allowing for the increase of weight by the chlorine absorbed) actually burned up and dissipated.

Many of the highly lignified bast fibres, like jute, manila, and hemp, are especially liable to chlorination, and fail to come to good color when subjected to the ordinary process of bleaching. These compounds of chlorine with the fibre substance range in color from bright yellow to orange, and develop a magnificent magenta when treated with a solution of bisulphite of soda. They are readily soluble in alkalies, and may be removed from the fibre by treatment with a 1 to 2 per cent. solution of soda-ash.

Besides the chlorination mentioned, which is a danger that care will usually avoid, there is always in bleaching a slight oxidation of the external layers of cellulose which is sufficient to affect the chemical relations of the fibre itself to certain coloring-matters. This change of relationship is mainly due, in the case of paper pulp, to the formation of a superficial layer of oxycellulose, which has a marked affinity for the basic coloring-matters and the power of withdrawing them from their solutions. If the oxidation extends into the substance of the fibre it occasions a considerable loss of strength.

The following analysis, made by ourselves, may be taken as indicative of the composition of well-bleached fibre:—

Analysis of Filter Paper
(Schleicher and Schull's No. 597)

	Per cent
Moisture, loss at 100° C	5.26
Mineral matter, ash	0.37
Hydrocellulose, etc. (soluble in alcohol)	0.73
Cellulose	93.69
Lignin, etc.	none
	100.05

We have obtained the following analytical and experimental figures from two samples of unbleached spruce pulp made by the sulphite process. A was a sample of what may be called normal pulp, whereas it had been found impossible in practice to bleach B to anything like good color. The latter sample contained, as will be noted, 0.34 per cent. of waxy material removable by carbon disulphide, and our examination showed that to this material the difficulty which had been experienced was mainly due. The material contained sulphur in combination, and was most probably formed during boiling by the action of the liquor upon some of the constituents of the wood. The presence in the liquor of the higher and easily decomposed sulphur acids is known to complicate the boiling process, and it is not impossible that this waxy material was the result of abnormal reactions thus occasioned. The objectionable substance was in any case so modified by the bleaching as to be removable by washing with very weak acid and alkali, and the color of the sample thus washed was beyond criticism.

	A	B
Moisture	7.00	7.89
Organic matter removed by bleaching	2.35	3.39
Waxy material removed by carbon disulphide after bleaching and drying	—	0.34
Hydrocellulose, gums, etc., remaining in bleached pulp, soluble in dilute caustic potash (1 per cent.)	2.76	2.17
Mineral matter removed by weak acid (1 per cent HCl)	0.60	1.10
Mineral matter remaining in bleached pulp after treatment with potash and acid	0.22	0.27
Cellulose	87.12	84.83
	100.05	99.99

		A	B
Apparent loss in bleaching		1.40	2.31
Mineral matter added by bleaching process		0.95	1.08
Actual organic matter lost in bleaching		2.35	3.39
Chlorination of fibre in bleaching		none	none
Bleaching-powder (35 per cent. available chlorine) consumed		16.90	18.80
Time of bleaching experiment, 4½ hours at about 50° C.			
Color obtained		good	bad (greenish)
Pulp, after bleaching and treatment with potash and acid, contained:—			
Cellulose		99.78	99.73
Mineral matter (ash)		0.22	0.27
		100.00	100.00
Ash of pulp as received		0.82	1.37
Ash of bleached pulp before treatment with potash and acid (original moisture basis)		1.79	2.51
Color of bleached pulp after purification with potash and acid		good	good

O'Neill gives the following interesting results of experiments made to determine the tensile strength of cotton threads before and after bleaching, by measuring the strain required to break the thread. The calico experimented on was of good quality, and had sixteen to eighteen threads to the ¼-inch; the length taken for testing varied from 0.25 inch to 3.1 inch.

	Average weight required to break a single thread.	
	Before bleaching.	After bleaching.
No. 1 cloth, weft threads	1714 grains	2785 grains
No. 1 " warp "	3140 "	2920 "
No. 2 " " "	3407 "	3708 "
No. 3 " " "	3512 "	4025 "

It is seen, says the author quoted, that in two cases out of three, the warp threads are stronger after bleaching than before, and in one case a little weaker. All that can be safely concluded from numerous trials made is, that the tensile strength of the cotton yarn is not injured by a careful but complete bleaching, and probably it may be strengthened by the wetting and pressure causing a more complete and effective binding of the separate cotton hairs or filaments, the twisting together of which makes the yarn.

There is a generally received opinion among the manufacturers of soda pulp that it is impossible to bleach their stock to good color, if more than a slight trace of alkali remains in the fibre. The difficulty is usually attributed to the presence of the alkali itself, but, as excellent results in bleaching may be obtained by the use of an alkaline solution of sodium hypochlorite, this is evidently an error. The trouble is really due to the presence of the organic matter in the small amount of black liquor still remaining in the pulp, and with which the alkali is associated.

We have made a large number of experiments in elucidation of this point, and find that a small proportion of such soluble organic matter remains in even very well washed brown pulp as taken from the mill. Forty grammes dry of such well washed poplar pulp required for its complete extraction 3800 cc of distilled water before the percolate failed to give a test for organic matter, and the total amount of chlorine consumed by the organic matter extracted amounted to 0.053836 grammes. When the washing has been well conducted at the mill, we find a remarkably close agreement in the figures which represent the amount of organic matter still remaining in the pulp of different mills. The amount of chlorine consumed by the organic matter extracted per 100 grammes dry pulp closely approximating 0.135 grammes.

In order to determine the effect of this small quantity of soluble organic matter upon the bleaching process, we have in a number of cases percolated several successive lots of pulp with the same water, after which another portion of pulp was mixed up with the percolate, and bleached in the usual way. For comparison, a quantity of pulp similar to the last was beaten up with distilled water and similarly bleached. We give the results of one experiment. Four lots of brown poplar pulp, amounting in all to 266 grammes dry, were successively percolated with the same water. Two fresh lots of pulp were then taken, each containing 88.6 grammes of dry pulp. Lot A was beaten up with water, while lot B

was beaten up with the percolate previously obtained. *A* bleached readily to good color in two and one-half hours, with a total chlorine consumption of 1.5954 grammes *B*, at that time, was far from being bleached, and at the end of five hours *B* was still inferior to *A* in color, although fairly well bleached. The chlorine consumed by *B* amounted to 2.1493 grammes. That is, the organic matter extracted from 266 grammes of dry pulp was sufficient so to retard the bleaching process that more than double the time was required, while there was an increase in the chlorine consumption of 28.07 per cent.

Where unfiltered water, or water highly colored by organic matter in solution, is used in bleaching, an appreciable quantity of bleaching-powder is required to bleach the water, and it will sometimes, especially in case of water colored by peat, be almost impossible to make the water entirely clear and colorless. This organic matter has, moreover, the same effect in retarding the bleaching of the pulp to color as that in brown liquor. We have made a number of experiments to determine the quantity of bleach consumed by different waters, and give a few of our results in the chapter on **Water**.

Cloudman has patented an apparatus especially adapted to the better bleaching and washing of soda pulp, which is thoroughly sound in principle, and which has proved itself very economical and efficient in practice. It is shown in Fig. 64, in which are sub-figures 1 and 2. Fig. 1 shows the apparatus in plan, and Fig. 2 is a vertical longitudinal section of a modified arrangement of two chests in line with one another, and with the conveyor for the material to be bleached and the passage through which the pulp passes from the top of one chest into the bottom of the next chest shown in the plane of section.

The apparatus consists of a series of chests fitted with agitators, washing-drums, and conveyors *f*. The bleach liquor is sent through the series in one direction, while the pulp is carried through in the opposite direction. The strong liquor entering the chest marked a^4 acts at first upon the pulp which has been nearly brought to color by contact with the weaker liquor in the other chests, while the nearly exhausted liquor entering the first chest *a*, expends its remaining strength upon the brown pulp which first passes into this chest.

Each chest is provided with an inlet passage *b*, the pulp entering the chest near the bottom through this passage, and, together with the pulp, the bleaching agent which has previously passed through the other chests of the series, is introduced so that both enter together at the lower portion of the first chest a of the series.

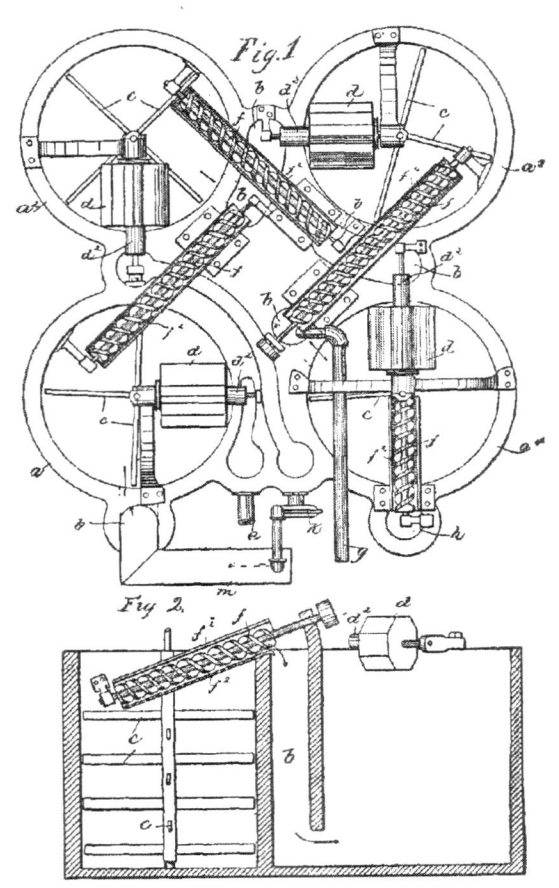

FIG. 64.—CLOUDMAN APPARATUS FOR WASHING AND BLEACHING.

A continuous flow of pulp and bleach liquor is maintained, so that, at each moment, the lower portion entering tends to displace that which has already entered, thus causing the mixture to rise gradually upward from the bottom to the top of the chest. By means of the conveyor and washing-drum at the top of the chest the pulp and liquor are partially separated when they reach the top.

The brown pulp enters at the bottom of the first chest a, through the inlet passage b. As it reaches the top of the chest it is raised by the conveyor f, and discharged into the top of the inlet passage b, leading to the chest a^2. It passes through this chest, and is similarly raised and discharged by the next conveyor in the inlet to the chest a^3. From the top of this chest it is again raised by the third conveyor and discharged into the inlet to the chest a^4. The bleached pulp is taken by the conveyor from the top of this chest and is discharged through the outlet h. Simultaneously with the above operations the strong bleach liquor has been passing through the chest in reverse order, entering through the inlet a^4, and being finally discharged as waste through the outlet e, leading from the chest a, into which the brown pulp has entered. The passage of the bleached liquor through the series is effected by means of the washing-drums d, which partially separate the liquor from the pulp, and which discharge into the inlet opening of the chest next preceding the one from which the liquor came. In this way, as bleaching progresses, the pulp meets stronger and stronger bleach liquor; while, as the proportion of available chlorine in the liquor decreases, the proportion of coloring-matter present in the pulp upon which the liquor is then acting increases. This is, of course, a reversal of the conditions obtaining in the usual methods of bleaching, where, as it becomes increasingly difficult to oxidize the last portion of coloring-matter, there is less and less available chlorine present for the purpose

Use of Acid. — The careful use of small quantities of hydrochloric or sulphuric acid in bleaching quickens the process by liberating hypochlorous acid, which is much more energetic in its action than bleaching-powder itself. The acid is best added after the pulp has nearly come to color, and should in all cases be diluted with several times its volume of water, and should then be poured into the chest or engine in a slow stream. A small amount of acid is as effective as a larger quantity; its action is more gradual, and there is less danger of chlorination of fibre and consequent loss of color. The first addition of acid neutralizes the lime present and decomposes the hypochlorite to form, if hydrochloric acid is used, chloride of calcium and free hypochlorous acid. The hypochlorous acid gives up its oxygen and is reduced to hydrochloric acid, which reacts with a fresh quantity of the hypochlorite as before, and the cycle of reactions continues until all of the hypochlorite has been decomposed. A small amount of hypochlorous acid is thus continuously liberated, but never enough to injure the fibre unless an excessive quantity of the stronger acid has been added. It is best to add the acid in several successive portions, and to stop, if any strong odor of hypochlorous acid persists.

Lunge recommended, several years ago, the use of small quantities of acetic acid in bleaching, in preference to the mineral acids, as its action is safer, while the amount required is so small that no objection can be made on account of cost. The acid has only recently been brought to the attention of the trade in a commercial way, but its use in the bleaching of paper stock is now growing rapidly. About one gallon of the commercial acid is added to a 1000-pound engine with the bleach liquor. It is stated, although the grounds for the claims are hardly apparent, that when used in connection with acetic acid, the amount of bleach may be reduced one-third, with the production of a cleaner and whiter half stuff. The results obtained in bleaching jute in this manner are said to be especially good.

Treating Jute. — Jute and similar materials derive their chief value as paper stock from the fact that the short ultimate fibres are bound together in the plant into filaments of great length and strength. In order that the stock may lend itself to the mechanical operations involved in the formation of a sheet of paper, it is necessary that these filaments be separated and partially broken down, but the methods of treatment are so regulated as to stop considerably short of such complete removal of the incrusting matter as would determine the separation of the ultimate fibres. The bleaching of such stock is therefore rarely carried beyond a good cream.

Jute butts, as received at the mill, usually contain from 12 to 18 per cent of moisture. They are first cut into three or four slabs or pieces, and violently "thrashed" for a few minutes to remove the coarser particles of adhering dirt. A further cutting and dusting follows, after which the stock is ready for boiling. The loss in weight caused by this preliminary treatment usually varies from 7 to 10 per cent.

The stock is boiled in rotaries for about twelve hours with milk of lime sufficient to rather more than half fill the rotary. The proportion of lime varies from 200 to 300 lbs. per ton of stock. In some mills the pressure is never allowed to exceed 15 lbs., while in others it is raised to 20 or even 30 lbs. The stock, after dumping from the rotary, is commonly allowed to remain on the floor for twenty-four to thirty-six hours to "temper," or soften, and is then thoroughly washed in an engine to remove all dirt and lime.

Bleaching, properly so-called, is done in the engine, the chloride of lime being generally added as powder in the proportion of from 10 to 20 per cent., according to the color desired and the thoroughness of the previous treatment. 4 or 5 per cent. of acid alum is sometimes added to hasten the action of the bleach, but in this case or if the stock is heated, there is much danger of chlorinating the fibre and forming yellow compounds, which defeat the object of the process. The stock, after running two or three hours in the engine, is often dumped into drainers, where the bleaching is allowed to continue slowly for about a week.

Bleaching Ground Wood. — Many paper-makers have expressed a desire for a process of bleaching ground wood, but the matter presents several difficulties which are not likely to be overcome. Ground wood contains, of course, all the constituents of the wood itself, except the small proportion which was soluble in water. There is, therefore, in all such pulp about 50 per cent. of incrusting matter to be destroyed by the hypochlorite solution before a white color can be obtained, and any process of true bleaching would entail a corresponding shrinkage in the weight of the fibre and an enormous consumption of bleach. The first effect of the bleach liquor is to lower the color of the pulp to red or brown, and this shade persists until nearly all the incrusting matter has been destroyed.

Although bleaching-powder is practically the only agent used for bleaching paper stock, various other bleach liquors have been proposed from time to time, and in some cases these possess advantages which would warrant their introduction, were it not for their greater cost. Among these liquors are: —

Magnesia Bleach Liquor. — This is prepared by adding Epsom salts to a solution of ordinary bleaching-powder, when calcium sulphate is precipitated and magnesium hypochlorite remains in solution. The clear liquor decanted from the precipitate is more unstable, but also more energetic in its action than the liquor made directly from bleaching-powder. It is less caustic, and does not turn straw, hemp, flax, etc., brown, as is done by hypochlorite of calcium solution. This liquor is also known as Ramsay's or Crouvelle's bleaching-liquor. A solution of magnesium hypochlorite, prepared by the electrolysis of a 5 per cent. solution of magnesium chloride, has been used on the large scale by Hermite in his electric bleaching process, and the efficiency claimed for his bleaching-liquor is undoubtedly due more to its composition than to the method of its manufacture.

Aluminum Bleach Liquor. — Sometimes called Wilson's bleach liquor, is prepared by treating a solution of bleaching-powder with one of alum. The reaction is similar to that which takes place in the preparation of the magnesium hypochlorite: that is, there is a precipitation of sulphate of lime, while the liquor consists of aluminum hypochlorite in solution. This liquor is exceedingly efficient, and the aluminum chloride which results from its decomposition is said to prevent the fungoid and other growths which sometimes appear as black specks upon bleached fibre. If this chloride is allowed to remain in the paper, however, it hastens the deterioration and yellowing of the sheet. Aluminum hypochlorite is formed, of course, when alum is added to the paper-engine, as is often the case in the ordinary process of bleaching; and where the alum used is a neutral one, the increased rapidity of the bleaching action is due to the aluminum hypochlorite which has been formed. With an acid alum there may be, in addition, some liberation of free hypochlorous acid.

Zinc Bleach Liquor. — By substituting zinc sulphate for the alum just mentioned, a solution of zinc hypochlorite is formed. This bleaches very rapidly, splitting up first into zinc oxide and hypochlorous acid. If the sulphate of zinc is added to the bleach liquor in the paper-engine, zinc oxide and sulphate of lime remain in the pulp. Zinc hypochlorite is sometimes called Varrentrapps' bleaching-salt.

In certain English mills and bleacheries which are in close proximity to plants manufacturing bleaching-powder, there is often used a bleach solution which is prepared by passing chlorine directly into milk of lime. In this way an excellent liquor is prepared, which is even more efficient than that made up from bleaching-powder. It is not improbable that, with the development of the electrolytic processes for the decomposition of salt, this liquor may find a use in this country in plants which are conveniently located to a source of chlorine.

Among the bleach liquors which are at present rarely or never used may be mentioned Eau de Javelle and Eau de Labarraque. The former is made by passing chlorine into a solution of potassium carbonate, and the latter by similarly treating a solution of carbonate of soda. In either case, the absorption of gas is continued until there is a slight effervescence, due to liberation of carbonic acid. If the caustic alkalies are substituted for the carbonates, similar but not identical liquors are prepared.

It has already been pointed out that the hypochlorites vary with respect to the ease with which they are decomposed in the presence of coloring-matter, and the rapidity of the bleaching action therefore varies in the different cases. The hypochlorites of alumina, zinc, and magnesia, are considerably more rapid in their action than hypochlorite of lime. Hypochlorite of soda is slowest of all, but when very slightly acidulated the action is as rapid as in case of any of the other hypochlorites named.

Liquid Chlorine. — The advent of this material as a bleaching agent affords a curious example of the manner in which the development of a process sometimes follows lines which apparently bring one back at last to the point of starting, although in reality the new point reached is on a higher plane. The early methods of gas bleaching were displaced by the simpler and more manageable processes involving the use of hypochlorites, and it now seems not improbable that the economies and improvements recently introduced in the methods of manufacture and transport of chlorine in its elementary form may re-establish gas bleaching.

The gas prepared from common salt, either by the well-known chemical methods or by the later ones which involve the use of electricity, is first dried and then brought to the liquid state by cooling and compression. The liquefied chlorine has a yellow color which is almost orange, and its specific gravity is 1.6602 at $-80°$ C., at $0°$ C. it is 1.4689, at $19°$ C., 1.4156; at $40°$ C., 1.3490; and at $77°$ C., 1.216. The coefficient of expansion is .00203 between $15°$ C. and $20°$ C., and what is called the *critical temperature* of the gas is $146°$ C., *i.e.*, at any temperature higher than the one given, it is impossible by any increase of pressure to condense the gas into the liquid.

The liquefaction is usually effected in stout wrought-iron drums, one form of which is shown in Fig. 65. This drum is provided with two valves; and when a quantity of gaseous chlorine is desired, the drum is set up vertically, and the protecting-cap A is unscrewed. The plug B, or B', of one of the valves, is then removed, and replaced by a screw-coupling C. To this coupling is best connected a lead pipe for conveying the gas to the point of use. It is necessary to open the valve very slowly, as otherwise a sudden rush of gas may burst the conveying-pipes. The conversion of the liquefied chlorine to the gaseous form is attended by so great an absorption of heat that the outside of the drum becomes heavily coated with frost, in which case, if a considerable amount of gas must be drawn off, it becomes necessary to raise the temperature of the drum, either by placing it in moderately warm water, or by wrapping it in hot cloths. The gas may be used for bleaching in the drainer, or it may be absorbed in water or in milk of lime. The latter method gives a liquor which is considerably more rapid and efficient in its action than any liquor made from bleaching-powder. Those who are interested in this new phase of bleaching will find an interesting and exhaustive paper on the subject by R. Kneitsch, in the "Annalen der Chemie," No. 259, page 100. He gives in the following table the pressure which the gas exerts on the inner surface of the cast-iron drums in which it is shipped. It will be noted that pressures are only for the ordinary temperatures which lie between 0° and 40° C.

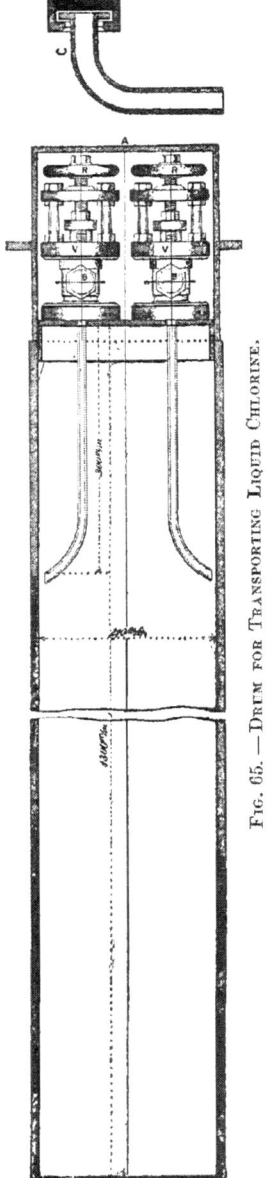

FIG. 65.—DRUM FOR TRANSPORTING LIQUID CHLORINE.

Temperature in °C	Pressure in Atmospheres	Temperature in °C	Pressure in Atmospheres
0	3 660	+ 21 67	6 960
+ 9 62	4 885	+ 29 70	8 652
+ 13 12	5 433	+ 33 16	9 470
+ 20 85	6 791	+ 38 72	10 889

Use of Oxygen. — The brothers Brin, who have successfully attacked the problem of producing oxygen on a commercial scale, have made a large number of experiments with a view to the use of the gas as an auxiliary agent in bleaching with chloride of lime. It does not appear that the high hopes at first entertained for the process have been realized, although under favorable conditions, and where the stock to be bleached was thoroughly cooked, some saving of bleaching-powder was shown. Contrary to what was claimed at the time by the advocates of oxygen, no improvement was noticed in either the feel, appearance, or felting qualities of the resulting bleached stock. Since these first experiments were made, the price of oxygen has been materially lowered, until to-day it can be made for 0 05 cent per cubic foot under favorable circumstances. It is now claimed by those who control this process that in bleaching esparto, with ordinary bleach liquor plus oxygen, the quantity of bleach required can be reduced in the proportion of 2 to 1 25, so that, in a case where a ton of stock requires ordinarily 224 lbs of 35 per cent. bleach, the use of 200 cubic feet of oxygen saves no less than 84 lbs.

Mr. Thorne, an expert in the use of oxygen for bleaching, claims that results can be obtained with oxygen which cannot be secured through the use of compressed air, and explains this rather curious phenomenon by the theory that the large amount of inert nitrogen which necessarily accompanies the oxygen when compressed air is used, carries away some oxygen and chlorine before the latter has time to act.

So far as we are aware, no thoroughly satisfactory theory has been advanced to explain the action of oxygen when used in this way. for oxygen in the gaseous form has no especial bleaching power

Ozone Bleach. — The Fahrig electrostatic process for the production of ozone on a commercial scale has placed this powerful bleaching agent in a position which encourages its advocates to claim that it may yet successfully compete with the hypochlorites in the bleaching of cellulose. It is already used with excellent effect for bleaching water; 20 grains per 1000 gallons is sufficient, it is claimed, to give a good result, and it is already being used upon a considerable scale as a bleaching and oxidizing agent in various lines of industry, which are, however, foreign to our subject. It is usually employed in the form of a 1 per cent. solution, although solutions containing 7 per cent. or 8 per cent. of ozone are sometimes made.

Hydrogen peroxide is closely similar to ozone in its action, and is also attracting some attention as a possible substitute for hypochlorites. It is employed in the form of a weak solution, to which magnesia is sometimes added.

Sulphurous Acid Bleach. — The bleaching action of sulphurous acid, as has been already pointed out elsewhere, differs essentially from that of the various oxidizing agents which have been considered. In those methods of bleaching which involve oxidation, the coloring-matters are split up into much more simple oxidation products, which are themselves colorless. Sulphurous acid in only a few cases bleaches by the destruction of the coloring-matter, so that whatever value it possesses as a bleaching agent depends mainly upon its property of combining with the coloring-matter to form colorless compounds, from which the unchanged coloring-matters may be again liberated by the action of a stronger acid, or merely by continued exposure to atmospheric influences. Many of the brightly colored flowers, for example, may be bleached by exposure to the gas; but if they are then dipped in very weak sulphuric acid, the original color is restored. Wool and other animal fibres are generally bleached by means of sulphurous acid, and the color reappears when the acid combines with the alkali of the soap used in washing.

In the best unbleached sulphite fibre the coloring-matters are merely masked, and more chloride of lime is required to bleach such fibre than is needed in the case of pulp which, through the use of higher temperatures, has had the incrusting matter more thoroughly removed, although its color is much poorer. The first effect of bleaching-powder, as is well known, is to cause a marked lowering of color, as the first products of the oxidation are usually more highly colored than the original materials. If now an excess of bisulphite liquor is added to the pulp, the latter immediately becomes nearly or quite white, not on account of any true bleaching action, but because the sulphurous acid arrests the process of oxidation and conceals the coloring-matters by combining with them. The subsequent addition of an excess of bleaching-powder solution oxidizes the acid and restores the color as the first step in the resumption of the true bleaching process. It is therefore evident that any bisulphite liquor or sulphite of lime which remains in sulphite pulp, as a result of imperfect washing, consumes its equivalent of hypochlorite, if the pulp is subsequently bleached, and adds proportionately to the cost of bleaching.

CHAPTER V.

SIZING AND LOADING.

THE infinite number of small spaces which exist within and between the fibres of a sheet of unsized paper, cause, by capillary action, a rapid spreading and absorption of any liquid with which the paper may come in contact. It is to this property that blotting paper owes its value, and there are a few other applications which require the use of an unsized or so-called "water-leaf" paper. Most of the uses to which paper is put, however, imply its contact with ink in one form or another, and it thus becomes necessary to so fill up the pores and coat the fibres with some material which shall offer sufficient resistance to the passage of fluid to prevent the spreading of the ink. This object is accomplished by the various methods of sizing which we propose to consider in this chapter.

The extent to which the sizing must be carried, and the nature of the sizing agents employed, depends upon the purpose for which the paper is to be used. Writing papers which are to come into contact with very fluid writing inks, require a much more perfect sizing than do printing papers for use with a thick and viscid printing ink. The division may be carried much farther, for while it is the object of some printing papers to retain the ink almost wholly upon the surface of the sheet, such papers as are used for other work in which quick absorption and rapid drying of the ink is necessary must have sufficient capillary power or "pull," as it is called, to accomplish these results.

In the days of hand-made paper practically the only material used for sizing was gelatine, which was called animal sizing from its source, and tub sizing from its method of application, the size being formerly contained in a tub into which the paper was dipped by hand.

With the advent of machine-made paper, and the application of the material to printing purposes, other methods of sizing came into use, until now the number of substances which have been more or less successfully adapted to the purpose is considerable. Practically, however, all sizing is still done either with gelatine or rosin. The materials used for rosin sizing are applied to the beaten stuff either in an engine or chest, and this form of treatment is therefore known as engine sizing.

Properties of Gelatine. — Pure gelatine is a colorless, odorless, almost transparent substance, having an insipid taste and being usually quite brittle. Its toughness, however, varies with its source. It softens and shrinks on heating, and gives off an unpleasant nitrogenous odor on burning. It is insoluble in cold water, but swells and absorbs three or four times its weight of the liquid. In hot water it is freely soluble, and the strong solution upon cooling sets to a firm clear jelly. A firm jelly is hardly formed unless the solution contains about 7 per cent. of gelatine. With the best material even so little as 1 per cent. gives a gelatinous mass on cooling

This power of gelatinizing is said to be destroyed by over-heating the solution, or if the solution is frequently heated and cooled The most conspicuous property of gelatine, and the one on which its value in the manufacture of leather depends, is found in its formation of an insoluble compound with tannic acid. Gelatine is also precipitated from its solution by alcohol, and is insoluble in ether and oils, but is dissolved by concentrated sulphuric acid in the cold. Alum does not precipitate it although it thickens the solution. If alkali is added to the mixture in sufficient quantity a precipitate is formed containing gelatine and a basic sulphate.

The purest commercial form of gelatine is isinglass prepared from the swimming bladders of certain fish, notably the sturgeon. Glue is a comparatively crude form of the material, and is made by boiling down scraps of hide, horn, and hoof. Bones yield a similar but inferior product. The yield from raw-hide is about 50 per cent.

The production of glue in a commercial form involves several distinct operations, but the preparation of size is simpler partly because the raw material as purchased by the paper-maker has already undergone the treatment with lime, and partly because he only needs the glue solution, and therefore does not prepare a solid glue. The scraps received at the mill are soaked for several days in water, which is changed from time to time. Sometimes the washing is finished in drums or other form of washing apparatus in which thorough agitation may be secured. Thorough washing is very important in order to remove traces of blood and any acid or lime remaining from the previous treatment to which the skins have been subjected. Arsenic, usually in the form of sulphide, is also sometimes present, it being brought into the skins by certain de-hairing processes. The washed pieces are next boiled with water, either in a tank, which may be lined with lead or copper, or else in a jacketed iron or copper vessel. Whatever the form of the vessel it is always fitted with a false bottom.

The mixture is then heated up to a temperature varying from 150° to 180° F., with the character of the material under treatment, and in about twelve hours extraction is completed. Any grease which is present will have come to the top of the liquid, and must be carefully removed or otherwise kept out of the size. The solution is cleared from suspended impurities and dirt either by settling or filtration.

Alum is added to the size partly as a preservative, and partly because it is thought to render the gelatine somewhat more efficient as a sizing agent. The first effect of the addition of the alum is to thicken up the gelatine solution until it becomes very stiff, but curiously enough this is corrected by the addition of a further quantity of alum. Arsenite of soda is sometimes added as a preservative, but its use must be condemned on account of the poisonous nature of the material.

In the process of animal sizing on the machine, which is now practically the only way in which this form of size is applied in this country, the web of paper is led through a trough filled with the size and to and from which a constant circulation of the liquid is maintained in order to prevent its becoming too cool for use. The drying of animal size in papers is a matter of nicety. If the best results are to be obtained, it is necessary that the drying be conducted slowly and at very moderate temperature. The commoner way in the preparation of writing papers is to subject the sized paper after cutting, to a process of loft drying, in which the sheets are suspended on poles in a loft which is kept warm by steam pipes. By this slow drying, the glue is gradually brought in great part to the surface of the sheet, where its presence is most required. Cheaper grades of paper are sometimes dried on the machine, but in this case a large number of skeleton driers are substituted for the steam drums which are ordinarily used as driers.

Each of these skeleton driers has within it a fan for keeping up the circulation of the air, and the total number of such driers may be thirty-five or more.

It is of the utmost importance that the size be entirely free from grease and acid; the former is liable to make unsightly streaks and spots, while even traces of acids are likely to affect delicate colors and cause deterioration of the paper. Animal size is sometimes used in moderate amount directly in the engine, but its value at this point is doubtful, and in the absence of any substances which will precipitate the gelatine the greater portion of it is lost in the wash water.

Engine Sizing.— We have already made reference on page 138 to the more prominent properties of rosin. Its use in size depends upon its acid character by virtue of which it forms soaps with the various metallic oxides, and of course most readily with potash or soda. Its salts, which are those of the various acids which occur in rosin, are collectively called resinates. The resinate of soda, which at present most concerns us, is made by boiling rosin with a moderately strong solution of soda-ash or soda crystals, and is soluble in water. All resinates of metals other than those of the alkalis, are for the most part insoluble. The older theory of engine sizing is, that after the size has been diluted with water and mixed with the stuff it is precipitated as resinate of aluminum upon the addition of alum, and that this alum soap is the true sizing agent, which by coating over the fibres prevents the absorption and spreading of liquid after the paper has been dried. The saponification of rosin in the preparation of size is rarely complete, and some free rosin is present in nearly all size. In some samples of white size as much as 25 per cent. of the rosin may be present as free rosin in a very fine state of subdivision. Commercial rosin contains also from 6 to 8 per cent. of unsaponifiable matter.

According to the later theory of rosin sizing, for which we are in large measure indebted to the researches and conclusions of Dr. Wurster, the precipitate produced by the addition of alum consists in the main of free rosin in a very fine state of division and mixed with a small proportion of resinate of aluminum. It is the view of Dr. Wurster and many other chemists who have studied the matter, that the sizing effect is due solely to the free rosin, the resinate of alumina being quite inactive. Engine sizing, according to this view, consists merely in mixing very finely divided rosin with the fibres, and then causing it to adhere and penetrate by the heat of the driers. We are ourselves disposed to adhere to the older view, for if free rosin alone is needed, equally good results should be obtained in sizing by the substitution of sulphuric acid for the alum usually employed. Our own results and those of Dr. Wurster indicate that such is not the case, but Lunge is said to have obtained good results by the use of sulphuric acid without alum. The true theory may perhaps lie between these two extremes, and define the office of the alumina as that of fixing the rosin upon the fibres.

Preparation of Rosin Size. — Nearly every mill has its own receipt for preparing rosin soap for use in sizing, but except as to proportions the general method of procedure is about the same in all cases. The powdered or finely broken rosin is boiled in an alkaline solution in an iron kettle, preferably heated by a steam coil, although sometimes live steam is used. The darker colored rosin is believed to be the best, and as we think with good reason, since it has been distilled at a higher temperature, and therefore contains less pitchy matter than the lighter grades. At the time when practically all soda was made by the LeBlanc process, soda crystals were generally used, because of their greater purity and even composition. At present 58 per cent. Solvay soda-ash is almost universally employed, and it is undoubtedly the best material to use. The common practice in this country calls for quantities of soda-ash, which range from 20 to 40 per cent. on the weight of the rosin taken.

Beadle, who has obtained the best results in sizing by the use of size containing 26 per cent. free rosin, recommends as the result of a large number of trials, the use of 1 lb. of soda-ash to every 7.65 lbs. of rosin, or for 1300 lbs. of rosin, 170 lbs. of soda-ash and 200 gals. of water, the whole to be boiled for seven hours and then made to the volume of 225 gals. by addition of water. Size made by the above receipt contained:—

	Per cent
Combined rosin	40.59
Free rosin	14.37
Combined soda	6.72
Free soda	1.34

During the boiling of size, considerable carbonic acid is evolved unless caustic soda is used, but the general experience has been that equally good results are not obtained with this material. The frothing due to liberation of carbonic acid when soda-ash is used, can generally be kept down if the sides of the kettle are not unduly heated, and for this reason where the steam jacket is used it should only cover the bottom of the kettle. In case the frothing becomes very violent, it may be checked by adding a little cold water through the sprinkler of a watering-pot, but even when the water is thus showered, it is apt to cause the formation of clots and make the size lumpy.

The amount of water used in making size is a matter of importance. With too much water the size sinks to the bottom with the dirt, whereas the aim of the size-maker should be to keep the solution of such density that the size will float, while the dirt sinks

New size is apt to make size spots, and it is, therefore, customary to keep a supply ahead, and to draw for use upon that which is at least a week, and better, two or three weeks old.

The following are our analyses of good average size as made by mills in this country:—

	A	B
Water	39.70	40.62
Free rosin	8.54	7.22
Dry size	51.76	52.16

Tallow is sometimes boiled up in small amounts with the rosin and is thought to improve the feel and finish of the sheet, but in the manner and small quantity in which it is used its value in these directions is doubtful

Action of Light on Rosin Size. — It has been known for a long time that both rosin and ground wood undergo some rather obscure changes on exposure to light and air, and that these changes were among the most important factors in causing the deterioration of paper by age. The subject has been investigated somewhat carefully by Herzberg Five kinds of engine-sized paper, the size of which was proved normal by testing, were exposed to direct sunshine and air for a period of two months; they were then tested, and exposed for another similar period At the end of the second exposure, four samples out of the five were no longer fit to write upon These were made of linen and cotton rags, some being with and some without ground wood pulp and straw. The fifth sample was made of ground wood and sulphite.

and gave an ash of 13.5 per cent. This was almost unaffected so far as the size was concerned, although the color was more altered than in case of any of the others. The exact nature of the change which takes place in rosin when exposed in this finely divided state to light, is not known, but Herzberg has proved that the change is due to light, rather than to the gases composing the atmosphere, since in other of his experiments, papers similarly exposed in tubes with oxygen and sulphuric acid were not affected so long as they were kept in diffused daylight. A piece of rosin kept for some time in direct sunlight loses its vitreous appearance and becomes covered with yellow powder.

Use of Aluminate of Soda.— Certain advantages have been claimed for a method of preparing rosin size in which the saponification of the rosin is effected by means of aluminate of soda, instead of carbonate of soda or caustic soda, as is usually the case. Aluminate of soda is a compound in which the alumina plays the part of a weak acid and enters into combination with the soda. From this compound alumina may be precipitated by the addition of acid or many salts.

The rosin soap is prepared by boiling rosin in the usual manner, except for the substitution of aluminate of soda for the customary alkali. One part by weight of aluminate of soda is dissolved in four times its weight of water and added to two parts by weight of rosin. It is only necessary to have sufficient alkali present to thoroughly saponify and hold the rosin in solution, and the proportion just given may be greatly varied so long as this condition is met. The soap is added to the pulp in the beating engine in the usual manner, and is decomposed with precipitation of the rosin and alumina upon the addition of a soluble salt of magnesium such as chloride or a sulphate. Chloride of calcium may also be used to advantage, or even ordinary alum, and the results in the latter case are said to be better with size prepared after the present method than are attainable through the use of a common rosin size. The strength of the solution used for the precipitation may be conveniently one part of the salt dissolved in twenty parts of water, but it is unnecessary to adhere closely to this formula. Where the magnesia salts are used the base is precipitated at the same time together with the rosin and alumina.

Casein Sizing. — Casein is a nitrogenous substance occurring in milk and closely resembling animal albumen in its composition and properties. One thousand parts of normal milk contain, according to Fownes, 48.20 parts of casein. A closely similar body is found in the vegetable kingdom, notably in pease, beans and lentils, and is called vegetable casein or legumin. Liebig, indeed, considers the two materials identical, but doubt has been thrown upon this view by later investigators. The name casein is derived from the Latin one for cheese, which is formed in large part of casein, and which bears a close resemblance to it.

Casein is prepared by coagulating the milk with dilute acid or with rennet, and washing the coagulum first with water, then with water containing a little acid, and finally with pure water again. It may then be brought down by drying to a friable mass, and usually appears in commerce as a dry granular powder of yellowish tinge. It dissolves readily in very weak alkaline solutions and is precipitated by many salts and especially by alum. The solution has not been used to any extent in this country for sizing paper, but experiments in this direction have been made by a number of German mills whose experience has been sufficiently favorable to warrant a trial of the material by American paper-makers. Its use depends upon the property possessed by casein of forming a bulky, gelatinous, insoluble compound with alum which adheres to the fibres and subsequently dries upon them, leaving the pores well filled.

The casein in the form of a 20 per cent. to 50 per cent. solution is commonly added to the engine just as rosin size would be, or it may be mixed with the size in any desired proportion. In either case alum is afterwards added to effect the precipitation as in case of rosin size. Paper sized with casein is said to be much more elastic than that sized with rosin. Practically all of the casein goes into the sheet. Paper so sized has an especially good feel and readily takes a high finish. Casein size also lessens the objectionable dust which often comes from papers carrying a large amount of mineral matter, and the percentage of filler retained is greater than with rosin size.

The most serious objection which has been raised against this material as a sizing agent, is that it is very liable, unless properly prepared and handled, to impart an unpleasant odor to the paper.

Silicate of Soda. — This material has been used from time to time by mills which desired to obtain a very hard sized paper which should rattle. It is commonly received in the form of a clear, very heavy liquid, containing about 50 per cent of the silicate dissolved in water. It is strongly caustic and may be used for preparing size in place of the carbonate usually employed, or any desired quantity may be mixed with the size itself or added directly to the engine. The addition of alum determines the formation of a bulky, gelatinous precipitate of hydrated silicic acid which is very similar in appearance to precipitated alumina. The same precipitation is brought about by the addition of acid to the engine, but this procedure is liable to bring the silica down in a gritty or sandy condition in which it is likely to cause trouble in various ways, and especially by leaving the surface of the sheet dusty. The only important advantage which the use of silicate of soda offers, is that it produces a harder paper and its use is in this country confined in the main to mills making writing papers.

Alum.—We have already pointed out (Part I., page 77,) that the term alum as employed in paper-making has come to refer almost entirely to sulphate of alumina, and we shall now use the word in this restricted sense. The use of alum in paper-making is due primarily to the fact that when a solution of alum comes in contact with one of rosin size, there is formed a bulky, adhesive, gelatinous precipitate, composed of alumina and rosin, which adheres to the fibres and dries down to a sort of water-repellent varnish. Other things being equal, the value of an alum for the purposes of paper-making is usually held to vary with the percentage of alumina present, but this is by no means a conclusive indication of the sizing power. The accompanying table brings out the great variations which appear in the composition of commercial alums, and the sizing power of the several samples is influenced by many factors other than the mere percentage of alumina. It will be noted in reference to these analyses that in a well-made alum the proportion of material insoluble in water is rarely above 0.50 per cent., and is often much below this figure. A much higher percentage, such as appears for instance in Samples VI., VIII., X., and XIV., generally indicates that the original raw material has not been thoroughly broken down by the acid. Such alums are apt to contain considerable free acid, and they find their chief use in bleaching or as a coagulant in the purification of water. They are only adapted for sizing in case of the cheapest papers. The alumina in these analyses varies from 11.64

ANALYSES OF ALUMS.

Griffin & Little.

	I.	II.	III.	IV.	V.	VI.	VII.	VIII.	IX.	X.	XI.	XII.	XIII.	XIV.	XV.	XVI.	XVII.	XVIII.
Insoluble in water	0.06	0.06	0.19	0.04	0.24	10.61	3.22	9.20	0.67	7.76	0.02	0.11	0.03	7.48	0.56	0.30	0.39	0.49
Alumina (Al_2O_3)	15.47	18.81	15.43	15.35	16.86	14.96	14.22	12.79	22.37	13.27	19.43	11.64	12.38	13.66	16.58	17.04	16.78	16.20
Iron protoxide (FeO)	0.02	0.13	0.02	0.11	1.02	0.13	0.11	0.09	0.46	0.46	0.44	0.06	0.50	0.66	—	0.48	—	—
Iron sesquioxide (Fe_2O_3)	0.00	0.66	0.03	1.06	0.66	1.08	0.72	0.49	0.08	0.52	0.05	1.17	0.36	0.09	0.04	0.04	0.01	0.06
Zinc oxide (ZnO)	—	—	—	—	—	—	—	—	3.80	—	0.38	—	—	—	—	4.43	—	—
Soda (Na_2O)	1.72	0.76	2.81	0.37	0.81	0.57	0.34	0.34	—	—	—	4.75	0.41	0.66	0.56	—	1.33	1.34
Magnesia (MgO)	—	—	—	—	—	—	—	—	—	—	—	0.46	—	—	—	—	—	—
Sulphuric acid (SO_3), combined	37.26	45.97	37.33	37.06	39.15	37.36	34.78	31.07	46.28	32.21	36.24	35.98	31.12	33.52	39.17	40.53	38.98	36.62
Sulphuric acid (SO_3), free	—	1.03	—	0.82	—	1.06	2.11	2.83	—	1.55	—	5.13	6.26	0.72	—	—	—	—
Water by difference	45.48	32.58	44.19	44.29	41.86	34.21	44.50	43.19	27.34	44.23	43.44	40.71	49.14	43.21	43.09	37.18	42.61	45.2
	100.00	100.00	100.00	100.00	100.00	100.00	100.00	100.00	100.00	100.00	100.00	100.00	100.00	100.00	100.00	100.00	100.00	100.00
Sizing test (parts of dry neutral rosin size precipitated by one part of the alum)	3.32	4.04	3.09	3.63	3.29	3.47	3.10	3.04	3.64	2.87	2.94	3.19	3.25	3.04	3.71	4.70	3.63	3.46

per cent. in Sample XII., to 22.37 per cent in Sample IX., but there is no corresponding variation in the sizing power. Sample IX is a very basic alum, and it is doubtful if the excess of alumina above that needed to form the neutral sulphate has much, if any, sizing value. The large quantity of free acid in XII. of course decomposes its equivalent of size, and, although objectionable in itself, increases the apparent sizing power of the alum. The maximum quantity of size is precipitated by XVI. with only 17.04 per cent. of alumina and no free acid, but after making proper allowance for the zinc and iron present in both cases, it appears that IX is made up more largely of basic sulphate than the stronger XVI

The deleterious effect of iron upon color makes the amount of this constituent a matter of importance in any alum intended for use in the paper engine. The total amount of iron oxides in the samples under discussion ranges from 0.02 per cent. in Sample I. to 1.23 per cent in the low grade Sample XII., and these figures may be taken as fairly representing the extremes. Since the salts of the protoxide of iron are comparatively colorless, it is the object of the alum manufacturer to convert as far as possible all the iron present to the ferrous state. This may be effected by the addition of metallic zinc which liberates nascent hydrogen as it goes into solution in the liquid alum, and to this fact is due the presence of the zinc oxide reported in certain analyses in the table. It should, however, be noted in this connection that while the color of an alum is improved by bringing the iron into the ferrous state, it does not follow that such iron is any the less objectionable, for it is rapidly oxidized during the processes of paper-making.

The soda which appears as a common constituent of the alums in the table is by itself without significance as to their value or character. Its presence is explained partly by the use of bicarbonate of soda in the manufacture of porous alums, and to neutralize the last portions of acid; but in some cases it may be derived from cryolite when this is used as the raw material.

The proportion of sulphuric acid deserves more attention than it usually receives from buyers of alum. Free acid, except on a bleaching alum, is objectionable not only because of its effect in color, but because it decomposes the size without at the same time precipitating alumina. If excessive quantities of a strongly acid alum are used there is the further danger of attacking the wires and felts, and injuring the strength of the paper as it passes over the driers.

From our own point of view a neutral, or slightly basic, alum should give the best results in sizing, but many paper-makers have a preference for a very basic or "concentrated" alum. Samples XIII and XI., which contain about the same amount of total acid, may be taken as representing the extremes in the proportion of acid to base.

The amount of alum used in sizing ranges in ordinary practice from 6 to 12 lbs. to an engine carrying 500 lbs. A larger quantity is sometimes added if the sizing is to be very hard, but the usual amount is about 10 lbs. It is best to put the size in first and allow it to become thoroughly distributed through the stock before the addition of alum, but some mills reverse this process. There is danger in this event that the size will be precipitated in small lumps, which come to the surface and make spots in the paper. In making manila paper the dry alum is added directly to the engine, but for better papers a stock solution is made up and cleared by settling or straining.

The quantity of alum used is always much in excess of that required to merely precipitate the size, but although there is a considerable waste of alum in most mills, good results in sizing cannot be obtained by use of the minimum amount of alum required by the size alone. A moderate proportion of free alum appears to be essential to good sizing, and portions of the alum added are neutralized by the water, by lime or other alkalis present in the stock, and by traces of bleach. By virtue of these decompositions the alum in the engine has an important clearing action similar to that which occurs during its use in purifying water. That is, it has a tendency to coagulate or gather together the fine suspended matter of any kind, such as particles of filler or bits of fibre which have been too finely beaten so that they might otherwise be lost.

Temperature has a noticeable effect on the quantity of alum required, particularly when ground wood is used, the amount required increasing with the rise in temperature. If the temperature of the contents of the engine exceeds 100° F. it is impossible to make a well-sized sheet, even though a large excess of alum be added.

Apart from its value as a sizing agent alum performs several important offices in the coloring of paper, and these will be considered in the chapter on Coloring

Sizing with Acid Sulphites. — Numerous attempts have been made by German chemists to size paper by using bisulphite liquor in place of alum to effect the decomposition of the rosin soap. This decomposition with precipitation of rosin can easily be brought about in this way, the extra acid combining with the soda and setting free the rosin. When a lime liquor is used there is thus formed sulphite of soda and sulphite of lime. As the last-named compound is insoluble, it serves to increase the proportion of filler in the sheet. This method of sizing is very cheap, and it is claimed by Kellner to have the important advantage, when applied to papers containing ground wood, of preventing or retarding very much the loss of color which usually takes place in such papers with age. This conclusion is rendered somewhat doubtful by the researches of Herzberg upon the action of light upon rosin size, which indicate that the change which gives the darkening in color is not one of simple oxidation. The addition of the sulphite liquor has undoubtedly some bleaching action which may be useful in case of papers made for immediate consumption, but such bleaching action is a very fugitive one. There is, moreover, considerable danger that if too much of the liquor is added to the engine, some of the free sulphurous acid may be oxidized to sulphuric acid as the paper passes over the heated driers. Any such action at this point would not only rust the driers, but would be apt to render the paper brittle through formation of hydrocellulose.

Any free sulphurous acid in the stock would corrode the wire as the sheet was formed on the machine. Another serious objection to this method of sizing is found in the action of the sulphurous acid upon many of the coloring matters which might be employed with it. It cannot be denied, in view of the results of Dr Kellner and others, that this method of sizing, when properly controlled, may be made to yield good results at a comparatively low cost but the process is one which is liable to involve in serious difficulty any less experienced workers.

The Mitscherlich Sizing Process. — Among the substances which occur in waste sulphite liquors are certain derivatives of the wood which are more or less closely allied to tannic acid, and which possess its property of precipitating gelatine. Dr. Mitscherlich has turned this to account in a process for engine-sizing with glue, and has made it a subject of a patent. In carrying out his process ordinary glue is digested at a temperature of about 60°, with ten times its weight of waste sulphite liquor, until dissolved. This requires several hours, and the mixture should be stirred from time to time. The solution thus prepared is then diluted with more waste liquor until the proportion of liquid to glue is about 50 to 1. The admixture must be made very gradually with constant stirring, and at the ordinary temperature of the air. The glue combines with the astringent material of the liquor to the extent of about 60 per cent. of its own weight, and is precipitated in flocks. The whole mixture is then allowed to stand for twenty-four hours. The liquor is then decanted from the precipitate, and the latter mixed with a quantity of water weighing about forty times as much as the glue originally taken. A small quantity of chalk or soda-ash, or other substances capable of neutralizing the free acid, is then added. The compound of glue and astringent matter goes into solution quickly, and a liquor so prepared may be added directly to the engine for use in size. Alum, or a weak acid, will then cause the precipitation of the gelatine compound throughout the fibre, and the solution may be therefore used when desired in connection with ordinary size.

The process just described is a development of the one first patented by Dr Mitscherlich in 1886, in which paper was sized by feeding in continuously on one side of the beating engine the waste sulphite liquor in a small stream, while ordinary glue solution was similarly fed in on the other side of the engine. As the two dilute solutions came together the gelatine compound was precipitated, and the action was, of course, continuous as long as the supply was kept up.

Loading. — The use of mineral fillers has come to have a recognized and legitimate place in paper-making, and the presence of such fillers in a sheet is not under ordinary circumstances to be regarded as evidence of adulteration. They are used quite as much for their beneficial effect upon the feel and finish of the paper as through a desire to lower the cost of production. Many of the best grades of book paper could not be made at all without the use of some filler in considerable amount to give the

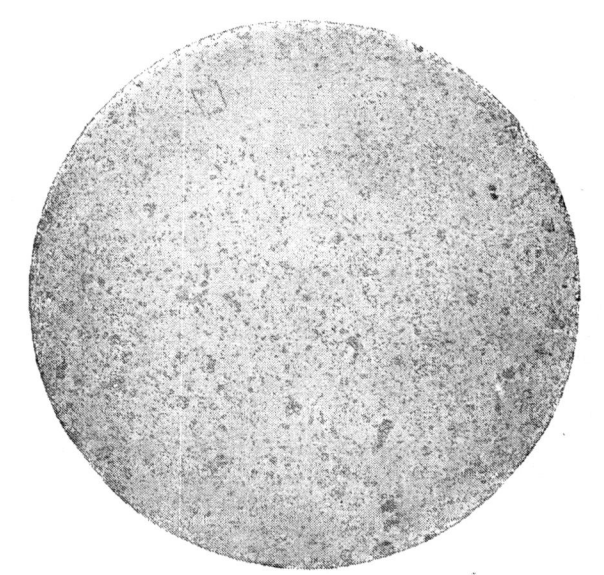

FIG. 66. — SOUTH CAROLINA CLAY.

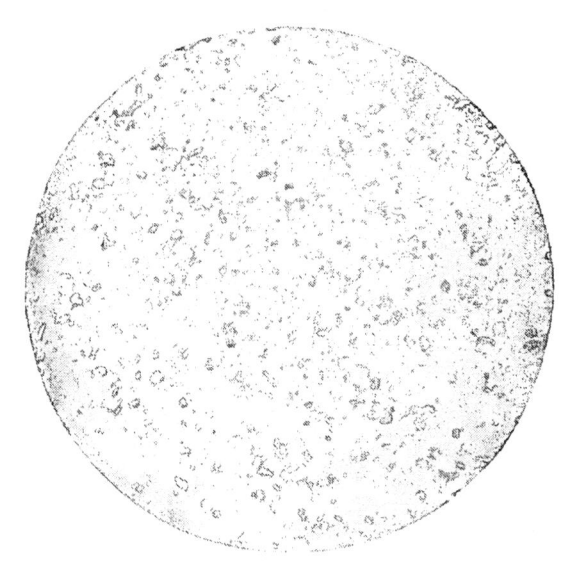

FIG. 67. — ENGLISH CHINA CLAY.

smoothness of surface required to bring out the fine lines of process cuts.

The materials commonly employed in this connection are some of the better sorts of china clay or kaolin, ground talc, and sulphate of lime. In preparing these for the paper-maker the clays are mixed with water to form a thin cream, which is then sent through long sluice ways or settling boxes with riffles to catch and retain the coarser particles which settle out. The water is then allowed to drain off from the finest particles, which alone are suitable for paper-making, and the clay comes to the market in the form of fairly dry lumps of moderate size.

The ground talc is usually not floated, but it is put instead through a fine bolting cloth. Sulphate of lime when used in the form of ground gypsum is similarly treated.

The value of the filling material for use in paper-making is dependent upon several factors, those of most importance being color and fineness. The suitability of the material is also largely determined by its specific gravity, as this of course affects the rate at which the particles of filler settle. The retention is thus likely to be low in case of a very heavy filler, and the paper is likely to be thin for weight. Solubility in water to any considerable extent of course unfits a material for use as a filler. Even the slight degree of solubility possessed by sulphate of lime is sufficient to cut down the retention appreciably.

A filler for use in high-grade papers should be almost entirely free from either grit or mica, since the former is apt to mark the calender rolls, while the shiny specks of the latter are very apparent in the finished sheet.

Clays. — These are formed by the weathering and disintegration of feldspathic rocks. The presence of mica indicates that the source of the clay was granite. With a moderate quantity of water they form a sticky plastic mass, with more or less soapy feel. Chemically considered they are essentially silicate of alumina. Since the value of clay for the uses of paper-making is so largely determined by color, only those sorts like the china clays, in which the content of iron is small, are suitable. The composition of the clays in general use by paper-makers is given below, and their microscopical appearance is shown in Figs 66, 67, and 68.

Analyses of Clays.

Griffin & Little.

	I.	II.	III.	IV.
Moisture, loss at 100° C.	0.30	10.15	7.09	9.10
Combined water, volatile at red heat	12.27	10.77	11.27	12.79
Silica (SiO_2)	47.56	42.72	43.50	41.16
Alumina (Al_2O_3)	38.12	33.44	35.48	35.84
Sesquioxide of iron (Fe_2O_3)	0.08	1.04	trace.	0.67
Lime (CaO)	0.39	1.61	0.17	0.42
Magnesia (MgO)	0.00	0.16	0.41	0.02
Alkalis	1.28	0.11	2.08	—
	100.00	100.00	100.00	100.00
Specific gravity of dry substance	2.8625	2.5585		2.5451
Grit by flotation test (per cent.)	0.65	6.83		0.10

Agalite. — This is a finely ground talc, and is, chemically, a silicate of magnesia. It has an especially good color, and a smooth, soapy feel. It is not nearly so finely reduced as clay, and the proportion of grit is much larger. It is, however, retained well in the paper, and large quantities of it are used. Its appearance under the microscope is shown in Fig. 69.

Analysis of Agalite.

Griffin & Little.

	Per cent.
Moisture and combined water, volatile at red heat	1.40
Silica (SiO_2)	61.89
Alumina (Al_2O_3)	1.36
Sesquioxide of iron (Fe_2O_3)	0.44
Lime (CaO)	4.21
Magnesia (MgO)	30.70
	100.10

Specific gravity, 2.6875.

Pearl Hardening. — Crystallized sulphate of lime, $CaSO_4, 2H_2O$, prepared by precipitating a solution of calcium chloride with one of acid sodium sulphate, or with dilute sulphuric acid,

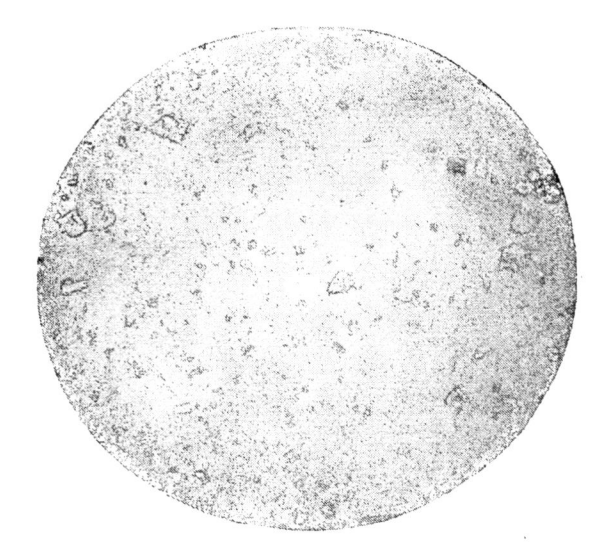

FIG. 68. — LEAMOUR CLAY.

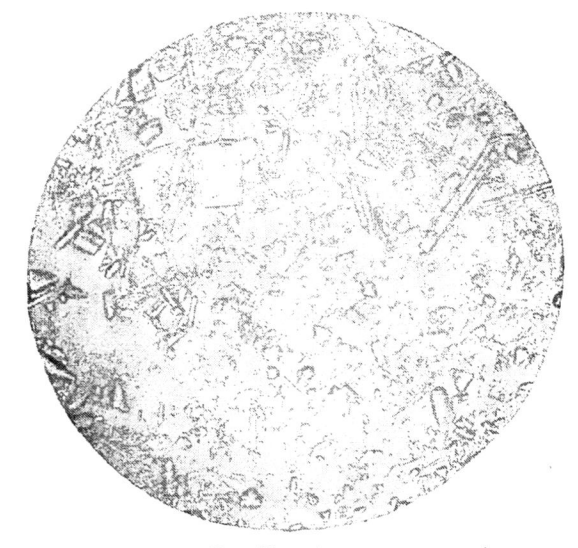

FIG. 69. — AGALITE.

has been largely imported, and used as a filler in the finer grades of paper under the name of *Pearl hardening*. Abroad it is sometimes called *Annaline*. *Crown filler* is another trade name for the same material.

The crystallized sulphate thus prepared is especially white, clean, and free from grit. As found in the market, in moist lumps, it contains a considerable percentage of water in addition to the water of crystallization. The latter amounts to 20.93 per cent on the chemically pure, and otherwise dry, substance; and this combined water remains with the filler to add to the weight of the air-dry paper. We give the following

ANALYSIS OF PEARL HARDENING.

Griffin & Little

	Per cent
Sand, etc., insoluble in acid	None.
Moisture	25.99
Combined water, driven off at red heat	15.31
Sulphate of lime ($CaSO_4$)[1]	57.85
Chloride of calcium ($CaCl_2$)	0.79
	99.94

Specific gravity of dry material, 2.3962

Under the microscope, Fig. 70, pearl hardening is seen to consist of minute needle-like crystals which have somewhat the appearance of short fibres. The crystals are soluble in about 400 parts of water, or to the extent of about 22 lbs. per 1000 gals. This fact, especially when the proportion of filler used is small, and when the return water is allowed to run away, has a considerable effect in cutting down retention.

Ground Gypsum is sometimes, though rarely, used as a filler. It answers to the same formula as pearl hardening, $CaSO_4, 2H_2O$, but in the grinding its crystalline structure is broken down, so that, in this regard, it is little different from any other finely pulverized mineral.

Fibrous Alumine. — A new filler, which has several important advantages, has lately been put upon the market under this name.

[1] Equivalent to crystallized sulphate of lime ($CaSO_4, 2H_2O$), 72.89

It is a fine, smooth, white powder almost entirely free from grit, and has the following composition : —

ANALYSIS OF FIBROUS ALUMINE.

Griffin & Little.

	Per cent
Insoluble in acid	0.32
Sulphate of lime (CaSO$_4$)[1]	82.55
Sulphate of alumina (Al$_2$(SO$_4$)$_3$)	5.92
Sulphate of iron (Fe$_2$(SO$_4$)$_3$)	0.22
Carbonate of lime (CaCO$_3$)	1.04
Carbonate of magnesia (MgCO$_3$)	0.34
Combined water	9.67
	100.06

[1] Equivalent to crystallized sulphate of lime (CaSO$_4$, 2H$_2$O), 104.40

Examination of the above analysis discloses the fact that the filler consists mainly of anhydrous sulphate of lime and that the alumina present is also combined as sulphate. This sulphate of alumina is, therefore, as readily available for use in sizing as though it were so much alum added directly to the engine. Upon agitation with water the anhydrous sulphate of lime combines with two molecules of water of crystallization, and assumes the fibrous, crystalline structure which is shown in Fig. 71, and from which the filler derives its name. Every 100 lbs. of the sulphate of lime as put in the engine forms 126 lbs. of the crystallized sulphate, and this fact, together with the fibrous character of the crystals, has an important bearing upon the quantity retained. Our comparative tests have shown that after hydration fibrous alumine settles much more slowly than other mineral fillers, and this not only aids retention but ensures a more even distribution of the filler through the paper. The sizing power of 100 lbs. of fibrous alumine is about equal to that of 12 lbs. of alum of good grade.

Retention. — Fillers are usually added to the engine after the stock has been well beaten, and before the addition of the size and alum, as the precipitation of the size tends to fix the filler in the fibre. Clays are made into a cream with water, and when intended for the better grades of paper are strained through a piece of Fourdrinier wire before going to the engine. Pearl hardening is

FIG. 70. — Pearl Hardening.

FIG. 71. — Fibrous Alumine.

similarly beaten up, although the straining is unnecessary. Agalite is put into the engine dry. Fibrous alumine is agitated briskly in a separate vessel with water for about one-half hour to bring about the desired crystallization, and is then run into the engine through a revolving strainer which holds back any of the larger crystals.

The quantity of filler retained by the paper may vary from 30 to 80 per cent. of that introduced into the engine. The higher figure is only reached under exceptional conditions, and a retention of 50 per cent. is usually regarded as satisfactory. A number of factors influence the retention, but although it is easy to point out in a general way the direction of their effect, it is impossible to lay down rules which shall apply to any one factor while the others are ignored. The kind of stock and the thoroughness with which it has been beaten and sized has much to do with the quantity of filler left in the sheet. Slow stuff holds the filler much better than that which is "quick" and allows the water to leave it rapidly on the wire. A heavy pull on the suction-boxes cuts down retention, and there is also, of course, a heavy loss in the return water when this is allowed to run to waste. This may amount to a pound of filler in every 30 gallons. Thick stuff and heavy papers generally show better retention than thin papers or stuff which is much diluted, and the percentage held varies also with the different fillers and the quantities used. With pearl hardening, for example, the proportion retained is usually greater when the quantity used is large than when it is inconsiderable.

Use of Starch. — J. Wiesner, who has examined some hundreds of ancient papers, finds that prior to the 13th century starch was the only material used for sizing. It is still used in small quantities as a filler and is thought to give a better feel and surface to the paper. It is either boiled up with the size or the boiled paste may be added directly to the engine. Often the starch is merely mixed with water and added after the mineral filler. Its value is doubtful, as many tests prove the retention to be extremely low.

CHAPTER VI.

COLORING

The great advances in textile-dyeing and color-printing which have resulted from the application of modern chemical methods of research to the problems of the art have by no means found their counterpart in the coloring of paper, which still remains a rather crude and empirical operation. Men whose knowledge of the different coloring-matters and the methods for their development or application is in any way coextensive with that of the best textile dyers are almost unknown in the paper trade. The coloring of an engine of stock is usually only a minor detail in the work of a busy superintendent, although brightness and evenness of color are among the most important factors in determining the quality of his product.

The term "color" as used in paper-making is applied much more generally to those nice distinctions in shade, tint, and general appearance which are to be observed in papers of the same class than to the actual color of the sheet in the ordinary sense of the word.

The materials directly concerned in coloring may be roughly classified as pigments and dyes. Pigments, of which ultramarine may be taken as a type, consist of fine, insoluble, intensely colored particles which are distributed through the sheet in quantity sufficient to give the desired tint. Dyes must, from their nature, be soluble until they are fixed or developed upon the fibre either by entering into loose combination with the substance of the fibre or through the intermediate action of some material called a mordant which has an affinity for both the fibre and the dye.

Dyes which are taken up by the fibre without a mordant are called substantive colors, while those which need a mordant are termed adjective colors. The classification is usually made with reference to silk or wool, as these fibres have much more affinity for colors than those of vegetable origin.

The number of pigments used by paper-makers is quite limited, and most of these are referred to in Chapter VIII. under Mineral Colors. The pigments may either be added directly to the stock in the engine, as in case of ultramarine, orange mineral, and Venetian red, or they may be formed upon the fibre, as when chrome yellow is produced by the addition of a solution of bichromate of potash followed by one of sugar of lead

Prussian blue was at one time always made at the mill by mixing a solution of copperas with one of yellow prussiate of potash, washing the precipitated color by decantation and oxidizing, either by exposure to the air or by addition of a solution of bleaching-powder. Prussian blue is apt to give a greenish tint to the paper, and should always be added after the alum and before the size, as the color is discharged by alkalis.

The complex and peculiar pigment known as ultramarine is largely used in paper-making, and the term is always understood to apply to the blue pigment, although red, green, yellow, and violet ultramarines are known. Common ultramarine often has a greenish cast. The color of a sample of the pigment is always made darker by moisture, and for this reason the low grades sometimes contain added water, glycerine, or molasses. They are lightened in color by admixture of clay, or sulphate of lime, or sulphate of barium.

Ultramarine is very sensitive to acid and to acid alums, but the different samples vary considerably in their power to withstand this action without loss of color. A little red is commonly used with the pigment to improve the shade. Owing to the difficulty of thoroughly wetting a dry powder, it is well to mix the ultramarine with a little glycerine, and to dilute with water before adding to the paper engine. Spots due to small lumps of the powder which break up under the calender rolls are otherwise likely to appear.

The yellow pigments are chromate of lead and yellow ochre. The former is used either as canary paste, or as a powder, but most commonly it is formed on the fibre in the engine. For this purpose a solution of bichromate of potash is added to the stock, and ten or fifteen minutes later one of sugar of lead. The usual proportion is one pound of bichromate to every two pounds of the lead salt. Alums, whether basic or acid, have no effect upon chrome yellow, but bleach residues and alkalis give it an orange tone, which may with sufficient alkali pass to red. The pigment is much used with blues to form green. With Venetian red it gives an orange.

Dyes.—Cochineal as a coloring-matter has been used for a very long time for tinting papers rose or scarlet. The dye is not so durable as some others of the same nature, but is of exceptional purity and of rare brilliance. It is most frequently used along with ultramarine or other blues, for whitening pulp in the production of high-class papers. Since the discovery of the coal-tar colors the use of cochineal has been largely superseded by fuchsine, or magenta, or eosin. Notwithstanding this, there are circumstances under which cochineal is still used, yielding rose, pink, or scarlet colors of any depth of shade, and remarkably pleasing to the eye. Its cost, judged from the standpoint of tinctorial power, is greater than other dyes of the same color, more especially those belonging to the aniline series.

Cochineal, as is well known, is the body of an insect found in Mexico and other parts of Central America, and is therefore, perhaps, the only dye of animal origin known to dyers. Although it was originally found in the central part of the American continent, successful attempts have been made to cultivate its growth in other hot countries; hence large consignments are sent to England and other parts of Europe, from Algeria, Teneriffe, Madeira, etc. The female insects, which yield a larger amount of coloring-matter than the males, are carefully gathered from the cactus plant, upon which they live, and are killed by roasting in a stove or by exposure on plates in the sun. The dried flies are then rubbed, sieved to free them from dirt, and finally sorted. The larger grained variety is the best. They present a somewhat shrivelled appearance of a dark brownish red color with frequent patches of a silvery lustre.

The coloring-matter contained in cochineal is called carminic acid. The behavior of this carminic acid toward chemical salts, etc., shows the paper-maker very clearly the various reactions which take place in the beater engine under the circumstances which usually prevail there, and therefore it is important that these reactions be known, so that he can regulate the shade and otherwise produce in the sheet of paper to be made, a good, clear color of uniform brilliant appearance. The aqueous extract of cochineal is a deep red liquid, which color is transformed into a deep violet on the addition of lime-water, while the addition of a solution of acetate of lead causes a deep violet blue lake to separate out in the form of a precipitate. If a solution of alum, cream of tartar, or acid oxalate of potash be added to it, the albuminous substance which is dissolved along with the coloring-matter from the flies, coagulates and carries down the carminic acid as a flocculent precipitate of a beautiful deep carmine color. This is the purest and strongest carmine. It is of great coloring-power, and in order to weaken it for industrial purposes, it is mixed with colorless substances, such as starch.

When carminic acid is separated from aqueous decoctions of cochineal by means of metallic oxides, the compounds formed are called carmine lakes. Thus, when an alkaline carbonate (carbonate of soda) dissolved in water is added to a decoction of cochineal which contains alum, a beautiful colored compound of the carminic acid and the alumina of the alum separates out, which is essentially a carmine lake. In the same way, when "tin crystals," previously dissolved in water, are added to a slightly alkaline decoction of cochineal, the oxide of tin combines with the carminic acid, forming, as above a beautiful carmine lake The aqueous extract of cochineal is unaltered by the addition of very dilute acids Alkalis, on the other hand, change the original crimson to a bluish red. These reactions show, in a general way, what will take place should any of these chemicals be brought into contact with the color when in the beater. An excess of free alkali (rosin size), for example, will impart a bluish shade to the pulp.

There are two decoctions of cochineal used when tinting papers with this dye; namely, the aqueous and ammoniacal extracts. The former is simply prepared by grinding the cochineal flies to powder in a large mortar and gently boiling them in pure soft water for half an hour in an ordinary copper. The first extract is then drawn off, and the boiling repeated several times with fresh portions of water The extracts are then mixed and carefully filtered through a close cotton bag

The ammoniacal extract is prepared by adding a known weight of the pulverized dye to spirits of ammonia in a carboy, with constant stirring, the proportions being 10 lbs of cochineal to three gallons of ammonia liquor of 66 per cent The carboy and contents are then closely corked up and laid aside for several days in a warm room, the temperature of which is kept constant until the liquor has thickened. The longer it is kept, the better its quality. Before adding this extract to the pulp in the beater, it must be diluted with water and carefully filtered.

Pulp which has been mordanted with alum and covered with cochineal produces a more durable tone than pulp not mordanted at all. But the color is somewhat dull, and is brightened by the use of a little oxalic acid. This acid imparts a yellowish shade to the crimson, especially if much of it be used. The presence of an excess of alkali (rosin size) changes the tone from red to blue, and therefore the size must not be in excess. Indeed, when sizing, the alum or sulphate of alumina must be added until the characteristic blue, produced by the alkali, has vanished. An addition of "tin crystals" brightens the color and develops its full brilliance. A much better reagent to use for the development and "fixing" of cochineal colors is the mordant known in trade as "scarlet liquor," and which is so extensively used in the dyeing and calico-printing industries. Scarlet liquor is a chloride of tin specially prepared in the liquid form and sold in carboys. Its action upon the pulp in the beater is much surer and quicker than "tin crystals," and on this account is to be preferred. A small quantity of tartaric acid is used along with it.

With the aqueous extract of cochineal it is somewhat difficult to obtain uniform results, and for this reason it is better to employ the ammoniacal extract, which, in conjunction with alum and tartaric acid, is the best way of coloring paper pulp with this dye. The alum and tartaric acid neutralize the ammoniacal cochineal and precipitate the carmine lake upon the pulp in a very uniform state. The pulp for this purpose should be well washed and free from bleach liquor. The alum and tartaric acid are then added, and when thoroughly incorporated with the fibre the ammoniacal cochineal is poured in in sufficient quantity to produce the depth of color required. Tin crystals slightly acidified with muriatic acid improve and brighten the color.

When coloring with this dye the "sizing" must be carried out with care. The pulp is usually colored before adding the size. The alum may then be added, and when thoroughly mixed, the rosin size, which should be largely diluted with water, is gradually poured in. The reason of this is obvious. If the size be added in the strong and concentrated state, the precipitated flakes of rosin may surround portions of the colored pulp, changing them to blue, which may not be affected by the acidity of the alum, even though this is in excess. For this reason the pulp is kept distinctly acid, with alum or the other mordants used, before running it into the stuff chest.

Papers colored with cochineal are very easily bleached by chlorine or bleach liquor, and are very susceptible to change under the influence of alkalis and acids. When heated in lime-water the crimson changes to violet. Dilute oil of vitriol transforms it into orange. Alcohol acidified with muriatic acid changes the color into a dirty yellow, while chloride of copper converts it into brown. By these tests cochineal colors may be known.

Since the discovery, by Perkins, in 1856, of mauvein, the list of materials available for the purposes of the dyer and paper-stainer has been enriched by a long series of very complex synthetical products derived from coal tar and known collectively as the coal-tar colors. These are generally the salts, as the hydrochloride or acetate, of colorless bases. For a time they were in some disrepute because of their want of fastness, but, as now made, some of them are more fast than indigo, while their brilliancy and convenience have enabled them to largely displace the older coloring-materials. The two most prominent classes of these dyes are those derived from aniline and the more recent azo dyes, which last form a whole series of fast and brilliant colors, all containing nitrogen.

As the study of the coal-tar colors forms one of the most difficult branches of chemistry, owing to their immense number and great complexity of composition, no attempt can be made in the present chapter to do more than refer, under their commercial names, to a few of those more commonly employed in paper-making.

The more prominent red dyes are magenta, eosin, the fast pinks, and saframine. These are called "straight colors," and many shades are made by their proper blending. They are mordanted with alum, or some extract like fustic containing tannin, or they may be fixed by sugar of lead. The magentas are salts of rosaniline, the hydrochloride being a common form, and they are also known commercially as fuchsine and aniline red. They occur as brilliant green crystals having the sheen noticed on the backs of certain beetles. The blue shades are purest, and well-crystallized samples should be preferred. They sometimes contain arsenic as an impurity. They dissolve readily in water to a magnificent crimson solution.

The eosins are a class of dyes derived from fluorescein. They are soluble in water and in alcohol, the latter solution being commonly fluorescent. They give a red which in some instances inclines to blue. They form lakes with alum.

Commercial safranine is a reddish-brown powder, which forms with water a red solution from which the color may be fixed by tannin extracts or tartar emetic. Under the head of the safranine dyes are comprised, however, a class of colors which range in shade from red to blue.

For the browns between red and yellow, paper brown and Bismarck brown are among the colors used, the tint being thrown to one side or the other by careful admixture of reds or yellows. These browns are soluble in water, and are best mordanted by means of tartar emetic

Auramine and naphthol are among the principal yellow dyes The former occurs as a sulphur-yellow powder, soluble in water and alcohol. It may be fixed by tartar emetic or by tannin.

The green coloring-matters derived from coal tar are especially rich and numerous. The straight colors, brilliant green, Victoria green, and malachite green, are those most used, and all three are soluble in water.

The blue dyes are also numerous, but the three most generally employed are soluble blue, paper blue, and cotton blue. Special shades are obtained in commercial anilines by the admixture of two or more of these. All are fixed by alum.

Methyl violet is the color most used for violet and the reddish shades of blue It occurs as a greenish powder or in crystals The tint of the commercial samples is made to range from very red to very blue. The color is precipitated by yellow prussiate of potash.

The commercial dyes which give the intermediate shades and colors are frequently, as has been already indicated, made by mixing two or more of the straight colors in proportions determined by careful experiment. Such admixture may often be detected by allowing a drop of the solution to fall upon filter paper, when, as the drop spreads out, differently colored zones appear. It is, in many cases, not difficult to match such a sample of mixed color by making up a solution containing a given quantity of the sample for a standard, and then mixing together, in carefully noted quantities, solutions of the other dyes which seem to be required, until the standard solution has been matched. From the strength and quantities of the other solutions used may then be calculated the proportions needed of the different dyes. All the solutions are best made rather dilute, and the tints are most easily compared in tubes such as are used for nesslerizing water.

The intense coloring power of these dyes makes them especially liable to adulteration or dilution by inert and valueless materials Sugar, dextrine, common salt, and sulphate of soda are commonly used for this purpose and are for the most part unobjectionable. except as they may carry dirt or diminish the tinctorial power of the sample. The salt and sulphate of soda, Glauber's salt, have a certain value as mordants, but when required they can be bought more cheaply under their common names. This sophistication has been the direct result of the demand by the buyers for cheap colors, and it may be taken as a general rule that the best colors will be found the cheapest when the cost is estimated, as it should be, on the ton of paper colored.

For use in the paper engine, it is customary to select those colors which are soluble in water, as the use of the alcohol colors involves considerable extra expense The best colors will stand boiling; those of lower grade should be dissolved in hot water. The solution, in either case. should be carefully strained through flannel and added to the engine before the size or alum. Many of the color manufacturers send out special formulas for guidance in the use of their colors, and it is well to consult and follow these. When the color has been properly fixed, either by the fibre or by the use of alum or other mordant, there should be no tinge to the water which runs away when a handful of the stuff is squeezed. It will be commonly found that the tints obtained from a given color will vary with the furnish, since the different fibres take the color differently. Ground wood is especially apt to change the tone of a color, but it is in any case impossible to lay down general rules which can replace experience.

The coloring of paper to the exact shade required by the buyer is somewhat complicated by the fact that the color of the stuff in the beater is never that of the finished paper, but always darker, mainly because of the large amount of water present, but also in some cases because of the effect which the heat of the dryers has upon certain delicate colors. It is, for this reason, often customary for superintendents to reduce to pulp the sheet they wish to match, and then to bring the stuff in the engine to this shade. By folding a sheet and looking into it. as into a partly opened book, the intensity of a faint tint is much increased, through multiple reflection of the light, and in this way a conclusion may often be reached as to the colors required to match the given shade.

A rough idea of what the color of the finished sheet will be may be obtained by squeezing a handful of the stuff and then beating it out between the hands and drying, but the thickness and unevenness of the cake introduce a considerable chance for error. When several engines of a given color have to be made up, it is a common practice to retain a bowl of the stuff from the first engine and to use this as the standard for comparison. The color of the stuff in the bowl is, however, apt to change on standing, and especially to grow darker. The better way is to squeeze out a handful of the stuff and match the next engine by it, the sample from the second engine then serving for the following one, and so on. Since it is a difficult thing at best to secure an exact match between two lots of paper, every care should be taken to have the conditions under which comparisons of color are made as nearly alike every time as possible. The character of the light coming through one window may be so far different from that at another one as to cause appreciable difference in the tint of colors examined at one place or the other. Light from the north is best.

Great differences in light are caused by reflection from the objects outside, and it is therefore advisable to select some one place in the mill where the light is good, and to do all the matching there. At night an arc light is best for showing colors, but wherever possible a change of colors should only be made in the daytime.

The kind of filler used has a considerable influence on the color of the sheet, and when changing onto a new filler or modifying the proportions of the old one it often becomes necessary to change the color furnish. The same observations of course apply when the mixture in the engine is modified by the addition of broken paper.

Numerous color furnishes are given by Dunbar, — *The Practical Paper-Maker*, London, 1887, — which will be found useful as indicating the proportions in which the various coloring-matters are employed in the production of colored papers. In the use of such general recipes, however, due allowance must always be made for the character of the stock and other materials in the furnish.

CHAPTER VII.

WATER

THE very large quantities of water which are required in the processes of paper-making, and the readiness with which the quality of the product is influenced by conditions which affect the character of the water-supply, make the subject one of the first importance to the manufacturer. Water which is pure in the strict chemical sense — that is, water which contains no foreign substance — is never obtained in nature, so that, from the manufacturing as well as from the sanitary standpoint, we have to consider waters with reference to the amount and character of the foreign constituents which they contain, and these include not only the mineral or inorganic substances which may be present, but also the various minute forms of plant and animal life.

Waters are broadly divided into surface and ground waters, surface waters comprising those of brooks, rivers, ponds, and lakes, while ground waters, as their name implies, are those which have percolated to some depth through the soil and the underlying porous strata. Although all these waters have a common origin in rain, and though surface waters become ground waters, and the reverse, there are yet certain broad distinctions between the classes, which are the result, in the main, of the action of light and air in the one case, and of the filtering and oxidizing power of porous earth, together with the solvent action of the water, in the other. Surface waters are apt to be more or less highly colored, and they contain plant and animal life, to which, in fact, much of their color is often due. Ground waters are clear and colorless, but they show a greater content of mineral matter.

Soft waters are such as contain comparatively little of those mineral constituents which have the power of decomposing soap, while hard waters are those in which this power is present in a marked degree. Lime salts are the most common cause of hardness in water, and of these the carbonate is most conspicuous, although in some localities hardness may be due to sulphate. Common salt and salts of magnesium, when present, have the same effect, the latter to an extent which is even more marked than in case of those of lime. The hardness of a water, as determined by the quantity of standard soap solution required to produce a permanent lather, is expressed in degrees, each degree indicating a hardness equivalent to that due to one grain of carbonate of lime in a gallon of water, or, better, one part of carbonate of lime to 100,000 parts of water.

For washing stock and for boiler purposes, a soft water is desirable, or even necessary, from its greater solvent power in the one case, and its slight tendency to form scale in the other. Its importance in the other departments of the manufacture is rather overestimated; for in boiling stock, bleaching, or furnishing an engine, the softest water is made hard by the materials employed in the operation. The use of a very hard water will, however, undoubtedly increase the quantity of size required, since the size is merely a soap, and the insoluble lime or magnesia soaps thrown down have little or no sizing power. Hardness due to sulphate of lime will also discharge the color of certain aniline blues, when these are used in the small amounts required in white papers.

The most important quality of water, from the paper-maker's standpoint, is that of color. The volume of water used in making a ton of paper is so great, — it is probably never less than 50,000, and sometimes as much as 200,000, gallons, — and the fibres form so perfect a filter, besides possessing the power of removing much of the dissolved coloring-matter, that the presence in the water of even minute quantities of material injurious to color may render impossible the manufacture of paper of high grade.

The purest natural waters are clear and colorless when examined in small quantities, but in the mass they have a bluish tint. Surface waters show every gradation in color, from this pellucid clearness through yellow and reddish tints to the dark brown of swamp waters. The only systematic attempt, within our knowledge, to apply a standard to the measurement of the depth of color found in waters, has been made by Dr Drown, chemist to the State Board of Health of Massachusetts, in the course of his exhaustive examination of the water-supplies of the State. The method adopted was that first suggested by Prof. Leeds. In the reports of the Board the color of the waters is expressed by numbers which increase with the amount of color. Water having a color of 1 0 is a decided yellowish brown. This color corresponds to that obtained by nesslerizing 1 c.c. of the standard ammonium chloride solution used in the determination of the ammonia in water. By this standard the average depth of color of the Connecticut River water at Turner's Falls is 0.30, though it ranges from 0.10 to 0.80. The Merrimac River at Lawrence shows a somewhat higher average, — 0.33, — though no single sample had a color above 0.70.

The color of water is due mainly to those substances which leach out from the ulmic matter formed by the decay of leaves, grasses, and similar material in the soil or on the surface of the ground. In other words, the cause in most cases or in greater part is decaying vegetation. If this decay has proceeded far, as in peaty swamps, the brown coloration thus derived is very permanent in character.

The immense number of microscopic plants which are developed in some surface waters at certain seasons of the year are an important cause of color in such waters. Such growths are most common in summer, though the periods of greatest abundance are often not coincident in case of the different genera. As a rule, however, the more important genera appear year after year in much the same order, so that where a particular organism has caused trouble at one time, a recurrence of the difficulty at about the same time may be expected the following year, if the conditions remain the same. The most important of these plants, from our present point of view, are the algæ. These are green or bluish green, and, like the larger plants, derive their color from chlorophyl and require light for their development. They do not occur to any extent in rapidly flowing streams, but thrive in ponds or reservoirs in which the water is comparatively stagnant. The fresh-water sponges, which occur as thin incrustations upon objects immersed in the water, or as a coating within the pipes, are doubtless, through their decomposition, a not infrequent cause of unpleasant tastes and odors in water. They thrive best in summer and in water which is in motion.

The suspended mineral matter, clay, silt, and such material, which a water carries has at times a marked effect upon the color of the water. This factor is a very variable one, and exerts its greatest influence after heavy rains, which wash the finely divided soil and earth into the streams. The soluble mineral constituents have, for the most part, no effect upon color. Even the soluble salts of iron are rarely or never present in amount sufficient to perceptibly color the water while they are present as such. It is when from any cause the iron is precipitated as hydrate that they cause trouble.

We have occasionally noticed, in case of mills using unfiltered water drawn from ponds, a gradual accumulation of a rust-like deposit in the water pipes, which sometimes was sufficient to nearly choke them up. It is probable that this difficulty is due to the microscopical plants known as iron bacteria, of which the commonest and most important is *Crenothrix Kuhniana*, or "well-thread." Although perhaps the largest among the bacteria, it is of course exceedingly minute, and quite invisible to the naked eye, until, by the accumulation of multitudes of cells, flocks or masses of visible size are formed. The cells are mainly cylindrical, and are united end to end to form threads or filaments. The presence of salts of iron in solution is necessary for their vigorous growth, and they have the curious power of withdrawing this iron from the water and depositing it in the form of ferric oxide as a sheath or tube around the filament. The color of this sheath, which at first is hardly noticeable, passes through this accumulation of iron from pale yellow to deep brown, and there is at the same time a gradual thickening of the wall. The thick and hard sheath then seems no longer suited to the activities of the plant, and is abandoned by the cells, which, as they work out from it, cause it to take on an increase of length or a structure which suggests branching.

Crenothrix has at several times been the cause of serious trouble in the water-supplies of European cities, notably at Berlin in 1878, and at Rotterdam in 1887. Its occurrence in this country is well established, and it is known to be common in Massachusetts. It may be removed and kept out of a water by thorough filtration, but may grow rapidly in an imperfectly filtered effluent. Light is not necessary for its growth, and in fact it thrives best in dark reservoirs or galleries and in systems of pipe.

All waters consume small quantities of bleaching-powder, the amount in each case depending upon that of the organic matter present in the water. Except in rare cases, the loss of bleach thus occasioned is inappreciable, as appears from our results given below.—

Volatile and inorganic matter in water	Bleaching-powder (36 per cent.) consumed
0 93 grains per gallon	1.77 grains per gallon.
0 35	1.16
1.167	3 87

The mineral constituents of a water affect its value for paper-making mainly as they bear upon the suitability of the water for boiler purposes. As already pointed out, a soft water is desirable for some of the operations of the mill, but its use in a boiler is almost essential if trouble from scale is to be avoided. According to Haswell, a coating of scale one-sixteenth of an inch in thickness causes a loss of fuel equal to 14 7 per cent., while we have seen samples of scale an inch and a quarter thick. When any considerable thickness of scale is present, there is much danger of overheating the boiler locally. This is often followed by blistering or cracking of the plates or collapsing of the tubes, and may even cause explosion, due to the breaking of the scale and the sudden contact of the water with the overheated plate below

Carbonate of lime is the most frequent cause of boiler scale. It is normally very slightly soluble in water; but if the water contains dissolved carbonic acid, the lime may be brought into solution as bicarbonate in very considerable amount. The bicarbonate is the cause of what is called *temporary hardness*, for upon boiling it is decomposed, with precipitation of the carbonate. According to Cousté, this precipitation is complete at 200° F., or under the conditions which obtain in most boilers Carbonate of magnesia, which is similarly soluble in the presence of dissolved carbonic acid, and similarly precipitated on boiling, is also likely to form scale Chloride of magnesia, although extremely soluble in water, is nevertheless objectionable, because at high pressures it is decomposed, with liberation of hydrochloric acid and formation of hydrate of magnesia, the latter acting as a sort of cement in binding together other scale-forming materials The precipitated carbonate of magnesia undergoes a like decomposition, carbonic acid being set free

The general character of a carbonate scale appears from the following analysis, but the proportions show considerable variation in different samples.

Analysis of a Carbonate Scale

(Silvester)

	Per cent
Carbonate of lime	75 85
Sulphate of lime	3 68
Hydrate of magnesia	2 56
Chloride of sodium	0 45
Silica	7 66
Oxides of iron and alumina	2 96
Organic matter	3 64
Moisture	3 20
	100 00

Sulphate of lime, although rather soluble in water, has its point of greatest solubility at 95° F., and from a solution saturated at this temperature, the salt is therefore gradually thrown out as the temperature rises. Moreover, the hydrated sulphate, $CaSO_4\ 2\ H_2O$, begins to lose its water of crystallization at about 260° F., and is converted into the anhydrous sulphate, $CaSO_4$, which is far more insoluble. Both these actions combine to produce a hard scale as the sulphate accumulates in the boiler, and the usual methods of softening water are of comparatively little value when sulphate of lime is present.

Much silica is troublesome in a water used for boiler purposes, as, when deposited, it serves as a binding material and causes the production of a very hard scale.

Acid waters are rarely met with in this country, where there is comparatively little contamination of streams by manufacturing waste; but in sulphite mills there is danger, if for any reason check-valves do not work properly, that some of the liquor from the digesters may find its way into the generating boilers and cause corrosion, which is more to be dreaded than scale. Cylinder oils not unfrequently contain free fatty acids, and when these are present, they pass with the feed water back into the boiler and corrode the metal. Very alkaline waters also are apt to attack the boiler fittings and cause leakage.

A 100-horse-power boiler evaporates 30,000 lbs. of water in 10 hours, or 900 tons in 25 days of continuous working. Since the mineral matters remain behind in the boiler as the evaporation of the water proceeds, it becomes obvious that apparently insignificant amounts of mineral impurity may, in this process of concentration, accumulate to such an extent as to cause serious inconvenience from mud and scale. A deposit of scale $\frac{1}{16}$ of an inch in thickness has already been said to cause a loss of fuel of 14 7 per cent., while if the scale is $\frac{1}{4}$-inch thick, the loss is said to amount to 38 per cent. A great many materials have been proposed for use in boilers as preventives of scale, but most of them are of doubtful value. Organic substances containing tannic acid, as, for instance, oak or hemlock bark, are sometimes used, their value depending on the tannic acid. Other materials, which either contain acetic acid, or which are of such a nature that the acid may be developed from them under the heat and pressure of the boiler, have also been used with some success, but are objectionable, from the danger that the acid due to them may corrode the boiler. Crude or refined petroleum has been recommended for use with waters containing large amounts of sulphate of lime. The refined oil is preferable, as the residuum from the crude oil is apt to cake on the plates and bind the scale more firmly. Abroad, sulphate waters are purified by the addition of carefully regulated amounts of either caustic soda or soda-ash, or, more rarely, barium chloride. Both the caustic soda and soda-ash result in precipitation of carbonate of lime, but the soda-ash is to be preferred. The barium chloride forms the very soluble chloride of calcium and the insoluble sulphate of barium. If the alkalis are used, much care is necessary to secure the proper amount, as an excess causes foaming.

The method for softening waters which is most generally used is that which is especially applicable to waters containing lime or magnesia as bicarbonates, and which is due to Dr. Clark. The Clark process depends upon the fact that when lime is added to such waters the extra equivalent of carbonic acid is neutralized, with the result that the lime originally present in the water, together with the added lime, is thrown down as the insoluble neutral carbonate, while the bicarbonate of magnesia is at the same time decomposed, with precipitation of the magnesia as hydroxide. Various modifications of the Clark process have appeared, which base their claims to improvement upon changes in the apparatus employed. The process is perhaps now most commonly worked under the form known as the Porter-Clark process, the apparatus for which is shown in Fig. 72.

The tank shown at the left of the figure is fitted with a mechanical agitator, and is used for preparing the lime-water by admixture of water and milk of lime, the latter being introduced through the funnel. The lime-water in a carefully regulated stream then flows over into the second tank, where it meets the water to be purified. The outflow from this tank is so controlled as to allow sufficient time for the completion of the desired reaction, and is

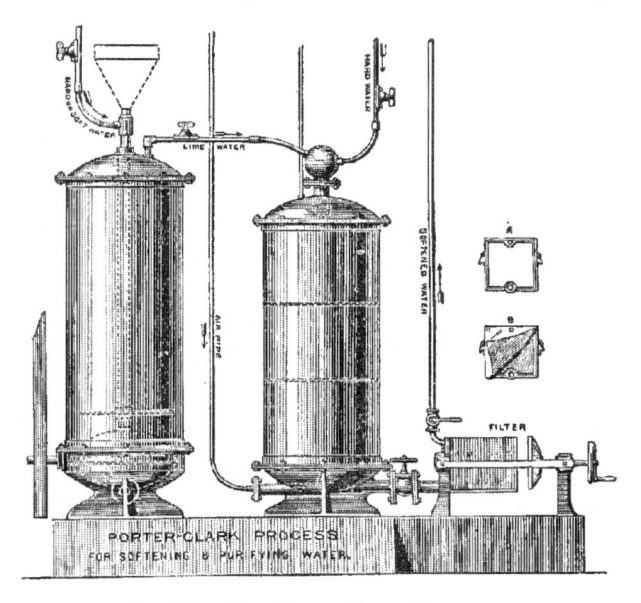

FIG. 72. — THE PORTER-CLARK PROCESS.

finally sent through a filter-pump, which retains the precipitated material and discharges the softened and clarified water.

Filtration. — The purification of water by filtration is a much more complex series of actions than a mere mechanical straining, though this is the most noticeable, and from our present point of view the most important, office of filtration. In the slow passage of water through a filtering medium, the principle of subsidence comes in play to hold back particles so fine that they would otherwise pass the interstices of the filter, and the water is at the same time subjected to influences which set up changes of both the chemical and biological order.

The primary action of a filter is, then, a straining one, to remove the coarser particles of suspended mineral and vegetable matter in the water. It is obvious, in addition, that if the water were standing in a tank, it would gradually clear itself of these impurities by the settling due to gravity. The length of time thus required would depend, other things being equal, upon the depth of water in the tank. If now the tank were divided by a midway horizontal partition, or false bottom, the average distance which each suspended particle must fall in order to find a resting-place is halved, and the time needed for the action similarly lessened. Within a filtering medium the number of shelves or surfaces upon which the finest particles may find lodgment as they settle is immensely great, and it is in large part to this fact that the efficiency of the medium is due.

The action of porous earth, when the passage of water through it is intermittent, is an oxidizing one of high order, from the fact that the water and the gas are brought so intimately into contact. In the natural filtration to which surface waters are subjected during their transformation into ground waters, this action may proceed so far under favorable conditions as to completely oxidize all the organic matter originally present. In this way not only is the suspended organic matter removed, together with the silt, by the process of straining, but the dissolved organic matter to which much of the color may have been due is consumed by oxidation, leaving the water, as in case of all perfectly filtered waters, entirely clear and colorless. The same process goes on to a considerable extent in artificial filtration, where the flow of water is intermittent and properly controlled. In continuous filtration there is little or no oxidation of organic matter, and other means are used to secure its removal.

The filtration of water has been mainly studied scientifically with reference to its sanitary aspect, and from this point of view the removal of bacteria and other organisms is the matter of first importance. It has been found that a layer of fine sand one inch in depth is sufficient to remove all algæ and animals from a water as rich in organisms as the Cochituate water of Boston.

In Europe open filter-beds are very generally used for the purification of water by filtration, and where the purification is for municipal purposes, the beds are sometimes of enormous extent. The filter-beds of the various London water companies cover an area of more than 100 acres. The continental cities have extensive and similar plants. The beds are built up of stones which decrease in size toward the top of the bed, and which are covered with a layer of fine sand, generally two inches in thickness. The average capacity of such filter beds is found to be 1,000,000 gallons per acre per twenty-four hours. Under these conditions there is formed upon the surface of the filter-bed a growth of bacteria which is called the bacteria jelly, and which prevents almost entirely the passage of bacteria through the filter, while of course at the same time holding back the suspended impurities in the water. The water of the Spree contains, for instance, under normal conditions, about 100,000 bacteria per cubic centimetre, while after passing through the filter-bed it has only 30–40 per cubic centimetre when the rate of flow is 1,000,000 gallons, and only 4–5 when the rate falls to 300,000 gallons per day.

The economic and climatic conditions which prevail in this country almost entirely preclude the operation of such extensive plants of relatively small capacity, so that most municipalities and factories requiring filtered water make use of some form of mechanical filter. These may be grouped under two systems, — gravity filters and pressure filters, — and we shall limit ourselves to the description of representative types of each system.

The efficiency of filters working under either of these systems is increased, and a partial chemical, as well as a complete mechanical, purification of the water effected by the introduction with the water of small quantities of alum or other coagulant. A crude sulphate of alumina is generally employed, and seems to give better results than crystallized alum. The alumina precipitated by the action of the alkaline water not only gathers the finely suspended material into flocks of appreciable size, but also removes the dissolved organic coloring-matter, and forms a film over the surface of the filter, which acts, as does the bacteria jelly before mentioned, in holding back minute organisms. The quantity of alum thus used varies from $\frac{1}{4}$-grain to 2 or 3 grains per gallon, the usual maximum being 2 grains. If very large amounts of loam are present in the water, small quantities of lime may sometimes be used first, and then alum.

The form of gravity filter which has been most generally introduced is the Warren filter, shown in Figs. 73 and 74. A Warren filter-plant usually consists of a settling-basin, one or more filters, and a weir for controlling the head, together with the necessary pipe connections. Each filter contains a bed of fine, sharp sand, C, two feet in depth, supported by a perforated copper bottom, B, and for cleaning this bed an agitator, D, is provided. This consists of a heavy rake containing 13 teeth 25 inches long, rotated by a system of gearing, K, and capable of being driven into the bed by means of suitable screw mechanism, LM, whereby the entire bed is thoroughly scoured.

The process of filtration is as follows: The water enters the settling-basin through a valve operated by a float, by which a

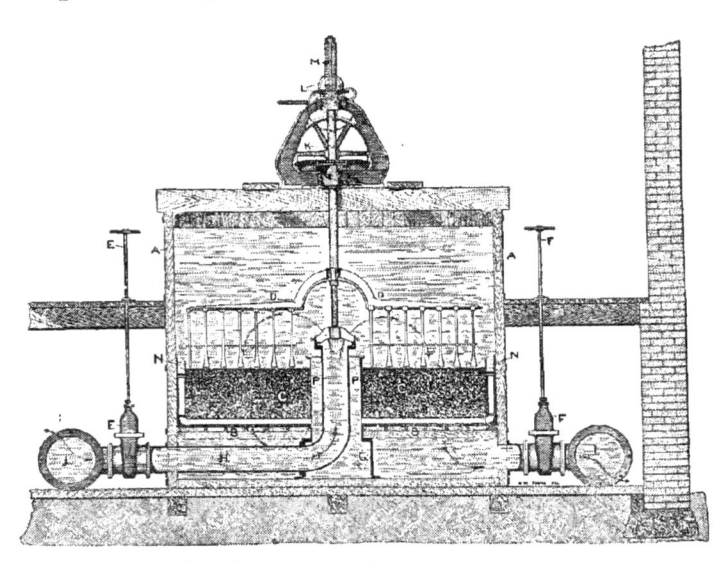

FIG. 73. — THE WARREN FILTER. — IN OPERATION.

constant level is maintained in the entire filter-system. The water entering through this valve passes through an 8-bladed propeller of brass, from 10 to 16 inches in diameter, so arranged as to revolve freely with the passage of the water. This, by means of two small bevel gears and an upright shaft, operates an alum pump, consisting of six hollow arms radiating from a chambered hub and bent in the direction of rotation. This pump revolves in a small tank containing a dilute standard solution of sulphate of alumina, or other coagulant, and by its revolution each arm takes up its modicum of alum water, passes it into the hub and to the deflector, which sends it down to the incoming water.

When the bed of a filter becomes clogged, and it seems best to clean it, the inlet and outlet valves EF are closed, and the washout G opened, allowing the contents of the tanks to escape to the sewer. The agitator D is then set in motion by means of the friction clutch with which it is equipped; and as the teeth on the rake begin to plough up the surface of the bed, a slight amount of filtered water is allowed to flow back up through the bed, in

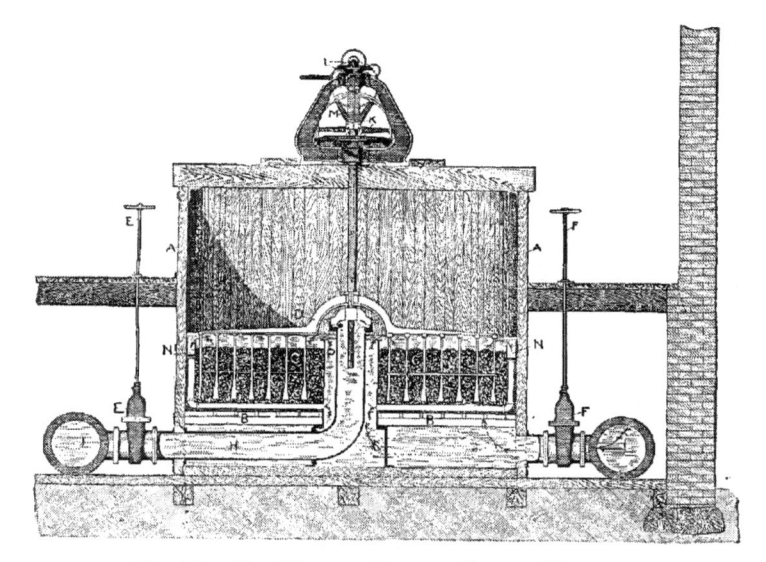

FIG. 74. — THE WARREN FILTER. — DURING WASHING.

order to rinse off the dirt loosened by the scouring action of the rake. This is kept up until the rake penetrates to the bottom of the bed, and thoroughly agitates every particle of material therein. As soon as the water flowing to the sewer appears to be clear, the motion of the rake is reversed, and it is slowly withdrawn from the bed. When the teeth are raised above the bed, the waste pipe is closed, the inlet valve E opened, and the filter-tank allowed to fill. After waiting a few minutes for the tank to resume its normal condition, the outlet valve F is slowly opened, and filtration is resumed.

The incoming water, having received its proportionate amount of coagulant, is then allowed to remain in the settling-basin from thirty to forty minutes, to enable the chemical reaction between the coagulant and the bases in the water to take place, and to permit of the heavier sediment, together with a portion of the coagulated matter, to settle by subsidence to the bottom of the tank, where it can be drawn off at intervals into the sewer.

The partially purified water then passes on through suitable piping and valves to the filter, and, filling the tank, passes down through the fine sand bed, leaving all the coagulated matter upon it. The filtered water makes its exit through the main I

The main, collecting the filtered water from the various filters, passes along between them to the head-box, or weir, over which the water is compelled to pass, and which controls the operation of the filters. The top of this weir is 20 inches below the water level maintained in the filter-system, and this head of 20 inches (equivalent to a pressure of three-fourths of a pound to a square inch) is the extreme pressure that can be brought to bear upon the filters, and it is claimed that they can at no time be pushed beyond the rate which experience has shown to yield the best results.

Two sizes of the Warren filter are built, both being 8 feet high. The smaller filter is 8 feet 8 inches in diameter, and has a capacity under alum of 200,000–250,000 gallons per twenty-four hours on a net area of 56 square feet. The large size is 10 feet 6 inches in diameter, its net area being 84 square feet, and its capacity 300,000–375,000 gallons. About 5 horse-power is required for each agitator; but as only one filter is washed at a time, the quantity of power required is irrespective of the size of the plant. The filters are usually washed every twelve hours.

The especial points of merit claimed for this system are, first, its cheapness, and, second, the thorough and rapid cleansing of the bed by the attrition of its particles set up by the mechanical stirring and scraping action of the rake.

The forms of pressure filter shown in Figs. 75 and 76, and built by the New York Filter Company, embody the best features of the numerous systems which, after being developed on somewhat divergent lines, have now been brought under the single control of this company. The filter shown in Fig. 75 consists of a cylindrical steel shell built to withstand any desired pressure. The water is introduced along a conduit running the entire length of the filter just beneath the crown. It filters through 4 feet of coke and sand, and passes out by the cone valves shown at the bottom. These valves are imbedded permanently in a cement floor and flush with it. They are filled with screened quartz gravel to prevent the passage of the filtering medium into the mains.

The method of cleansing the filter adopted by this company is that known as sectional washing, by which the entire force of the reversed current used in washing is directed against one-third of the bed only for about five minutes; it is then shut off, and the central third of the bed is scoured in the same manner; last, the remaining third is washed. No partitions are necessary to divide the bed, as the current is forced up nearly in a straight line. By

FIG. 75.—SECTIONAL WASHING PRESSURE FILTER.—NEW YORK FILTER COMPANY.

thus concentrating the force of the upward current against a small portion of the bed, thorough attrition and scouring of the particles composing the bed is accomplished, while the upward current carries away the separated impurities. The capacity of such a filter 8 feet in diameter and 20 feet long is about 500,000 gallons per twenty-four hours; or, in other words, two such filters have the capacity of a European filter-bed one acre in extent, when the latter is worked at the rate recommended by the Berlin authorities.

Fig. 76 shows a vertical washing-filter of essentially the same type. These are built in sizes ranging from 12 inches to 10 feet in diameter, and have a maximum capacity per twenty-four hours from about 4000 to 360,000 gallons. The filter consists of a vertical steel shell, the cone valves at the bottom being set on rubble grouting and imbedded in cement. The space above is about two-thirds filled with fine quartz sand and coke. The water to be purified is admitted under pressure to the filter at *A*, which delivers the water at the crown of the filter. It then passes down through the bed and out through the cone valves to the outlet *B*, leading to the service pipe. As often as may be necessary, usually once a day, the water is shut off from the inlet and allowed to enter the filter in the upward direction through the lower valves. These are so arranged as to admit the water to the cones under-

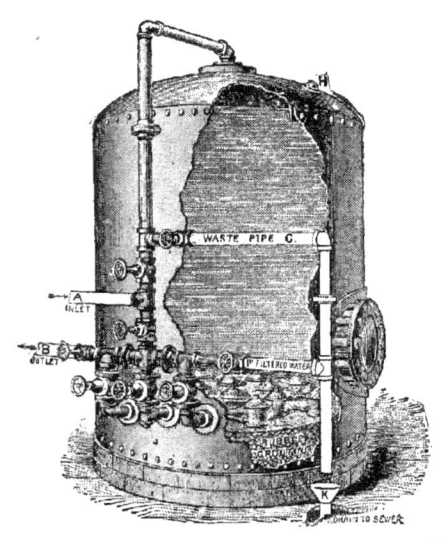

FIG. 76.—SECTIONAL WASHING PRESSURE FILTER.—NEW YORK FILTER COMPANY.

lying one-third of the bed at a time, and the waste water, carrying with it the impurities, passes to the sewer through *K*.

A minute quantity of alum solution is injected into the water passing to these filters, as in case of practically all systems of filtration in use in this country. In the present instance a special alum pump is employed which delivers a positive quantity of the solution, which is carefully regulated to suit the requirements of the water.

A novel form of plant is the Dervaux automatic water-purifying apparatus, shown in Fig. 77, for which we are indebted to the *Papier-Zeitung*. The action of the apparatus is a double one, cor-

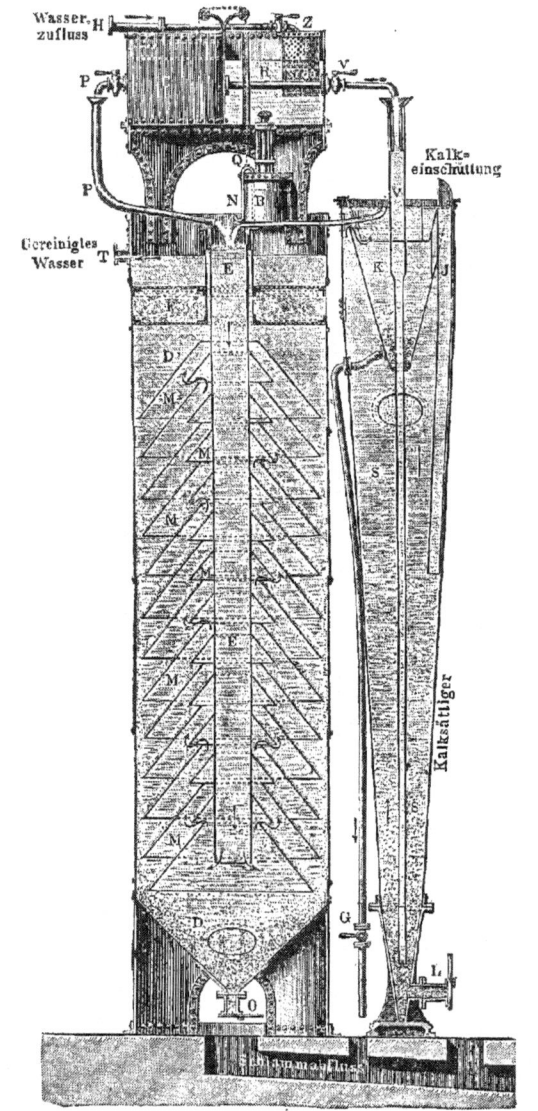

FIG. 77.—DERVAUX WATER-PURIFIER.

EXPLANATION OF TERMS.

Wasserzufluss	= Water inlet.	*Kalksättiger*	= Lime-saturator.
Gereinigtes Wasser	= Purified water.	*Soda*	= Carbonate of soda.
Kalkeinschüttung	= Inlet for lime.	*Schlammabfluss*	= Outlet for mechanical impurities.

responding to the double nature of the impurities present in the water; that is, it not only acts to precipitate the dissolved impurities, but also to separate such impurities as are in suspension. These last are caught and held in the tower-shaped holder D. The water enters from above, down through E, and is made to rise through a series of funnels or inclined funnel-shaped walls. On these walls the coarsest particles are caught, and from them they flow down to the bottom of the tower, where they collect together: the water then passes upwards through the filters F, which are made of wood shavings, and flows off, freed from its mechanical impurities, through the opening T. In the mean time, by the addition of lime and soda, the water has been chemically purified in the following way —

The water first flows in the reservoir C, through the pipe H. In C there is a float for regulating the flow of water. By the arrangement of the apparatus, a part of the water goes into E, through the pipe P, while the rest passes through the valve V into the lime-saturator S. S is filled with lime; the water first meets the lime at the bottom of the saturator and passes up through it; the conical shape of S causes the rise to be slower and slower as the water nears the top, so that the milk of lime at first formed has plenty of time to clarify itself. The lime-water usually contains some carbonate of lime in suspension; and as this is worthless for purpose of purification, it is eliminated by causing the water to flow over into the cone K, which is closed at the bottom. In this cone the carbonate settles out, and may be drawn off through G.

The clear, saturated lime-water, containing 1.3 grammes of lime to the litre, runs then directly into the mixing-tube E. A solution of soda-ash is made up of a strength always exactly the same, by taking a known weight of ash, which is placed in the cage Z, after which the tank R is filled to a definite mark with water. This solution slowly passes through the tube, provided with strainers: a float in the tube keeps the water in B at a constant level. The siphon N, one end of which dips to the bottom of B, allows the alkaline solution to flow into B. The regulation of the flow in E is done as follows: —

The siphon N is joined by a chain, Q, to the float in C. In case the flow of water through H to C is cut off, the float sinks, raising N and thus stopping the flow of the solution. At the same time the level in C sinks so low that the flow of water through P and V ceases, as soon as the flow of water through H recommences, the apparatus is again set in operation automatically.

The whole apparatus comes to a standstill as soon as the drawing off of the pure water at T stops; this is effected by a float in D not shown.

The chemical reaction going on in the apparatus was roughly this:—

The addition of the lime softens the water by precipitating any bicarbonate which may be present, and the excess of lime is thrown down by the carbonate of soda. This, by its precipitation, coagulates and throws out much of the finely divided organic impurity. The apparatus may be easily modified to work with alum where desirable. The water from T is said to be sufficiently free from chemical and mechanical impurity for all practical purposes. The yield of the apparatus varies, according to its size, from $\frac{1}{2}$ to 50 c. m. per hour. Larger sizes are also made and we are informed that 109 of these plants are in use in Europe at the present time.

In taking a sample of water for analysis, especially if any opinion as to its healthfulness is desired, much care must be observed to avoid contamination of the sample. A perfectly clean glass-stoppered bottle of about 1 gallon capacity should be used. The State Board of Health of Massachusetts has issued the following

Instructions for Collecting Samples of Water for Analysis.

1. **From a Water Tap.**—The water should run freely from the tap for a few minutes before it is collected. The bottle is then to be placed directly under the tap, and rinsed out with water three times, pouring out the water completely each time. It is then again to be placed under the tap, filled to overflowing, and a small quantity poured out, so that there shall be left an air-space under the stopper of about an inch. The stopper must be rinsed off with flowing water and inserted into the bottle while still wet, and secured by tying over it a clean piece of cotton cloth. The ends of the string must be sealed on the top of the stopper. Under no circumstances must the inside of the neck of

the bottle or the stem of the stopper be touched by the hand or wiped with a cloth

2. **From a Stream, Pond, or Reservoir.** — The bottle and stopper should be rinsed with the water, if this can be done without stirring up the sediment on the bottom. The bottle, with the stopper in place, should then be entirely submerged in the water, and the stopper taken out at a distance of 12 inches or more below the surface. When the bottle is full, the stopper is replaced below the surface if possible, and finally secured as above. It will be found convenient, in taking samples in this way, to have the bottle weighted, so that it will sink below the surface. It is important that the sample should be obtained free from the sediment on the bottom of a stream and from the scum on the surface. If a stream should not be deep enough to admit of this method of taking a sample, the water must be dipped off with an absolutely clean vessel, and poured into the bottle after it has been rinsed.

The sample of water should be collected immediately before shipping by express, so that as little time as possible shall intervene between the collection of the sample and its examination.

In case there are any abnormal or unusual conditions existing in the source of the water, mention the facts: as, for instance, if the streams or ponds are swollen by recent heavy rains; or are unusually low in consequence of prolonged drought; or if there is a great deal of vegetable growth in or on the surface of the water.

CHAPTER VIII.

CHEMICAL ANALYSIS.

Under this head we shall make no attempt to map out elaborate methods for the complete analysis of the different substances named, except in special instances, as such a course would clearly be beyond the scope of the present work. It would also, in many cases, call for more or less complicated and expensive apparatus, as well as a skill in chemical manipulation, which one could only expect to find in the well-equipped laboratory of the professional chemist.

There are, however, very many tests of value which may be readily applied by one not specially skilled in analytical methods, and which require for their application but a limited amount of apparatus. Such tests, if carefully carried out, will very often serve the manufacturer's purpose quite as well as a more extended analysis, and at other times may indicate the desirability of such analyses.

Our purpose here, then, is to bring together certain easily applied and reliable tests for ascertaining the purity or "strength" of the chemicals more or less directly concerned in the art of paper-making. In some few instances, for example, alums and sulphite liquors, we have thought it well to lay down a plan for the complete analysis of the substance.

The apparatus required for preparing the necessary solutions, and making the tests named, consists of:—

Fig. 78.—Analytical Balance.

1. A balance (Fig. 78), sensitive to $\frac{1}{4}$-milligramme, and capable of carrying a maximum load of 200 grammes in each pan. The

CHEMICAL ANALYSIS.

balance should be enclosed in a glass case to protect it from dust and acid vapors, as well as from drafts of air while weighing.

2. A set of weights ranging from a 100-gramme piece to a 1-milligramme piece. These should be kept in a box with a tight-fitting cover for protection from dust and dampness.

3. Measuring-flasks (Fig. 79), holding respectively 1000 c.c., 500 c.c., 250 c.c., 100 c.c., and 50 c.c., when filled to the mark engraved on the neck.

4. Two burettes, which are simply straight tubes of glass graduated into cubic centimetres and tenths of cubic centimetres. The most convenient size holds 50 c.c. One of these

FIG. 79.—MEASURING FLASKS.

(Fig. 80), is narrowed at its lower extremity, and is to be fitted with a piece of rubber tubing about 2 inches long, one end of which is slipped over the narrowed end of the burette, while the lower end of the tubing carries a short piece of glass tube which has been drawn out to a fine point. By means of a spring-clip, or pinch-cock, which pinches the rubber just above the glass tip, any desired quantity of the liquid in the tube may be run out.

The other burette should be provided with a glass cock, and is used to contain such liquids as would act upon rubber and be injuriously affected by it, as caustic soda or iodine solutions.

The manner of using these instruments will be shown farther on.

5. A burette stand like that shown in Fig. 80, or some arrangement for holding burettes firmly in a perpendicular position, and which will at the same time permit their ready removal for cleaning and filling. A simple screw clamp of wood or iron lined with cork fixed firmly

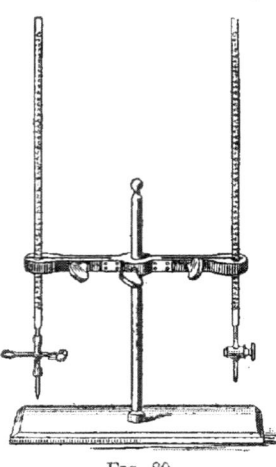

FIG. 80.

to an upright, or to the wall of the room, answers the purpose well.

6. Plain flasks, ungraduated, of different sizes, ranging in capacity, perhaps, from 2 or 4 oz. to 32 oz.

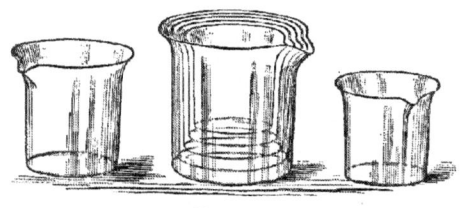

Fig. 81.

7. Beaker glasses (Fig. 81) of different sizes. These are by preference of the low wide form with lip for convenience in pouring. They are known as Griffin's beakers. They may best be obtained in nests as shown in the figure. Sizes holding from 4 oz. to 20 oz. are the most convenient.

8. Convex glasses known as clock glasses. These are to serve

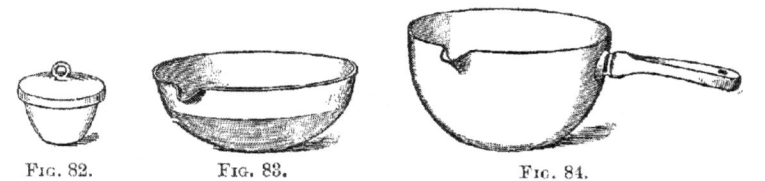

Fig. 82. Fig. 83. Fig. 84.

as covers for the beakers when required, and the sizes should be chosen with that end in view. They serve also for use in weighing such substances as iodine, which would injure the balance pan if placed directly upon it.

9. A number of pieces of solid glass rod 6 to 8 inches in length, with the ends rounded by fusing in a flame. These are for use as stirrers.

10. Crucibles, with covers, of Royal Berlin porcelain, $1\frac{1}{2}$ inch diameter (Fig. 82). Also 2 or 3 each of different sizes of evaporating-dishes (Fig. 83) of the same ware. Two or three casseroles (Fig. 84) will also be found convenient

Fig. 85.

CHEMICAL ANALYSIS. 351

11. A copper water-bath (Fig. 85), 6 inches in diameter, for use with the dishes last named.

12. A ring stand (Fig. 86) to support dishes and crucibles while being heated. An iron tripod is also needed to support the water-bath.

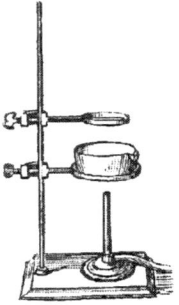

13. Two or three lamps for gas or alcohol, as the case may be. Where gas cannot be had, the Kellogg gasoline lamp for laboratory use gives excellent satisfaction, and with ordinary care is free from danger. Where alcohol is employed for heating, a Russian blast lamp, so-called, is a convenience and often almost a necessity.

14. Glass funnels of 60° angle. 2, 4, and 6-inch diameters are convenient sizes.

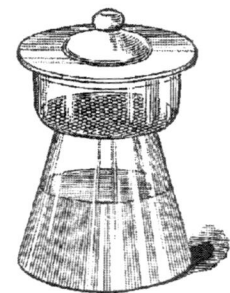

FIG. 86.

15. A 4-inch porcelain mortar for grinding samples, etc.

16. An evaporating-dish of platinum holding 50 to 100 c.c., and a crucible of the same metal of 15 to 20 c.c., capacity with a cover; also a triangle of stout platinum wire for supporting crucibles over the flame.

17. A set of reagent bottles, and several green glass bottles, holding $\frac{1}{2}$-gallon each, with glass stoppers, for holding standard solutions.

FIG. 87.

18. A dozen or two of 6-inch test-tubes, which for convenience in shaking should be not too wide to be easily covered by the thumb, some tubing of soft glass of about $\frac{1}{3}$-inch bore, with a few feet of rubber tubing to match; a desiccator (Fig. 87) and a pair of crucible tongs (Fig. 88) make up the list of apparatus. The manner in which these various pieces of apparatus are to be used will be explained as they are called for in the tests which follow.

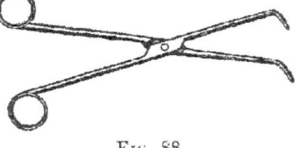

FIG. 88.

NORMAL SOLUTIONS

In the testing of certain substances, notably acids and alkalies, it is often most convenient to calculate their strength by ascertaining the quantity of a solution, the strength of which is known beforehand, it will take to neutralize or balance a definite quantity of the solution to be tested.

In such instances the test solution is called a standard solution, and is always either made and used of an exact and definite strength known as normal strength, or the actual volume employed of a strength other than normal is reduced in the calculation to the equivalent volume of normal strength by the use of a previously ascertained factor. Normal solutions then are always made on the simple and definite plan of having each 1000 c.c. of solution contain the number of grammes of pure substance represented by the molecular weight of that substance if its valency is one, one-half the molecular weight if the valency of the substance is two, one-third if the valency is three, etc. Thus, for example, to make a normal solution of sodium hydrate, NaHO, the valency of which is one, and its molecular weight 40 (Na $23+$ H $1+$ O $16=40$), 40 grammes of NaHO must be dissolved to make 1000 c.c. of solution.

To make normal sulphuric acid we dilute one-half the molecular weight in grammes to 1000 c.c., since sulphuric acid is a bivalent acid, or in figures $H_2SO_4=$ molecular weight 98, $\div 2=49$ grammes to the litre. The initial N is commonly used as an abbreviation for normal. When made upon this plan it will always be found that equal quantities by volume of any two normal solutions whose *chemical properties* are *opposite* will exactly balance or neutralize each other. For example, 100 c.c. N of soda solution will exactly neutralize 100 c.c. N of sulphuric, or a like amount of any other normal acid solution. Again, 50 c.c. of normal arsenic solution will exactly neutralize 50 c.c. of normal iodine. In practice it is difficult in most cases to make a *strictly* normal solution on account of slight impurities often present in so-called chemically pure chemicals, and the difficulty of accurately weighing many substances. It is usually much more convenient to weigh approximately the required number of grammes per litre of the substance in hand, and after the solution has been made up to volume, to accurately determine by appropriate means the actual amount of the given substance it contains per cubic centimetre, and this done it is easy to find a factor by means of which to reduce any number of c.c of this solution to equivalent c.c. of normal solution. For example, we have made up a solution of caustic soda (NaHO) and find that it contains 0.0398 grammes of NaHO per cubic centimetre, instead of 0.0400 grammes, which a strictly normal solution would contain

Then to find the factor for reducing this solution the proportion should be, as 0.04 (normal solution) is to 0.0398 (our solution), so is 1 c.c. to x ($0.04 : 0.0398 = 1 . x = 0.995$), and we find the factor to be 0.995. In other words, 100 c c of our solution equals $99\frac{1}{2}$ c.c. of normal solution.

The method of analysis by the use of normal solutions is called volumetric analysis, in distinction from gravimetric analysis, in which latter the substance to be estimated is converted into some definite compound insoluble in the given menstruum, and which is then separated, dried, and weighed, when, from the weight of the compound, that of the substance wanted is calculated. In gravimetric analysis, the exact strength of the reagent solutions employed is not necessarily known.

In every method of chemical analysis, cleanliness of apparatus employed, and the utmost care to guard against loss, and to secure accuracy in weighing and measuring, are essential in order to secure reliable results.

ACTUAL ANALYSIS

ACIDS.

Unite with alkalis and metallic salts — Solutions in water turn litmus red.

Sulphuric Acid (Oil of Vitriol).

Symbol, H_2SO_4 — Valency, II — Molecular weight, 98
For specific gravity of solutions of H_2SO_4, and percentage of actual H_2SO_4 contained, see **Appendix**

The presence of sulphuric acid, either free or in combination, may be recognized in solution by means of barium chloride solution, which forms, with sulphuric acid, or soluble sulphates, a heavy, white, very finely divided compound of barium sulphate

($BaSO_4$). This compound is insoluble in water, and very nearly so in dilute hydrochloric acid, even on boiling. It is soluble only very sparingly in strong boiling hydrochloric acid.

Free sulphuric acid in a solution not containing other free acids may be estimated volumetrically by means of standard soda solution as follows:—

Forty-nine grammes are weighed in a beaker, and made to 1000 c.c. with water, and the solution well shaken up. The beaker should be rinsed several times with water, and the rinsings poured into the 1000 c.c. flask, which is then filled to the mark, and shaken. 100 c.c of this solution are then measured out in the 100 c.c measuring flask, and transferred to a beaker, or porcelain dish, and the small flask rinsed several times with water, the rinsings being added to the liquid in the beaker. A few drops of litmus solution are added, and the whole warmed over the lamp. While the solution is warming, a burette with rubber tip should be filled just to the zero mark with standard soda solution. When the acid solution in the beaker has come to a boiling heat, the soda solution from the burette is run in, a little at a time, stirring the contents of the glass after each addition until the color of the solution has just changed from the red, which it has previously exhibited, to a purple tint. The number of cubic centimetres, and tenths of cubic centimetres, of soda solution used is now read off from the burette, and converted, by means of the appropriate factor, into normal cubic centimetres. The number of normal cubic centimetres employed represents directly the percentage of H_2SO_4 in the original solution, a portion of which was weighed out for the test. If the solution to be tested is weak, it is convenient to weigh twice, or three times, the amount named above (49 grammes), and dilute it to 1000 c.c., taking 100 c.c. of this solution, as before, for the actual test. In such case, of course, the number of normal cubic centimetres employed must be divided by 2, or 3, as the case may be, to give the per cent.

When free acids, other than sulphuric acid, are present with the latter in solution, the amount of this acid cannot be estimated by means of standard soda, but it must be separated and weighed, as in the estimation of sulphuric acid in **Sulphates** below, which see.

The impurities to be looked for in commercial oil of vitriol are lead, arsenic, nitric and nitrous acids, and occasionally ammonia.

Hydrochloric Acid (Muriatic Acid)

Symbol, HCl — Valency I — Molecular weight, 36.5
For specific gravity of solutions and percentage of HCl contained, see **Appendix**.

Hydrochloric acid may be recognized in solution, either when free or combined with bases, by means of solution of silver nitrate. When solution of silver nitrate is added to a solution containing HCl, or chlorides previously acidified by the addition of a *few drops only* of nitric acid, a white, curdy precipitate of silver chloride is formed which is insoluble in dilute nitric acid, either cold or hot. It is slightly soluble in strong nitric acid, and readily dissolved by ammonia water. The white chloride of silver precipitate, when exposed to strong daylight, rapidly turns purple, and after a little time becomes nearly black. If much organic matter is present in the solution tested, it often interferes with the above reaction, and may obscure it entirely by the formation of a black precipitate. In this case the solution must be evaporated to dryness, and gently ignited to carbonize the organic matter. It is then treated with water, and the resulting solution filtered and tested with silver nitrate.

Free hydrochloric acid in solution, other free acids not being present, may be estimated by means of standard soda solution. For this purpose 36.5 grammes of the solution are weighed out and made to 1000 c.c., as in testing **Sulphuric Acid** above, which see. 100 c.c. of the prepared solution are transferred to a beaker, or porcelain dish, as above, colored with litmus solution and standard soda solution run in from the burette, until *nearly* all the acid is neutralized. The solution is then heated to boiling, and the soda solution dropped in until the purple color appears. The number of cubic centimetres of soda solution used represents directly, after reduction to normal cubic centimetres by means of the appropriate factor, the percentage of HCl in the original solution weighed out.

To estimate HCl in solution with other free acids it must be separated and weighed as silver chloride, or, after neutralization, titrated with standard silver nitrate solution. For details of both these methods, see under **Chlorides**, below.

The impurities to be looked for in commercial muriatic acid are, sulphuric acid (sulphurous acid occasionally), iron, and other metals, and frequently arsenic in small amount.

Nitric Acid (Aqua fortis)

Symbol, HNO_3. — Valency, I — Molecular weight, 63
For specific gravity of solutions and percentage of HNO_3 contained, see **Appendix**.

Free or combined HNO_3 may be recognized in solution by means of ferrous sulphate. To test for HNO_3, a small amount of the liquid should be taken in a test-tube, and about an equal volume of strong H_2SO_4 added *cautiously*. The whole should then be mixed by means of a glass rod, and cooled quickly by placing the tube in water. When cool, a small piece of ferrous sulphate should be dropped into the tube, care being taken to select a fragment of crystal which is of a clear green color, with no powdery whitish substance upon it. If HNO_3 is present, a purplish zone will form after a few moments about the fragment of ferrous sulphate, while in the absence of HNO_3, the entire solution will remain unchanged. Instead of a fragment of the salt, a freshly made solution of ferrous sulphate may be employed. By inclining the tube containing the liquid to be tested, the ferrous solution may be carefully poured down the side so as not to mix with the solution in the tube. On again bringing the tube into an upright position, a purple zone will appear at the line of junction of the two liquids when HNO_3 is present, and on shaking the tube so as to mix the contents, the whole solution will be more or less darkened. A few experiments with solutions known to contain HNO_3, in comparison with those known not to contain it, will be useful in familiarizing one with the appearance of the test, and in enabling one to acquire the moderate skill necessary to make it successful.

Nitric acid in solution, when other free acids are absent, may be estimated with standard soda solution, the details of the process being precisely the same as in the case of **Hydrochloric Acid**, which see, the proper amount of solution to be weighed in this case being 63 grammes to be diluted to 1000 c.c.

The estimation of HNO_3 when mixed with other acids, or when in combination, presents certain difficulties and calls for special apparatus. When this estimation seems called for the sample had better be sent to a reliable analyst.

The impurities to be looked for in commercial nitric acid ("aqua fortis") are hydrochloric and sulphuric acids and metals.

ACETIC ACID.

Pyroligneous Acid (Wood Vinegar).

Symbol. $C_2H_4O_2$ — Valency, I — Molecular weight, 60
For specific gravity of solutions and percentage of $C_2H_4O_2$ contained, see
Appendix

Free acetic acid, unless present in quite small amount, may usually be recognized by its vinegar odor, more pronounced on warming. When present in too small a quantity to be recognizable by the above means, or when in combination, it may be converted into acetic ether, which is a very volatile substance having a very distinctive and penetrating though not unpleasant odor. To perform the test a small portion of the liquid to be tested is placed in a test-tube. About one-half its volume of alcohol is added, and an equal amount of strong sulphuric acid, and the whole well mixed. If acetic acid (or acetates) were present in the solution, the odor of acetic ether will be apparent either at once, or will become so on heating the contents of the tube to boiling over a lamp.

In order to familiarize oneself with the odor of acetic ether so as to be able to recognize it, it will be well to make the test as above upon a solution of sodium acetate containing from 2 to 5 grammes of the salt in 100 c.c.

Free acetic acid in solution, apart from other free acids, may be estimated by titration with standard soda solution in the manner given in detail under **Hydrochloric Acid**, above. The proper amount to be weighed in this case is 60 grammes to be made to 1000 c.c. The number of cubic centimetres of *normal* soda solution consumed or neutralized by 100 c.c. of the diluted solution then equals per cents. of $C_2H_4O_2$ in the original solution to be tested.

It should be borne in mind that in titrating acetic acid, when litmus solution is employed as the indicator of the saturation point, soda solution should be added until the liquid is a full blue, instead of stopping when the purple tint is reached, as in the titration of the acids previously mentioned

On this account, we prefer to employ a solution of phenolphtalein as indicator in the present case To make this solution, 0.200 grammes (about) of phenolphtalein should be dissolved in

100 c.c. of moderately strong alcohol, and the solution filtered if not clear. To this solution weak caustic soda solution is added until a very faint rose color remains after shaking. The solution is then ready for use. It should be kept well corked. About 10 to 15 drops of this solution are to be added to the portion of acid solution used for the titration. The soda solution should then be added until a brilliant rose purple coloration appears which remains permanent after stirring. This indicates that the acid has all been neutralized, since the color only appears in the presence of alkali, but the presence of even the most minute quantity of free alkali is sufficient to develop a brilliant color. For the estimation of acetic acid in combination, see **Acetates**.

Impurities in commercial acetic acid are muriatic acid, acetates of soda and lime, acetate of methyl, and empyreumatic (organic) matter.

Oxalic Acid

Symbol, $H_2C_2O_4 \cdot 2H_2O$ — Valency, II — Molecular weight, 126

Oxalic acid free, or in combination with *alkalis*, may be recognized in solution by means of calcium sulphate solution. The solution to be tested should be rendered alkaline by the addition of ammonia in excess. It is then filtered if necessary, and solution of calcium sulphate added. If oxalic acid, or an oxalate, is present, this will produce a fine white cloud or precipitate easily redissolved by hydrochloric acid in excess, and again appearing on addition of excess of ammonia water. Free oxalic acid may be estimated by titration with standard soda solution as in the preceding paragraphs.

The proper amount of the solution to be weighed is 63 grammes to be made to 1000 c.c.

If the crystallized acid is to be tested, it is as well to weigh one-half the above amount, and make to 1000 c.c., and take 100 c.c. of this solution for titration. Of course, in this case the number of cubic centimetres of *normal* soda used must be doubled to give the percentage of actual crystallized acid in the sample.

Either litmus or phenolphtalein solution may be employed as indicator with oxalic acid, and no precautions need be taken to nearly neutralize with soda solution before heating as in the case of hydrochloric and nitric acids, since this acid is not in the least volatile from its solution, as is the case with the acids last mentioned.

ALKALIS AND ALKALINE EARTHS.

Unite with acids to form salts — Solutions of the alkalis turn litmus blue

Sodium Hydrate (Caustic Soda).

Symbol, NaHO — Valency, I — Molecular weight, 40
For specific gravity of solutions and percentage of NaHO contained see **Appendix**.

It is difficult to apply tests to a solution of caustic soda or of soda salts which shall give direct evidence of the presence of soda as distinct from other alkalis. Perhaps the best ready qualitative test for soda lies in the intense yellow color given to the flame of an alcohol lamp or Bunsen burner when a platinum wire moistened with the solution to be tested is held in the flame. This test is, however, of such extreme delicacy, and the presence of compounds of soda in the minute quantities required to produce the yellow flame so well-nigh universal, as to render this test of little practical value. Probably the easiest way to prove the presence of soda in an alkaline solution is to work backwards and prove that it is *not* one of the other alkalis (appropriate tests for which will be described under their respective heads), and consequently must be soda.

There are several direct tests which can be applied to prove the presence of soda or its salts; but as they require very careful manipulation to render their indications reliable, we have thought it best not to describe them here.

Quantitative. — In a simple solution of caustic soda not containing other alkalis the percentage of soda, NaHO, may be easily determined by titration with standard *acid* solution. For this purpose a standard sulphuric acid of about normal strength (49 grammes H_2SO_4 per litre) is perhaps best. Standard oxalic acid also answers the purpose well.

Forty grammes of the soda solution or the solid substance caustic soda are to be weighed, and its solution made to 1000 c.c., 100 c.c. of this solution is, if not entirely clear, filtered through a *dry filter*, since, if the filter were previously wet with water, it would dilute to a certain extent the 100 c.c. passed through it. The filtrate is transferred to a beaker or casserole and colored with litmus solution. Standard acid is run in from the burette until the original blue color changes to purple. The liquid is then boiled, when the blue color will generally again appear. Acid is again dropped in from the burette, a drop at a time, boiling for a moment after each addition, until the liquid shows a full red color, and no trace of blue or purple appears after two or three minutes' boiling.

The number of cubic centimetres of acid employed, reduced to normal cubic centimetres by the use of the appropriate factor, represents the percentage of caustic soda, NaHO, in the sample tested.

In commercial transactions caustic soda is usually quoted as 60 or 70 per cent. *alkali*, as the case may be.

In this connection, as in the alkali trade generally, the term "alkali" does not have its proper *chemical* significance, but signifies sodium oxide, Na_2O, or we may call it anhydrous caustic soda. 31 parts by weight of this substance, Na_2O ("alkali") + 9 parts of water = 40 parts of sodium hydrate or caustic soda.

This being the case, if we wish to find the per cent of "alkali," Na_2O, in the sample tested as above, we must multiply the per cent. of caustic soda, NaHO, by 31 and divide the product by 40.

$$\frac{\%(NaHO) \times 31}{40} = \%(Na_2O), \text{ or "alkali"}$$

In Europe an arbitrary custom obtains of using the old numbers 32 and 41 in place of the corrected ones 31 and 40 respectively in all instances mentioned above. This is now entirely without right or reason, and is oftentimes annoying to the American buyer, who finds a caustic reported as 72 per cent alkali by the English chemist will be reported only 69.75 per cent by the American test, which gives its true value. Of course, when one is aware of the custom, it is easy to make the allowance; but in the interests of truth and fair dealing, every American buyer of alkali, either caustic or carbonated, should insist that payment be made on the basis of the American test.

The total amount of soda, Na_2O, present in a given solution, both as caustic and as salts of soda, is determined by means of a long and somewhat troublesome series of eliminations, by means of which the soda is finally obtained in the form either of pure sulphate or chloride, which may be weighed after ignition, and from its weight the soda calculated.

Potassium Hydrate (Caustic Potash)

Symbol, KHO — Valency, I — Molecular weight, 56.1
For specific gravities of solutions and per cent. of KHO, see **Appendix**

Potash may be recognized in solution by means of the color it imparts to the colorless Bunsen or alcohol flame. The color, except when the proportion of potash is very large, is usually masked to the naked eye by the intense yellow color of the sodium flame. By the use of a piece of blue (cobalt) glass of a moderately deep shade the yellow color of the sodium flame may be shut out, as it were, and the potash flame then appears through the glass of a beautiful rose color. The manner of applying the flame test is to dip the end of a small platinum wire in the solution to be tested, and then hold it in the flame until it becomes red hot.

Caustic potash in solutions not containing other free alkalis may be estimated by titration with standard acid in exactly the same way as caustic soda described above.

The amount to be weighed out is 56.1 grammes, to be diluted to 1000 c.c. The number of normal cubic centimetres of acid consumed by 100 c.c. of this solution equals per cents. of KHO.

If the percentage of K_2O anhydrous potash is required, it may be obtained by multiplying the per cents. of KHO by 47.1, and dividing the product by 56.1.

The process of determining accurately the total amount of potash in a solution containing salts of potash along with other substances, as with soda, is long and tedious to one not thoroughly conversant with chemical manipulations, and on that account we omit it here.

AMMONIUM HYDRATE.

Ammonia (Water of Ammonia)

Symbol, NH_4OH.

Ammonia is usually reckoned and reported in terms of anhydrous ammonia gas; and in accordance with this custom we shall so consider it in this paragraph.

Symbol, NH_3 — Valency, I — Molecular weight, 17
For tables of specific gravity of solutions and percentage of ammonia contained, see **Appendix**

Free, or caustic, ammonia, being a volatile alkali, reveals its presence, either at once, or on warming the solution, by its characteristic odor, and by turning a piece of filter paper, moistened with red litmus solution, blue, when held in the vapor arising from a warmed solution. It does not reveal its presence in this way when present in combination with an acid; but on the addition of a sufficient quantity of caustic soda solution to a solution containing any salt of ammonia it may be at once detected, as indicated above.

Caustic ammonia in solution not containing other free alkalis or alkali carbonates, may be titrated directly with standard acid, as indicated under **Soda**, above.

Ammonia being a volatile alkali, however, the solution must be titrated without heating.

The proper amount to be weighed out is 17 grammes to 1000 c.c.

For the determination of the combined ammonia in any liquid, it is sufficient, after having made up to 1000 c.c. as above, to take 100 c.c. and distil after adding an excess of magnesium oxide (caustic magnesia), MgO, so long as any ammonia continues to come over with the steam. This usually takes from one to two hours. The distillate is to be received in a flask containing a measured number of c.c of standard acid which must be more than sufficient to neutralize all the ammonia which may distil over. When all the ammonia has been distilled into the acid, the excess of acid remaining unneutralized is titrated by means of standard soda and litmus — the difference between the number of normal cubic centimetres of acid employed and the number of normal cubic centimetres of soda used to neutralize the excess remaining equals the number of normal cubic centimetres of acid neutralized by the ammonia, or per cents. of NH_3 in the sample

Calcium Hydrate (Slaked Lime)

Symbol, CaH_2O_2. — Valency, II — Molecular weight. 74
For specific gravity of solutions and milk of lime, see **Appendix**

Calcium Oxide. — Lime (Caustic Lime).

Symbol, CaO — Valency, II — Molecular weight, 56

The term "lime" or "caustic lime," as commonly employed, means burned lime or calcium oxide, CaO, in distinction from slaked lime. which is calcium hydrate, CaH_2O_2, or the former combined with water.

Lime may be recognized in solution by means of oxalate of ammonia solution with which it gives a fine white crystalline precipitate (compare **Oxalic Acid**, above). The solution to be tested should first be rendered alkaline with ammonia, filtered if ammonia has caused a precipitate, and the filtrate tested with a few drops of oxalate of ammonia.

If metallic salts, as lead acetate or zinc sulphate or chloride, are present, the metallic oxides must be removed by treatment of the solution, after the addition of ammonia, with ammonium sulphide solution and filtering. The filtrate is then tested with oxalate as above. A good method for testing a sample of burned lime or limestone, which is easily carried out and which with care will give results sufficiently accurate for all ordinary purposes, is as follows. A considerable amount, say a pound or two, of the lime should be picked out to represent as fairly as possible the average quality of the lot. This should be broken down into small bits not larger than peas. The whole is then well mixed, and an ounce or two taken out for the working sample. This small sample should be ground in a porcelain mortar sufficiently fine to pass a No. 24 sieve, and the resulting powder again well mixed and preserved in a well-closed bottle.

For the actual analysis, 5 grammes of the powder are to be weighed out and transferred to a beaker; about 50 c.c. of water are then poured on it, and sufficient hydrochloric acid to dissolve the sample (about 25 c.c. will be sufficient), and the whole boiled. This treatment will dissolve the entire sample with the exception of the silica, SiO_2, which is to be filtered out on a small filter, well washed with hot water, dried, transferred to a platinum crucible together with the filter, and ignited strongly, and after cooling weighed.

The weight found calculated to per cents. gives sand and silica, insoluble in acid, in the sample.

The solution filtered from the above, together with the washings from the same, is next to be heated, and ammonia water added cautiously until the odor of ammonia is just perceptible in the liquid after stirring. The solution is then to be kept very near to the boiling-point for some time until all the smell of ammonia has disappeared. This treatment separates the alumina and sesquioxide of iron present. The solution is next to be filtered, and the precipitate well washed with hot water. The residue of

Al_2O_3 and F_2O_3 on the filter is to be *thoroughly* dried and then ignited in the platinum crucible, together with the filter, and weighed after cooling, and the weight calculated into per cents.

The filtrate and washings from the alumina and iron oxide precipitate is next made to 500 c.c. Then 50 c.c. of this, which equals 0.5 grammes of the original sample, is transferred to the platinum evaporating-dish, which has been previously cleaned, ignited, and weighed. The contents of the dish are evaporated to dryness on the water-bath, and ignited (carefully, to avoid spattering and consequent loss) at a moderate heat until no more fumes come off. The dish is then cooled and a small amount of water added, together with two or three drops of hydrochloric acid. When all is dissolved, about 30 to 40 drops of strong sulphuric acid is added, and the whole again evaporated to dryness and ignited until no more fumes appear, and finally brought to a full red heat. It is absolutely necessary at this point that fumes do appear, otherwise it will be necessary to again add water with a few drops more sulphuric acid, evaporate, and ignite.

The residue in the dish now consists of the lime and magnesia present in the portion of the sample taken (with possibly sometimes traces of soda and potash, which may be here disregarded), now in the form of anhydrous sulphates. The residue here obtained should be of a pure white color. It is cooled in a desiccator and weighed as rapidly as possible, as, if there is much sulphate of magnesia present, it will rapidly absorb moisture from the air and gain in weight. Deducting the weight of the dish leaves the combined weights of the sulphate of lime and sulphate of magnesia, which can be formed from the amount of the sample taken for this estimation, 0.5 grammes.

After weighing, the substance in the dish is transferred by the aid of a little water from the washing-bottle to a small beaker. Any adhering particles may be removed by rubbing with the clean tip of the finger, and should afterward be rinsed into the beaker. Any lumps should be broken down with the end of a glass rod. Two or three drops of hydrochloric acid are next added and the solution well stirred. An undissolved portion will almost always remain. Next about two drops of sulphuric acid are added and stirred. Strong alcohol is next added equal in bulk to about twice the volume of the liquid in the beaker, the whole well stirred and allowed to stand, with occasional stirring, for two hours or more. It is then to be filtered and the filter washed two or three times with a mixture of two volumes of strong alcohol and one volume of water. It is then washed with a mixture of equal volumes of alcohol and water as long as the washing continues to remove anything, which may be ascertained by allowing a drop or two to fall from the funnel on a clean watch-glass and then evaporating it by gently moving the glass. If no appreciable residue is left on the glass, the washing may be considered finished. We now have on the filter all the lime as sulphate of lime, and all the magnesia in the solution. It only remains, then, to dry and ignite the precipitate of sulphate of lime and calculate the lime in it.

$$\text{Sulphate of Lime (CaSO}_4) \times 0.4118 = \text{Lime (CaO)}.$$

We next subtract the actual sulphate of lime, weighed as above, from the weight of the mixed sulphates of lime and magnesia found previously, the difference being sulphate of magnesia, which multiplied by $0.3333 =$ magnesia, MgO.

A good lime for building purposes or for causticising should be almost entirely free from magnesia. For the best results in making sulphite liquor it should carry at least 35 per cent. of magnesia.

Magnesium Hydrate.

Symbol, MgH_2O_2

Magnesia

Symbol, MgO — Valency II — Molecular weight, 40

The remarks above, in regard to calcium hydrate and lime, at the beginning of the last section, apply equally to magnesium hydrate and magnesia.

Magnesia is recognized in solution by means of solution of phosphate of soda. The solution to be tested must contain no metallic salts other than those of iron and alumina. Some ammonium chloride is first added to the solution, then ammonia in excess, the liquid boiled and filtered from the alumina and sesquioxide of iron precipitated. Oxalate of ammonia is added to the filtrate in considerable amount, and if a precipitate appears, the liquid is heated in a water-bath, and again filtered. More ammonia is added to the filtrate, and some phosphate of soda solution, and the liquid well stirred with a glass rod, allowing the rod to rub the sides and bottom of the glass. If magnesia is present, a precipitate soon appears as a fine, white crystalline powder, which soon settles, leaving the liquid clear. If very little MgO is present, it may appear only after a little time, and then only as white streaks at those places where the rod has marked the glass in stirring. If metallic salts are present, the slightly acid solution must first be treated with sulphuretted hydrogen gas, by bubbling the gas through the solution until it smells strongly of the gas after shaking. It is then to be filtered, and to the filtrate some ammonia is added, and then ammonium sulphide as long as the latter causes a precipitate. The liquid is again filtered, and an excess of oxalate of ammonia is added, to separate lime present. After warming for some time, the liquid is filtered from the lime precipitate, and is then ready, after cooling, to be tested for magnesia with phosphate of soda, after the manner first described.

Quantitative. — Magnesia is estimated by weighing it as magnesium pyrophosphate, $Mg_2P_2O_7$. This substance multiplied by 0.3604 gives the equivalent weight of magnesia, MgO.

The solution in which MgO is to be determined must be freed from all other substances except soda and potash and ammonia, as described above. To the solution thus prepared a large excess of ammonia is added, and phosphate of soda solution in excess. The liquid is well stirred, taking care, in this case, to *avoid* touching the sides and bottom of the glass with the rod, since this will cause the precipitate to adhere to the glass. The beaker is then covered, and allowed to rest for at least two hours. It is then filtered, and the precipitate rinsed on to the filter by the aid of a wash-bottle filled with water $8\frac{1}{2}$ parts, and ammonia, strong, $1\frac{1}{2}$ parts. It is necessary to employ this dilute ammonia for washing, instead of water, as the latter would dissolve the precipitate. The precipitate should be washed until a drop of the washings, to which a drop of nitric acid has been added, gives no cloud on the addition to it of a drop of a solution of silver nitrate. After the precipitate is thoroughly washed, it is dried, and transferred, as carefully as may be, to a small crucible (platinum by preference, though porcelain will answer), and ignited to a full red heat. The filter, with the remainder of the precipitate adhering, is then thrown into the crucible and ignited, until the carbon of the filter is entirely consumed, and the whole of a bright red heat. It is then cooled and weighed; and the weight of the precipitate multiplied by 0.3604 gives the actual weight of MgO in the portion of the sample operated on.

CARBONATES.

COMPOUNDS OF BASIC (ALKALINE) OXIDES WITH CARBONIC ACID.

Those which are soluble in water, carbonates of soda, potash, and ammonia, give solutions which show an alkaline reaction with litmus. All are decomposed by acids in general with liberation of carbonic acid gas and formation of that salt of the base corresponding to the acid employed.

SODIUM CARBONATE.

Sal Soda — Soda Crystals (Washing Soda) — Soda-Ash.

For specific gravity of solutions and per cent. of the salt contained see **Appendix**.
Soda crystals, or washing soda, is *crystallized* carbonate of soda.
Symbol, Na_2CO_3, 10 aq. — Valency, II. — Molecular weight, 286.

Carbonates of soda, potash, and ammonia all agree in being soluble in water; their solutions effervesce on the addition of an acid, and all give a white precipitate with solution of calcium chloride. Solution of ammonium carbonate is, however, distinguished from the other two by the strong smell of ammonia developed on the addition of caustic soda solution and warming. Carbonates of soda and potash are distinguished by the flame reaction (see under **Caustic Potash**), best applied after adding a slight excess of hydrochloric acid.

Soda-Ash.

Symbol, Na_2CO_3. — Valency, II. — Molecular weight, 106.

Soda-ash (Solvay) is nearly pure and nearly anhydrous carbonate of soda. Soda-ash may be formed from soda crystals by furnacing, which in this case serves simply to drive off, or dry out, the combined water, 10 aq., of the crystals; conversely, soda crystals are made from ash by simply dissolving and allowing to crystallize.

The amount of "alkali," Na_2O, in soda-ash or crystals may be estimated by titration with standard acid.

The proper amount to be weighed out for this purpose so that the number of normal cubic centimetres of acid consumed shall read per cents. of alkali direct is 31 grammes. This is to be dissolved, and the solution made to 1000 c.c. 100 c.c. of this solution are to be filtered through a dry (wet with the solution, and not with water) filter and titrated, the solution being colored with litmus solution, as under Caustic Soda (which see), the only additional precaution being to continue the boiling after the addition of acid sufficiently long to make sure that a red color has been obtained, which will not turn to blue or violet on longer boiling.

The percentage of carbonate of soda may be calculated to that of alkali by the proportion

$$\underset{62}{Na_2O} \quad \underset{106}{Na_2CO_3} = \% \ Na_2O \ \text{found} \ x,$$

and the percentage of soda crystals equivalent to the alkali found by the proportion

$$\underset{62}{Na_2O} \ . \ \underset{286}{Na_2CO_3 \, 10 \, aq} = \% \ Na_2O \ \text{found} \ x.$$

The soda-ash of the market is classified as carbonated or caustic ash, according as all the alkali in it exists as carbonate, or part as carbonate and part as caustic soda. The testing of carbonated ash for technical uses is commonly limited to the determination of the total alkali, Na_2O, it contains. Sometimes, however, in old process or "Leblanc" ash an estimation of the sulphate of soda may be useful, since for use in the manufacture of "soda pulp" a small percentage of sulphate of soda in the ash purchased is rather an advantage than otherwise.

The percentage of sulphate of soda present is easily calculated from the percentage of sulphuric anhydride, SO_3, contained.

This latter is determined as follows: —

100 c.c. of the solution prepared for titration, filtered as before through a dry filter, are transferred to a beaker, and hydrochloric acid cautiously added as long as each addition produces effervescence. A few drops more are added to render the solution strongly acid, and the solution covered with a glass and heated to boiling. Barium chloride solution is then added so long as it produces a precipitate, and the whole allowed to stand in a warm place until the precipitate has settled and the solution above it

become clear. The solution is then poured carefully on to a filter, taking care to disturb the precipitate as little as possible while pouring out the liquid. After all the liquid has passed through the filter, the precipitate is transferred to the filter by the aid of a wash-bottle filled with hot water, and the filter precipitate thoroughly washed with the water. It is then dried, transferred to the platinum crucible, the filter carefully folded and added, and the whole strongly ignited. The weight of the ignited barium sulphate, $BaSO_4$, multiplied by 0.3433, equals sulphuric anhydride, SO_3, which may then be calculated into per cents of the original ash.

The equivalent sulphate of soda may be found by the proportion

$$\underset{80}{SO_3} \quad \underset{142}{Na_2SO_4} = \% \text{ of } SO_3 \ x \% \text{ of } Na_2SO_4, \text{ sulphate of soda,}$$

and the percentage of alkali, Na_2O, which it can furnish on conversion by the proportion

$$\underset{142}{Na_2SO_4} \quad \underset{62}{Na_2O} = \% \text{ sulphate of soda} . x \ (\% \text{ of equivalent alkali}).$$

Caustic Ash.

The total alkali, Na_2O, in caustic ash and the sulphate present are to be estimated exactly as in carbonated ash just described. In addition to these determinations, however, a knowledge of the actual *caustic* alkali present is necessary to fix upon the value of the ash. This is determined as follows.

250 c.c. of the solution prepared for titration of the total alkali is transferred to a 500 c.c. flask, and the small flask well rinsed into the larger, using as little water as practicable for the purpose. A strong solution of barium chloride is then added, with shaking so long as it produces a precipitate. A little more of the barium chloride is added, and the flask filled to the mark with water and well shaken.

The flask is corked and allowed to rest until the white precipitate has settled and the solution above has become clear. 100 c.c. of this solution are then filtered through a dry filter, the funnel being kept covered with a glass during the filtration. This solution (100 c.c.) is then transferred to a beaker or dish, and litmus added and titrated with standard acid.

It is not necessary to heat the solution during this titration. The number of normal cubic centimetres of acid employed *multiplied by two*, since the 100 c.c. of the last solution is equal to only 50 c.c. of the original solution prepared, gives the percentage of alkali, Na_2O, existing as caustic soda, $NaHO$, in the sample.

Black Ash

This is a soda-ash containing a greater or less amount of finely divided carbon, from which it derives its black or dark gray color. It also contains ordinarily small amounts of sulphide of soda, which is formed from any sulphate which may have been present before furnacing the latter, being reduced by the carbon or organic matter at the high temperature of the furnace.

The valuation of black ash for technical purposes is, in most cases, limited to a determination of its total alkaline strength by titration, as under Soda-ash, above. This would include the alkali, Na_2O, present as sulphide as well as that present as actual carbonate. In testing a well-burned black ash no variation will be found to be necessary from the method given above for the titration of soda-ash, as the 100 c.c. of liquor filtered out for the test will be found to be practically colorless. If, however, the sample of black ash has not been thoroughly burned, the filtered solution may be quite dark, or even black, in color from partially carbonized matter dissolved.

In this case the simplest way out of the difficulty, perhaps, is to throw away the solution already prepared, and weigh out a new lot of 31 grammes. This is then transferred to a platinum dish (best to the evaporating-dish) and thoroughly ignited over the lamp. The whole is then transferred to the litre flask, the dish well rinsed in, and after the ash is dissolved made to the mark as before. If the ignition has been well performed, a sufficiently colorless solution will be obtained on filtering. The complete analysis of black ash is a problem of so complicated a nature as to be best performed by the professional chemist. Not infrequently, however, such an analysis may serve to point out an erroneous method of practice, or an avoidable waste in the manufacture, of which this black ash is a bye-product.

Bicarbonate of Soda (Baking-Soda).

Symbol, $NaHCO_3$ — Valency, 1 — Molecular weight, 84

This salt is much less soluble in water than the carbonate of soda. Its reactions in general are similar to those of the neutral carbonate, but less strong.

It contains about one-half as much alkali, Na_2O, as the simple carbonate, and about twice as much carbonic acid. On this account, and on account of its being very mildly alkaline, it is always employed in all baking-powders as the source of the gas required to "raise" the bread.

The testing of bicarbonate of soda requires a determination of the total alkali, Na_2O, and also a determination of the total carbonic anhydride, CO_2 (commonly called carbonic acid), present. From the data furnished by the two determinations, the actual amounts of bicarbonate and of carbonate of soda present may be calculated. Bicarbonate made by the "Solvay Process" also contains a small percentage of ammonia in combination with carbonic acid. When present, ammonia must also be determined.

The total alkali in bicarbonate, free from ammonia, may be determined by titration with standard acid.

3.100 grammes of the substance are to be weighed, transferred to a beaker or dish with about 100 c.c. of water, litmus added, and titrated direct with acid, care being taken to thoroughly boil the solution during the titration. The number of normal cubic centimetres of acid used gives the per cents. of alkali, Na_2O, present.

When ammonia is present, the sample weighed out for the titration must be ignited for some time at a moderate heat, which will expel all the ammonia, before dissolving it for titration.

The estimation of carbonic acid is conducted in a special form of apparatus, called the "Schroetter Carbonic Acid Apparatus." The use of this apparatus is as follows: The apparatus being clean and dry, 2 grammes to 5 grammes of the substance to be examined is weighed and transferred very carefully to the small flask forming the base of the apparatus. About 10 c.c. of water is then added and the cork carefully inserted. The stopcock between the flask and the bulb-tube directly above it is closed, and the bulb filled with hydrochloric or nitric acid, the neck carefully wiped.

and its stopper inserted. The other large bulb is next filled about one-half full of strong sulphuric acid, the neck wiped, and the stopper inserted. The whole apparatus with its contents is now weighed carefully and the weight recorded. The cock is next opened slightly so as to allow the acid in the bulb to very slowly drip into the flask. This at once frees carbonic acid gas from the carbonate there contained, which is forced to bubble through the bulb containing sulphuric acid. This acid serves to remove and retain all moisture which may be carried up by the gas, so that only pure, dry CO_2 gas finally escapes from the apparatus. After making certain that sufficient acid has been allowed to enter the flask to decompose the whole of the carbonate present, the cock is closed, and the contents of the flask heated cautiously to boiling and allowed to boil until steam *commences* to be driven over into the bulb containing the sulphuric acid. It is then removed from the heat and the cock *at once* opened to allow the remaining acid to run in or air to be drawn into the flask as the steam condenses and the apparatus allowed to become cold. It is then once more weighed, and this weight deducted from the previous weight leaves the loss of weight during the operation, which, if sufficient care has been employed, represents the weight of carbonic anhydride, CO_2, in the amount of substance operated upon. This weight may be easily figured into per cents.

The method of procedure described above may serve for the estimation of carbonic acid, CO_2, in any carbonate. The ammonia present in Solvay bicarbonate may be determined by placing a weighed amount, say about two or three grammes, of the bicarbonate in a tube of hard glass about six inches in length and a half-inch in diameter, known as an ignition tube. A loose plug of asbestos is placed near the mouth of the tube, which is fitted with a good cork. This in turn carries a piece of glass tube, passing just through the cork into the combustion tube, and bent downward in front of the tube, so as to pass through a cork fitted into one end of a U-tube. Two or three cubic centimetres of standard acid, accurately measured from a burette, are placed in the U-tube and colored with litmus. Enough water should be added so that the liquid in the tube may well cover the bend of the tube. The ignition tube should be held by a clasp in a nearly horizontal position and a gentle heat applied for some time to the portion of the tube containing the carbonate, and gradually increased nearly to redness. This will expel all the ammonia present, which will be driven into the U-tube, and there absorbed by the acid contained therein.

When no more bubbles are seen to pass through the liquid in the U-tube, and the substance in the ignition tube is very nearly or quite red hot, the connection between the two tubes may be broken and the lamp removed.

The liquid should next be transferred from the U-tube to a beaker, and the tube carefully rinsed, and the acid remaining in the liquid unneutralized titrated with standard soda. The number of normal cubic centimetres of soda employed, taken from the number of normal cubic centimetres of acid originally placed in the U-tube, leaves the normal cubic centimetres neutralized by the ammonia from the sample of bicarbonate weighed. This latter number multiplied by 0.017 will give the weight of ammonia, NH_3, obtained from the sample operated on, and this weight may be readily calculated into equivalent per cents.

If 1.7 grammes of the sample be weighed for the experiment, the number of normal cubic centimetres of acid neutralized by the ammonia driven off as above will represent per cents. of NH_3 in the sample analyzed.

Carbonate of Potash (Pearlash — Salt of Tartar).

Symbol, K_2CO_3 — Valency, II — Molecular weight, 138.2

This substance, though formerly much used in the arts, is now almost entirely discarded in favor of soda-ash, which has been found to answer the required purpose in a large majority of cases equally as well as the potash salt, and to offer in very many instances many advantages over the latter, not the least of which is its greater cheapness.

The methods for testing pearlash are precisely similar to those given in detail under **Carbonate of Soda**, which see.

The proper amount of pearlash to be weighed out for titration is 47.1 grammes to be made to 1000 c.c., and 100 c.c. employed for the test. The normal cubic centimetres used will then represent per cents. of potash, K_2O, present.

CARBONATE OF LIME.

Chalk (French White — Whiting — Marble — Limestone).

Symbol, $CaCO_3$. — Valency, II — Molecular weight, 100

Almost entirely insoluble in pure water — water containing alkaline salts and carbonic acid dissolves it in somewhat larger amounts.

The test required for chalk, French white, or whiting, is usually one for purity alone. and consists in dissolving a portion in dilute hydrochloric acid. A pure article should be entirely dissolved by the acid — absence of sand. or silicates (clay). The solution is next tested with barium chloride for presence of sulphates. A complete analysis of marble and limestone is frequently required. This may be performed with sufficient accuracy for most technical purposes in exactly the same way as described for the the analysis of **Lime** above, which see

The carbonic acid, CO_2. may be determined by the aid of the Schroetter apparatus. described above, when desired

CARBONATE OF MAGNESIA.

Magnesite.

Symbol, $MgCO_3$. — Valency, II — Molecular weight, 84

This substance is worth noting as being the crude base employed in making the solution used in the "Ekman Sulphite Pulp Process" An analysis of this substance for technical purposes may be made precisely as directed for the analysis of limestone The precaution, however, must be taken of weighing the ignited sulphates with the dish containing them covered with a glass, and the weighing must be performed as rapidly as possible, since ignited magnesium sulphate absorbs moisture very rapidly from the air, and increases in weight in consequence.

The ignition of the sulphates also should not be prolonged beyond the time necessary to expel all the free sulphuric acid or the heat raised beyond a moderate red heat, since sulphate of magnesia is not absolutely unalterable under prolonged and intense ignition.

CARBONATE OF ZINC.

Symbol, $ZnCO_3$ — Valency, II — Molecular weight, 125.

Impurities to be looked for: lead and lime carbonates, and sulphate of lime and insoluble matter.

The substance to be examined should be dissolved in hydrochloric acid, in which, if pure, it will be completely soluble. The solution nearly neutralized with carbonate of soda, but still distinctly acid, is treated with sulphuretted hydrogen by bubbling the gas through for a little time — any blackening of the solution, or the appearance of a black precipitate, indicates the presence of lead.

The solution, filtered if necessary, should then be rendered ammoniacal, and sulphide of ammonia added (best to the boiling solution) so long as it continues to cause a precipitate. The solution, filtered from this precipitate, may be tested for lime with oxalate of ammonia solution, as previously described.

SULPHATES

The sulphuric acid in sulphates is always determined in the same way; namely, by precipitating it by means of barium chloride solution from the solution rendered acid by hydrochloric acid, and weighing the barium sulphate produced.

For the details of the manipulation, see estimation of sulphate of soda in **Soda-Ash**.

ALUM.

Potash Alum,	$K_2Al_2\,4SO_4,\,24H_2O$	— Molecular weight,		948
Soda Alum,	$Na_2Al_2\,4SO_4,\,24H_2O$	— "	"	916
Ammonia Alum,	$(NH_4)_2Al_2\,4SO_4,\,24H_2O$ —	"	"	906
Sulphate of Alumina,	$Al_2\,3SO_4,\,18H_2O$	— "	"	666

Since the value of all alums for paper-makers' purposes depends on the amount of combined alumina they contain, and on the absence of free acid, of iron and of insoluble matter, it becomes necessary for our present purpose to give methods for the determination of these four things only.

The presence or absence of iron may be determined by the use of ferrocyanide of potash. For this purpose a considerable amount of alum should be dissolved in a moderate quantity of water, and the solution heated to boiling after the addition of a *few drops only* of nitric acid. The solution is then allowed to cool, and some freshly made solution of ferrocyanide of potash (yellow prussiate) added. If iron is present, a blue color will be developed of greater or less depth, according as there is more or less iron present. If no iron is present, the solution will remain colorless

Many methods have been proposed for testing an alum directly for the presence of free acid, but in our hands none have proved entirely satisfactory

For the valuation of an alum, then, we may proceed as follows: Weigh out 25 grammes and dissolve in about 200 c c. of warm water. When all is dissolved, filter from any insoluble matter into a 500 c.c measuring-flask and wash the residue on the filter thoroughly with hot water This residue dried, ignited, and weighed, gives the insoluble matter in the 25 grammes taken

The filtered solution is next made (after cooling) to 500 c c and well mixed. 100 c.c of this solution, equivalent to 5 grammes of the alum, are again made to 500 c.c. (solution No. 2).

100 c c of the latter (solution No 2), equivalent to 1 gramme of the alum, is taken for the estimation of total sulphuric acid present by precipitation with barium chloride (see **Sulphate in Soda-Ash**).

100 c.c of solution No. 2 is also taken for the determination of alumina. This is diluted to about 400 c.c. in a beaker, and some ammonia chloride solution added It is then heated nearly to boiling and ammonia solution added, drop by drop, until the smell of ammonia can just be distinctly detected in the solution It is then heated to just below the boiling-point for some time, until the odor of ammonia can no longer be detected in the solution. The volume of the solution should be kept nearly the same by the addition of hot water from time to time as the solution evaporates. This treatment precipitates all the alumina as well as all the sesquioxide of iron present in the form of the hydrated sesquioxides of alumina and of iron, a very bulky, gelatinous precipitate, white if no iron is present, but more or less colored if iron is present. The precipitate should be allowed to settle and the clear liquor carefully decanted through a good-sized filter Water is added to the precipitate in the beaker and brought to a

boil. It is again allowed to settle, and decanted through the same filter as before. The boiling up with water and decanting is best repeated a second time, and finally the precipitate is transferred to the filter and washed thereon with hot water until a drop of the washings gives at most only a very slight cloud when tested on a glass with a drop of silver nitrate solution

The precipitate is then dried thoroughly in the water oven, separated as completely as possible from the filter, and ignited in a platinum crucible tightly covered. Care must be taken to have the precipitate thoroughly dry before igniting, and to keep the crucible tightly covered until the substance is raised to a full red heat. The crucible is then allowed to cool, and the filter added, folded up, and again ignited — first with the cover on until all inflammable vapors cease to appear, and then with access of air until the carbon of the filter is entirely consumed. It is then cooled in the desiccator and weighed covered. The weight of the precipitate gives the weight of the alumina, Al_2O_3, and sesquioxide of iron, Fe_2O_3, in 1 gramme of the sample

To obtain the amount of alumina, the iron oxide must be separately determined, and its amount deducted from the total weight of precipitate, $Al_2O_3 + Fe_2O_3$, as found above

To find the amount of iron oxide present, we may take 100 c.c. of the original solution above, equal to 5 grammes of the sample This is transferred to a flask holding 200 or 300 c.c., and fitted with what is known as a Bunsen or Krooning valve. This consists merely of a rubber stopper for the neck of the flask, through the centre of which is slipped a short piece of glass tubing extending just through the stopper below and about one inch above the stopper

To the upper end is fitted a short piece of rubber tube about an inch in length, which has had a short slit cut in one side with a sharp knife, the upper end of the rubber tube being stopped with a bit of glass rod. This valve will open to relieve a pressure from within the flask, but will not admit air into the flask. Some pieces of pure iron-free zinc are added to the solution in the flask, and enough sulphuric acid to cause a moderately rapid evolution of gas.

The stopper fitted with the valve as above is then inserted, and the whole allowed to rest for an hour or two, taking care to keep up the evolution of gas during the time by the addition of zinc or acid as may be needed. The solution is then transferred to a large beaker and the flask rinsed in, taking care not to leave any undissolved bits of zinc behind

A solution of permanganate of potash is then dropped in from a burette drop by drop. with constant stirring, until a faint pink tint remains in the solution. The number of cubic centimetres of permanganate solution used is then read off, and the equivalent amount of sesquioxide of iron, Fe_2O_3, ascertained by multiplying by the appropriate factor.

The permanganate solution is made of appropriate strength by weighing about 3 grammes of the crystallized permanganate of potash and dissolving in water to make 1000 c.c

To obtain the value of this solution in terms of iron, Fe, we may dissolve about 0.200 grammes of fine piano wire by warming with a mixture of 3 volumes of water and 1 volume of sulphuric acid in a small flask fitted with a Krooning valve, as described above

When all is dissolved except some bits of carbon, the whole is transferred to a large beaker with 500 to 600 c.c. of water and titrated with the permanganate solution as above, until a pink color remains. Piano wire we may take as containing 99.7 per cent. of iron, Fe. Then, if we have dissolved 0 200 grammes, we shall in reality have a solution of ($0.200 \times 0.997 = 0.1994$) 0.1994 grammes of iron. Suppose this to have consumed. or decolorized, 20 c.c. of permanganate solution. Then 1 c.c. of permanganate will be equivalent to $\frac{0.1994}{20} = 0.00997$ grammes of iron, Fe, or 0 014243 grammes of Fe_2O_3

$$\begin{array}{cccc} 2\,Fe & Fe_2O_3 & Fe & Fe_2O_3 \\ 112 & 160 & = 0\,00997 & 0\,014243 \end{array}$$

The value of the permanganate solution must be determined each time directly before using, as it is apt to lose strength by keeping, with the formation of a brown precipitate. The solution of iron should always be tested before titrating by removing a small drop from the flask by means of a rod and bringing it in contact with a drop of a solution of potassium sulphocyanide, placed on a white surface, as a porcelain dish. If any reddish color appears *at once*, the iron has not all been dissolved to *proto-sulphate*, as is necessary before it can be titrated. The remedy is simply to allow it to remain longer in contact with zinc in the act of evolving hydrogen. When the reduction from the ferric to the ferrous condition is complete, the solution will give no red color with sulphocyanide solution. Certain "patent" or "concentrated" alums are met with, which contain a small percentage of zinc sulphate. This is formed from the use, at a certain stage of the manufacture, of zinc for the double purpose of neutralizing free acid and of rendering the alum more porous and consequently more easily dissolved.

A qualitative test for the presence of zinc may be made by adding an excess of ammonia solution to a moderately concentrated solution of the alum, heating to boiling and filtering from the alumina (and iron oxide) precipitated. The clear filtrate is then heated to boiling and a little ammonia sulphide solution added. If zinc is present, it will appear as a white flocculent precipitate, which on boiling for a few moments will readily settle.

When zinc is present in an alum, the iron may be determined as above; but for the estimation of alumina we must precipitate it along with the iron present as basic acetate of the sesquioxide, instead of the hydrate as in the former case.

To this end the solution must be largely diluted—about 1 gramme of alum in 500 c.c is proper. To the solution about 2 grammes of acetate of soda are added, and a few drops of acetic acid. The solution is then heated to boiling and kept in active ebullition for ten to fifteen minutes. By this means all the alumina and sesquioxide of iron are precipitated as basic acetates, while the zinc remains in solution. The precipitate is allowed to settle, and the liquid decanted through a filter as rapidly as possible. The precipitate is boiled up with water two or three times, allowed to settle, and the liquid decanted each time; and finally, the precipitate is thrown on the filter and the washing completed with boiling water, best containing a very little ammonium acetate. The filtrate and washings are to be evaporated to a moderate volume — say to about 200 c.c.; and if any precipitate separates during the concentration, as will usually be the case, it is to be filtered off, washed, ignited, and weighed with the main basic acetate precipitate.

The alumina precipitate is to be dried and ignited as above, and weighed as $Al_2O_3 + Fe_2O_3$. From this weight the weight of the Fe_2O_3 found by titration with permanganate as above is to be deducted, and the remainder will be the alumina present in the 1 gramme of alum taken.

The filtrate from the basic acetates of alumina and sesquioxide of iron is to be neutralized as nearly as possible with ammonia, heated to boiling, and ammonium sulphide added drop by drop so long as it continues to produce a precipitate. The boiling is to be continued for about fifteen or twenty minutes. The zinc sulphide is then allowed to settle, which it will do very rapidly. The clear liquor should then be tested with a single drop of ammonium sulphide. If this produces no cloud, the liquid may be filtered and the precipitate washed thoroughly with hot water.

If the addition of a drop of the reagent produces a precipitate, the liquid should be again boiled and tested, and so on until the reagent fails to give any further cloud in the solution.

The zinc sulphide is to be dried, removed as far as possible from the filter into a *porcelain* crucible, the filter added, and ignited with free access of air, gently at first, and finally as strongly as possible, with the addition now and then of a small piece of ammonium carbonate. The ignition should be continued until on cooling and weighing two consecutive weights are obtained alike. The strong ignition changes the zinc sulphide into zinc oxide, ZnO, and it is weighed as such.

In the foregoing we have constantly used the word "alum," but have really been describing the analysis or valuation of alum cake. The methods for the technical valuation of each is the same, however, so that a single description may serve for the whole class of sulphates commercially known as alums.

Free Acid in Alum.

Numerous methods have been proposed for the determination of free acid in alums, but after giving them an extended trial in our laboratory we have failed to find one which we can accept as even fairly accurate. Where this important point must be determined, we can, therefore, only recommend a complete analysis.

Sizing Test.

One of the most satisfactory tests to which an alum for papermakers' use can be subjected is that which we have worked out and called the "sizing test," by which the actual amount of rosin size which a given amount of alum will precipitate is determined. This is effected as follows.

A standard size solution is prepared by dissolving about 25 grammes of good ordinary rosin size in about 250 c.c. of strong alcohol. The solution is then filtered from insoluble matter, and diluted with a mixture of 500 c.c. of strong alcohol and 300 c.c. of water to nearly 1000 c.c. A little phenolphtalein solution is then added, and standard soda solution added drop by drop, shaking after each addition until a faint pink tinge is observed in the solution. This shows that all the rosin acids are combined with soda, and that the solution is one of *neutral* resinate of soda or neutral rosin size. The solution is now to be made to 1000 c.c. with the diluted alcohol mentioned above, and if not entirely clear, filtered again or allowed to stand until it settles clear. The clear alcoholic solution constitutes the standard size solution.

The value of this solution is next to be determined, best by means of a solution of pure crystallized ammonia alum, one part of which alum we have found to precipitate 2.46 parts of neutral rosin size.

For this purpose the clear, colorless crystals should be coarsely crushed in a mortar, and the resulting powder pressed between two sheets of filtering paper to remove any accidental moisture. Five grammes are then carefully weighed and dissolved to 500 c.c. Each cubic centimetre of this solution will then contain 0.01 gramme of alum.

Two burettes are next filled, one with the size solution, and one with the alum solution.

A flask of 150 to 200 c.c. capacity is filled about two-thirds full of water, and 20 c.c. of the size solution is run into it from the burette. The alum solution is next run in, a few drops at a time, the mouth of the flask being closed with the thumb and the flask *vigorously* shaken after each addition of alum, and allowed to rest until the flocculent precipitate formed has risen clear, which takes but a few moments. The addition of the alum solution should be continued until the precipitate on rising leaves the solution entirely clear, without the slightest trace of milkiness or opalescence.

The number of cubic centimetres of alum × 0.01 equals the amount of ammonia alum required to precipitate the size in the

20 c.c. of standard size employed. This multiplied by the factor for ammonia alum, as above, equals the quantity in grammes of neutral size in 20 c.c. of the standard solution.

The actual test of an alum is performed in exactly the same way, a solution of 5 grammes of the alum to 500 c.c. being employed, and, if necessary, filtered through a dry filter before titrating. 20 c.c. of the standard size solution are always employed, and the actual amount of neutral size it contains having been determined as above, it is easy to calculate from the data given by the titration the amount of size which one part of the alum tested will precipitate.

This test, as is evident, gives the absolute precipitating power of the alum, and does not discriminate between sulphates of alumina, iron, or other metallic oxides which may be present, or free acid, all of which have the power of precipitating size.

Moisture in Alum.

One other test as applied to alum should, however, be noticed before leaving the subject, and that is the determination of moisture. This, in the case of alums, cannot be determined, as in most instances, by drying or igniting a sample, and noting the loss which it sustains. Mere drying, even at a temperature considerably above 100° C., is not sufficient to expel all the moisture from an alum, while ignition drives off not only the water, but a portion of the sulphuric acid as well. To determine the moisture in this case, then, it is necessary that we ignite the sample, best in a platinum crucible, until fumes of SO_3 appear in abundance, then cool and weigh, and note the loss. We next treat the ignited sample with hot hydrochloric acid, until all lumps are broken down. If the ignition has not been too intense or prolonged, all will dissolve. It does not matter, however, if all does not dissolve, provided it is well broken down, so as to make sure that all soluble portions are brought into solution. The solution is filtered and the residue well washed on the filter with hot water. The filtrate and washings are next precipitated with barium chloride, and the sulphuric acid determined. The per cent of SO_3, here found, deducted from the total SO_3 contained in the sample, as determined above (see **Sulphate in Soda-Ash**), leaves the percentage of SO_3 driven off by the ignition. This taken from the total loss of weight by ignition, in per cents., leaves the percentage of moisture in the sample.

Pearl Hardening (Crystallized Sulphate of Lime).

Symbol, $CaSO_4$, 2 aq. — Molecular weight, 172.

Pearl hardening being made ordinarily by precipitating a soluble salt of lime as calcium chloride by means of sulphuric acid or sulphate of soda, washing and pressing in a filter press, the only tests which the substance calls for are tests for free acids, for chlorides, and for moisture.

Free acids may be recognized by mixing a portion of the sample with water and filtering. If no free acid is present, the filtered solution, when tested with litmus solution, should show no acid reaction. A portion of the filtered solution just mentioned may be tested for chlorides, by adding a drop *only* of nitric acid and some nitrate of silver solution. A slight cloud will usually be obtained, as it is difficult to remove all traces of chloride; but if any considerable precipitate forms, it will indicate that the pearl hardening has been incompletely washed.

Moisture may be determined by drying a sample at 100° C. in the water-oven until it ceases to lose weight. The total loss is equal to the moisture in the sample plus three-quarters of its water of crystallization. The remaining water of crystallization (one-quarter) can only be driven off at a heat approaching redness.

To obtain from these data the actual amount of moisture present in the sample apart from the combined water or water of crystallization, we must make the following calculation.

The molecular weight of anhydrous sulphate of lime, $CaSO_4$, is 136. Molecular weight of the crystallized salt, $CaSO_4$, 2 aq. $= 172$. Molecular weight of the salt dried at 100° C., $CaSO_4$, $\frac{2 \text{ aq.}}{4} = 145$.

From these figures we may form the proportion as 145, the molecular weight of the dried salt, is to 172, the molecular weight of the crystallized salt, so is (x), the weight of the dried sample to (y), the equivalent weight of crystallized salt actually present in the original sample. This weight (y) deducted from the original weight of the sample will leave the actual amount of moisture or water other than combined water which was expelled from the sample at 100° C.

Sulphate of Magnesia (Epsom Salts)

Symbol, $MgSO_4$, 7 aq — Molecular weight, 246

The only test called for by this substance is for the presence of metals, iron, and lime.

The former test may be made by slightly acidifying a solution of the salt with HCl and passing sulphuretted hydrogen gas through the solution. The formation of a colored precipitate indicates the presence of some of the heavy metals. The solution may be tested for iron sesquioxide by potassium ferrocyanide or sulphocyanide (see **Testing Alum for Iron** above).

If the sample is well crystallized and does not present a white, floury appearance, the presence of sulphate of lime in much more than traces can hardly be expected.

The solution may be tested for lime, however, by adding enough ammonium chloride solution to prevent the formation of a precipitate by ammonia. The latter is then added in excess and a little ammonia oxalate solution. The almost immediate formation of a fine white precipitate indicates the presence of lime.

Sulphate of Zinc (White Vitriol).

Symbol, $ZnSO_4$, 7 aq — Molecular weight, 287

Sulphate of iron is a common impurity in this salt and may be tested for as under **Sulphate of Magnesia**, which see, and the amount of iron oxide, F_2O_3, may be determined if desired, by precipitation, with excess of ammonia, and igniting the precipitate after careful washing and weighing as Fe_2O_3.

Sulphate of Copper (Blue Vitriol — Blue Stone).

Symbol, $CuSO_4$, 5 aq.— Molecular weight, 249.4

The "blue stone" of commerce almost always contains more or less sulphate of iron. This may be recognized by adding to a solution of the salt, ammonia sufficient to redissolve the precipitate of cupric hydrate first formed to form a clear, deep blue solution. The solution is then filtered, when any sesquioxide of iron present will remain on the filter, and may after washing be recognized by the appropriate tests.

The iron sulphate may nearly all be removed by dissolving the "blue stone" in hot water and recrystallizing.

Sulphate of Iron (Copperas — Green Vitriol).

Symbol, $FeSO_4$, 7 aq — Molecular weight, 278

The only test of this salt likely to be of use in a paper mill is a determination of the amount of bleaching-powder solution required to oxidize or rust a given amount. For this purpose a solution of the sulphate of iron is prepared containing 25 grammes to 1000 c.c. 100 c.c. of this solution, equal to 5 grammes of the sample, are diluted to at least 500 c.c. in a large beaker, and acidified strongly with sulphuric acid. The bleach solution it is proposed to use for "rusting" the "copperas" is then dropped in from a burette, with constant stirring, until a drop of the iron solution removed on a rod no longer gives a blue color when mixed on a porcelain plate with a drop of weak, freshly prepared solution of ferrocyanide of potassium. The number of cubic centimetres of bleach solution used is the measure of the amount of this solution required to oxidize or "rust" 5 grammes of the copperas. This process does not give strictly accurate results, but a sufficiently close approximation for practical work.

Salt Cake.

This is a residue left from the treating of common salt with sulphuric acid in the manufacture of muriatic acid, and consists for the most part of bisulphate of soda with varying amounts of neutral sulphate and chloride of sodium.

It is often of value to know the amount of free acid in the sample. By free acid in this connection is meant not only that which is actually free and uncombined with any base, but also that which is in excess of the amount required to form neutral sodium sulphate, Na_2SO_4, and which is, we may say, loosely combined as sodium bisulphate, $NaHSO_4$. This may be determined by titrating a solution of the salt directly with standard soda solution, as previously described (see **Determination of Strength of Sulphuric Acid**). For technical purposes it is rarely necessary to determine bases, other than soda present, in salt cake, as their amount is usually slight.

The total amount of neutral sulphate of soda, equivalent to the total base present, may be readily determined by adding a slight excess of ammonia to a solution of about 1 gramme of the substance, heating till the smell of ammonia can no longer be perceived, and filtering from any precipitate of alumina and iron oxides, which may, after washing, be ignited, and their weight determined if desired, and evaporating the filtrate and washings to dryness in a platinum dish over the water-bath. When thoroughly dry, the residue should be ignited, cautiously at first, and finally to redness. After cooling it should be moistened with dilute ammonia and again dried and ignited, cooled in a desiccator, and weighed as neutral sulphate of soda, Na_2SO_4.

CHLORIDES (MURIATES)

Chloride of Sodium (Common Salt).

Symbol, NaCl — Molecular weight, 58 5

For specific gravity of solutions and per cent of NaCl contained, see **Appendix**

Common salt usually contains, as impurities, small amounts of sulphate of lime and chloride (or sulphate) of magnesia, and frequently traces of salts of iron and alumina

The method of analysis of sodium chloride will serve in the main for all the commonly occurring chlorides. For the determination of the small amounts of impurities, a convenient quantity to weigh out is 20 grammes. This is dissolved in about 200 c.c. of water and acidified with a few drops of hydrochloric acid. The solution, filtered if necessary from any insoluble matter, is rendered alkaline by the addition of ammonia in slight excess, and heated to near boiling until all odor of ammonia has disappeared, the volume of the solution being maintained by the addition of hot distilled water from time to time as required The solution is filtered from the alumina and sesquioxide of iron precipitated, and the precipitate well washed, dried, ignited, and weighed. The lime is separated from the filtrate from the last precipitate by the addition of ammonia oxalate solution. This should be added to the hot liquid, and after boiling, the whole allowed to stand in a warm place until the precipitate has settled. It is then filtered and the precipitated oxalate of lime washed with hot water, dried, and ignited as strongly as possible for a quarter- to a half-hour or longer if the precipitate is in any considerable amount. It is well to guard against error at this point by igniting and weighing a second time, and repeating until two consecutive weights are obtained which are identical. The strong ignition changes the oxalate of lime into lime or calcium oxide, CaO, which is the substance weighed.

The filtrate from the oxalate of lime precipitate is rendered strongly alkaline by ammonia, and some phosphate of soda solution added, and after stirring, allowed to stand for some hours to separate magnesia as the double phosphate of ammonia and magnesia. This precipitate, filtered out and washed with a solution of ammonia ($1\frac{1}{2}$ volumes of strong ammonia to $8\frac{1}{2}$ volumes of water), is dried and ignited strongly, and weighed as magnesium pyrophosphate, which multiplied by 0.3604 gives the equivalent magnesia, MgO.

This completes the estimation of bases necessary.

Sulphuric acid is determined in a solution of 20 grammes acidified with hydrochloric acid, and filtered, if necessary, by precipitation with barium chloride (compare estimation of SO_3 in Soda-Ash).

For the determination of chlorine, 10 grammes of the sample are weighed and dissolved to 1000 c.c.

100 c.c. of this solution, containing 1 gramme of the sample, are diluted to 500 c.c. and 50 c.c. of the latter solution, equivalent to 0.1000 gramme of the sample, are taken for the test. This is placed in a beaker, and a small bit of neutral potassium chromate about the size of a pin-head added and dissolved, which should color the solution a light yellow. A $\frac{1}{10}$-normal solution of silver nitrate (prepared as below) is then dropped in from a burette (one with glass cock should be employed), with constant shaking or stirring. Each drop as it falls into the salt solution produces a brick-red spot of silver chromate, which, so long as any chlorine remains in the solution, disappears at once on stirring, being changed into white silver chloride. So soon, however, as all the chlorine present has been converted into silver chloride, the red silver chromate remains permanent, and a single drop of the silver nitrate solution is sufficient to give a perceptible

reddish tinge to the solution, and this is the end reaction. The cubic centimetres of silver solution used are then read off, and this number multiplied by 0.00355 gives the equivalent weight of chlorine, or by 0.00585 the equivalent weight of salt, NaCl, in substance taken (0.1000 gramme) for the titration.

The $\frac{1}{10}$-normal silver nitrate solution may be prepared with accuracy by weighing 16.966 grammes of pure silver nitrate and dissolving in *distilled* water to make 1000 c.c.

The silver nitrate should be very cautiously fused over a low flame in a porcelain crucible, employing only just sufficient heat to effect the fusion, since a high heat might decompose a portion of the salt. The mass after cooling should be coarsely powdered in a *clean* porcelain mortar, and the above-named weight of the powder taken to make the solution. Only pure distilled water must be used, since other water almost always contains either chlorides or organic matter, either of which would precipitate a portion of the silver, and consequently the solution would not be strictly $\frac{1}{10}$-normal.

The value of the solution may be tested, and if not strictly $\frac{1}{10}$-normal, a factor for its reduction to the latter may be found by titrating a weighed amount of pure NaCl with it in the same way as described above.

Pure salt may be readily prepared by evaporating a filtered solution of ordinary salt over the water-bath until only a small amount of liquid remains.

This is drained from the crystals of salt while hot, the crystals quickly rinsed with a little distilled water, and redissolved in distilled water, and the process repeated at least three times in all. The crystals are then dried at 100° C. and preserved for use.

To test the standard silver solution, a portion of the chemically pure salt should be powdered, and the powder heated nearly to redness to expel any moisture, and transferred while quite warm to a light bottle or tube having a well-fitting glass stopper. After tube and contents are entirely cold they are weighed, about 100 grammes are shaken into a beaker, and tube and contents weighed again. The difference between the first and second weights gives the amount taken for the titration. Suppose we have taken 0.095 grammes of salt and find that it takes 17.2 c.c. of the silver solution to give a *perceptible* red color to the solution (colored with chromate of potash). Then the value of our solution will be $\left(\frac{0.095}{17.2}=0.0055232\right)$ 0.0055232 grammes, NaCl, per cubic centimetre, or if we wish a factor to reduce our solution to $\frac{1}{10}$-normal cubic centimetres, we may find it by the proportion,

$$0.00585 : 0.0055232 = 1 : x,\text{ the required factor.}$$

For the estimation of chlorine by titration with standard silver solution, as above, it is necessary *always* that the solution be neutral in reaction. An acid solution may be rendered neutral by digestion for some time with powdered Iceland spar, which is pure calcium carbonate. An excess of the powder does not interfere in any way with the titration so that it need not be filtered out. In some cases it is preferable to precipitate the chlorine with an excess of silver nitrate and to weigh the silver chloride after gently igniting. For this purpose the solution of the chloride should not be too dilute, and should be *slightly* acidulated with *nitric* acid. The solution should be heated and the silver solution (quite strong) added in excess and the solution vigorously stirred. It should then be allowed to stand *in the dark* until the silver chloride has settled clear. It is then thrown on a filter and washed as rapidly as possible with hot water thoroughly. It is then dried, removed as thoroughly as possible from the filter to a small, weighed porcelain crucible, the filter burned separately, and the ash added to the silver chloride in the crucible. The whole is next moistened with a drop of nitric acid and warmed gently. A drop of HCl is then added and the crucible cautiously warmed with a low flame until the silver chloride *begins* to melt. It is then cooled and weighed. The weight of chloride of silver, AgCl, found multiplied by 0.2489 = chlorine, Cl, or multiplied by 0.40863 = chloride of sodium, NaCl.

Magnesium Chloride.

Symbol, $MgCl_2$ — Molecular weight, 95

Crystallized Magnesium Chloride.

Symbol, $MgCl_2$, aq.

This salt is of interest to the paper-maker mainly on account of its being the material employed in the Hermite electric bleaching process. It usually contains a little calcium chloride, $CaCl_2$, and frequently a little sodium chloride. These, however, do not unfit it for the above purpose. The only tests necessary for this substance are a determination of total chlorine, insoluble matter, and moisture.

The first may be determined by titration with standard silver solution, in the filtered solution as described, under **Sodium Chloride.**

The insoluble matter is determined by simply filtering out from the aqueous solution and weighing after ignition

The determination of moisture in this substance is somewhat difficult, since the salt does not part with all its water at 100° C., and on ignition it loses beside the water a portion of its chlorine. A method which is perhaps the simplest of all, and sufficiently accurate for technical purposes, is to first determine the total chlorine in a portion of the sample. A second portion is to be quite strongly ignited in a porcelain crucible and weighed after cooling. The loss will be the water together with more or less of the chlorine. The ignited sample is next boiled with water and filtered and the chlorine determined in the filtrate. The difference between the chlorine found in this and the original sample will represent the amount of chlorine which was expelled by ignition. This deducted from the total loss of the sample by ignition leaves the water in the sample.

Calcium Chloride

Symbol, $CaCl_2$. — Molecular weight, 111

This salt is rarely or never seen at present in a paper mill, but as it has also been proposed for use in electric bleaching, we note it here. It has a very great affinity for water, so great that a lump of the solid substance left exposed to the air will in a few hours attract so much moisture from the air as to liquefy itself.

Tests for free acid, total chlorine, insoluble matter, and moisture are required by this substance.

Free acid may be detected by means of litmus solution, and, if present, may be directly titrated with standard soda

Total chlorine is determined exactly as in the case of sodium chloride. In the absence of free acid, the moisture may be determined by the loss on careful ignition to a heat a little below redness. If free acid is present, the same procedure must be followed as described for the determination of moisture in magnesium chloride.

Sesquichloride of Iron.

Symbol, Fe_2Cl_6. — Molecular weight, 325

Solution of sesquichloride of iron, or ferric chloride, is occasionally employed to give a reddish tinge to paper. The salt always has an acid reaction, but in well-prepared samples the amount of free acid is slight, and the solution is so sparingly employed that it may usually be disregarded

It is frequently desirable to know the actual amount of iron contained in a solution of this salt or in the commercial article. This may be readily determined by reducing a solution of the salt with zinc and sulphuric acid and titrating the reduced solution, after diluting largely with distilled water, with standard permanganate solution. (Compare estimation of iron oxide in alum)

If it is desired to calculate the actual amount of ferric chloride equivalent to the sesquioxide of iron found, it may be done by the proportion —

$$\overset{Fe_2O_3}{160} : \overset{Fe_2Cl_6}{325} = Fe_2O_3 \text{ found} : Fe_2Cl_6 \text{ equivalent to same.}$$

The metal iron equivalent to the sesquioxide found may be found by the proportion —

$$\overset{Fe_2O_3}{160} \quad \overset{2Fe}{112} = Fe_2O_3 \text{ found} \quad \text{equivalent Fe.}$$

HYPOCHLORITES.

Calcium Hypochlorite (Chloride of Lime).

Symbol, Ca 2 ClO — Molecular weight, 143

Calcium hypochlorite constitutes the valuable ingredient in "bleaching-powder," and in a good article is present to the extent of from 65 to 75 per cent. The balance of "chloride of lime" consists of varying proportions of moisture, calcium hydrate, calcium carbonate, calcium chlorate, and calcium chloride. The only one of all these substances having any value as a bleaching agent in an *alkaline* solution such as a solution of bleaching-powder always is, is the calcium hypochlorite. The custom of the trade is, however, to reckon the value of bleaching-powder in terms of "available chlorine" instead of in terms of actual calcium hypochlorite. This "available chlorine" is in fact that portion of the total chlorine contained in the sample which is actually in combination as an integral part of the bleaching compound, which is, as we have said, calcium hypochlorite, and the percentage of "available chlorine" is to the equivalent amount of calcium hypochlorite as 71 is to 143.

Various methods have been proposed for the determination of 'available chlorine" in bleaching-powder. The method of simplest application, and all things considered the most satisfactory method for this determination, depends on the fact that hypochlorous acid, either free or in combination, has the power of converting arsenious acid (As_2O_3) into arsenic acid (As_2O_5), and in doing so it is itself reduced to hydrochloric acid or a chloride.

The carrying out of the process requires a deci-normal solution of arsenite of soda, and some starch paste having a small amount of potassium iodide dissolved in it.

The arsenite of soda solution is prepared by weighing roughly 30 grammes of pure crystallized carbonate of soda or about 12 grammes of the dry salt, and dissolving it with heat in about 100 c.c. of distilled water

4.95 grammes accurately weighed of chemically pure arsenious acid is added to the solution, and the whole heated nearly to boiling, best in a covered beaker, until the arsenic is entirely dissolved. This solution after cooling is to be diluted to exactly 1000 c.c. with distilled water, and forms the deci-normal solution of sodium arsenite, 1 c c of which will be changed to sodium arsenate by, or is equivalent to, 0.00355 grammes of active (bleaching or hypochlorous) chlorine.

The starch paste is made by adding a very little starch, previously rubbed up with a little water, to a considerable amount of boiling water, and after cooling, adding a very little potassium iodide and stirring well.

The bleaching-powder to be tested should be well mixed and the lumps broken down

3.55 grammes are then to be weighed on a glass accurately and transferred to a small porcelain mortar, and rubbed to a cream quickly with a little water. More water is then added, and well stirred with the pestle, allowed to stand for a moment for any lumps to settle, and the turbid liquid poured off into a litre flask. The residue in the mortar is again ground with water, allowed to settle for a moment, and the liquid decanted into the litre flask with the former, and the grinding and decanting repeated as long as any grains remain in the bottom of the mortar after decanting. The mortar and pestle are finally well rinsed and the rinsings added to the solution in the flask, which is finally made to the 1000 c.c. mark and well shaken.

100 c.c. of the turbid solution is then measured out, without filtering or allowing to settle, and transferred to a beaker, and the arsenic solution described above run in, slowly and with thorough stirring, from a burette. From time to time a drop of the solution should be removed from the beaker, by means of the glass stirrer, and brought in contact with a drop of the starch paste previously placed on a white porcelain surface. So long as a trace of hypochlorite remains in the solution, it will produce a more or less deep blue color with the iodized starch paste. The arsenic solution should be added, drop by drop, when the blue color given by a drop of the solution being titrated and a drop of the starch begins to fade, and the disappearance of the blue altogether marks the end of the reaction. The number of cubic centimetres of the arsenic used reads directly the percentage of available chlorine in the sample when the above weights and measures are adhered to.

In Europe it is customary to employ an *acid* solution of arsenic, made by dissolving the arsenious acid in hydrochloric acid and diluting, instead of in carbonate of soda, as above. The results obtained by the use of this solution are, however, apt to be too high, since the chlorate present acts in an *acid* solution to oxidize the arsenious acid in the same way as the hypochlorite, while the former is entirely without action on the arsenic so long as the solution remains alkaline.

The use of alkaline arsenic also corresponds more nearly to the conditions of practice in the use of bleaching-powder solutions, where the oxidizing or bleaching action takes place in strongly alkaline solutions.

Magnesium Hypochlorite.

Symbol, Mg 2 ClO — Molecular weight, 127

Magnesium hypochlorite is only known in solution and is chiefly interesting as being the bleaching agent in the Hermite electric bleaching process. It is the main product of the electrolysis of a solution of magnesium chloride under the conditions of this process. The strength of a solution of magnesium hypochlorite is measured in terms of available chlorine or active chlorine, as in the case of ordinary bleaching-powder solution and is determined in precisely the same way.

Potassium Hypochlorite.

Symbol, KClO — Molecular weight, 90 6

Sodium Hypochlorite.

Symbol, NaClO — Molecular weight, 74 5

Both these hypochlorites are known only in solution, and are made by decomposing a solution of hypochlorite of calcium by equivalent quantities of carbonate of potassium or sodium. The former is known in pharmacy as Javelle water, or "Eau de Javelle," and is chiefly employed for medicinal purposes.

Solution of hypochlorite of sodium is the "chlorinated soda" of the shops, and is also known as Labarraque's disinfectant solution. All the hypochlorite solutions possess bleaching and disinfecting properties, dependent upon the hypochlorous, or active, chlorine present. The strength of all is expressed in terms of available chlorine and is determined by titration with deci-normal solution of arsenite of soda, as described under **Hypochlorite of Calcium**

In testing solutions of hypochlorites, it is convenient to *weigh out* the number of grammes of the solution corresponding to the molecular weight of chlorine (35.5 grammes) and make up to 1000 c.c.

100 c.c. of this solution is measured and made again to 1000 c.c., and 100 c.c. of this second solution is taken up for the titration. The number of centimetres of deci-normal arsenic solution consumed will then indicate directly the per cents. of active chlorine in the original solution without any calculation.

ANTICHLORS.

Antichlors are of two kinds. The first, or antichlors proper, oppose the action of hypochlorous acid, either free or combined, by abstracting its oxygen and thus leaving the chlorine in the form of hydrochloric acid (or a chloride), whose chlorine is inactive.

This class is found in the lower oxides of sulphur, as sodium hyposulphite (or thiosulphate), $Na_2S_2O_3$, and sulphurous acid (SO_2) and its compounds, the sulphites and bisulphites.

These all serve to break up the hypochlorous compound as indicated above. They are all to be tested for their antichlorine strength, if we may be allowed the use of the term, by means of a deci-normal solution of iodine, the preparation and use of which will be explained under **Analysis of Bisulphite Solutions** below, which see.

The strength of an antichlor is conveniently expressed in terms of the chlorine which it will serve to "kill," reckoned in per cents. on the antichlor tested. 1 c.c. of deci-normal iodine solution is equivalent to 0.00355 grammes of active chlorine in this sense.

The second class of antichlors consists of substances which are capable of absorbing oxygen or chlorine, as the case may be, from the hypochlorous compound, and of combining directly with it.

To this class belong turpentine and essential oils in general which absorb oxygen directly. The caustic alkalis and ammonia are also antichlors to a degree, and act by combining directly with chlorine to produce chlorides.

NITRATES

Nitrate of Potash (Saltpetre).

Symbol, KNO_3. — Molecular weight, 101.1

The impurities in commercial saltpetre are small amounts of chloride of sodium and sulphate of potash, a little moisture, and organic matter.

The chloride of sodium is calculated from the chlorine found by titrating a solution of 10 grammes of the salt with standard silver nitrate solution. (Compare determination of chlorine in **Chloride of Sodium** — common salt.)

$$\overset{Cl}{35.5} : \overset{NaCl}{58.5} = \text{chlorine found} : \text{equivalent sodium chloride.}$$

Sulphate of potash is calculated from the sulphuric acid (SO_3) found by precipitating a solution of 10 grammes of the nitrate, acidified with a few drops of hydrochloric acid, with barium chloride. (Compare **Determination of Sulphuric Acid in Soda Ash**.) The proportion is —

$$\overset{SO_3}{80} : \overset{K_2SO_4}{174.2} = SO_3 \text{ found} : \text{equivalent sulphate of potash.}$$

The moisture and organic matter are determined from the loss on cautiously fusing 10 grammes of the sample in a porcelain crucible, covered, over a very low flame. As soon as the mass is completely fused, the heat should be removed, and the whole allowed to cool; and when completely cold, it is to be weighed. It is convenient to first weigh the crucible and cover, and then weigh into it 10 grammes of the nitrate for the fusion.

The actual KNO_3 is determined by difference between the percentage of the total impurities, determined as above, and 100 per cent.

Crude saltpetre often contains a small amount of nitrate of soda, but except in special instances its presence is unimportant.

Nitrate of Soda (Chili Saltpetre).

Symbol, $NaNO_3$ — Molecular weight, 85

What has been said above in regard to nitrate of potash applies equally to nitrate of soda, with the exception that in the latter salt the small amount of sulphuric acid present is to be considered as combined with soda instead of with potash. The formula, then, for converting the SO_3 found into equivalent sulphate of soda will be

$$\overset{SO_3}{80} : \overset{Na_2SO_4}{142} = \text{found} : \text{equivalent } Na_2SO_4$$

Nitrate of Iron.

Symbol, Fe 3 NO₃. — Molecular weight, 242

This always occurs in commerce as a solution.

It is frequently employed for the same purpose as ferric chloride (which see), and by dyers is employed in conjunction with different forms of tannin solutions in dyeing blacks, and hence is frequently called "black liquor."

The only test called for by this substance is a determination of the total iron oxide it contains. For the method compare **Sesquichloride of Iron.**

ACETATES

Acetate of Lead ("Sugar of Lead").

Symbol, Pb 2 C₂H₃O₂, 3 aq — Molecular weight, 379.

Acetate of lead is almost the only acetate ever employed in a paper mill. This is used in conjunction with a bichromate in the production of the canary-yellow chromate of lead. The test of this substance is for the total amount of soluble lead it contains, and this is calculated to the acetate. The method for determining the soluble lead present consists in adding to a filtered solution of the salt, which should be rather dilute and acidified with a few drops of acetic acid, a solution of bichromate of potash in excess. The liquid should be well stirred and allowed to stand in a warm place until the precipitate has settled, leaving the liquid clear. It is then to be filtered through a filter which has been previously balanced by means of another filter on the opposite scale-pan. The precipitate is well washed with hot water, the washing being continued until the washings come off colorless. The filter containing the precipitate is then dried, together with its companion filter, in the water-oven until it ceases to lose weight; and weighed, the empty filter being placed on the opposite scale-pan. The weight of the chromate of lead weighed, multiplied by 0.68947, equals oxide of lead, PbO. The equivalent acetate of lead may be found by the proportion —

PbO   Pb 2 C₂H₃O₂, 3 aq
222   378   = oxide of lead found : equivalent acetate of lead.

CHROMATES

Bichromate of Potash.

Symbol, $K_2Cr_2O_7$. — Molecular weight, 295.2

Bichromate of potash occurs in so great a state of purity as to hardly ever call for a test. If, however, this is desired, the total amount of chromic acid, CrO_3, may be determined by precipitating a solution containing a known amount of the sample by means of a solution of pure acetate of lead, acidified with acetic acid, and weighing the resultant lead chromate (compare **Acetate of Lead**). Chromate of lead, multiplied by 0.31053, equals chromic acid, CrO_3.

Bichromate of Soda.

Symbol, $Na_2Cr_2O_7$. — Molecular weight, 263

This salt is frequently employed for the same purpose as bichromate of potash on account of its less cost. It possesses the disadvantage, however, of being somewhat deliquescent. The proportion of actual chromic acid, CrO_3, may be determined as in bichromate of potash if desired. Theoretically, 263 parts of this salt will precipitate the same amount of lead acetate as 295.2 parts of the potassium bichromate.

MINERAL COLORS.

Chrome Yellow (Canary Yellow — Canary Paste).

Pure chrome yellow, or neutral chromate of lead, is found when solution of bichromate of potash or soda is mixed with a solution of a neutral salt of lead, such as the acetate or the nitrate of lead, as a bright yellow precipitate. It is entirely insoluble in pure water, and only slightly soluble in dilute mineral acids. In practice it is often formed in and on the fibre by first impregnating the fibre with a solution of sugar of lead in the beating engine, and then adding a solution of bichromate.

It occurs in commerce both as a dry powder and in the form of paste. The former is little liable to adulteration, as any addition would tend to change the shade of color.

The canary paste is, however, sometimes falsified by a judicious addition of ochre, clay, or barytes, with the aid of one of the brilliant yellow "aniline," or "azo" colors, or even picric acid. Mineral additions may be detected by treating a sample of the paste with weak caustic potash solution, which dissolves lead chromate to a clear yellow solution, while any of the mineral adulterants likely to be present would remain undissolved by the potash.

The presence of "azo" colors may be detected by treating a sample of the paste with strong alcohol. If only chromate of lead is present, the alcohol will remain colorless, while the other yellows will be dissolved and will appear in the alcohol.

Besides the canary or neutral chromate of lead there are basic lead chromates, varying in tint all the way to a brick-red or even crimson, some of them even rivalling vermilion in beauty and brilliancy.

Orange Mineral.

This is a manufactured lead pigment made by roasting the carbonate of lead under special conditions as regards temperature and access of air to the furnace.

On boiling with a considerable quantity of moderately dilute hydrochloric acid, orange mineral should dissolve without residue to a colorless solution. The solution should give no red color with potassium sulphocyanide, indicating that oxide of iron is absent.

Venetian Red.

Venetian red is a nearly pure sesquioxide of iron, and may be obtained in quite a variety of shades, the different shades being imparted to it by roasting at various temperatures and under various other conditions.

The pigment should be nearly all soluble in strong hydrochloric acid on heating with it. The small amount insoluble should be of a pure white color after washing.

The hydrochloric acid solution boiled with excess of ammonia and filtered from the ferric hydrate precipitated, should give, when tested with ammonium oxalate solution, only a small precipitate of oxalate of lime.

A portion of the hydrochloric acid solution tested with barium chloride solution should give but a slight precipitate.

Indian Red.

This is a mineral of complex composition which owes its color to a compound of ferric oxide. It should yield to boiling hydrochloric acid a moderate quantity of sesquioxide of iron.

Prussian Blue or Berlin Blue.

This is a ferrocyanide of iron. A pure Prussian blue should be odorless, of a bright blue color, with a coppery lustre. It should yield nothing to water or to dilute hydrochloric acid. On ignition, it should smoulder like tinder. The ignited residue should be entirely soluble in strong hydrochloric acid by continued heating with the same. The solution, after the precipitation of sesquioxide of iron by the addition of an excess of ammonia, should give no precipitate on the addition of ammonium oxalate solution.

Ultramarine.

Ultramarine is a peculiar compound of complex composition. The color is very sensitive to acids, being rapidly discharged by all the mineral acids even when very dilute. This character serves to distinguish it from Prussian blue. On the other hand, alkalis have no action on this color, while the color of Prussian blue is discharged by them.

An admixture of Prussian blue with ultramarine may be recognized by treating the sample with a moderately strong solution of caustic soda, and filtering. The filtered solution is then acidified with hydrochloric acid and a few drops of ferric chloride solution added. If Prussian blue were originally present, the addition of the ferric chloride will determine the formation of the same color in this solution.

Other Mineral Colors

of use to the paper-maker are certain colored clays known as ochres. These may be obtained of almost any shade from that of sienna and Vandyke brown to a cream-white. They all owe their color to sesquioxide of iron in varying proportions and combinations. In most instances the iron oxide may be all removed by treatment with boiling hydrochloric acid, leaving a pure white residual clay.

With these, as with clays proper, the technical test is more mechanical than chemical and relates to the fineness of the material and its freedom from grit. The presence of grit may be detected roughly by rubbing a bit of the sample between the teeth when the presence of gritty particles may be felt.

The character of the grit and its approximate amount may be determined by a flotation experiment as follows: —

A considerable quantity of the material, say 100 grammes, is well stirred with a pailful of water, best in a glazed earthenware jar. It is then allowed to stand at rest for a few moments, five minutes perhaps, for the heavier particles to deposit, and the milky portion carefully poured off from the sediment. This is again stirred with a fresh portion of water and poured off, and the process continued until the water becomes almost clear in the time allotted.

The sediment remaining is then transferred to a small beaker and allowed to deposit, and finally the water is drained off as closely as possible and the sediment dried and weighed. It may then be examined with a glass or otherwise as desired. If time enough is given for depositing each time, this sediment will contain all the grit of the sample.

In the matter of clays it is often of advantage, in judging of the character of a clay as to its suitableness for use in paper, to have a complete analysis of it, since what might pass as clay under an ordinary inspection an analysis might prove to be an entirely different substance and one which might not be well retained in the paper, or if retained might give an undesirable harshness or other quality to the sheet.

An analysis of this kind would, however, necessarily be made by a professional chemist.

All the mineral colors and clays are insoluble in water, and in the paper remain on the surface of and between the fibres of the sheet.

ANILINE COLORS

The "aniline colors," on the other hand, as well as carmine, are all soluble colors and *penetrate* the fibre. The only test to be applied to these colors is one which has in view to determine comparatively the intensity of the tinctorial power, or, in other words, the comparative strength of different samples relatively to their cost.

This is known as the "money-value test."

In applying this test, we do not weigh equal amounts of each sample if their price per pound is different, but that amount of each which the same amount of money will buy for the several amounts to be taken for the test. For example, if we wish to compare three different samples of soluble blue costing, say 16 cents, 20 cents, and $23\frac{1}{2}$ cents respectively, we would weigh 1.6 grammes of the first, $\frac{16}{20}$ of 1.6 grammes = 1.28 grammes of the second, and $\frac{16}{23\frac{1}{2}}$ of 1.6 grammes = 1.0893 grammes of the third, and dilute the solution of each of these amounts to 1000 c.c.

A convenient amount (say 10 or 20 c.c.) of the solution made from the lowest priced sample is next placed in a tall narrow bottle, or jar of clear glass, and diluted to a rather light tint with water, noting the amount of water added. The same amount of each of the other solutions is then measured and diluted in similar bottles or jars, until the depth of the tint of the solutions matches that of the first solution diluted, and the volume of the water required noted in each case. Then suppose we have diluted our first sample to 100 c.c., 10 c.c. of the strong solution being taken; the second requires 86 c.c. of water to match the shade, making 96 c.c. in this; and the third requires 120 c.c. — making 130 c.c. in all.

Then the tinctorial values of the three samples will be as 100, 96, and 130 per unit of cost, while their cost per unit of weight was as 16, 20, and $23\frac{1}{2}$, respectively. Graphically expressed, the result of the test we have cited would be: —

1 lb @ 16 cts will color to a given shade 100 lbs of pulp,
0.8 lb @ 20 cts will color to a given shade 96 lbs of pulp,
0.68 lb. @ $23\frac{1}{2}$ cts. will color to a given shade 130 lbs. of pulp,

and conversely, to color 100 lbs. of pulp to a given shade will require of

Sample 1, @ 16 cts, 1 lb, costing 16 cts.,
Sample 2, @ 20 cts, 0.833 lb, costing $16\frac{2}{3}$ cts.,
Sample 3, @ $23\frac{1}{2}$ cts, 0.523 lb, costing $12\frac{1}{3}$ cts;

showing that in the case we have taken for example the best is the cheapest to use, while that costing the lowest price per pound stands second in the list, and the sample at the medium price proves to be the most expensive of the three.

This method of "money-value testing" is largely adopted by dealers in dyes and extracts; and while not giving absolute values in per cents. of actual color present, it furnishes comparisons which could hardly be arrived at in any other way and which are often of much value.

WATER ANALYSIS.

No single element in the location of a paper mill is deserving of more consideration than that of the water supply. Not only for use in steam-generating boilers, but for the other purposes of the paper-maker, an abundant supply of water of good quality is of the highest importance.

The only means of judging beforehand of the character of a water lies in a more or less complete chemical examination. The color, smell, and taste of a water are, as far as they go, indications of its probable character, but it must be borne in mind that a water having the characteristics of good color, taste, and smell may be heavily charged with very troublesome mineral matters, while, on the other hand, one in which these characteristics are had, may still contain little which will interfere with the operations in which it is to be employed.

Hardness.

Considerable information in regard to the suitableness of a water for boiler use may be obtained by testing the "hardness," or, in other words, the soap-destroying power of a water.

Those mineral substances occurring in water which have a tendency to corrode a boiler, or to produce scale, have also the property, in general, of decomposing a solution of soap with the formation of an insoluble metallic soap, so that the measure of the soap-destroying power will be roughly a measure of the "scale-formers" in the water.

Free acids also have the power of decomposing soap solutions by combining with the alkali of the soap and setting free the fatty acids. All the results obtained in water analysis are from custom generally expressed in grains per gallon.

For the determination of the hardness of water, a standard

solution of soap is made by dissolving 10 grammes of good, white Castile soap in dilute alcohol (about 40 per cent) to make 1000 c.c. One cubic centimetre of this solution should be able to precipitate a soluble calcium salt equivalent to 0.001 gramme of carbonate of lime. On account of the varying amounts of moisture in Castile soap, however, it is only as we may say by accident that we are able to obtain from 10 grammes of soap a solution of exactly this strength. It is always necessary then to verify the soap solution by an actual experiment upon water containing a known amount of a calcium salt. For this purpose, we may weigh exactly 1 gramme of powdered marble, or Iceland spar, and dissolve it in a covered beaker, in a slight excess of dilute hydrochloric acid. The excess of acid is then neutralized by ammonia in very *slight* excess and the solution made to 1000 c.c. Each cubic centimetre of this solution will then contain lime equivalent to 0.001 gramme. In order to test the standard soap solution, 10 c.c. of the dilute lime solution just mentioned is measured accurately and placed in a wide bottle or flask holding about 200 c.c. 90 c.c. of distilled water are then added and the flask shaken. The standard soap solution is then run in from a burette, a little at a time, the stopper being inserted and the flask vigorously shaken after each addition until a distinct lather is formed which covers the surface of the liquid in the flask, and which will remain as a thin, unbroken pellicle for five minutes.

The lather should not be thick and frothy, but thin, and when it breaks, the liquid will show in patches beneath. When this point is reached, the number of cubic centimetres of soap solution used is read off, and the milligrammes of carbonate of lime equivalent to each cubic centimetre found by dividing 10, the milligrammes in the 10 c.c. of lime solution used, by the number of cubic centimetres of soap solution employed.

The standard soap solution will preserve its strength indefinitely if kept in a tightly stoppered bottle.

The total hardness of a sample of water is tested by measuring 100 c.c. of the sample, and treating it with soap solution as described above.

If 100 c.c. of the sample are found to consume more than 16 c.c. of the soap solution, a less quantity of the water must be taken and diluted to 100 c.c. with distilled water for the test, as the presence of any considerable amounts of lime or magnesia soaps interferes with lathering, and consequently with the accuracy of the test. The number of cubic centimetres of soap solution consumed, multiplied by the value per cubic centimetre, as above determined, gives the *equivalent* carbonate of lime in milligrammes in the amount of water taken for the test. This figure may be converted into equivalent grains per gallon by the proportion —

Cubic centimetres employed for test : cubic centimetres in 1 gallon (3785)
= grammes found × 15.4 grains per gallon.

It will be noted that we have used the term "equivalent" carbonate of lime above, and it must be borne in mind that this figure expresses not only the *actual* carbonate of lime present, but includes also the iron and alumina, and sulphate and chloride of calcium and magnesium present, expressed in terms of *equivalent* carbonate of lime.

Carbonate of lime, $CaCO_3$, is almost completely insoluble in pure water, but in those waters which hold carbonic acid in solution, as is the case with a majority of natural waters, especially those of springs and deep wells, it is soluble to no inconsiderable extent. The carbonate of lime thus held in solution by carbonic acid gives to a water what is called

Temporary Hardness.

The determination of the temporary hardness of a water is of even more importance in determining its fitness for boiler use than is the determination of the total hardness, especially if the water contains sulphate of lime, since on boiling the carbonic acid is driven off and the carbonate of lime previously held in solution by it falls in the shape of a fine powder. Now, if sulphate of lime is also present, it is gradually deposited as the water evaporates, being soluble only one part in one hundred parts at 60° F. and less soluble at higher temperatures, and serves to cement the particles of carbonate firmly together into a hard crust or scale.

The temporary hardness of a sample of water is determined by boiling 100 c.c. of the water in a flask for, at least, a half-hour. It is then cooled and again made to 100 c.c. with distilled water and titrated with the standard soap as described above. The number of cubic centimetres of standard soap used calculated to equivalent carbonate of lime, and this again to equivalent grains per gallon, gives the permanent hardness of the sample The difference between the permanent and the total hardness is the temporary hardness.

Clark's process for softening water consists in the removal of the *temporary* hardness by the addition of a small quantity of caustic lime, which combines with the carbonic acid present to remove it from solution as carbonate of lime. The removal of the carbonic acid also allows the carbonate of lime which it had previously held in solution to be precipitated, and thus destroys the temporary hardness

Clark's process is of no value as regards permanent hardness.

A water which shows by the soap test a permanent hardness of only two or three grains of $CaCO_3$ per gallon with no temporary hardness, and whose reaction is neutral or faintly alkaline to litmus, may with very little question be considered fit for use in a steam boiler

On the other hand, the hardness of a water as measured by the soap test does not necessarily condemn its use in a boiler. It indicates, however, the desirability of a more extended chemical examination before deciding on its fitness for that purpose. Sulphate of magnesium, for instance, would decompose soap, and, if this substance alone were present, a water might show almost any degree of hardness, but such a water would never, under ordinary circumstances, form scale in a boiler.

If the soap test has indicated that a further examination of the water is advisable, we next proceed to determine the

Total Solids.

For this purpose, having cleaned, ignited, and weighed a platinum dish, we place in it 100 c c of the water and evaporate it to dryness over the water-bath. If only a very little residue appears to be left, it is well to evaporate 150 c c. more, making $\frac{1}{4}$ litre in all, to dryness in the same dish. The residue is then heated to 130° C in an air-bath, and after cooling is weighed This gives, deducting the weight of the dish, the total solid matter in the amount of water evaporated, and this is to be calculated into grains per gallon by the proportion —

cubic centimetres evaporated cubic centimetres in 1 gallon = grammes weighed × 15 4 · grains per gallon

The dish is then ignited at a low red heat until the residue is white. After cooling, the residue is moistened with a solution of ammonium carbonate, or, better still, with a little carbonic acid water (a syphon of "soda water" answers the purpose well), to replace any carbonic acid which may have been driven off by the ignition, and again dried over the water-bath, heated to 130° C, cooled, and weighed. The weight of the last residue gives the total mineral matter present, and this deducted from the first residue, or the total solids, gives the organic and volatile matter by difference

The amount of the inorganic or mineral solids obtained from the portion evaporated as above will serve to determine how much of the sample must be concentrated for the examination of the mineral constituents. Enough should be taken to give at least 1 gramme of total mineral matter. Two grammes would be preferable, if the evaporation of the requisite amount of the sample is not too tedious. The sample to be evaporated for the latter purpose should be acidified with a few drops of hydrochloric acid, and evaporated in a platinum dish over the water-bath, adding a portion of the sample from time to time as it evaporates, until it has all been transferred to the dish. It is finally evaporated to dryness, and, after breaking down any lumps with a glass rod, is heated over the water-bath until the residue no longer smells of hydrochloric acid, in order to render insoluble any silica that may be present. After cooling, it is moistened with hydrochloric acid, and taken up with water, and the solution filtered from insoluble matter, which latter will consist of the silica and very likely a little organic matter. This is well washed over the filter with hot water and, after drying, ignited and weighed. The organic matter will, of course, be destroyed by the ignition leaving the silica pure white.

To the combined filtrate and washings from the silica ammonia is added in slight excess, and the whole heated very nearly to boiling for some time, until the odor of ammonia can no longer be detected. This serves to separate any alumina and sesquioxide of iron, and these should be filtered out and well washed with hot water, dried, ignited, and weighed. The filtrate and washings should next be concentrated to 100 c.c. or less, and an excess of ammonium oxalate solution added to separate the lime. Both the solutions should be hot before being mixed;

otherwise the oxalate of lime is apt to precipitate in a very finely divided condition and to give trouble by passing through the filter. The solution, after the oxalate is added, should be kept hot for a little time, until the precipitate has settled nearly clear. It is then filtered, and the precipitate washed with hot water. The oxalate of lime precipitate is dried, and ignited strongly for some time, and weighed. After weighing, it should again be ignited and weighed, and this repeated until a constant weight is obtained. The final weight is the weight of the lime, CaO, present. The filtrate and washings from the oxalate of lime are allowed to become cold, and then a large excess of ammonia is added and some solution of pure phosphate of ammonia to precipitate the magnesia. After stirring, this is allowed to stand for several hours for the precipitation of the magnesia to become complete. The precipitate is then filtered off, and washed with a mixture of $8\frac{1}{2}$ parts by volume of water and $1\frac{1}{2}$ parts of strong ammonia. The precipitate is dried and ignited strongly, and weighed as magnesium pyrophosphate, $Mg_2P_2O_7$, which multiplied by 0.3604 gives the equivalent magnesia, MgO.

This completes the separation of all the bases ordinarily present in water except the alkalis. For the determination of these, the filtrate from the magnesium phosphate precipitate is to be evaporated in the platinum dish to dryness and ignited gently until no more fumes appear, taking care only to barely fuse the residue. The residue is dissolved in water and filtered from any undissolved matter, and the filter well washed. The filtrate and washings are returned to the clean platinum dish, a few drops of ammonium chloride solution added, and again evaporated to dryness and ignited. It is cooled in the desiccator and weighed, and the weight of the dish deducted, leaving the weight of the mixed chlorides of sodium and potassium, $NaCl+KCl$. The chlorides are next dissolved in the dish with a *little* water and some solution of platinic chloride added, and the whole evaporated *almost* to dryness over the water-bath. It is then removed from the bath and some 80 per cent alcohol poured over the mass in the dish before it has had time to cool. It is covered and allowed to rest for some time and then filtered through a small filter, which has been tared by means of a similar filter placed on the opposite scale-pan, and trimmed until the two exactly balance.

The precipitate, which should consist of platinochloride of

potassium, $K_2Pt.Cl_6$, should be bright and crystalline It should be washed on the filter with 80 per cent. alcohol until the washings come off entirely colorless The precipitate and the tared filter should be dried in the water-oven and weighed, the tared filter being placed on the scale-pan opposite the one containing the filter carrying the precipitate. The weight of the precipitate multiplied by 0.1932 equals equivalent potash, K_2O, or multiplied by 0.3057 equals equivalent potassium chloride, KCl.

The weight of potassium chloride thus found, deducted from the weight of the mixed chlorides, as determined above, leaves the weight of the sodium chloride, NaCl, and this multiplied by 0.5306 gives the equivalent soda, Na_2O. This completes the determination of the bases.

A separate portion of 250 or 500 c c of the water should be measured and acidified with hydrochloric acid and evaporated to a small volume, say about 100 c.c. for the determination of sulphuric acid, SO_3 The concentrated water should be filtered if necessary and an excess of barium chloride solution added, and the SO_3 weighed as barium sulphate (compare determination of SO_3 in **Soda Ash**)

Still another portion of 250 or 500 c c is to be taken for the determination of chlorine, Cl. This portion should be evaporated *without* the addition of acid to about 50 c.c., and after cooling, titrated with standard silver nitrate solution by the aid of chromate of potash (compare estimation of chlorine in **Sodium Chloride**).

This completes the examination of the solid residue, it being rarely necessary to make a determination of carbonic acid directly. As yet, however, we have very little knowledge of the character of the mineral matter present in the water we have examined, and to obtain such knowledge, it is necessary to translate the language of our analytical data into that of the several compounds, as they exist in the original sample. Experience, coupled with direct experiment, has shown the manner of

Grouping the Constituents

to be as follows The chlorine is combined with soda as sodium chloride, NaCl. Any excess of chlorine over that required by the soda found is combined with potash, magnesia, and lime in turn. Any excess of soda over that required to form NaCl with the chlorine is calculated to sulphate of soda, Na_2SO_4, and the remainder of the sulphuric acid is to be combined with potash, magnesia, and lime in the order named. Any excess of bases yet remaining uncombined is to be calculated to neutral carbonates.

The sum of all these compounds, together with the iron oxide, alumina, and silica formed, expressed in grains per gallon should be equal to the grains per gallon calculated from the determination of the total inorganic solids to the fraction of a grain, otherwise the work must be repeated.

As before remarked, carbonate of lime is very nearly insoluble in water, and yet in the water-residue and in boiler scale we often find it present in considerable amount; the explanation of this seeming paradox being that the original water was a dilute solution of carbonic acid, and that in this solution, carbonate of lime is quite appreciably soluble. When, however, the water is heated, the free carbonic acid is driven out of the solution, and the water being no longer able to hold the carbonate in solution, it falls as a precipitate, and is found in the residue or in the scale, which is really the same thing. A water which contains even two or three grains of sulphate of lime per gallon is unfit for use in a boiler unless precautions are taken to guard against the formation of scale, and especially if it also shows temporary hardness under the soap test. Carbonate of lime alone (which is indicated by *temporary* hardness) makes mud rather than scale, but if sulphate of lime is also present, the latter seems to act as a cementing material to make the carbonate into stone on the boiler sheets, etc. The addition of soda-ash in the *proper proportion* to water showing temporary hardness and sulphate of lime will overcome the scaling tendency almost entirely, but will cause a large amount of *mud*, to get rid of which, the boilers must be blown out frequently.

Waters containing silica are especially troublesome, giving a hard, closely adherent scale, sometimes approaching feldspar in composition. Soda-ash may also be employed with advantage with waters of this class. In every case, however, soda-ash should be looked upon rather as a preventive than a cure, since it will only seldom serve to loosen up a scale already formed.

Many so-called scale preventers are in the market, and, like other patent medicines, some of them are probably of value. Petroleum oil, either crude or refined, is among the best of scale preventers, and is equally useful with almost every character of water which is likely to form scale. Its probable action is one of lubrication, preventing by its presence the cementation of the solid particles, and keeping the deposit in the form of mud, in which state it is easily gotten rid of. Organic impurities, unless present in very excessive amount, are of no very serious importance as regards the use of water in steam boilers, as they seldom form heavy deposits.

For Manufacturing Purposes.

For other purposes, a knowledge of the amount and character of the impurities in water is of even greater importance than for boiler use. Here, too, the soap test is of much value, since those substances which will precipitate soap, or which make a water "hard," will also precipitate rosin size, and the precipitate formed will have quite different properties from that formed by a salt of alumina or an alum. A given amount of size, for example, will not size a paper nearly so hard when a hard water is employed as it will with a soft water. Especially will this be the case when the size is added first and the alum later. When this order is followed, the size may even be entirely precipitated by the impurities of the water before the alum is added, and the alum have no effect whatever. In a case of this kind, a *little* soda-ash, added before the size and alum, will help the matter very much.

For use in paper-making, the absence of organic impurities, and especially of such as impart color to the water, is of great importance, both in the paper machine and in the bleaching. In using a colored water that must be bleached as well as the fibre, it often occurs that no small proportion of the bleach required to bring a chest or an engine of stock "up to color" is expended upon the organic impurities in the water.

A direct test of the amount of bleaching-powder, or available chlorine, a water will destroy may be easily made by adding a measured amount of bleaching-powder solution of known strength to a given volume of the water, and gently warming for an hour, and then determining the available chlorine remaining by means of standard arsenic solution. (Compare determination of strength of bleaching-powder, under **Hypochlorites**.) The difference between the available chlorine added and that remaining in the water will be the amount of available chlorine destroyed by the amount of water taken for the experiment, or the bleach-consuming power of the water.

Boiler Scales.

These are ordinarily residues left by the evaporation of the water used with the addition of iron oxide corroded from the boiler shell, and sometimes a little oil which has found its way into the boiler. The presence of the latter may be recognized by the odor on heating a sample, and if it is desired the amount may be determined by extracting the powdered scale with ether and weighing the oil after evaporation of the ether. The analysis of the oil-free residue is conducted as in examination of water residue (see under **Water Analysis**).

BISULPHITE SOLUTIONS

The bisulphite solutions are chiefly interesting as being in their several forms the basis of all the processes in use for the production of "Sulphite Pulp" from wood.

The oldest of these processes and the one first introduced into this country by Mr. Charles S. Wheelwright of Providence, R I, is known as the "Ekmann Process" and employs as the reducing agent a solution of bisulphite of magnesium

Without touching on the at present disputed point whether or not the bisulphites of the earth bases, as magnesia and lime, really exist, we may say that with the Ekmann process, at least, it has been proved by experiment that a solution which contains sulphurous acid, SO_2, and magnesia, MgO, most nearly in the proportions theoretically required to form magnesium bisulphite, MgS_2O_5, gives the best as well as the most economical results.

Estimation of Sulphurous Acid.

Symbol, SO_2 — Valency II — Molecular weight, 64

For the determination of the total sulphurous acid, SO_2, in a solution, we require a standard solution of iodine and some starch paste.

The solution of iodine is prepared by weighing accurately 12.7 grammes of chemically pure, resublimed iodine on a watch-glass and transferring the same to a flask. About 18 grammes roughly weighed of chemically pure potassium iodide is added to the iodine in the flask and about 100 c c of water. The whole is then allowed to rest with frequent gentle agitation until all the iodine is dissolved. Heat *must not* be used to hasten the solution of the iodine, and the flask should be covered or fitted with a glass stopper and kept in a cool place during solution. When the iodine has all been dissolved, the solution is to be diluted to exactly 1000 c.c. and well mixed. This will form a $\frac{1}{10}$-normal solution of iodine, each cubic centimetre of which is equivalent to 0.0032 gramme of sulphurous acid, SO_2. The strength of the solution may be verified by means of the standard arsenic solution mentioned under analysis of **Hypochlorites**, which see. The two solutions, if strictly deci-normal, should correspond or neutralize each other cubic centimetre for cubic centimetre.

The actual determination of sulphurous acid is made as follows, and the process is the same for all solutions containing sulphurous acid, free or combined: —

The specific gravity of the solutions at 15° C. (60° F.) is first ascertained.

Next, exactly 2 c.c. of the solution is measured and diluted with recently boiled water to about 100 c.c. Two or three grammes of bicarbonate of soda are added to the solution and a few drops of thin starch paste. The standard iodine solution is then run in gradually with constant stirring until a point is reached where the addition of a single drop of the iodine changes the entire liquid from colorless to a blue which does not disappear on stirring.

The number of cubic centimetres of iodine solution used is then read off from the burette. This number of cubic centimetres, multiplied by 0.0032, the value in SO_2 of one cubic centimetre, gives the grammes of SO_2 contained in the 2 c.c. of the solution used for the experiment.

In order to calculate this figure into per cents., we must take into account the specific gravity of the solution tested. Suppose we found the specific gravity to be 1.0425, then the 2 c.c. taken for the test would weigh (1.0425 × 2) 2.085 grammes, and the per centage of SO_2 would be found by the proportion —

$$2.085 : (SO_2) \text{ found in grammes} = 100 : x \text{ per cents.}$$

Determination of Sulphuric Acid.

Reported as SO_3 — Valency, II — Molecular weight, 80.

For this purpose at least 10 c.c. of the bisulphite solution, accurately measured, are placed in a covered beaker and an excess of strong hydrochloric acid added and the whole boiled for some time, the object of boiling with excess of hydrochloric acids being to free the solution entirely from sulphurous acid.

For this purpose more than enough HCl to combine with all the base present should be added and the boiling continued rapidly in a loosely covered beaker until no smell of sulphurous acid is perceptible. The liquid is then to be diluted to about 100 c.c., and the sulphuric acid precipitated with barium chloride solution, as in the estimation of sulphuric acid in Soda Ash (which see), being weighed as barium sulphate.

In calculating the grammes of sulphuric acid, SO_3, formed, regard must be had to the specific gravity of the solution tested, as explained under determination of sulphurous acid.

Determination of Bases.

In the determination of the bases in bisulphite solutions, attention must be paid to the presence of both lime and magnesia, even in the so-called magnesia liquors, since it is impossible to obtain magnesia (as magnesite) entirely free from lime, while, on the other hand, the lime used for making bisulphite of lime solutions always carries a greater or less proportion of magnesia.

When, as is sometimes the case, soda-ash is used in connection with lime or magnesia in making the liquors, soda is also present, which complicates the matter still further.

When only lime and magnesia are present, it is sufficient, in order to determine the amount of each, first to convert the entire amount of both the lime and the magnesia into sulphates and obtain the weight of the mixed sulphates.

For this purpose it is only necessary to measure out 10 or 20 c.c. of the sample with a pipette into a platinum dish (porcelain may be used if care is taken in igniting), add sulphuric acid in slight excess, and evaporate to dryness over the water-bath. The sulphuric acid will combine with all the bases present, while the sulphurous acid will be set free and will be volatilized with the water. It is well to cover the dish with a watch-glass until effervescence ceases. It may then be removed, rinsed into the dish, and the evaporation completed without fear of loss. After drying over the water-bath, the mass in the dish is to be heated over the naked flame, cautiously at first, to avoid spattering, until no more fumes of sulphuric acid appear, and finally to a full red heat. It is then cooled in the desiccator and weighed. Deducting the weight of the empty dish leaves the weight of the total sulphates of the bases present.

It is absolutely essential that white fumes of SO_3 should appear on ignition. If they do not appear, the mass must be again moistened with dilute sulphuric acid, and dried and ignited a second time. The ignited mass should be of a pure white color, or at most, only a trifle reddish from a trace of iron which is sometimes present. The ignited sulphates should be weighed quickly, since sulphate of magnesia after ignition absorbs water rapidly from the air, and rapidly increases in weight from that cause when exposed to the air. It will be found convenient to calculate the weight of the total sulphates of the bases found as above to per cents. on the weight of the sample as explained previously.

In order to separate the lime and magnesia present, the mixed sulphates obtained as above, after weighing. are treated with about 5 c.c. of water and one or two drops of hydrochloric acid, breaking down any lumps in the mass with a glass rod. This serves to dissolve all the sulphate of magnesia, together with a portion of the sulphate of lime. The whole is then rinsed into a beaker by the aid of the wash-bottle and the smallest possible amount of water; one or two drops of strong sulphuric acid added, and strong alcohol equal to twice the volume of the liquid in the beaker poured in. The whole is well stirred and left at rest for an hour or longer. It is then to be filtered and the precipitate washed two or three times with alcohol of 60 per cent. strength to remove acid, and then with alcohol of 40 per cent. strength so long as the latter removes anything. This latter point may be determined by evaporating a few drops of the filtrate on a piece of platinum or on glass, when the presence of any residue will indicate that the washing is not completed. When all soluble matter is removed by the 40 per cent. alcohol, the precipitate remaining on the filter may be taken as pure sulphate of lime. and may be dried, ignited, and weighed as such, $CaSO_4$. The weight of $CaSO_4 \times 0.4118$ gives the equivalent lime, CaO, which may be calculated to per cents. on the original sample. The weight of the sulphate of lime as above deducted from the weight of the mixed sulphates found, leaves the sulphate of magnesia, $MgSO_4$, which $\times 0.3333$ equals magnesia, MgO, which in turn is to be calculated to per cents. When soda is present as well as lime and magnesia, the best mode of procedure is as follows:—

First, evaporate 10 c.c., or a larger quantity, to dryness over the water-bath, with excess of hydrochloric acid. Take up the residue with a few drops of water, and transfer to a beaker, rinsing the dish with as little water as practicable to insure the removal of the entire substance. Add to the solution in the beaker gradually, with constant stirring, a slight excess of strong sulphuric acid, and then strong alcohol equal to twice the bulk of the liquid. Stir well and allow to stand for an hour or longer. This will precipitate all the lime as sulphate, which is to be washed on a filter with 60 per cent. alcohol to remove acid, and finally with 40 per cent. alcohol to remove all soluble matter, dried, ignited, and weighed as sulphate of lime, $CaSO_4$, as before.

The filtrate from the $CaSO_4$ precipitate is to be evaporated to a small volume over the water-bath to expel the alcohol. It is then allowed to cool, some ammonium chloride solution added, and a large excess of ammonia, and finally an excess of phosphate of soda solution, the whole well stirred without touching the sides or bottom of the glass with the stirrer, and allowed to rest for a couple of hours. This will precipitate the magnesium as phosphate of magnesium and ammonia. This is to be filtered off and washed thoroughly with dilute ammonia (15 c.c. of strong ammonia to the 100 c.c.). dried, ignited strongly, and weighed as magnesium pyrophosphate, $Mg_2P_2O_7$, which $\times 0.3604$ gives equivalent magnesia, MgO.

For the determination of soda, 10 c.c. or more should be placed in a platinum (or porcelain) dish, and baryta water added to alkaline reaction. The whole is then to be evaporated nearly to dryness, and filtered and washed thoroughly. The filtrate which contains all the soda is evaporated, with the addition of a few drops of ammonium chloride solution, to dryness over the water-bath, and the residue *gently* ignited, not to fusion, so long as fumes of ammonium chloride appear. The residue is dissolved in a very little water, and a few drops (excess) of ammonium oxalate added to precipitate the excess of baryta present added. The solution is to be again filtered, and the filtrate evaporated with ammonium chloride, and ignited, and the process repeated so long as the solution of the ignited substance continues to give any precipitate with ammonium oxalate solution. The final residue will consist of pure chloride of sodium, which is to be weighed after ignition to incipient fusion in the dish, and the weight of the dish deducted.

The chloride of sodium, NaCl, formed $\times 0.5306$ gives the equivalent soda, Na_2O, which is to be calculated to per cents. on the original sample, as previously explained. In calculating the composition of a bisulphite liquor from the results of analysis, the sulphuric acid formed is always combined with lime. When less than enough lime to saturate the sulphuric acid is present, the lime present is first saturated, and the balance of the SO_3 calculated to sulphate of magnesia, $MgSO_4$.

Excess of lime over that required to combine with sulphuric acid present is calculated to calcium bisulphite, CaS_2O_5, since monosulphite of calcium, $CaSO_3$, is almost entirely insoluble. The sulphurous acid, SO_2, still remaining goes first to form monosulphite of magnesia, $MgSO_3$, and any excess over the amount required for this to form magnesium bisulphite, MgS_2O_5. Any excess of SO_2 over the amount necessary to form bisulphite with all the lime and magnesia present is counted as free SO_2 unless soda is present. In the latter case it goes first to form sulphite of soda, Na_2SO_3, and second to form bisulphite of soda, $NaHSO_3$. Any excess over the amount necessary to form bisulphite with the total amount of all the bases present is counted as free SO_2. As we have said, the best and most economical liquor is that in which the bases and sulphurous acid are present in the exact proportions necessary to form the respective *bisulphites*, and these proportions can only vary within narrow limits without causing serious losses both in the manufacture of the solution and in the quality of the pulp produced, as well as serious difficulties both with the liquor apparatus and with the digesters employed.

ROSIN SIZE

Common rosin or colophony consists for the most part of a mixture of pinic and sylvic acids which, when boiled with soda-ash, gradually combine with the soda to form pinate and sylvate of the alkali, or, as we commonly term the whole compound. resinate of soda or rosin soap.

This rosin soap in a semi-solid state forms the common rosin size of the paper mill. As ordinarily met with in the mills, it contains from 40 per cent. to 60 per cent. of moisture. The amount in a given sample may be determined by drying a sample at 100° C. and noting the loss of weight. Rosin soap being hard to dry in a mass, a convenient mode of procedure is as follows:—

The sample (about 5 grammes) in which the moisture is to be determined is weighed in a porcelain dish. It is then dissolved in the smallest possible quantity of hot alcohol and about 50 grammes of sand previously dried and accurately weighed added. The alcohol may then be evaporated over the water-bath, and the residue dried in the water-oven and weighed.

Free Rosin.

If it is desired to estimate the free rosin in a rosin size, the sample, about 5 to 10 grammes of the thick size, should be first dissolved in strong, hot alcohol and filtered. This will give in the solution all the rosin free and combined with soda, while any excess of soda-ash which may be present, as well as other impurities. such as sulphate of soda, sand, etc , will remain insoluble in the alcohol, and may be dried and weighed after thorough washing with alcohol.

The solution should be freed from alcohol by evaporation over the water-bath and the residue taken up with 50 to 100 c c of water. The solution is next transferred to a separator, which consists of a pear-shaped or cylindrical glass vessel provided with a glass cock below and a glass stopper in the top. About 50 c c of strong ether is added, and the whole well (though not *too* vigorously) agitated, and the two liquids allowed to separate into two layers; the upper of the two layers of liquid being the ether which has dissolved out the free rosin, and the lower aqueous solution containing all the combined rosin. The aqueous solution is to be drawn off as closely as possible, and the ether solution washed once or twice with a small quantity of cold water. It is then transferred to a weighed vessel and the ether allowed to evaporate, and the residue heated to 100° C. for a few moments to drive off traces of moisture, cooled, and weighed

A white size may carry 25 to 30 per cent., or even more, of free rosin, on the dry basis, while a good brown size should carry scarcely any free rosin.

The amount of combined rosin may be readily determined by simply returning the water solution, from which the free rosin has been removed by shaking with ether as above, to the separator, adding an excess of dilute sulphuric acid, which serves to free the rosin from combination, and again washing out with ether, evaporating, and weighing, as in estimation of free rosin.

CHAPTER IX

PAPER-TESTING

COMPARATIVELY little attention has been paid in this country to the chemical and microscopical examination of papers, although in Germany much work in this direction has been done by Herzberg, Martens, Hartig, Weisner, and others who have so far developed their methods and brought their results into line with practical work that paper-testing is now one of the regular departments of the Königlichen Mechanish-Technischen Versuchs-Anstalt at Charlottenberg, and in similar institutions at Berlin and elsewhere. As a result of this work, official specifications are now prepared under a system of classification, to which papers must conform to be regarded as *Normal Papers*, so-called. According to their composition normal papers are divided into four classes : —

CLASS I. — Paper composed entirely of rags, and with 2 per cent of ash as a maximum

CLASS II — Paper composed of rags, with admixture of sulphite pulp, straw, or esparto but free from ground wood, and with not over 5 per cent of ash

CLASS III — Paper composed of various fibres, but without ground wood, and with 15 per cent of ash as a maximum

CLASS IV. — Paper composed of various fibres, whatever the per cent of ash

Each paper must be well sized, and without free acid

Upon the basis of physical character there is the following classification : —

CLASSES	1.	2	3	4	5	6
a Mean breaking length in metres	6000	5000	4000	3000	2000	1000
b Mean elasticity (per cent of stretch)	4 5	4 0	3 0	2 5	2 0	1 5
c Resistance to rubbing	6.	6	5.	4.	3	1

While these classifications may be useful as affording a means for the ready statement of the characteristics of a paper, it is impossible, in our opinion, to divide papers rigidly into a few classes in such a manner as to have the classification a direct exponent of their value; and there is always danger under any such system that, by a strict adherence to it, one may overlook in case of a given paper the special qualities which fit it for a given use. It is nevertheless true that these German methods have the advantage of giving greater definiteness to the statement of the factors upon which the value of a paper depends, and leave less to the caprice or personal equation of the buyers, and the classification may be disregarded without detracting in the least from the value of the methods upon which it depends. We shall, therefore, in the course of the present chapter consider these methods somewhat in detail.

Right and Wrong Sides of Paper. — Nearly all papers, except those which have been coated, have a different texture or surface upon their different sides, and the quality of printing done upon such papers depends largely upon which side the impression is made. In hand-made papers the wire side is regarded as the right side, although this is rather an anomaly, since the best impression is obtained upon the upper side. In machine-made papers the reverse is the case, so far as nomenclature is concerned, and the wire side is properly said to be the wrong side. It may usually, especially in wove papers, be detected by the small diamond-shaped depressions due to the wire, and called the wire mark. The roughest side is not invariably the wrong side, as, for instance, in case of paper for crayon and chalk drawing, where the right side is the roughest one. Upon opening a ream of unfolded or "flat" paper, the upper side is the right one; and if the paper is folded into quires, it is right side out. According to Parkinson, machine-made, azure laid, yellow wove, or blue papers are usually darker on the wrong side, while, if hand-made, the right side, so-called, is the darker.

Direction in which Paper came from the Machine. — This is sometimes important, especially when cutting strips to determine the strength of paper, since the sheet is always stronger in the direction in which it came from the machine than along its width. In case of paper made upon a cylinder machine, this point is very easily determined, since the fibres are so laid in such a paper that it tears in a straight line along the length of the machine, and in an irregular, jagged one at right angles to the line marking this direction. The direction in which a machine-made paper was run off, may be found by cutting from the sheet a circular piece about 10 cm. in diameter, floating this upon water for a few seconds, and then raising it carefully and placing upon the palm of the hand. The disc will begin to curl, until finally the opposite edges meet, forming a sort of tube. The direction of the axis of this tube or cylinder gives the direction in which the paper came from the machine. If water-leaf or unsized paper is taken for the test, it must first be dipped in a weak solution of rosin in absolute alcohol, and dried before placing in the water.

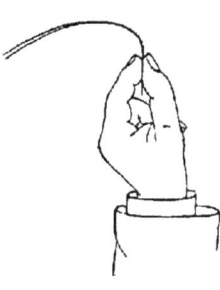

FIG. 89

Another and simpler method for determining this direction is to cut one strip about one-half an inch in width and four inches long from the paper lengthwise of the sheet, and a similar strip across the sheet. The strips should be marked when cut. If when held at one end by the thumb and forefinger, as shown in Fig. 89, the strips remain closely together, as there shown, the lower strip came from the direction in which the paper was run off. If the strips fall apart, as in Fig 90, the upper strip is the one which shows this direction.

Water Marks. — An examination of the water marks and the size and character of the wire marks is sometimes of the first importance in establishing the age or identity of a sample of paper, but the inferences drawn from such inspection are not always conclusive. It is, of course, not a difficult matter to imitate a water mark, and we have seen samples in which not only the marks, but the

FIG 90

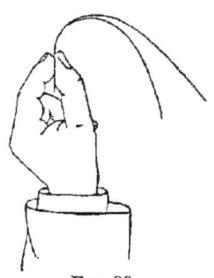

characteristics of the stock, and even of the dirt observed in ancient papers, were closely reproduced. Many designs having the appearance of a water mark, and which are in some cases of high artistic merit, are now produced in paper by subjecting the sheet to heavy pressure under a die. Legitimate water marks may, in this way, be closely imitated, so that occasions may arise when it becomes important to determine the manner in which the marks were made. The true water mark made by the dandy-roll, or by wires on the bottom of the mold, is thinner than the rest of the sheet, for the reason that there is actually less material where the lines occur than would be the case if they were absent. The spurious mark is thinner, merely because the material has been compressed; the lines contain as much fibre as any similar portion of the paper. Wetting the paper with strong caustic soda solution, therefore, renders the true mark more conspicuous, but obliterates the spurious one.

Finish and Evenness of Sheet. — There is no method of making a quantitative estimate of either of these factors which have so important a bearing in determining the market value of paper, and one can only gain the needful accuracy of judgment by the study and comparison of many different sheets with reference to their intended use. In general, smoothness and evenness of texture are more desirable in book papers than an extremely high gloss, which is apt to be trying to the eyes.

Papers in which the fibre is long and has been little beaten are usually rather uneven or "wild," as will be noticed on holding them to the light. In such papers the finish is higher on the thicker portions, and on looking across them at the light appears blotchy and uneven. This is a frequent characteristic of all-sulphite paper, and if unbleached sulphite has been used, the effect is heightened by the natural gloss of the hard fibre. A "hairy" look, due to the projection of the ends of fibres from the surface, is objectionable, as is also any tendency for the filler to leave the paper as "dust." This is noticed upon drawing the paper over a black coat-sleeve, and causes trouble in printing, by clogging and filling the type, and especially the fine lines of process cuts.

Dirt. — The common way of detecting dirt in paper is by holding the sheet to the light; but this method is not altogether fair to the paper-maker, since in use it is generally only the surface dirt which shows or is objectionable. This surface dirt may be brought into prominence by drawing a small circle around the larger specks. In this way the comparative cleanness of two or more sheets for the purposes of practical work may be determined at a glance. The character of the dirt is of more importance to the paper-maker than to the consumer. Shive and lumps of fibre are usually detected at once by their comparatively large size and general appearance. If due to uncooked wood, their color is intensified by a drop of aniline sulphate solution. Slime marks and size spots are more or less transparent, and if large, break the continuity of the sheet. Fine particles of iron from the engine rolls are far more numerous in paper than is commonly supposed. They may be distinguished from other dirt by moistening the paper with very weak hydrochloric acid, then allowing it to dry and dipping in a weak solution of ferrocyanide of potash. Each bit of iron then stands out surrounded by a blue zone. Spots due to filler or to calcium sulphite derived from sulphite pulp are usually nearly white, and break up under the point of a pin into many smaller particles. Mica in the filler is perhaps not properly dirt, but is equally noticeable from its shiny appearance, which causes it to stand out upon the surface.

Other dirt may consist of bits of bark or leaves or other vegetable matter derived from the water or the pulp. Particles of coal, tiny fragments of copper, and many other things find their way into the paper, either from the air or more commonly from the stock or chemicals. Their exact nature can usually be determined by simple chemical tests or by a microscopical examination, and not infrequently their source may be thus pointed out.

Mechanical Testing: *Thickness* — This is determined by means of an ordinary screw micrometer gauge with divisions giving thousandths of an inch, while the spaces between divisions may be read to one or two ten-thousandths. The ends of the micrometer which touch the paper should have rather wide disks or flanges, and care must be taken not to compress the paper in bringing them down upon it. It is often important to compare papers with reference to their so-called "thickness for weight." A direct numerical comparison may be made by first figuring the weights of the papers into sheets or reams of equal size and dividing the weight of each by the thickness in ten-thousandths of an inch. The weights of equal thicknesses of the papers are then directly proportional to the quotients obtained. Where other things are equal, laid papers are always thicker for weight than wove.

Mechanical Testing. *Strength and Stretch.* — The strength of a paper is the quality to which attention is usually first directed if its general appearance is in any way satisfactory. It is usually determined in this country either very roughly by tearing or more accurately by testing-machines which give only relative results useful for direct comparisons. The stretch which is of especial importance in papers used for lithographic work or for other purposes for which an accurate register is necessary is not determined at all. Several paper-testing machines which give both the strength and stretch of paper in absolute terms which permit of strict comparison without reference to the width or thickness of the samples are now in common use in Europe, and will be noted in some detail. The one which has found most general introduction in the institutions devoted to paper-testing is *the Wendler apparatus* shown in Fig. 91.

To obtain accurate information about the quality of paper with respect to strength and stretch, a strip of definite length and width is cut from the sheet, and is then strained either by weights or a spring of known strength, until it breaks. The measure of the strain gives the fracture weight, and the stretch of the strip up to the point of fracture is called the fracture stretch. For complete data, the paper should be thus tested both with the length of the machine and across it, since both the strength and elasticity of the paper vary with the direction in which the strip is cut. The power needed to tear the strip is no criterion of the strength of the stock from which the paper is made, as it gives merely the strength with which the fibres have felted, and varies also with thickness of the sheet. The strength of paper is expressed in Germany in terms of *fracture length*, the fracture length being the length of a strip of any width or thickness, which, if suspended by its upper end, would have just weight enough to cause the strip to break. The following example will show the method of calculating the fracture length. Ten strips were cut from the sheet, five being with the length of the machine and five across it:—

	WITH THE LENGTH.			ACROSS THE MACHINE.	
	Fracture Strength.	Fracture Stretch.		Fracture Strength.	Fracture Stretch.
1.	17.56 lbs.	1.9 per cent.	1.	10.80 lbs.	3.6 per cent.
2.	17.44 "	1.8 "	2.	10.88 "	3.6 "
3.	17.36 "	1.8 "	3.	10.60 "	3.4 "
4.	17.40 "	1.8 "	4.	10.76 "	3.5 "
5.	17.60 "	1.9 "	5.	10.80 "	3.5 "
	87.36 lbs.	9.2 per cent.		53.84 lbs.	17.6 per cent.
	Avg.....17.47 "	1.84 "		Avg... 10.768 "	3.52 "

These tests were made on the Wendler apparatus, and their close agreement will be noticed. The average weight of the strips was 0.0151 ounces, and in order to figure the fracture lengths, one has to determine the length of the strips of the same width which will weigh 17.47 lbs. and 10.768 lbs respectively. Calling the unknown length in the first case x, the length of the strip taken being 9 inches, we have the proportion:—

$$\tfrac{3}{4} \text{ ft.} : 0.0151 \text{ oz} = x : 279.52 \text{ oz.}$$

$$x = \frac{\tfrac{3}{4} \times 279.52}{0.0151} = 13884 \text{ ft}$$

Across the machine we have 10.768 lbs., or 172.280 ounces fracture strength; therefore —

$$\tfrac{3}{4} \text{ ft} : 0.0151 \text{ oz} = x : 172.288.$$

$$x = \frac{\tfrac{3}{4} \times 172.288}{0.0151} = 8557 \text{ ft.}$$

Our data may, therefore, be summed up as follows:—

With the length . .	13884 ft fract length	1.84 per cent. stretch.
Across the machine	8557 ft fract length	3.52 per cent stretch.
	22441 ft.	5.36 per cent.
Average . . .	11220 ft	2.68 "

Upon these figures the paper is classified in the official schedules. The calculation is greatly simplified by tables containing what are known in Germany as *fineness numbers;* that is, the quotients obtained by dividing the length of the strip by its weight. From these tables the number by which we should multiply the fracture weight in order to get the fracture length, can be at once obtained. Such well-known authorities as A. Martens, superintendent of the Berlin Royal Testing Institution, Professor Hartig, Professor Weisner, and W. Herzberg, have already, as has been stated, done much toward the classification of German papers, and the determination by this method of the influence of air, light, water, acids, sizing, and pressure upon the quality of paper.

The Wendler apparatus consists essentially of four main parts.—

1. The actuating mechanism.
2. The arrangement for holding the strip
3. The spring.
4. The mechanism for measuring the strength and stretch.

The first consists of a hand wheel, *E*, or a worm, *F*. The top of the wheel turns in the bearing block, which is cast in one piece with the bed. The screw *H* is tight with the sled *K*, and is led through the nut *G*, which consists of a shell containing a clutch which may be thrown in or out by turning the nut about 90°.

The arrangement for holding the strip consists of two clamps, *d* and *f*, the first being connected with the spring and the other with the sled. The strip is put between the jaws of the clamps, which are then pressed together by screws.

Two springs may be used, one of 20 lbs. strength, and the other of 40 lbs., the latter for heavy papers. The spring is

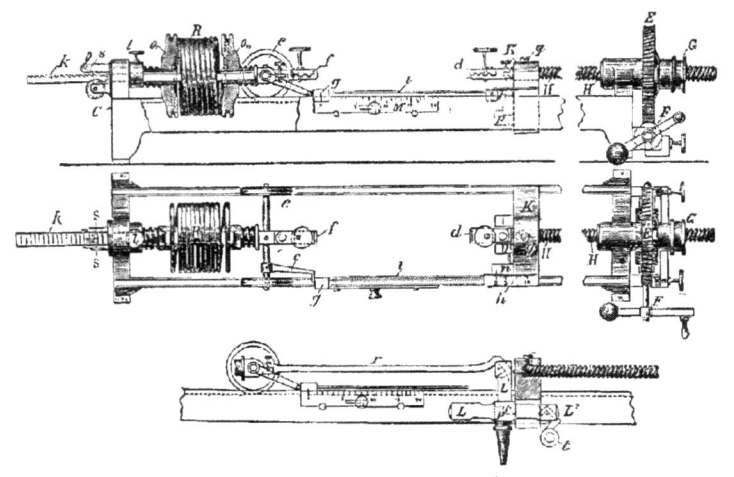

Fig. 91. — Wendler Paper-testing Apparatus.

supported at one end by the bed, and at the other end by the movable carriage. The rack is connected with the carriage and passes through the shell to the rear of the spring, where there are pawls which catch in the teeth of the rack and prevent the spring from flying back when the paper breaks.

The strain is measured as follows: The carriage pushes the indicator before itself by means of an angle rod. The indicator has a zero mark, under which is read on the scale the fracture strength after the strip breaks. The stretch is shown in per cents. of length by another indicator attached to the sled *K*. The scale above, which this indicator moves, goes forward at the same rate as the carriage, while, if the paper stretches, the indicator moves forward enough faster to take up the stretch, and from its position at the end of the test the stretch is read directly.

To test a paper with this apparatus, the strength scale is adjusted by raising the pawls s, bringing the indicator up against the angle rod, and the zero marks on scale and indicator together. Spring R is held in position by the screw l, which is tightened for the purpose. A strip of the paper to be tested is placed between the clamps f and d, the clutch G is thrown in, and the screw l loosened to free the spring, then by the hand, or better, by a little water or electric motor, the wheel E is slowly turned until the paper breaks. After tearing the strip the breaking strain and stretch are read from the scales, and the spring is made to resume its normal position by raising the pawls s and slowly letting the carriage back.

The Schopper Testing-Machine. — In using this machine, the samples required for testing have first to be prepared. This is done as follows. A piece of the sheet is taken and cut to a length of 12 inches, and then cut off in strips by the cutting blade, fixed upon the scale. The sheet of paper, when the correct length is once obtained, is simply put under the knife and rested against an edge, beyond which it cannot go. The knife is then lowered, thereby cutting off the strip to the needful size. Some little care is naturally required to see that this cutting of the paper is properly accomplished with due accuracy as to width. Thus the cutter arranges automatically, if carefully and methodically handled. After, say, ten or a dozen strips are cut off the sample, they are numbered in lead pencil from one to ten, or alphabetically, and the position in the sheet whence they come is also noted down on each strip. After having correctly obtained two sets of strips, one set across, and the other along the direction of the paper as it came from the machine, and each having been marked, they are next hung upon an ordinary paper scale, and the weight of each slip is taken and multiplied by two, which gives the equivalent weight of this sample of paper as a ream. It is then advisable to note down this figure upon the slip, and also, for safety sake, upon a separate sheet of paper. As soon as the weights equivalent to a ream have been duly noted, the samples are ready for testing.

The apparatus consists of a levelling stand, upon which there

PAPER-TESTING. 429

is a rod or pillar; near the top of the pillar there are two levers pivoted, the shorter and upper portions are curved or bent to facilitate the attaching of other parts thereto, and the lower or longer arms are each provided with an index pointer, so that when the material is being tested they each traverse graduated arcs. One of these arcs is fixed to the pillar and is graduated to indicate the pull exerted at the shorter end of the lever. The other arc is attached to the weight-indicating lever, and is graduated to show

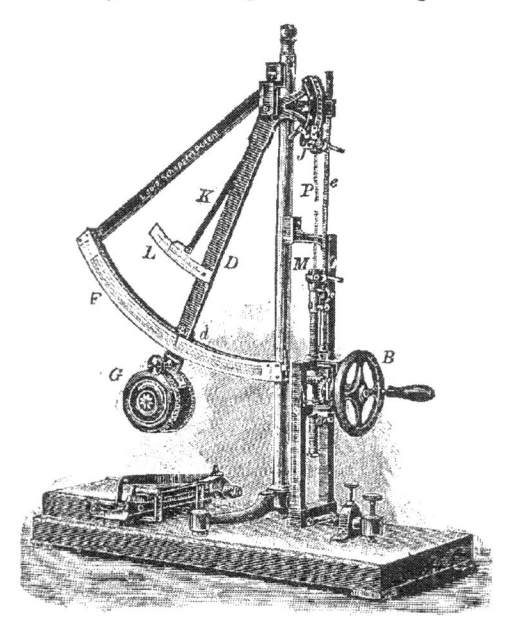

Fig. 92.—SHOPPER PAPER-TESTING MACHINE.

the per cent. of stretching prior to fracture by the breaking weight.

The weight-indicating arc is provided with ratchet teeth, and the lever with a series of pawls, so arranged that each tooth of the ratchet under the pawls is practically divided into fractional parts, thus securing strong teeth and avoiding shock by recoil when the paper breaks.

The bent or shorter arms of the lever have suitably pivoted connections. In case of the tension lever, or rod, the other end of which is connected with a slide. the weight lever has a clamp for the purpose of securing one end of the paper to be tested; the clamp for the other end is connected with the slide alluded to above; the slide is actuated with a screw, further connected with limit cog wheels and with hand-driving wheel, to communicate steady, continuous, slow motion to the slide.

To make the test, a definite length (according to the graduation of the tension arc) of paper is fixed between the clamps, in its normal straight condition, the index pointers adjusted to zero by means provided, then the wheel turned. The screw brings the slide down, stretching the paper until it breaks, then one of the series of pawls prevents recoil, and the breaking weight and tension can be read off.

The machine must stand level, and this can easily be arranged by ascertaining that the weight hangs true, and that the index pointer is exactly over the proper mark upon the curved scale board. Having settled this matter, and fixed the weight by inserting a small pin which rests in the stand, the wheel is duly set at its limit, and the screw controlling the tension rod is fastened. The sample slip is then inserted into the lower clamp and fastened thereby. This is very simply done, by merely bending the clamp back, and this causes the paper slip to become firmly held. The same is then arranged with the upper clamp, the slip of paper being gently but properly held taut by the two clamps.

All being ready, the pin holding the weight is withdrawn, and while the small wheel is set slowly revolving, the screw controlling the tension rod is unfastened. The weight at once begins to ascend the curved scale board, passing the numbered graduations en route. The back of the weight is provided with a set of four separate small pawls, which, as the weight ascends the scale board, move with it and drop into ratchet teeth in such a way that when the sample breaks the pawls stay the weight by their inability to move out of the teeth. The figure at which the weight drops is indicated by the pointer and denotes the number of pounds which represent the force of the strain. Meanwhile, above this pointer, and upon a smaller scale board, another pointer has been moving, and this indicates the tension of the sample, or the amount of stretch per cent. of which the sample is capable. This indicator also stops when the paper breaks, thereby permitting a perfectly accurate reading to be taken. As soon as this has been done, the small ratchet teeth are raised and the weight replaced in its primary position: the same is also done with the tension pointer, which, however, is without any ratchet teeth to control its movement.

The Rubbing Test. — The extent to which a paper will bear folding and rubbing without breaking has in many cases a considerable influence in determining its value. It may be tested in this respect by crumpling a half sheet strongly in the hand to form a sort of ball, then smoothing the paper and repeating the operation several times. Papers which, with reference to their power of resisting wear, would be classified as "extremely poor" on the following scale, which is that adopted by the Germans, soon develop holes under this treatment. As the paper succumbs to, or withstands, this treatment, or requires in addition, in order to make holes, more or less violent rubbing upon itself between the hands, it is given a number which has the significance shown below: —

    0 Extremely poor
    1 Very poor.
    2 Poor
    3 Medium.
    4 Rather good quality
    5 Good quality
    6 Very good quality
    7 Extremely good quality.

News and similar papers would be marked 0, while a Japanese or very strong pure jute paper would be given the number 7.

Determination of Size. — The methods employed in the laboratory of the Königlichen Mechanish-Technischen Versuchs-Anstalt at Charlottenburg, and which have been adopted with slight modification in our own laboratory, are thus described by Herzberg and others: —

The test for animal size with tannic acid depends on the formation of a precipitate of tannate of gelatine. When tannic acid is added to a solution of gelatine which is not too dilute, there will be formed a thick gelatinous precipitate. In a very dilute solution only a milky cloud will be seen, which will, after a short time, separate in flocks; the cloudy appearance without the separation of flocks shows the absence of animal size. In carrying out the test the paper is first treated, as described above, with distilled water, and the liquid concentrated as much as possible by evaporation, as then it is easier to see the reaction. When the solution is cold, a concentrated solution of tannic acid in water is added, and care must be taken to observe whether a precipitation and separation of flocks takes place.

When either very small amounts of material are available, as in the case of old manuscripts, or where it is necessary to determine the presence of very small quantities of animal size, this method cannot be used, and the reagent of Millon is alone available for the purpose. This reagent is a very delicate test for albumen, a substance always present in animal size, and is prepared as follows: To a weighed quantity of metallic quicksilver an equal weight of fuming nitric acid is added, and the whole allowed to stand in a cold place for a few hours; after which an equal volume of distilled water is added, and the whole left quiet for twenty-four hours. Prepared in this way the reagent will keep active for about four weeks.

A small piece of the paper to be tested is placed on a watch-glass and moistened with the reagent, and then brought on to a wire gauze and heated very gradually. If animal size is present, in a few minutes the paper will be colored red; the color will vary from rose to scarlet, according to the quantity of size which is present. As the red color gradually becomes brown, it is necessary to watch the paper during the whole reaction. The coloration can also be seen in the cold, but only after the reagent has acted for a considerable time on the paper, and the coloration will never be so distinct as when the paper is heated. It will be found advantageous to moisten a sample of the paper to be tested with distilled water, and to treat this in the same way as that moistened with the reagent, so as to compare the resulting colors. The reagent of Millon shows the presence of aromatic groups containing a simple hydroxyl; this being present in albuminoid bodies, it is consequently a test for albumen. As commercial glue always contains albumen (as does even the finest colorless gelatine), the reagent may be used as a test for animal size. However, it must be noted that chemically pure gelatine does not contain this group; for practical purposes, however, this is of no consequence, but the presence of animal size, as found by Millon's reagent, can only be considered as final under the following suppositions.—

1. That the paper does not contain albumen as such
2. That there are no free aromatic groups with hydroxyl

With regard to 1. Albuminoid bodies are very rarely found in paper fibres apart from size, and then only as traces. Further microscopical research will show whether the fibres give the albumen reaction, as in this case the coloration will be in the central canal of the cell, while the glue remains on the outside of the fibre. We need not take into consideration those cases in which the albumen has been added to the paper for special purposes, as in albumenized paper for photography. As regards the second supposition, it may be remarked that, apart from vanilline, we do not expect to find the forementioned aromatic groups in paper. If vanilline is present as a compound of wood, it can be found by phloroglucin and hydrochloric acid, which enables us to determine its origin. If the gelatine used for sizing is already decomposed, Millon's reagent will no longer show it. In testing old writing material, where fine parchment having the greatest similarity to paper is often found, it is also necessary to take the fibres into consideration; such parchment will, of course, at once be affected by Millon's reagent, not because it has been sized, but because it consists of substances containing gelatine.

As to whether the active sizing material in rosin size is free rosin, resinate of alumina, or a mixture of both, opinions are as yet divided. While Würster considers that the sizing of paper is caused by free rosin only, Tedesco and Rudel think that the active principle is a compound of rosin and alumina. That under all circumstances free rosin is present in rosin-sized paper, cannot be doubted, and indeed the test described below for rosin-sized paper depends on this.

Half a sheet of the paper to be tested is torn up into small pieces and absolute alcohol poured onto it; the vessel containing it is stood in hot water for about half an hour. When rosin is present, it is easily dissolved out by the alcohol, as is also resinate of alumina to some extent. If this solution is poured into a sufficient quantity of cold water, the rosin will be precipitated, as the dilute alcohol cannot dissolve it. The distilled water will assume a milky appearance, the intensity of which will depend on the quantity of rosin present.

In the method described by Schuman, a weighed quantity of paper is cut into the smallest pieces possible and warmed for a considerable time in a porcelain dish with a 4 to 5 per cent solution of caustic soda to 75° C.; by the action of the soda solution an easily soluble rosin soap is formed. The liquid is then filtered off and the paper well washed. To the filtrate a sufficient quantity of sulphuric acid is added to decompose the rosin soap. Sulphate of soda and free rosin being formed, the latter separates as a milky precipitate, which is filtered off through a weighed filter, well washed and dried at 100° C. To determine the weight of the rosin the weight of the filter should be deducted from the total weight found. If the milky precipitate at first runs through the pores of the filter, the filtrate is poured back onto the filter till the liquor runs clear through.

Starch is used in sizing to improve the appearance of paper and to give it a good finish. The use of starch alone for the purpose of sizing is far older than the use of rosin; starch sizing is but a thing of the past. For example, Weisner has found that all the papyrus belonging to the Archduke Rainer was prepared for writing on by means of starch paste. The first known use of animal sizing in paper was in the year 1377.

A solution of iodine is used for testing starch in paper; if a drop of this solution is applied to a paper containing starch, it will cause a blue or violet coloration. The iodine solution must be very dilute, or the coloration of the paper will be hidden by the brown color of the solution itself.

The quantitative determination of starch may be carried out according to a suggestion of Dr Wurster, as follows: A strip of the paper weighing from 0.5 to 1.5 gramme is boiled for a few minutes in absolute alcohol containing a drop or two of hydrochloric acid, when the rosin contained in the paper will go into solution. The strip is next washed in absolute alcohol, dried at 100° C., and the weight determined. The paper which has been thus freed from rosin is next boiled with 50 per cent alcohol containing a few drops of hydrochloric acid, until, when moistened with iodine solution, it no longer shows a light blue coloration; it is then washed in alcohol, dried at 100° C., and the weight determined. The loss in weight is the amount of starch present

The methods followed in our own laboratory, for the detection and estimation of starch in paper, differ from those given above and are as follows: —

In making a qualitative test for starch we do not apply the dilute iodine solution directly to the paper, as the distinctness of the reaction is apt to be impaired by the color which the paper itself takes on even when starch is absent. Instead we tear the paper into small bits and boil these for ten or fifteen minutes in water. The solution is then poured off and allowed to become cold, when a drop of dilute iodine solution is added. If starch is present, there is at once developed a pronounced blue coloration.

The determination of the amount of starch is effected by converting the starch into glucose by heating with dilute acid, and estimating the glucose by means of the well-known method with Fehling's solution. The glucose found multiplied by 0.9 gives the equivalent starch.

In the conversion of starch into glucose careful regard must be had to the strength of acid employed, and to the manner of heating, since under other circumstances cellulose itself is converted into glucose. We have found by experiment that a solution containing 2 per cent. by weight of sulphuric acid (H_2SO_4) does not attack cellulose appreciably when the heating is conducted in the water oven, while it converts starch completely under the same conditions. The best plan of procedure is to boil 5 grammes of the paper with about 500 cc. of water for some time to disintegrate the fibre and gelatinize all starch. The weight of the solution, which should be at least 500 grammes, is determined, and 2 per cent. of sulphuric acid added to it. It is then brought again to boiling and transferred to the water oven, where it is kept until a drop of the solution mixed with a drop of very dilute iodine solution gives no blue color. About three hours' heating is generally sufficient. It is then allowed to cool, transferred to a litre flask, and potash or soda added in excess. The whole is made to 1000 cc., and a portion filtered for the determination of glucose by Fehling's solution.

The extent to which a paper has been sized is usually determined in the mills and among buyers by pressing the tongue against the sheet and then holding the paper to the light. With a well-sized writing paper scarcely any difference is noticed between the portion thus moistened and the rest of the paper, but other papers appear more or less transparent where they have been wetted according to the extent to which the sizing has been carried. To replace this very crude test, Leonhardi has worked out a method which indicates with considerable definiteness the thoroughness with which the paper has been sized.

To carry out Leonhardi's method, a solution of ferric chloride of such strength as to contain 1.531 per cent. of iron is required. This solution is comparable in its power of penetrating the paper to the better grades of writing-inks. An ivory ruling-pen of the form used by draughtsmen, and with rounded tips 1 mm. apart, is used for drawing with the above solution a number of parallel lines upon the paper. The lines are allowed to dry, and then a weak solution of tannic acid in ether is poured upon the other side of the paper. This ether evaporates almost at once, leaving the tannic acid. If the paper has been badly sized, the ferric chloride solution will have so penetrated to the under side that upon pouring on the tannic acid solution dark lines due to tannate of iron appear, while with a very well-sized paper only the yellow lines caused by the ferric chloride will be noticed when the paper is held to the light.

An objection has been made to the ethereal solution of tannin, because it may dissolve rosin size to some extent, and a solution in water is therefore sometimes and perhaps better used instead. This is applied to the back of the paper by a bit of cloth or ball of cotton-wool, and the excess is taken up by blotting-paper.

It is not really necessary to use the ruling-pen for the ferric chloride solution, which may instead be dropped upon the paper to be tested from a pipette. To eliminate the error due to the thickness of the paper the drop may be allowed to remain as many seconds as the paper per square metre weighs in grammes. This of course is purely arbitrary, but when adhered to uniformly in all tests permits of comparison between different papers. At the end of the time the unabsorbed solution is removed by blotting-paper, and when the spot has dried, the tannic acid solution is applied to the other side. Care should be taken to have the drops from the pipette of a size as nearly uniform as possible.

Capillary Power of Blotting-papers. — This may be determined with considerable accuracy, by cutting a strip of the paper and marking upon it with a pencil the divisions of a millimetre scale. The paper is then suspended over water and lowered until it dips into the water sufficiently to bring the zero point on the scale at the surface of the water. The height in millimetres to which the water is drawn by the capillary action of the paper is then noted at short intervals up to ten minutes. This may range from about 100 mm. in case of the best samples, down to 20 mm. in case of especially poor ones.

Free Acids and Chlorides.—If the bleach is not thoroughly washed out of the half-stuff or neutralized by antichlor, it does not remain in the paper as hypochlorite for any length of time. The chlorides formed by its reduction are, however, believed to be objectionable, and to hasten the deterioration of the paper. They may be detected by cutting a piece about six inches square into small bits, covering these with water in a beaker and boiling. To the cold solution slightly acidified with nitric acid a few drops of silver nitrate solution are added, when chlorides, if present, determine the formation of a white precipitate or opalescence.

Free acid or an acid alum, if the last is present as such, weaken the paper in time through formation of hydrocellulose. It is difficult to determine free acid qualitatively in the presence of alum with certainty, since the alum itself affects the indicators used, but for practical purposes it is generally sufficient to boil up the paper as in the test for chlorides, and then to add litmus solution or congo-red.

Determination of Ash.—This is a matter of importance to both the maker and the buyer of paper, since it enables the one to determine what per cent. of the filler used has been retained in the sheet, while it points out to the other the extent to which the paper has been weighted. The test is very easily carried out although in unskilled hands it is apt to give too high results, owing to imperfect combustion. Two grammes of paper are taken, and after being folded into as small a compass as possible are placed in a crucible, and the cover put on. A moderate heat is then applied until no more smoke or inflammable vapor appears. The crucible is then placed on its side upon the triangle, and the cover is inclined so as to throw the heat well into the crucible. The whole is raised to bright redness, and this temperature is maintained until the ash is white, if the paper were not colored, or in any case until all carbon is burned off. The crucible and its contents are cooled in a desiccator and weighed. From this weight is taken the weight of the crucible, and the remainder is of course the weight of the ash. This divided by 2 gives the per cent. of ash, which for most practical purposes may be taken without correction as representing the percentage of the mineral filler in the sheet.

In very careful work, allowance may sometimes be made for the ash normally derived from the fibres composing the paper; the figures obtained by several chemists are given below. —

Ash in Commercial Pulps.

W. Herzberg

	Per cent
Sulphite (1)	0.48
Sulphite (2)	0.51
Sulphite, bleached	0.42
Soda	1.34
Soda, bleached	1.40
Straw	2.30
Straw, bleached	1.34
Ground wood (pine)	0.43
Ground wood (fir)	0.70
Ground wood (aspen)	0.44
Ground wood (lime)	0.40
Linen	0.76
Linen, bleached	0.94
Cotton	0.41
Cotton, bleached	0.76

Ash in Fibres.

Dr. Muller.

	Per cent
Cotton	0.12
Fine heckled Flemish flax	0.70
Italian hemp	0.82
China grass	2.87
Rhea	5.63
Jute	1.32
Phormium tenax	0.63
Best Manila hemp	1.02
Esparto	3.50–5.04
Adansonia	4.72–6.19
Sulphite fibre (Dr. Frank)	0.46–2.60
Soda fibre (Dr. Frank)	1.00–2.50

Various other determinations will be found in the chapter on **Fibres.** We have ourselves tested samples of cotton half-stuff in which the ash ranged from 0.13 to 0.57 per cent. Our figures for ground spruce wood are from 0.25–0.32 per cent., while in case of sulphite pulps the ash has varied from 0.22 per cent. to over 9.00 per cent.

The difficulty at once met in any attempt to correct the ash by means of the figures given above, is that these figures themselves are liable to vary so much according to the thoroughness of the different treatments to which the fibres have been subjected that there is danger of introducing a considerable error in attempting to guard against a slight one.

In order to obtain results which fairly represent the average of mineral matter in the paper, several samples should be tested. An uneven pull on the suction boxes may easily cause the amount of filler to vary by 2 per cent. on the different sides of the machine. Owing to settling and other causes, an even greater difference may appear in the different stages of a run.

Determination of the Kind of Filler. — This is necessary if one desires to know accurately the amount of weight actually added to the paper or the exact percentage of fibre which the paper carries.

A test showing the ash to contain large amounts of silica and alumina is all that is needed to prove the presence of clay. To make this test, transfer the ash to a porcelain dish, add sufficient hydrochloric acid to moisten thoroughly, and then bring the contents of the dish to a temperature of 120–130° C. on a sandbath until all the acid is driven off. The ash is then boiled up with water to which a few drops of hydrochloric acid are added, and the whole finally thrown on a filter. A white residue on the filter is silica. If ammonia added in very slight excess to the hot filtrate throws down a flocculent, bulky, white precipitate, alumina is present. The precipitate may be more or less colored if iron also is present.

To some of the above liquid cleared either by filtering or by decantation, add ammonium oxalate solution. If there is a slight cloudiness, it is doubtless due to lime derived from the clay, but a considerable precipitate indicates that the ash contains sulphate of lime, and that the filler used was either pearl hardening, fibrous alumine, or gypsum. Either of these fillers, if used without clay, should give a very white ash entirely soluble in water acidulated with hydrochloric acid: 300–400 c.c. of water in successive portions should be used in all. Such ash rarely contains grit, and often shows a needle-like crystalline structure when examined under a hand glass.

Agalite also gives a very white ash, but this rubbed between the teeth shows grit. It should give a test for silica and magnesia, both in large amounts. The test is made by fusing the ash in the crucible with about five times its weight of a mixture of potassium and sodium carbonates in equal amounts. The fused mass is dissolved in water, and after solution is complete, a few drops of hydrochloric acid are added. The solution is then run down to dryness in a porcelain dish, ignited at 130° C., until the acid is driven off, then boiled up with water and filtered.

A white residue on the paper is silica. The filtrate is tested for magnesia, as described under **Magnesia**.

The ash from any paper rarely contains a notable quantity of alumina derived from alum used in sizing.

If the examination outlined above shows the ash to consist of sulphate of lime, the percentage of ash found should be multiplied by 1.26 to find the percentage of the filler actually in the paper. This is because the sulphate of lime, as it exists in the paper, is combined with two molecules of water of crystallization, which add proportionately to the weight of the paper, but are driven off upon ignition of the ash. Clays also often have a definite percentage of combined water, which, although present in the paper to make weight, is similarly driven off on ignition. This percentage varies, however, in different clays, so that no general factor can be given for use in all cases. The amount of this combined water should be determined in the clay used and the proper factor found. The per cent. of ash multiplied by this factor gives the percentage of weight actually due to the clay in the paper. This corrected percentage subtracted from 100 gives the per cent. of fibre in the sheet. To figure retention, divide the pounds of fibre furnished by the per cent. of fibre in the paper. The quotient is the pounds of paper made from the engine. From this figure subtract the pounds of fibre furnished, and the balance is the pounds of filler retained. This figure divided by the pounds of filler furnished gives the percentage of the filler retained.

If mineral colors have been used in making the paper, something toward their recognition may be deduced from the character of the ash. Iron is recognized by the brown color of the ash, and may be determined by fusing as under **Agalite**, and treating the hot solution with ammonia. Its presence in considerable amount may indicate ochre, Venetian red, Indian red, or Prussian blue, the color of the paper being of course an aid in reaching a conclusion as to which of these colors is present. Chromium, if lead is absent, indicates chrome green. In the presence of lead it indicates chrome yellow, or if the paper is red, a basic chromate of lead. Lead alone, if the paper is buff, is probably derived from orange mineral. Ultramarine colors the ash blue, and its amount may be determined in many cases by carefully igniting a considerable quantity of the paper until all carbon has been burned off, then taking a quantity of ignited clay or sulphate of lime equal to the weight of the ash and finding how much of a standard sample of ultramarine must be mixed with this to produce the depth of color shown by the ash.

Microscopical Examination. — The study of the fibres used in paper-making can only be conducted by the aid of a good microscope, and a working knowledge of the instrument can be put to practical use in many ways by the paper-maker. The value of any particular microscope depends mainly upon the excellence of the lenses, but the purchaser should also have regard for the steadiness, ease of adjustment, and simplicity of construction of the stand. For present uses the preference should be given to an instrument having a short tube and low stand. Magnifying powers ranging from 70 to 500 diameters may be secured by the combinations of two eyepieces and two objectives, while in general one objective, giving with the eyepiece an enlargement of 70 diameters, will be found sufficient for most examinations. Low powers which bring out the details wanted are to be preferred to higher ones.

The sample for microscopical examination is prepared by cutting a few square inches from different portions of the sheet and tearing the pieces into little bits. These are boiled for about fifteen minutes in a 1 per cent. solution of caustic soda. The whole is then poured upon a sieve having a mesh which is at least as fine as 100 to the inch, and the paper which remains upon the sieve is gently rubbed with the finger to separate the fibres. To complete the separation, the pulpy mass is transferred to a bottle with a few garnets or bits of glass and sufficient water to about half fill the bottle. The bottle is shaken vigorously until all lumps are broken up and the material brought to about the consistency of stuff as it flows onto the paper machine.

The only way by which the student can fit himself for the microscopical examination of papers is by the careful study and comparison under the microscope of slides prepared from known samples of the different pulps and fibres and standard admixtures of them. Various standard papers in which the proportions of the different fibres are stated are made in Germany for use in this work, but it is safer to make up in the laboratory the different mixtures from the pulps and to preserve them for use as needed. Following the method given above for preparing paper samples for examination, the student should first prepare a set of standards from —

    1. Pure linen paper.
    2. Pure cotton rag paper.
    3. Bleached soda poplar fibre
    4. Bleached sulphite spruce
    5. Unbleached sulphite spruce
    6. Bleached straw fibre
    7. Bleached esparto fibre
    8. Half-bleached jute
    9. Ground wood (spruce)
   10. Ground wood (poplar).

After being properly pulped, the samples should be put in small bottles of uniform size and shape and marked with the number of the sample on a small label on the bottom of the bottle. There should then begin a thorough and systematic examination of slides made from the different samples, until the characteristics of each pulp become familiar. Attention should be paid not only to the length and relative diameter of the fibres, but to the thickenings and markings of the cell-wall and to characteristic cells, not fibres, which are found in the pulp. A frequent reference to Plate 1, and to the text in the chapter on **Fibres** will be found useful.

Besides the physical features above referred to, and upon which the main reliance must be placed for the recognition of the different fibres certain distinctive differences appear when the fibres are subjected to the action of various staining agents. The brown coloration noticed when a streak is made with nitric acid upon paper containing ground wood or other lignified fibre gives a rough example of the action of such a staining agent. Under the microscope similar methods of staining may be applied with sufficient refinement to permit of a rough classification of the different sorts of fibres by means of the colors which are thus developed. The most important of these reagents are —

1. *Iodine Solution.* — Made by dissolving 1 gramme of iodine and 5 grammes of potassium iodide in 100 c.c. of water. This solution is used alone or in connection with

2. *Sulphuric Acid.* — The acid is prepared of proper strength by mixing carefully, in order to avoid sudden heating, three volumes of sulphuric acid of specific gravity 1.84 with one volume of distilled water and two volumes of pure glycerine. It is ready for use when it has become cool.

3. *Aniline Sulphate.* — A saturated solution of the salt in alcohol. This stains ground wood and other lignified fibres yellow.

If, after being thoroughly beaten up and separated, a small quantity of the paper to be examined is placed on the slide with a drop of iodine solution, it will be found that the fibres may be grouped as follows according to the staining action of the iodine upon them : —

1. *Colorless Fibres.* — Bleached chemical wood fibre, bleached straw, and esparto.

2. *Fibres which are stained Yellow.* — Ground wood and jute.

3. *Fibres which are stained Brown.* — Cotton, linen, hemp.

The use of iodine in the identification of the different fibres may be further extended if the iodine is employed in connection with the diluted sulphuric acid above mentioned. In this case the iodine is allowed to act for a few minutes upon the fibres on the slide, and the excess of reagent is removed by carefully pressing down upon them a small square of blotting-paper. This is raised without disturbing the fibres, and after a drop of the diluted acid has been deposited upon them the preparation is covered with a thin cover-glass. The staining effects thus developed are not the same as those due to the action of the iodine alone, and are those to which occasional reference was made in the chapter on **Fibres**

Thus treated, fibres which consist of pure cellulose, like cotton, bleached linen, straw, esparto, and wood take on a color which may, in case of the different fibres, range from pure blue to purple or even to red slightly tinged with blue. Jute, ground wood, unbleached and poorly cooked sulphite, and other lignified fibres turn deep yellow. The staining also brings out more clearly those differences in structure which aid in the recognition of the fibres.

Aniline sulphate solution stains the lignified fibres yellow, and is especially useful for bringing ground wood into prominence.

Another very delicate reagent for detecting the presence of ground wood is phloroglucin. It is employed in solution prepared by dissolving 2 grammes of the reagent in 25 c.c. of alcohol and adding 5 c.c. of concentrated hydrochloric acid. It stains lignified fibres a brilliant red.

When the student has familiarized himself with the microscopical appearance of the standard samples, bottles should be selected at random from the set and examined until without reference to the number he finds himself able to identify any sample. Standard mixtures should then be prepared by weighing off and mixing the air-dry fibres in definite proportions and reducing to pulp as in case of paper. The following forms a convenient set of such mixed standards with which to begin:—

1. Linen 50 per cent., cotton 50 per cent.
2. Cotton 30 per cent., bleached poplar fibre 70 per cent.
3. Bleached sulphite spruce 30 per cent., bleached poplar 70 per cent.
4. Cotton 10 per cent., bleached sulphite spruce 20 per cent., bleached poplar 70 per cent.
5. Unbleached sulphite spruce 70 per cent., jute 30 per cent.
6. Unbleached sulphite spruce 50 per cent., spruce ground wood 50 per cent.
7. Unbleached sulphite spruce 50 per cent., poplar ground wood 50 per cent.
8. Unbleached sulphite spruce 20 per cent., spruce ground wood 80 per cent.
9. Unbleached sulphite spruce 20 per cent., poplar ground wood 80 per cent.
10. Bleached poplar 50 per cent., bleached straw 50 per cent.
11. Bleached straw 50 per cent., bleached esparto 50 per cent.

Besides enabling one to determine the proportions in which the different fibres are present in a paper, the microscope will also yield considerable information as to the manner in which these have been beaten. The action of a refining engine like the Jordan breaks or cuts many of the fibres, and leaves the ends blunt. Long beating in the common beating engine, on the other hand, breaks up the ends into little tendrils which curl off in every direction, and are often quite separated from the original fibre. If the fibres of one sort are found in this last condition, while the other fibres are nearly whole or broken sharply across, it is safe to assume that the much broken stock was put into the engine first and given a preliminary beating before the addition of the rest of the furnish.

Determination of Ground Wood.—Various qualitative methods of extreme delicacy have been worked out for the detection of ground wood in paper which do not require a resort to the microscope. The well-known nitric acid test, which consists merely in making a streak upon the paper with concentrated nitric acid, and noting whether the brown color which indicates the presence of uncooked wood is developed, is the test most frequently employed outside of laboratories.

A solution of aniline sulphate, prepared after the manner already described, is one of the best reagents for the detection of ground wood. If the paper is dipped in the solution and then allowed to dry, any ground wood which may be present is stained yellow, and from the depth of color thus obtained a rough idea may be formed of the proportion in which ground wood enters into the composition of the sheet.

Phloroglucin may be used either in the acid solution previously mentioned, or the paper may first be dipped in dilute hydrochloric acid, then dried and wet with a solution of phloroglucin in alcohol. The pink or red coloration due to lignified tissues is very characteristic, and the depth of color may serve here, as in case of aniline sulphate, to give an approximation to the quantity of ground wood in the paper.

It should be noted in connection with these tests, that what they really indicate is the presence of lignified fibre, and that this is not necessarily present in the condition of ground wood. Jute, for instance, gives a brilliant yellow with aniline sulphate, and sulphite fibre which has not been thoroughly reduced responds similarly to the reagent.

It has, moreover, been pointed out by F. v. Hohnel, that various carbohydrates, such as cane sugar, dextrins, etc., give reactions resembling the lignin reactions; for instance, Swedish filter paper, prepared from pure cellulose, impregnated with cane-sugar solution and tested with phloroglucin and hydrochloric acid at first gave no reaction, but when dry it becomes distinctly red just as if wood fibre were present. Again, wood cellulose, which tested in the ordinary way with phloroglucin and hydrochloric acid, showed only traces of lignin, became intensely red when, after treatment with the reagents, it was washed slightly and then quickly dried at 100°–110° C.

For these reasons the only conclusive evidence of the presence of ground wood is that furnished by the microscope. The fibre bundles which always occur in ground wood, and which are characterized by their broken ends and transverse markings, are then easily recognized. A surprisingly large proportion of the fibres are, however, well separated and unbroken, but these with the bundles stand out prominently when the material on the slide has first been stained with aniline sulphate.

A few chemical methods for the quantitative determination of ground wood have been proposed, but are rarely employed, as they entail more work than the matter usually warrants, while they are not much more accurate than a careful microscopical examination which gives an approximation sufficiently close for most practical purposes.

The most satisfactory of these chemical methods is that of Godeffroy and Coulon, which depends upon the fact that lignified wood fibre has the property of reducing gold from a solution of gold chloride while the purer forms of cellulose which constitute cotton, linen, chemical wood, straw, and similar fibres, do not have this power. The present method as simplified and otherwise improved by Godeffroy is as follows:—

Two equal portions of the paper are taken, and both are boiled for ten minutes in 10 per cent. aqueous ammonia, then thoroughly washed and dried. One portion is burned, and the ash determined. The other portion is boiled for ten minutes with a solution of gold chloride, then removed, washed, dried, and burned. From the weight of ash obtained, that found in the untreated paper is deducted, giving the weight of gold, which multiplied by 100 and divided by 21.2 gives the percentage of lignocellulose in the paper. The factor 21.2 represents the quantity of gold which 100 parts of ground wood will reduce under these conditions as determined by numerous experiments.

Testing Pulp for Moisture.—The determination of the amount of moisture in a given sample of pulp or paper is a very simple operation, as will appear from the method given below. The great chance for error lies in the manner in which the sample is drawn, and here too much care cannot be exercised. The following methods of sampling are those used in our own work, and long experience has shown us that they give a sample which fairly and accurately represents a lot of pulp.

If the pulp is coming from the machine, a uniform strip 2 inches wide should be taken every twenty minutes across its entire width. If the pulp is received at the mill in bales, and if these can be opened without too great inconvenience, one bale in ten should be taken at random from the lot and opened; from a sheet at about the centre of one of these bales a strip 1¼ inches wide is cut across the width of the sheet. A similar strip is cut from the fifth sheet of the next bale. The strip from the third bale is cut from the centre, but this time lengthwise of the sheet. The sample from the fourth bale is taken from the fifth, as is the case of the second bale, but lengthwise. The whole number of bales set aside for sampling — that is, one bale in every ten in the lot — is then sampled in this order.

For sampling pulp on dock, or where for many reasons it is impossible to open the bales, we employ a special tool similar to a washer cutter, but with a heavier and longer blade. This tool is used with a bit-stock, and enables the sampler to easily cut through 25 or 50 sheets, removing from each a disk 3 inches in diameter. The sampler first cuts through the bagging around the bale with a knife, and, if the pulp is fairly thick, drives the tool in until, on being withdrawn, it will remove 25 or more disks. The second, fifth, tenth, fifteenth, twentieth, and twenty-fifth disks are taken, and the others replaced in the bale. One bale in every ten is sampled in this manner, and, so far as possible, in different places. In all cases, and this point is one of the first importance, the moment the samples are cut they are at once placed in a tin pail or can with tightly fitting cover, which is only removed to admit a new portion of the sample. The can with its contents is weighed in the laboratory. Then, and not until then, is the pulp removed and the can weighed alone. The difference between the two weights gives the weight of the sample.

In sampling ground wood it is sufficient to cut one bale in every 20. The outside sheet of the first bale is cut, and the centre of the next one, and so on. It is sufficient to take a small triangular piece instead of a strip, but care should be taken that the pieces are about the same size.

Some form of water-oven is used for drying the sample; that is, a jacketed oven through which a circulation of air can be maintained. The jacket is about one-third filled with water, which is kept at the boiling point by a burner below the oven. In this way the pulp is dried at a temperature which never exceeds 100° C. The ovens are made with several compartments, so that no two samples are placed in the same compartment. The pulp is allowed to dry for at least one day, and is then quickly transferred to a tin can, which is then covered at once, and weighed as soon as cool. The pulp is again transferred to the oven, and the can weighed in order to determine by subtraction the weight of the pulp. A second drying for one half day follows; the pulp is again weighed as before. If the loss of the weight does not amount to more than $\frac{2}{10}$ of 1 per cent. on the weight of the original sample, the last weight is taken as the bone-dry weight, and when subtracted from the original weight of the sample gives the weight of the water which is then calculated into percentages. Should the difference between the two weights be greater than that indicated above, the pulp must again go into the oven for further drying, until two successive weights agree within the limit named.

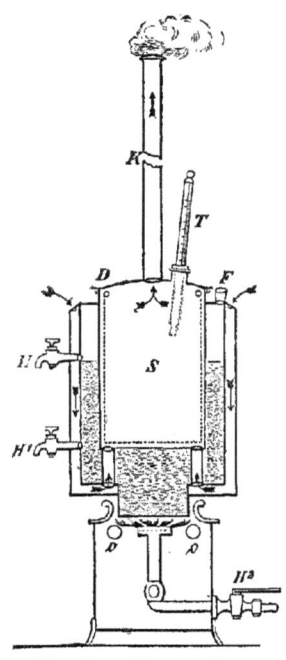

Fig. 93.—Drying-Oven.

A German drying oven which has many points of excellence is shown in Fig. 93. The top D may be removed for the introduction of the sample into the oven S, which is surrounded by a water and steam jacket, as shown. Around this water-jacket is a space with perforations at the top, open to the atmosphere and connected at the bottom by pipes leading to the oven. The air is heated during its passage down this space and then passes up through the oven to make its escape through pipe K, its course being shown by the arrows. The thermometer T is not really necessary. The dotted lines within the oven indicate a cylindrical cage of wire gauze into which the pulp may be placed. The Knöfler oven, shown in Fig. 94, is a very convenient form, and is so arranged that the weight of the pulp may be read off at any time. It is quite easy to determine when the pulp has become quite dry and to avoid overheating. It consists of a cylinder with a tightly fitting cover, and provided on the outside with a water gauge and a faucet, as shown. Space for the pulp in the oven proper is formed by two smaller cylinders concentric with the first; the innermost or third cylinder is open at the bottom and closed at the top so as to form a cylindrical steam chamber, the bottom of which is sealed by the water. A small pipe connects the top of this space with the upper portion of the second steam space outside the oven proper. The second cylinder projects down as far as the bottom of the innermost one, and the two are there joined. A section across the oven shows it therefore to be ring-shape, and by this shape the heating surface is enlarged. If pulp is to be dried, it is placed in the space between the two parts of the wire gauze cage shown in Figs. 95 and 96. This is suspended from a balance beam as shown in Fig. 94. If the material to be dried

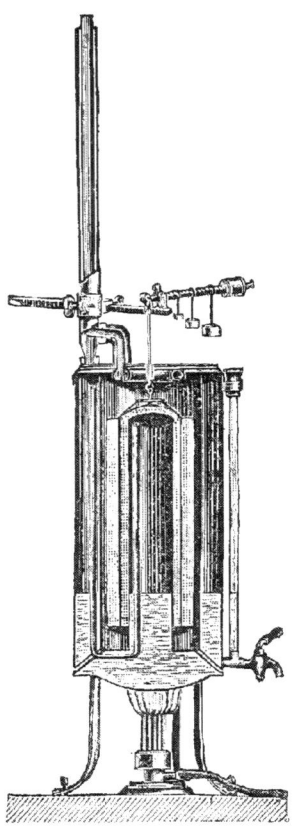

Fig. 94. — Knöfler Drying-Oven.

is a powder, the cage is replaced by the series of trays in Fig. 97.

Moisture in "Air-dry" Pulp. — This is usually determined by first drying the pulp to constant weight at the temperature of boiling water, and then allowing the sample to remain exposed to the air at the ordinary temperature for twenty-four or forty-eight hours, in order that it may take up what is supposed to be the amount of moisture normally present in the sample under ordinary atmospheric conditions. It is hardly necessary to point out that as atmospheric conditions are constantly subject to variation over wide ranges of temperature and humidity, there is really no such thing as a normal amount of moisture for any given sample of pulp or paper. The moisture in the sample is at all times varying with the atmospheric conditions, and these are never precisely the same in two places at once. The impossibility which thus arises of stating with any definiteness what "air-dry" pulp really is, makes the air-dry basis a most unsatisfactory one for sales, and is a source of constant dispute between buyer and seller.

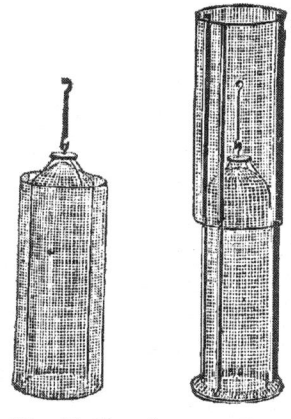

Figs. 95-96.—Cage for Holding Sample.

Many attempts have been made by chemists associated with the paper trade in this country and abroad to put the matter on a more definite, and therefore more satisfactory, basis. The experiments of Martin L. Griffin are of especial value, because of their large number and the length of time which they cover. These experiments were carried on for several years. During the year 1884, 10 samples of soda poplar fibre previously dried at 212° F. were exposed each day in a room having windows open and with no fire. The average gain in weight during the year amounted to 6.38 per cent., which represents the increase due to the absorption of the so-called atmospheric moisture. During 1886, from 3 to 5 samples previously dried as before, were exposed daily in a well-aired brick storehouse with cellar and good floor and allowed to remain there for a week. The monthly average which showed the greatest gain in weight was in November, when the moisture absorbed amounted to 9.39 per cent. The lowest was in June, when the gain was 5.40 per cent. The average gain for the year was 7.04 per cent. The method of test-

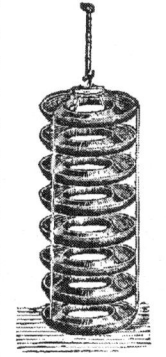

Fig. 97.

ing employed during the year 1888 was somewhat different, and consisted in keeping 20 samples in a sheet-iron closet so arranged that neither rain or snow could enter, although it permitted circulation of air. The samples were weighed each day and the fluctuations in moisture noted. The samples were changed about once in three months. The amount of moisture present ranged from 9.21 per cent. in November and December down to 5.66 per cent. in the previous January. The average for the year was 7.40 per cent.

Gemmell, in England, finds as the result of comparatively few experiments, that about 10 per cent. of moisture is absorbed. The Norwegian pulp-makers claim as much as 12 per cent.

Two ways of meeting the difficulty which arises from these variations have been proposed. The most logical one is, that pulp should be bought and sold upon the bone-dry basis, with no allowance for atmospheric moisture. This, of course, means a readjustment of prices to meet the new conditions of sale. The other and most generally adopted plan is for the buyer and seller to fix upon, by agreement, some arbitrary percentage which shall represent the air-dry moisture in the pulp. As a result of the experiments of Dr. Norton, 8 per cent. is commonly taken in case of ground wood, that is, 92 lbs. of the bone-dry pulp are said to represent 100 lbs. of the same pulp in the air-dry state. Soda pulp is commonly sold on the basis of its carrying 7.50 per cent. of atmospheric moisture, while in case of sulphite fibre the figure usually recognized by the trade is 10 per cent.

Where such a basis has been accepted, the method of figuring air-dry pulp is as follows: The sample is first made bone-dry by drying in a water oven to constant weight. The loss in weight represents the moisture in the sample, and is calculated into per cents; this figure, subtracted from 100, gives the per cent. of absolutely dry fibre. If now the pulp were sold on 10 per cent. basis, every 90 parts by weight of the bone-dry pulp represents 100 parts of air-dry. If the basis is 8 per cent., 92 parts of bone-dry pulp are required to make 100 of air-dry, while on the basis of 7.50 per cent., 92.50 parts of the dry pulp are required to make 100 of the air-dry. The percentage of bone-dry fibre found is, therefore, divided by 90 or 92 or 92.50, as the case may be, and the quotient multiplied by 100, the product being the percentage of air-dry pulp on the basis taken.

CHAPTER X.

ELECTROLYTIC PROCESSES

At the time electrolytic processes for the production of hypochlorites were first exploited in the large commercial way it was thought that they offered to the paper-maker a direct and simple method of preparing at the mill the liquors required for the bleaching of the stock, and this on such a basis of economy as to make it only a question of time when these so-called processes of electric bleaching would supplant the older method, which involved the use of chloride of lime. With the prospect that the paper-maker would have added to his other duties the superintendence of such electrolytic plants, it seemed desirable that a work on paper-making chemistry should set forth in some detail both the chemical and electrical principles involved in their operation. At the present time, however, the state of the art is such as to hold out little probability that the electrolytic production of bleaching agents will become a department of the paper-maker's work in any such general sense as the recovery of soda-ash or the manufacture of bisulphite solutions has already done. Any lengthy discussion of these electrolytic processes becomes, therefore, somewhat outside the scope of the present work, and it is, moreover, true that such of these processes as seem most likely to have a practical interest from the paper-maker's standpoint, through their probable effect upon the future price of bleaching-powder, are now so far from their final terms and subject to such rapid development that any description of the present forms of apparatus is likely within a short time to have only an historical interest. We shall for these reasons make no attempt to go into the subject in greater detail than to present briefly the more obvious principles which underlie the art, together with the general means involved in their application.

When a current of electricity passes along a metallic conductor, various magnetic and heating effects are observed, but the conductor itself does not apparently suffer change. Liquids, like other bodies, vary among themselves in their power to conduct electricity, some, like the oils, being among the best insulators, while others are excellent conductors, though never in this respect comparable to the metals. Those liquids which conduct electricity are termed "electrolytes," and it is the peculiarity of electrolytes that they suffer decomposition in direct proportion to the amount of current passing through them. The results or products of this decomposing action of the current are observed at those points called "poles" at which the current enters and leaves the liquid, and the operation itself is termed "electrolysis." The point or surface at which the current enters is called the "anode," and that at which it leaves the liquid is called the "cathode." The liquid or that component of it which is decomposed is, under the action of the current, split up into two constituents called "ions," one of which, the "anion," is liberated at the anode surface, while the other, the "cathion," is set free at the cathode surface. When, for example, a current is passed through slightly acidulated water, the products of the changes set up by the current are oxygen, which appears at the positive pole, or anode, and hydrogen, which is evolved at the negative pole, the cathode. The proportions of each evolved are those in which they unite to form the liquid. If the current is sent through fused sodium chloride, common salt, the chlorine is evolved at the anode, and metallic sodium at the cathode. This last is an example of the simplest form of electrolysis in which the products obtained are those directly due to the initial decomposition set up by the current. The electrolysis of a salt in solution is complicated by various secondary reactions which may or do take place between the liberated ions and the components of the liquid. If a solution of common salt in water is electrolyzed while the solution is at the same time mechanically agitated, the primary results of the electrolysis are, as in case of the fused salt, metallic sodium and chlorine, but as a result of the secondary reactions set up by contact of the liberated ions with the liquid the final and visible products are hydrogen, which escapes at the cathode, and sodium hypochlorite, which accumulates in the liquid.

If the two electrodes are separated by a porous partition, as, for example, one of unglazed earthenware, these secondary reactions do not go so far, and the final products are hydrogen and caustic soda at the cathode, and gaseous chlorine at the anode. Both the caustic soda and the hydrogen are, however, the result of secondary action between the metallic sodium originally set free and the water. The quantity of an electrolyte decomposed by the passage through it of a given quantity of electricity is always the same, but the course of the secondary reactions, and therefore the nature and quantities of the various final products, may be greatly modified by such conditions as the temperature and concentration of the solution, the size and character of the electrodes, and the strength of current. For these reasons, when a given product is desired, there may be, as the conditions of the work vary, corresponding variations in the quantity of the desired product obtained. The quantity found, divided by the theoretical amount, gives what is called the "current efficiency" of the process or apparatus.

In electro-chemical work, as in other departments of electricity, certain units are employed for measuring and expressing the strength and energy of the current, the resistance of the circuit around which it flows, and the power of the electromotive force.

As water, when in motion, possesses energy, while it would not when at rest and free from strain be said to have energy or be force, so electricity, though not to be regarded as a form of force or energy, possesses energy when in motion and will do work. Electricity in locomotion, or the electric current, presents many analogies to flowing water. They are crude analogies and must not be pushed too far, but bearing this in mind they may be safely used to obtain a clearer insight into the meaning and relations of common electrical terms. When water is pumped or carried from the sea-level to a higher one, a certain amount of work is done, and by virtue of its new position the water has an equal amount of potential energy, which reappears when the water is returning to the level from which it came. A difference of head is created, and the resulting pressure causes the water to flow. So, by properly directed work, what may be called a difference of electrical level may be set up, and this difference is termed a "difference of potential." Electricity tends to flow from a point of high potential to a point of low potential, and that which produces this tendency, or which causes electricity to flow, is known as "electromotive force," more briefly written E. M. F. The measure of electromotive force is the "volt." The E. M. F set up by an ordinary Daniell's cell, such as is used in telegraphing, is, roughly speaking, one volt. The measure of the quantity of electricity which flows is the "ampere." The measure of the resistance or opposition to its flow which the electric current encounters more or less in all conductors is the "ohm." It is the resistance of a column of pure mercury having a cross-section of one square millimetre and 106 centimetres long. One mile of ordinary telegraph wire has a resistance of about ten ohms. An E. M. F. of one volt will send a current of one ampere through a resistance of one ohm.

Electricity always flows in a closed circuit, the same quantity of electricity passing any cross-section of the circuit in the same time. The quantity of electricity which flows, measured in amperes, is equal to the E. M. F. in volts divided by the resistance of the circuit in ohms. This statement of the fact is known as Ohm's Law, and it expressed in the formula $C = \frac{E}{R}$, in which $C =$ the current in amperes, $E =$ the electromotive force in volts, and $R =$ the resistance of the circuit in ohms.

Small currents moving under a high electromotive force, and consequently through much resistance, are sometimes spoken of as intensity currents, while larger currents under a low electromotive force and through low resistance are sometimes called quantity currents. A small stream of water under great pressure will do as much work as a larger stream under correspondingly lower pressure, and so a small quantity of electricity propelled by a high electromotive force will do as much work as a much greater quantity moving under a proportionately lower E. M. F. The energy or power of the current in doing work is measured in "watts"; a current of one ampere under an E. M. F. of one volt has an energy of one watt. Seven hundred and forty-six watts are equal to one horse-power. The power of a circuit in watts is equal to the product of the number of amperes flowing multiplied by the E. M. F. in volts. The most efficient dynamos now in use generate a current having a power of about 680 watts for each horse-power at the dynamo pulley.

The points or terminals of a battery or dynamo to which the ends of the external circuit are joined are termed poles. the point of high potential, from which electricity flows into the circuit, being called the positive or + pole, while the point of low potential toward which electricity flows is known as the negative or − pole. A current is said to be continuous when it is flowing in one direction; when the relation of the poles, and consequently the direction of flow, is subject to rapid reversals, the current is said to be an alternating one. The ordinary rate of reversal in commercial alternating currents is 120 times per second. At present the continuous current is the only one which is adapted for electro-chemical work.

The theory of electrolysis is roughly this. It is assumed, and the assumption is justified by many experimental facts, that in all liquids which conduct electricity there is not only an incessant movement of the molecules of the liquid, but that probably, by virtue of this motion, certain of the molecules are split up into their component atoms, and that these free atoms, or ions, are moving about in every direction throughout the liquid, combining with other atoms as they come within the sphere of each other's attractive force, and again splitting up and recombining. Under ordinary conditions, when no current is passing, the motion of the ions may be in any direction, but under the influence of the current an attractive force comes into play which impels the ions toward one electrode or the other, according as they are positively or negatively charged.

Although as a laboratory experiment it has been for many years an easy matter to decompose solutions of the chlorides, with production of hypochlorite solutions or of free caustic and gaseous chlorine, the practical difficulties in the way of commercial operation have been very serious. It is necessary that the electrodes should have large surfaces and be near together, in order to cut down the resistance of the electrolyte to the lowest possible point, since that portion of the energy of the current spent in overcoming this resistance is wasted. For the same reason, if a diaphragm is used, it must be of such a nature as to be efficient in preventing diffusion and yet of low resistance, and the two qualities are in a measure contradictory. The chlorine and oxygen liberated at the anode have a powerfully corrosive action upon nearly all substances, and yet the anode must not be appreciably attacked, for the double reason that just so far as it is attacked the products of the electrolysis and the anode itself are lost.

In spite of these difficulties there has been within the last few years a great advance in the methods of commercial electrolysis, and especially in those having for their object the decomposition of chlorides. The number of these processes at the present time is large, and certain of them have unquestionably advanced beyond the experimental stage.

The first electrolytic process to be seriously considered by paper-makers was that of Hermite, although Becquerel, in 1843, noted that chlorine and soda are the products of the decomposition of salt, while Brandt, in 1848, claimed to have suggested as early as 1820 the application of electrolyzed sea-water to bleaching. Charles Watt, working with Hugh Burgess, was probably the first to demonstrate experimentally the possibilities of the method, but the crude means then available for generating the necessary current precluded any commercial development. The results of his researches are embodied in British patent No. 13,755, A.D. 1851.

Following Watt came numerous other experimenters, until in 1886 Hermite brought forward a well-considered system for the

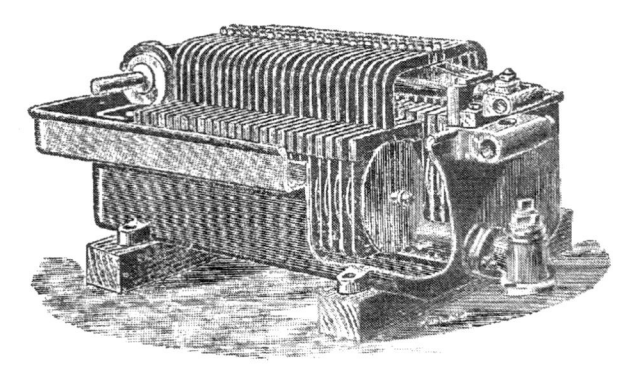

FIG. 98. — HERMITE ELECTROLYZER.

production of hypochlorite of magnesia, by electrolysis of a 5 per cent. solution of the chloride.

Hermite's apparatus consists of a dynamo capable of supplying a current of about 1250 amperes, one or more electrolyzers, a storage tank for liquor, the necessary pumps and piping for circulation, and two or more chests for holding the pulp to be bleached, and fitted with agitators. The electrolyzers, Fig. 98, consist of galvanized cast-iron boxes, having at the bottom a perforated pipe fitted with a cock, through which a 5 per cent. magnesium chloride solution is admitted from the storage tank to the electrolyzer; the top of each box is surrounded by a channel in which the solution is received on overflowing the sides of the box; from this channel it is carried away by a pipe, thus keeping up a continuous circulation. The negative electrodes are shown in the figure, and consist of a number of zinc discs arranged upon two spindles, which are caused to revolve slowly by means of worms and wheels. Between each of these discs is placed a positive plate, of which a view is shown in Fig. 99. The active surface of the plates is formed of platinum gauze, mounted in a frame of ebonite to give it stiffness, and each plate is connected to the copper casting shown above the box by means of a stud and nut, and can be removed at will. The positive terminal of the dynamo is connected to this copper casting, and the current distributes itself over the whole system of platinum plates, which thus form one large anode. It passes from them through the solution to the zinc discs, which form the cathode, as they are in contact with the iron box to which the negative pole of the dynamo is connected. In order to keep the negative plates clean and free from the magnesium hydrate which is deposited upon them, flexible knives are attached to the ebonite frames of the positive plates, and these knives scrape the surface of the slowly revolving zinc discs.

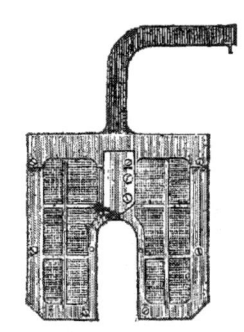

FIG. 99.—POSITIVE PLATE.

Several electrolyzers, commonly ten, are generally joined up in series, the negative terminal of the first being connected with the positive terminal of the second, and so on.

The solution of magnesium chloride passing into the electrolyzers is under the action of the current converted largely into one of magnesium hypochlorite, the practical effect of the reactions set up by the current being to add an atom of oxygen to the magnesium chloride molecule. The electrolyzed solution then passes directly upon the pulp contained in the first of a series of chests, or engines, the pulp in the first chest being that which is most nearly bleached. The solution is admitted at the bottom of the chest, and passes upward through the pulp, and is removed by a washing cylinder and transferred to the second chest. The number of such chests in series should be limited by the rate of flow of the solution, and the rapidity with which the active chlorine is exhausted. Two or three chests are usually sufficient. A small amount of soluble organic matter is extracted from the pulp by the solution, and as this is of such a nature that it requires a little time for its complete oxidation, the liquor passing from the last chest into the storage tank should contain a small residuum of active chlorine to destroy this dissolved organic matter, which would otherwise gradually accumulate in the solution and reduce the efficiency of the process. Under conditions properly regulated in the manner indicated the bleaching action of the solution is extremely rapid, and the pulp is bleached to good color without loss of strength. This is true of such refractory fibres as soda spruce.

In the process of bleaching the magnesium hypochlorite is of course reduced to the initial magnesium chloride, and the process thus involves a complete cycle of changes, in which, theoretically, only the coloring-matter of the fibre and the power needed to drive the dynamo are consumed. There is of necessity, in practice, a small loss of solution which is carried away in the bleached pulp.

Each electrolyzer working under this system requires an electromotive force of five volts. Nine or ten electrolyzers and an expenditure of about eighty horse-power are required to produce daily the equivalent in electrolyzed solution of one ton of bleaching-powder.

At the time of its first exploitation the great efficiency of the Hermite electrolyzed solution, when used according to his method, led to claims that its activity was largely due to the presence of new and hitherto unsuspected compounds developed by the electrolysis. Later experience has shown these claims to be unfounded, the superior efficiency of the solution being partly due to the fact that hypochlorite of magnesia is in itself a better bleaching agent than ordinary bleaching-powder, but still more to the method of circulation adopted, by which, as already stated, the fresh and strong solution passed directly upon the nearly bleached pulp and was finally exhausted by contact with the brown pulp. The solution now used by Hermite is practically one of common salt, only a small proportion of magnesium chloride being added. His process has met with gratifying success in France, but in this country and in England it has encountered difficulties which, though not inherent in the process, have proved a bar to its introduction.

The present tendency of development is toward those processes which have for their object the production of commercial bleach and alkali, and although certain to effect ultimately a material reduction in the price of these staples, they are not likely to introduce any radical changes into the chemical operations of the paper-mill. The most prominent of these processes are those of Greenwood, Andreoli, and Holland and Richardson in England, and of Cutten, Craney, Carmichael, and especially Le Sueur and Waite in this country. The fundamental principles underlying all these processes are the same, the differences being found in the design of the apparatus and in details of work. All of them work with saturated brine and employ some form of diaphragm between the electrodes to prevent diffusion and consequent recombination of the chlorine and caustic. Gas carbon has been almost universally adopted as the material for the anode, but the design and position of the anode and the means employed to secure contact with the conductors and to prevent too rapid disintegration of the carbon vary in the different processes. Similar variations are found in the general arrangement of the decomposing cell, the electrodes being sometimes placed horizontally, while in other cases, and much more commonly, they stand in a vertical position. The cathode is always of iron, although mercury has been proposed for certain forms of plant, and consists of a plate, a casting of special design, or wire gauze. In addition to variations in the material, form, and position of the diaphragm, the processes show important differences in the auxiliary means employed to further limit the losses caused by diffusion. Perhaps the best of these consists in maintaining a flow of the electrolyte through the diaphragm, either toward the cathode or to both electrodes.

Although such differences as have been noted may appear as minor ones, they are really what determine the success or failure of a process. A cell which requires six volts to send a given current through it cannot compete commercially with one which as a result of better design requires only four and one-half volts, for this apparently slight difference means that the former cell requires the expenditure of 33 per cent. more power than the latter for a given quantity of product.

It has been already pointed out that the present rapid development of these processes would soon make obsolete any detailed account of the several systems, but keeping in mind the differences in detail noted above, the following general description may be taken as applying to them all.

ELECTROLYTIC PROCESSES.

The dynamo for supplying the current is so wound as to deliver a continuous current of large volume under moderate voltage. One supplying 1250 amperes at 120 volts may be used to advantage, and requires about 225 horse-power. Large copper conductors carry the current to the decomposing cells, which are commonly arranged in multiple arc. That is, the cells are arranged in sets, the whole current going through each set and on to the next set, but only a fraction of the current going through a single cell. This fraction varies from 60 to 500 amperes, according to the size and construction of the cell, and the number of cells in a set varies accordingly. Each cell requires an electromotive force of from four and a half to six volts. The cells themselves consist of troughs, or vessels, which may be of iron or slate or earthenware, but such portions of them as come in contact with the chlorine must of course be of a material not corroded by the element, and this most commonly is slate or earthenware. Several cells, or at least several anode compartments, may open into a common trough, or each cell may be self-contained. They differ among themselves very much in size, appearance, and construction, but each embodies three essential elements,—an anode of gas carbon, a diaphragm or its equivalent, and an iron cathode. The whole cell is filled to such a point with saturated brine that both anode and cathode, with of course the diaphragm between them, are immersed in the liquid.

The current enters the cell through the conductor connected with the anode, and from the anode passes through the brine and the saturated diaphragm to the cathode, where it makes its exit by another conductor. The chlorine evolved at the anode leaves the liquid, and being confined by the walls of the anode compartment passes off into pipes leading to absorption chambers containing lime, or, if a solution is wanted for use at once, into agitating apparatus containing milk of lime. The hydrogen liberated at the cathode either passes off directly into the air, or the construction of the apparatus may be such that it is confined until it makes its way out through pipes. The caustic soda formed on the cathode by reaction of the water with the metallic sodium set free by the current gradually accumulates in the liquid, and either flows off automatically as a strong solution or is drawn off from time to time, either for use directly or for concentration by heat in order to separate the accompanying salt by crystallization and to secure the solid hydrate. Such plants have shown in practice an efficiency ranging, according to their type, from 50 to 90 per cent. of the theoretical, or, in other words, have produced from 18.12 grammes to 32 62 grammes of caustic, and from 16.08 grammes to 28 94 grammes of chlorine per ampere day, the theoretical yields being 36.24 grammes of caustic and 32 16 grammes of chlorine.

APPENDIX.

APPENDIX.

RULES FOR THE SPELLING AND PRONUNCIATION OF CHEMICAL TERMS

Adopted by the American Association for the Advancement of Science in 1891

GENERAL PRINCIPLES OF PRONUNCIATION

1 The pronunciation is as much in accord with the analogy of the English language as possible.

2 Derivatives retain as far as possible the accent and pronunciation of the root word.

3 Distinctly chemical compound words retain the accent and pronunciation of each portion

4 Similarly sounding endings for dissimilar compounds are avoided (hence -ĭd, -ite).

ACCENT

In polysyllabic chemical words the accent is generally on the antepenult, in words where the vowel of the penult is followed by two consonants, and in all words ending in -ic, the accent is on the penult

PREFIXES.

All prefixes in strictly chemical words are regarded as parts of compound words, and retain their own pronunciation unchanged (as ä'ceto-, ä'mīdo-, ä'zo-, hȳ'dro-, ī'so-, nī'tro-, nītrō'so-)

ELEMENTS

In words ending in -ium, the vowel of the antepenult is short if **i** (as ĭrĭ'dĭum), or **y** (as dĭdȳ'mĭum), or if before two consonants (as că'lcĭum), but long otherwise (as tĭtā'nĭum, sĕlē'nĭum, chrō'mĭum)

alū'mĭnum	că'dmĭum	cō'balt	germā'nĭum	iron
a'ntĭmony	că'lcĭum	colŭ'mbĭum	glū'cĭnum	lă'nthanum
a'rsĕnĭc	ca'rbon	co'pper	gold	lead
bā'rĭum	cē'rĭum	dĭdȳ'mĭum	hȳ'drogen	lĭ'thĭum
bĭ'smuth (bĭz)	cæsĭum	e'rbĭum	ĭ'ndĭum	magnē'sĭum (zhĭum)
bō'ron	chlō'rĭn	flū'orĭn	ĭ'odĭn	ma'nganese (eze)
brō'mĭn	chrō'mĭum	gă'llĭum	ĭrĭ'dĭum	me'rcury

465

molȳ'bdenum	plă'tinum	sĕlē'nium	tellū'rium	ū'rănium
nĭ'ckel	potă'ssium	sĭ'licon	te'rbium	vănā'dium
nĭ'trogen	rhō'dium	silver	thă'llium	ytte'rbium
ŏ'smium	rubĭ'dium	sō'dium	thō'rium	ў'ttrium
ŏ'xygen	ruthē'nium	strŏntium (shium)	tin	zinc
pallā'dium	samā'rium	sŭ'lfur	tītā'nium	zirco'nium
phŏs'phorus	scă'ndium	tă'ntalum	tŭ'ngsten	

Also: ămmō'nium, phosphō'nium, hă'logen, cȳă'nogen, ămȳ'dogen.

Note in the above list the spelling of the *halogens, cesium* and *sulfur*, f is used in the place of ph in all derivatives of *sulfur* (as *sulfuric, sulfite, sulfo-,* etc.).

TERMINATIONS IN -ic

The vowel of the penult in polysyllables is short (as *cȳă'nic, fŭmă'ric, arsĕ'nic, sulĭ'cic, ĭŏ'dic, bŭtȳ'ric*), except (1) u when not used before two consonants (as *mercū'ric, prŭ'ssic*), and (2) when the penult ends in a vowel (as *benzō'ic, olĕ'ic*), in dissyllables it is long except before two consonants (as *bō'ric, cĭ'tric*). Exception *acē'tic* or *acĕ'tic*.

The termination -ic is used for metals only where necessary to contrast with -ous (thus avoid *aluminic, ammonic,* etc.)

TERMINATIONS IN -ous

The accent follows the general rule (as *plă'tinous, sŭ'lfurous, phŏ'sphorous, cobă'ltous*). Exception *acē'tous*

TERMINATIONS IN -ate AND -ite

The accent follows the general rule (as *ă'cetate, vă'nadate*), in the following words the accent is thrown back, *ă'buetate, ă'lcoholate, ă'cetonate, ă'ntimonite*

TERMINATIONS IN -id (FORMERLY -ide)

The final e is dropped in every case and the syllable pronounced ĭd (as *chlō'rĭd, ĭ'odĭd, hȳ'drĭd, ŏ'xĭd, hȳ'droxĭd, sŭ'lfĭd, ă'mĭd, ă'nilĭd, mŭrē'xĭd*)

TERMINATIONS IN -ane, -ene, -ine, AND -one

The vowel of these syllables is invariably long (as *mĕ'thāne, ē'thāne, na'phthalēne, a'nthracēne, prō'pīne, quĭ'nōne, ă'cetōne, kē'tōne*)

A few dissyllables have no distinct accent (as *benzēne, xȳlēne, cētēne*)

The termination -ine is used only in the case of doubly unsaturated hydrocarbons, according to Hoffmann's grouping (as *propīne*)

TERMINATIONS IN -in

In names of chemical elements and compounds of this class, which includes all those formerly ending in -ine (except doubly unsaturated hydrocarbons) the final e is dropped, and the syllable pronounced -ĭn (as *chlō'rĭn, brō'mĭn*, etc., *ă'mĭn, ă'nilĭn, mo'rphĭn, quĭ'nĭn (kwĭ'nĭn), vanĭ'llĭn, alloxă'ntĭn, absĭ'nthĭn, emŭ'lsĭn, că'ffeĭn cŏ'caĭn*).

TERMINATIONS IN -ol

This termination, in the case of specific chemical compounds, is used *exclusively* for alcohols, and when so used is never followed by a final e. The last syllable is pronounced -ŏl (as glў'cŏl, phē'nŏl, crē'sŏl, thў'mŏl (ti), glў'cerŏl, quī'nŏl. Exceptions ălcohōl, a'rgŏl.

TERMINATIONS IN -ole

This termination is always pronounced -ōle, and its use is limited to compounds which are not alcohols (as ĭndōle).

TERMINATIONS IN -yl

No final e is used, the syllable is pronounced -ўl (as ă'cetўl, ă'mўl, cē'rotўl, cē'tўl, ē'thўl).

TERMINATIONS IN -yde

The y is long (as ă'ldehȳde).

TERMINATIONS IN -meter

The accent follows the general rule (as hydrŏ'meter, barŏ'meter, lactŏ'meter). Exception: words of this class used in the metric system are regarded as compound words, and each portion retains its own accent (as cĕn'time''ter, mĭlli-me''ter, kĭ'lome''ter).

MISCELLANEOUS WORDS WHICH DO NOT FALL UNDER THE PRECEDING RULES

Note the spelling: albumen, albuminous, albuminiferous, asbestos, gramme, radical.

Note the pronunciation: a'lkalīne, a'lloy (n and v), a'llotropy, a'llotropism, ī'somerism, pŏ'lymerism, apparā'tus (sing and plu), āqua regia, barȳ'ta, centĭgrade, co'ncentrated, crystallĭn or crystallīne, electrŏ'lysis, liter mŏ'lecule, mŏlē'cular, nō'men-clā''ture, olā'fiant, vā'lence, ū'nivā''lent, bi'vā''lent, tri'vā''lent, qua'drivā''lent, tī'trate

A LIST OF WORDS WHOSE USE SHOULD BE AVOIDED IN FAVOR OF THE ACCOMPANYING SYNONYMS

For —	Use —
sodic, calcic, zincic, nickelic, etc chlorid, etc	sodium, calcium, zinc, nickel, etc, chlorid, etc (vid terminations in -ic supra)
arsenetted hydrogen	arsin
antimonetted hydrogen	stibin
phosphoretted hydrogen	phosphin
sulfuretted hydrogen, etc	hydrogen sulfid, etc

For —	Use —	For —	Use —
beryllium	glucinum	furfurol	furfuraldehyde
niobium	columbium	fucusol	fucusaldehyde
glycerin	glycerol	anisol	methyl phenate

For—	Use—	For—	Use—
hydroquinone (and *hydrochinon*)	quinol	*phenetol*	ethyl phenate
		anethol	methyl allylphenol
pyrocatechin	catechol	*alkylogens*	alkyl haloids
resorcin, etc	resorcinol, etc	*titer* (n.)	strength or standard
mannite	mannitol	*titer* (v.)	titrate
dulcite, etc	dulcitol, etc	*monovalent*	univalent
benzol	benzene	*divalent* etc	bivalent, etc.
toluol, etc	toluene, etc	*quantivalence*	valence
thein	caffein		

Fāte, fŭt, făr, mēte, mĕt, pīne, pĭn, marine, nōte, nŏt, move, tūbe, tŭb, rule, mȳ, ў = ĭ

′ Primary accent, ″ secondary accent   N B — The accent follows the vowel of the syllable upon which the stress falls, but does not indicate the division of the word into syllables

---

NEW CELLULOSE DERIVATIVES.

The chemistry of cellulose has recently been enriched by the discovery by Cross, Bevan, and Beadle of the remarkable reaction which ensues when cellulose (as for example, in the form of bleached poplar fibre) is exposed to the action of caustic alkali and carbon bisulphide Many important industrial applications of the discovery have already been proposed as the new compound is plastic and soluble in water, and yields by its decomposition the original or slightly modified cellulose which may be thus brought into the form of films, sheets or masses without fibrous structure. We quote below from the original paper (Jour Chem Soc, London, 1893, p 837).

Cellulose Thiosulphocarbonic Acid. — When cellulose in any of its forms is treated with a concentrated solution of sodium hydrate (12 5 per cent. Na_2O), and the alkali cellulose thus obtained is exposed to the action of carbon bisulphide vapor, action ensues, and in the course of an hour or two a yellowish mass is obtained, which swells up enormously on treatment with water, and finally dissolves completely. This soluble compound is a cellulose thiocarbonate

The action proceeds rapidly when the agents are brought together in the ratio —

$$C_{12}H_{20}O_{10}, 2\,Na_2O, 2\,CS_2, 30 \text{ to } 40\,H_2O.$$

The most convenient conditions for laboratory experiment are with the alkali in the form of a 15 per cent aqueous solution of the hydrate (11 to 12 per cent Na_2O), the proportion by weight of this solution being from 3 5 to 4 times that of the cellulose

The crude solution obtained by dissolving the product in water, and containing yellow by-products (trithiocarbonate), yields the cellulose derivative in a pure state, on treating it with saturated brine or with strong alcohol. It is precipitated by the former in a flocculent condition, by the latter in leathery masses, which may then be further washed with a 13 per cent solution of sodium chloride or 65 per cent alcohol, respectively. On redissolving in water an almost colorless solution of extraordinary viscosity is obtained, which exhibits the following properties:—

(a) *Spontaneous Coagulation.*— After standing for a period, depending on the method of preparation and purification adopted, the solution "sets" to a firm coagulum of a hydrated cellulose of the same volume as the original solution; the coagulum then shrinks gradually, becoming surrounded with a yellow alkaline solution (trithiocarbonate). During shrinkage, the cellulose retains the form of the containing vessel.

(b) *Coagulation determined by Heat.*— The solution may be evaporated to dryness in thin layers at temperatures not exceeding 50°, without sensible decomposition, the dry substance obtained being perfectly soluble.

At 70 to 80°, however, the solution thickens rapidly, and at 80 to 90° the coagulation is almost instantaneous. These phenomena are due to the fact that the compound behaves as a product of association of cellulose, alkali, and carbon bisulphide, the coagulation above described being a dissociation of the compound into its constituents.

(c) *Coagulation determined by Reagents.*— From the foregoing it will be evident that the regeneration of cellulose will be determined by reagents, reacting either with the alkali or the sulphur group; thus acids and acid salts, sulphites, and metallic oxides all increase the rapidity of decomposition.

Characteristics of the Regenerated Cellulose.— We have assumed that the cellulose is obtained, in the main, unchanged from the solution as above described, and this is generally true. It shows a general agreement with the normal cellulose in regard to resistance to hydrolysis and oxidation, and it follows, from what has been said, that it is similar in its capacities for hydration, and also generally in its physical properties.

From the above it appears that carbon percentage is somewhat reduced, and it is to be noted also that the attraction of the product for moisture is increased, the normal hygroscopic moisture of the recovered cellulose amounting to 10 per cent as compared with 7 per cent. in the original cellulose. The original molecule, therefore, appears to have undergone hydration in the ratio $2\,C_{12}H_{20}O_{10}H_2O$, and we find that, like many other hydrates of the normal cellulose, it gives a blue coloration with iodine

We have also observed constitutional features differing from those of the normal type, as indicated by exceptional behavior in interactions such as those which determine solution and the production of the ethereal derivatives

The constitution of the derivative may be expressed by the general formula $CS < {OX \atop SNa}$, X representing the variable cellulose unit, that is, the acting residue. This is, however, not a cellulose residue pure and simple, but an alkali-cellulose, a fact which is to be expected *a priori*, and is proved by treating the solution with benzoyl chloride, when cellulose is eliminated as a cellulose benzoate

The formula, therefore, may be written $CS < {O(XONa) \atop SNa}$, which will be seen to be in harmony with the analytical data given above

The compound may therefore be described as the sodium salt of alkali-cellulosexanthic acid

The solutions of the compound give bright yellow precipitates with mercury and zinc salts, and a more orange yellow with lead salts. Moreover, as stated above, the purified compound in presence of a certain quantity of water changes spontaneously into cellulose, alkali, and carbon-bisulphide, which confirms this view of its constitution. Further, the solutions are precipitated by iodine, the precipitate being a thio-derivative which can readily be redissolved with formation of the original compound. This action carried out quantitatively gives fairly constant numbers.

LIST OF UNITED STATES PATENTS RELATING TO THE SULPHITE PROCESS.

Any of the patents in the following list may be obtained from the Patent Office, at Washington, on payment of 10 cents. Coupon books containing orders for 50 patents are issued by the office on payment of $5.00.

Akin, N P   127008   May 21, 1872.
    Manufacture of sulphurous acid
Albrecht, J   See Bernard, P L
Archbold George   274250   March 20, 1883
    Manufacture of paper pulp
Archbold, George   Reissue, 10328   May 22, 1883.
    Manufacture of paper pulp
Ball, Charles E   336078   Feb. 16, 1886
    Digester
Brion, Jean B   67041.   Aug 20, 1867
    Disintegrating wood to form paper pulp. Claims use of alkaline sulphides and sulphides of lime. Has been cited as anticipating Tilghman, but does not properly bear upon the sulphite process.
Bremaker, Charles   373810   Nov 29, 1887
    Digester
Bremaker, Charles   35373.   Dec 7, 1886
    Digester
Bremaker, Charles, and Michael Zier, Sr   333105   Dec. 29, 1885.
    Digester
Brungger, H   483828   Oct 4, 1892
    Digester
Brungger, H   483827   Oct 4, 1892.
    Digester lining
Brungger, H   483826   Oct 4, 1892.
    Digester lining
Burgess, T P   432692   July 15, 1890
    Apparatus for producing bisulphites
Carlisle, Frederick   395691.   Jan 8, 1889.
    Apparatus for absorbing gases
Carlisle, Frederick   284817   Sept 11, 1883.
    Manufacturing of hydrated sulphurous acid.
Catlin, Charles A   366153   July 5, 1887
    Sulphite solution for wood pulp
Catlin, Charles A   407818   July 30, 1889
    Process of charging liquids with gas
Clamer Francis J   283077   Aug 14, 1883
    Treating lead to impart to it the property of adhering to other metals.
Clapp, Eugene H   305740   Sept 30, 1884
    Digester and valve. Especially applicable to soda process, but valve is of interest

Closs, Gotthold   See Schurmann.
Comstock, W. O.   453076.   May 26, 1891.
    Digester lining
Cornwell, C   432604   July 15, 1890
    Apparatus for producing bisulphites.
Crocker, William O. and William P   339974   April 13, 1886.
    Producing sulphite or bisulphite of soda
Crocker, William O and William P.   406886   July 16, 1889.
    Digester.
Crocker, William O and William P.   339975   April 13, 1886
    Process of making bisulphites
Curtis, C. and N M Jones   485808.   Nov 8, 1892
    Digester.
Curtis, C , and N M Jones.   485809   Nov 8, 1892
    Digester
Curtis, C., and N M Jones.   485810.   Nov. 8, 1892.
    Digester
Curtis, C and N M Jones   484999   Oct 25, 1892
    Digester.
Curtis, C., and N M Jones   485000   Oct 25, 1892.
    Digester.
Denton, A A   339387   April 6, 1886
    Apparatus for exposing large surfaces of liquid to air, or vapor, or gas.
Drewsen, V.   492196   Feb. 21, 1893
    Recovery of gas
Eaton, A K   119224   Sept 26, 1871.
    Use of sulphite of sodium as a solvent in reducing wood to fibre.
Ekman, Carl D   253357   Feb 7, 1882
    Treating wood
Ekman, Carl D   Reissue, 10131   June 6, 1882.
    Method of treating wood
Ekman, Carl D   260749   July 11, 1882
    Treating fibrous vegetable substances to obtain fibre suitable for paper-making
Ekman, Carl D   307754   Nov 11, 1884
    Extraction of gelatine, fat, and similar substances. Patent covers the use of sulphite solution, as above
Ekman, Carl D , with George Fry and W B Espaut   286817   Oct 9 1883
    Extraction of saccharine matter from vegetable substances Boils the cane, sugar beet, etc , with sulphite solution
Ekman, Carl D   282971   Aug 14, 1883
    Obtaining coloring-matters.
Erwin, Franklin B   353056   Nov 23, 1886
    Apparatus   (Digester)
Fisher, Robert A   145496   Dec 16 1873
    Preventing corrosion of iron and steel.
Flodqvist, Carl W   348457   Aug 31, 1886.
    Digester.

Ford, H B. 363457 May 24, 1887
    Apparatus and process for manufacture of sulphurous acid
Frambach, Henry A , and Andrew J Volbrath 348159 Aug. 24, 1886
    Enamel lined digester.
Frank, Adolph 376189 and 376190 Jan. 10, 1888
    Production of sulphite solutions
Francke, David Otto 295865 March 25, 1884
    Manufacture of paper pulp
Francke, David Otto. 304092 Aug 26, 1884
    Digester.
Gamotis, L , and S Martin 17830 July 21, 1857.
    Apparatus for making acid sulphite of lime
Getchell, C. E 378673. Feb. 28, 1888.
    Apparatus for making sulphurous acid
Godfrey, C , and Reuben Lighthall 109508 Nov 22, 1870
    Protecting iron against corrosion by applying to iron an electropositive metal or alloy Same idea has recently been proposed for protecting sulphite digesters
Graham, James Anthony 280466 July 3, 1883
    Covering iron with lead
Graham, James Anthony 280171 June 26, 1883
    Treating fibrous substances
Hamish, E , and M Schroeder 376883 Jan. 24 1888
    Obtaining sulphurous acid
Haskell, J R 63044 March 19, 1867
    Treating and separating vegetable fibres Not on sulphite process, but claim covers first steaming the fibres and then condensing steam by shower of cold liquor so as to force liquor into the wood, as in later patents of Mitscherlich
Hatschek, Moritz 101011 March 22, 1870
    Tower apparatus for producing sulphurous acid
Hess, J 434272 August 12, 1890.
    Digester
Horsford, E N 39922 Sept 15, 1863
    Preparation of dry sulphite of lime.
Howell, W H. 487887 Dec 13, 1892
    Liquor apparatus
Hughes, H A 290642. Dec 18, 1883
    Apparatus for preparing sulphuretted cream of lime (sulphite of lime).
Jones, N M See Curtis Chas
Jones, W D 188801 March 27, 1877 197474 Nov 27 1877
    Apparatus for manufacture of hydrated sulphurous acid
Kellner, Carl or Charles. See also, Ritter, Eugen Baron
Kellner, Charles 352759 Nov 16 1886
    Method of sizing paper, to prevent sulphite and ground wood from turning yellow He precipitates the rosin size with a sulphite salt
Keys, William W , and N W. Williams 212077 Feb. 4, 1879.
    Deoxidized bronze

Keys, William W. 420275 Jan 28, 1890
    Sectional bronze digester
Ladd, William F. 115327. May 30, 1871
    Rotary digester without regard to process
Lavery, R 431267 July 1, 1890
    Digester
Little, Arthur D 351330 Oct. 19, 1886
    Enamel lining for digesters
Lovejoy, F C 429692 June 10, 1890
    Digester.
Lunge, George 344322 June 22, 1886
    Apparatus for treating liquids with gas
Mair, William 70588 Nov 5, 1867
    Manufacture of bisulphite of lime
Marshall, George E See Wheelwright, Charles S
Marshall, James F. 312875 Feb 24, 1885
    Digester.
Makin, John 335943 Feb 9, 1886
    Digester.
Makin, John 344120 June 22, 1886
    Lead-lined digester
Makin, John 312485 Feb 17, 1885
    Combined lead and iron plate
Marcehn, Paul 123713. Feb. 13, 1872.
    Manufacture of sulphurous acid
Martin, S See Gamotis L.
Maste, H. A. A. 480334 Aug. 9, 1892
    Preparation of cellulose from wood
Maynard, W 309968 Dec 30, 1884
    Apparatus for charging liquids with gas.
Maynard, W 180903 Aug 8, 1876 183185 Oct. 10, 1876
    Apparatus for manufacture of hydrated sulphurous acid
McDougall, Isaac S 298602. May 13, 1884
    Digester
McDougall, Isaac S 311595 Feb 3, 1885
    Manufacture of sulphurous acid
Minthorn, Daniel 307972. Nov. 11. 1884. 319295. June 2, 1885.
    Treating vegetable fibre
Mitscherlich, Alex. 395914 Jan 8, 1889
    Manufacturing thread from short fibre
Mitscherlich, Alex. 263797. Sept 5, 1882
    Manufacturing of tannic acid from waste sulphite liquors
Mitscherlich. Alex 284319 Sept 4, 1883
    Process and digester
Mitscherlich, Alex 377691 March 9, 1886
    Boiling fibres with sulphites (Preparation of liquor, process of treating wood)

APPENDIX.

Mitscherlich, Alex   336013   Feb. 9, 1886.
    Sizing paper (by material in waste liquor from sulphite boiling)
Mitscherlich, Alex   344328   June 22, 1886
    Paper pulp   (Process and apparatus for manufacturing)
Montgomery, T. W., and J. Warnke   433531   Aug 5 1890
    Apparatus for washing the fumes of sulphur (sulphurous acid)
Noble, G R   345168   July 6, 1886
    Making lead-lined digesters.
Noble, G R   427802   May 13, 1890
    Lining boilers with lead
Norton, J   480984   Aug 16, 1892
    Lining for tanks
Norton, J   496275   April 25, 1893.
    Digester
Phillips, George R   307587   Nov 4, 1884.
    Lining for digesters
Pictet, R P.   404431.   June 4, 1889.
    Process of disintegrating fibrous materials
Pictet. R. P.   191778.   June 12, 1877
    Apparatus for manufacture of sulphurous anhydride.
Pictet, R P.   331323.   Dec 1, 1885
    Manufacture of pulp from woody matter.
Pond, Goldsburg H   354931   Dec. 28, 1886
    Manufacture of paper pulp from wood
Pond, Goldsburg H   351067   Oct 19, 1886
    Machine for manufacture of wood pulp. Manufacture of bronze, and
        its use in digesters, etc , to resist chemicals, sulphuric acid, etc , in
        preparation of wood pulp
Pond, Goldsberg H   351068   Oct 19, 1886
    Manufacture of wood pulp
Radam, W   412664   Oct 8, 1889
    Apparatus for impregnating liquids with gases
Raudon, Francois   337197.   March 2, 1886
    Apparatus for production of pure sulphurous acid
Radford, B F   483942   Oct. 4, 1892
    Digester
Reynolds, Eli A   423531.   March 18, 1890
    Digester
Reynoso, A F C   185964   Jan 2, 1877.
    Apparatus for manufacture of sulphurous acid
Ritter, Eugen Baron, and Carl Kellner   328812   Oct 20 1885
    Apparatus for manufacture of cellulose from wood
Ritter, Eugen Baron, and Carl Kellner   329214   Oct. 27, 1885
    Apparatus (arrangement of tanks and digesters)
Ritter, Eugen Baron, and Carl Kellner   329215   Oct. 27, 1885
    Process of manufacturing cellulose.
Ritter, Eugen Baron, and Carl Kellner   329216   Oct. 27, 1885
    Making solutions of bisulphites

Ritter, Eugen Baron, and Carl Kellner   329217   Oct 27, 1885
    Digester
Ritter, Eugen Baron, and Carl Kellner   338557   March 23, 1886
    Apparatus for manufacture of sulphurous acid
Ritter, Eugen Baron, and Carl Kellner. 338558. March 23, 1886
    Process for manufacturing sulphites
Russell, G F   445235   Jan. 27, 1891.
    Digester
Russell, G F.   Reissue, 11282   Nov. 15, 1892
    Digester
Russell George W.   341434 and 341435   May 4, 1886.
    Digester
Saunders, John   234431   Nov 16, 1880
    Slide valve gate for digesters
Schenck Garrett   363173   May 17, 1887
    Process of, and apparatus for, charging liquids with gas
Schenck, Garrett   395082   Dec 25 1888
    Apparatus for preparing solutions of bisulphites.
Schnurmann Heinrich, and Gotthold Closs   360484   April 5, 1887.
    Apparatus (Digester, heater and circulation apparatus.)
Schroeder, M   See Hamsh, E
Smith, Sidney   428149   May 20, 1890.
    Lead lined digester.
Smith, Sidney.   421201   Feb 11, 1890.
    Sulphur burner
Smith S   428149.   May 20, 1890
    Digester
Smith, S   443922   Dec 30, 1890
    Digester.
Smith, S   443923   Dec 30, 1890.
    Digester.
Smith S   443924   Dec 30, 1890
    Digester
Spence, Peter   248511   Oct 18, 1881
    Furnace for burning pyrites
Spiro, J   See Wendler, A.
Springer, C C   411838   Oct 1, 1889
    Digester
Springer, C C.   335046.   Jan. 26 1886
    Digester
Stebbins, Henry W   405279   June 18, 1889
    Digester
Tilghman, B C.   70485.   Nov 5, 1867
    Treating vegetable substances for making paper pulp. The foundation patent
Tilghman, B C.   92229.   July 6, 1869
    Process of treating vegetable substances to obtain fibre.

Tompkins, John D.   401609.   April 16, 1889.
    Digester
Turner, Walter J   123799   Feb 20, 1872
    Apparatus for manufacture of bisulphites
Wagg, S. R   373703.   Nov 22, 1887.
    Digester
Wagg, S R   390727   Oct 9, 1888
    Lining for digesters
Wagg, S R   440242.   Nov 11, 1890.
    Digester
Wagg, S R   446041   Feb 10, 1891.
    Digester
Walker, G R   310753   Jan. 13, 1885
    Treating yucca to obtain fibre.   Uses borax liquor and sulphurous acid.
Warnke, J.   See Montgomery, T. W
Wendler, A , and J Spiro.   446652.
    Liquor apparatus
Wheelwright, Charles S   337720   337721   March 9, 1886
    Digester or converter.
Wheelwright, Charles S.   307608   Nov. 4, 1884.
    Digester
Wheelwright, Charles S , and George E Marshall   307609   Nov. 4, 1884.
    Apparatus for treating wood
Williams, N W.   See Keys, William W
Wurtz, Henry.   252287   Jan 10, 1882.
    Treating pyrites for manufacture of sulphurous acid
Zier, Michael   See Bremaker, Charles

METRIC WEIGHTS AND MEASURES

For the complicated system of weights and measures in use in this country and in England, most chemists substitute the very simple metric system. The unit of the system is the metre, a rod of platinum deposited in the Archives of France, which, when constructed was supposed to be one ten-millionth part of the quadrant of a great circle encompassing the earth on the meridian of Paris.

Measures of Length. — The metre measures 39 37 inches. It is multiplied and subdivided by 10 for the higher and lower measures of length.

	Metres	Inches
kilometre	1000 0	39370 0
hectometre	100 0	3937 0
decametre	10 0	393.70
metre	1 0	39 37
decimetre	0.1	3.937
centimetre	0 01	0.3937
millimetre	0 001	0 03937

The Greek prefixes *deca, hecto,* and *kilo* are used to represent the numbers 10, 100, and 1000, respectively, and the Latin *deci, centi,* and *milli* signify a tenth, hundredth, and thousandth. The prefixes are used with the same meaning in the other measures. The decimetre is very nearly 4 inches in length. This affords an easy method of roughly translating measures of the one denomination into those of the other.

Measures of Capacity. — The measure of capacity is derived from that of length by taking one cubic decimetre as the unit. This is named the litre, the capacity of which and that of its derivatives in the United States measures are appended: —

	Litres	Cubic inches	Pints (U S)
kilolitre	1000 0	61027 0	2113 1
hectolitre	100 0	6102 7	211 31
decalitre	10.0	610 27	21.131
litre	1 0	61 027	2 1131
decilitre	0 1	6 1027	0 2113
centilitre	0 01	0 61027	0 02113
millilitre	0 001	0 061027	0 002113

The litre being the capacity of a cubic decimetre, it is evident that the millilitre equals in volume a cubic centimetre, and this latter term, or its abbreviation (c.c.), is very frequently used in preference to millilitre; thus a pipette is said to contain 50 c.c., and a litre flask is often called a 1000 c.c. flask.

A cubic inch is equal to 16.3 cubic centimetres.

Measures of Weight. — The weight of one cubic centimetre of distilled water at its maximum density (4° C.) is taken as the unit of weight, and is called a gramme or gram. The subdivision and multiples are again the same.

	Grammes	Grains	Avoirdupois ounces
kilogramme	1000.0	15432.3	35.2739
hectogramme	100.0	1543.23	3.52739
decagramme	10.0	154.323	0.352739
gramme	1.0	15.4323	0.0352739
decigramme	0.1	1.5432	0.003527
centigramme	0.01	0.15432	0.0003527
milligramme	0.001	0.015432	0.00003527

A kilogramme is a little over 2 lbs. 3¼ oz., and a hectogramme 3½ oz. An ounce avoirdupois equals 28.35 grammes.

The relation between the weight and volume of water is seen to be a very simple one, the volume being the same number of cubic centimetres as the weight in grammes. With other liquids the volume in cubic centimetres × specific gravity = weight in grammes.

RELATIONS BETWEEN THERMOMETERS

In Fahrenheit's thermometer, the freezing-point of water is placed at 32°, and the boiling-point at 212°, and the number of intervening degrees is 180.

The Centigrade, or Celsius's thermometer, which is now recognized in the United States Pharmacopœia, and has been adopted generally by scientists, marks the freezing-point 0, and the boiling-point 100.

From the above statement it is evident that 180° of Fahrenheit are equal to 100° of Centigrade, or 1° of the first is equal to $\frac{5}{9}$ of a degree of the second. It is easy, therefore, to convert the degrees of one to the equivalent number of degrees of the other; but in ascertaining the corresponding point of the different scales it is necessary to take into consideration their different modes of graduation. Thus, as the 0 of Fahrenheit is at 32° below the point at which that of the Centigrade is placed, this number must be taken into account in the calculation.

If any degree on the Centigrade scale, either above or below 0, be multiplied by 1.8, the result will in either case be the number of degrees above or below 32, or the freezing-point, Fahrenheit.

The number of degrees between any point on the Fahrenheit scale and 32, if divided by 1.8, will give the corresponding point on the Centigrade.

Thermometric Equivalents,

According to the Centigrade and Fahrenheit Scales.

C.	F.	C.	F.	C.	F.
−40	−40.0	3	37.4	30	86.0
−35	−31.0	4	39.2	31	87.8
−30	−22.0	5	41.0	32	89.6
−25	−13.0	6	42.8	33	91.4
−20	− 4.0	7	44.6	34	93.2
−19	− 2.2	8	46.4	35	95.0
−18	− 0.4	9	48.2	36	96.8
−17	+ 1.4	10	50.0	37	98.6
−16	3.2	11	51.8	38	100.4
−15	5.0	12	53.6	39	102.2
−14	6.8	13	55.4	40	104.0
−13	8.6	14	57.2	41	105.8
−12	10.4	15	59.0	42	107.6
−11	12.2	16	60.8	43	109.4
−10	14.0	17	62.6	44	111.2
− 9	15.8	18	64.4	45	113.0
− 8	17.6	19	66.2	46	114.8
− 7	19.4	20	68.0	47	116.6
− 6	21.2	21	69.8	48	118.4
− 5	23.0	22	71.6	49	120.2
− 4	24.8	23	73.4	50	122.0
− 3	26.6	24	75.2	51	123.8
− 2	28.4	25	77.0	52	125.6
− 1	30.2	26	78.8	53	127.4
0	32.0	27	80.6	54	129.2
+ 1	33.8	28	82.4	55	131.0
2	35.6	29	84.2	56	132.8

THERMOMETRIC EQUIVALENTS (*continued*).

C.	F.	C.	F.	C.	F.
57	134.6	92	197.6	127	260.6
58	136.4	93	199.4	128	262.4
59	138.2	94	201.2	129	264.2
60	140.0	95	203.0	130	266.0
61	141.8	96	204.8	131	267.8
62	143.6	97	206.6	132	269.6
63	145.4	98	208.4	133	271.4
64	147.2	99	210.2	134	273.2
65	149.0	100	212.0	135	275.0
66	150.8	101	213.8	136	276.8
67	152.6	102	215.6	137	278.6
68	154.4	103	217.4	138	280.4
69	156.2	104	219.2	139	282.2
70	158.0	105	221.0	140	284.0
71	159.8	106	222.8	141	285.8
72	161.6	107	224.6	142	287.6
73	163.4	108	226.4	143	289.4
74	165.2	109	228.2	144	291.2
75	167.0	110	230.0	145	293.0
76	168.8	111	231.8	146	294.8
77	170.6	112	233.6	147	296.6
78	172.4	113	235.4	148	298.4
79	174.2	114	237.2	149	300.2
80	176.0	115	239.0	150	302.0
81	177.8	116	240.8	151	303.8
82	179.6	117	242.6	152	305.6
83	181.4	118	244.4	153	307.4
84	183.2	119	246.2	154	309.2
85	185.0	120	248.0	155	311.0
86	186.8	121	249.8	156	312.8
87	188.6	122	251.6	157	314.6
88	190.4	123	253.4	158	316.4
89	192.2	124	255.2	159	318.2
90	194.0	125	257.0	160	320.0
91	195.8	126	258.8		

Specific Gravity corresponding to Degrees of Baumé's Hydrometer for Liquids Lighter than Water

Degree of hydrometer	Specific gravity	Degree of hydrometer	Specific gravity	Degree of hydrometer	Specific gravity
10	1.000	33	0.862	56	0.758
11	0.993	34	0.857	57	0.754
12	0.986	35	0.852	58	0.750
13	0.979	36	0.847	59	0.746
14	0.973	37	0.842	60	0.742
15	0.966	38	0.837	61	0.738
16	0.960	39	0.832	62	0.735
17	0.953	40	0.827	63	0.731
18	0.947	41	0.823	64	0.727
19	0.941	42	0.818	65	0.724
20	0.935	43	0.813	66	0.720
21	0.929	44	0.809	67	0.716
22	0.923	45	0.804	68	0.713
23	0.917	46	0.800	69	0.709
24	0.911	47	0.795	70	0.706
25	0.905	48	0.791	71	0.702
26	0.900	49	0.787	72	0.699
27	0.894	50	0.783	73	0.696
28	0.889	51	0.778	74	0.692
29	0.883	52	0.774	75	0.689
30	0.878	53	0.770	76	0.686
31	0.872	54	0.766	77	0.682
32	0.867	55	0.762		

Percentage of Sodium Chloride in Solutions of Different Specific Gravities

Specific gravity	Per cent NaCl	Specific gravity	Per cent NaCl	Specific gravity	Per cent NaCl
1.00725	1	1.07335	10	1.14315	19
1.01450	2	1.08097	11	1.15107	20
1.02174	3	1.08859	12	1.15931	21
1.028999	4	1.09622	13	1.16755	22
1.03624	5	1.10384	14	1.17580	23
1.04366	6	1.11146	15	1.18404	24
1.05108	7	1.11938	16	1.19228	25
1.05851	8	1.12730	17	1.20098	26
1.06593	9	1.13523	18	1.20433	26.395

Specific Gravity corresponding to Degrees of Baumé's Hydrometer for Liquids Heavier than Water.

Degree of hydrometer.	Specific gravity.	Degree of hydrometer.	Specific gravity.	Degree of hydrometer.	Specific gravity.
0	1.000	26	1.221	52	1.566
1	1.007	27	1.231	53	1.583
2	1.014	28	1.242	54	1.601
3	1.022	29	1.252	55	1.618
4	1.029	30	1.261	56	1.637
5	1.036	31	1.275	57	1.656
6	1.044	32	1.286	58	1.676
7	1.052	33	1.298	59	1.695
8	1.060	34	1.309	60	1.715
9	1.067	35	1.321	61	1.736
10	1.075	36	1.334	62	1.758
11	1.083	37	1.346	63	1.779
12	1.091	38	1.359	64	1.801
13	1.100	39	1.372	65	1.823
14	1.108	40	1.384	66	1.847
15	1.116	41	1.398	67	1.872
16	1.125	42	1.412	68	1.897
17	1.134	43	1.426	69	1.921
18	1.143	44	1.440	70	1.946
19	1.152	45	1.454	71	1.974
20	1.161	46	1.470	72	2.002
21	1.171	47	1.485	73	2.031
22	1.180	48	1.501	74	2.059
23	1.190	49	1.516	75	2.087
24	1.199	50	1.532		
25	1.210	51	1.549		

Percentage of Oxalic Acid in Solutions of Different Specific Gravity at 15° C.

Specific gravity.	Per cent. $C_2H_2O_4 + 2H_2O$.	Specific gravity.	Per cent. $C_2H_2O_4 + 2H_2O$.	Specific gravity.	Per cent. $C_2H_2O_4 + 2H_2O$.
1.0032	1	1.0182	6	1.0271	10
1.0064	2	1.0204	7	1.0289	11
1.0096	3	1.0226	8	1.0309	12
1.0128	4	1.0248	9	1.0320	12.6
1.0160	5				

SPECIFIC GRAVITY CORRESPONDING TO DEGREES OF TWADDLE'S HYDROMETER.

Degrees Twaddle.	Specific gravity.	Degrees Twaddle.	Specific gravity.	Degrees Twaddle.	Specific gravity.
0	1.000	43	1.215	86	1.430
1	1.005	44	1.220	87	1.435
2	1.010	45	1.225	88	1.440
3	1.015	46	1.230	89	1.445
4	1.020	47	1.235	90	1.450
5	1.025	48	1.240	91	1.455
6	1.030	49	1.245	92	1.460
7	1.035	50	1.250	93	1.465
8	1.040	51	1.255	94	1.470
9	1.045	52	1.260	95	1.475
10	1.050	53	1.265	96	1.480
11	1.055	54	1.270	97	1.485
12	1.060	55	1.275	98	1.490
13	1.065	56	1.280	99	1.495
14	1.070	57	1.285	100	1.500
15	1.075	58	1.290	101	1.505
16	1.080	59	1.295	102	1.510
17	1.085	60	1.300	103	1.515
18	1.090	61	1.305	104	1.520
19	1.095	62	1.310	105	1.525
20	1.100	63	1.315	106	1.530
21	1.105	64	1.320	107	1.535
22	1.110	65	1.325	108	1.540
23	1.115	66	1.330	109	1.545
24	1.120	67	1.335	110	1.550
25	1.125	68	1.340	111	1.555
26	1.130	69	1.345	112	1.560
27	1.135	70	1.350	113	1.565
28	1.140	71	1.355	114	1.570
29	1.145	72	1.360	115	1.575
30	1.150	73	1.365	116	1.580
31	1.155	74	1.370	117	1.585
32	1.160	75	1.375	118	1.590
33	1.165	76	1.380	119	1.595
34	1.170	77	1.385	120	1.600
35	1.175	78	1.390	121	1.605
36	1.180	79	1.395	122	1.610
37	1.185	80	1.400	123	1.615
38	1.190	81	1.405	124	1.620
39	1.195	82	1.410	125	1.625
40	1.200	83	1.415	126	1.630
41	1.205	84	1.420	127	1.635
42	1.210	85	1.425	128	1.640

Specific Gravity corresponding to Degrees of Twaddle's Hydrometer (*continued*).

Degrees Twaddle.	Specific gravity.	Degrees Twaddle.	Specific gravity.	Degrees Twaddle.	Specific gravity.
129	1.645	153	1.765	177	1.885
130	1.650	154	1.770	178	1.890
131	1.655	155	1.775	179	1.895
132	1.660	156	1.780	180	1.900
133	1.665	157	1.785	181	1.905
134	1.670	158	1.790	182	1.910
135	1.675	159	1.795	183	1.915
136	1.680	160	1.800	184	1.920
137	1.685	161	1.805	185	1.925
138	1.690	162	1.810	186	1.930
139	1.695	163	1.815	187	1.935
140	1.700	164	1.820	188	1.940
141	1.705	165	1.825	189	1.945
142	1.710	166	1.830	190	1.950
143	1.715	167	1.835	191	1.955
144	1.720	168	1.840	192	1.960
145	1.725	169	1.845	193	1.965
146	1.730	170	1.850	194	1.970
147	1.735	171	1.855	195	1.975
148	1.740	172	1.860	196	1.980
149	1.745	173	1.865	197	1.985
150	1.750	174	1.870	198	1.990
151	1.755	175	1.875	199	1.995
152	1.760	176	1.880	200	2.000

Table of the Elements, together with their Symbols and Approximate Atomic Weights [1]

	Symbols	Atomic weight		Symbols	Atomic weight
Aluminum	Al	27.5	Molybdenum	Mo	96
Antimony	Sb	122	Nickel	Ni	59
Arsenic	As	75	Niobium	Nb	94
Barium	Ba	137	Nitrogen	N	14
Beryllium	Be	9.4	Osmium	Os	199
Bismuth	Bi	208	Oxygen	O	16
Boron	B	11	Palladium	Pd	106
Bromine	Br	80	Phosphorus	P	31
Cadmium	Cd	112	Platinum	Pt	197.18
Cæsium	Cs	133	Potassium	K	39
Calcium	Ca	40	Rhodium	Rh	104
Carbon	C	12	Rubidium	Rb	85
Cerium	Ce	137	Selenium	Se	79
Chlorine	Cl	35.5	Ruthenium	Ru	104
Chromium	Cr	52.5	Silicon	Si	28
Cobalt	Co	59	Silver	Ag	108
Copper	Cu	63.5	Sodium	Na	23
Didymium	Di	144	Strontium	Sr	87.5
Erbium	Er	170.6	Sulphur	S	32
Fluorine	F	19	Tantalum	Ta	182
Gold	Au	197	Tellurium	Te	125
Hydrogen	H	1	Thallium	Tl	204
Indium	In	113	Thorium	Tn	231.5
Iodine	I	127	Tin	Sn	118
Iridium	Ir	193	Titanium	Ti	48
Iron	Fe	56	Uranium	Ur	240
Lanthanum	La	139	Vanadium	V	51
Lead	Pb	207	Wolframium	W	184
Lithium	Li	7	Yttrium	Y	88
Magnesium	Mg	24	Zinc	Zn	65
Manganese	Mn	55	Zirconium	Zr	90
Mercury	Hg	200			

[1] The atomic weights here given are those used by Lunge in his "Alkali-Maker's Handbook."

TEMPERATURE OF SATURATED STEAM AT DIFFERENT PRESSURES.

Pressure per square inch.	Temperature. Degrees F.	Pressure per square inch.	Temperature. Degrees F.	Pressure per square inch.	Temperature. Degrees F.
1	102.1	34	257.6	68	300.9
2	126.3	35	259.3	69	301.9
3	141.6	36	260.9	70	302.9
4	153.1	37	262.6	71	303.9
5	162.3	38	264.2	72	304.8
6	170.2	39	265.8	73	305.7
7	176.9	40	267.3	74	306.6
8	182.9	41	268.7	75	307.5
9	188.3	42	270.2	76	308.4
10	193.3	43	271.6	77	309.3
11	197.8	44	273.0	78	310.2
12	202.0	45	274.4	79	311.1
13	205.9	46	275.8	80	312.0
14	209.6	47	277.1	81	312.8
14.7	212.0	48	278.4	82	313.6
15	213.1	49	279.7	83	314.5
16	216.3	50	281.0	84	315.3
17	219.6	51	282.3	85	316.1
18	222.4	52	283.5	86	316.9
19	225.3	53	284.7	87	317.8
20	228.0	54	285.9	88	318.6
21	230.6	55	287.1	89	319.4
22	233.1	56	288.2	90	320.2
23	235.5	57	289.3	91	321.0
24	237.8	58	290.4	92	321.7
25	240.1	59	291.6	93	322.5
26	242.3	60	292.7	94	323.3
27	244.4	61	293.8	95	324.1
28	246.4	62	294.8	96	324.8
29	248.4	63	295.9	97	325.6
30	250.4	64	296.9	98	326.3
31	252.2	65	298.0	99	327.1
32	254.1	66	299.0	100	327.9
33	255.9	67	300.0		

Percentage of Sulphuric Acid for Different Specific Gravities.

Specific gravity at 15° C.	Per cent. by weight c. p. sulphuric acid, H_2SO_4.	Specific gravity at 15° C.	Per cent. by weight c.p. sulphuric acid, H_2SO_4.
1.00	0.09	1.42	52.13
1.01	1.57	1.43	53.11
1.02	3.03	1.44	54.07
1.03	4.49	1.45	55.03
1.04	5.96	1.46	55.97
1.05	7.37	1.47	56.90
1.06	8.77	1.48	57.83
1.07	10.19	1.49	58.74
1.08	11.60	1.50	59.70
1.09	12.99	1.51	60.65
1.10	14.35	1.52	61.59
1.11	15.71	1.53	62.53
1.12	17.01	1.54	63.43
1.13	18.31	1.55	64.26
1.14	19.61	1.56	65.08
1.15	20.91	1.57	65.90
1.16	22.19	1.58	66.71
1.17	23.47	1.59	67.59
1.18	24.76	1.60	68.51
1.19	26.04	1.61	69.43
1.20	27.32	1.62	70.32
1.21	28.58	1.63	71.16
1.22	29.84	1.64	71.99
1.23	31.11	1.65	72.82
1.24	32.28	1.66	73.64
1.25	33.43	1.67	74.51
1.26	34.57	1.68	75.42
1.27	35.71	1.69	76.30
1.28	36.87	1.70	77.17
1.29	38.03	1.71	78.04
1.30	39.19	1.72	78.92
1.31	40.35	1.73	79.80
1.32	41.50	1.74	80.68
1.33	42.66	1.75	81.56
1.34	43.74	1.76	82.44
1.35	44.82	1.77	83.32
1.36	45.88	1.78	84.50
1.37	46.94	1.79	85.70
1.38	48.00	1.80	86.90
1.39	49.06	1.81	88.30
1.40	50.11	1.82	90.05
1.41	51.15	1.822	90.40

Percentage of Sulphuric Acid for Different Specific Gravities (continued).

Specific gravity at 15° C.	Per cent. by weight c.p. sulphuric acid, H_2SO_4.	Specific gravity at 15° C.	Per cent. by weight c.p. sulphuric acid, H_2SO_4.
1.824	90.80	1.840	95.60
1.826	91.25	1.8410	97.00
1.828	91.70	1.8415	97.70
1.830	92.10	1.8410	98.20
1.832	92.52	1.8400	99.20
1.834	93.05	1.8390	99.70
1.836	93.80	1.8385	99.95
1.838	94.60		

Table showing how to prepare Sulphuric Acid of Any Strength by mixing Different Proportions of Acid and Water.

Column a shows how many parts of oil of vitriol of 1.840 specific gravity (66° B, 168° Twaddle's) must be mixed with 100 parts water, at 15° or 20°, in order to obtain an acid of the specific gravity b.

a	b	a	b	a	b
1	1.009	130	1.456	370	1.723
2	1.015	140	1.473	380	1.727
5	1.035	150	1.490	390	1.730
10	1.060	160	1.510	400	1.733
15	1.090	170	1.530	410	1.737
20	1.113	180	1.543	420	1.740
25	1.140	190	1.556	430	1.743
30	1.165	200	1.568	440	1.746
35	1.187	210	1.580	450	1.750
40	1.210	220	1.593	460	1.754
45	1.229	230	1.606	470	1.757
50	1.248	240	1.620	480	1.760
55	1.265	250	1.630	490	1.763
60	1.280	260	1.640	500	1.766
65	1.297	270	1.648	510	1.768
70	1.312	280	1.654	520	1.770
75	1.326	290	1.667	530	1.772
80	1.340	300	1.678	540	1.774
85	1.357	310	1.689	550	1.776
90	1.372	320	1.700	560	1.777
95	1.386	330	1.705	580	1.778
100	1.398	340	1.710	590	1.780
110	1.420	350	1.714	600	1.782
120	1.438	360	1.719		

Percentage of Nitric Acid for Different Specific Gravities

Specific gravity	Per cent by weight of nitric acid	Specific gravity	Per cent by weight of nitric acid
1.000	0.10	1.215	34.55
1.005	1.00	1.220	35.28
1.010	1.90	1.225	36.03
1.015	2.80	1.230	36.78
1.020	3.70	1.235	37.53
1.025	4.60	1.240	38.29
1.030	5.50	1.245	39.05
1.035	6.38	1.250	39.82
1.040	7.26	1.255	40.58
1.045	8.13	1.260	41.34
1.050	8.99	1.265	42.10
1.055	9.84	1.270	42.87
1.060	10.68	1.275	43.64
1.065	11.51	1.280	44.41
1.070	12.33	1.285	45.18
1.075	13.15	1.290	45.95
1.080	13.95	1.295	46.72
1.085	14.74	1.300	47.49
1.090	15.53	1.305	48.26
1.095	16.32	1.310	49.07
1.100	17.11	1.315	49.89
1.105	17.89	1.320	50.71
1.110	18.67	1.325	51.53
1.115	19.45	1.330	52.37
1.120	20.23	1.335	53.22
1.125	21.00	1.340	55.07
1.130	21.77	1.345	54.93
1.135	22.54	1.350	55.79
1.140	23.31	1.355	56.66
1.145	24.08	1.360	57.57
1.150	24.81	1.365	58.48
1.155	25.60	1.370	59.39
1.160	26.36	1.375	60.30
1.165	27.12	1.380	61.27
1.170	27.88	1.385	62.24
1.175	28.63	1.390	63.23
1.180	29.38	1.395	64.25
1.185	30.13	1.400	65.30
1.190	30.88	1.405	66.40
1.195	31.62	1.410	67.50
1.200	32.36	1.415	68.63
1.205	33.09	1.420	69.80
1.210	33.82	1.425	70.98

APPENDIX.

PERCENTAGE OF NITRIC ACID FOR DIFFERENT SPECIFIC GRAVITIES (*continued*).

Specific gravity.	Per cent. by weight of nitric acid.	Specific gravity.	Per cent. by weight of nitric acid.
1.430	72.17	1.504	96.00
1.435	73.39	1.505	96.39
1.440	74.68	1.506	96.76
1.445	75.98	1.507	97.13
1.450	77.28	1.508	97.50
1.455	78.60	1.509	97.84
1.460	79.98	1.510	98.10
1.465	81.42	1.511	98.32
1.470	82.90	1.512	98.53
1.475	84.45	1.513	98.73
1.480	86.05	1.514	98.90
1.485	87.70	1.515	99.07
1.490	89.60	1.516	99.21
1.495	91.60	1.517	99.34
1.500	94.09	1.518	99.46
1.501	94.60	1.519	99.57
1.502	95.08	1.520	99.67
1.503	95.55		

PERCENTAGE OF HYDROCHLORIC ACID IN SOLUTIONS OF DIFFERENT SPECIFIC GRAVITIES AT 15° C.

Specific gravity.	Per cent. HCl.	Specific gravity.	Per cent. HCl.	Specific gravity.	Per cent. HCl.
1.000	0.16	1.070	14.17	1.140	27.66
1.005	1.15	1.075	15.16	1.145	28.61
1.010	2.14	1.080	16.15	1.150	29.57
1.015	3.12	1.085	17.13	1.155	30.55
1.020	4.13	1.090	18.11	1.160	31.52
1.025	5.15	1.095	19.06	1.165	32.49
1.030	6.15	1.100	20.01	1.170	33.46
1.035	7.15	1.105	20.97	1.175	34.42
1.040	8.16	1.110	21.92	1.180	35.39
1.045	9.16	1.115	22.86	1.185	36.31
1.050	10.17	1.120	23.82	1.190	37.23
1.055	11.18	1.125	24.78	1.195	38.16
1.060	12.19	1.130	25.75	1.200	39.11
1.065	13.19	1.135	26.70		

PERCENTAGE OF ABSOLUTE ACETIC ACID IN ACETIC ACID OF DIFFERENT DENSITIES (OUDEMANS) TEMPERATURE 15° C

Per cent	Specific gravity	Per cent	Specific gravity	Per cent	Specific gravity
100	1.0553	66	1.0717	33	1.0447
99	1.0580	65	1.0712	32	1.0436
98	1.0604	64	1.0707	31	1.0424
97	1.0625	63	1.0702	30	1.0412
96	1.0644	62	1.0697	29	1.0400
95	1.0660	61	1.0691	28	1.0388
94	1.0674	60	1.0685	27	1.0375
93	1.0686	59	1.0679	26	1.0363
92	1.0696	58	1.0673	25	1.0350
91	1.0705	57	1.0666	24	1.0337
90	1.0713	56	1.0660	23	1.0324
89	1.0720	55	1.0653	22	1.0311
88	1.0726	54	1.0646	21	1.0298
87	1.0731	53	1.0638	20	1.0284
86	1.0736	52	1.0631	19	1.0270
85	1.0739	51	1.0623	18	1.0256
84	1.0742	50	1.0615	17	1.0242
83	1.0744	49	1.0607	16	1.0228
82	1.0746	48	1.0598	15	1.0214
81	1.0747	47	1.0589	14	1.0201
80	1.0748	46	1.0580	13	1.0185
79	1.0748	45	1.0571	12	1.0171
78	1.0748	44	1.0562	11	1.0157
77	1.0748	43	1.0552	10	1.0142
76	1.0747	42	1.0543	9	1.0127
75	1.0746	41	1.0533	8	1.0113
74	1.0744	40	1.0523	7	1.0098
73	1.0742	39	1.0513	6	1.0083
72	1.0740	38	1.0502	5	1.0067
71	1.0737	37	1.0492	4	1.0052
70	1.0733	36	1.0481	3	1.0037
69	1.0729	35	1.0470	2	1.0022
68	1.0725	34	1.0459	1	1.0007
67	1.0721				

Percentage of Ammonia in Solutions of Different Specific Gravities at 15° C.

Specific gravity.	Per cent. NH_3.	Specific gravity.	Per cent. NH_3.	Specific gravity.	Per cent. NH_3.
0.880	35.60	0.925	20.18	0.965	8.59
0.885	33.67	0.930	18.64	0.970	7.31
0.890	31.73	0.935	17.12	0.975	6.05
0.895	30.03	0.940	15.63	0.980	4.80
0.900	28.33	0.945	14.17	0.985	3.55
0.905	26.64	0.950	12.74	0.990	2.31
0.910	24.99	0.955	11.32	0.995	1.14
0.915	23.35	0.960	9.91	1.000	0.00
0.920	21.75				

Percentage of Caustic Soda in Solutions of Different Specific Gravities at 15° C.

Specific gravity.	Per cent. NaOH.	Specific gravity.	Per cent. NaOH.	Specific gravity.	Per cent. NaOH.
1.007	0.61	1.142	12.64	1.308	27.80
1.014	1.20	1.152	13.55	1.320	28.83
1.022	2.00	1.162	14.37	1.332	29.93
1.029	2.71	1.171	15.13	1.345	31.22
1.036	3.35	1.180	15.91	1.357	32.47
1.045	4.00	1.190	16.77	1.370	33.69
1.052	4.64	1.200	17.67	1.383	34.96
1.060	5.29	1.210	18.58	1.397	36.25
1.067	5.87	1.220	19.58	1.410	37.47
1.075	6.55	1.231	20.59	1.424	38.80
1.083	7.31	1.241	21.42	1.438	39.99
1.091	8.00	1.252	22.64	1.453	41.41
1.100	8.68	1.263	23.67	1.468	42.83
1.108	9.42	1.274	24.81	1.498	46.15
1.116	10.06	1.285	25.80	1.514	47.60
1.125	10.97	1.297	26.83	1.530	49.02
1.134	11.84				

PERCENTAGE OF SODIUM CARBONATE IN SOLUTIONS OF DIFFERENT SPECIFIC GRAVITIES AT 15° C

Specific gravity	Per cent Na_2CO_3	Per cent $Na_2CO_3 + 10 H_2O$ (soda crystals)
1 007	0 67	1 807
1 014	1.33	3 587
1 022	2 09	5 637
1 029	2 76	7 444
1 036	3 43	9 251
1 045	4 29	11 570
1 052	4 94	13 323
1 060	5 71	15 400
1 067	6 37	17 180
1 075	7 12	19 203
1 083	7 88	21 252
1 091	8 62	23 248
1 100	9 43	25 432
1 108	10 19	27 482
1 116	10 95	29 532
1 125	11 81	31 851
1 134	12 61	34 009
1 142	13 16	35 493
1 152	14 24	38 405

PERCENTAGE OF ACETATE OF LEAD IN SOLUTIONS OF DIFFERENT SPECIFIC GRAVITIES AT 15° C

Specific gravity	Per cent $(C_2H_3O_2)_2Pb + 3 H_2O$	Specific gravity	Per cent $(C_2H_3O_2)_2Pb + 3 H_2O$	Specific gravity	Per cent $(C_2H_3O_2)_2Pb + 3 H_2O$
1 0127	2	1 1384	20	1 2768	36
1 0255	4	1 1544	22	1 2966	38
1.0386	6	1 1704	24	1 3163	40
1 0520	8	1 1869	26	1 3376	42
1 0654	10	1 2040	28	1 3588	44
1 0796	12	1 2211	30	1 3810	46
1 0939	14	1 2395	32	1 4041	48
1 1084	16	1 2578	34	1 4271	50
1 1234	18				

PERCENTAGE OF CAUSTIC POTASH IN SOLUTIONS OF DIFFERENT SPECIFIC GRAVITIES AT 15° C.

Specific gravity.	Per cent. KOH.	Specific gravity.	Per cent. KOH.
1.007	0.9	1.252	27.0
1.014	1.7	1.263	28.0
1.022	2.6	1.274	28.9
1.029	3.5	1.285	29.8
1.037	4.4	1.297	30.7
1.045	5.6	1.308	31.8
1.052	6.4	1.320	32.7
1.060	7.4	1.332	33.7
1.067	8.2	1.345	34.9
1.075	9.2	1.357	35.9
1.083	10.1	1.370	36.9
1.091	10.9	1.383	37.8
1.100	12.0	1.397	38.9
1.108	12.9	1.410	39.9
1.116	13.8	1.424	40.9
1.125	14.8	1.438	42.1
1.134	15.7	1.453	43.4
1.142	16.5	1.468	44.6
1.152	17.6	1.483	45.8
1.162	18.6	1.498	47.1
1.171	19.5	1.514	48.3
1.180	20.5	1.530	49.4
1.190	21.4	1.546	50.6
1.200	22.4	1.563	51.9
1.210	23.3	1.580	53.2
1.220	24.2	1.597	54.5
1.231	25.1	1.615	55.9
1.241	26.1	1.634	57.5

PER CENT. OF POTASH ALUM (CRYSTALS) IN SOLUTIONS OF DIFFERENT SPECIFIC GRAVITY AT 17.5° C.

Specific gravity.	Per cent. alum.	Specific gravity.	Per cent. alum.
1.007	1	1.022	4
1.010	2	1.027	5
1.017	3	1.032	6

THE CHEMISTRY OF PAPER-MAKING.

Density and Composition of Aluminium Sulphate Solutions (Chemically Pure). Temperature 15° C.

Specific gravity.	Degrees Beaumé.	100 kilos of solution contain kilos.					100 litres of solution contain kilos.				
		Al_2O_3.	SO_3.	Sulphate with 13 per cent. Al_2O_3.	Sulphate with 14 per cent. Al_2O_3.	Sulphate with 15 per cent. Al_2O_3.	Al_2O_3.	SO_3.	Sulphate with 13 per cent. Al_2O_3.	Sulphate with 14 per cent. Al_2O_3.	Sulphate with 15 per cent. Al_2O_3.
1.005	0.7	0.14	0.32	1.1	1.0	0.9	0.14	0.33	1.1	1	0.9
1.010	1.4	0.27	0.64	2.1	2.0	1.8	0.28	0.65	2.2	2	1.9
1.016	2.1	0.41	0.95	3.1	2.9	2.7	0.42	0.98	3.2	3	2.8
1.021	2.8	0.55	1.27	4.2	3.9	3.6	0.56	1.31	4.3	4	3.7
1.026	3.5	0.68	1.59	5.3	4.9	4.6	0.70	1.63	5.4	5	4.7
1.031	4.2	0.81	1.89	6.3	5.8	5.4	0.84	1.96	6.5	6	5.6
1.036	4.8	0.94	2.20	7.3	6.7	6.3	0.98	2.28	7.5	7	6.5
1.040	5.4	1.07	2.50	8.3	7.7	7.2	1.12	2.61	8.6	8	7.5
1.045	6.1	1.20	2.80	9.3	8.6	8.0	1.26	2.94	9.7	9	8.4
1.050	6.7	1.33	3.11	10.3	9.5	8.9	1.40	3.26	10.8	10	9.3
1.055	7.3	1.46	3.40	11.3	10.4	9.7	1.54	3.59	11.8	11	10.3
1.059	7.9	1.58	3.69	12.2	11.3	10.6	1.68	3.91	12.9	12	11.2
1.064	8.5	1.71	3.98	13.1	12.2	11.4	1.82	4.24	14.0	13	12.1
1.068	9.1	1.83	4.27	14.1	13.1	12.2	1.96	4.57	15.1	14	13.1
1.073	9.7	1.96	4.56	15.1	14.0	13.1	2.10	4.89	16.2	15	14.0
1.078	10.3	2.08	4.84	16.0	14.8	13.9	2.24	5.22	17.2	16	14.9
1.082	10.9	2.20	5.12	16.9	15.7	14.6	2.38	5.55	18.3	17	15.9
1.087	11.4	2.32	5.40	17.8	16.5	15.4	2.58	5.87	19.4	18	16.8
1.092	12.0	2.44	5.67	18.7	17.4	16.2	2.66	6.20	20.5	19	17.7
1.096	12.6	2.55	5.95	19.7	18.3	17.0	2.80	6.52	21.5	20	18.7
1.101	13.1	2.67	6.22	20.5	19.1	17.8	2.94	6.85	22.6	21	19.6
1.105	13.7	2.78	6.49	21.4	19.9	18.6	3.08	7.18	23.7	22	20.5
1.110	14.2	2.90	6.76	22.3	20.7	19.3	3.22	7.50	24.8	23	21.5
1.114	14.7	3.01	7.02	23.2	21.5	20.1	3.36	7.83	25.9	24	22.4
1.119	15.3	3.13	7.29	24.1	22.4	20.9	3.50	8.16	26.9	25	23.3
1.123	15.8	3.24	7.55	24.9	23.1	21.6	3.64	8.48	28.0	26	24.3
1.128	16.3	3.35	7.81	25.8	23.9	22.3	3.78	8.81	29.1	27	25.2
1.132	16.8	3.46	8.06	26.6	24.7	23.1	3.92	9.13	30.2	28	26.1
1.137	17.4	3.57	8.32	27.5	25.5	23.8	4.06	9.46	31.2	29	27.1
1.141	17.9	3.68	8.58	28.3	26.3	24.5	4.20	9.79	32.3	30	28.0
1.145	18.3	3.79	8.83	29.1	27.1	25.3	4.34	10.11	33.4	31	28.9
1.150	18.8	3.89	9.07	30.0	27.8	26.0	4.48	10.44	34.5	32	29.9
1.154	19.2	4.00	9.32	30.8	28.6	26.7	4.64	10.76	35.5	33	30.8
1.159	19.7	4.11	9.57	31.6	29.3	27.4	4.76	11.09	36.6	34	31.7
1.163	20.1	4.21	9.82	32.4	30.1	28.1	4.90	11.42	37.7	35	32.7
1.168	20.6	4.32	10.06	33.2	30.8	28.9	5.04	11.74	38.8	36	33.6
1.172	21.1	4.42	10.29	34.0	31.6	29.5	5.18	12.07	39.9	37	34.5
1.176	21.6	4.52	10.53	34.8	32.3	30.1	5.32	12.40	40.9	38	35.5
1.181	22.1	4.62	10.77	35.6	33.0	30.8	5.46	12.72	42.0	39	36.4

APPENDIX.

Density and Composition of Aluminium Sulphate Solutions (*continued*)

Specific gravity	Degrees Beaumé	100 kilos of solution contain kilos					100 litres of solution contain kilos				
		Al_2O_3	SO_3	Sulphate with 13 per cent Al_2O_3	Sulphate with 14 per cent Al_2O_3	Sulphate with 15 per cent Al_2O_3	Al_2O_3	SO_3	Sulphate with 13 per cent Al_2O_3	Sulphate with 14 per cent Al_2O_3	Sulphate with 15 per cent Al_2O_3
1 185	22 5	4 72	11 01	36.3	33 7	31 5	5 60	13 05	43 1	40	37 3
1 190	23 0	4 82	11 24	37 1	34 5	32 2	5 74	13 38	44 2	41	38 3
1 194	23 4	4 92	11 47	37 9	35 2	32 8	5 88	13 70	45 2	42	39 2
1 198	23.8	5 02	11 70	38 6	35 9	33 5	6 02	14 03	46 3	43	40 1
1 203	24.3	5 12	11 93	39 4	36 6	34 1	6 16	14 35	47 4	44	41 1
1 207	24 7	5.22	12 16	40 2	37 3	34 8	6 30	14 68	48 5	45	42 0
1 211	25 2	5 32	12 39	40 9	38 0	35 4	6 44	15 01	49 5	46	42 9
1 215	25 5	5 41	12 61	41 6	38 7	36 1	6 58	15 33	50 6	47	43 9
1 220	25 9	5 51	12 83	42 4	39 3	36 7	6.72	15 66	51 7	48	44 8
1 224	26 3	5 60	13 06	43 1	40 0	37 4	6 86	15 99	52 8	49	45 7
1 228	26 7	5 70	13 28	43 9	40 7	38 0	7.00	16 31	53 9	50	46 7
1 232	27.1	5 79	13 50	44 6	41 4	38 6	7 14	16 64	54 9	51	47 6
1 236	27 5	5 89	13 72	45 3	42 1	39 3	7 28	16 96	56 0	52	48 5
1 240	27.9	5 98	13 94	46 0	42 7	39 9	7 42	17 29	57 1	53	49 5
1 244	28 3	6 08	14 16	46 7	43 4	40 5	7 56	17 62	58 2	54	50 4
1 248	28 6	6 17	14 38	47 5	44 1	41 1	7 70	17 94	59 2	55	51 3
1 252	29.0	6 26	14 59	48 2	44 7	41 7	7 84	18 26	60 3	56	52 3
1 256	29 4	6.35	14 80	48 9	45 4	42 3	7.98	18 59	61 4	57	53.2
1 261	29 8	6 44	15 01	49 5	46 0	42 9	8 12	18 92	62 5	58	54 1
1 265	30 2	6 53	15 22	50 2	46 7	43 5	8 26	19.25	63 5	59	55 1
1 269	30 5	6.62	15 43	50.9	47 3	44 1	8 40	19 57	64 6	60	56 0
1 273	30 9	6 71	15 63	51 6	47 9	44 7	8 54	19 90	65 7	61	56 9
1 277	31 2	6 80	15 84	52 3	48 6	45 3	8.68	20 23	66 8	62	57 9
1.281	31 6	6 89	16.04	53 0	49 2	45 9	8 82	20 55	67 9	63	58 8
1 285	31 9	6.97	16 25	53.7	49 8	46 5	8 96	20 88	68 9	64	59 7
1 289	32 3	7 06	16 46	54 3	50 5	47 1	9 10	21 20	70 0	65	60 7
1 293	32 6	7 15	16.66	55 0*	51.1	47 7	9 24	21 53	71.1	66	61 6
1 297	33 0	7.23	16 85	55 6	51 7	48 2	9 38	21 86	72 2	67	62.5
1 301	33 3	7 32	17 05	56 3	52 3	48 8	9 52	22 18	73 2	68	63 5
1 305	33 7	7 40	17 25	57 0	52 9	49 4	9 66	22 51	74 3	69	64 4
1 309	34 0	7 49	17 45	57 6	53 5	49 9	9 80	22 84	75 4	70	65 3
1 312	34 4	7 57	17 65	58 3	54 1	50 5	9 94	23 16	76 5	71	66 3
1 316	34 7	7 66	17 84	58 9	54 5	51 1	10 08	23 49	77 5	72	67 2
1 320	35 0	7 74	18 04	59 6	55 3	51 6	10 22	23 81	78 6	73	68 1
1 324	35 3	7 83	18 23	60 2	55 9	52 2	10 36	24 14	79 7	74	69 1
1 328	35 6	7 91	18 43	60 8	56 5	52 7	10 50	24 47	80 8	75	70 0
1 331	35 9	7 99	18 62	61 5	57 1	53 3	10 64	24 79	81 8	76	70 9
1 335	36 2	8 07	18 81	62 1	57 7	53 8	10 78	25 12	82 9	77	71 9
1 339	36 5	8 16	19 00	62 7	58 3	54 4	10 92	25 45	84 0	78	72 8

Amount of Lime in Solutions of Milk of Lime of Different Specific Gravities.

Specific gravity.	Grammes CaO in 1 litre.	Specific gravity.	Grammes CaO in 1 litre.	Specific gravity.	Grammes CaO in 1 litre.
1.01	11.7	1.10	126.0	1.18	229.0
1.02	24.4	1.11	138.0	1.18	242.0
1.03	37.1	1.12	152.0	1.20	255.0
1.04	49.8	1.13	164.0	1.21	268.0
1.05	62.5	1.14	177.0	1.22	281.0
1.06	75.2	1.15	190.0	1.23	294.0
1.07	87.9	1.16	203.0	1.24	307.0
1.08	100.0	1.17	216.0	1.25	321.0
1.09	113.0				

Percentage of Glycerine in Solutions of Different Specific Gravities.

Specific gravity.	Per cent. glycerine.	Specific gravity.	Per cent. glycerine.	Specific gravity.	Per cent. glycerine.
1.0123	5	1.1320	50	1.2265	84
1.0245	10	1.1455	55	1.2318	86
1.0374	15	1.1582	60	1.2372	88
1.0498	20	1.1733	65	1.2425	90
1.0635	25	1.1889	70	1.2478	92
1.0771	30	1.2016	75	1.2531	94
1.0907	35	1.2106	78	1.2584	96
1.1045	40	1.2159	80	1.2637	98
1.1183	45	1.2212	82	1.2691	100

Specific Gravity of Different Solutions of Sulphurous Acid in Water.

Per cent. SO_2.	Specific gravity at 15° C.	Per cent. SO_2.	Specific gravity at 15° C.	Per cent. SO_2.	Specific gravity at 15° C.
0.5	1.0028	4.0	1.0221	7.5	1.0401
1.0	1.0056	4.5	1.0248	8.0	1.0426
1.5	1.0085	5.0	1.0275	8.5	1.0450
2.0	1.0113	5.5	1.0302	9.0	1.0474
2.5	1.0141	6.0	1.0328	9.5	1.0497
3.0	1.0168	6.5	1.0353	10.0	1.0520
3.5	1.0194	7.0	1.0377		

Per Cent. of Calcium Chloride in Solutions of Different Specific Gravities at 15° C.

Specific gravity.	Per cent. CaCl₂.	Specific gravity.	Per cent. CaCl₂.	Specific gravity.	Per cent. CaCl₂.
1.009	1	1.134	15	1.277	29
1.017	2	1.143	16	1.288	30
1.026	3	1.153	17	1.299	31
1.034	4	1.163	18	1.310	32
1.043	5	1.173	19	1.322	33
1.051	6	1.182	20	1.333	34
1.060	7	1.193	21	1.344	35
1.069	8	1.203	22	1.356	36
1.078	9	1.213	23	1.368	37
1.087	10	1.223	24	1.380	38
1.096	11	1.234	25	1.392	39
1.106	12	1.246	26	1.403	40
1.115	13	1.255	27	1.411	40.66 [1]
1.124	14	1.266	28		

[1] mother liquor.

Percentage of Alcohol for Different Specific Gravities.

Specific gravity at 15.5° C. (60° F.).	Per cent. by weight of absolute alcohol.	Per cent. by volume of absolute alcohol.	Specific gravity at 15.5° C. (60° F.).	Per cent. by weight of absolute alcohol.	Per cent. by volume of absolute alcohol.
1.000	0.00	0.00	0.972	19.67	24.08
0.998	0.79	0.99	0.970	21.31	26.04
0.996	2.28	2.86	0.968	22.85	27.80
0.994	3.41	4.27	0.966	24.38	29.67
0.992	4.62	5.78	0.964	25.86	31.40
0.990	5.87	7.32	0.962	27.21	32.98
0.988	7.27	9.04	0.960	28.56	34.54
0.986	8.64	10.73	0.958	29.87	36.04
0.984	10.08	12.49	0.956	31.00	37.34
0.982	11.62	14.37	0.954	32.25	38.75
0.980	13.15	16.24	0.952	33.47	40.14
0.978	14.82	18.25	0.950	34.52	41.32
0.976	16.46	20.24	0.948	35.50	42.40
0.974	18.08	22.18	0.946	36.56	43.56

PERCENTAGE OF ALCOHOL FOR DIFFERENT SPECIFIC GRAVITIES (*continued*)

Specific gravity at 15.5° C (90° F)	Per cent by weight of absolute alcohol	Per cent by volume of absolute alcohol	Specific gravity at 15.5° C (60° F)	Per cent by weight of absolute alcohol.	Per cent by volume of absolute alcohol
0.944	37.67	44.79	0.866	72.52	79.12
0.942	38.78	46.02	0.864	73.38	79.86
0.940	39.80	47.13	0.862	74.23	80.60
0.938	40.80	48.21	0.860	75.14	81.40
0.936	41.80	49.29	0.858	76.04	82.19
0.934	42.76	50.31	0.856	76.88	82.90
0.932	43.71	51.32	0.854	77.71	83.60
0.930	44.64	52.29	0.852	78.52	84.27
0.928	45.55	53.24	0.850	79.32	84.93
0.926	46.46	54.19	0.848	80.13	85.59
0.924	47.36	55.13	0.846	80.96	86.28
0.922	48.27	56.07	0.844	81.76	86.93
0.920	49.16	56.98	0.842	82.54	87.55
0.918	50.09	58.92	0.840	83.31	88.16
0.916	50.96	58.80	0.838	84.08	88.76
0.914	51.79	59.63	0.836	84.88	89.39
0.912	52.68	60.52	0.834	85.65	89.99
0.910	53.57	61.40	0.832	86.42	90.58
0.908	54.48	62.31	0.830	87.19	91.17
0.906	55.41	63.24	0.828	87.96	91.75
0.904	56.32	64.14	0.826	88.76	92.36
0.902	57.21	65.01	0.824	89.54	92.94
0.900	58.05	65.81	0.822	90.29	93.49
0.898	58.95	66.69	0.820	91.00	94.00
0.896	59.83	67.53	0.818	91.71	94.51
0.894	60.67	68.33	0.816	92.44	95.03
0.892	61.50	69.11	0.814	93.18	95.55
0.890	62.36	69.92	0.812	93.92	96.08
0.888	63.26	70.77	0.810	94.62	96.55
0.886	64.13	71.58	0.808	95.32	97.02
0.884	65.00	72.38	0.806	96.03	97.51
0.882	65.83	73.15	0.804	96.70	97.94
0.880	66.70	73.93	0.802	97.37	98.37
0.878	67.54	74.70	0.800	98.03	98.80
0.876	68.38	75.45	0.798	98.66	99.16
0.874	69.21	76.20	0.796	99.29	99.55
0.872	70.04	76.94	0.794	99.94	99.96
0.870	70.84	77.64	0.7938	100.00	100.00
0.868	71.67	78.38			

Per Cent. of Magnesium Chloride in Solutions of Different Specific Gravities at 15° C

Specific gravity	Per cent MgCl$_2$	Specific gravity	Per cent MgCl$_2$	Specific gravity	Per cent MgCl$_2$
1.008	1	1.113	13	1.228	25
1.017	2	1.122	14	1.238	26
1.025	3	1.131	15	1.248	27
1.033	4	1.140	16	1.259	28
1.042	5	1.150	17	1.269	29
1.052	6	1.159	18	1.270	30
1.060	7	1.169	19	1.290	31
1.068	8	1.178	20	1.301	32
1.077	9	1.188	21	1.312	33
1.086	10	1.198	22	1.323	34
1.095	11	1.208	23	1.334	35
1.104	12	1.218	24		

BIBLIOGRAPHY

ARCHER, T C —British Mfg Industries Vol. 8 Manufacture of Paper
— *Ibid*, Vol 15 The Industrial Classes and Industrial Statistics. Paper and Paper-making

ARNOT — Technology of the Paper Trade (Cantor Lecture, Society of Arts) London, 1877

BRIQUET, C M — Papiers et filigranes des archives de Genes 1154–1700. Geneva, 1888

CHRISTY, THOMAS — New Commercial Plants and Drugs, No 6, Part I, Fibres London, 1882.

CLAPPERTON, GEORGE — Practical Paper-making London, 1891 Crosby Lockwood & Son

CROSS, C F — Report on Miscellaneous Fibres London, 1886 William Clowes & Sons

CROSS AND BEVAN — Report on Pictet-Brelaz Process London, 1887 E & F N Spon

Cellulose. London, 1885 George Kenning

Chemistry of Hypochlorite Bleaching Jour Soc. Chem. Ind., May 31, 1890

Chemistry of Bast Fibres. Manchester, 1880 Palmer & Howe.

Reports on Hermite Process London, 1886

A Text-book of Paper-making London, 1888 E & F N Spon

Report on Indian Fibres and Fibrous Substances London, 1887. E & F N. Spon.

Davis, Charles Thomas — The Manufacture of Paper. Phila., 1886. Henry Carey Baird & Co

Dunbar, J — The Practical Paper-maker. London, 1881

Forestry and Forest Products. Edinburgh, 1884

Garcon, Jules. — Bibliographie de la Technologie Chimique des Fibres Textiles Paris, 1893. Gauthier-Villars et Fils

Griffin, Martin L — Remarks on Chemistry of Sulphite Processes. Trans Amer Soc. C E, 417 1889

Herzberg, W — Papier-Prüfung. Berlin 1888 Julius Springer

Hofmann, Carl — A Treatise on Paper-making Phila 1873 New and much enlarged edition, Howard Lockwood & Co, New York (*In press*)

Hohnel, Franz von — Die Mikroskopie der technisch verwendeten Faserstoffe. Vienna, 1887 Hartleben

Hoyer, Egbert — Fabrikation des Papiers Brunswick, 1886 F Vieweg & Sohn

Jagenberg, Ferdinand — Die Thierische Leimung für endloses Papier Berlin, 1878 Julius Springer

Japanese Papers — Boston Public Library *5024-18 contains 81 specimens of plain and tinted papers, *5021-20 has 64 specimens of ornamented papers

Le Normand, L S — Manuel du Fabricant des Papiers Paris, 1834

Michaelis, Major O E — Lime Sulphite Fibre Mfg in U. S. Trans Amer Soc C. E, 417 1889

Mierzinski, S — Handbuch der Papier-fabrikation Vienna, 1886

Muller, Dr A — Die Bestimmung des Holzschliffes im Papier Berlin, 1887 Julius Springer

Muller, Dr L — Die Fabrikation des Papiers. Berlin, 1877 Julius Springer

Muller, Hugo — Die Pflanzenfaser. Leipzig, 1873

Murray, J — Practical Remarks on Modern Paper Edinburgh, 1829

Normal-Papier — Pub by Die Papier-Zeitung Berlin, 1891

Parkinson, R — A Treatise on Paper Preston, 1886

Patents, British — Abridgements of specifications relating to Paper. 1636-1876

Planche, G — L'Industrie de la Papeterie Paris, 1853

Proteaux — The Manufacture of Paper and Boards Phila., 1873.

Routledge, Thomas. — Bamboo as a Paper-making Material London, 1875 E & F N Spon

Sadtler, Samuel P — Industrial Organic Chemistry pp 262-291 Phila, 1892. J. B Lippincott Co.

Sargeant, Charles S — Forest Trees of North America Tenth U S Census

Schubert, Max — Die Cellulosefabrikation. Berlin, 1892 Fischer & Heilmann

Tomlinson — The Manufacture of Paper

Vetillart — Études sur les Fibres Végétales Paris, 1876.

Watt, Alex — The Art of Paper-making. London, 1890

Wiesner, Dr. Julius — Die Mikroscopische Untersuchung des Papiers Vienna, 1887

INDEX.

REFERENCES ARE TO PAGES

Absorption apparatus, 203
   Behrend, 223.
   Catlin 217
   Ekman, 210
   Frank, 223
   Francke, 218
   McDougall, 214, 216
   Mitscheilich, 205
   Némethy 220
   Partington, 213
   Ritter-Kellner,
     tank apparatus, 212
     towers, 218
   tower systems, 204
   Wendler-Spiro, 221
   Wheelwright, 215
Accent of chemical terms, 465, 468
Acetate of alumina, 77
   lead, 92, 397
   density of solutions, 494
Acetates, analysis of, 397
Acetic acid, analysis, 357
   density of solutions, 492
   use in bleaching 293
Acid, acetic, analysis 357
   density of solutions, 492
   use in bleaching, 293
   alkali-cellulosexanthic, 470
   antimonic, 89
   arsenic, 61
   arsenious, 60
   benzoic, 139
   boracic, 57
   boric, 57
   carbonic, 32
   carminic, 322
   cellulose-thiosulphocarbonic, 468
   chloric, 54
   chlorous, 54
   cinnamic, 139
   cyanhydric, 35
   free, action on cellulose, 282
     in alum 311
       det of, 380
     in paper, 437
     in sulphite liquor, 209, 225
   hydrochloric, 49
     analysis, 355
     density of solutions, 491

Acid hydrofluoric 56
   hypochlorous 51
   hyposulphurous, 44
   muriatic, 49
     analysis, 355
     density of solutions, 491
   nitric, 30
     analysis, 356
     density of solutions, 490
   Nordhausen, 47
   oxalic, analysis, 358
     density of solutions, 483
   perchloric, 55
   polythionic, 47
   pyroligneous, analysis, 357
   sulphites, 41
   sulphuric, 45
     analysis, 353
     density of solutions, 488
     in burner gas, 197
     in paper-testing, 443
     prep of different strengths, 488
     in sulphite liquor, 414
   sulphurous, 40
     action upon life 274
     action upon throat and lungs, 274
     analysis, 412
     density of solutions, 498
   sylvic, 139
   thionic, 47
   thiosulphuric, 45
   waters, 334
Acids, analysis of, 353
   definition, 13
Adansonia, composition of bast, 128
Agalite (Fig 69), 316, 140
Agate, 58
Agave, 129
Air, 29
   in wood cells, 137
Air-dry pulp, 440
   calculation of, 451
Alabaster, 73
Alcohol 106
   density of solutions, 499
Alfa, 131.
Algæ, 331-337
Alkali, analysis, 359
   by electrolysis 400

Alkali, cellulose 468
  manufacturing, 65
  metals, 63
  in soda pulp, 289
Alkaline earths, analysis, 359
  metals of 69
Aloe fibre, 129
Alternating current, 456
Alum 77
  ammonia 78
  potash, 78
    density of solutions 495
Alum (sulphate of alumina) 309
  analyses of, 310
  analysis of, 375
  density of solutions, 496, 497
  free acid, det. of, 380
  manufacture of, 77
  moisture in, 382
  preservative effect on size 303
  sizing test for 380
Alumina, 76
Aluminate of soda, 307
Alumine, fibrous, 317
Aluminum, 76
  acetate, 77
  bleach liquor, 295
  chloride, action on cellulose, 282
  hydrate, 77
  hydroxide, 77
  oxide, 76
  sulphate, see Alum
Amalgams 63 97
Amethyst, 58
  color of, 82
Ammonia, 30, 69
  analysis of, 361
  density of solutions, 493
  water, 30, 69
Ammonia alum, 77
Ammonium, 68
  hydrate analysis, 361
    density of solutions, 493
  hydroxide, 69
  sulphate, 69
Ampère, 454, 455
  law of, 7
Amyloid 107
Analysis, chemical, 348
  volumetric, 353
Anion, def., 453
Anode, def 453
  use of gas carbon for, 460.
Andreoli process, 460
Anatase, 86
Anhydrides, def., 16
Anhydrite, 73
Aniline colors 325
  analysis of, 401.
  red, 325
  sulphate, 445

Aniline sulphate for paper-testing, 443
Animal size, 301
  first use of, 434
Annaline, 317
Antichlor, 251, 283
  analysis of, 395
  Hosford's 284
Antimonic anhydride, 89
  chloride, 88
  sulphide, 88
Antimonous antimonate, 88.
  chloride, 88
  hydride, 88
  oxide, 88
  oxychloride 88
  sulphide 88
Antimony, 88
  group 88
Apatite, 73
Apparatus for analysis, 348
Aqua ammonia, 30
  density of solutions, 493
Aqua fortis, 30
  density of solutions, 490
Arithmetic, chemical, 18
Argentic oxide, 95
Argentous oxide, 95.
Arsenic, 60
  acid, 61
  in aniline colors, 60
  in hides 303
  in wall paper, 60
Arsenide of cobalt, 83
Arsenite of soda, preservative for size, 303
Arsenious acid, 60.
Artificial silk, 111
Asbestos, 74
Ash in paper, 437
  in pulp, 438
Aspen, 145
Atomic theory, 5
  weights, 8
    table of, 486
Atoms 5
Auramine, 326

Bacteria, 338
  iron, 332
  jelly, 338
Baeyer cellulose and chlorine, 113
Bagasse 132
Baking soda 65
Balsam 113
Balsams, 138, 139
Bamboo, 132
Barium, 70
  hydrate, 70
  hydroxide, 70
  oxide, 70
  peroxide, 70
  sulphate 70

INDEX

Bark, 140
   coloring matter of, 141
   mulberry, 128
   tannin, 141
Baryta, caustic, 70
Bases, def., 15
   det. of in sulphite liquors, 414
Basic alum, 312
   lead chromate, 92
Bass wood, 147
Bast fibres, 121
   characteristics of, 122
Bauxite, 77
Beadle, cellulose, derivatives, 468
   formula for size, 305
Beaumé hydrometer, 482, 483
Becquerel, electrolysis of chlorides, 457
Beech, 146
Belgian flax, 124
Benzoic acid, 139
Berlin blue, 400
Beryllium, 75
Bevan, cellulose derivatives, 468
Bibliography, 501
Bicarbonate, ferrous, 81
   of soda, 371
Bichromate of potash, 85, 398
   of soda, 398
Birch, paper, 147
   white, 147
Bismuth, 89
   nitrate, 89
   terchloride, 89
Bisulphide of carbon, 48
   action on cellulose, 468
Bisulphites, 41
Bisulphite of lime, 181
   liquor, analyses of, 226–228
      analysis 412
      mfg. 190
   of magnesia, 184
   of soda, 184
Black ash, analysis of, 370
Black liquor, analysis of, 165
Black spruce, 142
Black willow, 148
Blast furnace, 80
   lamp, Russian, 351
Bleach, consumed by water, 332
   liquid chlorine, 296
   liquor, 279
      aluminum, 295
      Crouvelle's, 295
      magnesium, 294
      Ramsey's, 295
      Wilson's, 295
      zinc, 295
   oxygen, 298
   ozone, 298
   removal from cellulose, 282
   sulphurous acid, 299

Bleaching, 275
   acid, use of in, 292
   chlorination of cellulose in, 285
   Cloudman process, 290
   ground wood, 294
   Hermite process, 457
   hot, 281
Bleaching jute, 294
   rags, 281
   wood fibre, 281
Bleaching-powder, 275
   analysis of, 391
   composition of, 278
   consumption of, 280
   deterioration of, 277
   introduction of, 276
   manufacture of, 52
      by electrolysis, 460
   preparation of solution, 279
   properties, 276
   strength of, 277
Bleaching-salt, Varrentrapp's, 295
Blotting-paper, capillary power, 436
Blowpipe, oxyhydrogen, 28
"Blue Billy," 40
   composition of, 177
Blue dyes, 326
   stone, 93, 384
   vitriol, 93
Boiler, sulphite, see Digester
   vomiting, 157
Boiler scale, 333, 412
   composition of, 334
Boiling-point of water, 165
Boiling rags, 151.
Boiling wood by sulphite process, 250
Boracic acid, 57
Borax, 57, 65
Boric acid, 57
Boron, 57
Boron fluoride, 57
Bottger and Otto, discovery of guncotton, 108
Brandt, electrolysis of sea-water, 457
Britannia metal, 85
Bromine, 55
Brookite, 86
Bronze, 86
   digesters, 239
Brown dyes, 326
Buckeye, 148
Buddeus, waste sulphite liquors, 271
Burette, 349
Burgess, Hugh, electrolysis of chlorides, 457
Burnett's disinfecting solution, 75
Burning of pulp, 252

Cadmium, 75
Cæsium, 68
Calamine, 74

INDEX.

Calcium, 71
  carbonate, 72
    see also Carbonate of Lime
  chloride, 72, 390
    density of solutions, 499
    in paper, 437
    in pulp, 283
  hydrate, 71, 72
    analysis of, 362
    density of milk of lime, 498
  hydroxide, 71
  hypochlorite, 391
    see also Bleaching-powder
  hyposulphite, 45
Carbon, 31
  bisulphide, 48
    action on cellulose, 468
  dioxide, 32
  monoxide, 32
  and nitrogen, 35
  and oxygen, 32
  and sulphur, 48
Carbonate of iron, 80
  of lime, 72
    analysis, 374
    formation in causticizing, 174
    in towers, 204
    water, 333
  of magnesia, 74
    analysis, 374
    in water, 330
  of potash, 64
    analysis, 373
Calcium oxide, 71, 72
  analysis, 362
  see also Lime
  phosphate, 73
  sulphate, 73
    filler for paper, 316-318
    see also Lime, Sulphate of
  sulphite, 42
    use as antichlor, 284
    in pulp, 270
    see also Lime, Sulphite of
  thiosulphate, use as antichlor, 285
Calomel, 97
Cambium layer, 135
Canary paste, 398
  yellow 85 398
Capacity, measures of, 478
Carbohydrates, 34, 104
Carbonate of soda, 65
  analysis, 367
  causticizing, 173-175
  density of solutions, 494
  mfg , 65
  use in treating picker seed, 156
    rag-boiling, 153
    sulphate process, 178
    sulphite process, 230
  of zinc, 75

Carbonate of zinc, analysis, 375
Carbonates, 33
  analysis, 367
Carbonic acid, 32.
  anhydride, 32
Carbonizing wood 114
Carmichael process, 460
Carminic acid, 323
Carnelian, 58
Casein sizing, 307
Casserole, 350
Cassiterite, 86.
Cast-iron digester, 232
Cathion, def , 453
Cathode, def , 453
  use of iron for, 460
Caustic ash, analysis, 369
  baryta, 70
  potash, 64
    analysis, 361
  soda, 64
    analysis, 359
    density of solutions, 493
Caustic soda, mfg , 65
  use in making size, 304
    preventing boiler-scale, 335.
    soda process, 161.
    sulphate process, 179
    treating rags, 155
      straw, 159
Celestine, 47
Cellulose, 103
  and chlorine, 112
    oxygen, 113.
  effect of heat upon, 115
  fermentation of, 115
  Mercerized, 113
  processes for isolating, 151
Cellulose acetate, 108
  benzoate, 470
  nitrates, 109
  thiocarbonates, 468
Celsius thermometer, 479
Cement, 72
Cement linings, 246
  Curtis & Jones, 250
  Kellner, 246
  Russell 247
  Wenzel, 246
Centigrade thermometer 479
Century plant, fibre of, 129
Cerium, 79
Chalk, analysis, 374
Chalybeate waters, 81
Chemical changes, def , 3
Chemistry, def , 3
  organic, def , 35
Chestnut, 148
Chili saltpetre, 65, 396.
China glass, 128
Chloric acid, 54

INDEX

Chloride of aluminum, action on cellulose, 282
  of calcium, 390
    density of solutions, 499
  ferric, 391
  of gold, 98
"Chloride of Lime," 275
  see also Bleaching-powder.
Chloride of magnesium, 389
  in Hermite process, 457
  in water, 333
  of potash, 64
  of platinum, 98
  of sodium, 65
    analysis of, 386
    density of solutions, 482
  of zinc, 75
Chlorides, action on cellulose, 282
  analysis of, 386
  in paper, 437
Chlorine, 49
  action upon coloring matters, 276
  liquid, 296
  mfg by electrolysis, 453
Chlorine and cellulose, 112
  and hydrogen, 49
  and nitrogen, 55
  and oxygen, 50
  and sulphur, 55
Chlorine, anhydrides of, 51
  dioxide, 51
  hydrate, 49
Chlorates, 54
Chlorinated compounds in bleached cellulose, 285
Chlorinated soda, 394
Chlorites, 54
Chlorophyll, 117
Chlorous acid, 54
Choke-damp, 32
Chrome yellow, 321, 398
Chromate of lead, 85, 92, 321, 398
  of potassium, 84
Chromates, analysis of, 398
Chromium, 84
  compounds, 84
Cinnabar, 37
Cinnamic acid, in resins, 139
Clark process, 335, 406
Classification of papers, 420
Clay, 58, 77
  composition of, 316
  determination of in paper, 439
  use as paper-filler, 315
Clay iron-stone, 80.
Cloudman's bleaching apparatus, 290
Coal-tar colors, 325
Cobalt, 83
  compounds of, 83
Cochineal, 322
Cocoanut fibre, 128.

Cohesion, 6.
Coir fibre, 128.
Coke, 31
Collodion, 111
Colophony, 139
Color furnishes, 328
  of paper, 320
  of pulp, 266
  of water, 330
Coloring 320
Coloring matter of bark, 141
  of cotton, 121
  of knots, 141
Colors, ash of mineral, 440
  substantive, 320
Columbium, 90
Combined rosin, 419
Combustion, 26, 38
  spontaneous, 26
Compounds, 7, 10
Condensed water in sulphite process, 255
Coniferous trees, wood of, 134
Connecticut River, color of water, 331
Conservation of energy, 3
Continuous current, 455
Copper, 92
  pyrites, 198
  sulphate, 384
Copperas, 81, 385
Coprolites, 73
Cork, 141
Corundum, 76
Cotton, 121
  threads, strength of 289
  waste, 157
Cottonwood, 145
Craney process, 460
Cream of tartar, 64
Crenothrix, 332
Crocker process, 230
Cross and Bevan, action of chlorine on cellulose, 112
  exam of fibres, 123, 124
  lignification, 118
Cross, Bevan, and Beadle, new cellulose derivatives, 468
Crouvelle's bleaching-liquor, 295
Crown filler, 317
Cryolite, 57, 77
Current, electric, 454
Current efficiency, 454
Curtis & Jones lining, 250
Cutton process, 460
Cyanhydric acid, 35
Cyanogen, 35
Cypress, 146

Dalton, atomic theory, 5
De Chardonnet, artificial silk, 111
Definite proportions, 9
Deliquescence, 64.

Density of woods 137
Dervaux filter, 344
Desiccator, 351
Dextrin, 106, 114
Diamond, 31
Diaphragm, use in electrolysis, 460
Didymium, 79
Difference of potential, 454
Digesters, 162, 232
    bronze, 239
    cement-lined, 246
    emptying of, 260 263
    enamel-lined, 243
    experimental, 269
    lead-lined 232
    Mitscherlich, 242
    Salomon-Brungger, 243
    valves for 240
Dinitrocellulose 110
Dirt in paper 423
    in pulp 267
Discs use of in Mitscherlich process, 190
Dithionates 47
Dolomite, 227
Drying, loft, 303
Duramen, 136
Durin, cellulosic fermentation, 116
Dyes, 320–322
    dilutions of, 327
    testing of, 326

Earth metals. 76
Eau de Javelle, 296, 391
    de Labarraque 296
Eder, nitrogen in pyroxylins 110
    prep of cellulose penta-nitrate, 110
Edge-runner for working straw, 161
Ekman furnace 194
    modified, 193
    lining 237
    process, 185
    towers 210
Electric bleaching, 452
Electricity, conduction by liquids, 452
Electric current, analogy to flowing water, 454
    effect of, 452
Electrical units, 454
Electrolysis, 453
    conditions of, 456
    theory of, 456
Electrolytes def., 453
Electrolytic processes 452
    efficiency of, 462
    general features of 460
Electrolyzer, Hermite, 457
Electromotive force, 454
Elements, chemical, 5, 7
    metallic, 62
    non-metallic, 25
    table of, 486

Elements of wood, 133
Emerald, 75
Emery, 76
E M F , 454
Energy, conservation of, 3
Engine sizing, 304
English test for alkali 360
Eosin, 326
Epsom salts, 47
Equations, 17
Equivalents, 13
Erbium, 79
Esparto, 131
    treatment of, 157
Euchlorine, 51
Evaporation, multiple effect, 166
    open pan, 165
Evaporator, Gaunt, 169
    Porion, 172
    Yaryan, 166
Examples in chemical arithmetic, 19
Expansion of lead, 232
Experimental digester, 269

Fahrenheit's thermometer, 479
Fermentation, decomposition of cellulose by, 115
    formation of cellulose by, 116
Ferric chloride, 81
    nitrate, 397
    oxide, 81
    salts, def 15
Ferricyanide of potassium, 35
Ferrocyanide of potassium, 35
Ferrous bicarbonate, 81
    salts def , 15
    sulphate, 385
Fibres, 117
    bast 121
    chemical examination, 124
    derived from whole stems or leaves, 129
    from wood, 132
    fungoid growth on, 269
    microscopical examination, 441
    staining effects, 443
    standard mixtures, 444
Fibrous alumine, 317
    tests for in paper, 439
Fillers, mineral, 314
Filter Dervaux, 344
    gravity, 338
    New York, 311
    pressure, 341
    Warren, 338
Filter paper, analysis of, 287
Filter-beds, 337
Filtration, 336
Filaments, 123
Fir, white 143
Flax, 124
Flax, New Zealand, 127

INDEX

Flint, 58
Flint glass, 92.
Flowers of sulphur, 36
Fluoride of boron, 57
Fluorine, 56
Fluorspar, 56
"Fool's gold," 38
Fracture length of paper, 425
   how calculated 426
Frank, Dr, action of waste sulphite liquors on animal life, 273
   sulphite liquor apparatus, 223
Free acid in alum 311
   in sulphite liquor, 208
   rosin, determination of, 418
Freiberg pyrites burner 198
French white analysis of 374
Fuchsine, 325
Fuel value of woods, 133
Fungoid growth in fibre, 269

Galena, 37, 91
Gallium 94
Gas-cooler, Wheelwright, 203
Gas pressure, 7
   in sulphite process, 252
Gas recovery, 261
Gelatine, 302
Gemmell, moisture in pulp, 451
German silver, 84
Girard, hydration of cellulose, 114
Gladstone, action of soda upon cellulose, 115
Glass, 58
Glauber's salt, 65
Glucinum, 75
Glucose, 106, 114
Glue, 302
Glycerine, density of solutions, 498
Godeffroy det of ground wood, 446
Gold, 98
Goodale, bast-fibres, 122
Graham digester, 238
Graphite, 31
Graphic symbols, 11
Gravity filters, 338.
Gray pine, 142
Green dyes, 326
   vitriol, 81
Greenwood process, 460
Griffin, Martin L, moisture in pulp, 450
Grit in paper-fillers, 315
Ground wood, bleaching of, 294
   sampling, 447
   tests for, 445
Growth of wood, 135
Gum resins, 138
Gum, sweet, 145
Gums, 120
Guncotton, 109
Gypsum, 47, 73

Gypsum paper-filler, 317
   det of, 439
Hackmatack, 144
Haermatite, 80
Halogens, 57
   compounds of, 57
Hard water, 72, 329
Hardness, test for, in water, 408
Heart wood, 136
Heat, 6
   latent, 7
   relations of atoms to, 8
   specific, 7
   unit of, 7
   units developed by combustion, 33
Heavy spar, 47, 70
"Heavy lead ore," 91
Hemlock, 144
Hemp, 126
   sisal, 129
   sunn, 127
Henequin, 129
Hermite process, 457
Herzberg, ash in pulps, 438
   plate of fibres, 132
Hewitt and Mond, causticizing process, 175
Hexanitrocellulose, 110
Hohnel, lignin reactions, 445
Holland and Richardson process, 460
Horse power, electrical, 456
Hosford's antichlor, 284
Hydrate of aluminum, 77.
   of calcium, 71
   of magnesium 74
Hydrates, def, 15
Hydraulic lime, 72
Hydrocarbons, 31
Hydrocellulose, 114, 437.
Hydrochloric acid, 49
   analysis of, 355
   density of solutions, 491.
   use in bleaching, 292
Hydrofluoric acid, 56
Hydrogen, 27
   and chlorine, 49
   peroxide, 29.
      mfg, 70
      use as antichlor, 285
   sulphide, 38
Hydrolysis, def, 182
Hydrometer, Beaumé, 482, 483
   Twaddle's, 484
Hydroxide of alumina, 77
   of zinc, 74
Hypochlorite of aluminum, 295
   of calcium, 275, 391
   of magnesium, 294, 394
   of potash, 296, 394
   of soda, 296, 394
   of zinc, 295
Hypochlorites, prep by electrolysis, 452

Hypochlorous acid, 51, 292
Hyposulphite of soda, 15, 283
Hyposulphurous acid, 44

Indian red, 400
Indium, 94
Injectors for transferring liquor, 231
Iodine, 56
   solution for paper-testing, 143
Ion, def., 453
Intensity currents, 455
Iridium, 100
Irish flax, 124
Iron, 80
   in alum, 311
   bacteria, 332
   pyrites, 198
   wood, 138
Isinglass, 302
Italian hemp, 126

Javelle water, 394
Jung and Lindig lining, 245
Jute, 125
   bleaching of, 291
   treatment of, 293
Kaolin, 58
Kellner, cement lining, 246
   filtering-tower, 201
   sizing, 313
Kellogg lamp, 351
Kier, the Mather, 153
Knofler oven, 449
Knots, 140
   removing from wood, 189
Kupfer-nickel, 84

Labarraque's solution, 394
Lampblack, 31
Lanthanum, 79
Larch, 144
Latent heat, 7
Lavoisier, 3
Law of Ampère, 7
   of definite proportions, 9
   of multiple proportions, 12
   Ohm's, 455
Lead, 91
   action of acids upon, 233
   burning, 241
   linings, 232
      Ekman, 237
      Francke, 234
      Graham, 238
      Makin, 235
      Mitscherlich, 242
      Partington, 234, 236
      Ritter-Kellner, 237
      Russell, 233
      Springer, 236
      Wheelwright, 238

Lead acetate, 92, 397
   density of solutions, 494
   chromate, 85, 92
   testing, 398
   use in coloring paper, 321
   sugar of, 92, 397
   density of solutions, 494
Leblanc process, 65
Length, measures of, 478
Leonhardi's test for sizing, 436
Le Sueur and Waite process, 460
Liber-fibres, 123
Light, action on rosin size, 306
Liquified fibre, tests for, 445
Lignification, 118
Lignin, 118
Ligmeose, 119
Lignite, 31
Lignone, 119
Lignose, 119
Lime, 71
   analysis of, 362
   composition of, for causticizing, 174.
   for rag-boiling, 152
   for sulphite liquor, 227
   det. of in sulphite liquor, 414
   hydraulic, 72
   milk of, 71
      density 498
   reclaimer, 175
   water, 71
Lime, carbonate of, 72
   analysis, 374
   in water, 333
   sulphate of, 73, 191
   sulphite of, 191, 229, 253
Limestone, 72
   analysis of, 374
   use in tanks, 212
   in towers, 204
Linen, 124
Liquor-making, sulphite, 190
Litharge, 91
Lithium, 68
Loading paper, 314
Locust, 145
Lunar caustic, 96

Mactear, tabulated view of alkali mfg., 67
Magenta, 325
Magnesia, 74
   analysis, 365
   bleach liquor, 294
   det. of in sulphite liquors, 414
   use in Ekman process, 187, 210
Magnesite, analysis, 374
Magnesium, 73
   carbonate, analysis, 374
   chloride, 389
      density of solutions, 501
      electrolysis of, 458

Magnesium hydrate, 74, 365
  hypochlorite, 294, 394
    by electrolysis, 458
  oxide, 74, 187, 210
  silicate, 74
    use as paper-filler, 316, 440
  sulphate, 74, 381
Magnetic iron ore, 80.
  metals, 79
Magnetite, 80
Makin lining, 235
Malachite green, 326
Manganese, 82
Manganite, 82
Manila, 126
Maple, silver, 146
Marble analysis, 374
Marsh gas from cellulose, 116
Mass, def., 4
Mather, Kiel, 153
Matter, 3
  conservation of, 3
  properties of, 5
  states of, 6
Mauvein, 325
McDougall, digester lining, 235
  liquor apparatus, 212, 217
Measures, metric system, 1, 478
Meerschaum, 74
Mercerized cellulose, 115
Mercury, 97
  compounds of, 97
Merrimac River, color of water, 331
Metals, 62
  alkali group, 63
  antimony group, 88
  of alkaline earths, 69
  earth, 76
  iron group, 79.
  lead group, 90
  magnesium group, 73
  magnetic, 79
  noble, 95
  silver group, 95
  tin group, 85
Metantimonic acid, 89.
Methyl violet, 326
Metric system, 478
Microscope, 441
Microscopical examination of fibres, 441
  of paper-fillers, 314
Milk of lime, 71
  density of, 498
Millon's reagent, test for animal size, 432
Mineral colors, 321, 398
Mineralization of cell-wall, 117
Minium, 91
Mitscherlich process, digester, 242
  gas recovery, 262
  boiling, 256
  pulp, 267

Mitscherlich process, pyrites burner, 199
  stamp mill, 263
  sulphur furnace, 196
  tower system, 205
Mitscherlich sizing process, 313
Mixtures and compounds, 10
Moisture in pulp, 446
Molecules, 5
Molybdenite, 87
Molybdenum, 87
"Money value" test for dyes, 402
Monosulphite of calcium, formation of, 228, 253
  incrustation, 229, 253
  removal of, 230
Mordants, 320
Mortars, 72
Mosaic gold, 86
Mulberry tree, 128
Mulder, formation of glucose, 115
Muller, A., ash in fibres, 438
Muller, Hugo, analysis of cotton, 121
  esparto, 131
  flax, 124
  jute, 125
  hemp, 126
  manila, 127
  sunn hemp, 127
  woods, 140
Multiple-effect evaporation, 166
Muriatic acid, 49
  analysis, 355
  density of solutions, 491

Naphthol, 326
Nascent state, 17
Negative pole, 455
Némethy liquor apparatus, 220
New York Filter Co.'s filter, 341
New Zealand flax, 127
Nickel, and compounds of, 84
Nitrates, 31
  analysis of, 395
Nitrate of iron, 397
  of lead, 92
  of potash, 64, 395
  of silver, 96.
  of soda, 65, 396.
Nitric acid, 30
  analysis of, 356
  density of solutions, 490
Nitrogen, 29
  and carbon, 35
  and chlorine, 55
  and oxygen, 30
  and sulphur, 48
Noble metals, 95
Nomenclature, 14
Nordhausen acid, 47
Normal paper, 420
Normal solutions, 352

Norton, Dr. L. M., moisture in pulp, 451

Ochres, 400
Ohm, def., 455
Ohm's law, 455
Oil of vitriol, 45
Oleo-resins, 138
Onyx, 58
Open-pan evaporation, 165
Orange mineral, 91, 399
Osmium, 100
Ovens, drying-, 448
Oxalic acid, analysis, 358
    density of solutions, 483
Oxides 26
    of aluminum, 76
    of antimony, 88
    of arsenic, 60
    of barium, 70
    of cadmium, 75
    of calcium, 71
    of carbon, 32
    of chlorine, 50
    of cobalt, 83
    of copper, 92
    of chromium, 84
    of iridium, 94
    of iron, 80
    of lead, 91
    of magnesium, 74
    of manganese, 82
    of mercury, 97
    of molybdenum, 87
    of nickel, 84
    of nitrogen, 30
    of potassium, 63
    of silicon, 58
    of silver, 95
    of sodium, 360
    of sulphur, 39
    of tin, 85
    of tungsten, 87
    of vanadium, 90
    of zinc, 74
Oxidizing flame, 34
Oxycellulose, 113
Oxygen, 25
    mfg. of, 70
    use in bleaching, 298
Oxyhydrogen flame, 28
Ozone, 27
    bleach, 298

Palladium, 99
Paper, ash in, 437
    capillary power of blotting, 436
    chlorides in, 437
    classification of, 420
    direction on machine, 421
    dirt in, 423

Paper filler, det. of kind, 439
    filter, analysis of, 287
    finish of, 423
    fracture length of, 425
    free acid in, 437
    ground wood in, 445
    microscopical examination of, 441
    normal, 120
    parchment, 107
    right and wrong sides, 421
    starch in, 434
    strength of, 424
    stretch of, 424
    testing, 420
    thickness of, 421
    water marks, 422
Paper birch, 147
    mulberry, 128
Parchment paper, 107
Paris green, 60, 93.
Paris, plaster of, 73
Partington lining, 234, 236
    liquor apparatus, 215
Partition, use of porous, in electrolysis, 453
Paste, 92
Patents, list of sulphite, 471
Pearlash, analysis of, 373
Pearl hardening, 316, 439
    analysis of, 383
    composition of, 317
Pelouze, action of nitric acid on cellulose, 108
Penta-nitro-cellulose, 110
Perchloric acid, 55
Permanganate of potash, 83
Peroxide of barium, 70
    of hydrogen, 29
    use as antichlor, 285
Pewter, 85
Phloroglucin, for paper-testing, 444, 445
Phosphate of lime, 73
Phosphate rock, 73
Phosphides, 59
Phosphor bronze, 60, 86
Phosphorus, 59
Photography, 96
Physical change, 3
Physical properties, 5
Picker seed, treatment of, 156
Picker waste, treatment of, 156
Pig iron, 81
Pine, gray, 142
    white, 143
Plaster of Paris, 73
Platinum, 98
Plumbago, 31
Poles, def., 453
    of dynamo, 455
Polythionic acids, 197
Poplar, 144
Porion evaporator, 172

INDEX

Porter-Clark process, 335
Potash, 63
  caustic, 64
    analysis, 361
    density of solutions, 495
Potash alum, 77
  density of solutions, 495
Potassium, 65
  bichromate, 85, 398
  carbonate, 64
  chlorate, 54, 64
  chloride, 64
  chromate, 84
  ferricyanide, 35
  ferrocyanide, 35
  hydrate, 64, 361, 495
  hypochlorite, 296, 394
  nitrate, 64, 395
  oxide, 63, 361
  permanganate, 85
  tartrate, 64
Potential, 454
Prefixes, use in chemical terms, 465
Preparing wood, 188
Pronunciation of chemical terms, 465
Prussian blue, 35, 321, 400
Prussic acid, 35
Pulp, "air-dry," moisture in, 419
  sampling, 447
  testing for moisture, 446
Pulp, soda, 161
  cause of bad odors in, 38
  effect of traces of black liquor, 289
  yields, 149
  sulphate, mfg, 178
  sulphite, analysis of, bleached, 287
    analysis of Mitscherlich, 267
    analysis of quick cooked, 268
    bleaching, loss in, 288
    blue, addition of, to bleached, 285
    burned, 266
    cause of bad odors in, 38
    chlorinated cellulose in, 286
    dirt in, 267
    fungoid growth on, 269
    quality, conditions affecting, 261, 266
    yellow discoloration on, 283
    yields, 149, 269
Pumping sulphite liquor, 230
Pyrites, 37, 38
  copper, 198
  iron, 198
Pyrites burner, Freiberg, 198
  Mitscherlich, 199
Pyrolusite, 82
Pyroxylin, 109

Quantity currents, 455
Quantivalence, 13
Quartz, 58
Quicklime, 71

Radicle der., 69
Rags, boiling, etc., 151
Ramie, 127
Ramsay's bleach liquor, 295
Reactions, 17
  analytical, 18
  secondary, 453
  synthetical, 18
Recovered lime, 175
Recovery of gas, 261
  of soda, 158, 164
Red dyes, 325
Reducing flame, 34
Resins, 120, 138
Retention of fillers, 318, 440
Retort sulphur furnace, 193
Rhea, 128
Rhodium, 99
Ritter-Kellner filtering-tower, 200
  lining, 237
  tank apparatus, 211
  tower system, 218
Rock crystal, 58
Rosin, 139
  combined, det. of, 419
  free, in size, 304
Rosin size, analysis of, 417
  composition of, 303
  preparation, 305
  test for, 438
Rotary furnaces, 170
  rag boilers, 151
  sulphite digesters, 236
Rubbing test for paper, 431
Rubidium, 68
Ruby, 76
Ruby copper ore, 93
Russell cement lining, 217
  lead lining, 235
Russian blast lamp, 351
Ruthenium, 99
Rutile, 86

Safranine, 326
Salomon-Brunggei digester, 243
Salt cake, 385
Salt, common, 65
  analysis of, 386
  density of solutions, 482
  electrolysis of, 453
Salt of tartar, 373
Saltpetre, 64
  analysis of, 395
Salts, 15
Sampling pulp, 447
Sapphire, 76
Sapwood, 136
Scale boiler, 333
  preventives, 335
Scarlet liquor, 324
Schenck digester metal, 239

514 *INDEX*

Schonbein, discovery of explosive cotton, 108
Schopper paper-tester, 428
Schuman, det of rosin size, 434
Schunck, wax, etc., in raw cotton, 121
Schweizer's reagent, 104
Sea-water, 40
Secondary reactions, 153
Seed-hairs 121
Selenite, 73
Selenium, 48
Serpentine, 74
Sesquichloride of iron, 391.
Sesquioxide of alumina, 77
    of iron 81
Silver, 95
Silver maple 146
Silvering mirrors, 97
Silica, 58
    in water, 334
Silicate of magnesia, 74
    of soda, 58, 308
Silicon, 58
Sisal hemp, 129
Size, det of in paper 431
    rosin, 304
        action of light on, 306
        analysis of, 417
        composition of, 305, 306
        prep of, 305
            with aluminate of soda, 307
            with silicate of soda, 308
Sizing, 301
    use of acid sulphites, 313
        casein, 307
        starch, 319
Smalt, 83
Soapstone, 74
Soda, 65
    analysis of, 367.
    density of solutions, 494
    det of in sulphite liquor 416
    recovery of, 158 164
    sources of loss in 177
Soda alum, 77
Soda, aluminate of, 307
Soda ash, 65
    analysis of, 367
    causticizing, 173-175
    density of solutions, 494
Soda, caustic, 64
    analysis of 359
    density of solutions, 493
Soda process for wood fibre 161
    boiling, 162
    causticizing, 173
        Hewitt & Mond process, 175
    recovery, 164
    sources of loss, 177
Sodium, 64
    by electrolysis, 453

Sodium aluminum fluoride 77
    biborate, 57, 65
    bicarbonate, 65
        analysis of, 371
    bichromate, 398
    carbonate, 65
        analysis of, 367
        density of solutions, 494
    chloride 65
        analysis of, 386
        density of solutions, 432
        electrolysis of, 453-459
        use in Hermite process, 459
    hydrate, 64
        analysis of, 359
        density of solutions, 493
    hypochlorite, 290, 394
    hyposulphite, 44
        use as antichlor, 283
    nitrate, 65
        analysis of, 396
    silicate, 58
        use in sizing, 308
    sulphate, 385
    sulphite, use as antichlor, 284
    thiosulphate, 45
        use as antichlor, 283
    tungstate, 87
Soft water, 329
Solder, 86
Solids, mineral in water, 407
    total in water, 406
Solutions, normal, 352
Solvay ash, use in sulphite process, 230
Solvay process, 68
Sorghum, 132
Specific gravity, 4
    and degrees Beaumé 482, 483
    and degrees Twaddle, 484
Specific heat, 7
Specular iron ore, 80
Speiss cobalt, 83
Spelling of chemical terms, 465
Sponges, fresh-water 331
Spontaneous combustion, 26
Springer lining, 236
Spruce, 142
    analysis of, 140
    preparation, 188
    specific gravity etc., 138
    yields, 149, 269
Spruce pulp, ground wood, 142
    soda, 164
    sulphate, 178
    sulphite, 267
        analyses of, 267, 268, 287
Stamp mill 263
Standard papers 442
Standard solutions 352
Stannate of soda, 86
Starch 319, 434

INDEX.

Steam, temperature of, 487
Steel, 81
Stibine, 88
Stoichiometry, 18
Stock in normal papers, 420
Storage tanks, 231
Stores, fixing of nitrogen by humus, 116
Straw, 129
    treatment of, 158
Strontium, 71
Suberin, 141
Sublimation of sulphur, 197
Substantive colors, 320
Sugar of lead, 92
    analysis of, 397
    density of solutions, 494
Sulphates, 47
    analysis of, 375
Sulphate of alumina, 77, 309.
    analysis of, 375
    composition of, 310
Sulphate of ammonia, 69
    of barium, 70
    of calcium, 73, 228
    of copper, 93, 384
    of iron, 81, 385
    of lead, 91, 233
    of lime, 73
        in ash of paper, 439
        in sulphite liquor 191, 221, 228
        in towers, 207
        in water, 334
        paper-filler, 316
    of magnesia, 74, 384
    of soda, 65, 384
    of zinc, 75, 384
Sulphate process, 178
Sulphides 37
Sulphites, 41
Sulphite of lime, 43
    antichlor, 284
    cause of leaky tanks, 231
    cause of leaky valves, 230
    in liquor, 209
    in Frank apparatus, 225
    in Jung & Lindig lining, 245
    in Salomon-Brungger lining, 243
    in sediment, 228
    in towers, 207
    incrustation in digester, 253
        liquor apparatus, 229
    precipitation of, 253
    solubility, 191
Sulphite of magnesia, 43
    in towers, 188
Sulphite of soda, 184
    antichlor, 284
Sulphite liquors, analysis of, 412
    composition of, 208, 209 210, 226, 228
    preparation of, 190
        absorption apparatus, 203

Sulphite liquors, lime for, 227
    pumping, 230
    storage, 231
    sulphur burning, 192
    waste, 270
    action on life, 273, 274.
Sulphite process, 179
    boiling, 250
    digesters and linings, 232
    gas recovery, 201.
    history, 185
    liquor-making, 190
    patents, 471
    preparing wood, 188
    theory, 182
    waste liquor 270
Sulpho-arsenides, 60
Sulphur, 35
    action of SO_2 on 197.
    analyses of, 192.
    burning, 190, 192
    filtering-tower, 201
    flowers of, 36
    grades 37, 192
    loss of, 228
    sublimation 197
    yield of SO_2, 225
Sulphur and carbon 48.
    and chlorine, 55
    and nitrogen, 48
    and oxygen, 39
Sulphur, compounds of, 37
Sulphur dioxide, 40
Sulphuretted hydrogen, 39
Sulphuric acid, 45
    action on lead, 233
        on wood, 182
    analysis of, 353
    cause of loss of sulphur, 229.
    density of solutions, 488
    det. of in sulphite liquor, 414
    formation during boiling, 181, 185
        during sulphur burning, 190, 191, 196, 214
    in alum, 311
    prep of different strengths 489
    removal from gas, 200, 203
    use in bleaching 292
    in paper-testing, 443
Sulphuric anhydride, 47
Sulphurous acid, 40
    action on life, 274
        on sulphur, 197
    available, 209
    bleach, 44, 299
    blowing off, 252
    combined, 209
    density of solutions, 498
    determination of 412
    free, 209.
    gas pressure, 252

Sulphurous acid in burner gas, 208
    in furnace gas, 190
    in sulphite liquor, 210, 226, 228
    in waste liquor, 273
    use in pulp-making, 179
Sulphurous anhydride, 40.
Sunn hemp, 127
Surface waters, 329
Sylvic acid, in resins, 139
Symbols, 10
    graphic, 14
Synthetical reactions, 18
Sweet gum, 145

Talc, 74
Tamarack, 144
Tannic acid, test for animal size, 431
Tannin in bark, 141
Tappeiner, fermentation of cellulose, 115
Tartar emetic 88
Tartar, salt of, analysis, 373.
Tauss, effect of hot water on cellulose, 115
Tellurium, 48
Temperature, 6
    effect on sizing 312
Temporary hardness, 405
Terminations of chemical terms, 466
Tetranitro-cellulose, 110
Thallium, 92
Thermometers, relations between, 479
Thio-derivatives of cellulose, 468
Thionic acids, 47
Thiosulphate of calcium, use as antichlor, 285
    of soda, 45
Thiosulphuric acid, 45
Thorium, 87
Tilghman, inventor of sulphite process, 179
Tin, 85
Tinstone, 86
Titanium, 86
Tracheids, 132
    measurements of, 137
Trinitro-cellulose, 110
Tungsten, 87
Turpeth mineral, 97
Turquoise, 77
Twaddle's hydrometer, 484

Ulbricht, distribution of resin in wood, 139
Ultramarine, 321, 400
Unit of atomic weights, 8
    of heat, 7, 33
Units, electrical, 454
    of weights and measures, 478
Uranium, 85

Vanadium, 89
    attraction of cellulose for compounds of, 104

Vanadium, attraction of oxycellulose for compounds of, 113
Vanillin, test for, 433
    in waste liquors, 271.
Varrentrapp's bleaching-salt, 295
Vegetable cell, 117
Venetian red, 399
Verdigris, 93
Vermilion, 97
Victoria green, 326
Vinegar, analysis of wood, 357
Violet dyes, 326
Vitriol, blue, 93, 384
    green, 81, 385
    white, 75, 384
Vitriol, oil of, 45
    analysis, 353
    density of solutions, 488
    prep of different strengths, 489
Volt, def , 454
Volume, def , 4
Volumetric analysis, 353
Vomiting boiler, 157

Warren filters, 338
    rotary furnace, 170
Washing and bleaching apparatus, Cloudman, 290
Washing-soda, 65
Waste sulphite liquor, 270
Water, 29, 329
    acid, 334
    analysis, 403
    Clark's softening process, 406
    collecting samples, 316
    color of, 330
    effect upon bleaching, 290
    for manufacturing purposes, 411.
    hardness of, 329, 333, 403
    in wood, 137
    organic and volatile matter in, 407
    scale-forming, 333
    sea, 49
    total solids, 406
    volume used per ton of paper, 330
Water-bath, 351
    gas, 32
    marks, 422
Water of ammonia, 69
    analysis, 361.
Waters, chalybeate, 81
    surface and ground, 329
Wax in raw cotton, 121
    in straw, 131
Weigelt-Reufach, action of waste liquors on life, 273
Weight, def , 4
Weights, atomic, 8
    metric system, 478
Well-thread, 332
Wendler paper-tester, 425

Wendler-Spiro liquor apparatus, 221
Wenzel cement lining, 246
Wheelwright cooler, 203
    digester, 238
    liquor apparatus, 215
White arsenic, 60
    birch, 147
    fir, 143.
    lead, 91
    pine, 143
Whiting, 374
Wiesner, starch in ancient papers, 319
Willesden paper, 105
Willow, 148
Wilson's bleach liquor, 295
Witherite, 70
Witz, action of oxidizing agents on cellulose, 113.
Wood, 132
    density of, 137
    elements of, 133
    growth of, 135
    heaviest, 138

Wood, moisture in, 137
    of coniferous trees, 134
    preparing, 161, 188
    resin in, 139
Wood-cells, air and water in, 137
Wood-fibres, 133
Wood-vinegar, 357
Woods, analyses of, 140
    fuel value, 138
Woods used in pulp-making, 141, 149, 150
Wurster, determination of starch, 434
    theory of sizing, 304, 433

Yaryan evaporator, 166
Yellow dyes, 326
Yttrium, 79.

Zinc, 74
    bleach liquor, 295
    compounds of, 74, 75
    sulphate, analysis of, 384
Zirconium, 86
Zylonite, 111

· NATRONA POROUS ALUM ·

FOR PAPER MAKERS' USE.

THE Original "Porous" Alum and the only Alum made from KRYOLITH ALUMINA. Do not be deceived by parties offering so-called Porous, but buy and take no other than Natrona Porous Alum.

PENNA. SALT MFG. CO.,

SOLE MANUFACTURERS,

115 CHESTNUT ST., PHILADELPHIA, PA.

THE READY FAMILY SOAP MAKER.

LEWIS' 98% LYE

POWDERED AND PERFUMED
(PATENTED).

The strongest and purest Lye made. Will make the best Perfumed Hard Soap in twenty minutes *without boiling*.
The best water softener made. The best disinfectant.

SOME OF THE ADVANTAGES OBTAINED BY USING LEWIS' 98 PER CENT. POWDERED LYE ARE:

Unlike other Lye, it is packed in an iron can with a removable lid, easily taken off, thereby saving trouble and danger (from flying particles). It being a fine powder, and the lid easily removed, the contents are always ready for use. A teaspoonful can be used, in scrubbing, etc., and the lid replaced, saving the balance. With other Lyes all must be used quickly, or the strength is gone. Absolute *purity*. The best soap can be made in from ten to twenty minutes with this Lye. In making soap no failure is possible if the simple directions are followed. One can is equal to 20 pounds of Washing Soda; is 28 per cent. stronger, and will saponify one pound more grease than any other preparation. One teaspoonful will thoroughly cleanse waste pipes, sinks, drains or closets, and is invaluable for killing insects, etc.

PENNA. SALT MFG. CO., General Agents, PHILADELPHIA, PA.

THE HELLER & MERZ CO.,

PROPRIETORS OF THE

American Ultramarine and Globe Aniline Works,

55 MAIDEN LANE,

P. O. BOX 1094.   NEW YORK.

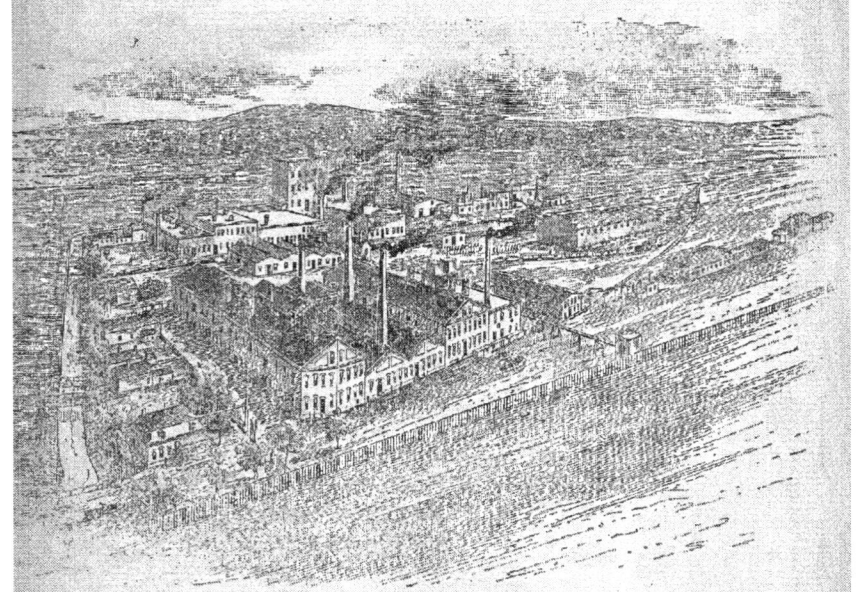

WORKS, NEWARK, N. J.

Ultramarine for Paper Makers.

R. C. No. 4.   R. S. xx.   A. P. R. x.

ANILINE COLORS OF ALL SHADES.

SAMPLES MATCHED.   ✧   SAMPLES MATCHED.

This Sheet Made and Colored in Our Laboratory.

[OVER].

THE HELLER & MERZ CO.,

NEW YORK,

MANUFACTURERS AND IMPORTERS OF

Ultramarine Blues

AND

Aniline Colors.

SAMPLES FOR ALL INDUSTRIES
CAREFULLY MATCHED.

ULTRAMARINE FOR PAPER MAKERS.

BROMO FLUORESCEIN,	VIOLETS,
ROSE BENGALE,	ANILINE BLUES,
PHLOXINES,	NIGROSINES,
ERYTHROSINES,	ORANGE, CARMOSINES,
SAFROSINE,	SCARLETS,
EOSINES,	BISMARCK BROWNS,
MAGENTAS,	NANKING BROWNS,
GARNETS,	CHRYSOIDINES, Etc.

P. O. BOX 1094,
NEW YORK.

WORKS:
NEWARK, N. J.

[OVER.]

MATHIESON ALKALI WORKS,

SALTVILLE, VA.

58 Per Cent. PURE ALKALI,

CAUSTIC SODA, All Strengths,

BLEACHING POWDERS,

SULPHATE OF SODA for Glass Makers.

THE unexcelled quality of merchandise turned out by Messrs. N. MATHIESON & Co., of Widnes, is well known among all consumers in the United States, Mathieson's Bleaching Powders especially commanding the highest price of any offered on this market for many years. Alkali and Caustic Soda as well, bearing Mr. Mathieson's name, have earned a reputation excelled by no other large maker. Mr. Mathieson is a large stockholder in this company, and Mr. T. T. Mathieson, for many years past having sole supervision of N. Mathieson & Co.'s Works in England, has entire charge of the Mathieson Alkali Works in this country.

These Works are rapidly approaching completion, and goods will be in the market within a few months.

Correspondence solicited by

MASON, CHAPIN & CO.,

PROVIDENCE,   NEW YORK,   BOSTON

A. D. LITTLE,

(GRIFFIN & LITTLE)

Consulting and Analytical Chemist,

EXPERT IN PATENT CAUSES,

103 Milk Street, Boston.

Particular attention given to all Chemical Matters pertaining to the Treatment of Fibres and the Manufacture of Pulp and Paper. Chemical and Microscopical Analyses of Paper and Paper-Making Materials. Commercial Analyses of every description.

NEW PROCESSES INVESTIGATED AND DEVELOPED.

Alum of all kinds for every possible purpose of the paper-maker.

Paste Yellow of fine Canary Tint; stands calender heat without change.

Paste Rose stands alum, acids, alkali, calenders and sunlight. COSTLY, but the only permanent and delicate rose tint known.

Paste Blue, perfectly even in tinting strength and absolutely uniform.

Paints, the best it is possible to manufacture for house, mill or machinery.

HARRISON BROS. & CO.,
PHILADELPHIA,
NEW YORK,
CINCINNATI.

ALUM! ♦ ♦ ♦ ♦

Bleaching, Sizing and Filtering Alums

Made Expressly for Paper Makers' Use.

Those requiring a strictly neutral and pure Alum for the highest grades of paper should try the

MERRIMAC POROUS ALUM

(either lump or ground, as preferred). Samples and prices of the different grades sent on application. Our works being on the Boston and Maine Railroad system, we are well situated for reaching all parts of New England.

Merrimac Chemical Co.,

13 Pearl Street,
Boston, Mass.

♦ ♦ ♦ ♦ ♦

[COPY.]
OFFICE OF STATE ASSAYER.
BOSTON, June 30, 1894.

We have examined a number of samples of the MERRIMAC POROUS ALUM, and have found this Alum to be of excellent quality both in respect to purity and strength, and suitable for the highest grades of paper.
(Signed) GRIFFIN & LITTLE.

The United Alkali Co., Ltd.,

OF GREAT BRITAIN,

Head Office, Exchange Buildings,   LIVERPOOL, ENGLAND.

Paid up Capital, - - $42,000,000.
Undivided Surplus, - - 2,500,000.

MANUFACTURERS OF

SODA ASH (All strengths, by Ammonia and Le Blanc Processes, Carbonated and Caustic),

CAUSTIC SODA,
(All strengths from 60 per cent. to Double Refined 98 per cent.),

HIGH TEST BLEACHING POWDER, Slow and Quick Acting

PEARL HARDENING,

SULPHATE OF ALUMINA
(Special quality free from Iron)

J. L. & D. S. RIKER,

Importers and Manufacturers' Agents,

45 CEDAR STREET, NEW YORK,

SOLE AGENTS FOR THE UNITED STATES AND CANADA OF

THE UNITED ALKALI CO., LIMITED,

OF GREAT BRITAIN,

For the sale of their various brands of Bleaching Powder and other articles of their manufacture.

THE SOLVAY PROCESS CO.,

SYRACUSE, N. Y.

Works at GEDDES, N. Y., three miles West of Syracuse.

PURE SODA. . . . — 58 per cent. actual Alkali, equals 99.16 per cent. Carbonate Soda; of uniform strength and purity.

AMMONIA SODA. — 48 per cent. actual Alkali, specially prepared for the glass trade; stronger than the so-called 48 per cent. Soda Ash.

BICARBONATE SODA. — The basis of Baking Powders, Rochelle Salts and carbonated beverages.

CAUSTIC SODA. . . — In all usual strengths for making Paper, Soap, Oil, Glycerine, Sugar, Starch, Etc.

CRYSTAL PAPER FILLER. — Superior to the Pearl Hardening in common use for surfacing paper stock.

HYDRATE OF ALUMINA. — A superior basis for making Alum and Salts of Alumina and other mordants.

OXIDE OF ALUMINA. — Refined from Bauxite, 98 per cent. pure; well suited for making pure Aluminum and its alloys.

Aggregate Finished Product, 500 Tons Daily.

NEW YORK SELLING AGENTS:

WING & EVANS,

54 William St., New York City.